Thine truly

John G. Whittier

THE

POETICAL WORKS

OF

JOHN GREENLEAF WHITTIER

Household Edition

WITH ILLUSTRATIONS

BOSTON AND NEW YORK

HOUGHTON, MIFFLIN AND COMPANY

The Riverside Press, Cambridge

The Riverside Press, Cambridge, Mass., U. S. A.
Electrotyped and Printed by H. O. Houghton & Company.

NOTE BY THE AUTHOR

TO THE EDITION OF 1857.

In these volumes, for the first time, a complete collection of my poetical writings has been made. While it is satisfactory to know that these scattered children of my brain have found a home, I cannot but regret that I have been unable, by reason of illness, to give that attention to their revision and arrangement, which respect for the opinions of others and my own afterthought and experience demand.

That there are pieces in this collection which I would "willingly let die," I am free to confess. But it is now too late to disown them, and I must submit to the inevitable penalty of poetical as well as other sins. There are others, intimately connected with the author's life and times, which owe their tenacity of vitality to the circumstances under which they were written, and the events by which they were suggested.

The long poem of Mogg Megone was in a great measure composed in early life ; and it is scarcely necessary to say that its subject is not such as the writer would have chosen at any subsequent period.

J. G. W.

Amesbury, 18th 3d mo., 1857.

PROEM.

I LOVE the old melodious lays
Which softly melt the ages through,
 The songs of Spenser's golden days,
 Arcadian Sidney's silvery phrase,
Sprinkling our noon of time with freshest morning dew.

Yet, vainly in my quiet hours
To breathe their marvellous notes I try ;
 I feel them, as the leaves and flowers
 In silence feel the dewy showers,
And drink with glad still lips the blessing of the sky.

The rigor of a frozen clime,
The harshness of an untaught ear,
 The jarring words of one whose rhyme
 Beat often Labor's hurried time,
Or Duty's rugged march through storm and strife, are here.

Of mystic beauty, dreamy grace,
No rounded art the lack supplies ;
 Unskilled the subtle lines to trace,
 Or softer shades of Nature's face,
I view her common forms with unanointed eyes.

Nor mine the seer-like power to show
The secrets of the heart and mind ;
 To drop the plummet-line below
 Our common world of joy and woe,
A more intense despair or brighter hope to find.

Yet here at least an earnest sense
Of human right and weal is shown ;
 A hate of tyranny intense,
 And hearty in its vehemence,
As if my brother's pain and sorrow were my own.

O Freedom ! if to me belong
Nor mighty Milton's gift divine,
 Nor Marvell's wit and graceful song,
 Still with a love as deep and strong
As theirs, I lay, like them, my best gifts on thy shrine !

AMESBURY, 11th mo., 1847

CONTENTS

CONTENTS.

CONTENTS.

LIST OF ILLUSTRATIONS.

MOGG MEGONE.

[The story of MOGG MEGONE has been considered by the author only as a framework for sketches of the scenery of New England, and of its early inhabitants. In portraying the Indian character, he has followed, as closely as his story would admit, the rough but natural delineations of Church, Mayhew, Charlevoix, and Roger Williams; and in so doing he has necessarily discarded much of the romance which poets and novelists have thrown around the ill-fated red man.]

PART I.

WHO stands on that cliff, like a figure
  of stone,
  Unmoving and tall in the light of the
    sky,
  Where the spray of the cataract spar-
    kles on high,
Lonely and sternly, save Mogg Me-
  gone ? [1]
Close to the verge of the rock is he,
  While beneath him the Saco its work
    is doing,
Hurrying down to its grave, the sea,
  And slow through the rock its path-
    way hewing !
Far down, through the mist of the fall-
  ing river,
Which rises up like an incense ever,
The splintered points of the crags are
  seen,
With water howling and vexed between,
While the scooping whirl of the pool be-
  neath
Seems an open throat, with its granite
  teeth !

But Mogg Megone never trembled yet
Wherever his eye or his foot was set.
He is watchful : each form in the moon-
  light dim,
Of rock or of tree, is seen of him :
He listens ; each sound from afar is
  caught,
The faintest shiver of leaf and limb :
But he sees not the waters, which foam
  and fret,
Whose moonlit spray has his moccasin
  wet, —
And the roar of their rushing, he hears
  it not.

The moonlight, through the open bough
  Of the gnarl'd beech, whose naked
    root
  Coils like a serpent at his foot,
Falls, checkered, on the Indian's brow.
His head is bare, save only where
Waves in the wind one lock of hair,
  Reserved for him, whoe'er he be,
More mighty than Megone in strife,
  When breast to breast and knee to
    knee,
Above the fallen warrior's life
Gleams, quick and keen, the scalping-
  knife.

Megone hath his knife and hatchet and
  gun,
And his gaudy and tasselled blanket
  on :
His knife hath a handle with gold inlaid,
And magic words on its polished blade, —
'T was the gift of Castine [2] to Mogg Me-
  gone,
For a scalp or twain from the Yengees
  torn :
His gun was the gift of the Tarrantine,
  And Modocawando's wives had strung
The brass and the beads, which tinkle
  and shine
On the polished breach, and broad bright
  line
  Of beaded wampum around it hung.

What seeks Megone ?   His foes are
            near, —
    Grey Jocelyn's [3] eye is never sleeping,
And the garrison lights are burning
    clear,
    Where Phillips' [4] men their watch are
            keeping.
Let him hie him away through the dank
    river fog,
    Never rustling the boughs nor dis-
            placing the rocks,
For the eyes and the ears which are
            watching for Mogg
    Are keener than those of the wolf or
            the fox.

He starts, — there 's a rustle among the
            leaves :
    Another, — the click of his gun is
            heard !
A footstep, — is it the step of Cleaves,
    With Indian blood on his English
            sword ?
Steals Harmon [5] down from the sands of
            York,
With hand of iron and foot of cork ?
Has Scamman, versed in Indian wile,
For vengeance left his vine-hung isle ? [6]
Hark ! at that whistle, soft and low,
    How lights the eye of Mogg Megone !
A smile gleams o'er his dusky brow, —
    " Boon welcome, Johnny Bonython !"

Out steps, with cautious foot and slow,
And quick, keen glances to and fro,
    The hunted outlaw, Bonython ! [7]
A low, lean, swarthy man is he,
With blanket-garb and buskined knee,
    And naught of English fashion on ;
For he hates the race from whence he
            sprung,
And he couches his words in the Indian
            tongue.

" Hush, — let the Sachem's voice be
            weak ;
The water-rat shall hear him speak, —
The owl shall whoop in the white man's
            ear,
That Mogg Megone, with his scalps, is
            here !"
He pauses, — dark, over cheek and
            brow,
A flush, as of shame, is stealing now :
" Sachem !" he says, " let me have the
            land,
Which stretches away upon either hand,

As far about as my feet can stray
In the half of a gentle summer's day,
    From the leaping brook [8] to the Saco
            river,
    And the fair-haired girl, thou hast sought
            of me,
Shall sit in the Sachem's wigwam, and be
    The wife of Mogg Megone forever."

There 's a sudden light in the Indian's
            glance,
    A moment's trace of powerful feeling,
Of love or triumph, or both perchance,
    Over his proud, calm features steal-
            ing.
"The words of my father are very good ;
He shall have the land, and water, and
            wood ;
And he who harms the Sagamore John,
Shall feel the knife of Mogg Megone ;
But the fawn of the Yengees shall sleep
            on my breast,
And the bird of the clearing shall sing
            in my nest."

"But, father !" — and the Indian's hand
    Falls gently on the white man's arm,
And with a smile as shrewdly bland
    As the deep voice is slow and calm, —
" Where is my father's singing-bird, —
    The sunny eye, and sunset hair ?
I know I have my father's word,
    And that his word is good and fair ;
    But will my father tell me where
Megone shall go and look for his
            bride ? —
For he sees her not by her father's side."

The dark, stern eye of Bonython
    Flashes over the features of Mogg Me-
            gone,
    In one of those glances which search
            within ;
But the stolid calm of the Indian alone
    Remains where the trace of emotion
            has been.
" Does the Sachem doubt ?   Let him
            go with me,
And the eyes of the Sachem his bride
            shall see."

Cautious and slow, with pauses oft,
And watchful eyes and whispers soft,
The twain are stealing through the wood,
Leaving the downward-rushing flood,
Whose deep and solemn roar behind
Grows fainter on the evening wind.

Hark ! — is that the angry howl
  Of the wolf, the hills among ? —
Or the hooting of the owl,
  On his leafy cradle swung ? —
Quickly glancing, to and fro,
Listening to each sound they go
Round the columns of the pine,
  Indistinct, in shadow, seeming
Like some old and pillared shrine ;
With the soft and white moonshine,
  Round the foliage-tracery shed
Of each column's branching head,
  For its lamps of worship gleaming !
And the sounds awakened there,
  In the pine-leaves fine and small,
  Soft and sweetly musical,
By the fingers of the air,
For the anthem's dying fall
Lingering round some temple's wall !
Niche and cornice round and round
Wailing like the ghost of sound !
Is not Nature's worship thus,
  Ceaseless ever, going on ?
Hath it not a voice for us
  In the thunder, or the tone
Of the leaf-harp faint and small,
  Speaking to the unsealed ear
  Words of blended love and fear,
Of the mighty Soul of all ?

Naught had the twain of thoughts like
  these
As they wound along through the
  crowded trees,
Where never had rung the axeman's stroke
On the gnarled trunk of the rough-barked
  oak ; —
Climbing the dead tree's mossy log,
  Breaking the mesh of the bramble fine,
  Turning aside the wild grapevine,
And lightly crossing the quaking bog
Whose surface shakes at the leap of the
  frog,
And out of whose pools the ghostly fog
  Creeps into the chill moonshine !
Yet, even that Indian's ear had heard
The preaching of the Holy Word :
Sanchekantacket's isle of sand
Was once his father's hunting land,
Where zealous Hiacoomes [9] stood, —
The wild apostle of the wood,
Shook from his soul the fear of harm,
And trampled on the Powwaw's charm ;
Until the wizard's curses hung
Suspended on his palsying tongue,
And the fierce warrior, grim and tall,
Trembled before the forest Paul !

A cottage hidden in the wood, —
  Red through its seams a light is glowing,
On rock and bough and tree-trunk rude,
  A narrow lustre throwing.
" Who 's there ? " a clear, firm voice
  demands ;
  " Hold, Ruth, — 't is I, the Saga-
  more ! "
Quick, at the summons, hasty hands
  Unclose the bolted door ;
And on the outlaw's daughter shine
The flashes of the kindled pine.

Tall and erect the maiden stands,
  Like some young priestess of the wood,
  The freeborn child of Solitude,
  And bearing still the wild and rude,
Yet noble trace of Nature's hands.
Her dark brown cheek has caught its stain
More from the sunshine than the rain ;
Yet, where her long fair hair is parting,
A pure white brow into light is starting ;
And, where the folds of her blanket sever,
Are a neck and bosom as white as ever
The foam-wreaths rise on the leaping river.
But in the convulsive quiver and grip
Of the muscles around her bloodless lip,
  There is something painful and sad to
  see ;
And her eye has a glance more sternly
  wild
Than even that of a forest child
  In its fearless and untamed freedom
  should be.
Yet, seldom in hall or court are seen
So queenly a form and so noble a mien,
  As freely and smiling she welcomes
  them there, —
Her outlawed sire and Mogg Megone :
  " Pray, father, how does thy hunting
  fare ?
  And, Sachem, say, — does Scamman
  wear,
In spite of thy promise, a scalp of his
  own ? "
Hurried and light is the maiden's tone ;
  But a fearful meaning lurks within
Her glance, as it questions the eye of
  Megone, —
  An awful meaning of guilt and sin ! —
The Indian hath opened his blanket, and
  there
Hangs a human scalp by its long damp
  hair !
With hand upraised, with quick drawn
  breath,
She meets that ghastly sign of death.

In one long, glassy, spectral stare
The enlarging eye is fastened there,
As if that mesh of pale brown hair
  Had power to change at sight alone,
Even as the fearful locks which wound
Medusa's fatal forehead round,
  The gazer into stone.
With such a look Herodias read
The features of the bleeding head,
So looked the mad Moor on his dead,
Or the young Cenci as she stood,
O'er-dabbled with a father's blood !

Look !—feeling melts that frozen glance,
It moves that marble countenance,
As if at once within her strove
Pity with shame, and hate with love.
The Past recalls its joy and pain,
Old memories rise before her brain, —
The lips which love's embraces met,
The hand her tears of parting wet,
The voice whose pleading tones beguiled
The pleased ear of the forest-child, —
And tears she may no more repress
Reveal her lingering tenderness.

O, woman wronged can cherish hate
  More deep and dark than manhood may ;
But when the mockery of Fate
  Hath left Revenge its chosen way,
And the fell curse, which years have
    nursed,
Full on the spoiler's head hath burst, —
When all her wrong, and shame, and pain,
Burns fiercely on his heart and brain, —
Still lingers something of the spell
  Which bound her to the traitor's
    bosom, —
Still, midst the vengeful fires of hell,
  Some flowers of old affection blossom.

John Bonython's eyebrows together are
    drawn
With a fierce expression of wrath and
    scorn, —
He hoarsely whispers, " Ruth, beware !
  Is this the time to be playing the fool, —
Crying over a paltry lock of hair,
  Like a love-sick girl at school ? —
Curse on it !—an Indian can see and
    hear :
Away, — and prepare our evening cheer !"

How keenly the Indian is watching now
Her tearful eye and her varying brow, —
  With a serpent eye, which kindles
    and burns,

Like a fiery star in the upper air :
On sire and daughter his fierce glance
    turns : —
  " Has my old white father a scalp to
    spare ?
  For his young one loves the pale
    brown hair
Of the scalp of an English dog far more
Than Mogg Megone, or his wigwam floor ;
  Go, — Mogg is wise : he will keep his
    land, —
  And Sagamore John, when he feels
    with his hand,
Shall miss his scalp where it grew before.'

The moment's gust of grief is gone, —
  The lip is clenched, — the tears are
    still, —
God pity thee, Ruth Bonython !
  With what a strength of will
Are nature's feelings in thy breast,
As with an iron hand, repressed !
And how, upon that nameless woe,
Quick as the pulse can come and go,
While shakes the unsteadfast knee, and
    yet
The bosom heaves, — the eye is wet, —
Has thy dark spirit power to stay
The heart's wild current on its way ?
  And whence that baleful strength of
    guile,
Which over that still working brow
And tearful eye and cheek can throw
  The mockery of a smile ?
Warned by her father's blackening frown,
With one strong effort crushing down
Grief, hate, remorse, she meets again
  The savage murderer's sullen gaze,
  And scarcely look or tone betrays
How the heart strives beneath its chain.

" Is the Sachem angry, — angry with
    Ruth,
Because she cries with an ache in her
    tooth,[10]
Which would make a Sagamore jump
    and cry,
And look about with a woman's eye ?
No, — Ruth will sit in the Sachem's
    door
And braid the mats for his wigwam floor,
And broil his fish and tender fawn,
And weave his wampum, and grind his
    corn, —
For she loves the brave and the wise,
    and none
Are braver and wiser than Mogg Megone !"

The Indian's brow is clear once more :
　　With grave, calm face, and half-shut
　　　eye,
He sits upon the wigwam floor,
　　And watches Ruth go by,
Intent upon her household care ;
　　And ever and anon, the while,
Or on the maiden, or her fare,
Which smokes in grateful promise there,
　　Bestows his quiet smile.

Ah, Mogg Megone ! — what dreams are
　　thine,
　　But those which love's own fancies
　　　dress, —
　　The sum of Indian happiness ! —
A wigwam, where the warm sunshine
Looks in among the groves of pine, —
A stream, where, round thy light canoe,
The trout and salmon dart in view,
And the fair girl, before thee now,
Spreading thy mat with hand of snow,
Or plying, in the dews of morn,
Her hoe amidst thy patch of corn,
Or offering up, at eve, to thee,
Thy birchen dish of hominy !

From the rude board of Bonython,
Venison and succotash have gone, —
For long these dwellers of the wood
Have felt the gnawing want of food.
But untasted of Ruth is the frugal cheer, —
With head averted, yet ready ear,
She stands by the side of her austere
　　sire,
Feeding, at times, the unequal fire
With the yellow knots of the pitch-pine
　　tree,
Whose flaring light, as they kindle, falls
On the cottage-roof, and its black log
　　walls,
And over its inmates three.

From Sagamore Bonython's hunting flask
　　The fire-water burns at the lip of Me-
　　　gone :
" Will the Sachem hear what his father
　　shall ask ?
　　Will he make his mark, that it may
　　　be known,
On the speaking-leaf, that he gives the
　　land,
From the Sachem's own, to his father's
　　hand ? "
The fire-water shines in the Indian's eyes,
　　As he rises, the white man's bidding
　　　to do :

" Wuttamuttata — weekan ! [11] Mogg is
　　wise, —
　　For the water he drinks is strong and
　　　new, —
Mogg's heart is great ! — will he shut his
　　hand,
When his father asks for a little land ?" —
With unsteady fingers, the Indian has
　　drawn
　　On the parchment the shape of a
　　　hunter's bow,
" Boon water, — boon water, — Saga-
　　more John !
　　Wuttamuttata, — weekan ! our hearts
　　will grow ! "
He drinks yet deeper, — he mutters
　　low, —
He reels on his bear-skin to and fro, —
His head falls down on his naked
　　breast, —
He struggles, and sinks to a drunken rest.

" Humph — drunk as a beast ! " — and
　　Bonython's brow
　　Is darker than ever with evil thought —
" The fool has signed his warrant ; but
　　how
　　And when shall the deed be wrought ?
Speak, Ruth ! why, what the devil is
　　there,
To fix thy gaze in that empty air ? —
Speak, Ruth ! by my soul, if I thought
　　that tear,
Which shames thyself and our purpose
　　here,
Were shed for that cursed and pale-
　　faced dog,
Whose green scalp hangs from the belt
　　of Mogg,
　　And whose beastly soul is in Satan's
　　keeping, —
This — this ! " — he dashes his hand
　　upon
The rattling stock of his loaded gun, —
　　" Should send thee with him to do
　　　thy weeping ! "

" Father ! " — the eye of Bonython
Sinks at that low, sepulchral tone,
Hollow and deep, as it were spoken
By the unmoving tongue of death, —
Or from some statue's lips had broken, —
　　A sound without a breath !
" Father ! — my life I value less
Than yonder fool his gaudy dress ;
And how it ends it matters not,
By heart-break or by rifle-shot ;

But spare awhile the scoff and threat, —
Our business is not finished yet."

"True, true, my girl, — I only meant
To draw up again the bow unbent.
Harm thee, my Ruth ! I only sought
To frighten off thy gloomy thought ;
Come, — let 's be friends ! "   He seeks
        to clasp
His daughter's cold, damp hand in his.
Ruth startles from her father's grasp,
As if each nerve and muscle felt,
Instinctively, the touch of guilt,
Through all their subtle sympathies.

He points her to the sleeping Mogg :
" What shall be done with yonder dog ?
Scamman is dead, and revenge is thine, —
The deed is signed and the land is mine ;
    And this drunken fool is of use no more,
Save as thy hopeful bridegroom, and
        sooth,
'T were Christian mercy to finish him,
        Ruth,
Now, while he lies like a beast on our
        floor, —
If not for thine, at least for his sake,
Rather than let the poor dog awake
To drain my flask, and claim as his bride
Such a forest devil to run by his side, —
Such a Wetuomanit [12] as thou wouldst
        make ! "

He laughs at his jest.   Hush — what is
        there ? —
    The sleeping Indian is striving to rise,
    With his knife in his hand, and glar-
        ing eyes ! —
" Wagh ! — Mogg will have the pale-
        face's hair,
    For his knife is sharp, and his fingers
        can help
The hair to pull and the skin to peel, —
Let him cry like a woman and twist like
        an eel,
    The great Captain Scamman must lose
        his scalp !
And Ruth, when she sees it, shall dance
        with Mogg."
His eyes are fixed, — but his lips draw
        in, —
With a low, hoarse chuckle, and fiendish
        grin, —
    And he sinks again, like a senseless log.

Ruth does not speak, — she does not stir ;
But she gazes down on the murderer,

Whose broken and dreamful slumbers tell
Too much for her ear of that deed of hell
She sees the knife, with its slaughter red,
And the dark fingers clenching the bear-
        skin bed !
What thoughts of horror and madness
        whirl
Through the burning brain of that fallen
        girl !

John Bonython lifts his gun to his eye,
    Its muzzle is close to the Indian's ear, —
But he drops it again.   " Some one may
        be nigh,
    And I would not that even the wolves
        should hear."

He draws his knife from its deer-skin
        belt, —
    Its edge with his fingers is slowly felt ;—
Kneeling down on one knee, by the In-
        dian's side,
From his throat he opens the blanket
        wide ;
And twice or thrice he feebly essays
A trembling hand with the knife to raise.

"I cannot," — he mutters, — " did he
        not save
My life from a cold and wintry grave,
When the storm came down from Agioo-
        chook,
And the north-wind howled, and the
        tree-tops shook, —
And I strove, in the drifts of the rush-
        ing snow,
Till my knees grew weak and I could
        not go,
And I felt the cold to my vitals creep,
And my heart's blood stiffen, and pulses
        sleep !
I cannot strike him — Ruth Bonython !
In the Devil's name, tell me — what 's
        to be done ?"

O, when the soul, once pure and high,
Is stricken down from Virtue's sky,
As, with the downcast star of morn,
Some gems of light are with it drawn, —
And, through its night of darkness, play
Some tokens of its primal day, —
Some lofty feelings linger still, —
    The strength to dare, the nerve to meet
    Whatever threatens with defeat
Its all-indomitable will ! —
But lacks the mean of mind and heart,
    Though eager for the gains of crime,
    Oft, at his chosen place and time,

The strength to bear his evil part ;
And, shielded by his very Vice,
Escapes from Crime by Cowardice.

Ruth starts erect, — with bloodshot eye,
And lips drawn tight across her teeth,
Showing their locked embrace beneath,
In the red firelight :— "Mogg must die !
Give me the knife !" — The outlaw turns,
Shuddering in heart and limb, away, —
But, fitfully there, the hearth-fire burns,
And he sees on the wall strange shad-
ows play.
A lifted arm, a tremulous blade.
Are dimly pictured in light and shade,
Plunging down in the darkness. Hark,
that cry
Again — and again — he sees it fall, —
That shadowy arm down the lighted wall !
He hears quick footsteps — a shape
flits by —
The door on its rusted hinges creaks :—
"Ruth — daughter Ruth !" the outlaw
shrieks.
But no sound comes back, — he is stand-
ing alone
By the mangled corse of Mogg Megone !

PART II.

'T is morning over Norridgewock, —
On tree and wigwam, wave and rock.
Bathed in the autumnal sunshine, stirred
At intervals by breeze and bird,
And wearing all the hues which glow
In heaven's own pure and perfect bow,
That glorious picture of the air,
Which summer's light-robed angel forms
On the dark ground of fading storms,
With pencil dipped in sunbeams
there, —
And, stretching out, on either hand,
O'er all that wide and unshorn land,
Till, weary of its gorgeousness,
The aching and the dazzled eye
Rests, gladdened, on the calm blue sky, —
Slumbers the mighty wilderness !
The oak, upon the windy hill,
Its dark green burthen upward
heaves —
The hemlock broods above its rill,
Its cone-like foliage darker still,
Against the birch's graceful stem,
And the rough walnut-bough receives
The sun upon its crowded leaves,
Each colored like a topaz gem ,

And the tall maple wears with them
The coronal, which autumn gives,
The brief, bright sign of ruin near,
The hectic of a dying year !

The hermit priest, who lingers now
On the Bald Mountain's shrubless brow,
The gray and thunder-smitten pile
Which marks afar the Desert Isle,[13]
While gazing on the scene below,
May half forget the dreams of home,
That nightly with his slumbers come, —
The tranquil skies of sunny France,
The peasant's harvest song and dance,
The vines around the hillsides wreathing
The soft airs midst their clusters breath-
ing,
The wings which dipped, the stars which
shone
Within thy bosom, blue Garonne !
And round the Abbey's shadowed wall,
At morning spring and even-fall,
Sweet voices in the still air singing, —
The chant of many a holy hymn, —
The solemn bell of vespers ringing, —
And hallowed torchlight falling dim
On pictured saint and seraphim !
For here beneath him lies unrolled,
Bathed deep in morning's flood of gold,
A vision gorgeous as the dream
Of the beatified may seem,
When, as his Church's legends say,
Borne upward in ecstatic bliss,
The rapt enthusiast soars away
Unto a brighter world than this :
A mortal's glimpse beyond the pale, —
A moment's lifting of the veil !

Far eastward o'er the lovely bay,
Penobscot's clustered wigwams lay ;
And gently from that Indian town
The verdant hillside slopes adown,
To where the sparkling waters play
Upon the yellow sands below ;
And shooting round the winding shores
Of narrow capes, and isles which lie
Slumbering to ocean's lullaby, —
With birchen boat and glancing oars,
The red men to their fishing go ;
While from their planting ground is borne
The treasure of the golden corn,
By laughing girls, whose dark eyes glow
Wild through the locks which o'er them
flow.
The wrinkled squaw, whose toil is done,
Sits on her bear-skin in the sun,
Watching the huskers, with a smile

For each full ear which swells the pile ;
And the old chief, who nevermore
May bend the bow or pull the oar,
Smokes gravely in his wigwam door,
Or slowly shapes, with axe of stone,
The arrow-head from flint and bone.

Beneath the westward turning eye
A thousand wooded islands lie, —
Gems of the waters ! — with each hue
Of brightness set in ocean's blue.
Each bears aloft its tuft of trees
    Touched by the pencil of the frost,
And, with the motion of each breeze,
    A moment seen, — a moment lost, —
    Changing and blent, confused and
        tossed,
The brighter with the darker crossed,
Their thousand tints of beauty glow
Down in the restless waves below,
    And tremble in the sunny skies,
As if, from waving bough to bough,
    Flitted the birds of paradise.
There sleep Placentia's group, — and
        there
Père Breteaux marks the hour of prayer ;
And there, beneath the sea-worn cliff,
    On which the Father's hut is seen,
The Indian stays his rocking skiff,
    And peers the hemlock-boughs be-
        tween,
Half trembling, as he seeks to look
Upon the Jesuit's Cross and Book.[14]
There, gloomily against the sky
The Dark Isles rear their summits high ;
And Desert Rock, abrupt and bare,
Lifts its gray turrets in the air, —
Seen from afar, like some stronghold
Built by the ocean kings of old ;
And, faint as smoke-wreath white and
        thin,
Swells in the north vast Katahdin :
And, wandering from its marshy feet,
The broad Penobscot comes to meet
    And mingle with his own bright bay.
Slow sweep his dark and gathering floods,
Arched over by the ancient woods,
Which Time, in those dim solitudes,
    Wielding the dull axe of Decay,
    Alone hath ever shorn away.

Not thus, within the woods which hide
The beauty of thy azure tide,
    And with their falling timbers block
Thy broken currents, Kennebec !
Gazes the white man on the wreck
    Of the down-trodden Norridgewock, —

In one lone village hemmed at length,
In battle shorn of half their strength,
Turned, like the panther in his lair,
    With his fast-flowing life-blood wet,
For one last struggle of despair,
    Wounded and faint, but tameless yet ¹
Unreaped, upon the planting lands,
The scant, neglected harvest stands :
    No shout is there, — no dance, — no
        song :
The aspect of the very child
Scowls with a meaning sad and wild
    Of bitterness and wrong.
The almost infant Norridgewock
Essays to lift the tomahawk ;
And plucks his father's knife away,
To mimic, in his frightful play,
    The scalping of an English foe :
Wreathes on his lip a horrid smile,
Burns, like a snake's, his small eye, while
    Some bough or sapling meets his blow.
The fisher, as he drops his line,
Starts, when he sees the hazels quiver
Along the margin of the river,
Looks up and down the rippling tide,
And grasps the firelock at his side.
For Bomazeen [15] from Tacconock
Has sent his runners to Norridgewock,
With tidings that Moulton and Harmon
        of York
    Far up the river have come :
They have left their boats, — they have
        entered the wood,
And filled the depths of the solitude
    With the sound of the ranger's drum.

On the brow of a hill, which slopes to
        meet
The flowing river, and bathe its feet, —
The bare-washed rock, and the drooping
        grass,
And the creeping vine, as the waters
        pass, —
A rude and unshapely chapel stands,
Built up in that wild by unskilled hands,
Yet the traveller knows it a place of
        prayer,
For the holy sign of the cross is there :
And should he chance at that place to be,
    Of a Sabbath morn, or some hallowed
        day,
When prayers are made and masses are
        said,
Some for the living and some for the dead,
Well might that traveller start to see
    The tall dark forms, that take their way
From the birch canoe, on the river-shore,

And the forest paths, to that chapel door;
And marvel to mark the naked knees
   And the dusky foreheads bending there,
While, in coarse white vesture, over these
   In blessing or in prayer,
Stretching abroad his thin pale hands,
Like a shrouded ghost, the Jesuit[16] stands.

Two forms are now in that chapel dim,
   The Jesuit, silent and sad and pale,
   Anxiously heeding some fearful tale,
Which a stranger is telling him.
That stranger's garb is soiled and torn,
And wet with dew and loosely worn ;
Her fair neglected hair falls down
O'er cheeks with wind and sunshine
      brown ;
Yet still, in that disordered face,
The Jesuit's cautious eye can trace
Those elements of former grace
Which, half effaced, seem scarcely less,
Even now, than perfect loveliness.

With drooping head, and voice so low
   That scarce it meets the Jesuit's ears, —
While through her clasped fingers flow,
From the heart's fountain, hot and slow,
   Her penitential tears, —
She tells the story of the woe
   And evil of her years.

"O father, bear with me ; my heart
   Is sick and death-like, and my brain
   Seems girdled with a fiery chain,
Whose scorching links will never part,
   And never cool again.
Bear with me while I speak, — but turn
   Away that gentle eye, the while, —
The fires of guilt more fiercely burn
   Beneath its holy smile ;
For half I fancy I can see
My mother's sainted look in thee.

"My dear lost mother ! sad and pale,
   Mournfully sinking day by day,
And with a hold on life as frail
   As frosted leaves, that, thin and gray,
   Hang feebly on their parent spray,
And tremble in the gale ;
Yet watching o'er my childishness
With patient fondness, — not the less
For all the agony which kept
Her blue eye wakeful, while I slept ;
And checking every tear and groan
That haply might have waked my own,
And bearing still, without offence,
My idle words, and petulance ;

Reproving with a tear, — and, while
The tooth of pain was keenly preying
Upon her very heart, repaying
   My brief repentance with a smile.

"O, in her meek, forgiving eye
   There was a brightness not of mirth.
A light whose clear intensity
   Was borrowed not of earth.
Along her cheek a deepening red
Told where the feverish hectic fed ;
   And yet, each fatal token gave
To the mild beauty of her face
A newer and a dearer grace,
   Unwarning of the grave.
'T was like the hue which Autumn gives
To yonder changed and dying leaves,
   Breathed over by his frosty breath ;
Scarce can the gazer feel that this
Is but the spoiler's treacherous kiss,
   The mocking-smile of Death !

"Sweet were the tales she used to tell
   When summer's eve was dear to us,
And, fading from the darkening dell,
The glory of the sunset fell
   On wooded Agamenticus, —
When, sitting by our cottage wall,
The murmur of the Saco's fall,
   And the south-wind's expiring sighs,
Came, softly blending, on my ear,
With the low tones I loved to hear :
   Tales of the pure, — the good, — the
      wise, —
The holy men and maids of old,
In the all-sacred pages told ; —
Of Rachel, stooped at Haran's fount-
   ains,
   Amid her father's thirsty flock,
Beautiful to her kinsman seeming
As the bright angels of his dreaming,
   On Padan-aran's holy rock ;
Of gentle Ruth, — and her who kept
Her awful vigil on the mountains,
By Israel's virgin daughters wept ;
Of Miriam, with her maidens, singing
   The song for grateful Israel meet,
While every crimson wave was bringing
   The spoils of Egypt at her feet ;
Of her, — Samaria's humble daughter,
Who paused to hear, beside her well,
   Lessons of love and truth, which fell
Softly as Shiloh's flowing water ;
   And saw, beneath his pilgrim guise,
The Promised One, so long foretold
By holy seer and bard of old,
   Revealed before her wondering eyes!

"Slowly she faded.   Day by day
Her step grew weaker in our hall,
And fainter, at each even-fall,
    Her sad voice died away.
Yet on her thin, pale lip, the while,
Sat Resignation's holy smile :
And even my father checked his tread,
And hushed his voice, beside her bed :
Beneath the calm and sad rebuke
Of her meek eye's imploring look,
The scowl of hate his brow forsook,
    And in his stern and gloomy eye,
At times, a few unwonted tears
Wet the dark lashes, which for years
    Hatred and pride had kept so dry.

"Calm as a child to slumber soothed,
As if an angel's hand had smoothed
    The still, white features into rest,
Silent and cold, without a breath
    To stir the drapery on her breast,
Pain, with its keen and poisoned fang,
The horror of the mortal pang,
The suffering look her brow had worn,
The fear, the strife, the anguish gone, —
    She slept at last in death !

"O, tell me, father, _can_ the dead
    Walk on the earth, and look on us,
And lay upon the living's head
    Their blessing or their curse ?
For, O, last night she stood by me,
    As I lay beneath the woodland tree ! "

The Jesuit crosses himself in awe, —
"Jesu ! what was it my daughter saw ? "

"_She_ came to me last night.
    The dried leaves did not feel her
        tread ;
She stood by me in the wan moonlight,
    In the white robes of the dead !
Pale, and very mournfully
She bent her light form over me.
I heard no sound, I felt no breath
Breathe o'er me from that face of death :
Its blue eyes rested on my own,
Rayless and cold as eyes of stone ;
Yet, in their fixed, unchanging gaze,
Something, which spoke of early days, —
A sadness in their quiet glare,
As if love's smile were frozen there, —
Came o'er me with an icy thrill ;
O God ! I feel its presence still ! "

The Jesuit makes the holy sign, —
"How passed the vision, daughter mine ? "

"All dimly in the wan moonshine,
As a wreath of mist will twist and twine,
And scatter, and melt into the light, —
So scattering, — melting on my sight,
    The pale, cold vision passed ;
But those sad eyes were fixed on mine
    Mournfully to the last."

"God help thee, daughter, tell me why
That spirit passed before thine eye ! "

"Father, I know not, save it be
    That deeds of mine have summoned her
    From the unbreathing sepulchre,
To leave her last rebuke with me.
Ah, woe for me ! my mother died
Just at the moment when I stood
Close on the verge of womanhood,
A child in everything beside ;
And when my wild heart needed most
Her gentle counsels, they were lost.

"My father lived a stormy life,
Of frequent change and daily strife ;
And — God forgive him ! — left his child
To feel, like him, a freedom wild ;
To love the red man's dwelling-place,
    The birch boat on his shaded floods.
The wild excitement of the chase
    Sweeping the ancient woods,
The camp-fire, blazing on the shore
    Of the still lakes, the clear stream where
The idle fisher sets his wear,
Or angles in the shade, far more
    Than that restraining awe I felt
Beneath my gentle mother's care,
    When nightly at her knee I knelt,
With childhood's simple prayer.

"There came a change.   The wild, glad
        mood
    Of unchecked freedom passed.
Amid the ancient solitude
Of unshorn grass and waving wood,
    And waters glancing bright and fast,
A softened voice was in my ear,
Sweet as those lulling sounds and fine
The hunter lifts his head to hear,
Now far and faint, now full and near —
    The murmur of the wind-swept pine.
A manly form was ever nigh,
A bold, free hunter, with an eye
    Whose dark, keen glance had power
        to wake
Both fear and love, — to awe and charm ;
    'T was as the wizard rattlesnake,
Whose evil glances lure to harm —

Whose cold and small and glittering
    eye,
And brilliant coil, and changing dye,
Draw, step by step, the gazer near,
With drooping wing and cry of fear,
Yet powerless all to turn away,
A conscious, but a willing prey !

"Fear, doubt, thought, life itself, erelong
Merged in one feeling deep and strong.
Faded the world which I had known,
    A poor vain shadow, cold and waste ;
In the warm present bliss alone
    Seemed I of actual life to taste.
Fond longings dimly understood,
The glow of passion's quickening blood,
And cherished fantasies which press
The young lip with a dream's caress, —
The heart's forecast and prophecy
Took form and life before my eye,
Seen in the glance which met my own,
Heard in the soft and pleading tone,
Felt in the arms around me cast,
And warm heart-pulses beating fast.
Ah ! scarcely yet to God above
With deeper trust, with stronger love,
Has prayerful saint his meek heart
    lent,
Or cloistered nun at twilight bent,
Than I, before a human shrine,
As mortal and as frail as mine,
With heart, and soul, and mind, and form,
Knelt madly to a fellow-worm.

"Full soon, upon that dream of sin,
An awful light came bursting in.
The shrine was cold at which I knelt,
    The idol of that shrine was gone ;
A humbled thing of shame and guilt,
    Outcast, and spurned and lone,
Wrapt in the shadows of my crime,
    With withering heart and burning
    brain,
    And tears that fell like fiery rain,
I passed a fearful time.

"There came a voice — it checked the
    tear —
    In heart and soul it wrought a change ; —
My father's voice was in my ear ;
    It whispered of revenge !
A new and fiercer feeling swept
    All lingering tenderness away ;
And tiger passions, which had slept
    In childhood's better day,
Unknown, unfelt, arose at length
In all their own demoniac strength.

"A youthful warrior of the wild,
By words deceived, by smiles beguiled,
Of crime the cheated instrument,
Upon our fatal errands went.
    Through camp and town and wilderness
He tracked his victim ; and, at last,
Just when the tide of hate had passed,
And milder thoughts came warm and fast,
Exulting, at my feet he cast
    The bloody token of success.

"O God ! with what an awful power
    I saw the buried past uprise,
And gather, in a single hour,
    Its ghost-like memories !
And then I felt — alas ! too late —
That underneath the mask of hate,
That shame and guilt and wrong had
    thrown
O'er feelings which they might not own,
    The heart's wild love had known no
    change ;
And still that deep and hidden love,
With its first fondness, wept above
    The victim of its own revenge !
There lay the fearful scalp, and there
The blood was on its pale brown hair !
I thought not of the victim's scorn,
    I thought not of his baleful guile,
My deadly wrong, my outcast name,
The characters of sin and shame
On heart and forehead drawn ;
    I only saw that victim's smile, —
The still, green places where we met, —
    The moonlit branches, dewy wet ;
I only felt, I only heard
The greeting and the parting word, —
The smile, — the embrace, — the tone,
    which made
An Eden of the forest shade.

"And oh, with what a loathing eye,
    With what a deadly hate, and deep,
I saw that Indian murderer lie
    Before me, in his drunken sleep !
What though for me the deed was done,
And words of mine had sped him on !
Yet when he murmured, as he slept,
    The horrors of that deed of blood,
The tide of utter madness swept
    O'er brain and bosom, like a flood.
And, father, with this hand of mine —"
    "Ha ! what didst thou ?" the Jesuit
    cries,
Shuddering, as smitten with sudden pain,
    And shading, with one thin hand, his
    eyes,

With the other he makes the holy sign.
" — I smote him as I would a worm ; —
With heart as steeled, with nerves as
    firm :
He never woke again !"

"Woman of sin and blood and shame,
Speak, — I would know that victim's
    name."

"Father," she gasped, "a chieftain,
    known
As Saco's Sachem, — MOGG MEGONE !"

Pale priest ! What proud and lofty
    dreams,
What keen desires, what cherished
    schemes,
What hopes, that time may not recall,
Are darkened by that chieftain's fall !
Was he not pledged, by cross and vow,
To lift the hatchet of his sire,
And, round his own, the Church's foe,
To light the avenging fire ?
Who now the Tarrantine shall wake,
For thine and for the Church's sake ?
Who summon to the scene
Of conquest and unsparing strife,
And vengeance dearer than his life,
The fiery-souled Castine ? [17]
Three backward steps the Jesuit takes, —
His long, thin frame as ague shakes ;
And loathing hate is in his eye,
As from his lips these words of fear
Fall hoarsely on the maiden's ear, —
    "The soul that sinneth shall surely
    die !"

She stands, as stands the stricken deer,
    Checked midway in the fearful chase,
When bursts, upon his eye and ear,
The gaunt, gray robber, baying near,
    Between him and his hiding-place ;
While still behind, with yell and blow,
Sweeps, like a storm, the coming foe.
"Save me, O holy man !" — her cry
    Fills all the void, as if a tongue,
Unseen, from rib and rafter hung,
Thrilling with mortal agony ;
Her hands are clasping the Jesuit's
    knee,
    And her eye looks fearfully into his
    own ; —
"Off, woman of sin ! — nay, touch not
    me
    With those fingers of blood ; — be-
    gone !"

With a gesture of horror, he spurns the
    form
That writhes at his feet like a trodden
    worm.

Ever thus the spirit must,
    Guilty in the sight of Heaven,
    With a keener woe be riven,
For its weak and sinful trust
In the strength of human dust ;
    And its anguish thrill afresh,
For each vain reliance given
    To the failing arm of flesh.

PART III.

AH, weary Priest ! — with pale hands
    pressed
    On thy throbbing brow of pain,
Baffled in thy life-long quest,
    Overworn with toiling vain,
How ill thy troubled musings fit
    The holy quiet of a breast
    With the Dove of Peace at rest,
Sweetly brooding over it.
Thoughts are thine which have no part
With the meek and pure of heart,
Undisturbed by outward things,
Resting in the heavenly shade,
By the overspreading wings
    Of the Blessed Spirit made.
Thoughts of strife and hate and wrong
Sweep thy heated brain along,
Fading hopes for whose success
    It were sin to breathe a prayer ; —
Schemes which Heaven may never
    bless, —
    Fears which darken to despair.
Hoary priest ! thy dream is done
Of a hundred red tribes won
    To the pale of Holy Church ;
And the heretic o'erthrown,
And his name no longer known,
And thy weary brethren turning,
Joyful from their years of mourning,
'Twixt the altar and the porch.
Hark ! what sudden sound is heard
    In the wood and in the sky,
Shriller than the scream of bird, —
    Than the trumpet's clang more
    high !
Every wolf-cave of the hills, —
    Forest arch and mountain gorge,
    Rock and dell, and river verge, —
With an answering echo thrills.
Well does the Jesuit know that cry.

Which summons the Norridgewock to
   die,
And tells that the foe of his flock is nigh.
He listens, and hears the rangers come,
With loud hurrah, and jar of drum,
And hurrying feet (for the chase is hot),
And the short, sharp sound of rifle shot,
And taunt and menace, — answered well
By the Indians' mocking cry and yell, —
The bark of dogs, — the squaw's mad
   scream, —
The dash of paddles along the stream, —
The whistle of shot as it cuts the leaves
Of the maples around the church's
   eaves, —
And the gride of hatchets fiercely
   thrown,
On wigwam-log and tree and stone.
Black with the grime of paint and dust,
  Spotted and streaked with human
   gore,
A grim and naked head is thrust
  Within the chapel-door.
"Ha — Bomazeen! — In God's name say,
What mean these sounds of bloody fray?"
Silent, the Indian points his hand
  To where across the echoing glen
Sweep Harmon's dreaded ranger-band,
  And Moulton with his men.
"Where are thy warriors, Bomazeen?
Where are De Rouville [18] and Castine,
And where the braves of Sawga's queen?"
"Let my father find the winter snow
Which the sun drank up long moons ago!
Under the falls of Tacconock,
The wolves are eating the Norridgewock;
Castine with his wives lies closely hid
Like a fox in the woods of Pemaquid!
On Sawga's banks the man of war
Sits in his wigwam like a squaw, —
Squando has fled, and Mogg Megone,
Struck by the knife of Sagamore John,
Lies stiff and stark and cold as a stone."

Fearfully over the Jesuit's face,
Of a thousand thoughts, trace after trace,
Like swift cloud-shadows, each other
  chase.
One instant, his fingers grasp his knife,
For a last vain struggle for cherished
  life, —
The next, he hurls the blade away,
And kneels at his altar's foot to pray;
Over his beads his fingers stray,
And he kisses the cross, and calls aloud
On the Virgin and her Son;
For terrible thoughts his memory crowd

Of evil seen and done, —
Of scalps brought home by his savage
  flock
From Casco and Sawga and Sagadahock
  In the Church's service won.

No shrift the gloomy savage brooks,
As scowling on the priest he looks:
"Cowesass — cowesass — tawhich wessa
  seen? [19]
Let my father look upon Bomazeen, —
My father's heart is the heart of a squaw,
But mine is so hard that it does not thaw;
Let my father ask his God to make
  A dance and a feast for a great saga-
   more,
When he paddles across the western lake,
  With his dogs and his squaws to the
   spirit's shore.
"Cowesass — cowesass — tawhich wessa-
  seen?
Let my father die like Bomazeen!"

Through the chapel's narrow doors,
  And through each window in the walls,
Round the priest and warrior pours
  The deadly shower of English balls.
Low on his cross the Jesuit falls;
While at his side the Norridgewock,
With failing breath, essays to mock
And menace yet the hated foe, —
Shakes his scalp-trophies to and fro
  Exultingly before their eyes, —
Till, cleft and torn by shot and blow,
  Defiant still, he dies.

"So fare all eaters of the frog!
Death to the Babylonish dog!
  Down with the beast of Rome!"
With shouts like these, around the dead,
Unconscious on his bloody bed,
  The rangers crowding come.
Brave men! the dead priest cannot hear
The unfeeling taunt, — the brutal jeer;—
Spurn — for he sees ye not — in wrath,
The symbol of your Saviour's death;
  Tear from his death-grasp, in your zeal,
And trample, as a thing accursed,
The cross he cherished in the dust:
  The dead man cannot feel!

Brutal alike in deed and word,
  With callous heart and hand of strife,
How like a fiend may man be made,
Plying the foul and monstrous trade
  Whose harvest-field is human life,
  Whose sickle is the reeking sword!

Quenching, with reckless hand in blood,
Sparks kindled by the breath of God ;
Urging the deathless soul, unshriven,
  Of open guilt or secret sin,
Before the bar of that pure Heaven
  The holy only enter in !
O, by the widow's sore distress,
The orphan's wailing wretchedness,
By Virtue struggling in the accursed
Embraces of polluting Lust,
By the fell discord of the Pit,
And the pained souls that people it,
And by the blessed peace which fills
  The Paradise of God forever,
Resting on all its holy hills,
  And flowing with its crystal river, —
Let Christian hands no longer bear
  In triumph on his crimson car
  The foul and idol god of war ;
No more the purple wreaths prepare
To bind amid his snaky hair ;
Nor Christian bards his glories tell,
Nor Christian tongues his praises swell.

Through the gun-smoke wreathing white,
Glimpses on the soldiers' sight
A thing of human shape I ween,
For a moment only seen,
With its loose hair backward streaming,
And its eyeballs madly gleaming,
Shrieking, like a soul in pain,
  From the world of light and breath,
Hurrying to its place again,
  Spectre-like it vanisheth !

Wretched girl ! one eye alone
Notes the way which thou hast gone.
That great Eye, which slumbers never,
Watching o'er a lost world ever,
Tracks thee over vale and mountain,
By the gushing forest-fountain,
Plucking from the vine its fruit,
Searching for the ground-nut's root,
Peering in the she-wolf's den,
Wading through the marshy fen,
Where the sluggish water-snake
Basks beside the sunny brake,
Coiling in his slimy bed,
Smooth and cold against thy tread, —
Purposeless, thy mazy way
Threading through the lingering day.
And at night securely sleeping
Where the dogwood's dews are weeping !
Still, though earth and man discard thee,
Doth thy Heavenly Father guard thee :
He who spared the guilty Cain,
  Even when a brother's blood,

Crying in the ear of God,
Gave the earth its primal stain, —
He whose mercy ever liveth,
Who repenting guilt forgiveth,
And the broken heart receiveth, —
Wanderer of the wilderness,
  Haunted, guilty, crazed, and wild,
He regardeth thy distress,
  And careth for his sinful child !

'T is springtime on the eastern hills !
Like torrents gush the summer rills ;
Through winter's moss and dry dead
    leaves
The bladed grass revives and lives,
Pushes the mouldering waste away,
And glimpses to the April day.
In kindly shower and sunshine bud
The branches of the dull gray wood ;
Out from its sunned and sheltered nooks
The blue eye of the violet looks ;
  The southwest wind is warmly blowing,
And odors from the springing grass,
The pine-tree and the sassafras,
  Are with it on its errands going.

A band is marching through the wood
Where rolls the Kennebec his flood, —
The warriors of the wilderness,
Painted, and in their battle dress ;
And with them one whose bearded cheek,
And white and wrinkled brow, bespeak
  A wanderer from the shores of France.
A few long locks of scattering snow
Beneath a battered morion flow,
And from the rivets of the vest
Which girds in steel his ample breast,
  The slanted sunbeams glance.
In the harsh outlines of his face
Passion and sin have left their trace ;
Yet, save worn brow and thin gray hair,
No signs of weary age are there.
  His step is firm, his eye is keen,
Nor years in broil and battle spent,
Nor toil, nor wounds, nor pain have bent
  The lordly frame of old Castine.

No purpose now of strife and blood
  Urges the hoary veteran on :
The fire of conquest and the mood
  Of chivalry have gone.
A mournful task is his, — to lay
  Within the earth the bones of those
Who perished in that fearful day,
When Norridgewock became the prey
  Of all unsparing foes.
Sadly and still, dark thoughts between,

Of coming vengeance mused Castine,
Of the fallen chieftain Bomazeen,
Who bade for him the Norridgewocks
Dig up their buried tomahawks
    For firm defence or swift attack ;
And him whose friendship formed the tie
    Which held the stern self-exile back
From lapsing into savagery ;
Whose garb and tone and kindly glance
    Recalled a younger, happier day,
    And prompted memory's fond essay,
    To bridge the mighty waste which lay
    Between his wild home and that gray,
Tall chateau of his native France,
Whose chapel bell, with far-heard din,
Ushered his birth-hour gayly in,
And counted with its solemn toll
The masses for his father's soul.

Hark ! from the foremost of the band
    Suddenly bursts the Indian yell ;
For now on the very spot they stand
    Where the Norridgewocks fighting fell.
No wigwam smoke is curling there ;
The very earth is scorched and bare :
And they pause and listen to catch a sound
    Of breathing life, — but there comes
        not one,
Save the fox's bark and the rabbit's bound ;
But here and there, on the blackened
        ground,
    White bones are glistening in the sun.
And where the house of prayer arose,
And the holy hymn, at daylight's close,

And the aged priest stood up to bless
The children of the wilderness,
There is naught save ashes sodden and
        dank ;
    And the birchen boats of the Nor-
        ridgewock,
    Tethered to tree and stump and rock,
Rotting along the river bank !

Blessed Mary ! who is she
Leaning against that maple-tree ?
The sun upon her face burns hot,
But the fixed eyelid moveth not ;
The squirrel's chirp is shrill and clear
From the dry bough above her ear ;
Dashing from rock and root its spray,
    Close at her feet the river rushes ;
    The blackbird's wing against her
        brushes,
    And sweetly through the hazel-bushes
    The robin's mellow music gushes ; —
God save her ! will she sleep alway ?

Castine hath bent him over the sleeper :
    "Wake, daughter, — wake !" — but
        she stirs no limb :
    The eye that looks on him is fixed and
        dim ;
And the sleep she is sleeping shall be no
        deeper,
    Until the angel's oath is said,
And the final blast of the trump goes forth
To the graves of the sea and the graves
        of earth.
    RUTH BONYTHON IS DEAD !

THE BRIDAL OF PENNACOOK.[20]

WE had been wandering for many days
Through the rough northern country.
        We had seen
The sunset, with its bars of purple cloud,
Like a new heaven, shine upward from
        the lake
Of Winnepiseogee ; and had felt
The sunrise breezes, midst the leafy isles
Which stoop their summer beauty to the
        lips
Of the bright waters.   We had checked
    our steeds,

Silent with wonder, where the mountain
        wall
Is piled to heaven ; and, through the
        narrow rift
Of the vast rocks, against whose rugged
        feet
Beats the mad torrent with perpetual roar,
Where noonday is as twilight, and the
        wind
Comes burdened with the everlasting
        moan
Of forests and of far-off waterfalls,

We had looked upward where the sum-
mer sky,
Tasselled with clouds light-woven by
the sun,
Sprung its blue arch above the abutting
crags
O'er-roofing the vast portal of the land
Beyond the wall of mountains. We had
passed
The high source of the Saco ; and be-
wildered
In the dwarf spruce-belts of the Crystal
Hills,
Had heard above us, like a voice in the
cloud,
The horn of Fabyan sounding ; and atop
Of old Agioochook had seen the mountains
Piled to the northward, shagged with
wood, and thick
As meadow mole-hills, — the far sea of
Casco,
A white gleam on the horizon of the east ;
Fair lakes, embosomed in the woods
and hills ;
Moosehillock's mountain range, and
Kearsarge
Lifting his Titan forehead to the sun !

And we had rested underneath the oaks
Shadowing the bank, whose grassy spires
are shaken
By the perpetual beating of the falls
Of the wild Ammonoosuc. We had
tracked
The winding Pemigewasset, overhung
By beechen shadows, whitening down
its rocks,
Or lazily gliding through its intervals,
From waving rye-fields sending up the
gleam
Of sunlit waters. We had seen the moon
Rising behind Umbagog's eastern pines,
Like a great Indian camp-fire ; and its
beams
At midnight spanning with a bridge of
silver
The Merrimack by Uncanoonuc's falls.

There were five souls of us whom trav-
el's chance
Had thrown together in these wild
north hills : —
A city lawyer, for a month escaping
From his dull office, where the weary eye
Saw only hot brick walls and close
thronged streets, —
Briefless as yet, but with an eye to see

Life's sunniest side, and with a heart to
take
Its chances all as godsends ; and his
brother,
Pale from long pulpit studies, yet re-
taining
The warmth and freshness of a genial
heart,
Whose mirror of the beautiful and true,
In Man and Nature, was as yet un
dimmed
By dust of theologic strife, or breath
Of sect, or cobwebs of scholastic lore ;
Like a clear crystal calm of water, taking
The hue and image of o'erleaning flowers,
Sweet human faces, white clouds of the
noon,
Slant starlight glimpses through the
dewy leaves,
And tenderest moonrise. 'T was, in
truth, a study,
To mark his spirit, alternating between
A decent and professional gravity
And an irreverent mirthfulness, which
often
Laughed in the face of his divinity,
Plucked off the sacred ephod, quite un-
shrined
The oracle, and for the pattern priest
Left us the man. A shrewd, sagacious
merchant,
To whom the soiled sheet found in
Crawford's inn,
Giving the latest news of city stocks
And sales of cotton, had a deeper meaning
Than the great presence of the awful
mountains
Glorified by the sunset ; — and his
daughter
A delicate flower on whom had blown
too long
Those evil winds, which, sweeping from
the ice
And winnowing the fogs of Labrador,
Shed their cold blight round Massachu-
setts Bay,
With the same breath which stirs
Spring's opening leaves
And lifts her half-formed flower-bell on
its stem,
Poisoning our seaside atmosphere.

It chanced
That as we turned upon our homeward way,
A drear northeastern storm came howl-
ing up
The valley of the Saco ; and that girl

Who had stood with us upon Mount
  Washington,
Her brown locks ruffled by the wind
  which whirled
In gusts around its sharp cold pinnacle,
Who had joined our gay trout-fishing in
  the streams
Which lave that giant's feet ; whose
  laugh was heard
Like a bird's carol on the sunrise breeze
Which swelled our sail amidst the lake's
  green islands,
Shrank from its harsh, chill breath, and
  visibly drooped
Like a flower in the frost. So, in that
  quiet inn
Which looks from Conway on the moun-
  tains piled
Heavily against the horizon of the north,
Like summer thunder-clouds, we made
  our home :
And while the mist hung over dripping
  hills,
And the cold wind-driven rain-drops all
  day long
Beat their sad music upon roof and pane,
We strove to cheer our gentle invalid.

The lawyer in the pauses of the storm
Went angling down the Saco, and, re-
  turning,
Recounted his adventures and mishaps ;
Gave us the history of his scaly clients,
Mingling with ludicrous yet apt citations
Of barbarous law Latin, passages
From Izaak Walton's Angler, sweet and
  fresh
As the flower-skirted streams of Stafford-
  shire,
Where, under aged trees, the southwest
  wind
Of soft June mornings fanned the thin,
  white hair
Of the sage fisher. And, if truth be told,
Our youthful candidate forsook his ser-
  mons,
His commentaries, articles and creeds,
For the fair page of human loveliness, —
The missal of young hearts, whose sa-
  cred text
Is music, its illumining sweet smiles.
He sang the songs she loved ; and in
  his low,
Deep, earnest voice, recited many a page
Of poetry, — the holiest, tenderest lines
Of the sad bard of Olney, — the sweet
  songs,

Simple and beautiful as Truth and Na-
  ture,
Of him whose whitened locks on Rydal
  Mount
Are lifted yet by morning breezes blowing
From the green hills, immortal in his lays.
And for myself, obedient to her wish,
I searched our landlord's proffered li-
  brary, —
A well-thumbed Bunyan, with its nice
  wood pictures
Of scaly fiends and angels not unlike
  them, —
Watts' unmelodious psalms, — Astrol-
  ogy's
Last home, a musty pile of almanacs,
And an old chronicle of border wars
And Indian history. And, as I read
A story of the marriage of the Chief
Of Saugus to the dusky Weetamoo,
Daughter of Passaconaway, who dwelt
In the old time upon the Merrimack,
Our fair one, in the playful exercise
Of her prerogative, — the right divine
Of youth and beauty, — bade us versify
The legend, and with ready pencil
  sketched
Its plan and outlines, laughingly as-
  signing
To each his part, and barring our excuses
With absolute will. So, like the cavaliers
Whose voices still are heard in the Ro-
  mance
Of silver-tongued Boccaccio, on the banks
Of Arno, with soft tales of love beguiling
The ear of languid beauty, plague-exiled
From stately Florence, we rehearsed our
  rhymes
To their fair auditor, and shared by turns
Her kind approval and her playful cen-
  sure.

It may be that these fragments owe alone
To the fair setting of their circum-
  stances, —
The associations of time, scene, and
  audience, —
Their place amid the pictures which
  fill up
The chambers of my memory. Yet I trust
That some, who sigh, while wandering
  in thought,
Pilgrims of Romance o'er the olden world,
That our broad land, — our sea-like
  lakes and mountains
Piled to the clouds, — our rivers over-
  hung

2

By forests which have known no other
   change
For ages, than the budding and the fall
Of leaves, — our valleys lovelier than
   those
Which the old poets sang of, — should
   but figure
On the apocryphal chart of speculation
As pastures, wood-lots, mill-sites, with
   the privileges,
Rights, and appurtenances, which make
   up
A Yankee Paradise, — unsung, unknown,
To beautiful tradition ; even their names,
Whose melody yet lingers like the last
Vibration of the red man's requiem,
Exchanged for syllables significant
Of cotton-mill and rail-car, will look
   kindly
Upon this effort to call up the ghost
Of our dim Past, and listen with pleased
   ear
To the responses of the questioned Shade.

I. THE MERRIMACK.

O CHILD of that white-crested mountain
   whose springs
Gush forth in the shade of the cliff-eagle's
   wings,
Down whose slopes to the lowlands thy
   wild waters shine,
Leaping gray walls of rock, flashing
   through the dwarf pine.

From that cloud-curtained cradle so cold
   and so lone,
From the arms of that wintry-locked
   mother of stone,
By hills hung with forests, through
   vales wide and free,
Thy mountain-born brightness glanced
   down to the sea !

No bridge arched thy waters save that
   where the trees
Stretched their long arms above thee
   and kissed in the breeze :
No sound save the lapse of the waves on
   thy shores,
The plunging of otters, the light dip of
   oars.

Green-tufted, oak-shaded, by Amoskeag's fall
Thy twin Uncanoonucs rose stately and
   tall,

Thy Nashua meadows lay green and unshorn,
And the hills of Pentucket were tasselled
   with corn.

But thy Pennacook valley was fairer
   than these,
And greener its grasses and taller its trees,
Ere the sound of an axe in the forest
   had rung,
Or the mower his scythe in the meadows
   had swung.

In their sheltered repose looking out
   from the wood
The bark-builded wigwams of Pennacook
   stood,
There glided the corn-dance, the coun-
   cil-fire shone,
And against the red war-post the hatchet
   was thrown.

There the old smoked in silence their
   pipes, and the young
To the pike and the white-perch their
   baited lines flung ;
There the boy shaped his arrows, and
   there the shy maid
Wove her many-hued baskets and bright
   wampum braid.

O Stream of the Mountains ! if answer
   of thine
Could rise from thy waters to question
   of mine,
Methinks through the din of thy
   thronged banks a moan
Of sorrow would swell for the days which
   have gone.

Not for thee the dull jar of the loom and
   the wheel,
The gliding of shuttles, the ringing of
   steel ;
But that old voice of waters, of bird and
   of breeze,
The dip of the wild-fowl, the rustling of
   trees !

II. THE BASHABA.[21]

LIFT we the twilight curtains of the Past,
And, turning from familiar sight and
   sound,
Sadly and full of reverence let us cast
   A glance upon Tradition's shadowy
   ground,

Led by the few pale lights which, glim-
  mering round
  That dim, strange land of Eld, seem
    dying fast ;
And that which history gives not to the
    eye,
The faded coloring of Time's tapestry,
Let Fancy, with her dream-dipped brush,
    supply.

Roof of bark and walls of pine,
Through whose chinks the sunbeams
    shine,
Tracing many a golden line
  On the ample floor within ;
Where, upon that earth-floor stark,
Lay the gaudy mats of bark,
With the bear's hide, rough and dark,
  And the red-deer's skin.

Window-tracery, small and slight,
Woven of the willow white,
Lent a dimly checkered light,
  And the night-stars glimmered down,
Where the lodge-fire's heavy smoke,
Slowly through an opening broke,
In the low roof, ribbed with oak,
  Sheathed with hemlock brown.

Gloomed behind the changeless shade,
By the solemn pine-wood made ;
Through the rugged palisade,
  In the open foreground planted,
Glimpses came of rowers rowing,
Stir of leaves and wild-flowers blow-
    ing,
Steel-like gleams of water flowing,
  In the sunlight slanted.

Here the mighty Bashaba
Held his long-unquestioned sway,
From the White Hills, far away,
  To the great sea's sounding shore ;
Chief of chiefs, his regal word
All the river Sachems heard,
At his call the war-dance stirred,
  Or was still once more.

There his spoils of chase and war,
Jaw of wolf and black bear's paw,
Panther's skin and eagle's claw,
  Lay beside his axe and bow ;
And, adown the roof-pole hung,
Loosely on a snake-skin strung,
In the smoke his scalp-locks swung
  Grimly to and fro.

Nightly down the river going,
Swifter was the hunter's rowing,
When he saw that lodge-fire glowing
  O'er the waters still and red ;
And the squaw's dark eye burned brighter,
And she drew her blanket tighter,
As, with quicker step and lighter,
  From that door she fled.

For that chief had magic skill,
And a Panisee's dark will,
Over powers of good and ill,
  Powers which bless and powers which
    ban, —
Wizard lord of Pennacook,
Chiefs upon their war-path shook,
When they met the steady look
  Of that wise dark man.

Tales of him the gray squaw told,
When the winter night-wind cold
Pierced her blanket's thickest fold,
  And her fire burned low and small,
Till the very child abed,
Drew its bear-skin over head,
Shrinking from the pale lights shed
  On the trembling wall.

All the subtle spirits hiding
Under earth or wave, abiding
In the caverned rock, or riding
  Misty clouds or morning breeze ;
Every dark intelligence,
Secret soul, and influence
Of all things which outward sense
  Feels, or hears, or sees, —

These the wizard's skill confessed,
At his bidding banned or blessed,
Stormful woke or lulled to rest
  Wind and cloud, and fire and flood
Burned for him the drifted snow,
Bade through ice fresh lilies blow,
And the leaves of summer grow
  Over winter's wood !

Not untrue that tale of old !
Now, as then, the wise and bold
All the powers of Nature hold
  Subject to their kingly will ;
From the wondering crowds ashore,
Treading life's wild waters o'er,
  As upon a marble floor,
    Moves the strong man still.

Still, to such, life's elements
With their sterner laws dispense,

And the chain of consequence
  Broken in their pathway lies ;
Time and change their vassals making,
Flowers from icy pillows waking,
Tresses of the sunrise shaking
  Over midnight skies.

Still, to th' earnest soul, the sun
Rests on towered Gibeon,
And the moon of Ajalon
  Lights the battle-grounds of life ;
To his aid the strong reverses
Hidden powers and giant forces,
And the high stars, in their courses,
  Mingle in his strife !

III. THE DAUGHTER.

THE soot-black brows of men, — the
    yell
  Of women thronging round the bed,—
The tinkling charm of ring and shell, —
  The Powah whispering o'er the
    dead ! —
All these the Sachem's home had
    known,
  When, on her journey long and wild
To the dim World of Souls, alone,
  In her young beauty passed the mother
    of his child.

Three bow-shots from the Sachem's
    dwelling
  They laid her in the walnut shade,
Where a green hillock gently swelling
  Her fitting mound of burial made.
There trailed the vine in summer hours,
  The tree-perched squirrel dropped
    his shell, —
On velvet moss and pale-hued flowers,
Woven with leaf and spray, the softened
    sunshine fell !

The Indian's heart is hard and cold, —
  It closes darkly o'er its care,
And formed in Nature's sternest mould,
  Is slow to feel, and strong to bear.
The war-paint on the Sachem's face,
  Unwet with tears, shone fierce and
    red,
And, still in battle or in chase,
Dry leaf and snow-rime crisped beneath
    His foremost tread.

Yet when her name was heard no more,
  And when the robe her mother gave,

And small, light moccasin she wore,
  Had slowly wasted on her grave,
Unmarked of him the dark maids sped
  Their sunset dance and moonlit play;
No other shared his lonely bed,
No other fair young head upon his
    bosom lay.

A lone, stern man. Yet, as sometimes
  The tempest-smitten tree receives
From one small root the sap which
    climbs
  Its topmost spray and crowning
    leaves,
So from his child the Sachem drew
  A life of Love and Hope, and felt
His cold and rugged nature through
The softness and the warmth of her
    young being melt.

A laugh which in the woodland rang
  Bemocking April's gladdest bird, —
A light and graceful form which sprang
  To meet him when his step was
    heard, —
Eyes by his lodge-fire flashing dark,
  Small fingers stringing bead and shell
Or weaving mats of bright-hued bark,—
With these the household-god [22] had
    graced his wigwam well.

Child of the forest ! — strong and free,
  Slight-robed, with loosely flowing
    hair,
She swam the lake or climbed the tree,
  Or struck the flying bird in air.
O'er the heaped drifts of winter's moon
  Her snow-shoes tracked the hunter's
    way ;
And dazzling in the summer noon
The blade of her light oar threw off its
    shower of spray !

Unknown to her the rigid rule,
  The dull restraint, the chiding frown,
The weary torture of the school,
  The taming of wild nature down.
Her only lore, the legends told
  Around the hunter's fire at night ;
Stars rose and set, and seasons rolled,
Flowers bloomed and snow-flakes fell,
    unquestioned in her sight.

Unknown to her the subtle skill
  With which the artist-eye can trace
In rock and tree and lake and hill
  The outlines of divinest grace ;

Unknown the fine soul's keen unrest,
  Which sees, admires, yet yearns
    alway ;
Too closely on her mother's breast
To note her smiles of love the child of
    Nature lay !

It is enough for such to be
  Of common, natural things a part,
To feel, with bird and stream and tree,
  The pulses of the same great heart ;
But we, from Nature long exiled
    In our cold homes of Art and
      Thought,
Grieve like the stranger-tended child,
Which seeks its mother's arms, and sees
  , but feels them not.

The garden rose may richly bloom
  In cultured soil and genial air
To cloud the light of Fashion's room
  Or droop in Beauty's midnight hair,
In lonelier grace, to sun and dew
  The sweetbrier on the hillside shows
Its single leaf and fainter hue,
Untrained and wildly free, yet still a
    sister rose !

Thus o'er the heart of Weetamoo
  Their mingling shades of joy and ill
The instincts of her nature threw, —
  The savage was a woman still.
Midst outlines dim of maiden schemes,
  Heart-colored prophecies of life,
Rose on the ground of her young dreams
The light of a new home, — the lover
    and the wife.

IV. THE WEDDING.

Cool and dark fell the autumn night,
But the Bashaba's wigwam glowed with
    light,
For down from its roof by green withes
    hung
Flaring and smoking the pine-knots
    swung.

And along the river great wood-fires
Shot into the night their long red spires,
Showing behind the tall, dark wood,
Flashing before on the sweeping flood.

In the changeful wind, with shimmer
    and shade,
Now high, now low, that firelight played,

On tree-leaves wet with evening dews,
On gliding water and still canoes.

The trapper that night on Turee's brook,
And the weary fisher on Contoocook,
Saw over the marshes and through the
    pine,
And down on the river the dance-lights
    shine.

For the Saugus Sachem had come to woo
The Bashaba's daughter Weetamoo,
And laid at her father's feet that night
His softest furs and wampum white.

From the Crystal Hills to the far south-
    east
The river Sagamores came to the feast ;
And chiefs whose homes the sea-winds
    shook,
Sat down on the mats of Pennacook.

They came from Sunapee's shore of rock,
From the snowy sources of Snooganock,
And from rough Coös whose thick woods
    shake
Their pine-cones in Umbagog Lake.

From Ammonoosuc's mountain pass,
Wild as his home, came Chepewass ;
And the Keenomps of the hills which
    throw
Their shade on the Smile of Manito.

With pipes of peace and bows unstrung,
Glowing with paint came old and young,
In wampum and furs and feathers arrayed,
To the dance and feast the Bashaba made.

Bird of the air and beast of the field,
All which the woods and waters yield,
On dishes of birch and hemlock piled,
Garnished and graced that banquet wild.

Steaks of the brown bear fat and large
From the rocky slopes of the Kearsarge ;
Delicate trout from Babboosuck brook,
And salmon speared in the Contoocook ;

Squirrels which fed where nuts fell thick
In the gravelly bed of the Otternic ;
And small wild-hens in reed-snares caught
From the banks of Sondagardee brought ;

Pike and perch from the Suncook taken,
Nuts from the trees of the Black Hills
    shaken,

Cranberries picked in the Squamscot bog,
And grapes from the vines of Piscataquog:

And, drawn from that great stone vase
        which stands
In the river scooped by a spirit's hands,[23]
Garnished with spoons of shell and horn,
Stood the birchen dishes of smoking corn.

Thus bird of the air and beast of the field,
All which the woods and the waters yield,
Furnished in that olden day
The bridal feast of the Bashaba.

And merrily when that feast was done
On the fire-lit green the dance begun,
With squaws' shrill stave, and deeper hum
Of old men beating the Indian drum.

Painted and plumed, with scalp-locks
        flowing,
And red arms tossing and black eyes
        glowing,
Now in the light and now in the shade
Around the fires the dancers played.

The step was quicker, the song more shrill,
And the beat of the small drums louder still
Whenever within the circle drew
The Saugus Sachem and Weetamoo.

The moons of forty winters had shed
Their snow upon that chieftain's head,
And toil and care, and battle's chance
Had seamed his hard dark countenance.

A fawn beside the bison grim, —
Why turns the bride's fond eye on him,
In whose cold look is naught beside
The triumph of a sullen pride ?

Ask why the graceful grape entwines
The rough oak with her arm of vines ;
And why the gray rock's rugged cheek
The soft lips of the mosses seek :

Why, with wise instinct, Nature seems
To harmonize her wide extremes,
Linking the stronger with the weak,
The haughty with the soft and meek !

V. THE NEW HOME.

A WILD and broken landscape, spiked
        with firs,
    Roughening the bleak horizon's north-
        ern edge,

Steep, cavernous hillsides, where black
        hemlock spurs
    And sharp, gray splinters of the wind-
        swept ledge
Pierced the thin-glazed ice, or bristling
        rose,
Where the cold rim of the sky sunk down
        upon the snows.

And eastward cold, wide marshes
        stretched away,
    Dull, dreary flats without a bush or
        tree,
O'er-crossed by icy creeks, where twice a
        day
    Gurgled the waters of the moon-struck
        sea ;
And faint with distance came the stifled
        roar,
The melancholy lapse of waves on that
        low shore.

No cheerful village with its mingling
        smokes,
    No laugh of children wrestling in the
        snow,
No camp-fire blazing through the hill-
        side oaks,
    No fishers kneeling on the ice below ;
Yet midst all desolate things of sound
        and view,
Through the long winter moons smiled
        dark-eyed Weetamoo.

Her heart had found a home ; and freshly
        all
    Its beautiful affections overgrew
Their rugged prop. As o'er some granite
        wall
    Soft vine-leaves open to the moisten-
        ing dew
And warm bright sun, the love of that
        young wife
Found on a hard cold breast the dew
        and warmth of life.

The steep bleak hills, the melancholy
        shore,
    The long dead level of the marsh be-
        tween,
A coloring of unreal beauty wore
    Through the soft golden mist of young
        love seen.
For o'er those hills and from that dreary
        plain,
Nightly she welcomed home her hunter
        chief again.

No warmth of heart, no passionate burst
of feeling,
  Repaid her welcoming smile and parting kiss,
No fond and playful dalliance half concealing,
  Under the guise of mirth, its tenderness ;
But, in their stead, the warrior's settled
pride,
And vanity's pleased smile with homage
satisfied.

Enough for Weetamoo, that she alone
  Sat on his mat and slumbered at his
side ;
That he whose fame to her young ear
had flown
  Now looked upon her proudly as his
bride ;
That he whose name the Mohawk trembling heard
Vouchsafed to her at times a kindly look
or word.

For she had learned the maxims of her
race,
  Which teach the woman to become a
slave
And feel herself the pardonless disgrace
  Of love's fond weakness in the wise
and brave, —
The scandal and the shame which they
incur,
Who give to woman all which man requires of her.

So passed the winter moons. The sun
at last
  Broke link by link the frost chain of
the rills,
And the warm breathings of the southwest passed
  Over the hoar rime of the Saugus hills,
The gray and desolate marsh grew green
once more,
And the birch-tree's tremulous shade fell
round the Sachem's door.

Then from far Pennacook swift runners
came,
  With gift and greeting for the Saugus
chief ;
Beseeching him in the great Sachem's
name,
  That, with the coming of the flower
and leaf,

The song of birds, the warm breeze and
the rain,
Young Weetamoo might greet her lonely
sire again.

And Winnepurkit called his chiefs to-
gether,
  And a grave council in his wigwam
met,
Solemn and brief in words, considering
whether
  The rigid rules of forest etiquette
Permitted Weetamoo once more to look
Upon her father's face and green-banked
Pennacook.

With interludes of pipe-smoke and
strong water,
  The forest sages pondered, and at
length,
Concluded in a body to escort her
  Up to her father's home of pride and
strength,
Impressing thus on Pennacook a sense
Of Winnepurkit's power and regal con-
sequence.

So through old woods which Aukeeta-
mit's [24] hand,
  A soft and many-shaded greenness lent,
Over high breezy hills, and meadow land
  Yellow with flowers, the wild proces-
sion went,
Till, rolling down its wooded banks be-
tween,
A broad, clear, mountain stream, the
Merrimack was seen.

The hunter leaning on his bow undrawn,
  The fisher lounging on the pebbled
shores,
Squaws in the clearing dropping the
seed-corn,
  Young children peering through the
wigwam doors,
Saw with delight, surrounded by her
train
Of painted Saugus braves, their Weetamoo
again.

VI. AT PENNACOOK.

THE hills are dearest which our childish
feet
Have climbed the earliest ; and the
streams most sweet

Are ever those at which our young lips
    drank,
Stooped to their waters o'er the grassy
    bank :

Midst the cold dreary sea-watch, Home's
    hearth-light
Shines round the helmsman plunging
    through the night ;
And still, with inward eye, the traveller
    sees
In close, dark, stranger streets his native
    trees.

The home-sick dreamer's brow is nightly
    fanned
By breezes whispering of his native land,
And on the stranger's dim and dying
    eye
The soft, sweet pictures of his child-
    hood lie.

Joy then for Weetamoo, to sit once more
A child upon her father's wigwam floor !
Once more with her old fondness to be-
    guile
From his cold eye the strange light of a
    smile.

The long bright days of summer swiftly
    passed,
The dry leaves whirled in autumn's ris-
    ing blast,
And evening cloud and whitening sun-
    rise rime
Told of the coming of the winter-time.

But vainly looked, the while, young
    Weetamoo,
Down the dark river for her chief's canoe ;
No dusky messenger from Saugus brought
The grateful tidings which the young
    wife sought.

At length a runner from her father sent,
To Winnepurkit's sea-cooled wigwam
    went :
" Eagle of Saugus, — in the woods the
    dove
Mourns for the shelter of thy wings of
    love."

But the dark chief of Saugus turned aside
In the grim anger of hard-hearted pride ;
" I bore her as became a chieftain's
    daughter,
Up to her home beside the gliding water.

" If now no more a mat for her is found
Of all which line her father's wigwam
    round,
Let Pennacook call out his warrior train,
And send her back with wampum gifts
    again."

The baffled runner turned upon his track,
Bearing the words of Winnepurkit back.
" Dog of the Marsh," cried Pennacook,
    " no more
Shall child of mine sit on his wigwam
    floor.

" Go, — let him seek some meaner squaw
    to spread
The stolen bear-skin of his beggar's bed :
Son of a fish-hawk ! — let him dig his
    clams
For some vile daughter of the Agawams,

" Or coward Nipmucks ! — may his scalp
    dry black
In Mohawk smoke, before I send her
    back."
He shook his clenched hand towards the
    ocean wave,
While hoarse assent his listening coun-
    cil gave.

Alas poor bride ! — can thy grim sire
    impart
His iron hardness to thy woman's heart ?
Or cold self-torturing pride like his atone
For love denied and life's warm beauty
    flown ?

On Autumn's gray and mournful grave
    the snow
Hung its white wreaths ; with stifled
    voice and low
The river crept, by one vast bridge o'er-
    crossed,
Built by the hoar-locked artisan of Frost.

And many a Moon in beauty newly born
Pierced the red sunset with her silver
    horn,
Or, from the east, across her azure field
Rolled the wide brightness of her full-
    orbed shield.

Yet Winnepurkit came not, — on the mat
Of the scorned wife her dusky rival sat ;
And he, the while, in Western woods afar,
Urged the long chase, or trod the path
    of war.

Dry up thy tears, young daughter of a
    chief !
Waste not on him the sacredness of grief;
Be the fierce spirit of thy sire thine own,
His lips of scorning, and his heart of stone.

What heeds the warrior of a hundred
    fights,
The storm-worn watcher through long
    hunting nights,
Cold, crafty, proud of woman's weak
    distress,
Her home-bound grief and pining lone-
    liness ?

VII. THE DEPARTURE.

THE wild March rains had fallen fast and
    long
The snowy mountains of the North among,
Making each vale a watercourse, — each
    hill
Bright with the cascade of some new-
    made rill.

Gnawed by the sunbeams, softened by
    the rain,
Heaved underneath by the swollen cur-
    rent's strain,
The ice-bridge yielded, and the Merri-
    mack
Bore the huge ruin crashing down its
    track.

On that strong turbid water, a small boat
Guided by one weak hand was seen to
    float ;
Evil the fate which loosed it from the
    shore,
Too early voyager with too frail an oar !

Down the vexed centre of that rushing
    tide,
The thick huge ice-blocks threatening
    either side,
The foam-white rocks of Amoskeag in
    view,
With arrowy swiftness sped that light
    canoe.

The trapper, moistening his moose's meat
On the wet bank by Uncanoonuc's feet,
Saw the swift boat flash down the trou-
    bled stream —
Slept he, or waked he ? — was it truth
    o dream ?

The straining eye bent fearfully before,
The small hand clenching on the useless
    oar,
The bead-wrought blanket trailing o'er
    the water —
He knew them all — woe for the Sachem's
    daughter !

Sick and aweary of her lonely life,
Heedless of peril the still faithful wife
Had left her mother's grave, her father's
    door,
To seek the wigwam of her chief once
    more.

Down the white rapids like a sear leaf
    whirled,
On the sharp rocks and piled-up ices
    hurled,
Empty and broken, circled the canoe
In the vexed pool below — but, where
    was Weetamoo ?

VIII. SONG OF INDIAN WOMEN.

THE Dark eye has left us,
    The Spring-bird has flown ;
On the pathway of spirits
    She wanders alone.
The song of the wood-dove has died on
    our shore, —
Mat wonck kunna-monee ! [25] — We hear
    it no more !

O dark water Spirit !
    We cast on thy wave
These furs which may never
    Hang over her grave ;
Bear down to the lost one the robes that
    she wore, —
Mat wonck kunna-monee ! — We see her
    no more !

Of the strange land she walks in
    No Powah has told :
It may burn with the sunshine,
    Or freeze with the cold.
Let us give to our lost one the robes that
    she wore,
Mat wonck kunna-monee ! — We see her
    no more !

The path she is treading
    Shall soon be our own ;
Each gliding in shadow
    Unseen and alone ! —

In vain shall we call on the souls gone
    before, —
Mat wonck kunna-monee ! — They hear
    us no more !

O mighty Sowanna ! [26]
    Thy gateways unfold,
From thy wigwam of sunset
    Lift curtains of gold !
Take home the poor Spirit whose journey
    is o'er, —
Mat wonck kunna-monee ! — We see her
    no more !

So sang the Children of the Leaves beside
The broad, dark river's coldly flowing tide,
Now low, now harsh, with sob-like
    pause and swell,
On the high wind their voices rose and fell.
Nature's wild music, — sounds of wind-
    swept trees,
The scream of birds, the wailing of the
    breeze,
The roar of waters, steady, deep, and
    strong, —
Mingled and murmured in that farewell
    song.

LEGENDARY.

THE MERRIMACK.

["The Indians speak of a beautiful river, far
to the south, which they call Merrimack." —
SIEUR DE MONTS : 1604.]

STREAM of my fathers ! sweetly still
The sunset rays thy valley fill ;
Poured slantwise down the long defile,
Wave, wood, and spire beneath them
    smile.
I see the winding Powow fold
The green hill in its belt of gold,
And following down its wavy line,
Its sparkling waters blend with thine.
There 's not a tree upon thy side,
Nor rock, which thy returning tide
As yet hath left abrupt and stark
Above thy evening water-mark ;
No calm cove with its rocky hem,
No isle whose emerald swells begem
Thy broad, smooth current ; not a sail
Bowed to the freshening ocean gale ;
No small boat with its busy oars,
Nor gray wall sloping to thy shores ;
Nor farm-house with its maple shade,
Or rigid poplar colonnade,
But lies distinct and full in sight,
Beneath this gush of sunset light.
Centuries ago, that harbor-bar,
Stretching its length of foam afar,
And Salisbury's beach of shining sand,
And yonder island's wave-smoothed
    strand,
Saw the adventurer's tiny sail,

Flit, stooping from the eastern gale ; [27]
And o'er these woods and waters broke
The cheer from Britain's hearts of oak,
As brightly on the voyager's eye,
Weary of forest, sea, and sky,
Breaking the dull continuous wood,
The Merrimack rolled down his flood ;
Mingling that clear pellucid brook,
Which channels vast Agioochook
When spring-time's sun and shower un-
    lock
The frozen fountains of the rock,
And more abundant waters given
From that pure lake, "The Smile of
    Heaven," [28]
Tributes from vale and mountain-side, —
With ocean's dark, eternal tide !

On yonder rocky cape, which braves
The stormy challenge of the waves,
Midst tangled vine and dwarfish wood,
The hardy Anglo-Saxon stood,
Planting upon the topmost crag
The staff of England's battle-flag ;
And, while from out its heavy fold
Saint George's crimson cross unrolled,
Midst roll of drum and trumpet blare,
And weapons brandishing in air,
He gave to that lone promontory
The sweetest name in all his story ; [29]
Of her, the flower of Islam's daughters,
Whose harems look on Stamboul's
    waters, —
Who, when the chance of war had bound

The Moslem chain his limbs around,
Wreathed o'er with silk that iron chain,
Soothed with her smiles his hours of pain,
And fondly to her youthful slave
A dearer gift than freedom gave.

But look ! — the yellow light no more
Streams down on wave and verdant shore ;
And clearly on the calm air swells
The twilight voice of distant bells.
From Ocean's bosom, white and thin,
The mists come slowly rolling in ;
Hills, woods, the river's rocky rim,
Amidst the sea-like vapor swim,
While yonder lonely coast-light, set
Within its wave-washed minaret,
Half quenched, a beamless star and pale,
Shines dimly through its cloudy veil !

Home of my fathers ! — I have stood
Where Hudson rolled his lordly flood :
Seen sunrise rest and sunset fade
Along his frowning Palisade ;
Looked down the Apalachian peak
On Juniata's silver streak;
Have seen along his valley gleam
The Mohawk's softly winding stream ;
The level light of sunset shine
Through broad Potomac's hem of pine ;
And autumn's rainbow-tinted banner
Hang lightly o'er the Susquehanna ;
Yet wheresoe'er his step might be,
Thy wandering child looked back to thee !
Heard in his dreams thy river's sound
Of murmuring on its pebbly bound,
The unforgotten swell and roar
Of waves on thy familiar shore ;
And saw, amidst the curtained gloom
And quiet of his lonely room,
Thy sunset scenes before him pass ;
As, in Agrippa's magic glass,
The loved and lost arose to view,
Remembered groves in greenness grew,
Bathed still in childhood's morning dew,
Along whose bowers of beauty swept
Whatever Memory's mourners wept,
Sweet faces, which the charnel kept,
Young, gentle eyes, which long had slept ;
And while the gazer leaned to trace,
More near, some dear familiar face,
He wept to find the vision flown, —
A phantom and a dream alone !

THE NORSEMEN.[30]

GIFT from the cold and silent Past !
A relic to the present cast ;
Left on the ever-changing strand
Of shifting and unstable sand,
Which wastes beneath the steady chime
And beating of the waves of Time !
Who from its bed of primal rock
First wrenched thy dark, unshapely block ?
Whose hand, of curious skill untaught,
Thy rude and savage outline wrought ?

The waters of my native stream
Are glancing in the sun's warm beam :
From sail-urged keel and flashing oar
The circles widen to its shore :
And cultured field and peopled town
Slope to its willowed margin down.
Yet, while this morning breeze is bringing
The home-life sound of school-bells ringing,
And rolling wheel, and rapid jar
Of the fire-winged and steedless car,
And voices from the wayside near
Come quick and blended on my ear, —
A spell is in this old gray stone,
My thoughts are with the Past alone !

A change ! — The steepled town no more
Stretches along the sail-thronged shore :
Like palace-domes in sunset's cloud,
Fade sun-gilt spire and mansion proud :
Spectrally rising where they stood,
I see the old, primeval wood :
Dark, shadow-like, on either hand
I see its solemn waste expand :
It climbs the green and cultured hill,
It arches o'er the valley's rill,
And leans from cliff and crag, to throw
Its wild arms o'er the stream below.
Unchanged, alone, the same bright river
Flows on, as it will flow forever !
I listen, and I hear the low
Soft ripple where its waters go ;
I hear behind the panther's cry,
The wild-bird's scream goes thrilling by,
And shyly on the river's brink
The deer is stooping down to drink.

But hark ! — from wood and rock flung back,
What sound comes up the Merrimack ?
What sea-worn barks are those which throw
The light spray from each rushing prow ?

Have they not in the North Sea's blast
Bowed to the waves the straining mast ?
Their frozen sails the low, pale sun
Of Thulé's night has shone upon ;
Flapped by the sea-wind's gusty sweep
Round icy drift, and headland steep.
Wild Jutland's wives and Lochlin's
          daughters
Have watched them fading o'er the waters,
Lessening through driving mist and spray,
Like white-winged sea-birds on their way !

Onward they glide, — and now I view
Their iron-armed and stalwart crew ;
Joy glistens in each wild blue eye,
Turned to green earth and summer sky :
Each broad, seamed breast has cast aside
Its cumbering vest of shaggy hide ;
Bared to the sun and soft warm air,
Streams back the Norsemen's yellow hair.
I see the gleam of axe and spear,
The sound of smitten shields I hear,
Keeping a harsh and fitting time
To Saga's chant, and Runic rhyme ;
Such lays as Zetland's Scald has sung,
His gray and naked isles among ;
Or muttered low at midnight hour
Round Odin's mossy stone of power.
The wolf beneath the Arctic moon
Has answered to that startling rune ;
The Gael has heard its stormy swell,
The light Frank knows its summons well ;
Iona's sable-stoled Culdee
Has heard it sounding o'er the sea,
And swept, with hoary beard and hair,
His altar's foot in trembling prayer !

'T is past, — the 'wildering vision dies
In darkness on my dreaming eyes !
The forest vanishes in air, —
Hill-slope and vale lie starkly bare ;
I hear the common tread of men,
And hum of work-day life again :
The mystic relic seems alone
A broken mass of common stone ;
And if it be the chiselled limb
Of Berserker or idol grim, —
A fragment of Valhalla's Thor,
The stormy Viking's god of War,
Or Praga of the Runic lay,
Or love-awakening Siona,
I know not, — for no graven line,
Nor Druid mark, nor Runic sign,
Is left me here, by which to trace
Its name, or origin, or place.
Yet, for this vision of the Past,
This glance upon its darkness cast,

My spirit bows in gratitude
Before the Giver of all good,
Who fashioned so the human mind,
That, from the waste of Time behind
A simple stone, or mound of earth,
Can summon the departed forth ;
Quicken the Past to life again, —
The Present lose in what hath been,
And in their primal freshness show
The buried forms of long ago.
As if a portion of that Thought
By which the Eternal will is wrought,
Whose impulse fills anew with breath
The frozen solitude of Death,
To mortal mind were sometimes lent,
To mortal musings sometimes sent,
To whisper — even when it seems
But Memory's fantasy of dreams —
Through the mind's waste of woe and
          sin,
Of an immortal origin !

CASSANDRA SOUTHWICK.

1658.

To the God of all sure mercies let my
          blessing rise to-day,
From the scoffer and the cruel He hath
          plucked the spoil away, —
Yea, He who cooled the furnace around
          the faithful three,
And tamed the Chaldean lions, hath set
          his handmaid free !

Last night I saw the sunset melt through
          my prison bars,
Last night across my damp earth-floor
          fell the pale gleam of stars ;
In the coldness and the darkness all
          through the long night-time,
My grated casement whitened with au-
          tumn's early rime.

Alone, in that dark sorrow, hour after
          hour crept by ;
Star after star looked palely in and sank
          adown the sky ;
No sound amid night's stillness, save that
          which seemed to be
The dull and heavy beating of the pulses
          of the sea ;

All night I sat unsleeping, for I knew
          that on the morrow
The ruler and the cruel priest would mock
          me in my sorrow,

Dragged to their place of market, and
   bargained for and sold,
Like a lamb before the shambles, like a
   heifer from the fold !

the weakness of the flesh was there, —
   the shrinking and the shame ;
And the low voice of the Tempter like
   whispers to me came :
" Why sit'st thou thus forlornly ! " the
   wicked murmur said,
" Damp walls thy bower of beauty, cold
   earth thy maiden bed ?

" Where be the smiling faces, and voices
   soft and sweet,
Seen in thy father's dwelling, heard in
   the pleasant street ?
Where be the youths whose glances, the
   summer Sabbath through,
Turned tenderly and timidly unto thy
   father's pew ?

" Why sit'st thou here, Cassandra ? —
   Bethink thee with what mirth
Thy happy schoolmates gather around the
   warm bright hearth ;
How the crimson shadows tremble on
   foreheads white and fair,
On eyes of merry girlhood, half hid in
   golden hair.

" Not for thee the hearth-fire brightens,
   not for thee kind words are spoken,
Not for thee the nuts of Wenham woods
   by laughing boys are broken,
No first-fruits of the orchard within thy
   lap are laid,
For thee no flowers of autumn the youthful hunters braid.

" O, weak, deluded maiden ! — by crazy
   fancies led,
With wild and raving railers an evil path
   to tread ;
To leave a wholesome worship, and teaching pure and sound ;
And mate with maniac women, loose-
   haired and sackcloth bound.

" Mad scoffers of the priesthood, who
   mock at things divine,
Who rail against the pulpit, and holy
   bread and wine ;
Sore from their cart-tail scourgings, and
   from the pillory lame,
Rejoicing in their wretchedness, and
   glorying in their shame.

" And what a fate awaits thee ? — a sadly
   toiling slave,
Dragging the slowly lengthening chain
   of bondage to the grave !
Think of thy woman's nature, subdued
   in hopeless thrall,
The easy prey of any, the scoff and scorn
   of all ! "

O, ever as the Tempter spoke, and feeble
   Nature's fears
Wrung drop by drop the scalding flow
   of unavailing tears,
I wrestled down the evil thoughts, and
   strove in silent prayer,
To feel, O Helper of the weak ! that
   Thou indeed wert there !

I thought of Paul and Silas, within
   Philippi's cell,
And how from Peter's sleeping limbs the
   prison-shackles fell,
Till I seemed to hear the trailing of an
   angel's robe of white,
And to feel a blessed presence invisible
   to sight.

Bless the Lord for all his mercies ! — for
   the peace and love I felt,
Like dew of Hermon's holy hill, upon
   my spirit melt ;
When " Get behind me, Satan ! " was
   the language of my heart,
And I felt the Evil Tempter with all his
   doubts depart.

Slow broke the gray cold morning ; again
   the sunshine fell,
Flecked with the shade of bar and grate
   within my lonely cell ;
The hoar-frost melted on the wall, and
   upward from the street
Came careless laugh and idle word, and
   tread of passing feet.

At length the heavy bolts fell back, my
   door was open cast,
And slowly at the sheriff's side, up the
   long street I passed ;
I heard the murmur round me, and felt,
   but dared not see,
How, from every door and window, the
   people gazed on me.

And doubt and fear fell on me, shame
   burned upon my cheek,
Swam earth and sky around me, my
   trembling limbs grew weak :

"O Lord! support thy handmaid; and
from her soul cast out
The fear of man, which brings a snare, —
the weakness and the doubt."

Then the dreary shadows scattered, like
a cloud in morning's breeze,
And a low deep voice within me seemed
whispering words like these :
"Though thy earth be as the iron, and
thy heaven a brazen wall,
Trust still His loving-kindness whose
power is over all."

We paused at length, where at my feet
the sunlit waters broke
On glaring reach of shining beach, and
shingly wall of rock ;
The merchant-ships lay idly there, in
hard clear lines on high,
Tracing with rope and slender spar their
network on the sky.

And there were ancient citizens, cloak-
wrapped and grave and cold,
And grim and stout sea-captains with
faces bronzed and old,
And on his horse, with Rawson, his cruel
clerk at hand,
Sat dark and haughty Endicott, the
ruler of the land.

And poisoning with his evil words the
ruler's ready ear,
The priest leaned o'er his saddle, with
laugh and scoff and jeer ;
It stirred my soul, and from my lips the
seal of silence broke,
As if through woman's weakness a warning spirit spoke.

I cried, "The Lord rebuke thee, thou
smiter of the meek,
Thou robber of the righteous, thou tram-
pler of the weak !
Go light the dark, cold hearth-stones, —
go turn the prison lock
Of the poor hearts thou hast hunted, thou
wolf amid the flock !"

Dark lowered the brows of Endicott,
and with a deeper red
O'er Rawson's wine-empurpled cheek the
flush of anger spread ;
"Good people," quoth the white-lipped
priest, "heed not her words so wild,
Her Master speaks within her, — the
Devil owns his child !"

But gray heads shook, and young brows
knit, the while the sheriff read
That law the wicked rulers against the
poor have made,
Who to their house of Rimmon and idol
priesthood bring
No bended knee of worship, nor gainful
offering.

Then to the stout sea-captains the sher-
iff, turning, said, —
"Which of ye, worthy seamen, will take
this Quaker maid ?
In the Isle of fair Barbadoes, or on Vir-
ginia's shore,
You may hold her at a higher price than
Indian girl or Moor."

Grim and silent stood the captains ; and
when again he cried,
"Speak out, my worthy seamen !" — no
voice, no sign replied ;
But I felt a hard hand press my own,
and kind words met my ear, —
"God bless thee, and preserve thee, my
gentle girl and dear !"

A weight seemed lifted from my heart, —
a pitying friend was nigh,
I felt it in his hard, rough hand, and saw
it in his eye ;
And when again the sheriff spoke, that
voice, so kind to me,
Growled back its stormy answer like the
roaring of the sea, —

"Pile my ship with bars of silver, — pack
with coins of Spanish gold,
From keel-piece up to deck-plank, the
roomage of her hold,
By the living God who made me ! — I
would sooner in your bay
Sink ship and crew and cargo, than bear
this child away !"

"Well answered, worthy captain, shame
on their cruel laws !"
Ran through the crowd in murmurs loud
the people's just applause.
"Like the herdsman of Tekoa, in Israel
of old,
Shall we see the poor and righteous again
for silver sold ?"

I looked on haughty Endicott ; with
weapon half-way drawn,
Swept round the throng his lion glare of
bitter hate and scorn ;

"The solemn pines along its shore."   Page 31.

Fiercely he drew his bridle-rein, and
  turned in silence back,
And sneering priest and baffled clerk
  rode murmuring in his track.

Hard after them the sheriff looked, in
  bitterness of soul ;
Thrice smote his staff upon the ground,
  and crushed his parchment roll.
"Good friends," he said, "since both
  have fled, the ruler and the priest,
Judge ye, if from their further work I
  be not well released."

Loud was the cheer which, full and
  clear, swept round the silent bay,
As, with kind words and kinder looks,
  he bade me go my way ;
For He who turns the courses of the
  streamlet of the glen,
And the river of great waters, had
  turned the hearts of men.

O, at that hour the very earth seemed
  changed beneath my eye,
A holier wonder round me rose the blue
  walls of the sky,
A lovelier light on rock and hill and
  stream and woodland lay,
And softer lapsed on sunnier sands the
  waters of the bay.

Thanksgiving to the Lord of life ! — to
  Him all praises be,
Who from the hands of evil men hath
  set his handmaid free ;
All praise to Him before whose power
  the mighty are afraid,
Who takes the crafty in the snare
  which for the poor is laid !

Sing, O my soul, rejoicingly, on evening's twilight calm
Uplift the loud thanksgiving, — pour
  forth the grateful psalm ;
Let all dear hearts with me rejoice, as
  did the saints of old,
When of the Lord's good angel the
  rescued Peter told.

And weep and howl, ye evil priests and
  mighty men of wrong,
The Lord shall smite the proud, and
  lay his hand upon the strong.
Woe to the wicked rulers in his avenging hour !
Woe to the wolves who seek the flocks
  to raven and devour !

But let the humble ones arise, — the poor
  in heart be glad,
And let the mourning ones again with
  robes of praise be clad,
For He who cooled the furnace, and
  smoothed the stormy wave,
And tamed the Chaldean lions, is mighty
  still to save !

FUNERAL TREE OF THE SOKOKIS.

1756.

AROUND Sebago's lonely lake
There lingers not a breeze to break
The mirror which its waters make.

The solemn pines along its shore,
The firs which hang its gray rocks o'er,
Are painted on its glassy floor.

The sun looks o'er, with hazy eye,
The snowy mountain-tops which lie
Piled coldly up against the sky.

Dazzling and white ! save where the bleak,
Wild winds have bared some splintering
  peak,
Or snow-slide left its dusky streak.

Yet green are Saco's banks below,
And belts of spruce and cedar show,
Dark fringing round those cones of snow.

The earth hath felt the breath of spring,
Though yet on her deliverer's wing
The lingering frosts of winter cling.

Fresh grasses fringe the meadow-brooks,
And mildly from its sunny nooks
The blue eye of the violet looks.

And odors from the springing grass,
The sweet birch and the sassafras,
Upon the scarce-felt breezes pass.

Her tokens of renewing care
Hath Nature scattered everywhere,
In bud and flower, and warmer air.

But in their hour of bitterness,
What reck the broken Sokokis,
Beside their slaughtered chief, of this?

The turf's red stain is yet undried, —
Scarce have the death-shot echoes died
Along Sebago's wooded side :

And silent now the hunters stand,
Grouped darkly, where a swell of land
Slopes upward from the lake's white
    sand.

Fire and the axe have swept it bare,
Save one lone beech, unclosing there
Its light leaves in the vernal air.

With grave, cold looks, all sternly mute,
They break the damp turf at its foot,
And bare its coiled and twisted root.

They heave the stubborn trunk aside,
The firm roots from the earth divide, —
The rent beneath yawns dark and wide.

And there the fallen chief is laid,
In tasselled garbs of skins arrayed,
And girded with his wampum-braid.

The silver cross he loved is pressed
Beneath the heavy arms, which rest
Upon his scarred and naked breast.

'Tis done : the roots are backward sent,
The beechen-tree stands up unbent, —
The Indian's fitting monument !

When of that sleeper's broken race
Their green and pleasant dwelling-place
Which knew them once, retains no trace ;

O, long may sunset's light be shed
As now upon that beech's head, —
A green memorial of the dead !

There shall his fitting requiem be,
In northern winds, that, cold and free,
Howl nightly in that funeral tree.

To their wild wail the waves which break
Forever round that lonely lake
A solemn undertone shall make !

And who shall deem the spot unblest,
Where Nature's younger children rest,
Lulled on their sorrowing mother's breast ?

Deem ye that mother loveth less
These bronzed forms of the wilderness
She foldeth in her long caress ?

As sweet o'er them her wild-flowers
    blow
As if with fairer hair and brow
The blue-eyed Saxon slept below.

What though the places of their rest
No priestly knee hath ever pressed, —
No funeral rite nor prayer hath blessed !

What though the bigot's ban be there,
And thoughts of wailing and despair,
And cursing in the place of prayer !

Yet Heaven hath angels watching round
The Indian's lowliest forest-mound, —
And *they* have made it holy ground.

There ceases man's frail judgment ; all
His powerless bolts of cursing fall
Unheeded on that grassy pall.

O, peeled, and hunted, and reviled,
Sleep on, dark tenant of the wild !
Great Nature owns her simple child !

And Nature's God, to whom alone
The secret of the heart is known, —
The hidden language traced thereon ;

Who from its many cumberings
Of form and creed, and outward things,
To light the naked spirit brings ;

Not with our partial eye shall scan,
Not with our pride and scorn shall
    ban,
The spirit of our brother man !

ST. JOHN.

1647.

"To the winds give our banner !
    Bear homeward again !"
Cried the Lord of Acadia,
    Cried Charles of Estienne ;
From the prow of his shallop
    He gazed, as the sun,
From its bed in the ocean,
    Streamed up the St. John.

O'er the blue western waters
    That shallop had passed,
Where the mists of Penobscot
    Clung damp on her mast.
St. Saviour had looked
    On the heretic sail,
As the songs of the Huguenot
    Rose on the gale.

The pale, ghostly fathers
    Remembered her well,

And had cursed her while passing,
  With taper and bell,
But the men of Monhegan,
  Of Papists abhorred,
Had welcomed and feasted
  The heretic Lord.

They had loaded his shallop
  With dun-fish and ball,
With stores for his larder,
  And steel for his wall.
Pemequid, from her bastions
  And turrets of stone,
Had welcomed his coming
  With banner and gun.

And the prayers of the elders
  Had followed his way,
As homeward he glided,
  Down Pentecost Bay.
O, well sped La Tour !
  For, in peril and pain,
His lady kept watch,
  For his coming again.

O'er the Isle of the Pheasant
  The morning sun shone,
On the plane-trees which shaded
  The shores of St. John.
"Now, why from yon battlements
  Speaks not my love !
Why waves there no banner
  My fortress above ?"

Dark and wild, from his deck
  St. Estienne gazed about,
On fire-wasted dwellings,
  And silent redoubt ;
From the low, shattered walls
  Which the flame had o'errun,
There floated no banner,
  There thundered no gun !

But beneath the low arch
  Of its doorway there stood
A pale priest of Rome,
  In his cloak and his hood.
With the bound of a lion,
  La Tour sprang to land,
On the throat of the Papist
  He fastened his hand.

"Speak, son of the Woman
  Of scarlet and sin ! •
What wolf has been prowling
  My castle within ?"
3

From the grasp of the soldier
  The Jesuit broke,
Half in scorn, half in sorrow,
  He smiled as he spoke :

"No wolf, Lord of Estienne,
  Has ravaged thy hall,
But thy red-handed rival,
  With fire, steel, and ball !
On an errand of mercy
  I hitherward came,
While the walls of thy castle
  Yet spouted with flame.

"Pentagoet's dark vessels
  Were moored in the bay,
Grim sea-lions, roaring
  Aloud for their prey."
"But what of my lady ?"
  Cried Charles of Estienne :
"On the shot-crumbled turret
  Thy lady was seen :

"Half-veiled in the smoke-cloud,
  Her hand grasped thy pennon,
While her dark tresses swayed
  In the hot breath of cannon !
But woe to the heretic,
  Evermore woe !
When the son of the church
  And the cross is his foe !

"In the track of the shell,
  In the path of the ball,
Pentagoet swept over
  The breach of the wall !
Steel to steel, gun to gun,
  One moment, — and then
Alone stood the victor,
  Alone with his men !

"Of its sturdy defenders,
  Thy lady alone
Saw the cross-blazoned banner
  Float over St. John."
"Let the dastard look to it !"
  Cried fiery Estienne,
"Were D'Aulney King Louis,
  I 'd free her again !"

"Alas for thy lady !
  No service from thee
Is needed by her
  Whom the Lord hath set free :
Nine days, in stern silence,
  Her thraldom she bore,

But the tenth morning came,
　And Death opened her door ! ''

As if suddenly smitten
　La Tour staggered back ;
His hand grasped his sword-hilt,
　His forehead grew black.
He sprang on the deck
　Of his shallop again.
" We cruise now for vengeance !
　Give way ! " cried Estienne.

" Massachusetts shall hear
　Of the Huguenot's wrong,
And from island and creekside
　Her fishers shall throng !
Pentagoet shall rue
　What his Papists have done,
When his palisades echo
　The Puritan's gun ! "

O, the loveliest of heavens
　Hung tenderly o'er him,
There were waves in the sunshine,
　And green isles before him :
But a pale hand was beckoning
　The Huguenot on ;
And in blackness and ashes
　Behind was St. John !

PENTUCKET.

1708.

How sweetly on the wood-girt town
The mellow light of sunset shone !
Each small, bright lake, whose waters still
Mirror the forest and the hill,
Reflected from its waveless breast
The beauty of a cloudless west,
Glorious as if a glimpse were given
Within the western gates of heaven,
Left, by the spirit of the star
Of sunset's holy hour, ajar !

Beside the river's tranquil flood
The dark and low-walled dwellings stood,
Where many a rood of open land
Stretched up and down on either hand,
With corn-leaves waving freshly green
The thick and blackened stumps between.
Behind, unbroken, deep and dread,
The wild, untravelled forest spread,
Back to those mountains, white and cold,
Of which the Indian trapper told,
Upon whose summits never yet
Was mortal foot in safety set.

Quiet and calm, without a fear
Of danger darkly lurking near,
The weary laborer left his plough, —
The milkmaid carolled by her cow, —
From cottage door and household hearth
Rose songs of praise, or tones of mirth.
At length the murmur died away,
And silence on that village lay, —
So slept Pompeii, tower and hall,
Ere the quick earthquake swallowed all,
Undreaming of the fiery fate
Which made its dwellings desolate !

Hours passed away. By moonlight sped
The Merrimack along his bed.
Bathed in the pallid lustre, stood
Dark cottage-wall and rock and wood,
Silent, beneath that tranquil beam,
As the hushed grouping of a dream.
Yet on the still air crept a sound, —
No bark of fox, nor rabbit's bound,
Nor stir of wings, nor waters flowing,
Nor leaves in midnight breezes blowing.

Was that the tread of many feet,
Which downward from the hillside beat ?
What forms were those which darkly
　　stood
Just on the margin of the wood ? —
Charred tree-stumps in the moonlight
　　dim,
Or paling rude, or leafless limb ?
No, — through the trees fierce eyeballs
　　glowed,
Dark human forms in moonshine showed,
Wild from their native wilderness,
With painted limbs and battle-dress !

A yell the dead might wake to hear
Swelled on the night air, far and clear, —
Then smote the Indian tomahawk
On crashing door and shattering lock, —
Then rang the rifle-shot, -- and then
The shrill death-scream of stricken
　　men, —
Sank the red axe in woman's brain,
And childhood's cry arose in vain, —
Bursting through roof and window came,
Red, fast, and fierce, the kindled flame ;
And blended fire and moonlight glared
On still dead men and weapons bared.

The morning sun looked brightly through
The river willows, wet with dew.
No sound of combat filled the air, —
No shout was heard, — nor gunshot there :
Yet still the thick and sullen smoke

From smouldering ruins slowly broke ;
And on the greensward many a stain,
And, here and there, the mangled slain,
Told how that midnight bolt had sped
Pentucket, on thy fated head !

Even now the villager can tell
Where Rolfe beside his hearthstone fell,
Still show the door of wasting oak,
Through which the fatal death-shot broke,
And point the curious stranger where
De Rouville's corse lay grim and bare, —
Whose hideous head, in death still feared,
Bore not a trace of hair or beard, —
And still, within the churchyard ground,
Heaves darkly up the ancient mound,
Whose grass-grown surface overlies
The victims of that sacrifice.

THE FAMILIST'S HYMN.

FATHER ! to thy suffering poor
  Strength and grace and faith impart,
And with thy own love restore
  Comfort to the broken heart !
O, the failing ones confirm
  With a holier strength of zeal ! —
Give thou not the feeble worm
  Helpless to the spoiler's heel !

Father ! for thy holy sake
  We are spoiled and hunted thus ;
Joyful, for thy truth we take
  Bonds and burthens unto us :
Poor, and weak, and robbed of all,
  Weary with our daily task,
That thy truth may never fall
  Through our weakness, Lord, we ask.

Round our fired and wasted homes
  Flits the forest-bird unscared,
And at noon the wild beast comes
  Where our frugal meal was shared ;
For the song of praises there
  Shrieks the crow the livelong day ;
For the sound of evening prayer
  Howls the evil beast of prey !

Sweet the songs we loved to sing
  Underneath thy holy sky, —
Words and tones that used to bring
  Tears of joy in every eye, —
Dear the wrestling hours of prayer,
  When we gathered knee to knee,
Blameless youth and hoary hair,
  Bowed, O God, alone to thee.

As thine early children, Lord,
  Shared their wealth and daily bread,
Even so, with one accord,
  We, in love, each other fed.
Not with us the miser's hoard,
  Not with us his grasping hand ;
Equal round a common board,
  Drew our meek and brother band !

Safe our quiet Eden lay
  When the war-whoop stirred the
    land
And the Indian turned away
  From our home his bloody hand.
Well that forest-ranger saw,
  That the burthen and the curse
Of the white man's cruel law
  Rested also upon us.

Torn apart, and driven forth
  To our toiling hard and long,
Father ! from the dust of earth
  Lift we still our grateful song !
Grateful, — that in bonds we share
  In thy love which maketh free ;
Joyful, — that the wrongs we bear,
  Draw us nearer, Lord, to thee !

Grateful ! — that where'er we toil, —
  By Wachuset's wooded side,
On Nantucket's sea-worn isle,
  Or by wild Neponset's tide, —
Still, in spirit, we are near,
  And our evening hymns, which rise
Separate and discordant here,
  Meet and mingle in the skies !

Let the scoffer scorn and mock,
  Let the proud and evil priest
Rob the needy of his flock,
  For his wine-cup and his feast, —
Redden not thy bolts in store
  Through the blackness of thy skies ?
For the sighing of the poor
  Wilt Thou not, at length, arise ?

Worn and wasted, oh ! how long
  Shall thy trodden poor complain ?
In thy name they bear the wrong,
  In thy cause the bonds of pain !
Melt oppression's heart of steel,
  Let the haughty priesthood see,
And their blinded followers feel,
  That in us they mock at Thee !

In thy time, O Lord of hosts,
  Stretch abroad that hand to save

Which of old, on Egypt's coasts,
  Smote apart the Red Sea's wave !
Lead us from this evil land,
  From the spoiler set us free,
And once more our gathered band,
  Heart to heart, shall worship thee !

THE FOUNTAIN.

TRAVELLER ! on thy journey toiling
  By the swift Powow,
With the summer sunshine falling
  On thy heated brow,
Listen, while all else is still,
To the brooklet from the hill.

Wild and sweet the flowers are blowing
  By that streamlet's side,
And a greener verdure showing
  Where its waters glide, —
Down the hill-slope murmuring on,
Over root and mossy stone.

Where yon oak his broad arms flingeth
  O'er the sloping hill,
Beautiful and freshly springeth
  That soft-flowing rill,
Through its dark roots wreathed and
    bare,
Gushing up to sun and air.

Brighter waters sparkled never
  In that magic well,
Of whose gift of life forever
  Ancient legends tell, —
In the lonely desert wasted,
And by mortal lip untasted.

Waters which the proud Castilian [31]
  Sought with longing eyes,
Underneath the bright pavilion
  Of the Indian skies ;
Where his forest pathway lay
Through the blooms of Florida.

Years ago a lonely stranger,
  With the dusky brow
Of the outcast forest-ranger,
  Crossed the swift Powow ;
And betook him to the rill
And the oak upon the hill.

O'er his face of moody sadness
  For an instant shone
Something like a gleam of gladness,
  As he stooped him down

To the fountain's grassy side,
And his eager thirst supplied.

With the oak its shadow throwing
  O'er his mossy seat,
And the cool, sweet waters flowing
  Softly at his feet,
Closely by the fountain's rim
That lone Indian seated him.

Autumn's earliest frost had given
  To the woods below
Hues of beauty, such as heaven
  Lendeth to its bow ;
And the soft breeze from the west
Scarcely broke their dreamy rest.

Far behind was Ocean striving
  With his chains of sand ;
Southward, sunny glimpses giving,
  'Twixt the swells of land,
Of its calm and silvery track,
Rolled the tranquil Merrimack.

Over village, wood, and meadow
  Gazed that stranger man,
Sadly, till the twilight shadow
  Over all things ran,
Save where spire and westward pane
Flashed the sunset back again.

Gazing thus upon the dwelling
  Of his warrior sires,
Where no lingering trace was telling
  Of their wigwam fires,
Who the gloomy thoughts might know
Of that wandering child of woe ?

Naked lay, in sunshine glowing,
  Hills that once had stood
Down their sides the shadows throw
    ing
  Of a mighty wood,
Where the deer his covert kept,
And the eagle's pinion swept !

Where the birch canoe had glided
  Down the swift Powow,
Dark and gloomy bridges strided
  Those clear waters now ;
And where once the beaver swam,
Jarred the wheel and frowned the dam

For the wood-bird's merry singing,
  And the hunter's cheer,
Iron clang and hammer's ringing
  Smote upon his ear ;

And the thick and sullen smoke
From the blackened forges broke.

Could it be his fathers ever
    Loved to linger here ?
These bare hills, this conquered river, —
    Could they hold them dear,
With their native loveliness
Tamed and tortured into this ?

Sadly, as the shades of even
    Gathered o'er the hill,
While the western half of heaven
    Blushed with sunset still,
From the fountain's mossy seat
Turned the Indian's weary feet.

Year on year hath flown forever,
    But he came no more
To the hillside or the river
    Where he came before.
But the villager can tell
Of that strange man's visit well.

And the merry children, laden
    With their fruits or flowers, —
Roving boy and laughing maiden,
    In their school-day hours,
Love the simple tale to tell
Of the Indian and his well.

THE EXILES.

1660.

THE goodman sat beside his door
    One sultry afternoon,
With his young wife singing at his side
    An old and goodly tune.

A glimmer of heat was in the air ;
    The dark green woods were still ;
And the skirts of a heavy thunder-cloud
    Hung over the western hill.

Black, thick, and vast arose that cloud
    Above the wilderness,
As some dark world from upper air
    Were stooping over this.

At times the solemn thunder pealed,
    And all was still again,
Save a low murmur in the air
    Of coming wind and rain.

Just as the first big rain-drop fell,
    A weary stranger came,

And stood before the farmer's door,
    With travel soiled and lame.

Sad seemed he, yet sustaining hope
    Was in his quiet glance,
And peace, like autumn's moonlight, clothed
    His tranquil countenance.

A look, like that his Master wore
    In Pilate's council-hall :
It told of wrongs, — but of a love
    Meekly forgiving all.

"Friend ! wilt thou give me shelter
    here ?"
    The stranger meekly said ;
And, leaning on his oaken staff,
    The goodman's features read.

" My life is hunted, — evil men
    Are following in my track ;
The traces of the torturer's whip
    Are on my aged back.

" And much, I fear, 't will peril thee
    Within thy doors to take
A hunted seeker of the Truth,
    Oppressed for conscience' sake."

O, kindly spoke the goodman's wife, —
    " Come in, old man !" quoth she, —
" We will not leave thee to the storm,
    Whoever thou mayst be."

Then came the aged wanderer in,
    And silent sat him down ;
While all within grew dark as night
    Beneath the storm-cloud's frown.

But while the sudden lightning's blaze
    Filled every cottage nook,
And with the jarring thunder-roll
    The loosened casements shook,

A heavy tramp of horses' feet
    Came sounding up the lane,
And half a score of horse, or more,
    Came plunging through the rain.

"Now, Goodman Macey, ope thy door, —
    We would not be house-breakers ;
A rueful deed thou 'st done this day,
    In harboring banished Quakers."

Out looked the cautious goodman then,
    With much of fear and awe,

For there, with broad wig drenched with
        rain,
    The parish priest he saw.

"Open thy door, thou wicked man,
    And let thy pastor in,
And give God thanks, if forty stripes
    Repay thy deadly sin."

"What seek ye?" quoth the goodman, —
    "The stranger is my guest:
He is worn with toil and grievous
        wrong, —
    Pray let the old man rest."

"Now, out upon thee, canting knave!"
    And strong hands shook the door.
"Believe me, Macey," quoth the
        priest, —
    "Thou 'lt rue thy conduct sore."

Then kindled Macey's eye of fire:
    "No priest who walks the earth,
Shall pluck away the stranger-guest
    Made welcome to my hearth."

Down from his cottage wall he caught
    The matchlock, hotly tried
At Preston-pans and Marston-moor,
    By fiery Ireton's side;

Where Puritan, and Cavalier,
    With shout and psalm contended;
And Rupert's oath, and Cromwell's
        prayer,
    With battle-thunder blended.

Up rose the ancient stranger then:
    "My spirit is not free
To bring the wrath and violence
    Of evil men on thee:

"And for thyself, I pray forbear, —
    Bethink thee of thy Lord,
Who healed again the smitten ear,
    And sheathed his follower's sword.

"I go, as to the slaughter led:
    Friends of the poor, farewell!"
Beneath his hand the oaken door
    Back on its hinges fell.

"Come forth, old graybeard, yea and
        nay,"
    The reckless scoffers cried,
As to a horseman's saddle-bow
    The old man's arms were tied.

And of his bondage hard and long
    In Boston's crowded jail,
Where suffering woman's prayer was
        heard,
    With sickening childhood's wail,

It suits not with our tale to tell:
    Those scenes have passed away, —
Let the dim shadows of the past
    Brood o'er that evil day.

"Ho, sheriff!" quoth the ardent
        priest, —
    "Take Goodman Macey too;
The sin of this day's heresy
    His back or purse shall rue."

"Now, goodwife, haste thee!" Macey
        cried,
    She caught his manly arm: —
Behind, the parson urged pursuit,
    With outcry and alarm.

Ho! speed the Maceys, neck or naught, —
    The river-course was near: —
The plashing on its pebbled shore
    Was music to their ear.

A gray rock, tasselled o'er with birch,
    Above the waters hung,
And at its base, with every wave,
    A small light wherry swung.

A leap — they gain the boat — and there
    The goodman wields his oar:
"Ill luck betide them all," — he cried, —
    "The laggards upon the shore."

Down through the crashing underwood,
    The burly sheriff came: —
"Stand, Goodman Macey, — yield thy-
        self;
    Yield in the King's own name."

"Now out upon thy hangman's face!"
    Bold Macey answered then, —
"Whip *women*, on the village green,
    But meddle not with *men*."

The priest came panting to the shore, —
    His grave cocked hat was gone;
Behind him, like some owl's nest, hung
    His wig upon a thorn.

"Come back, — come back!" the par-
        son cried,
    "The church's curse beware."

"Curse, an' thou wilt," said Macey, "but
    Thy blessing prithee spare."

"Vile scoffer !" cried the baffled priest, —
    "Thou 'lt yet the gallows see."
"Who 's born to be hanged, will not be
        drowned,"
    Quoth Macey, merrily ;

"And so, sir sheriff and priest, good by !"
    He bent him to his oar,
And the small boat glided quietly
    From the twain upon the shore.

Now in the west, the heavy clouds
    Scattered and fell asunder,
While feebler came the rush of rain,
    And fainter growled the thunder.

And through the broken clouds, the sun
    Looked out serene and warm,
Painting its holy symbol-light
    Upon the passing storm.

O, beautiful ! that rainbow span,
    O'er dim Crane-neck was bended ; —
One bright foot touched the eastern hills,
    And one with ocean blended.

By green Pentucket's southern slope
    The small boat glided fast, —
The watchers of "the Block-house" saw
    The strangers as they passed.

That night a stalwart garrison
    Sat shaking in their shoes,
To hear the dip of Indian oars, —
    The glide of birch canoes.

The fisher-wives of Salisbury,
    (The men were all away,)
Looked out to see the stranger oar
    Upon their waters play.

Deer-Island's rocks and fir-trees threw
    Their sunset-shadows o'er them,
And Newbury's spire and weathercock
    Peered o'er the pines before them.

Around the Black Rocks, on their left,
    The marsh lay broad and green ;
And on their right, with dwarf shrubs
        crowned,
    Plum Island's hills were seen.

With skilful hand and wary eye
    The harbor-bar was crossed ; —

A plaything of the restless wave,
    The boat on ocean tossed.

The glory of the sunset heaven
    On land and water lay, —
On the steep hills of Agawam,
    On cape, and bluff, and bay.

They passed the gray rocks of Cape Ann,
    And Gloucester's harbor-bar ;
The watch-fire of the garrison
    Shone like a setting star.

How brightly broke the morning
    On Massachusetts Bay !
Blue wave, and bright green island,
    Rejoicing in the day.

On passed the bark in safety
    Round isle and headland steep, —
No tempest broke above them,
    No fog-cloud veiled the deep.

Far round the bleak and stormy Cape
    The vent'rous Macey passed,
And on Nantucket's naked isle
    Drew up his boat at last.

And how, in log-built cabin,
    They braved the rough sea-weather ;
And there, in peace and quietness,
    Went down life's vale together :

How others drew around them,
    And how their fishing sped,
Until to every wind of heaven
    Nantucket's sails were spread ;

How pale Want alternated
    With Plenty's golden smile ;
Behold, is it not written
    In the annals of the isle ?

And yet that isle remaineth
    A refuge of the free,
As when true-hearted Macey
    Beheld it from the sea.

Free as the winds that winnow
    Her shrubless hills of sand, —
Free as the waves that batter
    Along her yielding land.

Than hers, at duty's summons,
    No loftier spirit stirs, —
Nor falls o'er human suffering
    A readier tear than hers.

God bless the sea-beat island ! —
  And grant forevermore,
That charity and freedom dwell
  As now upon her shore !

THE NEW WIFE AND THE OLD.

DARK the halls, and cold the feast, —
Gone the bridemaids, gone the priest :
All is over, — all is done,
Twain of yesterday are one !
Blooming girl and manhood gray,
Autumn in the arms of May !

Hushed within and hushed without,
Dancing feet and wrestlers' shout ;
Dies the bonfire on the hill ;
All is dark and all is still,
Save the starlight, save the breeze
Moaning through the graveyard trees ;
And the great sea-waves below,
Pulse of the midnight beating slow.

From the brief dream of a bride
She hath wakened, at his side.
With half-uttered shriek and start, —
Feels she not his beating heart ?
And the pressure of his arm,
And his breathing near and warm ?

Lightly from the bridal bed
Springs that fair dishevelled head,
And a feeling, new, intense,
Half of shame, half innocence,
Maiden fear and wonder speaks
Through her lips and changing cheeks.

From the oaken mantel glowing
Faintest light the lamp is throwing
On the mirror's antique mould,
High-backed chair, and wainscot old,
And, through faded curtains stealing,
His dark sleeping face revealing.

Listless lies the strong man there,
Silver-streaked his careless hair ;
Lips of love have left no trace
On that hard and haughty face ;
And that forehead's knitted thought
Love's soft hand hath not unwrought.

"Yet," she sighs, "he loves me well,
More than these calm lips will tell.
Stooping to my lowly state,
He hath made me rich and great,
And I bless him, though he be
Hard and stern to all save me !"

While she speaketh, falls the light
O'er her fingers small and white ;
Gold and gem, and costly ring
Back the timid lustre fling, —
Love's selectest gifts, and rare,
His proud hand had fastened there.

Gratefully she marks the glow
From those tapering lines of snow ;
Fondly o'er the sleeper bending
His black hair with golden blending,
In her soft and light caress,
Cheek and lip together press.

Ha ! — that start of horror ! — Why
That wild stare and wilder cry,
Full of terror, full of pain ?
Is there madness in her brain ?
Hark ! that gasping, hoarse and low,
" Spare me, — spare me, — let me
      go ! "

God have mercy ! — Icy cold
Spectral hands her own enfold,
Drawing silently from them
Love's fair gifts of gold and gem,
"Waken ! save me !" still as death
At her side he slumbereth.

Ring and bracelet all are gone,
And that ice-cold hand withdrawn ;
But she hears a murmur low,
Full of sweetness, full of woe,
Half a sigh and half a moan :
" Fear not ! give the dead her own ! "

Ah ! — the dead wife's voice she knows !
That cold hand, whose pressure froze,
Once in warmest life had borne
Gem and band her own hath worn.
"Wake thee ! wake thee !" Lo, his
          eyes
Open with a dull surprise.

In his arms the strong man folds her,
Closer to his breast he holds her ;
Trembling limbs his own are meeting,
And he feels her heart's quick beating :
" Nay, my dearest, why this fear ?"
"Hush !" she saith, "the dead is here !"

" Nay, a dream, — an idle dream."
But before the lamp's pale gleam
Tremblingly her hand she raises, —
There no more the diamond blazes,
Clasp of pearl, or ring of gold, —
"Ah !" she sighs, "her hand was cold !"

Broken words of cheer he saith,
But his dark lip quivereth,
And as o'er the past he thinketh,
From his young wife's arms he shrinketh;
Can those soft arms round him lie,
Underneath his dead wife's eye?

She her fair young head can rest
Soothed and childlike on his breast,
And in trustful innocence
Draw new strength and courage thence;
He, the proud man, feels within
But the cowardice of sin!

She can murmur in her thought
Simple prayers her mother taught,
And His blessed angels call,
Whose great love is over all;
He, alone, in prayerless pride,
Meets the dark Past at her side!

One, who living shrank with dread
From his look, or word, or tread,
Unto whom her early grave
Was as freedom to the slave,
Moves him at this midnight hour,
With the dead's unconscious power!

Ah, the dead, the unforgot!
From their solemn homes of thought,
Where the cypress shadows blend
Darkly over foe and friend,
Or in love or sad rebuke,
Back upon the living look.

And the tenderest ones and weakest,
Who their wrongs have borne the meekest,
Lifting from those dark, still places,
Sweet and sad-remembered faces,
O'er the guilty hearts behind
An unwitting triumph find.

VOICES OF FREEDOM.

TOUSSAINT L'OUVERTURE.[32]

'T WAS night. The tranquil moonlight smile
  With which Heaven dreams of Earth, shed down
Its beauty on the Indian isle, —
  On broad green field and white-walled town;
And inland waste of rock and wood,
In searching sunshine, wild and rude,
Rose, mellowed through the silver gleam,
Soft as the landscape of a dream,
All motionless and dewy wet,
Tree, vine, and flower in shadow met:
The myrtle with its snowy bloom,
Crossing the nightshade's solemn gloom, —
The white cecropia's silver rind
Relieved by deeper green behind, —
The orange with its fruit of gold, —
The lithe paullinia's verdant fold, —
The passion-flower, with symbol holy,
Twining its tendrils long and lowly, —
The rhexias dark, and cassia tall,
And proudly rising over all,
The kingly palm's imperial stem,
Crowned with its leafy diadem,

Star-like, beneath whose sombre shade,
The fiery-winged cucullo played!
Yes, — lovely was thine aspect, then,
  Fair island of the Western Sea!
Lavish of beauty, even when
Thy brutes were happier than thy men,
  For they, at least, were free!
Regardless of thy glorious clime,
  Unmindful of thy soil of flowers,
The toiling negro sighed, that Time
  No faster sped his hours.
For, by the dewy moonlight still,
He fed the weary-turning mill,
Or bent him in the chill morass,
To pluck the long and tangled grass,
And hear above his scar-worn back
The heavy slave-whip's frequent crack:
While in his heart one evil thought
In solitary madness wrought,
One baleful fire surviving still
  The quenching of the immortal mind,
  One sterner passion of his kind,
Which even fetters could not kill, —
The savage hope, to deal, erelong,
A vengeance bitterer than his wrong!

Hark to that cry! — long, loud, and shrill,
From field and forest, rock and hill,

Thrilling and horrible it rang,
  Around, beneath, above ; —
The wild beast from his tavern sprang,
  The wild bird from her grove !
Nor fear, nor joy, nor agony
Were mingled in that midnight cry ;
But like the lion's growl of wrath,
When falls that hunter in his path
Whose barbed arrow, deeply set,
Is rankling in his bosom yet,
It told of hate, full, deep, and strong,
Of vengeance kindling out of wrong ;
It was as if the crimes of years —
The unrequited toil, the tears,
The shame and hate, which liken well
Earth's garden to the nether hell —
Had found in nature's self a tongue,
On which the gathered horror hung ;
As if from cliff, and stream, and glen
Burst on the startled ears of men
That voice which rises unto God,
Solemn and stern, — the cry of blood !
It ceased, — and all was still once more,
Save ocean chafing on his shore,
The sighing of the wind between
The broad banana's leaves of green,
Or bough by restless plumage shook,
Or murmuring voice of mountain brook.

Brief was the silence.   Once again
  Pealed to the skies that frantic yell,
Glowed on the heavens a fiery stain,
  And flashes rose and fell ;
And painted on the blood-red sky,
Dark, naked arms were tossed on high ;
And, round the white man's lordly hall,
  Trod, fierce and free, *the brute he made ;*
And those who crept along the wall,
And answered to his lightest call
  With more than spaniel dread, —
The creatures of his lawless beck, —
Were trampling on his very neck !
And on the night-air, wild and clear,
Rose woman's shriek of more than fear ;
For bloodied arms were round her thrown,
And dark cheeks pressed against her own !

Then, injured Afric ! — for the shame
Of thy own daughters, vengeance came
Full on the scornful hearts of those,
Who mocked thee in thy nameless woes,
And to thy hapless children gave
One choice, — pollution or the grave !
Where then was he whose fiery zeal
Had taught the trampled heart to feel,
Until despair itself grew strong,
And vengeance fed its torch from wrong ?

Now, when the thunderbolt is speeding ;
Now, when oppression's heart is bleed-
    ing ;
Now, when the latent curse of Time
  Is raining down in fire and blood, —
That curse which, through long years of
    crime,
Has gathered, drop by drop, its flood, —
Why strikes he not, the foremost one,
Where murder's sternest deeds are done !

He stood the aged palms beneath,
  That shadowed o'er his humble door,
Listening, with half-suspended breath,
To the wild sounds of fear and death,
  Toussaint l'Ouverture !
What marvel that his heart beat high !
  The blow for freedom had been given,
And blood had answered to the cry
  Which Earth sent up to Heaven !
What marvel that a fierce delight
Smiled grimly o'er his brow of night, —
As groan and shout and bursting flame
Told where the midnight tempest came,
With blood and fire along its van,
And death behind ! — he was a Man !

Yes, dark-souled chieftain ! — if the light
  Of mild Religion's heavenly ray
Unveiled not to thy mental sight
  The lowlier and the purer way,
In which the Holy Sufferer trod,
  Meekly amidst the sons of crime, —
That calm reliance upon God
For justice in his own good time, —
That gentleness to which belongs
Forgiveness for its many wrongs,
Even as the primal martyr, kneeling
For mercy on the evil-dealing, —
Let not the favored white man name
Thy stern appeal, with words of blame.
Has *he* not, with the light of heaven
  Broadly around him, made the same ?
Yea, on his thousand war-fields striven,
  And gloried in his ghastly shame ? —
Kneeling amidst his brother's blood,
To offer mockery unto God,
As if the High and Holy One
Could smile on deeds of murder done ! —
As if a human sacrifice
Were purer in his Holy eyes,
Though offered up by Christian hands,
Than the foul rites of Pagan lands !

*   *   *   *   *

Sternly, amidst his household band,
His carbine grasped within his hand,

The white man stood, prepared and still,
Waiting the shock of maddened men,
Unchained, and fierce as tigers, when
    The horn winds through their caverned
        hill.
And one was weeping in his sight, —
    The sweetest flower of all the isle, —
The bride who seemed but yesternight
    Love's fair embodied smile.
And, clinging to her trembling knee,
Looked up the form of infancy,
With tearful glance in either face
The secret of its fear to trace.

"Ha! stand or die!" The white man's
        eye
    His steady musket gleamed along,
As a tall Negro hastened nigh,
    With fearless step and strong.
"What, ho, Toussaint!" A moment
        more,
His shadow crossed the lighted floor.
"Away!" he shouted; "fly with me, —
The white man's bark is on the sea; —
Her sails must catch the seaward wind,
For sudden vengeance sweeps behind.
Our brethren from their graves have
        spoken,
The yoke is spurned, — the chain is
        broken;
On all the hills our fires are glowing, —
Through all the vales red blood is flowing!
No more the mocking White shall rest
His foot upon the Negro's breast;
No more, at morn or eve, shall drip
The warm blood from the driver's whip:
Yet, though Toussaint has vengeance
        sworn
For all the wrongs his race have borne, —
Though for each drop of Negro blood
The white man's veins shall pour a flood;
Not all alone the sense of ill
Around his heart is lingering still,
Nor deeper can the white man feel
The generous warmth of grateful zeal.
Friends of the Negro! fly with me, —
The path is open to the sea:
Away, for life!" — He spoke, and pressed
The young child to his manly breast,
As, headlong, through the cracking cane,
Down swept the dark insurgent train, —
Drunken and grim, with shout and yell
Howled through the dark, like sounds
        from hell.

Far out, in peace, the white man's sail
Swayed free before the sunrise gale.

Cloud-like that island hung afar,
    Along the bright horizon's verge,
O'er which the curse of servile war
    Rolled its red torrent, surge on surge;
And he—the Negro champion—where
    In the fierce tumult struggled he?
Go trace him by the fiery glare
Of dwellings in the midnight air, —
The yells of triumph and despair, —
    The streams that crimson to the sea!

Sleep calmly in thy dungeon-tomb,
    Beneath Besançon's alien sky,
Dark Haytien!—for the time shall come,
    Yea, even now is nigh, —
When, everywhere, thy name shall be
Redeemed from *color's infamy*;
And men shall learn to speak of thee,
As one of earth's great spirits, born
In servitude, and nursed in scorn,
Casting aside the weary weight
And fetters of its low estate,
In that strong majesty of soul
    Which knows no color, tongue, or
        clime, —
Which still hath spurned the base control
    Of tyrants through all time!
Far other hands than mine may wreathe
The laurel round thy brow of death,
And speak thy praise, as one whose word
A thousand fiery spirits stirred, —
Who crushed his foeman as a worm, —
Whose step on human hearts fell firm:—[33]
Be mine the better task to find
A tribute for thy lofty mind,
Amidst whose gloomy vengeance shone
Some milder virtues all thine own, —
Some gleams of feeling pure and warm,
Like sunshine on a sky of storm, —
Proofs that the Negro's heart retains
Some nobleness amidst its chains, —
That kindness to the wronged is never
    Without its excellent reward, —
Holy to human-kind and ever
    Acceptable to God.

THE SLAVE-SHIPS.[34]

> "That fatal, that perfidious bark,
> Built i' the eclipse, and rigged with curses dark."
> *Milton's Lycidas.*

"ALL ready?" cried the captain;
    "Ay, ay!" the seamen said;
"Heave up the worthless lubbers, —
    The dying and the dead."
Up from the slave-ship's prison
    Fierce, bearded heads were thrust:

" Now let the sharks look to it, —
  Toss up the dead ones first ! "

Corpse after corpse came up, —
  Death had been busy there ;
Where every blow is mercy,
  Why should the spoiler spare ?
Corpse after corpse they cast
  Sullenly from the ship,
Yet bloody with the traces
  Of fetter-link and whip.

Gloomily stood the captain,
  With his arms upon his breast,
With his cold brow sternly knotted,
  And his iron lip compressed.
"Are all the dead dogs over ?"
  Growled through that matted lip, —
" The blind ones are no better,
  Let 's lighten the good ship."

Hark ! from the ship's dark bosom,
  The very sounds of hell !
The ringing clank of iron, —
  The maniac's short, sharp yell ! —
The hoarse, low curse, throat-stifled, —
  The starving infant's moan, —
The horror of a breaking heart
  Poured through a mother's groan.

Up from that loathsome prison
  The stricken blind ones came :
Below, had all been darkness, —
  Above, was still the same.
Yet the holy breath of heaven
  Was sweetly breathing there,
And the heated brow of fever
  Cooled in the soft sea air.

" Overboard with them, shipmates ! "
  Cutlass and dirk were plied ;
Fettered and blind, one after one,
  Plunged down the vessel's side.
The sabre smote above, —
  Beneath, the lean shark lay,
Waiting with wide and bloody jaw
  His quick and human prey.

God of the earth ! what cries
  Rang upward unto thee ?
Voices of agony and blood,
  From ship-deck and from sea.
The last dull plunge was heard, —
  The last wave caught its stain, —
And the unsated shark looked up
  For human hearts in vain.

*   *   *   *   *

Red glowed the western waters, —
  The setting sun was there,
Scattering alike on wave and cloud
  His fiery mesh of hair.
Amidst a group in blindness,
  A solitary eye
Gazed, from the burdened slaver's deck,
  Into that burning sky.

" A storm," spoke out the gazer,
  " Is gathering and at hand, —
Curse on 't — I 'd give my other eye
  For one firm rood of land."
And then he laughed, — but only
  His echoed laugh replied, —
For the blinded and the suffering
  Alone were at his side.

Night settled on the waters,
  And on a stormy heaven,
While fiercely on that lone ship's track
  The thunder-gust was driven.
" A sail ! — thank God, a sail ! "
  And as the helmsman spoke,
Up through the stormy murmur
  A shout of gladness broke.

Down came the stranger vessel,
  Unheeding on her way,
So near that on the slaver's deck
  Fell off her driven spray.
" Ho ! for the love of mercy, —
  We 're perishing and blind ! "
A wail of utter agony
  Came back upon the wind :

" Help *us !* for we are stricken
  With blindness every one ;
Ten days we 've floated fearfully,
  Unnoting star or sun.
Our ship 's the slaver Leon, —
  We 've but a score on board, —
Our slaves are all gone over, —
  Help, — for the love of God ! "

On livid brows of agony
  The broad red lightning shone, —
But the roar of wind and thunder
  Stifled the answering groan ;
Wailed from the broken waters
  A last despairing cry,
As, kindling in the stormy light,
  The stranger ship went by.

*   *   *   *   *

In the sunny Guadaloupe
  A dark-hulled vessel lay, —

With a crew who noted never
    The nightfall or the day.
The blossom of the orange
    Was white by every stream,
And tropic leaf, and flower, and bird
    Were in the warm sunbeam.

And the sky was bright as ever,
    And the moonlight slept as well,
On the palm-trees by the hillside,
    And the streamlet of the dell :
And the glances of the Creole
    Were still as archly deep,
And her smiles as full as ever
    Of passion and of sleep.

But vain were bird and blossom,
    The green earth and the sky,
And the smile of human faces,
    To the slaver's darkened eye ;
At the breaking of the morning,
    At the star-lit evening time,
O'er a world of light and beauty
    Fell the blackness of his crime.

STANZAS.

[" The despotism which our fathers could not
bear in their native country is expiring, and the
sword of justice in her reformed hands has ap-
plied its exterminating edge to slavery. Shall
the United States — the free United States,
which could not bear the bonds of a king —
cradle the bondage which a king is abolishing ?
Shall a Republic be less free than a Monarchy ?
Shall we, in the vigor and buoyancy of our
manhood, be less energetic in righteousness than
a kingdom in its age ?" — *Dr. Follen's Address.*

" Genius of America ! — Spirit of our free in-
stitutions ! — where art thou ? — How art thou
fallen, O Lucifer ! son of the morning, — how
art thou fallen from Heaven ! Hell from beneath
is moved for thee, to meet thee at thy coming !
— The kings of the earth cry out to thee, Aha !
Aha ! — ART THOU BECOME LIKE UNTO US ?" —
Speech of Samuel J. May.]

OUR fellow-countrymen in chains !
    Slaves — in a land of light and law !
Slaves — crouching on the very plains
    Where rolled the storm of Freedom's
        war !
A groan from Eutaw's haunted wood, —
    A wail where Camden's martyrs fell, —
By every shrine of patriot blood,
    From Moultrie's wall and Jaspar's well !

By storied hill and hallowed grot,
    By mossy wood and marshy glen,
Whence rang of old the rifle-shot,
    And hurrying shout of Marion's men !

The groan of breaking hearts is there, —
    The failing lash, — the fetter's clank !
Slaves, — SLAVES are breathing in that
        air,
    Which old De Kalb and Sumter drank !

What, ho ! — *our* countrymen in chains !
    The whip on WOMAN's shrinking flesh !
Our soil yet reddening with the stains
    Caught from her scourging, warm and
        fresh !
What ! mothers from their children
        riven !
    What ! God's own image bought and
        sold !
AMERICANS to market driven,
    And bartered as the brute for gold !

Speak ! shall their agony of prayer
    Come thrilling to our hearts in vain ?
To us whose fathers scorned to bear
    The paltry *menace* of a chain ;
To us, whose boast is loud and long
    Of holy Liberty and Light, —
Say, shall these writhing slaves of Wrong
    Plead vainly for their plundered Right ?

What ! shall we send, with lavish breath,
    Our sympathies across the wave,
Where Manhood, on the field of death,
    Strikes for his freedom or a grave ?
Shall prayers go up, and hymns be sung
    For Greece, the Moslem fetter spurning,
And millions hail with pen and tongue
    Our light on all her altars burning ?

Shall Belgium feel, and gallant France,
    By Vendome's pile and Schoenbrun's
        wall,
And Poland, gasping on her lance,
    The impulse of our cheering call ?
And shall the SLAVE, beneath our eye,
    Clank o'er *our* fields his hateful chain ?
And toss his fettered arms on high,
    And groan for Freedom's gift, in vain ?

O, say, shall Prussia's banner be
    A refuge for the stricken slave ?
And shall the Russian serf go free
    By Baikal's lake and Neva's wave ?
And shall the wintry-bosomed Dane
    Relax the iron hand of pride,
And bid his bondmen cast the chain,
    From fettered soul and limb, aside ?

Shall every flap of England's flag
    Proclaim that all around are free,

From "farthest Ind" to each blue crag
  That beetles o'er the Western Sea?
And shall we scoff at Europe's kings,
  When Freedom's fire is dim with us,
And round our country's altar clings
  The damning shade of Slavery's curse?

Go — let us ask of Constantine
  To loose his grasp on Poland's throat;
And beg the lord of Mahmoud's line
  To spare the struggling Suliote, —
Will not the scorching answer come
  From turbaned Turk, and scornful
    Russ :
" Go, loose your fettered slaves at home,
  Then turn, and ask the like of us !"

Just God ! and shall we calmly rest,
  The Christian's scorn, — the heathen's
    mirth, —
Content to live the lingering jest
  And by-word of a mocking Earth ?
Shall our own glorious land retain
  That curse which Europe scorns to bear?
Shall our own brethren drag the chain
  Which not even Russia's menials wear?

Up, then, in Freedom's manly part,
  From graybeard eld to fiery youth,
And on the nation's naked heart
  Scatter the living coals of Truth !
Up, — while ye slumber, deeper yet
  The shadow of our fame is growing !
Up, — while ye pause, our sun may set
  In blood, around our altars flowing !

Oh ! rouse ye, ere the storm comes
    forth, —
  The gathered wrath of God and man, —
Like that which wasted Egypt's earth,
  When hail and fire above it ran.
Hear ye no warnings in the air ?
  Feel ye no earthquake underneath ?
Up, — up ! why will ye slumber where
  The sleeper only wakes in death ?

Up *now* for Freedom ! — not in strife
  Like that your sterner fathers saw, —
The awful waste of human life, —
  The glory and the guilt of war :
But break the chain, — the yoke remove,
  And smite to earth Oppression's rod,
With those mild arms of Truth and Love,
  Made mighty through the living God !

Down let the shrine of Moloch sink,
  And leave no traces where it stood ;

Nor longer let its idol drink
  His daily cup of human blood ;
But rear another altar there,
  To Truth and Love and Mercy given,
And Freedom's gift, and Freedom's prayer,
  Shall call an answer down from
    Heaven !

THE YANKEE GIRL.

SHE sings by her wheel at that low cot-
    tage-door,
Which the long evening shadow is
  stretching before,
With a music as sweet as the music
  which seems
Breathed softly and faint in the ear of
  our dreams !

How brilliant and mirthful the light of
  her eye,
Like a star glancing out from the blue
  of the sky !
And lightly and freely her dark tresses
  play
O'er a brow and a bosom as lovely as they !

Who comes in his pride to that low cot-
    tage-door, —
The haughty and rich to the humble and
  poor ?
'T is the great Southern planter, — the
  master who waves
His whip of dominion o'er hundreds of
  slaves.

" Nay, Ellen, — for shame ! Let those
  Yankee fools spin,
Who would pass for our slaves with a
  change of their skin ;
Let them toil as they will at the loom
  or the wheel,
Too stupid for shame, and too vulgar to
  feel !

" But thou art too lovely and precious a
    gem
To be bound to their burdens and sullied by them, —
For shame, Ellen, shame, — cast thy
  bondage aside,
And away to the South, as my blessing
  and pride.

" O, come where no winter thy footsteps
  can wrong,

But where flowers are blossoming all the
  year long,
Where the shade of the palm-tree is
  over my home,
And the lemon and orange are white in
  their bloom !

"O, come to my home, where my servants shall all
Depart at thy bidding and come at thy
  call ;
They shall heed thee as mistress with
  trembling and awe,
And each wish of thy heart shall be felt
  as a law."

O, could ye have seen her — that pride
  of our girl's —
Arise and cast back the dark wealth of
  her curls,
With a scorn in her eye which the gazer
  could feel,
And a glance like the sunshine that
  flashes on steel !

"Go back, haughty Southron ! thy
  treasures of gold
Are dim with the blood of the hearts thou
  hast sold ;
Thy home may be lovely, but round it
  I hear
The crack of the whip and the footsteps
  of fear !

"And the sky of thy South may be
  brighter than ours,
And greener thy landscapes, and fairer
  thy flowers ;
But dearer the blast round our mountains which raves,
Than the sweet summer zephyr which
  breathes over slaves !

"Full low at thy bidding thy negroes
  may kneel,
With the iron of bondage on spirit and
  heel ;
Yet know that the Yankee girl sooner
  would be
In fetters with them, than in freedom
  with thee !"

TO W. L. G.

CHAMPION of those who groan beneath
  Oppression's iron hand :
In view of penury, hate, and death,
  I see thee fearless stand.

Still bearing up thy lofty brow,
  In the steadfast strength of truth,
In manhood sealing well the vow
  And promise of thy youth.

Go on, — for thou hast chosen well ;
  On in the strength of God !
Long as one human heart shall swell
  Beneath the tyrant's rod.
Speak in a slumbering nation's ear,
  As thou hast ever spoken,
Until the dead in sin shall hear, —
  The fetter's link be broken !

I love thee with a brother's love,
  I feel my pulses thrill,
To mark thy spirit soar above
  The cloud of human ill.
My heart hath leaped to answer thine,
  And echo back thy words,
As leaps the warrior's at the shine
  And flash of kindred swords !

They tell me thou art rash and vain, —
  A searcher after fame ;
That thou art striving but to gain
  A long-enduring name ;
That thou hast nerved the Afric's hand
  And steeled the Afric's heart,
To shake aloft his vengeful brand,
  And rend his chain apart.

Have I not known thee well, and read
  Thy mighty purpose long ?
And watched the trials which have made
  Thy human spirit strong ?
And shall the slanderer's demon breath
  Avail with one like me,
To dim the sunshine of my faith
  And earnest trust in thee ?

Go on, — the dagger's point may glare
  Amid thy pathway's gloom, —
The fate which sternly threatens there
  Is glorious martyrdom !
Then onward with a martyr's zeal ;
  And wait thy sure reward
When man to man no more shall kneel,
  And God alone be Lord !
  1833.

SONG OF THE FREE.

PRIDE of New England !
  Soul of our fathers !
Shrink we all craven-like,
  When the storm gathers ?

What though the tempest be
    Over us lowering,
Where 's the New-Englander
    Shamefully cowering ?
Graves green and holy
    Around us are lying, —
Free were the sleepers all,
    Living and dying !

Back with the Southerner's
    Padlocks and scourges !
Go, — let him fetter down
    Ocean's free surges !
Go, — let him silence
    Winds, clouds, and waters, —
Never New England's own
    Free sons and daughters !
Free as our rivers are
    Ocean-ward going, —
Free as the breezes are
    Over us blowing.

Up to our altars, then,
    Haste we, and summon
Courage and loveliness,
    Manhood and woman !
Deep let our pledges be :
    Freedom forever !
Truce with oppression,
    Never, O, never !
By our own birthright-gift,
    Granted of Heaven, —
Freedom for heart and lip,
    Be the pledge given !

If we have whispered truth,
    Whisper no longer ;
Speak as the tempest does,
    Sterner and stronger ;
Still be the tones of truth
    Louder and firmer,
Startling the haughty South
    With the deep murmur ;
God and our charter's right,
    Freedom forever !
Truce with oppression,
    Never, O, never !
1836.

THE HUNTERS OF MEN.

HAVE ye heard of our hunting, o'er
        mountain and glen,
Through cane-brake and forest, — the
    hunting of men ?
The lords of our land to this hunting
    have gone,
As the fox-hunter follows the sound of
    the horn ;
Hark ! — the cheer and the hallo ! — the
    crack of the whip,
And the yell of the hound as he fastens
    his grip !
All blithe are our hunters, and noble
    their match, —
Though hundreds are caught, there are
    millions to catch.
So speed to their hunting, o'er mountain
    and glen,
Through cane-brake and forest, — the
    hunting of men !

Gay luck to our hunters ! — how nobly
    they ride
In the glow of their zeal, and the strength
    of their pride ! —
The priest with his cassock flung back
    on the wind,
Just screening the politic statesman be-
    hind, —
The saint and the sinner, with cursing
    and prayer,
The drunk and the sober, ride merrily
    there.
And woman, — kind woman, — wife,
    widow, and maid,
For the good of the hunted, is lending
    her aid :
Her foot 's in the stirrup, her hand on
    the rein,
How blithely she rides to the hunting of
    men !

O, goodly and grand is our hunting to
    see,
In this "land of the brave and this
    home of the free."
Priest, warrior, and statesman, from
    Georgia to Maine,
All mounting the saddle, — all grasping
    the rein, —
Right merrily hunting the black man,
    whose sin
Is the curl of his hair and the hue of
    his skin !
Woe, now, to the hunted who turns him
    at bay !
Will our hunters be turned from their
    purpose and prey ?
Will their hearts fail within them ? —
    their nerves tremble, when
All roughly they ride to the hunting of
    men ?

Ho ! — ALMS for our hunters ! all weary
    and faint,
Wax the curse of the sinner and prayer
    of the saint.
The horn is wound faintly, — the echoes
    are still,
Over cane-brake and river, and forest
    and hill.
Haste, — alms for our hunters ! the
    hunted once more
Have turned from their flight with their
    backs to the shore :
What right have *they* here in the home
    of the white,
Shadowed o'er by *our* banner of Free-
    dom and Right ?
Ho ! — alms for the hunters ! or never
    again
Will they ride in their pomp to the
    hunting of men !

ALMS, — ALMS for our hunters ! why
    will ye delay,
When their pride and their glory are
    melting away ?
The parson has turned ; for, on charge
    of his own,
Who goeth a warfare, or hunting, alone ?
The politic statesman looks back with a
    sigh, —
There is doubt in his heart, — there is
    fear in his eye.
O, haste, lest that doubting and fear
    shall prevail,
And the head of his steed take the place
    of the tail.
O, haste, ere he leave us ! for who will
    ride then,
For pleasure or gain, to the hunting of
    men ?
1835.

CLERICAL OPPRESSORS.

[In the report of the celebrated proslavery
meeting in Charlestown, S. C., on the 4th of
the 9th month, 1835, published in the Courier
of that city, it is stated : " *The* CLERGY *of all
denominations attended in a body*, LENDING THEIR
SANCTION TO THE PROCEEDINGS, and adding by
their presence to the impressive character of the
scene ! "]

JUST God ! — and these are they
Who minister at thine altar, God of Right !
Men who their hands with prayer and
    blessing lay
On Israel's Ark of light !

What ! preach and kidnap men ?
Give thanks, — and rob thy own af-
    flicted poor ?
Talk of thy glorious liberty, and then
    Bolt hard the captive's door ?

What ! servants of thy own
Merciful Son, who came to seek and
    save
The homeless and the outcast, — fetter-
    ing down
The tasked and plundered slave !

Pilate and Herod, friends !
Chief priests and rulers, as of old, com-
    bine !
Just God and holy ! is that church,
    which lends
Strength to the spoiler, thine ?

Paid hypocrites, who turn
Judgment aside, and rob the Holy Book
Of those high words of truth which
    search and burn
In warning and rebuke ;

Feed fat, ye locusts, feed !
And, in your tasselled pulpits, thank
    the Lord
That, from the toiling bondman's utter
    need,
Ye pile your own full board.

How long, O Lord ! how long
Shall such a priesthood barter truth away,
And in thy name, for robbery and wrong
    At thy own altars pray ?

Is not thy hand stretched forth
Visibly in the heavens, to awe and smite ?
Shall not the living God of all the
    earth,
And heaven above, do right ?

Woe, then, to all who grind
Their brethren of a common Father
    down !
To all who plunder from the immortal
    mind
Its bright and glorious crown !

Woe to the priesthood ! woe
To those whose hire is with the price of
    blood, —
Perverting, darkening, changing, as they
    go,
The searching truths of God !

Their glory and their might
Shall perish ; and their very names
    shall be
Vile before all the people, in the light
    Of a world's liberty.

O, speed the moment on
When Wrong shall cease, and Liberty
    and Love
And Truth and Right throughout the
    earth be known
As in their home above.

THE CHRISTIAN SLAVE.

[In a late publication of L. F. Tasistro —
"Random Shots and Southern Breezes " — is a
description of a slave auction at New Orleans, at
which the auctioneer recommended the woman
on the stand as " A GOOD CHRISTIAN ! "]

A CHRISTIAN ! going, gone !
Who bids for God's own image ? — for
    his grace,
Which that poor victim of the market-
    place
Hath in her suffering won ?

My God ! can such things be ?
Hast thou not said that whatsoe'er is done
Unto thy weakest and thy humblest one
    Is even done to thee ?

In that sad victim, then,
Child of thy pitying love, I see thee
    stand, —
Once more the jest-word of a mocking
    band,
    Bound, sold, and scourged again !

A Christian up for sale !
Wet with her blood your whips, o'er-
    task her frame,
Make her life loathsome with your wrong
    and shame,
    Her patience shall not fail !

A heathen hand might deal
Back on your heads the gathered wrong
    of years :
But her low, broken prayer and nightly
    tears,
    Ye neither heed nor feel.

Con well thy lesson o'er,
Thou prudent teacher, — tell the toiling
    slave

No dangerous tale of Him who came to
    save
    The outcast and the poor.

But wisely shut the ray
Of God's free Gospel from her simple heart,
And to her darkened mind alone impart
    One stern command, — OBEY !

So shalt thou deftly raise
The market price of human flesh ; and
    while
On thee, their pampered guest, the
    planters smile,
    Thy church shall praise.

Grave, reverend men shall tell
From Northern pulpits how thy work
    was blest,
While in that vile South Sodom first
    and best,
    Thy poor disciples sell.

O, shame ! the Moslem thrall,
Who, with his master, to the Prophet
    kneels,
While turning to the sacred Kebla feels
    His fetters break and fall.

Cheers for the turbaned Bey
Of robber-peopled Tunis ! he hath torn
The dark slave-dungeons open, and hath
    borne
    Their inmates into day :

But our poor slave in vain
Turns to the Christian shrine his aching
    eyes, —
Its rites will only swell his market price,
    And rivet on his chain.

God of all right ! how long
Shall priestly robbers at thine altar stand,
Lifting in prayer to thee, the bloody hand
    And haughty brow of wrong ?

O, from the fields of cane,
From the low rice-swamp, from the
    trader's cell, —
From the black slave-ship's foul and
    loathsome hell,
    And coffle's weary chain, —

Hoarse, horrible, and strong,
Rises to Heaven that agonizing cry,
Filling the arches of the hollow sky,
    HOW LONG, O GOD, HOW LONG ?

STANZAS FOR THE TIMES.

Is this the land our fathers loved,
   The freedom which they toiled to win ?
Is this the soil whereon they moved ?
   Are these the graves they slumber in ?
Are *we* the sons by whom are borne
The mantles which the dead have worn ?

And shall we crouch above these graves,
   With craven soul and fettered lip ?
Yoke in with marked and branded slaves,
   And tremble at the driver's whip ?
Bend to the earth our pliant knees,
And speak — but as our masters please ?

Shall outraged Nature cease to feel ?
   Shall Mercy's tears no longer flow ?
Shall ruffian threats of cord and steel, —
   The dungeon's gloom, — the assas-
      sin's blow,
Turn back the spirit roused to save
The Truth, our Country, and the Slave ?

Of human skulls that shrine was made,
   Round which the priests of Mexico
Before their loathsome idol prayed ; —
   Is Freedom's altar fashioned so ?
And must we yield to Freedom's God,
As offering meet, the negro's blood ?

Shall tongues be mute, when deeds are
      wrought
   Which well might shame extremest
      hell ?
Shall freemen lock the indignant thought ?
   Shall Pity's bosom cease to swell ?
Shall Honor bleed ? — shall Truth suc-
      cumb ?
Shall pen, and press, and soul be dumb ?

No ; — by each spot of haunted ground,
   Where Freedom weeps her children's
      fall, —
By Plymouth's rock, and Bunker's
      mound, —
   By Griswold's stained and shattered
      wall, —
By Warren's ghost, — by Langdon's
      shade, —
By all the memories of our dead !

By their enlarging souls, which burst
   The bands and fetters round them
      set, —
By the free Pilgrim spirit nursed
   Within our inmost bosoms, yet, —

By all above, around, below,
Be ours the indignant answer, — NO !

No ; — guided by our country's laws,
   For truth, and right, and suffering man,
Be ours to strive in Freedom's cause,
   As Christians *may*, — as freemen *can !*
Still pouring on unwilling ears
That truth oppression only fears.

What ! shall we guard our neighbor still,
   While woman shrieks beneath his rod,
And while he tramples down at will
   The image of a common God !
Shall watch and ward be round him set,
Of Northern nerve and bayonet ?

And shall we know and share with him
   The danger and the growing shame ?
And see our Freedom's light grow dim,
   Which should have filled the world
      with flame ?
And, writhing, feel, where'er we turn,
A world's reproach around us burn ?

Is 't not enough that this is borne ?
   And asks our haughty neighbor more ?
Must fetters which his slaves have worn
   Clank round the Yankee farmer's door ?
Must he be told, beside his plough,
What he must speak, and when, and
      how ?

Must he be told his freedom stands
   On Slavery's dark foundations
      strong, —
On breaking hearts and fettered hands,
   On robbery, and crime, and wrong ?
That all his fathers taught is vain, —
That Freedom's emblem is the chain ?

Its life, its soul, from slavery drawn ?
   False, foul, profane ! Go, — teach a
      well
Of holy Truth from Falsehood born !
   Of Heaven refreshed by airs from Hell !
Of Virtue in the arms of Vice !
Of Demons planting Paradise !

Rail on, then, " brethren of the
      South," —
   Ye shall not hear the truth the less ; —
No seal is on the Yankee's mouth,
   No fetter on the Yankee's press !
From our Green Mountains to the sea,
One voice shall thunder, — WE ARE
   FREE !

LINES,

WRITTEN ON READING THE MESSAGE
OF GOVERNOR RITNER, OF PENN-
SYLVANIA, 1836.

THANK God for the token ! — one lip is
    still free, —
One spirit untrammelled, — unbending
    one knee !
Like the oak of the mountain, deep-
    rooted and firm,
Erect, when the multitude bends to the
    storm ;
When traitors to Freedom, and Honor,
    and God,
Are bowed at an Idol polluted with
    blood ;
When the recreant North has forgotten
    her trust,
And the lip of her honor is low in the
    dust, —
Thank God, that one arm from the
    shackle has broken !
Thank God, that one man as a *freeman*
    has spoken !

O'er thy crags, Alleghany, a blast has
    been blown !
Down thy tide, Susquehanna, the mur-
    mur has gone !
To the land of the South, — of the char-
    ter and chain, —
Of Liberty sweetened with Slavery's
    pain ;
Where the cant of Democracy dwells on
    the lips
Of the forgers of fetters, and wielders of
    whips !
Where "chivalric" honor means really
    no more
Than scourging of women, and robbing
    the poor !
Where the Moloch of Slavery sitteth on
    high,
And the words which he utters, are —
    WORSHIP, OR DIE !

Right onward, O speed it ! Wherever
    the blood
Of the wronged and the guiltless is cry-
    ing to God ;
Wherever a slave in his fetters is pining ;
Wherever the lash of the driver is twin-
    ing ;
Wherever from kindred, torn rudely
    apart,

Comes the sorrowful wail of the broken
    of heart ;
Wherever the shackles of tyranny bind,
In silence and darkness, the God-given
    mind ;
There, God speed it onward ! — its truth
    will be felt, —
The bonds shall be loosened, — the iron
    shall melt !

And O, will the land where the free soul
    of PENN
Still lingers and breathes over mountain
    and glen, —
Will the land where a BENEZET'S spirit
    went forth
To the peeled and the meted, and outcast
    of Earth, —
Where the words of the Charter of Lib-
    erty first
From the soul of the sage and the pa-
    triot burst, —
Where first for the wronged and the weak
    of their kind,
The Christian and statesman their efforts
    combined, —
Will that land of the free and the good
    wear a chain ?
Will the call to the rescue of Freedom
    be vain ?

No, RITNER ! — her "Friends" at thy
    warning shall stand
Erect for the truth, like their ancestral
    band ;
Forgetting the feuds and the strife of
    past time,
Counting coldness injustice, and silence
    a crime ;
Turning back from the cavil of creeds,
    to unite
Once again for the poor in defence of the
    Right ;
Breasting calmly, but firmly, the full
    tide of Wrong,
Overwhelmed, but not borne on its surges
    along ;
Unappalled by the danger, the shame,
    and the pain,
And counting each trial for Truth as
    their gain !

And that bold-hearted yeomanry, hon-
    est and true,
Who, haters of fraud, give to labor its due;
Whose fathers, of old, sang in concert
    with thine,

On the banks of Swetara, the songs of
  the Rhine, —
The German-born pilgrims, who first
  dared to brave
The scorn of the proud in the cause of
  the slave : —
Will the sons of such men yield the
  lords of the South
One brow for the brand, — for the pad-
  lock one mouth ?
They cater to tyrants ? — They rivet the
  chain,
Which their fathers smote off, on the
  negro again ?

No, never ! — one voice, like the sound
  in the cloud,
When the roar of the storm waxes loud
  and more loud,
Wherever the foot of the freeman hath
  pressed
From the Delaware's marge to the Lake
  of the West,
On the South-going breezes shall deepen
  and grow
Till the land it sweeps over shall tremble
  below !
The voice of a PEOPLE, — uprisen, —
  awake, —
Pennsylvania's watchword, with Free-
  dom at stake,
Thrilling up from each valley, flung
  down from each height,
" OUR COUNTRY AND LIBERTY ! — GOD
  FOR THE RIGHT ! "

THE PASTORAL LETTER.

So, this is all, — the utmost reach
  Of priestly power the mind to fetter !
When laymen think — when women
  preach —
  A war of words — a "Pastoral Let-
  ter !"
Now, shame upon ye, parish Popes !
  Was it thus with those, your prede-
  cessors,
Who sealed with racks, and fire, and
  ropes
  Their loving-kindness to transgressors ?

A "Pastoral Letter," grave and dull —
  Alas ! in hoof and horns and features,
How different is your Brookfield bull,
  From him who bellows from St. Pe-
  ter's !

Your pastoral rights and powers from
  harm,
Think ye, can words alone preserve
  them ?
Your wiser fathers taught the arm
  And sword of temporal power to serve
  them.

O, glorious days, — when Church and
  State
Were wedded by your spiritual fathers !
And on submissive shoulders sat
  Your Wilsons and your Cotton Ma-
  thers.
No vile "itinerant" then could mar
  The beauty of your tranquil Zion,
But at his peril of the scar
  Of hangman's whip and branding-iron.

Then, wholesome laws relieved the Church
  Of heretic and mischief-maker,
And priest and bailiff joined in search,
  By turns, of Papist, witch, and Qua-
  ker !
The stocks were at each church's door,
  The gallows stood on Boston Common,
A Papist's ears the pillory bore, —
  The gallows-rope, a Quaker woman !

Your fathers dealt not as ye deal
  With "non-professing" frantic teach-
  ers ;
They bored the tongue with red-hot steel,
  And flayed the backs of "female
  preachers."
Old Newbury, had her fields a tongue,
  And Salem's streets could tell their
  story,
Of fainting woman dragged along,
  Gashed by the whip, accursed and
  gory!

And will ye ask me, why this taunt
  Of memories sacred from the scorner ?
And why with reckless hand I plant
  A nettle on the graves ye honor ?
Not to reproach New England's dead
  This record from the past I summon,
Of manhood to the scaffold led,
  And suffering and heroic woman.

No, — for yourselves alone, I turn
  The pages of intolerance over,
That, in their spirit, dark and stern,
  Ye haply may your own discover !
For, if ye claim the "pastoral right,"
  To silence Freedom's voice of warning,

And from your precincts shut the light
  Of Freedom's day around ye dawn-
    ing ;

If when an earthquake voice of power,
  And signs in earth and heaven, are
    showing
That forth, in its appointed hour,
  The Spirit of the Lord is going ! ˙
And, with that Spirit, Freedom's light
  On kindred, tongue, and people break-
    ing,
Whose slumbering millions, at the sight,
  In glory and in strength are waking !

When for the sighing of the poor,
  And for the needy, God hath risen,
And chains are breaking, and a door
  Is opening for the souls in prison !
If then ye would, with puny hands,
  Arrest the very work of Heaven,
And bind anew the evil bands
  Which God's right arm of power hath
    riven, —

What marvel that, in many a mind,
  Those darker deeds of bigot madness
Are closely with your own combined,
  Yet " less in anger than in sadness " ?
What marvel, if the people learn
  To claim the right of free opinion ?
What marvel, if at times they spurn
  The ancient yoke of your dominion ?

A glorious remnant linger yet,
  Whose lips are wet at Freedom's foun-
    tains,
The coming of whose welcome feet
  Is beautiful upon our mountains !
Men, who the gospel tidings bring
  Of Liberty and Love forever,
Whose joy is an abiding spring,
  Whose peace is as a gentle river !

But ye, who scorn the thrilling tale
  Of Carolina's high-souled daughters,
Which echoes here the mournful wail
  Of sorrow from Edisto's waters,
Close while ye may the public ear, —
  With malice vex, with slander wound
    them, —
The pure and good shall throng to hear,
  And tried and manly hearts surround
    them.

O, ever may the power which led
  Their way to such a fiery trial,

And strengthened womanhood to tread
  The wine-press of such self-denial,
Be round them in an evil land,
  With wisdom and with strength from
    Heaven,
With Miriam's voice, and Judith's hand,
  And Deborah's song, for triumph given !

And what are ye who strive with God
  Against the ark of his salvation,
Moved by the breath of prayer abroad,
  With blessings for a dying nation ?
What, but the stubble and the hay
  To perish, even as flax consuming,
With all that bars his glorious way,
  Before the brightness of his coming ?

And thou, sad Angel, who so long
  Hast waited for the glorious token,
That Earth from all her bonds of wrong
  To liberty and light has broken, —
Angel of Freedom ! soon to thee
  The sounding trumpet shall be given,
And over Earth's full jubilee
  Shall deeper joy be felt in Heaven !

LINES,

WRITTEN FOR THE MEETING OF THE
ANTISLAVERY SOCIETY, AT CHAT-
HAM STREET CHAPEL, N. Y., HELD
ON THE 4TH OF THE 7TH MONTH,
1834.

O Thou, whose presence went before
  Our fathers in their weary way,
As with thy chosen moved of yore
  The fire by night, the cloud by day !

When from each temple of the free,
  A nation's song ascends to Heaven,
Most Holy Father ! unto thee
  May not our humble prayer be given ?

Thy children all, — though hue and form
  Are varied in thine own good will, —
With thy own holy breathings warm,
  And fashioned in thine image still.

We thank thee, Father ! — hill and plain
  Around us wave their fruits once more,
And clustered vine, and blossomed grain,
  Are bending round each cottage door.

And peace is here ; and hope and love
  Are round us as a mantle thrown,

And unto Thee, supreme above,
  The knee of prayer is bowed alone.

But O, for those this day can bring,
  As unto us, no joyful thrill, —
For those who, under Freedom's wing,
  Are bound in Slavery's fetters still :

For those to whom thy living word
  Of light and love is never given, —
For those whose ears have never heard
  The promise and the hope of Heaven !

For broken heart, and clouded mind,
  Whereon no human mercies fall, —
O, be thy gracious love inclined,
  Who, as a Father, pitiest all !

And grant, O Father ! that the time
  Of Earth's deliverance may be near,
When every land and tongue and clime
  The message of thy love shall hear, —

When, smitten as with fire from heaven,
  The captive's chain shall sink in dust,
And to his fettered soul be given
  The glorious freedom of the just !

LINES,

WRITTEN FOR THE CELEBRATION OF
THE THIRD ANNIVERSARY OF BRIT-
ISH EMANCIPATION AT THE BROAD-
WAY TABERNACLE, N. Y., "FIRST OF
AUGUST," 1837.

O HOLY FATHER ! — just and true
  Are all thy works and words and ways,
And unto thee alone are due
    Thanksgiving and eternal praise !
As children of thy gracious care,
  We veil the eye, we bend the knee,
With broken words of praise and prayer,
  Father and God, we come to thee.

For thou hast heard, O God of Right,
  The sighing of the island slave ;
And stretched for him the arm of might,
  Not shortened that it could not save.
The laborer sits beneath his vine,
  The shackled soul and hand are free, —
Thanksgiving ! — for the work is thine !
  Praise ! — for the blessing is of thee !

And O, we feel thy presence here, —
  Thy awful arm in judgment bare !

Thine eye hath seen the bondman's tear,—
  Thine ear hath heard the bondman's
    prayer.
Praise ! — for the pride of man is low,
  The counsels of the wise are naught,
The fountains of repentance flow ;
  What hath our God in mercy wrought ?

Speed on thy work, Lord God of Hosts !
  And when the bondman's chain is
    riven,
And swells from all our guilty coasts
  The anthem of the free to Heaven,
O, not to those whom thou hast led,
  As with thy cloud and fire before,
But unto thee, in fear and dread,
  Be praise and glory evermore.

LINES,

WRITTEN FOR THE ANNIVERSARY CEL-
 EBRATION OF THE FIRST OF AUGUST,
AT MILTON, 1846.

A FEW brief years have passed away
  Since Britain drove her million slaves
Beneath the tropic's fiery ray :
God willed their freedom ; and to-day
  Life blooms above those island graves !

He spoke ! across the Carib Sea,
  We heard the clash of breaking chains,
And felt the heart-throb of the free,
The first, strong pulse of liberty
  Which thrilled along the bondman's
    veins.

Though long delayed, and far, and slow,
  The Briton's triumph shall be ours :
Wears slavery here a prouder brow
Than that which twelve short years ago
  Scowled darkly from her island bow-
    ers ?

Mighty alike for good or ill
  With mother-land, we fully share
The Saxon strength, — the nerve of
    steel, —
The tireless energy of will, —
  The power to do, the pride to dare.

What she has done can we not do ?
  Our hour and men are both at hand ;
The blast which Freedom's angel blew
O'er her green islands, echoes through
  Each valley of our forest land.

Hear it, old Europe ! we have sworn
  The death of slavery. — When it falls,
Look to your vassals in their turn,
Your poor dumb millions, crushed and
    worn,
  Your prisons and your palace walls !

O kingly mockers ! — scoffing show
  What deeds in Freedom's name we do ;
Yet know that every taunt ye throw
Across the waters, goads our slow
  Progression towards the right and
    true.

Not always shall your outraged poor,
  Appalled by democratic crime,
Grind as their fathers ground before, —
The hour which sees our prison door
  Swing wide shall be *their* triumph time.

On then, my brothers ! every blow
  Ye deal is felt the wide earth through ;
Whatever here uplifts the low
Or humbles Freedom's hateful foe,
  Blesses the Old World through the
    New.

Take heart ! The promised hour draws
    near, —
  I hear the downward beat of wings,
And Freedom's trumpet sounding clear :
" Joy to the people ! — woe and fear
  To   new-world   tyrants,   old-world
    kings ! "

THE FAREWELL

OF A VIRGINIA SLAVE MOTHER TO HER
DAUGHTERS SOLD INTO SOUTHERN
BONDAGE.

GONE, gone, — sold and gone,
  To the rice-swamp dank and lone.
Where the slave-whip ceaseless swings,
Where the noisome insect stings,
Where the fever demon strews
Poison with the falling dews,
Where the sickly sunbeams glare
Through the hot and misty air, —
  Gone, gone, — sold and gone,
  To the rice-swamp dank and lone,
  From Virginia's hills and waters, —
  Woe is me, my stolen daughters !

Gone, gone, — sold and gone,
  To the rice-swamp dank and lone.

There no mother's eye is near them,
There no mother's ear can hear them ;
Never, when the torturing lash
Seams their back with many a gash,
Shall a mother's kindness bless them,
Or a mother's arms caress them.
  Gone, gone, — sold and gone,
  To the rice-swamp dank and lone,
  From Virginia's hills and waters, —
  Woe is me, my stolen daughters !

Gone, gone, — sold and gone,
  To the rice-swamp dank and lone.
O, when weary, sad, and slow,
From the fields at night they go,
Faint with toil, and racked with pain,
To their cheerless homes again,
There no brother's voice shall greet
    them, —
There no father's welcome meet them.
  Gone, gone, — sold and gone,
  To the rice-swamp dank and lone,
  From Virginia's hills and waters, —
  Woe is me, my stolen daughters !

Gone, gone, — sold and gone,
  To the rice-swamp dank and lone.
From the tree whose shadow lay
On their childhood's place of play, —
From the cool spring where they drank, —
Rock, and hill, and rivulet bank, —
From the solemn house of prayer,
And the holy counsels there, —
  Gone, gone, — sold and gone,
  To the rice-swamp dank and lone,
  From Virginia's hills and waters, —
  Woe is me, my stolen daughters !

Gone, gone, — sold and gone,
  To the rice-swamp dank and lone, —
Toiling through the weary day,
And at night the spoiler's prey.
O that they had earlier died,
Sleeping calmly, side by side,
Where the tyrant's power is o'er,
And the fetter galls no more !
  Gone, gone, — sold and gone,
  To the rice-swamp dank and lone,
  From Virginia's hills and waters, —
  Woe is me, my stolen daughters !

Gone, gone, — sold and gone,
  To the rice-swamp dank and lone.
By the holy love He beareth, —
By the bruised reed He spareth —
O, may He, to whom alone
All their cruel wrongs are known,

Still their hope and refuge prove,
With a more than mother's love.
  Gone, gone, — sold and gone,
  To the rice-swamp dank and lone,
  From Virginia's hills and waters, —
  Woe is me, my stolen daughters !

THE MORAL WARFARE.

WHEN Freedom, on her natal day,
Within her war-rocked cradle lay,
An iron race around her stood,
Baptized her infant brow in blood ;
And, through the storm which round her
    swept,
Their constant ward and watching kept.

Then, where our quiet herds repose,
The roar of baleful battle rose,
And brethren of a common tongue
To mortal strife as tigers sprung,
And every gift on Freedom's shrine
Was man for beast, and blood for wine !

Our fathers to their graves have gone ;
Their strife is past, — their triumph won ;
But sterner trials wait the race
Which rises in their honored place, —
A moral warfare with the crime
And folly of an evil time.

So let it be. In God's own might
We gird us for the coming fight,
And, strong in Him whose cause is ours
In conflict with unholy powers,
We grasp the weapons He has given, —
The Light, and Truth, and Love of
    Heaven.

THE WORLD'S CONVENTION

OF THE FRIENDS OF EMANCIPATION,
HELD IN LONDON IN 1840.

YES, let them gather ! — Summon forth
The pledged philanthropy of Earth,
From every land, whose hills have heard
  The bugle blast of Freedom waking ;
Or shrieking of her symbol-bird
  From out his cloudy eyrie breaking :
Where Justice hath one worshipper,
Or truth one altar built to her ;
Where'er a human eye is weeping
  O'er wrongs which Earth's sad chil-
    dren know, —

Where'er a single heart is keeping
  Its prayerful watch with human woe :
Thence let them come, and greet each
    other,
And know in each a friend and brother !

Yes, let them come ! from each green vale
  Where England's old baronial halls
Still bear upon their storied walls
The grim crusader's rusted mail,
Battered by Paynim spear and brand
On Malta's rock or Syria's sand !
And mouldering pennon-staves once set
  Within the soil of Palestine,
By Jordan and Genesaret ;
  Or, borne with England's battle line,
O'er Acre's shattered turrets stooping,
Or, midst the camp their banners droop-
    ing,
  With dews from hallowed Hermon wet,
A holier summons now is given
  Than that gray hermit's voice of old,
Which unto all the winds of heaven
  The banners of the Cross unrolled !
Not for the long-deserted shrine, —
  Not for the dull unconscious sod,
Which tells not by one lingering sign
  That there the hope of Israel trod ; —
But for that TRUTH, for which alone
  In pilgrim eyes are sanctified
The garden moss, the mountain stone,
  Whereon his holy sandals pressed, —
The fountain which his lip hath
    blessed, —
Whate'er hath touched his garment's hem
At Bethany or Bethlehem,
  Or Jordan's river-side.
For FREEDOM, in the name of Him
  Who came to raise Earth's drooping
    poor,
To break the chain from every limb,
The bolt from every prison door !
For these, o'er all the earth hath passed
An ever-deepening trumpet blast,
As if an angel's breath had lent
Its vigor to the instrument.

And Wales, from Snowden's mountain
    wall,
Shall startle at that thrilling call,
  As if she heard her bards again ;
And Erin's "harp on Tara's wall"
  Give out its ancient strain,
Mirthful and sweet, yet sad withal, —
  The melody which Erin loves,
When o'er that harp, 'mid bursts of glad-
    ness

And slogan cries and lyke-wake sadness,
  The hand of her O'Connell moves !
Scotland, from lake and tarn and rill,
And mountain hold, and heathery hill,
  Shall catch and echo back the note,
As if she heard upon her air
Once more her Cameronian's prayer
  And song of Freedom float.
And cheering echoes shall reply
From each remote dependency,
Where Britain's mighty sway is known,
In tropic sea or frozen zone ;
Where'er her sunset flag is furling,
Or morning gun-fire's smoke is curling ;
From Indian Bengal's groves of palm
And rosy fields and gales of balm,
Where Eastern pomp and power are rolled
Through regal Ava's gates of gold ;
And from the lakes and ancient woods
And dim Canadian solitudes,
Whence, sternly from her rocky throne,
Queen of the North, Quebec looks down ;
And from those bright and ransomed
    Isles
Where all unwonted Freedom smiles,
And the dark laborer still retains
The scar of slavery's broken chains !

From the hoar Alps, which sentinel
The gateways of the land of Tell,
Where morning's keen and earliest glance
On Jura's rocky wall is thrown,
And from the olive bowers of France
    And vine groves garlanding the
    Rhone, —
"Friends of the Blacks," as true and
    tried
As those who stood by Oge's side,
And heard the Haytien's tale of wrong,
Shall gather at that summons strong, —
Broglie, Passy, and him whose song
Breathed over Syria's holy sod,
And in the paths which Jesus trod,
And murmured midst the hills which hem
Crownless and sad Jerusalem,
Hath echoes whereso'er the tone
Of Israel's prophet-lyre is known.

Still let them come, — from Quito's
    walls,
  And from the Orinoco's tide,
From Lima's Inca-haunted halls,
From Santa Fe and Yucatan, —
  Men who by swart Guerrero's side
Proclaimed the deathless RIGHTS OF MAN,
  Broke every bond and fetter off,
  And hailed in every sable serf

A free and brother Mexican !
Chiefs who across the Andes' chain
  Have followed Freedom's flowing
    pennon,
And seen on Junin's fearful plain,
Glare o'er the broken ranks of Spain
  The fire-burst of Bolivar's cannon !
And Hayti, from her mountain land,
  Shall send the sons of those who hurled
Defiance from her blazing strand, —
The war-gage from her Petion's hand,
  Alone against a hostile world.

Nor all unmindful, thou, the while,
Land of the dark and mystic Nile ! —
  Thy Moslem mercy yet may shame
  All tyrants of a Christian name, —
When in the shade of Gizeh's pile,
Or, where from Abyssinian hills
El Gerek's upper fountain fills,
Or where from Mountains of the Moon
El Abiad bears his watery boon,
Where'er thy lotus blossoms swim
    Within their ancient hallowed wa-
    ters, —
Where'er is heard the Coptic hymn,
  Or song of Nubia's sable daughters, —
The curse of SLAVERY and the crime,
Thy bequest from remotest time,
At thy dark Mehemet's decree
Forevermore shall pass from thee ;
  And chains forsake each captive's limb
Of all those tribes, whose hills around
Have echoed back the cymbal sound
  And victor horn of Ibrahim.

And thou whose glory and whose crime
To earth's remotest bound and clime,
In mingled tones of awe and scorn,
The echoes of a world have borne,
My country ! glorious at thy birth,
A day-star flashing brightly forth, —
  The herald-sign of Freedom's dawn !
O, who could dream that saw thee then,
  And watched thy rising from afar,
That vapors from oppression's fen
  Would cloud the upward tending star ?
Or, that earth's tyrant powers, which
    heard,
  Awe-struck, the shout which hailed
    thy dawning,
Would rise so soon, prince, peer, and
    king,
To mock thee with their welcoming,
Like Hades when her thrones were stirred
  To greet the down-cast Star of Morn-
    ing !

"Aha ! and art thou fallen thus ?
Art THOU become as one of *us ?*"

Land of my fathers ! — there will stand,
Amidst that world-assembled band,
Those owning thy maternal claim
Unweakened by thy crime and shame, —
The sad reprovers of thy wrong, —
The children thou hast spurned so long.
Still with affection's fondest yearning
To their unnatural mother turning.
No traitors they ! — but tried and leal,
Whose own is but thy general weal,
Still blending with the patriot's zeal
The Christian's love for human kind,
To caste and climate unconfined.

A holy gathering ! — peaceful all :
No threat of war, — no savage call
    For vengeance on an erring brother !
But in their stead the godlike plan
To teach the brotherhood of man
    To love and reverence one another,
As sharers of a common blood,
The children of a common God ! —
Yet, even at its lightest word,
Shall Slavery's darkest depths be stirred :
Spain, watching from her Moro's keep
Her slave-ships traversing the deep,
And Rio, in her strength and pride,
Lifting, along her mountain-side,
Her snowy battlements and towers, —
Her lemon-groves and tropic bowers,
With bitter hate and sullen fear
Its freedom-giving voice shall hear ;
And where my country's flag is flow-
    ing,
On breezes from Mount Vernon blowing
    Above the Nation's council halls,
Where Freedom's praise is loud and long,
    While close beneath the outward walls
The driver plies his reeking thong, —
    The hammer of the man-thief falls,
O'er hypocritic cheek and brow
The crimson flush of shame shall glow :
And all who for their native land
Are pledging life and heart and hand, —
Worn watchers o'er her changing weal,
Who for her tarnished honor feel, —
Through cottage door and council-hall
Shall thunder an awakening call.
The pen along its page shall burn
With all intolerable scorn, —
An eloquent rebuke shall go
On all the winds that Southward blow, —
From priestly lips, now sealed and dumb,
Warning and dread appeal shall come,

Like those which Israel heard from him,
The Prophet of the Cherubim, —
Or those which sad Esaias hurled
Against a sin-accursed world !
Its wizard leaves the Press shall fling
Unceasing from its iron wing,
With characters inscribed thereon,
    As fearful in the despot's hall
As to the pomp of Babylon
    The fire-sign on the palace wall !
And, from her dark iniquities,
Methinks I see my country rise :
Not challenging the nations round
    To note her tardy justice done, —
Her captives from their chains unbound,
    Her prisons opening to the sun : —
But tearfully her arms extending
Over the poor and unoffending ;
Her regal emblem now no longer
A bird of prey, with talons reeking,
Above the dying captive shrieking,
But, spreading out her ample wing, —
A broad, impartial covering, —
    The weaker sheltered by the stron-
        ger ! —
O, then to Faith's anointed eyes
    The promised token shall be given ;
And on a nation's sacrifice,
Atoning for the sin of years,
And wet with penitential tears, —
    The fire shall fall from Heaven !
        1839.

NEW HAMPSHIRE.

1845.

GOD bless New Hampshire ! — from her
    granite peaks
Once more the voice of Stark and
    Langdon speaks.
The long-bound vassal of the exulting
    South
    For very shame her self-forged chain
        has broken, —
Torn the black seal of slavery from her
    mouth,
    And in the clear tones of her old time
        spoken !
O, all undreamed-of, all unhoped-for
    changes ! —
    The tyrant's ally proves his sternest
        foe ;
To all his biddings, from her mountain
    ranges,
    New Hampshire thunders an indig-
        nant No !

Who is it now despairs? O, faint of heart,
  Look upward to those Northern moun-
    tains cold,
  Flouted by Freedom's victor-flag un-
    rolled,
And gather strength to bear a manlier
  part !
All is not lost. The angel of God's
  blessing
  Encamps with Freedom on the field
    of fight ;
Still to her banner, day by day, are
  pressing,
  Unlooked-for allies, striking for the
    right !
Courage, then, Northern hearts ! — Be
  firm, be true :
What one brave State hath done, can ye
  not also do ?

THE NEW YEAR :

ADDRESSED TO THE PATRONS OF THE
PENNSYLVANIA FREEMAN.

THE wave is breaking on the shore, —
  The echo fading from the chime, —
Again the shadow moveth o'er
  The dial-plate of time !

O, seer-seen Angel ! waiting now
  With weary feet on sea and shore,
Impatient for the last dread vow
  That time shall be no more !

Once more across thy sleepless eye
  The semblance of a smile has passed :
The year departing leaves more nigh
  Time's fearfullest and last.

O, in that dying year hath been
  The sum of all since time began, —
The birth and death, the joy and pain,
  Of Nature and of Man.

Spring, with her change of sun and
  shower,
  And streams released from Winter's
    chain,
And bursting bud, and opening flower,
  And greenly growing grain ;

And Summer's shade, and sunshine warm,
  And rainbows o'er her hill-tops bowed,
And voices in her rising storm, —
  God speaking from his cloud ! —

And Autumn's fruits and clustering
  sheaves,
  And soft, warm days of golden light,
The glory of her forest leaves,
  And harvest-moon at night ;

And Winter with her leafless grove,
  And prisoned stream, and drifting
    snow,
The brilliance of her heaven above
  And of her earth below : —

And man, — in whom an angel's mind
  With earth's low instincts finds
    abode, —
The highest of the links which bind
  Brute nature to her God ;

His infant eye hath seen the light,
  His childhood's merriest laughter rung,
And active sports to manlier might
  The nerves of boyhood strung !

And quiet love, and passion's fires,
  Have soothed or burned in manhood's
    breast,
And lofty aims and low desires
  By turns disturbed his rest.

The wailing of the newly-born
  Has mingled with the funeral knell ;
And o'er the dying's ear has gone
  The merry marriage-bell.

And Wealth has filled his halls with
  mirth,
  While Want, in many a humble shed,
Toiled, shivering by her cheerless hearth,
  The live-long night for bread.

And worse than all, — the human
  slave, —
  The sport of lust, and pride, and
    scorn !
Plucked off the crown his Maker gave, —
  His regal manhood gone !

O, still, my country ! o'er thy plains,
  Blackened with slavery's blight and
    ban,
That human chattel drags his chains, —
  An uncreated man !

And still, where'er to sun and breeze,
  My country, is thy flag unrolled,
With scorn, the gazing stranger sees
  A stain on every fold.

O, tear the gorgeous emblem down !
　It gathers scorn from every eye,
And despots smile and good men frown
　Whene'er it passes by.

Shame ! shame ! its starry splendors
　　glow
Above the slaver's loathsome jail, —
Its folds are ruffling even now
　His crimson flag of sale.

Still round our country's proudest hall
　The trade in human flesh is driven,
And at each careless hammer-fall
　A human heart is riven.

And this, too, sanctioned by the men
　Vested with power to shield the right,
And throw each vile and robber den
　Wide open to the light.

Yet, shame upon them ! — there they sit,
　Men of the North, subdued and still ;
Meek, pliant poltroons, only fit
　To work a master's will.

Sold, — bargained off for Southern
　　votes, —
　A passive herd of Northern mules,
Just braying through their purchased
　　throats
　Whate'er their owner rules.

And he,[35] — the basest of the base,
　The vilest of the vile, — whose name,
Embalmed in infinite disgrace,
　Is deathless in its shame ! —

A tool, — to bolt the people's door
　Against the people clamoring there,
An ass, — to trample on their floor
　A people's right of prayer !

Nailed to his self-made gibbet fast,
　Self-pilloried to the public view, —
A mark for every passing blast
　Of scorn to whistle through ;

There let him hang, and hear the boast
　Of Southrons o'er their pliant tool, —
A new Stylites on his post,
　" Sacred to ridicule ! "

Look we at home ! — our noble hall,
　To Freedom's holy purpose given,
Now rears its black and ruined wall,
　Beneath the wintry heaven, —

Telling the story of its doom, —
　The fiendish mob, — the prostrate
　　law, —
The fiery jet through midnight's gloom,
　Our gazing thousands saw.

Look to our State, — the poor man's right
　Torn from him : — and the sons of
　　those
Whose blood in Freedom's sternest fight
　Sprinkled the Jersey snows,

Outlawed within the land of Penn,
　That Slavery's guilty fears might cease,
And those whom God created men
　Toil on as brutes in peace.

Yet o'er the blackness of the storm
　A bow of promise bends on high,
And gleams of sunshine, soft and warm,
　Break through our clouded sky.

East, West, and North, the shout is
　　heard,
　Of freemen rising for the right :
Each valley hath its rallying word, —
　Each hill its signal light.

O'er Massachusetts' rocks of gray,
　The strengthening light of freedom
　　shines,
Rhode Island's Narragansett Bay, —
　And Vermont's snow-hung pines !

From Hudson's frowning palisades
　To Alleghany's laurelled crest,
O'er lakes and prairies, streams and glades,
　It shines upon the West.

Speed on the light to those who dwell
　In Slavery's land of woe and sin,
And through the blackness of that hell,
　Let Heaven's own light break in.

So shall the Southern conscience quake
　Before that light poured full and
　　strong,
So shall the Southern heart awake
　To all the bondman's wrong.

And from that rich and sunny land
　The song of grateful millions rise,
Like that of Israel's ransomed band
　Beneath Arabia's skies :

And all who now are bound beneath
　Our banner's shade, our eagle's wing,

From Slavery's night of moral death
  To light and life shall spring.

Broken the bondman's chain, and gone
  The master's guilt, and hate, and fear,
And unto both alike shall dawn
  A New and Happy Year.
    1839.

MASSACHUSETTS TO VIRGINIA.

[Written on reading an account of the proceedings of the citizens of Norfolk, Va., in reference to GEORGE LATIMER, the alleged fugitive slave, the result of whose case in Massachusetts will probably be similar to that of the negro SOMERSET in England, in 1772.]

THE blast from Freedom's Northern
  hills, upon its Southern way,
Bears greeting to Virginia from Massachusetts Bay :—
No word of haughty challenging, nor
  battle bugle's peal,
Nor steady tread of marching files, nor
  clang of horsemen's steel.

No trains of deep-mouthed cannon along
  our highways go, —
Around our silent arsenals untrodden
  lies the snow ;
And to the land-breeze of our ports, upon
  their errands far,
A thousand sails of commerce swell, but
  none are spread for war.

We hear thy threats, Virginia ! thy
  stormy words and high,
Swell harshly on the Southern winds
  which melt along our sky ;
Yet, not one brown, hard hand foregoes
  its honest labor here,
No hewer of our mountain oaks suspends
  his axe in fear.

Wild are the waves which lash the reefs
  along St. George's bank, —
Cold on the shore of Labrador the fog
  lies white and dank ;
Through storm, and wave, and blinding
  mist, stout are the hearts which man
The fishing-smacks of Marblehead, the
  sea-boats of Cape Ann.

The cold north light and wintry sun
  glare on their icy forms,
Bent grimly o'er their straining lines or
  wrestling with the storms ;

Free as the winds they drive before,
  rough as the waves they roam,
They laugh to scorn the slaver's threat
  against their rocky home.

What means the Old Dominion ? Hath
  she forgot the day
When o'er her conquered valleys swept
  the Briton's steel array ?
How side by side, with sons of hers, the
  Massachusetts men
Encountered Tarleton's charge of fire,
  and stout Cornwallis, then ?

Forgets she how the Bay State, in answer to the call
Of her old House of Burgesses, spoke out
  from Faneuil Hall ?
When, echoing back her Henry's cry,
  came pulsing on each breath
Of Northern winds, the thrilling sounds
  of " LIBERTY OR DEATH ! "

What asks the Old Dominion ? If now
  her sons have proved
False to their fathers' memory, — false
  to the faith they loved,
If she can scoff at Freedom, and its great
  charter spurn,
Must we of Massachusetts from truth
  and duty turn ?

We hunt your bondmen, flying from
  Slavery's hateful hell, —
Our voices, at your bidding, take up the
  bloodhound's yell, —
We gather, at your summons, above our
  fathers' graves,
From Freedom's holy altar-horns to tear
  your wretched slaves !

Thank God ! not yet so vilely can Massachusetts bow ;
The spirit of her early time is with her
  even now ;
Dream not because her Pilgrim blood
  moves slow and calm and cool,
She thus can stoop her chainless neck,
  a sister's slave and tool !

All that a *sister* State should do, all that
  a *free* State may,
Heart, hand, and purse we proffer, as in
  our early day ;
But that one dark loathsome burden ye
  must stagger with alone,
And reap the bitter harvest which ye
  yourselves have sown !

Hold, while ye may, your struggling
　　slaves, and burden God's free air
With woman's shriek beneath the lash,
　　and manhood's wild despair ;
Cling closer to the "cleaving curse" that
　　writes upon your plains
The blasting of Almighty wrath against
　　a land of chains.

Still shame your gallant ancestry, the
　　cavaliers of old,
By watching round the shambles where
　　human flesh is sold, —
Gloat o'er the new-born child, and count
　　his market value, when
The maddened mother's cry of woe shall
　　pierce the slaver's den !

Lower than plummet soundeth, sink the
　　Virginia name ;
Plant, if ye will, your fathers' graves
　　with rankest weeds of shame ;
Be, if ye will, the scandal of God's fair
　　universe, —
We wash our hands forever of your sin
　　and shame and curse.

A voice from lips whereon the coal from
　　Freedom's shrine hath been,
Thrilled, as but yesterday, the hearts of
　　Berkshire's mountain men :
The echoes of that solemn voice are sadly
　　lingering still
In all our sunny valleys, on every wind-
　　swept hill.

And when the prowling man-thief came
　　hunting for his prey
Beneath the very shadow of Bunker's
　　shaft of gray,
How, through the free lips of the son,
　　the father's warning spoke ;
How, from its bonds of trade and sect,
　　the Pilgrim city broke !

A hundred thousand right arms were
　　lifted up on high, —
A hundred thousand voices sent back
　　their loud reply ;
Through the thronged towns of Essex
　　the startling summons rang,
And up from bench and loom and wheel
　　her young mechanics sprang !

The voice of free, broad Middlesex, — of
　　thousands as of one, —
The shaft of Bunker calling to that of
　　Lexington, —

From Norfolk's ancient villages, from
　　Plymouth's rocky bound
To where Nantucket feels the arms of
　　ocean close her round ; —

From rich and rural Worcester, where
　　through the calm repose
Of cultured vales and fringing woods the
　　gentle Nashua flows,
To where Wachuset's wintry blasts the
　　mountain larches stir,
Swelled up to Heaven the thrilling cry
　　of "God save Latimer !"

And sandy Barnstable rose up, wet with
　　the salt sea spray, —
And Bristol sent her answering shout
　　down Narragansett Bay !
Along the broad Connecticut old Hamp-
　　den felt the thrill,
And the cheer of Hampshire's woodmen
　　swept down from Holyoke Hill.

The voice of Massachusetts ! Of her free
　　sons and daughters, —
Deep calling unto deep aloud, — the
　　sound of many waters !
Against the burden of that voice what
　　tyrant power shall stand ?
*No fetters in the Bay State ! No slave
　　upon her land !*

Look to it well, Virginians ! In calm-
　　ness we have borne,
In answer to our faith and trust, your
　　insult and your scorn ;
You've spurned our kindest counsels, —
　　you've hunted for our lives, —
And shaken round our hearths and
　　homes your manacles and gyves !

We wage no war, — we lift no arm, —
　　we fling no torch within
The fire-damps of the quaking mine be-
　　neath your soil of sin ;
We leave ye with your bondmen, to
　　wrestle, while ye can,
With the strong upward tendencies and
　　godlike soul of man !

But for us and for our children, the vow
　　which we have given
For freedom and humanity is registered
　　in heaven ;
*No slave-hunt in our borders, — no pirate
　　on our strand !
No fetters in the Bay State, — no slave
　　upon our land !*

THE RELIC.

[PENNSYLVANIA HALL, dedicated to Free Discussion and the cause of human liberty, was destroyed by a mob in 1838. The following was written on receiving a cane wrought from a fragment of the wood-work which the fire had spared.]

TOKEN of friendship true and tried,
    From one whose fiery heart of youth
With mine has beaten, side by side,
    For Liberty and Truth ;
With honest pride the gift I take,
And prize it for the giver's sake.

But not alone because it tells
    Of generous hand and heart sincere ;
Around that gift of friendship dwells
    A memory doubly dear, —
Earth's noblest aim, — man's holiest
        thought,
With that memorial frail inwrought !

Pure thoughts and sweet, like flowers
        unfold,
    And precious memories round it cling,
Even as the Prophet's rod of old
    In beauty blossoming :
And buds of feeling pure and good
Spring from its cold unconscious wood.

Relic of Freedom's shrine ! — a brand
    Plucked from its burning ! — let it be
Dear as a jewel from the hand
    Of a lost friend to me ! —
Flower of a perished garland left,
Of life and beauty unbereft !

O, if the young enthusiast bears,
    O'er weary waste and sea, the stone
Which crumbled from the Forum's stairs,
    Or round the Parthenon ;
Or olive-bough from some wild tree
Hung over old Thermopylæ :

If leaflets from some hero's tomb,
    Or moss-wreath torn from ruins
        hoary, —
Or faded flowers whose sisters bloom
    On fields renowned in story, —
Or fragment from the Alhambra's crest,
Or the gray rock by Druids blessed ;

Sad Erin's shamrock greenly growing
    Where Freedom led her stalwart kern,
Or Scotia's " rough bur thistle " blowing
    On Bruce's Bannockburn, —

Or Runnymede's wild English rose,
Or lichen plucked from Sempach's
    snows : —

If it be true that things like these
    To heart and eye bright visions bring,
Shall not far holier memories
    To this memorial cling ?
Which needs no mellowing mist of
        time
To hide the crimson stains of crime !

Wreck of a temple, unprofaned, —
    Of courts where Peace with Freedom
        trod,
Lifting on high, with hands unstained,
    Thanksgiving unto God ;
Where Mercy's voice of love was pleading
For human hearts in bondage bleeding ! —

Where, midst the sound of rushing feet
    And curses on the night-air flung,
That pleading voice rose calm and sweet
    From woman's earnest tongue ;
And Riot turned his scowling glance,
Awed, from her tranquil countenance !

That temple now in ruin lies ! —
    The fire-stain on its shattered wall,
And open to the changing skies
    Its black and roofless hall,
It stands before a nation's sight,
A gravestone over buried Right !

But from that ruin, as of old,
    The fire-scorched stones themselves
        are crying,
And from their ashes white and cold
    Its timbers are replying !
A voice which slavery cannot kill
Speaks from the crumbling arches still !

And even this relic from thy shrine,
    O holy Freedom ! hath to me
A potent power, a voice and sign
    To testify of thee ;
And, grasping it, methinks I feel
A deeper faith, a stronger zeal.

And not unlike that mystic rod,
    Of old stretched o'er the Egyptian
        wave,
Which opened, in the strength of God,
    A pathway for the slave,
It yet may point the bondman's way,
And turn the spoiler from his prey.

THE BRANDED HAND.

1846.

WELCOME home again, brave seaman ! with thy thoughtful brow and gray,
And the old heroic spirit of our earlier, better day, —
With that front of calm endurance, on whose steady nerve in vain
Pressed the iron of the prison, smote the fiery shafts of pain !

Is the tyrant's brand upon thee ? Did the brutal cravens aim
To make God's truth thy falsehood, his holiest work thy shame ?
When, all blood-quenched, from the torture the iron was withdrawn,
How laughed their evil angel the baffled fools to scorn !

They change to wrong the duty which God hath written out
On the great heart of humanity, too legible for doubt !
They, the loathsome moral lepers, blotched from footsole up to crown,
Give to shame what God hath given unto honor and renown !

Why, that brand is highest honor ! — than its traces never yet
Upon old armorial hatchments was a prouder blazon set ;
And thy unborn generations, as they tread our rocky strand,
Shall tell with pride the story of their father's BRANDED HAND !

As the Templar home was welcome, bearing back from Syrian wars
The scars of Arab lances and of Paynim scymitars,
The pallor of the prison, and the shackle's crimson span,
So we meet thee, so we greet thee, truest friend of God and man.

He suffered for the ransom of the dear Redeemer's grave,
Thou for his living presence in the bound and bleeding slave ;
He for a soil no longer by the feet of angels trod,
Thou for the true Shechinah, the present home of God !

For, while the jurist, sitting with the slave-whip o'er him swung,
From the tortured truths of freedom the lie of slavery wrung,
And the solemn priest to Moloch, on each God-deserted shrine,
Broke the bondman's heart for bread, poured the bondman's blood for wine, —

While the multitude in blindness to a far-off Saviour knelt,
And spurned, the while, the temple where a present Saviour dwelt ;
Thou beheld'st him in the task-field, in the prison shadows dim,
And thy mercy to the bondman, it was mercy unto him !

In thy lone and long night-watches, sky above and wave below,
Thou didst learn a higher wisdom than the babbling schoolmen know ;
God's stars and silence taught thee, as his angels only can,
That the one sole sacred thing beneath the cope of heaven is Man !

That he who treads profanely on the scrolls of law and creed,
In the depth of God's great goodness may find mercy in his need ;
But woe to him who crushes the SOUL with chain and rod,
And herds with lower natures the awful form of God !

Then lift that manly right-hand, bold ploughman of the wave !
Its branded palm shall prophesy, " SALVATION TO THE SLAVE ! "
Hold up its fire-wrought language, that whoso reads may feel
His heart swell strong within him, his sinews change to steel.

Hold it up before our sunshine, up against our Northern air, —
Ho ! men of Massachusetts, for the love of God, look there !
Take it henceforth for your standard, like the Bruce's heart of yore,
In the dark strife closing round ye, let that hand be seen before !

And the tyrants of the slave-land shall tremble at that sign,

5

When it points its finger Southward
    along the Puritan line :
Woe to the State-gorged leeches and the
    Church's locust band,
When they look from slavery's ramparts
    on the coming of that hand !

TEXAS.

VOICE OF NEW ENGLAND.

Up the hillside, down the glen,
Rouse the sleeping citizen ;
Summon out the might of men !

Like a lion growling low, —
Like a night-storm rising slow, —
Like the tread of unseen foe, —

It is coming, — it is nigh !
Stand your homes and altars by ;
On your own free thresholds die.

Clang the bells in all your spires ;
On the gray hills of your sires
Fling to heaven your signal-fires.

From Wachuset, lone and bleak,
Unto Berkshire's tallest peak,
Let the flame-tongued heralds speak.

O, for God and duty stand,
Heart to heart and hand to hand,
Round the old graves of the land.

Whoso shrinks or falters now,
Whoso to the yoke would bow,
Brand the craven on his brow !

Freedom's soil hath only place
For a free and fearless race, —
None for traitors false and base.

Perish party, — perish clan ;
Strike together while ye can,
Like the arm of one strong man.

Like that angel's voice sublime,
Heard above a world of crime,
Crying of the end of time, —

With one heart and with one mouth,
Let the North unto the South
Speak the word befitting both :

" What though Issachar be strong !
Ye may load his back with wrong
Overmuch and over long :

" Patience with her cup o'errun,
With her weary thread outspun,
Murmurs that her work is done.

" Make our Union-bond a chain,
Weak as tow in Freedom's strain
Link by link shall snap in twain.

" Vainly shall your sand-wrought rope
Bind the starry cluster up,
Shattered over heaven's blue cope !

" Give us bright though broken rays,
Rather than eternal haze,
Clouding o'er the full-orbed blaze.

" Take your land of sun and bloom ;
Only leave to Freedom room
For her plough, and forge, and loom ;

" Take your slavery-blackened vales ;
Leave us but our own free gales,
Blowing on our thousand sails.

" Boldly, or with treacherous art,
Strike the blood-wrought chain apart ;
Break the Union's mighty heart ;

" Work the ruin, if ye will ;
Pluck upon your heads an ill
Which shall grow and deepen still.

" With your bondman's right arm bare,
With his heart of black despair,
Stand alone, if stand ye dare !

" Onward with your fell design ;
Dig the gulf and draw the line :
Fire beneath your feet the mine :

" Deeply, when the wide abyss
Yawns between your land and this,
Shall ye feel your helplessness.

" By the hearth, and in the bed,
Shaken by a look or tread,
Ye shall own a guilty dread.

" And the curse of unpaid toil,
Downward through your generous soil
Like a fire shall burn and spoil.

" Our bleak hills shall bud and blow,
Vines our rocks shall overgrow,
Plenty in our valleys flow ; —

" And when vengeance clouds your skies,
Hither shall ye turn your eyes,
As the lost on Paradise !

" We but ask our rocky strand,
Freedom's true and brother band,
Freedom's strong and honest hand, —

"Valleys by the slave untrod,
And the Pilgrim's mountain sod,
Blessed of our fathers' God ! "

TO FANEUIL HALL.

1844.

MEN ! — if manhood still ye claim,
  If the Northern pulse can thrill,
Roused by wrong or stung by shame,
  Freely, strongly still, —
Let the sounds of traffic die :
  Shut the mill-gate, — leave the stall, —
Fling the axe and hammer by, —
  Throng to Faneuil Hall !

Wrongs which freemen never brooked, —
  Dangers grim and fierce as they,
Which, like couching lions, looked
  On your fathers' way, —
These your instant zeal demand,
Shaking with their earthquake-call
Every rood of Pilgrim land,
  Ho, to Faneuil Hall !

From your capes and sandy bars, —
  From your mountain-ridges cold,
Through whose pines the westering stars
  Stoop their crowns of gold, —
Come, and with your footsteps wake
  Echoes from that holy wall ;
Once again, for Freedom's sake,
  Rock your fathers' hall !

Up, and tread beneath your feet
  Every cord by party spun :
Let your hearts together beat
  As the heart of one.
Banks and tariffs, stocks and trade,
  Let them rise or let them fall :
Freedom asks your common aid, —
  Up, to Faneuil Hall !

Up, and let each voice that speaks
  Ring from thence to Southern plains,
Sharply as the blow which breaks
  Prison-bolts and chains !
Speak as well becomes the free :
  Dreaded more than steel or ball,
Shall your calmest utterance be,
  Heard from Faneuil Hall !

Have they wronged us ? Let us then
  Render back nor threats nor prayers ;
Have they chained our free-born men ?
  LET US UNCHAIN THEIRS !
Up, your banner leads the van,
  Blazoned, " Liberty for all ! "
Finish what your sires began !
  Up, to Faneuil Hall !

TO MASSACHUSETTS.

1844.

WHAT though around thee blazes
  No fiery rallying sign ?
From all thy own high places,
  Give heaven the light of thine !
What though unthrilled, unmoving,
  The statesman stand apart,
And comes no warm approving
  From Mammon's crowded mart ?

Still, let the land be shaken
  By a summons of thine own !
By all save truth forsaken,
  Why, stand with that alone !
Shrink not from strife unequal !
  With the best is always hope ;
And ever in the sequel
  God holds the right side up !

But when, with thine uniting,
  Come voices long and loud,
And far-off hills are writing
  Thy fire-words on the cloud ;
When from Penobscot's fountains
  A deep response is heard,
And across the Western mountains
  Rolls back thy rallying word ;

Shall thy line of battle falter,
  With its allies just in view ?
O, by hearth and holy altar,
  My fatherland, be true !
Fling abroad thy scrolls of Freedom !
  Speed them onward far and fast !
Over hill and valley speed them,
  Like the sibyl's on the blast !

Lo ! the Empire State is shaking
  The shackles from her hand ;
With the rugged North is waking
  The level sunset land !
On they come, — the free battalions !
  East and West and North they come,
And the heart-beat of the millions
  Is the beat of Freedom's drum.

"To the tyrant's plot no favor !
No heed to place-fed knaves !
Bar and bolt the door forever
Against the land of slaves !"
Hear it, mother Earth, and hear it,
The Heavens above us spread !
The land is roused, — its spirit
Was sleeping, but not dead !

THE PINE–TREE.

1846.

Lift again the stately emblem on the
Bay State's rusted shield,
Give to Northern winds the Pine-Tree
on our banner's tattered field.
Sons of men who sat in council with their
Bibles round the board,
Answering England's royal missive with
a firm, "THUS SAITH THE LORD !"
Rise again for home and freedom ! — set
the battle in array ! —
What the fathers did of old time we
their sons must do to-day.

Tell us not of banks and tariffs, — cease
your paltry pedler cries, —
Shall the good State sink her honor that
your gambling stocks may rise ?
Would ye barter man for cotton ? — That
your gains may sum up higher,
Must we kiss the feet of Moloch, pass
our children through the fire ?
Is the dollar only real ? — God and truth
and right a dream ?
Weighed against your lying ledgers must
our manhood kick the beam ?

O my God ! — for that free spirit, which
of old in Boston town
Smote the Province House with terror,
struck the crest of Andros down ! —
For another strong-voiced Adams in the
city's streets to cry,
"Up for God and Massachusetts ! — Set
your feet on Mammon's lie !
Perish banks and perish traffic, — spin
your cotton's latest pound, —
But in Heaven's name keep your honor, —
keep the heart o' the Bay State
sound !"

Where 's the MAN for Massachusetts ? —
Where 's the voice to speak her
free ? —

Where 's the hand to light up bonfires
from her mountains to the sea ?
Beats her Pilgrim pulse no longer ? —
Sits she dumb in her despair ? —
Has she none to break the silence ? —
Has she none to do and dare ?
O my God ! for one right worthy to lift
up her rusted shield,
And to plant again the Pine-Tree in her
banner's tattered field !

LINES,

SUGGESTED BY A VISIT TO THE CITY OF
WASHINGTON, IN THE 12TH MONTH
OF 1845.

With a cold and wintry noon-light,
On its roofs and steeples shed,
Shadows weaving with the sunlight
From the gray sky overhead,
Broadly, vaguely, all around me, lies the
half-built town outspread.

Through this broad street, restless ever,
Ebbs and flows a human tide,
Wave on wave a living river ;
Wealth and fashion side by side :
Toiler, idler, slave and master, in the
same quick current glide.

Underneath yon dome, whose coping
Springs above them, vast and tall,
Grave men in the dust are groping
For the largess, base and small,
Which the hand of Power is scattering.
crumbs which from its table fall.

Base of heart ! They vilely barter
Honor's wealth for party's place :
Step by step on Freedom's charter
Leaving footprints of disgrace ;
For to-day's poor pittance turning from
the great hope of their race.

Yet, where festal lamps are throwing
Glory round the dancer's hair,
Gold-tressed, like an angel's, flowing
Backward on the sunset air ;
And the low quick pulse of music beats
its measure sweet and rare :

There to-night shall woman's glances,
Star-like, welcome give to them,
Fawning fools with shy advances
Seek to touch their garments' hem,
With the tongue of flattery glozing deeds
which God and Truth condemn

From this glittering lie my vision
Takes a broader, sadder range,
Full before me have arisen
Other pictures dark and strange ;
From the parlor to the prison must the
scene and witness change.

Hark ! the heavy gate is swinging
On its hinges, harsh and slow ;
One pale prison lamp is flinging
On a fearful group below
Such a light as leaves to terror whatso-
e'er it does not show.

Pitying God ! — Is that a WOMAN
On whose wrist the shackles clash ?
Is that shriek she utters human,
Underneath the stinging lash ?
Are they MEN whose eyes of madness
from that sad procession flash ?

Still the dance goes gayly onward !
What is it to Wealth and Pride
That without the stars are looking
On a scene which earth should hide ?
That the SLAVE-SHIP lies in waiting,
rocking on Potomac's tide !

Vainly to that mean Ambition
Which, upon a rival's fall,
Winds above its old condition,
With a reptile's slimy crawl,
Shall the pleading voice of sorrow, shall
the slave in anguish call.

Vainly to the child of Fashion,
Giving to ideal woe
Graceful luxury of compassion,
Shall the stricken mourner go ;
Hateful seems the earnest sorrow, beau-
tiful the hollow show !

Nay, my words are all too sweeping :
In this crowded human mart,
Feeling is not dead, but sleeping ;
Man's strong will and woman's heart,
In the coming strife for Freedom, yet
shall bear their generous part.

And from yonder sunny valleys,
Southward in the distance lost,
Freedom yet shall summon allies
Worthier than the North can boast,
With the Evil by their hearth-stones
grappling at severer cost.

Now, the soul alone is willing :
Faint the heart and weak the knee ;

And as yet no lip is thrilling
With the mighty words, "BE FREE!"
Tarrieth long the land's Good Angel,
but his advent is to be !

Meanwhile, turning from the revel
To the prison-cell my sight,
For intenser hate of evil,
For a keener sense of right,
Shaking off thy dust, I thank thee, City
of the Slaves, to-night !

"To thy duty now and ever !
Dream no more of rest or stay ;
Give to Freedom's great endeavor
All thou art and hast to-day " : —
Thus, above the city's murmur, saith a
Voice, or seems to say.

Ye with heart and vision gifted
To discern and love the right,
Whose worn faces have been lifted
To the slowly-growing light,
Where from Freedom's sunrise drifted
slowly back the murk of night ! —

Ye who through long years of trial
Still have held your purpose fast,
While a lengthening shade the dial
From the westering sunshine cast,
And of hope each hour's denial seemed
an echo of the last ! —

O my brothers ! O my sisters !
Would to God that ye were near,
Gazing with me down the vistas
Of a sorrow strange and drear ;
Would to God that ye were listeners to
the Voice I seem to hear !

With the storm above us driving,
With the false earth mined below, —
Who shall marvel if thus striving
We have counted friend as foe ;
Unto one another giving in the darkness
blow for blow.

Well it may be that our natures
Have grown sterner and more hard,
And the freshness of their features
Somewhat harsh and battle-scarred,
And their harmonies of feeling over-
tasked and rudely jarred.

Be it so.   It should not swerve us
From a purpose true and brave ;

Dearer Freedom's rugged service
    Than the pastime of the slave ;
Better is the storm above it than the
    quiet of the grave.

Let us then, uniting, bury
    All our idle feuds in dust,
And to future conflicts carry
    Mutual faith and common trust ;
Always he who most forgiveth in his
    brother is most just.

From the eternal shadow rounding
    All our sun and starlight here,
Voices of our lost ones sounding
    Bid us be of heart and cheer,
Through the silence, down the spaces,
    falling on the inward ear.

Know we not our dead are looking
    Downward with a sad surprise,
All our strife of words rebuking
    With their mild and loving eyes ?
Shall we grieve the holy angels ?   Shall
    we cloud their blessed skies ?

Let us draw their mantles o'er us
    Which have fallen in our way ;
Let us do the work before us,
    Cheerly, bravely, while we may,
Ere the long night-silence cometh, and
    with us it is not day !

LINES,

FROM A LETTER TO A YOUNG CLERI-
CAL FRIEND.

A STRENGTH Thy service cannot tire, —
    A faith which doubt can never dim, —
A heart of love, a lip of fire, —
    O Freedom's God ! be thou to him !

Speak through him words of power and
    fear,
    As through thy prophet bards of old,
And let a scornful people hear
    Once more thy Sinai-thunders rolled.

For lying lips thy blessing seek,
    And hands of blood are raised to Thee,
And on thy children, crushed and weak,
    The oppressor plants his kneeling knee.

Let then, O God ! thy servant dare
    Thy truth in all its power to tell,
Unmask the priestly thieves, and tear
    The Bible from the grasp of hell !

From hollow rite and narrow span
    Of law and sect by Thee released,
O, teach him that the Christian man
    Is holier than the Jewish priest.

Chase back the shadows, gray and old,
    Of the dead ages, from his way,
And let his hopeful eyes behold
    The dawn of thy millennial day ; —

That day when fettered limb and mind
    Shall know the truth which maketh
        free,
And he alone who loves his kind
    Shall, childlike, claim the love of Thee !

YORKTOWN.[36]

FROM Yorktown's ruins, ranked and still,
Two lines stretch far o'er vale and hill :
Who curbs his steed at head of one ?
Hark ! the low murmur : Washington !
Who bends his keen, approving glance
Where down the gorgeous line of France
Shine knightly star and plume of snow ?
Thou too art victor, Rochambeau !

The earth which bears this calm array
Shook with the war-charge yesterday,
Ploughed deep with hurrying hoof and
    wheel,
Shot-sown and bladed thick with steel ;
October's clear and noonday sun
Paled in the breath-smoke of the gun,
And down night's double blackness fell,
Like a dropped star, the blazing shell.

Now all is hushed : the gleaming lines
Stand moveless as the neighboring pines ;
While through them, sullen, grim, and
    slow,
The conquered hosts of England go :
O'Hara's brow belies his dress,
Gay Tarleton's troop rides bannerless :
Shout, from thy fired and wasted homes,
Thy scourge, Virginia, captive comes !

Nor thou alone : with one glad voice
Let all thy sister States rejoice ;
Let Freedom, in whatever clime
She waits with sleepless eye her time,
Shouting from cave and mountain wood
Make glad her desert solitude,

While they who hunt her quail with fear ;
The New World's chain lies broken here !

But who are they, who, cowering, wait
Within the shattered fortress gate ?
Dark tillers of Virginia's soil,
Classed with the battle's common spoil,
With household stuffs, and fowl, and
    swine,
With Indian weed and planters' wine,
With stolen beeves, and foraged corn, —
Are they not men, Virginian born ?

O, veil your faces, young and brave !
Sleep, Scammel, in thy soldier grave !
Sons of the Northland, ye who set
Stout hearts against the bayonet,
And pressed with steady footfall near
The moated battery's blazing tier,
Turn your scarred faces from the sight,
Let shame do homage to the right !

Lo ! threescore years have passed ; and
    where
The Gallic timbrel stirred the air,
With Northern drum-roll, and the clear,
Wild horn-blow of the mountaineer,
While Britain grounded on that plain
The arms she might not lift again,
As abject as in that old day
The slave still toils his life away.

O, fields still green and fresh in story,
Old days of pride, old names of glory,
Old marvels of the tongue and pen,
Old thoughts which stirred the hearts
    of men,
Ye spared the wrong ; and over all
Behold the avenging shadow fall !
Your world-wide honor stained with
    shame,
Your freedom's self a hollow name !

Where 's now the flag of that old war ?
Where flows its stripe ? Where burns
    its star ?
Bear witness, Palo Alto's day,
Dark Vale of Palms, red Monterey,
Where Mexic Freedom, young and weak,
Fleshes the Northern eagle's beak ;
Symbol of terror and despair,
Of chains and slaves, go seek it there !

Laugh, Prussia, midst thy iron ranks !
Laugh, Russia, from thy Neva's banks !
Brave sport to see the fledgling born
Of Freedom by its parent torn !

Safe now is Speilberg's dungeon cell,
Safe drear Siberia's frozen hell :
With Slavery's flag o'er both unrolled,
What of the New World fears the Old ?

LINES,

ON page of thine I cannot trace
The cold and heartless commonplace, —
A statue's fixed and marble grace.

For ever as these lines I penned,
Still with the thought of thee will blend
That of some loved and common friend, —

Who in life's desert track has made
His pilgrim tent with mine, or strayed
Beneath the same remembered shade.

And hence my pen unfettered moves
In freedom which the heart approves, —
The negligence which friendship loves.

And wilt thou prize my poor gift less
For simple air and rustic dress,
And sign of haste and carelessness ? —

O, more than specious counterfeit
Of sentiment or studied wit,
A heart like thine should value it.

Yet half I fear my gift will be
Unto thy book, if not to thee,
Of more than doubtful courtesy.

A banished name from fashion's sphere,
A lay unheard of Beauty's ear,
Forbid, disowned, — what do they
    here ? —

Upon my ear not all in vain
Came the sad captive's clanking chain, —
The groaning from his bed of pain.

And sadder still, I saw the woe
Which only wounded spirits know
When Pride's strong footsteps o'er them
    go.

Spurned not alone in walks abroad,
But from the " temples of the Lord "
Thrust out apart, like things abhorred.

Deep as I felt, and stern and strong,
In words which Prudence smothered long,
My soul spoke out against the wrong ;

Not mine alone the task to speak
Of comfort to the poor and weak,
And dry the tear on Sorrow's cheek ;

But, mingled in the conflict warm,
To pour the fiery breath of storm
Through the harsh trumpet of Reform ;

To brave Opinion's settled frown,
From ermined robe and saintly gown,
While wrestling reverenced Error down.

Founts gushed beside my pilgrim way,
Cool shadows on the greensward lay,
Flowers swung upon the bending spray.

And, broad and bright, on either hand,
Stretched the green slopes of Fairy-land,
With Hope's eternal sunbow spanned ;

Whence voices called me like the flow,
Which on the listener's ear will grow,
Of forest streamlets soft and low.

And gentle eyes, which still retain
Their picture on the heart and brain,
Smiled, beckoning from that path of
      pain.

In vain ! — nor dream, nor rest, nor
      pause
Remain for him who round him draws
The battered mail of Freedom's cause.

From youthful hopes, — from each green
      spot
Of young Romance, and gentle Thought,
Where storm and tumult enter not, —

From each fair altar, where belong
The offerings Love requires of Song
In homage to her bright-eyed throng, —

With soul and strength, with heart and
      hand,
I turned to Freedom's struggling band, —
To the sad Helots of our land.

What marvel then that Fame should
      turn
Her notes of praise to those of scorn, —
Her gifts reclaimed, — her smiles with-
      drawn ?

What matters it ! — a few years more,
Life's surge so restless heretofore
Shall break upon the unknown shore !

In that far land shall disappear
The shadows which we follow here, —
The mist-wreaths of our atmosphere !

Before no work of mortal hand,
Of human will or strength expand
The pearl gates of the Better Land ;

Alone in that great love which gave
Life to the sleeper of the grave,
Resteth the power to "seek and save."

Yet, if the spirit gazing through
The vista of the past can view
One deed to Heaven and virtue true, —

If through the wreck of wasted powers,
Of garlands wreathed from Folly's
      bowers,
Of idle aims and misspent hours, —

The eye can note one sacred spot
By Pride and Self profaned not, —
A green place in the waste of thought, —

Where deed or word hath rendered less
"The sum of human wretchedness,"
And Gratitude looks forth to bless, —

The simple burst of tenderest feeling
From sad hearts worn by evil-dealing,
For blessing on the hand of healing, —

Better than Glory's pomp will be
That green and blessed spot to me,
A palm-shade in Eternity ! —

Something of Time which may invite
The purified and spiritual sight
To rest on with a calm delight.

And when the summer winds shall
      sweep
With their light wings my place of sleep,
And mosses round my headstone creep, —

If still, as Freedom's rallying sign,
Upon the young heart's altars shine
The very fires they caught from mine, —

If words my lips once uttered still,
In the calm faith and steadfast will
Of other hearts, their work fulfil, —

Perchance with joy the soul may learn
These tokens, and its eye discern
The fires which on those altars burn, —

A marvellous joy that even then,
The spirit hath its life again,
In the strong hearts of mortal men.

Take, lady, then, the gift I bring,
No gay and graceful offering, —
No flower-smile of the laughing spring.

Midst the green buds of Youth's fresh
    May,
With Fancy's leaf-enwoven bay,
My sad and sombre gift I lay.

And if it deepens in thy mind
A sense of suffering human-kind, —
The outcast and the spirit-blind :

Oppressed and spoiled on every side,
By Prejudice, and Scorn, and Pride,
Life's common courtesies denied ;

Sad mothers mourning o'er their trust,
Children by want and misery nursed,
Tasting life's bitter cup at first ;

If to their strong appeals which come
From fireless hearth, and crowded room,
And the close alley's noisome gloom, —

Though dark the hands upraised to thee
In mute beseeching agony,
Thou lend'st thy woman's sympathy, —

Not vainly on thy gentle shrine,
Where Love, and Mirth, and Friendship
    twine
Their varied gifts, I offer mine.

PÆAN.

1848.

Now, joy and thanks forevermore !
    The dreary night has wellnigh passed,
The slumbers of the North are o'er,
    The Giant stands erect at last !

More than we hoped in that dark time
    When, faint with watching, few and
        worn,
We saw no welcome day-star climb
    The cold gray pathway of the morn !

O weary hours ! O night of years !
    What storms our darkling pathway
        swept,
Where, beating back our thronging fears,
    By Faith alone our march we kept.

How jeered the scoffing crowd behind,
    How mocked before the tyrant train,
As, one by one, the true and kind
    Fell fainting in our path of pain !

They died, — their brave hearts breaking
        slow, —
But, self-forgetful to the last,
In words of cheer and bugle blow
    Their breath upon the darkness passed.

A mighty host, on either hand,
    Stood waiting for the dawn of day
To crush like reeds our feeble band ;
    The morn has come, — and where are
        they ?

Troop after troop their line forsakes ;
    With peace-white banners waving
        free,
And from our own the glad shout breaks,
    Of Freedom and Fraternity !

Like mist before the growing light,
    The hostile cohorts melt away ;
Our frowning foemen of the night
    Are brothers at the dawn of day !

As unto these repentant ones
    We open wide our toil-worn ranks,
Along our line a murmur runs
    Of song, and praise, and grateful
        thanks.

Sound for the onset ! — Blast on blast !
    Till Slavery's minions cower and
        quail ;
One charge of fire shall drive them fast
    Like chaff before our Northern gale !

O prisoners in your house of pain,
    Dumb, toiling millions, bound and
        sold,
Look ! stretched o'er Southern vale and
        plain,
    The Lord's delivering hand behold !

Above the tyrant's pride of power,
    His iron gates and guarded wall,
The bolts which shattered Shinar's
        tower
    Hang, smoking, for a fiercer fall.

Awake ! awake ! my Fatherland !
    It is thy Northern light that shines ;
This stirring march of Freedom's band
    The storm-song of thy mountain pines.

Wake, dwellers where the day expires !
  And hear, in winds that sweep your
    lakes
And fan your prairies' roaring fires,
  The signal-call that Freedom makes !

TO THE MEMORY OF THOMAS SHIPLEY.

GONE to thy Heavenly Father's rest !
  The flowers of Eden round thee blow-
    ing,
And on thine ear the murmurs blest
  Of Siloa's waters softly flowing !
Beneath that Tree of Life which gives
To all the earth its healing leaves
In the white robe of angels clad,
  And wandering by that sacred river,
Whose streams of holiness make glad
  The city of our God forever !

Gentlest of spirits ! — not for thee
  Our tears are shed, our sighs are given ;
Why mourn to know thou art a free
  Partaker of the joys of Heaven ?
Finished thy work, and kept thy faith
In Christian firmness unto death ;
And beautiful as sky and earth,
  When autumn's sun is downward go-
    ing,
The blessed memory of thy worth
  Around thy place of slumber glowing !

But woe for us ! who linger still
  With feebler strength and hearts less
    lowly,
And minds less steadfast to the will
  Of Him whose every work is holy.
For not like thine, is crucified
The spirit of our human pride :
And at the bondman's tale of woe,
  And for the outcast and forsaken,
Not warm like thine, but cold and slow,
  Our weaker sympathies awaken.

Darkly upon our struggling way
  The storm of human hate is sweeping ;
Hunted and branded, and a prey,
  Our watch amidst the darkness keep-
    ing,
O for that hidden strength which can
Nerve unto death the inner man !
O for thy spirit, tried and true,
  And constant in the hour of trial,
Prepared to suffer, or to do,
  In meekness and in self-denial.

O for that spirit, meek and mild,
  Derided, spurned, yet uncomplain-
    ing, —
By man deserted and reviled,
  Yet faithful to its trust remaining.
Still prompt and resolute to save
From scourge and chain the hunted
    slave ;
Unwavering in the Truth's defence,
  Even where the fires of Hate were
    burning,
The unquailing eye of innocence
  Alone upon the oppressor turning !

O loved of thousands ! to thy grave,
  Sorrowing of heart, thy brethren bore
    thee.
The poor man and the rescued slave
  Wept as the broken earth closed o'er
    thee ;
And grateful tears, like summer rain,
Quickened its dying grass again !
And there, as to some pilgrim-shrine,
  Shall come the outcast and the lowly,
Of gentle deeds and words of thine
  Recalling memories sweet and holy !

O for the death the righteous die !
  An end, like autumn's day declining,
On human hearts, as on the sky,
  With holier, tenderer beauty shining ;
As to the parting soul were given
The radiance of an opening Heaven !
As if that pure and blessed light,
  From off the Eternal altar flowing,
Were bathing, in its upward flight,
  The spirit to its worship going !

TO A SOUTHERN STATESMAN.

1846.

Is this thy voice, whose treble notes of
    fear
Wail in the wind ?   And dost thou shake
    to hear,
Actæon-like, the bay of thine own
    hounds,
Spurning the leash, and leaping o'er
    their bounds ?
Sore-baffled statesman ! when thy eager
    hand,
With game afoot, unslipped the hungry
    pack,
To hunt down Freedom in her chosen
    land,

Hadst thou no fear, that, erelong,
 doubling back,
These dogs of thine might snuff on
 Slavery's track ?
Where 's now the boast, which even thy
 guarded tongue,
Cold, calm, and proud, in the teeth o'
 the Senate flung,
O'er the fulfilment of thy baleful plan,
Like Satan's triumph at the fall of man ?
How stood'st thou then, thy feet on
 Freedom planting,
And pointing to the lurid heaven afar,
Whence all could see, through the south
 windows slanting,
Crimson as blood, the beams of that
 Lone Star !
The Fates are just ; they give us but our
 own ;
Nemesis ripens what our hands have
 sown.
There is an Eastern story, not unknown,
Doubtless, to thee, of one whose magic
 skill
Called demons up his water-jars to fill ;
Deftly and silently, they did his will,
But, when the task was done, kept
 pouring still.
In vain with spell and charm the wizard
 wrought,
Faster and faster were the buckets
 brought,
Higher and higher rose the flood around,
Till the fiends clapped their hands above
 their master drowned !
So, Carolinian, it may prove with thee,
For God still overrules man's schemes,
 and takes
Craftiness in its self-set snare, and
 makes
The wrath of man to praise Him. It
 may be,
That the roused spirits of Democracy
May leave to freer States the same wide
 door
Through which thy slave-cursed T xas
 entered in,
From out the blood and fire, the wrong
 and sin,
Of the stormed city and the ghastly
 plain,
Beat by hot hail, and wet with bloody
 rain,
A myriad-handed Aztec host may pour,
And swarthy South with pallid North
 combine
Back on thyself to turn thy dark design.

LINES,

WRITTEN ON THE ADOPTION OF PINCK-
NEY'S RESOLUTIONS, IN THE HOUSE
OF REPRESENTATIVES, AND THE PAS-
SAGE OF CALHOUN'S "BILL FOR EX-
CLUDING PAPERS WRITTEN OR PRINT-
ED, TOUCHING THE SUBJECT OF
SLAVERY, FROM THE U. S. POST-
OFFICE," IN THE SENATE OF THE
UNITED STATES.

MEN of the North-land ! where 's the
 manly spirit
  Of the true-hearted and the unshackled
   gone ?
Sons of old freemen, do we but inherit
  Their names alone ?

Is the old Pilgrim spirit quenched within us,
  Stoops the strong manhood of our
   souls so low,
That Mammon's lure or Party's wile can
 win us
    To silence now ?

Now, when our land to ruin's brink is
 verging,
  In God's name, let us speak while
   there is time !
Now, when the padlocks for our lips
 are forging,
    Silence is crime !

What ! shall we henceforth humbly ask
 as favors
  Rights all our own ? In madness
   shall we barter,
For treacherous peace, the freedom
 Nature gave us,
    God and our charter ?

Here shall the statesman forge his human fetters,
  Here the false jurist human rights
   deny,
And, in the church, their proud and
 skilled abettors
    Make truth a lie ?

Torture the pages of the hallowed Bible,
  To sanction crime, and robbery, and
   blood ?
And, in Oppression's hateful service,
 libel
    Both man and God ?

Shall our New England stand erect no
    longer,
  But stoop in chains upon her down-
      ward way,
Thicker to gather on her limbs and
    stronger
        Day after day ?

O no ; methinks from all her wild, green
    mountains, —
  From valleys where her slumbering
      fathers lie, —
From her blue rivers and her welling
    fountains,
        And clear, cold sky, —

From her rough coast, and isles, which
    hungry Ocean
  Gnaws with his surges, — from the
      fisher's skiff,
With white sail swaying to the billows'
    motion
        Round rock and cliff, —

From the free fireside of her unbought
    farmer, —
  From her free laborer at his loom and
      wheel, —
From the brown smith-shop, where, be-
    neath the hammer,
        Rings the red steel, —

From each and all, if God hath not
    forsaken
  Our land, and left us to an evil choice,
Loud as the summer thunderbolt shall
    waken
        A People's voice.

Startling and stern ! the Northern winds
    shall bear it
  Over Potomac's to St. Mary's wave ;
And buried Freedom shall awake to
    hear it
        Within her grave.

O, let that voice go forth ! The bond-
    man sighing
  By Santee's wave, in Mississippi's
      cane,
Shall feel the hope, within his bosom
    dying,
        Revive again.

Let it go forth ! The millions who are
    gazing
  Sadly upon us from afar, shall smile,

And unto God devout thanksgiving
    raising,
        Bless us the while.

O for your ancient freedom, pure and
    holy,
  For the deliverance of a groaning earth,
For the wronged captive, bleeding,
    crushed, and lowly,
        Let it go forth !

Sons of the best of fathers ! will ye falter
  With all they left ye perilled and at
      stake ?
Ho ! once again on Freedom's holy altar
        The fire awake !

Prayer-strengthened for the trial, come
    together,
  Put on the harness for the moral fight,
And, with the blessing of your Heav-
    enly Father,
        MAINTAIN THE RIGHT !

THE CURSE OF THE CHARTER-
BREAKERS.[37]

IN Westminster's royal halls,
Robed in their pontificals,
England's ancient prelates stood
For the people's right and good.

Closed around the waiting crowd,
Dark and still, like winter's cloud ;
King and council, lord and knight,
Squire and yeoman, stood in sight, —

Stood to hear the priest rehearse,
In God's name, the Church's curse,
By the tapers round them lit,
Slowly, sternly uttering it.

" Right of voice in framing laws,
Right of peers to try each cause ;
Peasant homestead, mean and small,
Sacred as the monarch's hall, —

" Whoso lays his hand on these,
England's ancient liberties, —
Whoso breaks, by word or deed,
England's vow at Runnymede, —

" Be he Prince or belted knight,
Whatsoe'er his rank or might,
If the highest, then the worst,
Let him live and die accursed.

"Thou, who to thy Church hast given
Keys alike, of hell and heaven,
Make our word and witness sure,
Let the curse we speak endure!"

Silent, while that curse was said,
Every bare and listening head
Bowed in reverent awe, and then
All the people said, Amen!

Seven times the bells have tolled,
For the centuries gray and old,
Since that stoled and mitred band
Cursed the tyrants of their land.

Since the priesthood, like a tower,
Stood between the poor and power;
And the wronged and trodden down
Blessed the abbot's shaven crown.

Gone, thank God, their wizard spell,
Lost, their keys of heaven and hell;
Yet I sigh for men as bold
As those bearded priests of old.

Now, too oft the priesthood wait
At the threshold of the state, —
Waiting for the beck and nod
Of its power as law and God.

Fraud exults, while solemn words
Sanctify his stolen hoards;
Slavery laughs, while ghostly lips
Bless his manacles and whips.

Not on them the poor rely,
Not to them looks liberty,
Who with fawning falsehood cower
To the wrong, when clothed with power.

O, to see them meanly cling,
Round the master, round the king,
Sported with, and sold and bought, —
Pitifuller sight is not!

Tell me not that this must be:
God's true priest is always free;
Free, the needed truth to speak,
Right the wronged, and raise the weak.

Not to fawn on wealth and state,
Leaving Lazarus at the gate, —
Not to peddle creeds like wares, —
Not to mutter hireling prayers, —

Nor to paint the new life's bliss
On the sable ground of this, —

Golden streets for idle knave,
Sabbath rest for weary slave!

Not for words and works like these,
Priest of God, thy mission is;
But to make earth's desert glad,
In its Eden greenness clad;

And to level manhood bring
Lord and peasant, serf and king;
And the Christ of God to find
In the humblest of thy kind!

Thine to work as well as pray,
Clearing thorny wrongs away;
Plucking up the weeds of sin,
Letting heaven's warm sunshine in, —

Watching on the hills of Faith;
Listening what the spirit saith,
Of the dim-seen light afar,
Growing like a nearing star.

God's interpreter art thou,
To the waiting ones below;
'Twixt them and its light midway
Heralding the better day, —

Catching gleams of temple spires,
Hearing notes of angel choirs,
Where, as yet unseen of them,
Comes the New Jerusalem!

Like the seer of Patmos gazing,
On the glory downward blazing;
Till upon Earth's grateful sod
Rests the City of our God!

THE SLAVES OF MARTINIQUE.

SUGGESTED BY A DAGUERREOTYPE FROM
A FRENCH ENGRAVING.

BEAMS of noon, like burning lances,
     through the tree-tops flash and
     glisten,
As she stands before her lover, with raised
     face to look and listen.

Dark, but comely, like the maiden in the
     ancient Jewish song:
Scarcely has the toil of task-fields done
     her graceful beauty wrong.

He, the strong one and the manly, with
     the vassal's garb and hue,

Holding still his spirit's birthright, to
　　his higher nature true ;

Hiding deep the strengthening purpose
　　of a freeman in his heart,
As the greegree holds his Fetich from
　　the white man's gaze apart.

Ever foremost of his comrades, when the
　　driver's morning horn
Calls away to stifling mill-house, to the
　　fields of cane and corn :

Fall the keen and burning lashes never
　　on his back or limb ;
Scarce with look or word of censure, turns
　　the driver unto him.

Yet, his brow is always thoughtful, and
　　his eye is hard and stern ;
Slavery's last and humblest lesson he has
　　never deigned to learn.

And, at evening, when his comrades
　　dance before their master's door,
Folding arms and knitting forehead,
　　stands he silent evermore.

God be praised for every instinct which
　　rebels against a lot
Where the brute survives the human, and
　　man's upright form is not !

As the serpent-like bejuco winds his
　　spiral fold on fold
Round the tall and stately ceiba, till it
　　withers in his hold ; —

Slow decays the forest monarch, closer
　　girds the fell embrace,
Till the tree is seen no longer, and the
　　vine is in its place, —

So a base and bestial nature round the
　　vassal's manhood twines,
And the spirit wastes beneath it, like the
　　ceiba choked with vines.

God is Love, saith the Evangel ; and our
　　world of woe and sin
Is made light and happy only when a
　　Love is shining in.

Ye whose lives are free as sunshine, find-
　　ing, wheresoe'er ye roam,
Smiles of welcome, looks of kindness,
　　making all the world like home ;

In the veins of whose affections kindred
　　blood is but a part,
Of one kindly current throbbing from the
　　universal heart ;

Can ye know the deeper meaning of a
　　love in Slavery nursed,
Last flower of a lost Eden, blooming in
　　that Soil accursed ?

Love of Home, and Love of Woman ! —
　　dear to all, but doubly dear
To the heart whose pulses elsewhere
　　measure only hate and fear.

All around the desert circles, underneath
　　a brazen sky,
Only one green spot remaining where the
　　dew is never dry !

From the horror of that desert, from its
　　atmosphere of hell,
Turns the fainting spirit thither, as the
　　diver seeks his bell.

'T is the fervid tropic noontime ; faint
　　and low the sea-waves beat ;
Hazy rise the inland mountains through
　　the glimmer of the heat, —

Where, through mingled leaves and blos-
　　soms, arrowy sunbeams flash and
　　glisten,
Speaks her lover to the slave-girl, and she
　　lifts her head to listen : —

" We shall live as slaves no longer !
　　Freedom's hour is close at hand !
Rocks her bark upon the waters, rests the
　　boat upon the strand !

" I have seen the Haytien Captain ; I
　　have seen his swarthy crew,
Haters of the pallid faces, to their race
　　and color true.

" They have sworn to wait our coming
　　till the night has passed its noon,
And the gray and darkening waters roll
　　above the sunken moon ! "

O the blessed hope of freedom ! how with
　　joy and glad surprise,
For an instant throbs her bosom, for an
　　instant beam her eyes !

But she looks across the valley, where
  her mother's hut is seen,
Through the snowy bloom of coffee, and
  the lemon-leaves so green.

And she answers, sad and earnest : "It
  were wrong for thee to stay ;
God hath heard thy prayer for freedom,
  and his finger points the way.

" Well I know with what endurance, for
  the sake of me and mine,
Thou hast borne too long a burden never
  meant for souls like thine.

" Go ; and at the hour of midnight, when
  our last farewell is o'er,
Kneeling on our place of parting, I will
  bless thee from the shore.

" But for me, my mother, lying on her
  sick-bed all the day,
Lifts her weary head to watch me, coming
  through the twilight gray.

"Should I leave her sick and helpless, even
  freedom, shared with thee,
Would be sadder far than bondage, lonely
  toil, and stripes to me.

" For my heart would die within me, and
  my brain would soon be wild ;
I should hear my mother calling through
  the twilight for her child ! "

Blazing upward from the ocean, shines
  the sun of morning-time,
Through the coffee-trees in blossom, and
  green hedges of the lime.

Side by side, amidst the slave-gang, toil
  the lover and the maid ;
Wherefore looks he o'er the waters, leaning forward on his spade ?

Sadly looks he, deeply sighs he : 't is the
  Haytien's sail he sees,
Like a white cloud of the mountains,
  driven seaward by the breeze !

But his arm a light hand presses, and he
  hears a low voice call :
Hate of Slavery, hope of Freedom, Love
  is mightier than all.

THE CRISIS.

WRITTEN ON LEARNING THE TERMS OF
THE TREATY WITH MEXICO.

ACROSS the Stony Mountains, o'er the
  desert's drouth and sand,
The circles of our empire touch the West-
  ern Ocean's strand ;
From slumberous Timpanogos, to Gila,
  wild and free,
Flowing down from Nuevo-Leon to Cali-
  fornia's sea ;
And from the mountains of the East, to
  Santa Rosa's shore,
The eagles of Mexitli shall beat the air
  no more.

O Vale of Rio Bravo ! Let thy simple
  children weep ;
Close watch about their holy fire let maids
  of Pecos keep ;
Let Taos send her cry across Sierra Madre's
  pines,
And Algodones toll her bells amidst her
  corn and vines ;
For lo ! the pale land-seekers come, with
  eager eyes of gain,
Wide scattering, like the bison herds on
  broad Salada's plain.

Let Sacramento's herdsmen heed what
  sound the winds bring down
Of footsteps on the crisping snow, from
  cold Nevada's crown !
Full hot and fast the Saxon rides, with
  rein of travel slack,
And, bending on his saddle, leaves the
  sunrise at his back ;
By many a lonely river, and gorge of fir
  and pine,
On many a wintry hill-top, his nightly
  camp-fires shine.

O countrymen and brothers ! that land
  of lake and plain,
Of salt wastes alternating with valleys
  fat with grain ;
Of mountains white with winter, looking
  downward, cold, serene,
On their feet with spring-vines tangled
  and lapped in softest green ;
Swift through whose black volcanic gates,
  o'er many a sunny vale,
Wind-like the Arapahoe sweeps the bison's dusty trail !

Great spaces yet untravelled, great lakes
    whose mystic shores
The Saxon rifle never heard, nor dip of
    Saxon oars ;
Great herds that wander all unwatched,
    wild steeds that none have tamed,
Strange fish in unknown streams, and
    birds the Saxon never named ;
Deep mines, dark mountain crucibles,
    where Nature's chemic powers
Work out the Great Designer's will ; —
    all these ye say are ours !

Forever ours ! for good or ill, on us the
    burden lies ;
God's balance, watched by angels, is hung
    across the skies.
Shall Justice, Truth, and Freedom turn
    the poised and trembling scale ?
Or shall the Evil triumph, and robber
    Wrong prevail ?
Shall the broad land o'er which our flag
    in starry splendor waves,
Forego through us its freedom, and bear
    the tread of slaves ?

The day is breaking in the East of which
    the prophets told,
And brightens up the sky of Time the
    Christian Age of Gold ;
Old Might to Right is yielding, battle
    blade to clerkly pen,
Earth's monarchs are her peoples, and
    her serfs stand up as men ;
The isles rejoice together, in a day are
    nations born,
And the slave walks free in Tunis, and
    by Stamboul's Golden Horn !

Is this, O countrymen of mine ! a day for
    us to sow
The soil of new-gained empire with
    slavery's seeds of woe ?
To feed with our fresh life-blood the Old
    World's cast-off crime,
Dropped, like some monstrous early birth,
    from the tired lap of Time ?
To run anew the evil race the old lost
    nations ran,
And die like them of unbelief of God, and
    wrong of man ?

Great Heaven ! Is this our mission ?
    End in this the prayers and tears,
The toil, the strife, the watchings of our
    younger, better years ?
Still as the Old World rolls in light, shall
    ours in shadow turn,
A beamless Chaos, cursed of God, through
    outer darkness borne ?
Where the far nations looked for light, a
    blackness in the air ?
Where for words of hope they listened
    the long wail of despair ?

The Crisis presses on us ; face to face
    with us it stands,
With solemn lips of question, like the
    Sphinx in Egypt's sands !
This day we fashion Destiny, our web
    of Fate we spin ;
This day for all hereafter choose we
    holiness or sin ;
Even now from starry Gerizim, or Ebal's
    cloudy crown,
We call the dews of blessing or the bolts
    of cursing down !

By all for which the martyrs bore their
    agony and shame ;
By all the warning words of truth with
    which the prophets came ;
By the Future which awaits us ; by all
    the hopes which cast
Their faint and trembling beams across
    the blackness of the Past ;
And by the blessed thought of Him who
    for Earth's freedom died,
O my people ! O my brothers ! let us
    choose the righteous side.

So shall the Northern pioneer go joyful
    on his way ;
To wed Penobscot's waters to San Fran-
    cisco's bay ;
To make the rugged places smooth, and
    sow the vales with grain ;
And bear, with Liberty and Law, the
    Bible in his train :
The mighty West shall bless the East,
    and sea shall answer sea,
And mountain unto mountain call,
    PRAISE GOD, FOR WE ARE FREE !

MISCELLANEOUS.

THE KNIGHT OF ST. JOHN.

Ere down yon blue Carpathian hills
  The sun shall sink again,
Farewell to life and all its ills,
  Farewell to cell and chain.

These prison shades are dark and cold, —
  But, darker far than they,
The shadow of a sorrow old
  Is on my heart alway.

For since the day when Warkworth wood
  Closed o'er my steed and I,
An alien from my name and blood,
  A weed cast out to die, —

When, looking back in sunset light,
  I saw her turret gleam,
And from its casement, far and white,
  Her sign of farewell stream,

Like one who, from some desert shore,
  Doth home's green isles descry,
And, vainly longing, gazes o'er
  The waste of wave and sky ;

So from the desert of my fate
  I gaze across the past ;
Forever on life's dial-plate
  The shade is backward cast !

I 've wandered wide from shore to shore,
  I 've knelt at many a shrine ;
And bowed me to the rocky floor
  Where Bethlehem's tapers shine ;

And by the Holy Sepulchre
  I 've pledged my knightly sword
To Christ, his blessed Church, and her,
  The Mother of our Lord.

O, vain the vow, and vain the strife !
  How vain do all things seem !
My soul is in the past, and life
  To-day is but a dream !

In vain the penance strange and long,
  And hard for flesh to bear ;
The prayer, the fasting, and the thong
  And sackcloth shirt of hair.

The eyes of memory will not sleep,-
  Its ears are open still ;
And vigils with the past they keep
  Against my feeble will.

And still the loves and joys of old
  Do evermore uprise ;
I see the flow of locks of gold,
  The shine of loving eyes !

Ah me ! upon another's breast
  Those golden locks recline ;
I see upon another rest
  The glance that once was mine.

"O faithless priest ! O perjured knight!"
  I hear the Master cry ;
"Shut out the vision from thy sight,
  Let Earth and Nature die.

" The Church of God is now thy spouse,
  And thou the bridegroom art ;
Then let the burden of thy vows
  Crush down thy human heart !

In vain ! This heart its grief must
    know,
  Till life itself hath ceased,
And falls beneath the self-same blow
  The lover and the priest !

O pitying Mother ! souls of light,
  And saints, and martyrs old !
Pray for a weak and sinful knight,
  A suffering man uphold.

Then let the Paynim work his will,
  And death unbind my chain,
Ere down yon blue Carpathian hill
  The sun shall fall again.

THE HOLY LAND.

FROM LAMARTINE.

I have not felt, o'er seas of sand,
  The rocking of the desert bark ;
Nor laved at Hebron's fount my hand,
  By Hebron's palm-trees cool and
    dark ;

6

Nor pitched my tent at even-fall,
  On dust where Job of old has lain,
Nor dreamed beneath its canvas wall,
  The dream of Jacob o'er again.

One vast world-page remains unread ;
  How shine the stars in Chaldea's
    sky,
How sounds the reverent pilgrim's tread,
  How beats the heart with God so
    nigh ! —
How round gray arch and column lone
  The spirit of the old time broods,
And sighs in all the winds that moan
  Along the sandy solitudes !

In thy tall cedars, Lebanon,
  I have not heard the nations' cries,
Nor seen thy eagles stooping down
  Where buried Tyre in ruin lies.
The Christian's prayer I have not said
  In Tadmor's temples of decay,
Nor startled, with my dreary tread,
  The waste where Memnon's empire lay.

Nor have I, from thy hallowed tide,
  O Jordan ! heard the low lament,
Like that sad wail along thy side
  Which Israel's mournful prophet sent !
Nor thrilled within that grotto lone
  Where, deep in night, the Bard of
    Kings
Felt hands of fire direct his own,
  And sweep for God the conscious
    strings.

I have not climbed to Olivet,
  Nor laid me where my Saviour lay,
And left his trace of tears as yet
  By angel eyes unwept away ;
Nor watched, at midnight's solemn time,
  The garden where his prayer and
    groan,
Wrung by his sorrow and our crime,
  Rose to One listening ear alone.

I have not kissed the rock-hewn grot
  Where in his Mother's arms he lay,
Nor knelt upon the sacred spot
  Where last his footsteps pressed the
    clay ;
Nor looked on that sad mountain head,
  Nor smote my sinful breast, where
    wide
His arms to fold the world he spread,
  And bowed his head to bless — and
    died !

PALESTINE.

BLEST land of Judæa ! thrice hallowed
    of song,
Where the holiest of memories pilgrim-
    like throng ;
In the shade of thy palms, by the shores
    of thy sea,
On the hills of thy beauty, my heart is
    with thee.

With the eye of a spirit I look on that
    shore,
Where pilgrim and prophet have lin-
    gered before ;
With the glide of a spirit I traverse the
    sod
Made bright by the steps of the angels
    of God.

Blue sea of the hills ! — in my spirit I
    hear
Thy waters, Genesaret, chime on my ear ;
Where the Lowly and Just with the peo-
    ple sat down,
And thy spray on the dust of his san-
    dals was thrown.

Beyond are Bethulia's mountains of
    green,
And the desolate hills of the wild Gad-
    arene ;
And I pause on the goat-crags of Tabor
    to see
The gleam of thy waters, O dark Galilee !

Hark, a sound in the valley ! where,
    swollen and strong,
Thy river, O Kishon, is sweeping along ;
Where the Canaanite strove with Je-
    hovah in vain,
And thy torrent grew dark with the
    blood of the slain.

There down from his mountains stern
    Zebulon came,
And Naphtali's stag, with his eyeballs
    of flame,
And the chariots of Jabin rolled harm-
    lessly on,
For the arm of the Lord was Abinoam's
    son !

There sleep the still rocks and the cav-
    erns which rang
To the song which the beautiful proph-
    etess sang,

"And throned on her hills sits Jerusalem yet."   Page 83.

When the princes of Issachar stood by
her side,
And the shout of a host in its triumph
replied.

Lo, Bethlehem's hill-site before me is
seen,
With the mountains around, and the
valleys between ;
There rested the shepherds of Judah,
and there
The song of the angels rose sweet on
the air.

And Bethany's palm-trees in beauty still
throw
Their shadows at noon on the ruins
below ;
But where are the sisters who hastened
to greet
The lowly Redeemer, and sit at his feet ?

I tread where the TWELVE in their way-
faring trod ;
I stand where they stood with the
CHOSEN OF GOD, —
Where his blessing was heard and his
lessons were taught,
Where the blind were restored and the
healing was wrought.

O, here with his flock the sad Wanderer
came, —
These hills he toiled over in grief are
the same, —
The founts where he drank by the wayside still flow,
And the same airs are blowing which
breathed on his brow !

And throned on her hills sits Jerusalem
yet,
But, with dust on her forehead, and
chains on her feet ;
For the crown of her pride to the mocker
hath gone,
And the holy Shechinah is dark where
it shone.

But wherefore this dream of the earthly
abode
Of Humanity clothed in the brightness
of God ?
Were my spirit but turned from the
outward and dim,
It could gaze, even now, on the presence
of Him !

Not in clouds and in terrors, but gentle
as when,
In love and in meekness, He moved
among men ;
And the voice which breathed peace to
the waves of the sea
In the hush of my spirit would whisper
to me !

And what if my feet may not tread
where He stood,
Nor my ears hear the dashing of Galilee's flood,
Nor my eyes see the cross which He
bowed him to bear,
Nor my knees press Gethsemane's garden of prayer.

Yet, Loved of the Father, thy Spirit is
near
To the meek, and the lowly, and penitent here ;
And the voice of thy love is the same
even now
As at Bethany's tomb or on Olivet's
brow.

O, the outward hath gone ! — but in
glory and power,
The SPIRIT surviveth the things of an
hour ;
Unchanged, undecaying, its Pentecost
flame
On the heart's secret altar is burning
the same !

EZEKIEL.

CHAPTER XXXIII. 30 – 33.

THEY hear thee not, O God ! nor see ;
Beneath thy rod they mock at thee ;
The princes of our ancient line
Lie drunken with Assyrian wine ;
The priests around thy altar speak
The false words which their hearers seek ;
And hymns which Chaldea's wanton
maids
Have sung in Dura's idol-shades
Are with the Levites' chant ascending,
With Zion's holiest anthems blending !

On Israel's bleeding bosom set,
The heathen heel is crushing yet ;
The towers upon our holy hill
Echo Chaldean footsteps still.

Our wasted shrines, — who weeps for
   them ?
Who mourneth for Jerusalem ?
Who turneth from his gains away ?
Whose knee with mine is bowed to pray ?
Who, leaving feast and purpling cup,
Takes Zion's lamentation up ?

A sad and thoughtful youth, I went
With Israel's early banishment ;
And where the sullen Chebar crept,
The ritual of my fathers kept.
The water for the trench I drew,
The firstling of the flock I slew,
And, standing at the altar's side,
I shared the Levites' lingering pride,
That still, amidst her mocking foes,
The smoke of Zion's offering rose.

In sudden whirlwind, cloud and flame,
The Spirit of the Highest came !
Before mine eyes a vision passed,
A glory terrible and vast ;
With dreadful eyes of living things,
And sounding sweep of angel wings,
With circling light and sapphire throne,
And flame-like form of One thereon,
And voice of that dread Likeness sent
Down from the crystal firmament !

The burden of a prophet's power
Fell on me in that fearful hour ;
From off unutterable woes
The curtain of the future rose ;
I saw far down the coming time
The fiery chastisement of crime ;
With noise of mingling hosts, and jar
Of falling towers and shouts of war,
I saw the nations rise and fall,
Like fire-gleams on my tent's white
   wall.

In dream and trance, I saw the slain
Of Egypt heaped like harvest grain.
I saw the walls of sea-born Tyre
Swept over by the spoiler's fire ;
And heard the low, expiring moan
Of Edom on his rocky throne ;
And, woe is me ! the wild lament
From Zion's desolation sent ;
And felt within my heart each blow
Which laid her holy places low.

In bonds and sorrow, day by day,
Before the pictured tile I lay ;
And there, as in a mirror, saw
The coming of Assyria's war, —

Her swarthy lines of spearmen pass
Like locusts through Bethhoron's grass ;
I saw them draw their stormy hem
Of battle round Jerusalem ;
And, listening, heard the Hebrew wail
Blend with the victor-trump of Baal !

Who trembled at my warning word ?
Who owned the prophet of the Lord ?
How mocked the rude, — how scoffed
   the vile, —
How stung the Levites' scornful smile,
As o'er my spirit, dark and slow,
The shadow crept of Israel's woe
As if the angel's mournful roll
Had left its record on my soul,
And traced in lines of darkness there
The picture of its great despair !

Yet ever at the hour I feel
My lips in prophecy unseal.
Prince, priest, and Levite gather near,
And Salem's daughters haste to hear,
On Chebar's waste and alien shore,
The harp of Judah swept once more.
They listen, as in Babel's throng
The Chaldeans to the dancer's song,
Or wild sabbeka's nightly play,
As careless and as vain as they.

And thus, O Prophet-bard of old,
Hast thou thy tale of sorrow told !
The same which earth's unwelcome seers
Have felt in all succeeding years.
Sport of the changeful multitude,
Nor calmly heard nor understood,
Their song has seemed a trick of art,
Their warnings but the actor's part.
With bonds, and scorn, and evil will,
The world requites its prophets still.

So was it when the Holy One
The garments of the flesh put on !
Men followed where the Highest led
For common gifts of daily bread,
And gross of ear, of vision dim,
Owned not the godlike power of him.
Vain as a dreamer's words to them
His wail above Jerusalem,
And meaningless the watch he kept
Through which his weak disciples slept

Yet shrink not thou, whoe'er thou art,
For God's great purpose set apart,
Before whose far-discerning eyes,
The Future as the Present lies !

Beyond a narrow-bounded age
Stretches thy prophet-heritage,
Through Heaven's dim spaces angel-trod,
Through arches round the throne of
    God !
Thy audience, worlds ! — all Time to be
The witness of the Truth in thee !

THE WIFE OF MANOAH TO HER
HUSBAND.

AGAINST the sunset's glowing wall
The city towers rise black and tall,
Where Zorah, on its rocky height,
Stands like an armed man in the light.

Down Eshtaol's vales of ripened grain
Falls like a cloud the night amain,
And up the hillsides climbing slow
The barley reapers homeward go.

Look, dearest ! how our fair child's head
The sunset light hath hallowed,
Where at this olive's foot he lies,
Uplooking to the tranquil skies.

O, while beneath the fervent heat
Thy sickle swept the bearded wheat,
I've watched, with mingled joy and
    dread,
Our child upon his grassy bed.

Joy, which the mother feels alone
Whose morning hope like mine had
    flown,
When to her bosom, over-blessed,
A dearer life than hers is pressed.

Dread, for the future dark and still,
Which shapes our dear one to its will ;
Forever in his large calm eyes,
I read a tale of sacrifice. —

The same foreboding awe I felt
When at the altar's side we knelt,
And he, who as a pilgrim came,
Rose, winged and glorious, through the
    flame.

I slept not, though the wild bees made
A dreamlike murmuring in the shade,
And on me the warm-fingered hours
Pressed with the drowsy smell of flowers.

Before me, in a vision, rose
The hosts of Israel's scornful foes, —

Rank over rank, helm, shield, and spear,
Glittered in noon's hot atmosphere.

I heard their boast, and bitter word,
Their mockery of the Hebrew's Lord,
I saw their hands his ark assail,
Their feet profane his holy veil.

No angel down the blue space spoke,
No thunder from the still sky broke ;
But in their midst, in power and awe,
Like God's waked wrath, OUR CHILD I
    saw !

A child no more ! — harsh-browed and
    strong,
He towered a giant in the throng,
And down his shoulders, broad and bare,
Swept the black terror of his hair.

He raised his arm ; he smote amain ;
As round the reaper falls the grain,
So the dark host around him fell,
So sank the foes of Israel !

Again I looked.   In sunlight shone
The towers and domes of Askelon.
Priest, warrior, slave, a mighty crowd,
Within her idol temple bowed.

Yet one knelt not ; stark, gaunt, and
    blind,
His arms the massive pillars twined, —
An eyeless captive, strong with hate,
He stood there like an evil Fate.

The red shrines smoked, — the trumpets
    pealed :
He stooped, — the giant columns
    reeled, —
Reeled tower and fane, sank arch and
    wall,
And the thick dust-cloud closed o'er
    all !

Above the shriek, the crash, the groan
Of the fallen pride of Askelon,
I heard, sheer down the echoing sky,
A voice as of an angel cry, —

The voice of him, who at our side
Sat through the golden eventide, —
Of him who, on thy altar's blaze,
Rose fire-winged, with his song of praise.

" Rejoice o'er Israel's broken chain,
Gray mother of the mighty slain !

Rejoice !" it cried, "he vanquisheth !
The strong in life is strong in death !

"To him shall Zorah's daughters raise
Through coming years their hymns of
　praise,
And gray old men at evening tell
Of all he wrought for Israel.

"And they who sing and they who
　hear
Alike shall hold thy memory dear,
And pour their blessings on thy head,
O mother of the mighty dead !"

It ceased ; and though a sound I heard
As if great wings the still air stirred,
I only saw the barley sheaves
And hills half hid by olive leaves.

I bowed my face, in awe and fear,
On the dear child who slumbered near.
"With me, as with my only son,
O God," I said, "THY WILL BE DONE !"

THE CITIES OF THE PLAIN.

"GET ye up from the wrath of God's
　terrible day !
Ungirded, unsandalled, arise and away !
'T is the vintage of blood, 't is the ful-
　ness of time,
And vengeance shall gather the harvest
　of crime !"

The warning was spoken ; the righteous
　had gone,
And the proud ones of Sodom were
　feasting alone ;
All gay was the banquet ; the revel was
　long,
With the pouring of wine and the
　breathing of song.

'T was an evening of beauty ; the air was
　perfume,
The earth was all greenness, the trees
　were all bloom ;
And softly the delicate viol was heard,
Like the murmur of love or the notes of
　a bird.

And beautiful maidens moved down in
　the dance,
With the magic of motion and sunshine
　of glance ;

And white arms wreathed lightly, and
　tresses fell free
As the plumage of birds in some tropical
　tree.

Where the shrines of foul idols were
　lighted on high,
And wantonness tempted the lust of the
　eye ;
Midst rites of obsceneness, strange,
　loathsome, abhorred,
The blasphemer scoffed at the name of
　the Lord.

Hark ! the growl of the thunder, — the
　quaking of earth !
Woe, woe to the worship, and woe to
　the mirth !
The black sky has opened, — there 's
　flame in the air, —
The red arm of vengeance is lifted and
　bare !

Then the shriek of the dying rose wild
　where the song
And the low tone of love had been whis-
　pered along ;
For the fierce flames went lightly o'er
　palace and bower,
Like the red tongues of demons, to blast
　and devour !

Down, — down on the fallen the red
　ruin rained,
And the reveller sank with his wine-cup
　undrained ;
The foot of the dancer, the music's loved
　thrill,
And the shout and the laughter grew
　suddenly still.

The last throb of anguish was fearfully
　given ;
The last eye glared forth in its madness
　on Heaven !
The last groan of horror rose wildly and
　vain,
And death brooded over the pride of the
　Plain !

THE CRUCIFIXION.

SUNLIGHT upon Judæa's hills !
　And on the waves of Galilee, —
On Jordan's stream, and on the rills
　That feed the dead and sleeping sea !

Most freshly from the green wood springs
The light breeze on its scented wings ;
And gayly quiver in the sun
The cedar tops of Lebanon !

A few more hours, — a change hath
    come !
  The sky is dark without a cloud !
The shouts of wrath and joy are dumb,
    And proud knees unto earth are
      bowed.
A change is on the hill of Death,
The helmed watchers pant for breath,
And turn with wild and maniac eyes
From the dark scene of sacrifice !

That Sacrifice ! — the death of Him, —
    The High and ever Holy One !
Well may the conscious Heaven grow
    dim,
And blacken the beholding Sun.
The wonted light hath fled away,
Night settles on the middle day,
And earthquake from his caverned bed
Is waking with a thrill of dread !

The dead are waking underneath !
    Their prison door is rent away !
And, ghastly with the seal of death,
    They wander in the eye of day !
The temple of the Cherubim,
The House of God is cold and dim ;
A curse is on its trembling walls,
Its mighty veil asunder falls !

Well may the cavern-depths of Earth
    Be shaken, and her mountains nod ;
Well may the sheeted dead come forth
    To gaze upon a suffering God !
Well may the temple-shrine grow dim,
And shadows veil the Cherubim,
When He, the chosen one of Heaven,
A sacrifice for guilt is given !

And shall the sinful heart, alone,
    Behold unmoved the atoning hour,
When Nature trembles on her throne,
    And Death resigns his iron power ?
O, shall the heart — whose sinfulness
Gave keenness to his sore distress,
And added to his tears of blood —
Refuse its trembling gratitude !

THE STAR OF BETHLEHEM.

WHERE Time the measure of his hours
  By changeful bud and blossom keeps,

And, like a young bride crowned with
      flowers,
    Fair Shiraz in her garden sleeps ;

Where, to her poet's turban stone,
    The Spring her gift of flowers imparts,
Less sweet than those his thoughts have
      sown
    In the warm soil of Persian hearts :

There sat the stranger, where the shade
    Of scattered date-trees thinly lay,
While in the hot clear heaven delayed
    The long and still and weary day.

Strange trees and fruits above him hung,
    Strange odors filled the sultry air,
Strange birds upon the branches swung,
    Strange insect voices murmured there.

And strange bright blossoms shone
      around,
    Turned sunward from the shadowy
      bowers,
As if the Gheber's soul had found
    A fitting home in Iran's flowers.

Whate'er he saw, whate'er he heard,
    Awakened feelings new and sad, —
No Christian garb, nor Christian word,
    Nor church with Sabbath-bell chimes
      glad,

But Moslem graves, with turban stones,
    And mosque-spires gleaming white, in
      view,
And graybeard Mollahs in low tones
    Chanting their Koran service through.

The flowers which smiled on either
      hand,
    Like tempting fiends, were such as
      they
Which once, o'er all that Eastern land,
    As gifts on demon altars lay.

As if the burning eye of Baal
    The servant of his Conqueror knew,
From skies which knew no cloudy veil,
    The Sun's hot glances smote him
      through.

"Ah me !" the lonely stranger said,
  "The hope which led my footsteps on,
And light from heaven around them
      shed,
    O'er weary wave and waste, is gone !

"Where are the harvest fields all
        white,
    For Truth to thrust her sickle in ?
Where flock the souls, like doves in
        flight,
    From the dark hiding-place of sin ?

" A silent horror broods o'er all, —
    The burden of a hateful spell, —
The very flowers around recall
    The hoary magi's rites of hell !

" And what am I, o'er such a land
    The banner of the Cross to bear ?
Dear Lord, uphold me with thy hand,
    Thy strength with human weakness
        share ! "

He ceased ; for at his very feet
    In mild rebuke a floweret smiled, —
How thrilled his sinking heart to greet
    The Star-flower of the Virgin's child !

Sown by some wandering Frank, it
        drew
    Its life from alien air and earth,
And told to Paynim sun and dew
    The story of the Saviour's birth.

From scorching beams, in kindly mood,
    The Persian plants its beauty screened,
And on its pagan sisterhood,
    In love, the Christian floweret leaned.

With tears of joy the wanderer felt
    The darkness of his long despair
Before that hallowed symbol melt,
    Which God's dear love had nurtured
        there.

From Nature's face, that simple flower
    The lines of sin and sadness swept ;
And Magian pile and Paynim bower
    In peace like that of Eden slept.

Each Moslem tomb, and cypress old,
    Looked holy through the sunset air ;
And, angel-like, the Muezzin told
    From tower and mosque the hour of
        prayer.

With cheerful steps, the morrow's dawn
    From Shiraz saw the stranger part ;
The Star-flower of the Virgin-Born
    Still blooming in his hopeful heart !

HYMNS.

FROM THE FRENCH OF LAMARTINE.

ONE hymn more, O my lyre !
    Praise to the God above,
    Of joy and life and love,
Sweeping its strings of fire !

O, who the speed of bird and wind
    And sunbeam's glance will lend to me,
That, soaring upward, I may find
    My resting-place and home in Thee ?—
Thou, whom my soul, midst doubt and
        gloom,
    Adoreth with a fervent flame, —
Mysterious spirit ! unto whom
    Pertain nor sign nor name !

Swiftly my lyre's soft murmurs go,
    Up from the cold and joyless earth,
Back to the God who bade them flow,
    Whose moving spirit sent them forth.
But as for me, O God ! for me,
    The lowly creature of thy will,
Lingering and sad, I sigh to thee,
    An earth-bound pilgrim still !

Was not my spirit born to shine
    Where yonder stars and suns are glow-
        ing ?
To breathe with them the light divine
    From God's own holy altar flowing ?
To be, indeed, whate'er the soul
    In dreams hath thirsted for so long, —
A portion of Heaven's glorious whole
    Of loveliness and song ?

O, watchers of the stars at night,
    Who breathe their fire, as we the air, —
Suns, thunders, stars, and rays of light,
    O, say, is He, the Eternal, there ?
Bend there around his awful throne
    The seraph's glance, the angel's knee ?
Or are thy inmost depths his own,
    O wild and mighty sea ?

Thoughts of my soul, how swift ye go !
    Swift as the eagle's glance of fire,
Or arrows from the archer's bow,
    To the far aim of your desire !
Thought after thought, ye thronging
        rise,
    Like spring-doves from the startled
        wood,
Bearing like them your sacrifice
    Of music unto God !

And shall these thoughts of joy and love
  Come back again no more to me ? —
Returning like the Patriarch's dove
  Wing-weary from the eternal sea,
To bear within my longing arms
  The promise-bough of kindlier skies,
Plucked from the green, immortal palms
  Which shadow Paradise ?

All-moving spirit ! — freely forth
  At thy command the strong wind
    goes :
Its errand to the passive earth,
  Nor art can stay, nor strength oppose,
Until it folds its weary wing
  Once more within the hand divine ;
So, weary from its wandering,
  My spirit turns to thine !

Child of the sea, the mountain stream,
  From its dark caverns, hurries on,
Ceaseless, by night and morning's beam,
  By evening's star and noontide's sun,
Until at last it sinks to rest,
  O'erwearied, in the waiting sea,
And moans upon its mother's breast, —
  So turns my soul to Thee !

O Thou who bidd'st the torrent flow,
  Who lendest wings unto the wind, —
Mover of all things ! where art thou ?
  O, whither shall I go to find
The secret of thy resting-place ?
  Is there no holy wing for me,
That, soaring, I may search the space
  Of highest heaven for Thee ?

O, would I were as free to rise
  As leaves on autumn's whirlwind
    borne, —
The arrowy light of sunset skies,
  Or sound, or ray, or star of morn,
Which melts in heaven at twilight's
    close,
  Or aught which soars unchecked and
    free
Through Earth and Heaven ; that I
    might lose
  Myself in finding Thee !

———

When the breath divine is flowing,
Zephyr-like o'er all things going,
And, as the touch of viewless fingers,
Softly on my soul it lingers,
Open to a breath the lightest,

Conscious of a touch the slightest, —
As some calm, still lake, whereon
Sinks the snowy-bosomed swan,
And the glistening water-rings
Circle round her moving wings :
When my upward gaze is turning
Where the stars of heaven are burning
Through the deep and dark abyss, —
Flowers of midnight's wilderness,
Blowing with the evening's breath
Sweetly in their Maker's path :

When the breaking day is flushing
All the east, and light is gushing
Upward through the horizon's haze,
Sheaf-like, with its thousand rays,
Spreading, until all above
Overflows with joy and love,
And below, on earth's green bosom,
All is changed to light and blossom :

When my waking fancies over
Forms of brightness flit and hover,
Holy as the seraphs are,
Who by Zion's fountains wear
On their foreheads, white and broad,
" Holiness unto the Lord ! "
When, inspired with rapture high,
It would seem a single sigh
Could a world of love create, —
That my life could know no date,
And my eager thoughts could fill
Heaven and Earth, o'erflowing still ! —

Then, O Father ! thou alone,
From the shadow of thy throne,
To the sighing of my breast
And its rapture answerest.
All my thoughts, which, upward wing-
    ing,
Bathe where thy own light is spring-
    ing, —
All my yearnings to be free
Are as echoes answering thee !

Seldom upon lips of mine,
Father ! rests that name of thine, —
Deep within my inmost breast,
  In the secret place of mind,
  Like an awful presence shrined,
Doth the dread idea rest !
Hushed and holy dwells it there, —
Prompter of the silent prayer,
Lifting up my spirit's eye
And its faint, but earnest cry,
From its dark and cold abode,
Unto thee, my Guide and God !

THE FEMALE MARTYR.

[MARY G——, aged 18, a " SISTER OF CHARITY,"
died in one of our Atlantic cities, during the
prevalence of the Indian cholera, while in volun-
tary attendance upon the sick.]

"BRING out your dead !" The mid-
    night street
  Heard and gave back the hoarse, low
    call ;
Harsh fell the tread of hasty feet, —
Glanced through the dark the coarse
    white sheet, —
  Her coffin and her pall.
" What — only one !" the brutal hack-
    man said,
As, with an oath, he spurned away the
    dead.

How sunk the inmost hearts of all,
  As rolled that dead-cart slowly by,
With creaking wheel and harsh hoof-
    fall !
The dying turned him to the wall,
  To hear it and to die ! —
Onward it rolled ; while oft its driver
    stayed,
And hoarsely clamored, " Ho ! — bring
    out your dead."

It paused beside the burial-place ;
  "Toss in your load !" — and it was
    done. —
With quick hand and averted face,
Hastily to the grave's embrace
  They cast them, one by one, —
Stranger and friend, — the evil and the
    just,
Together trodden in the churchyard dust !

And thou, young martyr ! — thou wast
    there, —
  No white-robed sisters round thee
    trod, —
Nor holy hymn, nor funeral prayer
Rose through the damp and noisome air,
  Giving thee to thy God ;
Nor flower, nor cross, nor hallowed taper
    gave
Grace to the dead, and beauty to the
    grave !

Yet, gentle sufferer ! there shall be,
  In every heart of kindly feeling,
A rite as holy paid to thee
As if beneath the convent-tree
  Thy sisterhood were kneeling,

At vesper hours, like sorrowing angels,
    keeping
Their tearful watch around thy place of
    sleeping.

For thou wast one in whom the light
  Of Heaven's own love was kindled
    well.
Enduring with a martyr's might,
Through weary day and wakeful night
  Far more than words may tell :
Gentle, and meek, and lowly, and un-
    known, —
Thy mercies measured by thy God alone !

Where manly hearts were failing, —
    where
  The throngful street grew foul with
    death,
O high-souled martyr ! — thou wast
    there,
Inhaling, from the loathsome air,
  Poison with every breath.
Yet shrinking not from offices of dread
For the wrung dying, and the uncon-
    scious dead.

And, where the sickly taper shed
  Its light through vapors, damp, con-
    fined,
Hushed as a seraph's fell thy tread, —
A new Electra by the bed
  Of suffering human-kind !
Pointing the spirit, in its dark dismay,
To that pure hope which fadeth not away.

Innocent teacher of the high
  And holy mysteries of Heaven !
How turned to thee each glazing eye,
In mute and awful sympathy,
  As thy low prayers were given ;
And the o'er-hovering Spoiler wore, the
    while,
An angel's features, — a deliverer's
    smile !

A blessed task ! — and worthy one
  Who, turning from the world, as thou,
Before life's pathway had begun
To leave its spring-time flower and sun,
  Had sealed her early vow ;
Giving to God her beauty and her youth,
Her pure affections and her guileless
    truth.

Earth may not claim thee. Nothing here
  Could be for thee a meet reward ;

Thine is a treasure far more dear, —
Eye hath not seen it, nor the ear
    Of living mortal heard, —
The joys prepared, — the promised bliss
    above, —
The holy presence of Eternal Love !

Sleep on in peace. The earth has not
    A nobler name than thine shall be.
The deeds by martial manhood wrought,
The lofty energies of thought,
    The fire of poesy, —
These have but frail and fading hon-
    ors ; — thine
Shall Time unto Eternity consign.

Yea, and when thrones shall crumble
    down,
    And human pride and grandeur fall, —
The herald's line of long renown, —
The mitre and the kingly crown, —
    Perishing glories all !
The pure devotion of thy generous heart
Shall live in Heaven, of which it was a
    part.

THE FROST SPIRIT.

He comes, — he comes, — the Frost Spirit
    comes ! You may trace his foot-
    steps now
On the naked woods and the blasted fields
    and the brown hill's withered brow.
He has smitten the leaves of the gray
    old trees where their pleasant
    green came forth,
And the winds, which follow wherever
    he goes, have shaken them down
    to earth.

He comes, — he comes, — the Frost
    Spirit comes ! — from the frozen
    Labrador, —
From the icy bridge of the Northern
    seas, which the white bear wan-
    ders o'er, —
Where the fisherman's sail is stiff with
    ice, and the luckless forms below
In the sunless cold of the lingering night
    into marble statues grow !

He comes, — he comes, — the Frost
    Spirit comes ! — on the rushing
    Northern blast,
And the dark Norwegian pines have
    bowed as his fearful breath went
    past.

With an unscorched wing he has hur-
    ried on, where the fires of Hecla
    glow
On the darkly beautiful sky above and
    the ancient ice below.

He comes, — he comes, — the Frost
    Spirit comes ! — and the quiet
    lake shall feel
The torpid touch of his glazing breath,
    and ring to the skater's heel ;
And the streams which danced on the
    broken rocks, or sang to the lean-
    ing grass,
Shall bow again to their winter chain,
    and in mournful silence pass.

He comes, — he comes, — the Frost
    Spirit comes ! — let us meet him
    as we may,
And turn with the light of the parlor-
    fire his evil power away ;
And gather closer the circle round, when
    that firelight dances high,
And laugh at the shriek of the baffled
    Fiend as his sounding wing goes
    by !

THE VAUDOIS TEACHER.[38]

" O lady fair, these silks of mine are
    beautiful and rare, —
The richest web of the Indian loom,
    which beauty's queen might wear ;
And my pearls are pure as thy own fair
    neck, with whose radiant light
    they vie ;
I have brought them with me a weary
    way, — will my gentle lady buy ?"

And the lady smiled on the worn old man
    through the dark and clustering
    curls
Which veiled her brow as she bent to
    view his silks and glittering pearls ;
And she placed their price in the old
    man's hand, and lightly turned
    away,
But she paused at the wanderer's earnest
    call, — " My gentle lady, stay ! "

" O lady fair, I have yet a gem which a
    purer lustre flings,
Than the diamond flash of the jewelled
    crown on the lofty brow of
    kings, —

A wonderful pearl of exceeding price,
  whose virtue shall not decay,
Whose light shall be as a spell to thee
  and a blessing on thy way ! "

The lady glanced at the mirroring steel
  where her form of grace was seen,
Where her eye shone clear, and her dark
  locks waved their clasping pearls
  between ;
" Bring forth thy pearl of exceeding
  worth, thou traveller gray and
  old, —
And name the price of thy precious gem,
  and my page shall count thy gold."

The cloud went off from the pilgrim's
  brow, as a small and meagre book,
Unchased with gold or gem of cost, from
  his folding robe he took !
" Here, lady fair, is the pearl of price,
  may it prove as such to thee !
Nay — keep thy gold — I ask it not, for
  the word of God is free ! "

The hoary traveller went his way, but
  the gift he left behind
Hath had its pure and perfect work on
  that high-born maiden's mind,
And she hath turned from the pride of
  sin to the lowliness of truth,
And given her human heart to God in
  its beautiful hour of youth !

And she hath left the gray old halls,
  where an evil faith had power,
The courtly knights of her father's train,
  and the maidens of her bower ;
And she hath gone to the Vaudois vales
  by lordly feet untrod,
Where the poor and needy of earth are
  rich in the perfect love of God !

THE CALL OF THE CHRISTIAN.

  NOT always as the whirlwind's rush
    On Horeb's mount of fear,
  Not always as the burning bush
    To Midian's shepherd seer,
  Nor as the awful voice which came
    To Israel's prophet bards,
  Nor as the tongues of cloven flame,
    Nor gift of fearful words, —

  Not always thus, with outward sign
    Of fire or voice from Heaven,

The message of a truth divine,
  The call of God is given !
Awaking in the human heart
  Love for the true and right, —
Zeal for the Christian's better part,
  Strength for the Christian's fight.

Nor unto manhood's heart alone
  The holy influence steals :
Warm with a rapture not its own,
  The heart of woman feels !
As she who by Samaria's wall
  The Saviour's errand sought, —
As those who with the fervent Paul
  And meek Aquila wrought :

Or those meek ones whose martyrdom
  Rome's gathered grandeur saw :
Or those who in their Alpine home
  Braved the Crusader's war,
When the green Vaudois, trembling,
  heard,
  Through all its vales of death,
The martyr's song of triumph poured
  From woman's failing breath.

And gently, by a thousand things
  Which o'er our spirits pass,
Like breezes o'er the harp's fine strings,
  Or vapors o'er a glass,
Leaving their token strange and new
  Of music or of shade,
The summons to the right and true
  And merciful is made.

O, then, if gleams of truth and light
  Flash o'er thy waiting mind,
Unfolding to thy mental sight
  The wants of human-kind ;
If, brooding over human grief,
  The earnest wish is known
To soothe and gladden with relief
  An anguish not thine own ;

Though heralded with naught of fear,
  Or outward sign or show ;
Though only to the inward ear
  It whispers soft and low ;
Though dropping, as the manna fell,
  Unseen, yet from above,
Noiseless as dew-fall, heed it well, —
  Thy Father's call of love !

MY SOUL AND I.

STAND still, my soul, in the silent dark
  I would question thee,

Alone in the shadow drear and stark
    With God and me !

What, my soul, was thy errand here ?
    Was it mirth or ease,
Or heaping up dust from year to year ?
    " Nay, none of these ! "

Speak, soul, aright in His holy sight
    Whose eye looks still
And steadily on thee through the night :
    " To do his will ! "

What hast thou done, O soul of mine,
    That thou tremblest so ? —
Hast thou wrought his task, and kept
        the line
    He bade thee go ?

What, silent all ! — art sad of cheer ?
    Art fearful now ?
When God seemed far and men were near,
    How brave wert thou !

Aha ? thou tremblest ! — well I see
    Thou 'rt craven grown.
Is it so hard with God and me
    To stand alone ? —

Summon thy sunshine bravery back,
    O wretched sprite !
Let me hear thy voice through this deep
        and black
    Abysmal night.

What hast thou wrought for Right and
        Truth,
    For God and Man,
From the golden hours of bright-eyed
        youth
    To life's mid span ?

Ah, soul of mine, thy tones I hear,
    But weak and low,
Like far sad murmurs on my ear
    They come and go.

" I have wrestled stoutly with the
        Wrong,
    And borne the Right
From beneath the footfall of the throng
    To life and light.

" Wherever Freedom shivered a chain,
    God speed, quoth I ;
To Error amidst her shouting train
    I gave the lie."

Ah, soul of mine ? ah, soul of mine !
    Thy deeds are well :
Were they wrought for Truth's sake or
        for thine ?
    My soul, pray tell.

" Of all the work my hand hath wrought
    Beneath the sky,
Save a place in kindly human thought,
    No gain have I."

Go to, go to ! — for thy very self
    Thy deeds were done :
Thou for fame, the miser for pelf,
    Your end is one !

And where art thou going, soul of mine ?
    Canst see the end ?
And whither this troubled life of thine
    Evermore doth tend ?

What daunts thee now ? — what shakes
        thee so ?
    My sad soul say.
" I see a cloud like a curtain low
    Hang o'er my way.

" Whither I go I cannot tell :
    That cloud hangs black,
High as the heaven and deep as hell
    Across my track.

" I see its shadow coldly enwrap
    The souls before.
Sadly they enter it, step by step,
    To return no more.

" They shrink, they shudder, dear God!
        they kneel
    To thee in prayer.
They shut their eyes on the cloud, but
        feel
    That it still is there.

"In vain they turn from the dread Before
    To the Known and Gone ;
For while gazing behind them evermore
    Their feet glide on.

" Yet, at times, I see upon sweet pale
        faces
    A light begin
To tremble, as if from holy places
    And shrines within.

" And at times methinks their cold lips
        move
    With hymn and prayer,

As if somewhat of awe, but more of love
  And hope were there.

" I call on the souls who have left the
     light
  To reveal their lot ;
I bend mine ear to that wall of night,
  And they answer not.

" But I hear around me sighs of pain
  And the cry of fear,
And a sound like the slow sad dropping
    of rain,
  Each drop a tear !

" Ah, the cloud is dark, and day by day
  I am moving thither :
I must pass beneath it on my way —
  God pity me ! — WHITHER ? "

Ah, soul of mine ! so brave and wise
  In the life-storm loud,
Fronting so calmly all human eyes
  In the sunlit crowd !

Now standing apart with God and me
  Thou art weakness all,
Gazing vainly after the things to be
  Through Death's dread wall.

But never for this, never for this
  Was thy being lent ;
For the craven's fear is but selfishness,
  Like his merriment.

Folly and Fear are sisters twain :
  One closing her eyes,
The other peopling the dark inane
  With spectral lies.

Know well, my soul, God's hand controls
  Whate'er thou fearest ;
Round him in calmest music rolls
  Whate'er thou hearest.

What to thee is shadow, to him is day,
  And the end he knoweth,
And not on a blind and aimless way
  The spirit goeth.

Man sees no future, — a phantom show
  Is alone before him :
Past Time is dead, and the grasses grow,
  And flowers bloom o'er him.

Nothing before, nothing behind ;
  The steps of Faith

Fall on the seeming void, and find
  The rock beneath.

The Present, the Present is all thou hast
  For thy sure possessing ;
Like the patriarch's angel hold it fast
  Till it gives its blessing.

Why fear the night ? why shrink from
    Death,
  That phantom wan ?
There is nothing in heaven or earth be-
    neath
  Save God and man.

Peopling the shadows we turn from Him
  And from one another ;
All is spectral and vague and dim
  Save God and our brother !

Like warp and woof all destinies
  Are woven fast,
Linked in sympathy like the keys
  Of an organ vast.

Pluck one thread, and the web ye mar ·
  Break but one
Of a thousand keys, and the paining jar
  Through all will run.

O restless spirit ! wherefore strain
  Beyond thy sphere ?
Heaven and hell, with their joy and pain,
  Are now and here.

Back to thyself is measured well
  All thou hast given ;
Thy neighbor's wrong is thy present hell,
  His bliss, thy heaven.

And in life, in death, in dark and light,
  All are in God's care :
Sound the black abyss, pierce the deep
    of night,
  And he is there !

All which is real now remaineth,
  And fadeth never :
The hand which upholds it now sustaineth
  The soul forever.

Leaning on him, make with reverent
    meekness
  His own thy will,
And with strength from Him shall thy
    utter weakness
  Life's task fulfil ;

And that cloud itself, which now before
    thee
    Lies dark in view,
Shall with beams of light from the inner
    glory
    Be stricken through.

And like meadow mist through autumn's
    dawn
    Uprolling thin,
Its thickest folds when about thee drawn
    Let sunlight in.

Then of what is to be, and of what is done,
    Why queriest thou ? —
The past and the time to be are one,
    And both are NOW !

TO A FRIEND,

ON HER RETURN FROM EUROPE.

How smiled the land of France
Under thy blue eye's glance,
    Light-hearted rover !
Old walls of chateaux gray,
Towers of an early day,
Which the Three Colors play
    Flauntingly over.

Now midst the brilliant train
Thronging the banks of Seine :
    Now midst the splendor
Of the wild Alpine range,
Waking with change on change
Thoughts in thy young heart strange,
    Lovely, and tender.

Vales, soft Elysian,
Like those in the vision
    Of Mirza, when, dreaming,
He saw the long hollow dell,
Touched by the prophet's spell,
Into an ocean swell
    With its isles teeming.

Cliffs wrapped in snows of years,
Splintering with icy spears
    Autumn's blue heaven :
Loose rock and frozen slide,
Hung on the mountain-side,
Waiting their hour to glide
    Downward, storm-driven !

Rhine-stream, by castle old,
Baron's and robber's hold,

Peacefully flowing ;
Sweeping through vineyards green,
Or where the cliffs are seen
O'er the broad wave between
    Grim shadows throwing.

Or, where St. Peter's dome
Swells o'er eternal Rome,
    Vast, dim, and solemn, —
Hymns ever chanting low, —
Censers swung to and fro, —
Sable stoles sweeping slow
    Cornice and column !

O, as from each and all
Will there not voices call
    Evermore back again ?
In the mind's gallery
Wilt thou not always see
Dim phantoms beckon thee
    O'er that old track again ?

New forms thy presence haunt, —
New voices softly chant, —
    New faces greet thee ! —
Pilgrims from many a shrine
Hallowed by poet's line,
At memory's magic sign,
    Rising to meet thee.

And when such visions come
Unto thy olden home,
    Will they not waken
Deep thoughts of Him whose hand
Led thee o'er sea and land
Back to the household band
    Whence thou wast taken ?

While, at the sunset time,
Swells the cathedral's chime,
    Yet, in thy dreaming,
While to thy spirit's eye
Yet the vast mountains lie
Piled in the Switzer's sky,
    Icy and gleaming :

Prompter of silent prayer,
Be the wild picture there
    In the mind's chamber,
And, through each coming day
Him who, as staff and stay,
Watched o'er thy wandering way,
    Freshly remember.

So, when the call shall be
Soon or late unto thee,
    As to all given,

Still may that picture live,
All its fair forms survive,
And to thy spirit give
  Gladness in Heaven !

THE ANGEL OF PATIENCE.

A FREE PARAPHRASE OF THE GERMAN.

To weary hearts, to mourning homes,
God's meekest Angel gently comes :
No power has he to banish pain,
Or give us back our lost again ;
And yet in tenderest love, our dear
And Heavenly Father sends him here.

There's quiet in that Angel's glance,
There's rest in his still countenance !
He mocks no grief with idle cheer,
Nor wounds with words the mourner's ear ;
But ills and woes he may not cure
He kindly trains us to endure.

Angel of Patience ! sent to calm
Our feverish brows with cooling palm ;
To lay the storms of hope and fear,
And reconcile life's smile and tear ;
The throbs of wounded pride to still,
And make our own our Father's will !

O thou who mournest on thy way,
With longings for the close of day ;
He walks with thee, that Angel kind,
And gently whispers, " Be resigned :
Bear up, bear on, the end shall tell
The dear Lord ordereth all things well ! "

FOLLEN.

ON READING HIS ESSAY ON THE " FU-
TURE STATE."

FRIEND of my soul ! — as with moist eye
I look up from this page of thine,
Is it a dream that thou art nigh,
  Thy mild face gazing into mine ?

That presence seems before me now,
  A placid heaven of sweet moonrise,
When, dew-like, on the earth below
  Descends the quiet of the skies.

The calm brow through the parted hair,
  The gentle lips which knew no guile,
Softening the blue eye's thoughtful care
  With the bland beauty of their smile.

Ah me ! — at times that last dread scene
  Of Frost and Fire and moaning Sea,
Will cast its shade of doubt between
  The failing eyes of Faith and thee.

Yet, lingering o'er thy charmed page,
  Where through the twilight air of earth,
Alike enthusiast and sage,
  Prophet and bard, thou gazest forth ;

Lifting the Future's solemn veil ;
  The reaching of a mortal hand
To put aside the cold and pale
  Cloud-curtains of the Unseen Land ;

In thoughts which answer to my own,
  In words which reach my inward ear,
Like whispers from the void Unknown,
  I feel thy living presence here.

The waves which lull thy body's rest,
  The dust thy pilgrim footsteps trod,
Unwasted, through each change, attest
  The fixed economy of God.

Shall these poor elements outlive
  The mind whose kingly will they
    wrought ?
Their gross unconsciousness survive
  Thy godlike energy of thought ?

THOU LIVEST, FOLLEN ! — not in vain
  Hath thy fine spirit meekly borne
The burthen of Life's cross of pain,
  And the thorned crown of suffering
    worn.

O, while Life's solemn mystery glooms
  Around us like a dungeon's wall, —
Silent earth's pale and crowded tombs,
  Silent the heaven which bends o'er
    all ! —

While day by day our loved ones glide
  In spectral silence, hushed and lone,
To the cold shadows which divide
  The living from the dread Unknown ;

While even on the closing eye,
  And on the lip which moves in vain,
The seals of that stern mystery
  Their undiscovered trust retain ; —

And only midst the gloom of death,
  Its mournful doubts and haunting
    fears,
Two pale, sweet angels, Hope and Faith,
  Smile dimly on us through their tears ;

'T is something to a heart like mine
  To think of thee as living yet ;
To feel that such a light as thine
  Could not in utter darkness set.

Less dreary seems the untried way
  Since thou hast left thy footprints there,
And beams of mournful beauty play
  Round the sad Angel's sable hair.

Oh ! — at this hour when half the sky
  Is glorious with its evening light,
And fair broad fields of summer lie
  Hung o'er with greenness in my sight ;

While through these elm-boughs wet with
  rain
  The sunset's golden walls are seen,
With clover-bloom and yellow grain
  And wood-draped hill and stream be-
  tween ;

I long to know if scenes like this
  Are hidden from an angel's eyes ;
If earth's familiar loveliness
  Haunts not thy heaven's serener skies.

For sweetly here upon thee grew
  The lesson which that beauty gave,
The ideal of the Pure and True
  In earth and sky and gliding wave.

And it may be that all which lends
  The soul an upward impulse here,
With a diviner beauty blends,
  And greets us in a holier sphere.

Through groves where blighting never fell
  The humbler flowers of earth may
  twine ;
And simple draughts from childhood's
  well
  Blend with the angel-tasted wine.

But be the prying vision veiled,
  And let the seeking lips be dumb, —
Where even seraph eyes have failed
  Shall mortal blindness seek to come ?

We only know that thou hast gone,
  And that the same returnless tide
Which bore thee from us still glides on,
  And we who mourn thee with it glide.

On all thou lookest we shall look,
  And to our gaze erelong shall turn
That page of God's mysterious book
  We so much wish, yet dread to learn.

7

With Him, before whose awful power
  Thy spirit bent its trembling knee ; —
Who, in the silent greeting flower,
  And forest leaf, looked out on thee, —

We leave thee, with a trust serene,
  Which Time, nor Change, nor Death
  can move,
While with thy childlike faith we lean
  On Him whose dearest name is Love !

TO THE REFORMERS OF ENG-
LAND.

GOD bless ye, brothers ! — in the fight
  Ye 're waging now, ye cannot fail,
For better is your sense of right
  Than king-craft's triple mail.

Than tyrant's law, or bigot's ban,
  More mighty is your simplest word ;
The free heart of an honest man
  Than crosier or the sword.

Go, — let your bloated Church rehearse
  The lesson it has learned so well ;
It moves not with its prayer or curse
  The gates of heaven or hell.

Let the State scaffold rise again, —
  Did Freedom die when Russell died ?
Forget ye how the blood of Vane
  From earth's green bosom cried ?

The great hearts of your olden time
  Are beating with you, full and strong
All holy memories and sublime
  And glorious round ye throng.

The bluff, bold men of Runnymede
  Are with ye still in times like these
The shades of England's mighty dead,
  Your cloud of witnesses !

The truths ye urge are borne abroad
  By every wind and every tide ;
The voice of Nature and of God
  Speaks out upon your side.

The weapons which your hands have
  found
  Are those which Heaven itself has
  wrought,
Light, Truth, and Love ; — your battle-
  ground
  The free, broad field of Thought.

No partial, selfish purpose breaks
  The simple beauty of your plan,
Nor lie from throne or altar shakes
  Your steady faith in man.

The languid pulse of England starts
  And bounds beneath your words of
      power,
The beating of her million hearts
  Is with you at this hour !

O ye who, with undoubting eyes,
  Through present cloud and gathering
      storm,
Behold the span of Freedom's skies,
  And sunshine soft and warm, —

Press bravely onward ! — not in vain
  Your generous trust in human-kind ;
The good which bloodshed could not gain
  Your peaceful zeal shall find.

Press on ! — the triumph shall be won
  Of common rights and equal laws,
The glorious dream of Harrington,
  And Sidney's good old cause.

Blessing the cotter and the crown,
  Sweetening worn Labor's bitter cup ;
And, plucking not the highest down,
  Lifting the lowest up.

Press on ! — and we who may not share
  The toil or glory of your fight
May ask, at least, in earnest prayer,
  God's blessing on the right !

THE QUAKER OF THE OLDEN
TIME.

The Quaker of the olden time ! —
  How calm and firm and true,
Unspotted by its wrong and crime,
  He walked the dark earth through.
The lust of power, the love of gain,
  The thousand lures of sin
Around him, had no power to stain
  The purity within.

With that deep insight which detects
  All great things in the small,
And knows how each man's life affects
  The spiritual life of all,
He walked by faith and not by sight,
  By love and not by law ;
The presence of the wrong or right
  He rather felt than saw.

He felt that wrong with wrong partakes,
  That nothing stands alone,
That whoso gives the motive, makes
  His brother's sin his own.
And, pausing not for doubtful choice
  Of evils great or small,
He listened to that inward voice
  Which called away from all.

O Spirit of that early day,
  So pure and strong and true,
Be with us in the narrow way
  Our faithful fathers knew.
Give strength the evil to forsake,
  The cross of Truth to bear,
And love and reverent fear to make
  Our daily lives a prayer !

THE REFORMER.

All grim and soiled and brown with
     tan,
  I saw a Strong One, in his wrath,
Smiting the godless shrines of man
     Along his path.

The Church, beneath her trembling dome,
  Essayed in vain her ghostly charm :
Wealth shook within his gilded home
     With strange alarm.

Fraud from his secret chambers fled
  Before the sunlight bursting in :
Sloth drew her pillow o'er her head
     To drown the din.

"Spare," Art implored, " yon holy pile ;
  That grand, old, time-worn turret
     spare " ;
Meek Reverence, kneeling in the aisle,
     Cried out, " Forbear ! "

Gray-bearded Use, who, deaf and blind,
  Groped for his old accustomed stone,
Leaned on his staff, and wept to find
     His seat o'erthrown.

Young Romance raised his dreamy eyes,
  O'erhung with paly locks of gold, —
" Why smite," he asked in sad surprise,
     " The fair, the old ? "

Yet louder rang the Strong One's stroke,
  Yet nearer flashed his axe's gleam ;
Shuddering and sick of heart I woke,
     As from a dream.

I looked : aside the dust-cloud rolled, —
  The Waster seemed the Builder too ;
Up springing from the ruined Old
    I saw the New.

'T was but the ruin of the bad, —
  The wasting of the wrong and ill ;
Whate'er of good the old time had
    Was living still.

Calm grew the brows of him I feared ;
  The frown which awed me passed away,
And left behind a smile which cheered
    Like breaking day.

The grain grew green on battle-plains,
  O'er swarded war-mounds grazed the
      cow ;
The slave stood forging from his chains
    The spade and plough.

Where frowned the fort, pavilions gay
  And cottage windows, flower-entwined,
Looked out upon the peaceful bay
    And hills behind.

Through vine-wreathed cups with wine
    once red,
  The lights on brimming crystal fell,
Drawn, sparkling, from the rivulet head
    And mossy well.

Through prison walls, like Heaven-sent
    hope,
  Fresh breezes blew, and sunbeams
    strayed,
And with the idle gallows-rope
    The young child played.

Where the doomed victim in his cell
  Had counted o'er the weary hours,
Glad school-girls, answering to the bell,
    Came crowned with flowers.

Grown wiser for the lesson given,
  I fear no longer, for I know
That, where the share is deepest driven,
    The best fruits grow.

The outworn rite, the old abuse,
  The pious fraud transparent grown,
The good held captive in the use
    Of wrong alone,

These wait their doom, from that great law
  Which makes the past time serve to-
    day ;

And fresher life the world shall draw
    From their decay.

O, backward-looking son of time !
  The new is old, the old is new,
The cycle of a change sublime
    Still sweeping through.

So wisely taught the Indian seer ;
  Destroying Seva, forming Brahm,
Who wake by turns Earth's love and
    fear,
    Are one, the same.

Idly as thou, in that old day
  Thou mournest, did thy sire repine ;
So, in his time, thy child grown gray
    Shall sigh for thine.

But life shall on and upward go ;
  Th' eternal step of Progress beats
To that great anthem, calm and slow,
    Which God repeats.

Take heart ! — the Waster builds again, —
  A charmed life old Goodness hath ;
The tares may perish, — but the grain
    Is not for death.

God works in all things ; all obey
  His first propulsion from the night :
Wake thou and watch ! — the world is
    gray
    With morning light !

THE PRISONER FOR DEBT.

Look on him ! — through his dungeon
    grate
  Feebly and cold, the morning light
Comes stealing round him, dim and
    late,
  As if it loathed the sight.
Reclining on his strawy bed,
His hand upholds his drooping head, —
His bloodless cheek is seamed and hard,
Unshorn his gray, neglected beard ;
And o'er his bony fingers flow
His long, dishevelled locks of snow.

No grateful fire before him glows,
  And yet the winter's breath is chill ;
And o'er his half-clad person goes
  The frequent ague thrill !
Silent, save ever and anon,
A sound, half murmur and half groan,

Forces apart the painful grip
Of the old sufferer's bearded lip ;
O sad and crushing is the fate
Of old age chained and desolate !

Just God ! why lies that old man there ?
  A murderer shares his prison bed,
Whose eyeballs, through his horrid hair,
  Gleam on him, fierce and red ;
And the rude oath and heartless jeer
Fall ever on his loathing ear,
And, or in wakefulness or sleep,
Nerve, flesh, and pulses thrill and creep
Whene'er that ruffian's tossing limb,
Crimson with murder, touches him !

What has the gray-haired prisoner done ?
• Has murder stained his hands with
      gore ?
Not so ; his crime's a fouler one ;
  GOD MADE THE OLD MAN POOR !
For this he shares a felon's cell, —
The fittest earthly type of hell !
For this, the boon for which he poured
His young blood on the invader's sword,
And counted light the fearful cost, —
His blood-gained liberty is lost !

And so, for such a place of rest,
    Old prisoner, dropped thy blood as
      rain
On Concord's field, and Bunker's crest,
    And Saratoga's plain ?
Look forth, thou man of many scars,
Through thy dim dungeon's iron bars ;
It must be joy, in sooth, to see
Yon monument upreared to thee, —
Piled granite and a prison cell, —
The land repays thy service well !

Go, ring the bells and fire the guns,
    And fling the starry banner out ;
Shout "Freedom !" till your lisping
      ones
    Give back their cradle-shout ;
Let boastful eloquence declaim
Of honor, liberty, and fame ;
Still let the poet's strain be heard,
With glory for each second word,
And everything with breath agree
To praise "our glorious liberty !"

But when the patron cannon jars
    That prison's cold and gloomy wall,
And through its grates the stripes and
      stars
    Rise on the wind, and fall, —

Think ye that prisoner's aged ear
Rejoices in the general cheer ?
Think ye his dim and failing eye
Is kindled at your pageantry ?
Sorrowing of soul, and chained of limb,
What is your carnival to him ?

Down with the LAW that binds him
      thus !
  Unworthy freemen, let it find
No refuge from the withering curse
  Of God and human kind !
Open the prison's living tomb,
And usher from its brooding gloom
The victims of your savage code
To the free sun and air of God ;
No longer dare as crime to brand
The chastening of the Almighty's hand.

LINES,

WRITTEN   ON   READING   PAMPHLETS
PUBLISHED BY CLERGYMEN AGAINST
THE ABOLITION OF THE GALLOWS.

I.

THE suns of eighteen centuries have
      shone
    Since the Redeemer walked with man,
      and made
The fisher's boat, the cavern's floor of
      stone,
    And mountain moss, a pillow for his
      head ;
And He, who wandered with the peas-
      ant Jew,
    And broke with publicans the bread
      of shame,
    And drank, with blessings in his Fa-
      ther's name,
The water which Samaria's outcast drew,
Hath now his temples upon every shore,
    Altar and shrine and priest, — and in-
      cense dim
    Evermore rising, with low prayer and
      hymn,
From lips which press the temple's mar-
      ble floor,
Or kiss the gilded sign of the dread
      Cross He bore.

II.

Yet as of old, when, meekly "doing
      good,"
He fed a blind and selfish multitude,

And even the poor companions of his lot
With their dim earthly vision knew him
not,
How ill are his high teachings under-
stood !
Where He hath spoken Liberty, the
priest
At his own altar binds the chain
anew ;
Where He hath bidden to Life's equal
feast,
The starving many wait upon the few ;
Where He hath spoken Peace, his name
hath been
The loudest war-cry of contending men ;
Priests, pale with vigils, in his name
have blessed
The unsheathed sword, and laid the
spear in rest,
Wet the war-banner with their sacred
wine,
And crossed its blazon with the holy
sign ;
Yea, in his name who bade the erring
live,
And daily taught his lesson, — to for-
give ! —
Twisted the cord and edged the mur-
derous steel ;
And, with his words of mercy on their
lips,
Hung gloating o'er the pincer's burning
grips,
And the grim horror of the straining
wheel ;
Fed the slow flame which gnawed the
victim's limb,
Who saw before his searing eyeballs
swim
The image of *their* Christ in cruel
zeal,
Through the black torment-smoke, held
mockingly to him !

III.

The blood which mingled with the des-
ert sand,
And beaded with its red and ghastly
dew
The vines and olives of the Holy Land, —
The shrieking curses of the hunted
Jew, —
The white-sown bones of heretics,
where'er
They sank beneath the Crusade's holy
spear, —

Goa's dark dungeons, — Malta's sea-
washed cell,
Where with the hymns the ghostly
fathers sung
Mingled the groans by subtle torture
wrung,
Heaven's anthem blending with the
shriek of hell !
The midnight of Bartholomew, — the
stake
Of Smithfield, and that thrice-ac-
cursed flame
Which Calvin kindled by Geneva's
lake, —
New England's scaffold, and the priestly
sneer
Which mocked its victims in that hour
of fear,
When guilt itself a human tear might
claim, —
Bear witness, O thou wronged and merciful One !
That Earth's most hateful crimes have
in thy name been done !

IV.

Thank God ! that I have lived to see
the time
When the great truth begins at last to
find
An utterance from the deep heart of
mankind,
Earnest and clear, that ALL REVENGE IS
CRIME !
That man is holier than a creed, — that
all
Restraint upon him must consult his
good,
Hope's sunshine linger on his prison
wall,
And Love look in upon his soli-
tude.
The beautiful lesson which our Saviour
taught
Through long, dark centuries its way
hath wrought
Into the common mind and popular
thought ;
And words, to which by Galilee's lake
shore
The humble fishers listened with hushed
oar,
Have found an echo in the general
heart,
And of the public faith become a living
part.

v.

Who shall arrest this tendency ? — Bring
    back
The cells of Venice and the bigot's rack ?
Harden the softening human heart again
To cold indifference to a brother's pain ?
Ye most unhappy men ! — who, turned
    away
From the mild sunshine of the Gospel
    day,
    Grope in the shadows of Man's twi-
        light time,
What mean ye, that with ghoul-like
    zest ye brood,
O'er those foul altars streaming with
    warm blood,
    Permitted in another age and clime ?
Why cite that law with which the bigot
    Jew
Rebuked the Pagan's mercy, when he
    knew
No evil in the Just One ? — Wherefore
    turn
To the dark cruel past ? — Can ye not
    learn
From the pure Teacher's life, how mildly
    free
Is the great Gospel of Humanity ?
The Flamen's knife is bloodless, and no
    more
Mexitli's altars soak with human gore,
No more the ghastly sacrifice smoke
Through the green arches of the Druid's
    oak ;
And ye of milder faith, with your high
    claim
Of prophet-utterance in the Holiest
    name,
Will ye become the Druids of our time !
Set up your scaffold-altars in our land,
And, consecrators of Law's darkest
    crime,
    Urge to its loathsome work the hang-
        man's hand ?
Beware, — lest human nature, roused at
    last,
From its peeled shoulder your encum-
    brance cast,
    And, sick to loathing of your cry for
        blood,
Rank ye with those who led their vic-
    tims round
The Celt's red altar and the Indian's
    mound,
    Abhorred of Earth and Heaven, — a
        pagan brotherhood !

THE HUMAN SACRIFICE.

I.

FAR from his close and noisome cell,
    By grassy lane and sunny stream,
Blown clover field and strawberry dell,
And green and meadow freshness, fell
    The footsteps of his dream.
Again from careless feet the dew
    Of summer's misty morn he shook ;
Again with merry heart he threw
    His light line in the rippling brook.
Back crowded all his school-day joys, —
    He urged the ball and quoit again,
And heard the shout of laughing boys
    Come ringing down the walnut glen.
Again he felt the western breeze,
    With scent of flowers and crisping
        hay ;
And down again through wind-stirred
        trees
    He saw the quivering sunlight play.
An angel in home's vine-hung door,
    He saw his sister smile once more ;
Once more the truant's brown-locked
        head
Upon his mother's knees was laid,
And sweetly lulled to slumber there,
With evening's holy hymn and prayer !

II.

He woke.   At once on heart and brain
The present Terror rushed again, —
Clanked on his limbs the felon's chain !
He woke, to hear the church-tower tell
Time's footfall on the conscious bell,
And, shuddering, feel that clanging din
His life's LAST HOUR had ushered in ;
To see within his prison-yard,
Through the small window, iron barred,
The gallows shadow rising dim
Between the sunrise heaven and him, —
A horror in God's blessed air, —
    A blackness in his morning light, —
Like some foul devil-altar there
    Built up by demon hands at night.
And, maddened by that evil sight,
Dark, horrible, confused, and strange,
A chaos of wild, weltering change,
All power of check and guidance gone,
Dizzy and blind, his mind swept on.
In vain he strove to breathe a prayer,
    In vain he turned the Holy Book,
He only heard the gallows-stair
    Creak as the wind its timbers shook.
No dream for him of sin forgiven,
    While still that baleful spectre stood,

With its hoarse murmur, "*Blood for
     Blood!*"
Between him and the pitying Heaven!

III.

Low on his dungeon floor he knelt,
     And smote his breast, and on his
          chain,
Whose iron clasp he always felt,
     His hot tears fell like rain;
And near him, with the cold, calm look
     And tone of one whose formal part,
     Unwarmed, unsoftened of the heart,
Is measured out by rule and book,
With placid lip and tranquil blood,
The hangman's ghostly ally stood,
Blessing with solemn text and word
The gallows-drop and strangling cord;
Lending the sacred Gospel's awe
And sanction to the crime of Law.

IV.

He saw the victim's tortured brow, —
     The sweat of anguish starting there, —
The record of a nameless woe
     In the dim eye's imploring stare,
     Seen hideous through the long, damp
          hair, —
Fingers of ghastly skin and bone
Working and writhing on the stone! —
And heard, by mortal terror wrung
From heaving breast and stiffened tongue,
     The choking sob and low hoarse prayer;
As o'er his half-crazed fancy came
A vision of the eternal flame, —
Its smoking cloud of agonies, —
Its demon-worm that never dies, —
The everlasting rise and fall
Of fire-waves round the infernal wall;
While high above that dark red flood,
Black, giant-like, the gallows stood;
Two busy fiends attending there:
One with cold mocking rite and prayer,
The other with impatient grasp,
Tightening the death-rope's strangling
     clasp.

V.

The unfelt rite at length was done, —
     The prayer unheard at length was
          said, —
An hour had passed: — the noonday sun
     Smote on the features of the dead!
And he who stood the doomed beside,
Calm gauger of the swelling tide
Of mortal agony and fear,
Heeding with curious eye and ear

Whate'er revealed the keen excess
Of man's extremest wretchedness:
And who in that dark anguish saw
     An earnest of the victim's fate,
The vengeful terrors of God's law,
     The kindlings of Eternal hate, —
The first drops of that fiery rain
Which beats the dark red realm of pain,
Did he uplift his earnest cries
     Against the crime of Law, which gave
     His brother to that fearful grave,
Whereon Hope's moonlight never lies,
     And Faith's white blossoms never wave
To the soft breath of Memory's sighs; —
Which sent a spirit marred and stained,
By fiends of sin possessed, profaned,
In madness and in blindness stark,
Into the silent, unknown dark?
No, — from the wild and shrinking dread
With which he saw the victim led
     Beneath the dark veil which divides
Ever the living from the dead,
     And Nature's solemn secret hides,
The man of prayer can only draw
New reasons for his bloody law;
New faith in staying Murder's hand
By murder at that Law's command;
New reverence for the gallows-rope,
As human nature's latest hope;
Last relic of the good old time,
When Power found license for its crime,
And held a writhing world in check
By that fell cord about its neck;
Stifled Sedition's rising shout,
Choked the young breath of Freedom out,
And timely checked the words which
     sprung
From Heresy's forbidden tongue;
While in its noose of terror bound,
The Church its cherished union found,
Conforming, on the Moslem plan,
The motley-colored mind of man,
Not by the Koran and the Sword,
But by the Bible and the Cord!

VI.

O Thou! at whose rebuke the grave
Back to warm life its sleeper gave,
Beneath whose sad and tearful glance
The cold and changed countenance
Broke the still horror of its trance,
And, waking, saw with joy above,
A brother's face of tenderest love;
Thou, unto whom the blind and lame,
The sorrowing and the sin-sick came,
And from thy very garment's hem
Drew life and healing unto them.

The burden of thy holy faith
Was love and life, not hate and death,
Man's demon ministers of pain,
    The fiends of his revenge were sent
    From thy pure Gospel's element
To their dark home again.
Thy name is Love ! What, then, is he,
    Who in that name the gallows rears,
An awful altar built to thee,
    With sacrifice of blood and tears ?
O, once again thy healing lay
    On the blind eyes which knew thee not,
And let the light of thy pure day
    Melt in upon his darkened thought.
Soften his hard, cold heart, and show
    The power which in forbearance lies,
And let him feel that mercy now
    Is better than old sacrifice !

VII.

As on the White Sea's charmed shore,
    The Parsee sees his holy hill
With dunnest smoke-clouds curtained
        o'er,
Yet knows beneath them, evermore,
    The low, pale fire is quivering still ;
So, underneath its clouds of sin,
    The heart of man retaineth yet
Gleams of its holy origin ;
    And half-quenched stars that never set,
Dim colors of its faded bow,
    And early beauty, linger there,
And o'er its wasted desert blow
    Faint breathings of its morning air,
O, never yet upon the scroll
Of the sin-stained, but priceless soul,
    Hath Heaven inscribed " DESPAIR ! "
Cast not the clouded gem away,
Quench not the dim but living ray, —
    My brother man, Beware !
With that deep voice which from the
        skies
Forbade the Patriarch's sacrifice,
    God's angel cries, FORBEAR !

RANDOLPH OF ROANOKE.

O MOTHER EARTH ! upon thy lap
    Thy weary ones receiving,
And o'er them, silent as a dream,
    Thy grassy mantle weaving,
Fold softly in thy long embrace
    That heart so worn and broken,
And cool its pulse of fire beneath
    Thy shadows old and oaken.

Shut out from him the bitter word
    And serpent hiss of scorning ;
Nor let the storms of yesterday
    Disturb his quiet morning.
Breathe over him forgetfulness
    Of all save deeds of kindness,
And, save to smiles of grateful eyes,
    Press down his lids in blindness.

There, where with living ear and eye
    He heard Potomac's flowing,
And, through his tall ancestral trees,
    Saw autumn's sunset glowing,
He sleeps, — still looking to the west,
    Beneath the dark wood shadow,
As if he still would see the sun
    Sink down on wave and meadow.

Bard, Sage, and Tribune ! — in himself
    All moods of mind contrasting, —
The tenderest wail of human woe,
    The scorn-like lightning blasting ;
The pathos which from rival eyes
    Unwilling tears could summon,
The stinging taunt, the fiery burst
    Of hatred scarcely human !

Mirth, sparkling like a diamond shower,
    From lips of life-long sadness ;
Clear picturings of majestic thought
    Upon a ground of madness ;
And over all Romance and Song
    A classic beauty throwing,
And laurelled Clio at his side
    Her storied pages showing.

All parties feared him : each in turn
    Beheld its schemes disjointed,
As right or left his fatal glance
    And spectral finger pointed.
Sworn foe of Cant, he smote it down
    With trenchant wit unsparing,
And, mocking, rent with ruthless hand
    The robe Pretence was wearing.

Too honest or too proud to feign
    A love he never cherished,
Beyond Virginia's border line
    His patriotism perished.
While others hailed in distant skies
    Our eagle's dusky pinion,
He only saw the mountain bird
    Stoop o'er his Old Dominion !

Still through each change of fortune
        strange,
    Racked nerve, and brain all burning,

His loving faith in Mother-land
  Knew never shade of turning ;
By Britain's lakes, by Neva's wave,
  Whatever sky was o'er him,
He heard her rivers' rushing sound,
  Her blue peaks rose before him.

He held his slaves, yet made withal
  No false and vain pretences,
Nor paid a lying priest to seek
  For Scriptural defences.
His harshest words of proud rebuke,
  His bitterest taunt and scorning,
Fell fire-like on the Northern brow
  That bent to him in fawning.

He held his slaves ; yet kept the while
  His reverence for the Human ;
In the dark vassals of his will
  He saw but Man and Woman !
No hunter of God's outraged poor
  His Roanoke valley entered ;
No trader in the souls of men
  Across his threshold ventured.

And when the old and wearied man
  Lay down for his last sleeping,
And at his side, a slave no more,
  His brother-man stood weeping,
His latest thought, his latest breath,
  To Freedom's duty giving,
With failing tongue and trembling hand
  The dying blest the living.

O, never bore his ancient State
  A truer son or braver !
None trampling with a calmer scorn
  On foreign hate or favor.
He knew her faults, yet never stooped
  His proud and manly feeling
To poor excuses of the wrong
  Or meanness of concealing.

But none beheld with clearer eye
  The plague-spot o'er her spreading,
None heard more sure the steps of
    Doom
  Along her future treading.
For her as for himself he spake,
  When, his gaunt frame upbracing,
He traced with dying hand "REMORSE :"
  And perished in the tracing.

As from the grave where Henry sleeps,
  From Vernon's weeping willow,
And from the grassy pall which hides
  The Sage of Monticello,

So from the leaf-strewn burial-stone
  Of Randolph's lowly dwelling,
Virginia ! o'er thy land of slaves
  A warning voice is swelling !

And hark ! from thy deserted fields
  Are sadder warnings spoken,
From quenched hearths, where thy ex
    iled sons
  Their household gods have broken.
The curse is on thee, — wolves for men,
  And briers for corn-sheaves giving !
O, more than all thy dead renown
  Were now one hero living !

DEMOCRACY.

All things whatsoever ye would that men
should do to you, do ye even so to them. —
Matthew vii. 12.

BEARER of Freedom's holy light,
  Breaker of Slavery's chain and rod,
The foe of all which pains the sight,
  Or wounds the generous ear of God !

Beautiful yet thy temples rise,
  Though there profaning gifts are
    thrown ;
And fires unkindled of the skies
  Are glaring round thy altar-stone.

Still sacred, — though thy name be
    breathed
  By those whose hearts thy truth de-
    ride ;
And garlands, plucked from thee, are
    wreathed
  Around the haughty brows of Pride.

O, ideal of my boyhood's time !
  The faith in which my father stood,
Even when the sons of Lust and Crime
  Had stained thy peaceful courts with
    blood !

Still to those courts my footsteps turn,
  For through the mists which darken
    there,
I see the flame of Freedom burn, —
  The Kebla of the patriot's prayer !

The generous feeling, pure and warm,
  Which owns the rights of *all* divine, —
The pitying heart, — the helping arm, —
  The prompt self-sacrifice, — are thine.

Beneath thy broad, impartial eye,
　How fade the lines of caste and birth !
How equal in their suffering lie
　The groaning muititudes of earth !

Still to a stricken brother true,
　Whatever clime hath nurtured him ;
As stooped to heal the wounded Jew
　The worshipper of Gerizim.

By misery unrepelled, unawed
　By pomp or power, thou seest a MAN
In prince or peasant, — slave or lord, —
　Pale priest, or swarthy artisan.

Through all disguise, form, place, or
　name,
　Beneath the flaunting robes of sin,
Through poverty and squalid shame,
　Thou lookest on *the man* within.

On man, as man, retaining yet,
　Howe'er debased, and soiled, and dim,
The crown upon his forehead set, —
　The immortal gift of God to him.

And there is reverence in thy look ;
　For that frail form which mortals wear
The Spirit of the Holiest took,
　And veiled his perfect brightness there.

Not from the shallow babbling fount
　Of vain philosophy thou art ;
He who of old on Syria's mount
　Thrilled, warmed, by turns, the lis-
　　tener's heart,

In holy words which cannot die,
　In thoughts which angels leaned to
　　know,
Proclaimed thy message from on high, —
　Thy mission to a world of woe.

That voice's echo hath not died !
　From the blue lake of Galilee,
And Tabor's lonely mountain-side,
　It calls a struggling world to thee.

Thy name and watchword o'er this land
　I hear in every breeze that stirs,
And round a thousand altars stand
　Thy banded party worshippers.

Not to these altars of a day,
　At party's call, my gift I bring ;
But on thy olden shrine I lay
　A freeman's dearest offering :

The voiceless utterance of his will, —
　His pledge to Freedom and to Truth,
That manhood's heart remembers still
　The homage of his generous youth.

Election Day, 1843.

TO RONGE.

STRIKE home, strong - hearted man !
　Down to the root
Of old oppression sink the Saxon steel.
Thy work is to hew down. In God's
　name then
Put nerve into thy task. Let other men
Plant, as they may, that better tree
　whose fruit
The wounded bosom of the Church shall
　heal.
Be thou the image-breaker. Let thy
　blows
Fall heavy as the Suabian's iron hand,
On crown or crosier, which shall inter-
　pose
Between thee and the weal of Father-
　land.
Leave creeds to closet idlers. First of
　all,
Shake thou all German dream-land with
　the fall
Of that accursed tree, whose evil trunk
Was spared of old by Erfurt's stalwart
　monk.
Fight not with ghosts and shadows.
　Let us hear
The snap of chain-links. Let our glad-
　dened ear
Catch the pale prisoner's welcome, as
　the light
Follows thy axe-stroke, through his cell
　of night.
Be faithful to both worlds ; nor think to
　feed
Earth's starving millions with the husks
　of creed.
Servant of Him whose mission high and
　holy
Was to the wronged, the sorrowing, and
　the lowly,
Thrust not his Eden promise from our
　sphere,
Distant and dim beyond the blue sky's
　span ;
Like him of Patmos, see it, now and
　here, —
The New Jerusalem comes down to
　man !

Be warned by Luther's error. Nor like
   him,
When the roused Teuton dashes from his
   limb
The rusted chain of ages, help to bind
His hands for whom thou claim'st the
   freedom of the mind !

CHALKLEY HALL.[39]

How bland and sweet the greeting of
   this breeze
    To him who flies
From crowded street and red wall's
   weary gleam,
Till far behind him like a hideous dream
    The close dark city lies !

Here, while the market murmurs, while
   men throng
    The marble floor
Of Mammon's altar, from the crush and
   din
Of the world's madness let me gather in
    My better thoughts once more.

O, once again revive, while on my ear
    The cry of Gain
And low hoarse hum of Traffic die away,
Ye blessed memories of my early day
    Like sere grass wet with rain ! —

Once more let God's green earth and
   sunset air
    Old feelings waken ;
Through weary years of toil and strife
   and ill,
O, let me feel that my good angel still
    Hath not his trust forsaken.

And well do time and place befit my
   mood :
    Beneath the arms
Of this embracing wood, a good man
   made
His home, like Abraham resting in the
   shade
    Of Mamre's lonely palms.

Here, rich with autumn gifts of countless years,
    The virgin soil
Turned from the share he guided, and
   in rain
And summer sunshine throve the fruits
   and grain
    Which blessed his honest toil.

Here, from his voyages on the stormy
   seas,
    Weary and worn,
He came to meet his children and to
   bless
The Giver of all good in thankfulness
    And praise for his return.

And here his neighbors gathered in to
   greet
    Their friend again,
Safe from the wave and the destroying
   gales,
Which reap untimely green Bermuda's
   vales,
    And vex the Carib main.

To hear the good man tell of simple truth,
    Sown in an hour
Of weakness in some far-off Indian isle,
From the parched bosom of a barren
   soil,
    Raised up in life and power :

How at those gatherings in Barbadian
   vales,
    A tendering love
Came o'er him, like the gentle rain from
   heaven,
And words of fitness to his lips were
   given,
    And strength as from above :

How the sad captive listened to the
   Word,
    Until his chain
Grew lighter, and his wounded spirit
   felt
The healing balm of consolation melt
    Upon its life-long pain :

How the armed warrior sat him down to
   hear
    Of Peace and Truth,
And the proud ruler and his Creole
   dame,
Jewelled and gorgeous in her beauty
   came,
    And fair and bright-eyed youth.

O, far away beneath New England's
   sky,
    Even when a boy,
Following my plough by Merrimack's
   green shore,
His simple record I have pondered o'er
    With deep and quiet joy.

And hence this scene, in sunset glory
    warm, —
      Its woods around,
Its still stream winding on in light and
    shade,
Its soft, green meadows and its upland
    glade, —
      To me is holy ground.

And dearer far than haunts where
    Genius keeps
      His vigils still ;
Than that where Avon's son of song is
    laid,
Of Vaucluse hallowed by its Petrarch's
    shade,
      Or Virgil's laurelled hill.

To the gray walls of fallen Paraclete,
    To Juliet's urn,
Fair Arno and Sorrento's orange-grove,
Where Tasso sang, let young Romance
    and Love
      Like brother pilgrims turn.

But here a deeper and serener charm
    To all is given ;
And blessed memories of the faithful
    dead
O'er wood and vale and meadow-stream
    have shed
      The holy hues of Heaven !

TO J. P.

NOT as a poor requital of the joy
    With which my childhood heard that
    lay of thine,
Which, like an echo of the song divine
At Bethlehem breathed above the Holy
    Boy,
    Bore to my ear the Airs of Palestine, —
Not to the poet, but the man I bring
In friendship's fearless trust my offering :
How much it lacks I feel, and thou wilt
    see,
Yet well I know that thou hast deemed
    with me
Life all too earnest, and its time too
    short
For dreamy ease and Fancy's graceful
    sport ;
    And girded for thy constant strife with
    wrong,
Like Nehemiah fighting while he
    wrought

The broken walls of Zion, even thy
    song
Hath a rude martial tone, a blow in
    every thought !

THE CYPRESS-TREE OF CEYLON.

[IBN BATUTA, the celebrated Mussulman traveller of the fourteenth century, speaks of a cy-
press-tree in Ceylon, universally held sacred by
the natives, the leaves of which were said to fall
only at certain intervals, and he who had the
happiness to find and eat one of them was restored, at once, to youth and vigor. The traveller saw several venerable JOGEES, or saints, sitting silent and motionless under the tree, patiently waiting the falling of a leaf.]

THEY sat in silent watchfulness
    The sacred cypress-tree about,
And, from beneath old wrinkled brows,
    Their failing eyes looked out.

Gray Age and Sickness waiting there
    Through weary night and lingering
    day, —
Grim as the idols at their side,
    And motionless as they.

Unheeded in the boughs above
    The song of Ceylon's birds was sweet ;
Unseen of them the island flowers
    Bloomed brightly at their feet.

O'er them the tropic night-storm swept,
    The thunder crashed on rock and hill ;
The cloud-fire on their eyeballs blazed,
    Yet there they waited still !

What was the world without to them ?
    The Moslem's sunset-call, — the dance
Of Ceylon's maids, — the passing gleam
    Of battle-flag and lance ?

They waited for that falling leaf
    Of which the wandering Jogees sing :
Which lends once more to wintry age
    The greenness of its spring.

O, if these poor and blinded ones
    In trustful patience wait to feel
O'er torpid pulse and failing limb
    A youthful freshness steal ;

Shall we, who sit beneath that Tree
    Whose healing leaves of life are shed,
In answer to the breath of prayer,
    Upon the waiting head ;

Not to restore our failing forms,
    And build the spirit's broken shrine,
But on the fainting SOUL to shed
    A light and life divine ;

Shall we grow weary in our watch,
    And murmur at the long delay ?
Impatient of our Father's time
    And his appointed way ?

Or shall the stir of outward things
    Allure and claim the Christian's eye,
When on the heathen watcher's ear
    Their powerless murmurs die ?

Alas ! a deeper test of faith
    Than prison cell or martyr's stake,
The self-abasing watchfulness
    Of silent prayer may make.

We gird us bravely to rebuke
    Our erring brother in the wrong, —
And in the ear of Pride and Power
    Our warning voice is strong.

Easier to smite with Peter's sword
    Than " watch one hour " in humbling
        prayer.
Life's " great things," like the Syrian
        lord,
    Our hearts can do and dare.

But oh ! we shrink from Jordan's side,
    From waters which alone can save ;
And murmur for Abana's banks
    And Pharpar's brighter wave.

O Thou, who in the garden's shade
    Didst wake thy weary ones again,
Who slumbered at that fearful hour
    Forgetful of thy pain ;

Bend o'er us now, as over them,
    And set our sleep-bound spirits free,
Nor leave us slumbering in the watch
    Our souls should keep with Thee !

A DREAM OF SUMMER.

BLAND as the morning breath of June
    The southwest breezes play ;
And, through its haze, the winter noon
    Seems warm as summer's day.
The snow-plumed Angel of the North
    Has dropped his icy spear ;
Again the mossy earth looks forth,
    Again the streams gush clear.

The fox his hillside cell forsakes,
    The muskrat leaves his nook,
The bluebird in the meadow brakes
    Is singing with the brook.
" Bear up, O Mother Nature ! " cry
    Bird, breeze, and streamlet free ;
" Our winter voices prophesy
    Of summer days to thee ! "

So, in those winters of the soul,
    By bitter blasts and drear
O'erswept from Memory's frozen pole,
    Will sunny days appear.
Reviving Hope and Faith, they show
    The soul its living powers,
And how beneath the winter's snow
    Lie germs of summer flowers !

The Night is mother of the Day,
    The Winter of the Spring,
And ever upon old Decay
    The greenest mosses cling.
Behind the cloud the starlight lurks,
    Through showers the sunbeams fall ;
For God, who loveth all his works,
    Has left his Hope with all !
        4th 1st month, 1847.

TO ———,

WITH A COPY OF WOOLMAN'S JOURNAL.

" Get the writings of John Woolman by
heart." — *Essays of Elia.*

MAIDEN ! with the fair brown tresses
    Shading o'er thy dreamy eye,
Floating on thy thoughtful forehead
    Cloud wreaths of its sky.

Youthful years and maiden beauty,
    Joy with them should still abide, —
Instinct take the place of Duty,
    Love, not Reason, guide.

Ever in the New rejoicing,
    Kindly beckoning back the Old,
Turning, with the gift of Midas,
    All things into gold.

And the passing shades of sadness
    Wearing even a welcome guise,
As, when some bright lake lies open
    To the sunny skies,

Every wing of bird above it,
    Every light cloud floating on,

Glitters like that flashing mirror
  In the self-same sun.

But upon thy youthful forehead
  Something like a shadow lies ;
And a serious soul is looking
  From thy earnest eyes.

With an early introversion,
  Through the forms of outward things,
Seeking for the subtle essence,
  And the hidden springs.

Deeper than the gilded surface
  Hath thy wakeful vision seen,
Farther than the narrow present
  Have thy journeyings been.

Thou hast midst Life's empty noises
  Heard the solemn steps of Time,
And the low mysterious voices
  Of another clime.

All the mystery of Being
  Hath upon thy spirit pressed, —
Thoughts which, like the Deluge wan-
    derer,
  Find no place of rest :

That which mystic Plato pondered,
  That which Zeno heard with awe,
And the star-rapt Zoroaster
  In his night-watch saw.

From the doubt and darkness springing
  Of the dim, uncertain Past,
Moving to the dark still shadows
  O'er the Future cast,

Early hath Life's mighty question
  Thrilled within thy heart of youth,
With a deep and strong beseeching :
  WHAT and WHERE IS TRUTH ?

Hollow creed and ceremonial,
  Whence the ancient life hath fled,
Idle faith unknown to action,
  Dull and cold and dead.

Oracles, whose wire-worked meanings
  Only wake a quiet scorn, —
Not from these thy seeking spirit
  Hath its answer drawn.

But, like some tired child at even,
  On thy mother Nature's breast,
Thou, methinks, art vainly seeking
  Truth, and peace, and rest.

O'er that mother's rugged features
  Thou art throwing Fancy's veil,
Light and soft as woven moonbeams,
  Beautiful and frail !

O'er the rough chart of Existence,
  Rocks of sin and wastes of woe,
Soft airs breathe, and green leaves tremble,
  And cool fountains flow.

And to thee an answer cometh
  From the earth and from the sky,
And to thee the hills and waters
  And the stars reply.

But a soul-sufficing answer
  Hath no outward origin ;
More than Nature's many voices
  May be heard within.

Even as the great Augustine
  Questioned earth and sea and sky,[40]
And the dusty tomes of learning
  And old poesy.

But his earnest spirit needed
  More than outward Nature taught, —
More than blest the poet's vision
  Or the sage's thought.

Only in the gathered silence
  Of a calm and waiting frame
Light and wisdom as from Heaven
  To the seeker came.

Not to ease and aimless quiet
  Doth that inward answer tend,
But to works of love and duty
  As our being's end, —

Not to idle dreams and trances,
  Length of face, and solemn tone,
But to Faith, in daily striving
  And performance shown.

Earnest toil and strong endeavor
  Of a spirit which within
Wrestles with familiar evil
  And besetting sin ;

And without, with tireless vigor,
  Steady heart, and weapon strong,
In the power of truth assailing
  Every form of wrong.

Guided thus, how passing lovely
  Is the track of WOOLMAN's feet !

And his brief and simple record
  How serenely sweet !

O'er life's humblest duties throwing
  Light the earthling never knew,
Freshening all its dark waste places
  As with Hermon's dew.

All which glows in Pascal's pages, —
  All which sainted Guion sought,
Or the blue-eyed German Rahel
  Half-unconscious taught : —

Beauty, such as Goethe pictured,
  Such as Shelley dreamed of, shed
Living warmth and starry brightness
  Round that poor man's head.

Not a vain and cold ideal,
  Not a poet's dream alone,
But a presence warm and real,
  Seen and felt and known.

When the red right-hand of slaughter
  Moulders with the steel it swung,
When the name of seer and poet
  Dies on Memory's tongue,

All bright thoughts and pure shall gather
  Round that meek and suffering one, —
Glorious, like the seer-seen angel
  Standing in the sun !

Take the good man's book and ponder
  What its pages say to thee, —
Blessed as the hand of healing
  May its lesson be.

If it only serves to strengthen
  Yearnings for a higher good,
For the fount of living waters
  And diviner food ;

If the pride of human reason
  Feels its meek and still rebuke,

Quailing like the eye of Peter
  From the Just One's look ! —

If with readier ear thou heedest
  What the Inward Teacher saith,
Listening with a willing spirit
  And a childlike faith, —

Thou mayst live to bless the giver,
  Who, himself but frail and weak,
Would at least the highest welfare
  Of another seek ;

And his gift, though poor and lowly
  It may seem to other eyes,
Yet may prove an angel holy
  In a pilgrim's guise.

LEGGETT'S MONUMENT.

" Ye build the tombs of the prophets."
                           Holy Writ

YES, — pile the marble o'er him ! It is
  well
  That ye who mocked him in his long
    stern strife,
  And planted in the pathway of his life
The ploughshares of your hatred hot
    from hell,
  Who clamored down the bold reformer
    when
  He pleaded for his captive fellow-men,
Who spurned him in the market-place,
    and sought
  Within thy walls, St. Tammany, to
    bind   ·
In party chains the free and honest
    thought,
  The angel utterance of an upright mind,
Well is it now that o'er his grave ye raise
The stony tribute of your tardy praise,
For not alone that pile shall tell to Fame
Of the brave heart beneath, but of th
    builders' shame !

SONGS OF LABOR,

AND OTHER POEMS.

DEDICATION.

I WOULD the gift I offer here
  Might graces from thy favor take,
And, seen through Friendship's at-
    mosphere,
On softened lines and coloring, wear
The unaccustomed light of beauty, for
    thy sake.

Few leaves of Fancy's spring remain :
  But what I have I give to thee, —
The o'er-sunned bloom of summer's
    plain,
And paler flowers, the latter rain
Calls from the westering slope of life's
    autumnal lea.

Above the fallen groves of green,
  Where youth's enchanted forest
    stood,
Dry root and mosséd trunk between,
A sober after-growth is seen,
As springs the pine where falls the gay-
    leafed maple wood !

Yet birds will sing, and breezes play
  Their leaf-harps in the sombre tree ;
And through the bleak and wintry day
It keeps its steady green alway, —
So, even my after-thoughts may have a
    charm for thee.

Art's perfect forms no moral need,
  And beauty is its own excuse ; [41]
But for the dull and flowerless weed
Some healing virtue still must plead,
And the rough ore must find its honors
    in its use.

So haply these, my simple lays
  Of homely toil, may serve to show
The orchard bloom and tasselled maize
That skirt and gladden duty's ways,
The unsung beauty hid life's common
    things below.

Haply from them the toiler, bent
  Above his forge or plough, may gain,
A manlier spirit of content,
  And feel that life is wisest spent
Where the strong working hand makes
    strong the working brain.

The doom which to the guilty pair
  Without the walls of Eden came,
Transforming sinless ease to care
And rugged toil, no more shall bear
The burden of old crime, or mark of
    primal shame.

A blessing now, — a curse no more ;
  Since He, whose name we breathe
    with awe,
The coarse mechanic vesture wore, —
A poor man toiling with the poor,
In labor, as in prayer, fulfilling the same
    law.

THE SHIP-BUILDERS.

THE sky is ruddy in the east,
  The earth is gray below,
And, spectral in the river-mist,
  The ship's white timbers show.
Then let the sounds of measured stroke
  And grating saw begin ;
The broad-axe to the gnarléd oak,
  The mallet to the pin !

Hark ! — roars the bellows, blast on blast,
  The sooty smithy jars,
And fire-sparks, rising far and fast,
  Are fading with the stars.
All day for us the smith shall stand
  Beside that flashing forge ;
All day for us his heavy hand
  The groaning anvil scourge.

From far-off hills, the panting team
  For us is toiling near ;
For us the raftsmen down the stream
  Their island barges steer.
Rings out for us the axe-man's stroke
  In forests old and still, —
For us the century-circled oak
  Falls crashing down his hill.

Up ! — up ! — in nobler toil than ours
 No craftsmen bear a part :
We make of Nature's giant powers
 The slaves of human Art.
Lay rib to rib and beam to beam,
 And drive the treenails free ;
Nor faithless joint nor yawning seam
 Shall tempt the searching sea !

Where'er the keel of our good ship
 The sea's rough field shall plough, —
Where'er her tossing spars shall drip
 With salt-spray caught below, —
That ship must heed her master's beck,
 Her helm obey his hand,
And seamen tread her reeling deck
 As if they trod the land.

Her oaken ribs the vulture-beak
 Of Northern ice may peel ;
The sunken rock and coral peak
 May grate along her keel ;
And know we well the painted shell
 We give to wind and wave,
Must float, the sailor's citadel,
 Or sink, the sailor's grave !

Ho ! — strike away the bars and blocks,
 And set the good ship free !
Why lingers on these dusty rocks
 The young bride of the sea ?
Look ! how she moves adown the grooves,
 In graceful beauty now !
How lowly on the breast she loves
 Sinks down her virgin prow !

God bless her ! wheresoe'er the breeze
 Her snowy wing shall fan,
Aside the frozen Hebrides,
 Or sultry Hindostan !
Where'er, in mart or on the main,
 With peaceful flag unfurled,
She helps to wind the silken chain
 Of commerce round the world !

Speed on the ship ! — But let her bear
 No merchandise of sin,
No groaning cargo of despair
 Her roomy hold within ;
No Lethean drug for Eastern lands,
 Nor poison-draught for ours ;
But honest fruits of toiling hands
 And Nature's sun and showers.

Be hers the Prairie's golden grain,
 The Desert's golden sand,
The clustered fruits of sunny Spain,
 The spice of Morning-land !

8

Her pathway on the open main
 May blessings follow free,
And glad hearts welcome back again
 Her white sails from the sea !

THE SHOEMAKERS.

Ho ! workers of the old time styled
 The Gentle Craft of Leather !
Young brothers of the ancient guild,
 Stand forth once more together !
Call out again your long array,
 In the olden merry manner !
Once more, on gay St. Crispin's day,
 Fling out your blazoned banner !

Rap, rap ! upon the well-worn stone
 How falls the polished hammer !
Rap, rap ! the measured sound has grown
 A quick and merry clamor.
Now shape the sole ! now deftly curl
 The glossy vamp around it,
And bless the while the bright-eyed girl
 Whose gentle fingers bound it !

For you, along the Spanish main
 A hundred keels are ploughing ;
For you, the Indian on the plain
 His lasso-coil is throwing ;
For you, deep glens with hemlock dark
 The woodman's fire is lighting ;
For you, upon the oak's gray bark,
 The woodman's axe is smiting.

For you, from Carolina's pine
 The rosin-gum is stealing ;
For you, the dark-eyed Florentine
 Her silken skein is reeling ;
For you, the dizzy goatherd roams
 His rugged Alpine ledges ;
For you, round all her shepherd homes,
 Bloom England's thorny hedges.

The foremost still, by day or night,
 On moated mound or heather,
Where'er the need of trampled right
 Brought toiling men together ;
Where the free burghers from the wall
 Defied the mail-clad master,
Than yours, at Freedom's trumpet-call,
 No craftsmen rallied faster.

Let foplings sneer, let fools deride, —
 Ye heed no idle scorner ;
Free hands and hearts are still your pride,
 And duty done, your honor.

Ye dare to trust, for honest fame,
　　The jury Time empanels,
And leave to truth each noble name
　　Which glorifies your annals.

Thy songs, Han Sachs, are living yet,
　　In strong and hearty German ;
And Bloomfield's lay, and Gifford's wit,
　　And patriot fame of Sherman ;
Still from his book, a mystic seer,
　　The soul of Behmen teaches,
And England's priestcraft shakes to hear
　　Of Fox's leathern breeches.

The foot is yours ; where'er it falls,
　　It treads your well-wrought leather,
On earthen floor, in marble halls,
　　On carpet, or on heather.
Still there the sweetest charm is found
　　Of matron grace or vestal's,
As Hebe's foot bore nectar round
　　Among the old celestials !

Rap, rap !—your stout and bluff brogan,
　　With footsteps slow and weary,
May wander where the sky's blue span
　　Shuts down upon the prairie.
On Beauty's foot your slippers glance,
　　By Saratoga's fountains,
Or twinkle down the summer dance
　　Beneath the Crystal Mountains !

The red brick to the mason's hand,
　　The brown earth to the tiller's,
The shoe in yours shall wealth command,
　　Like fairy Cinderella's !
As they who shunned the household maid
　　Beheld the crown upon her,
So all shall see your toil repaid
　　With hearth and home and honor.

Then let the toast be freely quaffed,
　　In water cool and brimming, —
"All honor to the good old Craft,
　　Its merry men and women !"
Call out again your long array,
　　In the old time's pleasant manner :
Once more, on gay St. Crispin's day,
　　Fling out his blazoned banner !

THE DROVERS.

Through heat and cold, and shower
　　　　and sun,
　　Still onward cheerly driving !
There 's life alone in duty done,
　　And rest alone in striving.

But see ! the day is closing cool,
　　The woods are dim before us ;
The white fog of the wayside pool
　　Is creeping slowly o'er us.

The night is falling, comrades mine,
　　Our footsore beasts are weary,
And through yon elms the tavern sign
　　Looks out upon us cheery.
The landlord beckons from his door,
　　His beechen fire is glowing ;
These ample barns, with feed in store,
　　Are filled to overflowing.

From many a valley frowned across
　　By brows of rugged mountains ;
From hillsides where, through spongy
　　　　moss,
　　Gush out the river fountains ;
From quiet farm-fields, green and low,
　　And bright with blooming clover ;
From vales of corn the wandering crow
　　No richer hovers over ;

Day after day our way has been,
　　O'er many a hill and hollow ;
By lake and stream, by wood and glen,
　　Our stately drove we follow.
Through dust-clouds rising thick and dun,
　　As smoke of battle o'er us,
Their white horns glisten in the sun,
　　Like plumes and crests before us.

We see them slowly climb the hill,
　　As slow behind it sinking ;
Or, thronging close, from roadside rill,
　　Or sunny lakelet, drinking.
Now crowding in the narrow road,
　　In thick and struggling masses,
They glare upon the teamster's load,
　　Or rattling coach that passes.

Anon, with toss of horn and tail,
　　And paw of hoof, and bellow,
They leap some farmer's broken pale,
　　O'er meadow-close or fallow.
Forth comes the startled goodman ; forth
　　Wife, children, house-dog, sally,
Till once more on their dusty path
　　The baffled truants rally.

We drive no starvelings, scraggy grown,
　　Loose-legged, and ribbed and bony,
Like those who grind their noses down
　　On pastures bare and stony, —
Lank oxen, rough as Indian dogs,
　　And cows too lean for shadows,

Disputing feebly with the frogs
  The crop of saw-grass meadows !

In our good drove, so sleek and fair,
  No bones of leanness rattle ;
No tottering hide-bound ghosts are there,
  Or Pharaoh's evil cattle.
Each stately beeve bespeaks the hand
  That fed him unrepining ;
The fatness of a goodly land
  In each dun hide is shining.

We 've sought them where, in warmest
      nooks,
  The freshest feed is growing,
By sweetest springs and clearest brooks
  Through honeysuckle flowing ;
Wherever hillsides, sloping south,
  Are bright with early grasses,
Or, tracking green the lowland's drouth,
  The mountain streamlet passes.

But now the day is closing cool,
  The woods are dim before us,
The white fog of the wayside pool
  Is creeping slowly o'er us.
The cricket to the frog's bassoon
  His shrillest time is keeping ;
The sickle of yon setting moon
  The meadow-mist is reaping.

The night is falling, comrades mine,
  Our footsore beasts are weary,
And through yon elms the tavern sign
  Looks out upon us cheery.
To-morrow, eastward with our charge
  We 'll go to meet the dawning,
Ere yet the pines of Kéarsarge
  Have seen the sun of morning.

When snow-flakes o'er the frozen earth,
  Instead of birds, are flitting ;
When children throng the glowing
      hearth,
  And quiet wives are knitting ;
While in the fire-light strong and clear
  Young eyes of pleasure glisten,
To tales of all we see and hear
  The ears of home shall listen.

By many a Northern lake and hill,
  From many a mountain pasture,
Shall Fancy play the Drover still,
  And speed the long night faster.
Then let us on, through shower and sun,
  And heat and cold, be driving ;
There 's life alone in duty done,
  And rest alone in striving.

THE FISHERMEN.

HURRAH ! the seaward breezes
  Sweep down the bay amain ;
Heave up, my lads, the anchor !
  Run up the sail again !
Leave to the lubber landsmen
  The rail-car and the steed ;
The stars of heaven shall guide us,
  The breath of heaven shall speed.

From the hill-top looks the steeple,
  And the lighthouse from the sand ;
And the scattered pines are waving
  Their farewell from the land.
One glance, my lads, behind us,
  For the homes we leave one sigh,
Ere we take the change and chances
  Of the ocean and the sky.

Now, brothers, for the icebergs
  Of frozen Labrador,
Floating spectral in the moonshine,
  Along the low, black shore !
Where like snow the gannet's feathers
  On Brador's rocks are shed,
And the noisy murr are flying,
  Like black scuds, overhead ;

Where in mist the rock is hiding,
  And the sharp reef lurks below,
And the white squall smites in sum-
      mer,
  And the autumn tempests blow ;
Where, through gray and rolling vapor,
  From evening unto morn,
A thousand boats are hailing,
  Horn answering unto horn.

Hurrah ! for the Red Island,
  With the white cross on its crown !
Hurrah ! for Meccatina,
  And its mountains bare and brown !
Where the Caribou's tall antlers
  O'er the dwarf-wood freely toss,
And the footstep of the Mickmack
  Has no sound upon the moss.

There we 'll drop our lines, and gather
  Old Ocean's treasures in,
Where'er the mottled mackerel
  Turns up a steel-dark fin.
The sea 's our field of harvest,
  Its scaly tribes our grain ;
We 'll reap the teeming waters
  As at home they reap the plain !

Our wet hands spread the carpet,
  And light the hearth of home ;
From our fish, as in the old time,
  The silver coin shall come.
As the demon fled the chamber
  Where the fish of Tobit lay,
So ours from all our dwellings
  Shall frighten Want away.

Though the mist upon our jackets
  In the bitter air congeals,
And our lines wind stiff and slowly
  From off the frozen reels ;
Though the fog be dark around us,
  And the storm blow high and loud,
We will whistle down the wild wind,
  And laugh beneath the cloud !

In the darkness as in daylight,
  On the water as on land,
God's eye is looking on us,
  And beneath us is his hand !
Death will find us soon or later,
  On the deck or in the cot ;
And we cannot meet him better
  Than in working out our lot.

Hurrah ! — hurrah ! — the west-wind
  Comes freshening down the bay,
The rising sails are filling, —
  Give way, my lads, give way !
Leave the coward landsman clinging
  To the dull earth, like a weed, —
The stars of heaven shall guide us,
  The breath of heaven shall speed !

THE HUSKERS.

It was late in mild October, and the
    long autumnal rain
Had left the summer harvest-fields all
    green with grass again ;
The first sharp frosts had fallen, leaving
    all the woodlands gay
With the hues of summer's rainbow, or
    the meadow-flowers of May.

Through a thin, dry mist, that morning,
    the sun rose broad and red,
At first a rayless disk of fire, he bright-
    ened as he sped ;
Yet, even his noontide glory fell chas-
    tened and subdued,
On the cornfields and the orchards, and
    softly pictured wood.

And all that quiet afternoon, slow slop-
    ing to the night,
He wove with golden shuttle the haze
    with yellow light ;
Slanting through the painted beeches,
    he glorified the hill ;
And, beneath it, pond and meadow lay
    brighter, greener still.

And shouting boys in woodland haunts
    caught glimpses of that sky,
Flecked by the many-tinted leaves, and
    laughed, they knew not why ;
And school-girls, gay with aster-flowers,
    beside the meadow brooks,
Mingled the glow of autumn with the
    sunshine of sweet looks.

From spire and barn looked westerly the
    patient weathercocks ;
But even the birches on the hill stood
    motionless as rocks.
No sound was in the woodlands, save the
    squirrel's dropping shell,
And the yellow leaves among the boughs,
    low rustling as they fell.

The summer grains were harvested ; the
    stubble-fields lay dry,
Where June winds rolled, in light and
    shade, the pale green waves of rye ;
But still, on gentle hill-slopes, in valleys
    fringed with wood,
Ungathered, bleaching in the sun, the
    heavy corn crop stood.

Bent low, by autumn's wind and rain,
    through husks that, dry and sere,
Unfolded from their ripened charge, shone
    out the yellow ear ;
Beneath, the turnip lay concealed, in
    many a verdant fold,
And glistened in the slanting light the
    pumpkin's sphere of gold.

There wrought the busy harvesters ; and
    many a creaking wain
Bore slowly to the long barn-floor its load
    of husk and grain ;
Till broad and red, as when he rose, the
    sun sank down, at last,
And like a merry guest's farewell, the
    day in brightness passed.

And lo ! as through the western pines, on
    meadow, stream, and pond,
Flamed the red radiance of a sky, set all
    afire beyond,

Slowly o'er the eastern sea-bluffs a milder
glory shone,
And the sunset and the moonrise were
mingled into one !

As thus into the quiet night the twilight
lapsed away,
And deeper in the brightening moon the
tranquil shadows lay ;
From many a brown old farm-house, and
hamlet without name,
Their milking and their home-tasks done,
the merry huskers came.

Swung o'er the heaped-up harvest, from
pitchforks in the mow,
Shone dimly down the lanterns on the
pleasant scene below ;
The growing pile of husks behind, the
golden ears before,
And laughing eyes and busy hands and
brown cheeks glimmering o'er.

Half hidden in a quiet nook, serene of
look and heart,
Talking their old times over, the old men
sat apart ;
While, up and down the unhusked pile,
or nestling in its shade,
At hide-and-seek, with laugh and shout,
the happy children played.

Urged by the good host's daughter, a
maiden young and fair,
Lifting to light her sweet blue eyes and
pride of soft brown hair,
The master of the village school, sleek of
hair and smooth of tongue,
To the quaint tune of some old psalm, a
husking-ballad sung.

THE CORN-SONG.

HEAP high the farmer's wintry hoard !
Heap high the golden corn !
No richer gift has Autumn poured
From out her lavish horn !

Let other lands, exulting, glean
The apple from the pine,
The orange from its glossy green,
The cluster from the vine ;

We better love the hardy gift
Our rugged vales bestow,

To cheer us when the storm shall drift
Our harvest-fields with snow.

Through vales of grass and meads of
flowers,
Our ploughs their furrows made,
While on the hills the sun and show-
ers
Of changeful April played.

We dropped the seed o'er hill and
plain,
Beneath the sun of May,
And frightened from our sprouting
grain
The robber crows away.

All through the long, bright days of
June
Its leaves grew green and fair,
And waved in hot midsummer's noon
Its soft and yellow hair.

And now, with autumn's moonlit eves,
Its harvest-time has come,
We pluck away the frosted leaves,
And bear the treasure home.

There, richer than the fabled gift
Apollo showered of old,
Fair hands the broken grain shall sift,
And knead its meal of gold.

Let vapid idlers loll in silk
Around their costly board ;
Give us the bowl of samp and milk,
By homespun beauty poured !

Where'er the wide old kitchen hearth
Sends up its smoky curls,
Who will not thank the kindly earth,
And bless our farmer girls !

Then shame on all the proud and vain,
Whose folly laughs to scorn
The blessing of our hardy grain,
Our wealth of golden corn !

Let earth withhold her goodly root,
Let mildew blight the rye,
Give to the worm the orchard's fruit,
The wheat-field to the fly :

But let the good old crop adorn
The hills our fathers trod ;
Still let us, for his golden corn,
Send up our thanks to God !

THE LUMBERMEN.

WILDLY round our woodland quarters,
　Sad-voiced Autumn grieves ;
Thickly down these swelling waters
　Float his fallen leaves.
Through the tall and naked timber,
　Column-like and old,
Gleam the sunsets of November,
　From their skies of gold.

O'er us, to the southland heading,
　Screams the gray wild-goose ;
On the night-frost sounds the treading
　Of the brindled moose.
Noiseless creeping, while we 're sleeping,
　Frost his task-work plies ;
Soon, his icy bridges heaping,
　Shall our log-piles rise.

When, with sounds of smothered thun-
　　der,
　On some night of rain,
Lake and river break asunder
　Winter's weakened chain,
Down the wild March flood shall bear
　　them
　To the saw-mill's wheel,
Or where Steam, the slave, shall tear
　　them
　With his teeth of steel.

Be it starlight, be it moonlight,
　In these vales below,
When the earliest beams of sunlight
　Streak the mountain's snow,
Crisps the hoar-frost, keen and early,
　To our hurrying feet,
And the forest echoes clearly
　All our blows repeat.

Where the crystal Ambijejis
　Stretches broad and clear,
And Millnoket's pine-black ridges
　Hide the browsing deer :
Where, through lakes and wide morasses,
　Or through rocky walls,
Swift and strong, Penobscot passes
　White with foamy falls ;

Where, through clouds, are glimpses
　　given
　Of Katahdin's sides, —
Rock and forest piled to heaven,
　Torn and ploughed by slides !
Far below, the Indian trapping,
　In the sunshine warm ;

Far above, the snow-cloud wrapping
　Half the peak in storm !

Where are mossy carpets better
　Than the Persian weaves,
And than Eastern perfumes sweeter
　Seem the fading leaves ;
And a music wild and solemn,
　From the pine-tree's height,
Rolls its vast and sea-like volume
　On the wind of night ;

Make we here our camp of winter ;
　And, through sleet and snow,
Pitchy knot and beechen splinter
　On our hearth shall glow.
Here, with mirth to lighten duty,
　We shall lack alone
Woman's smile and girlhood's beauty,
　Childhood's lisping tone.

But their hearth is brighter burning
　For our toil to-day ;
And the welcome of returning
　Shall our loss repay,
When, like seamen from the waters,
　From the woods we come,
Greeting sisters, wives, and daughters,
　Angels of our home !

Not for us the measured ringing
　From the village spire,
Not for us the Sabbath singing
　Of the sweet-voiced choir :
Ours the old, majestic temple,
　Where God's brightness shines
Down the dome so grand and ample,
　Propped by lofty pines !

Through each branch-enwoven skylight,
　Speaks He in the breeze,
As of old beneath the twilight
　Of lost Eden's trees !
For his ear, the inward feeling
　Needs no outward tongue ;
He can see the spirit kneeling
　While the axe is swung.

Heeding truth alone, and turning
　From the false and dim,
Lamp of toil or altar burning
　Are alike to Him.
Strike, then, comrades ! — Trade is
　　waiting
　On our rugged toil ;
Far ships waiting for the freighting
　Of our woodland spoil !

"Down the wild March flood shall bear them." Page 118.

Ships, whose traffic links these highlands,
  Bleak and cold, of ours,
With the citron-planted islands
  Of a clime of flowers ;
To our frosts the tribute bringing
  Of eternal heats ;
In our lap of winter flinging
  Tropic fruits and sweets.

Cheerly, on the axe of labor,
  Let the sunbeams dance,
Better than the flash of sabre
  Or the gleam of lance !
Strike ! —With every blow is given
  Freer sun and sky,
And the long-hid earth to heaven
  Looks, with wondering eye !

Loud behind us grow the murmurs
  Of the age to come ;
Clang of smiths, and tread of farmers,
  Bearing harvest home !
Here her virgin lap with treasures
  Shall the green earth fill ;
Waving wheat and golden maize-ears
  Crown each beechen hill.

Keep who will the city's alleys,
  Take the smooth-shorn plain, —
Give to us the cedar valleys,
  Rocks and hills of Maine !
In our North-land, wild and woody,
  Let us still have part :
Rugged nurse and mother sturdy,
  Hold us to thy heart !

O, our free hearts beat the warmer
  For thy breath of snow ;
And our tread is all the firmer
  For thy rocks below.
Freedom, hand in hand with labor,
  Walketh strong and brave ;
On the forehead of his neighbor
  No man writeth Slave !

Lo, the day breaks ! old Katahdin's
  Pine-trees show its fires,
While from these dim forest gardens
  Rise their blackened spires.
Up, my comrades ! up and doing !
  Manhood's rugged play
Still renewing, bravely hewing
  Through the world our way !

MISCELLANEOUS.

THE ANGELS OF BUENA VISTA.

SPEAK and tell us, our Ximena, looking
    northward far away,
O'er the camp of the invaders, o'er the
    Mexican array,
Who is losing ? who is winning ? are they
    far or come they near ?
Look abroad, and tell us, sister, whither
    rolls the storm we hear.

"Down the hills of Angostura still the
    storm of battle rolls ;
Blood is flowing, men are dying ; God
    have mercy on their souls ! "
Who is losing ? who is winning ? —
    "Over hill and over plain,
I see but smoke of cannon clouding
    through the mountain rain."

Holy Mother ! keep our brothers ! Look,
    Ximena, look once more.
"Still I see the fearful whirlwind rolling
    darkly as before,

Bearing on, in strange confusion, friend
    and foeman, foot and horse,
Like some wild and troubled torrent
    sweeping down its mountain
    course."

Look forth once more, Ximena ! "Ah !
    the smoke has rolled away ;
And I see the Northern rifles gleaming
    down the ranks of gray.
Hark ! that sudden blast of bugles ! there
    the troop of Minon wheels ;
There the Northern horses thunder, with
    the cannon at their heels.

"Jesu, pity ! how it thickens ! now re-
    treat and now advance !
Right against the blazing cannon shivers
    Puebla's charging lance !
Down they go, the brave young riders ;
    horse and foot together fall ;
Like a ploughshare in the fallow, through
    them ploughs the Northern ball."

Nearer came the storm and nearer, rolling fast and frightful on !
Speak, Ximena, speak and tell us, who
has lost, and who has won ?
" Alas ! alas ! I know not ; friend and foe
together fall,
O'er the dying rush the living : pray, my
sisters, for them all !

" Lo ! the wind the smoke is lifting :
Blessed Mother, save my brain !
I can see the wounded crawling slowly
out from heaps of slain.
Now they stagger, blind and bleeding ;
now they fall, and strive to rise ;
Hasten, sisters, haste and save them, lest
they die before our eyes !

" O my heart's love ! O my dear one !
lay thy poor head on my knee :
Dost thou know the lips that kiss thee ?
Canst thou hear me ? canst thou
see ?
O my husband, brave and gentle ! O my
Bernal, look once more
On the blessed cross before thee ! Mercy !
mercy ! all is o'er ! "

Dry thy tears, my poor Ximena ; lay thy
dear one down to rest ;
Let his hands be meekly folded, lay the
cross upon his breast ;
Let his dirge be sung hereafter, and his
funeral masses said :
To-day, thou poor bereaved one, the
living ask thy aid.

Close beside her, faintly moaning, fair
and young, a soldier lay,
Torn with shot and pierced with lances,
bleeding slow his life away ;
But, as tenderly before him the lorn
Ximena knelt,
She saw the Northern eagle shining on
his pistol-belt.

With a stifled cry of horror straight she
turned away her head ;
With a sad and bitter feeling looked she
back upon her dead ;
But she heard the youth's low moaning,
and his struggling breath of pain,
And she raised the cooling water to his
parching lips again.

Whispered low the dying soldier, pressed
her hand and faintly smiled :
Was that pitying face his mother's ? did
she watch beside her child ?
All his stranger words with meaning her
woman's heart supplied ;
With her kiss upon his forehead,
" Mother ! " murmured he, and
died !

" A bitter curse upon them, poor boy,
who led thee forth,
From some gentle, sad-eyed mother,
weeping, lonely, in the North ! "
Spake the mournful Mexic woman, as
she laid him with her dead,
And turned to soothe the living, and
bind the wounds which bled.

Look forth once more, Ximena ! " Like
a cloud before the wind
Rolls the battle down the mountains,
leaving blood and death behind ;
Ah ! they plead in vain for mercy ; in
the dust the wounded strive ;
Hide your faces, holy angels ! O thou
Christ of God, forgive ! "

Sink, O Night, among thy mountains ;
let the cool, gray shadows fall ;
Dying brothers, fighting demons, drop
thy curtain over all !
Through the thickening winter twilight,
wide apart the battle rolled,
In its sheath the sabre rested, and the
cannon's lips grew cold.

But the noble Mexic women still their
holy task pursued,
Through that long, dark night of sorrow,
worn and faint and lacking food.
Over weak and suffering brothers, with
a tender care they hung,
And the dying foeman blessed them in
a strange and Northern tongue.

Not wholly lost, O Father ! is this evil
world of ours ;
Upward, through its blood and ashes,
spring afresh the Eden flowers ;
From its smoking hell of battle, Love
and Pity send their prayer,
And still thy white-winged angels hover
dimly in our air !

FORGIVENESS.

My heart was heavy, for its trust had been
  Abused, its kindness answered with
      foul wrong ;
So, turning gloomily from my fellow-
      men,
  One summer Sabbath day I strolled
      among
The green mounds of the village burial-
      place ;
  Where, pondering how all human love
      and hate
  Find one sad level ; and how, soon or
      late,
Wronged and wrongdoer, each with
      meekened face,
  And cold hands folded over a still heart,
Pass the green threshold of our common
      grave,
  Whither all footsteps tend, whence
      none depart,
Awed for myself, and pitying my race,
  Our common sorrow, like a mighty wave,
Swept all my pride away, and trembling
      I forgave !

BARCLAY OF URY.[42]

Up the streets of Aberdeen,
By the kirk and college green,
    Rode the Laird of Ury ;
Close behind him, close beside,
Foul of mouth and evil-eyed,
    Pressed the mob in fury.

Flouted him the drunken churl,
Jeered at him the serving-girl,
    Prompt to please her master ;
And the begging carlin, late
Fed and clothed at Ury's gate,
    Cursed him as he passed her.

Yet, with calm and stately mien,
Up the streets of Aberdeen
    Came he slowly riding :
And, to all he saw and heard,
Answering not with bitter word,
    Turning not for chiding.

Came a troop with broadswords swinging,
Bits and bridles sharply ringing,
    Loose and free and froward ;
Quoth the foremost, " Ride him down !
Push him ! prick him ! through the town
    Drive the Quaker coward ! "

But from out the thickening crowd
Cried a sudden voice and loud :
    " Barclay ! Ho ! a Barclay ! "
And the old man at his side
Saw a comrade, battle tried,
    Scarred and sunburned darkly ;

Who with ready weapon bare,
Fronting to the troopers there,
    Cried aloud : " God save us,
Call ye coward him who stood
Ankle deep in Lutzen's blood,
    With the brave Gustavus ? "

" Nay, I do not need thy sword,
Comrade mine," said Ury's lord ;
    " Put it up, I pray thee :
Passive to his holy will,
Trust I in my Master still,
    Even though he slay me.

" Pledges of thy love and faith,
Proved on many a field of death,
    Not by me are needed."
Marvelled much that henchman bold,
That his laird, so stout of old,
    Now so meekly pleaded.

" Woe 's the day ! " he sadly said,
With a slowly shaking head,
    And a look of pity ;
" Ury's honest lord reviled,
Mock of knave and sport of child,
    In his own good city !

" Speak the word, and, master mine,
As we charged on Tilly's line,
    And his Walloon lancers,
Smiting through their midst we 'll teach
Civil look and decent speech
    To these boyish prancers ! "

" Marvel not, mine ancient friend,
Like beginning, like the end " :
    Quoth the Laird of Ury,
" Is the sinful servant more
Than his gracious Lord who bore
    Bonds and stripes in Jewry ?

" Give me joy that in his name
I can bear, with patient frame,
    All these vain ones offer ;
While for them He suffereth long,
Shall I answer wrong with wrong,
    Scoffing with the scoffer ?

" Happier I, with loss of all,
Hunted, outlawed, held in thrall,
    With few friends to greet me,
Than when reeve and squire were seen,
Riding out from Aberdeen,
    With bared heads to meet me.

" When each goodwife, o'er and o'er,
Blessed me as I passed her door ;
    And the snooded daughter,
Through her casement glancing down,
Smiled on him who bore renown
    From red fields of slaughter.

" Hard to feel the stranger's scoff,
Hard the old friend's falling off,
    Hard to learn forgiving :
But the Lord his own rewards,
And his love with theirs accords,
    Warm and fresh and living.

" Through this dark and stormy night
Faith beholds a feeble light
    Up the blackness streaking ;
Knowing God's own time is best,
In a patient hope I rest
    For the full day-breaking ! "

So the Laird of Ury said,
Turning slow his horse's head
    Towards the Tolbooth prison,
Where, through iron grates, he heard
Poor disciples of the Word
    Preach of Christ arisen !

Not in vain, Confessor old,
Unto us the tale is told
    Of thy day of trial ;
Every age on him, who strays
From its broad and beaten ways,
    Pours its sevenfold vial.

Happy he whose inward ear
Angel comfortings can hear,
    O'er the rabble's laughter ;
And while Hatred's fagots burn,
Glimpses through the smoke discern
    Of the good hereafter.

Knowing this, that never yet
Share of Truth was vainly set
    In the world's wide fallow ;
After hands shall sow the seed,
After hands from hill and mead
    Reap the harvests yellow.

Thus, with somewhat of the Seer,
Must the moral pioneer

From the Future borrow ;
Clothe the waste with dreams of grain,
And, on midnight's sky of rain,
    Paint the golden morrow !

WHAT THE VOICE SAID.

MADDENED by Earth's wrong and evil,
    " Lord ! " I cried in sudden ire,
" From thy right hand, clothed with
        thunder,
    Shake the bolted fire !

" Love is lost, and Faith is dying ;
    With the brute the man is sold ;
And the dropping blood of labor
    Hardens into gold.

" Here the dying wail of Famine,
    There the battle's groan of pain ;
And, in silence, smooth-faced Mammon
    Reaping men like grain.

" ' Where is God, that we should fear
        Him ?'
    Thus the earth-born Titans say ;
' God ! if thou art living, hear us !'
    Thus the weak ones pray."

"Thou, the patient Heaven upbraid-
        ing,"
    Spake a solemn Voice within ;
" Weary of our Lord's forbearance,
    Art thou free from sin ?

" Fearless brow to Him uplifting,
    Canst thou for his thunders call,
Knowing that to guilt's attraction
    Evermore they fall ?

" Know'st thou not all germs of evil
    In thy heart await their time ?
Not thyself, but God's restraining,
    Stays their growth of crime.

" Couldst thou boast, O child of weak-
        ness !
    O'er the sons of wrong and strife,
Were their strong temptations planted
    In thy path of life ?

" Thou hast seen two streamlets gush-
        ing
    From one fountain, clear and free,
But by widely varying channels
    Searching for the sea.

" Glideth one through greenest valleys,
  Kissing them with lips still sweet ;
One, mad roaring down the mountains,
  Stagnates at their feet.

" Is it choice whereby the Parsee
  Kneels before his mother's fire ?
In his black tent did the Tartar
  Choose his wandering sire ?

" He alone, whose hand is bounding
  Human power and human will,
Looking through each soul's surrounding,
  Knows its good or ill.

" For thyself, while wrong and sorrow
  Make to thee their strong appeal,
Coward wert thou not to utter
  What the heart must feel.

" Earnest words must needs be spoken
  When the warm heart bleeds or burns
With its scorn of wrong, or pity
  For the wronged, by turns.

" But, by all thy nature's weakness,
  Hidden faults and follies known,
Be thou, in rebuking evil,
  Conscious of thine own.

" Not the less shall stern-eyed Duty
  To thy lips her trumpet set,
But with harsher blasts shall mingle
  Wailings of regret."

Cease not, Voice of holy speaking,
  Teacher sent of God, be near,
Whispering through the day's cool silence,
  Let my spirit hear !

So, when thoughts of evil-doers
  Waken scorn, or hatred move,
Shall a mournful fellow-feeling
  Temper all with love.

TO DELAWARE.

[Written during the discussion in the Legislature of that State, in the winter of 1846 – 47, of a bill for the abolition of slavery.]

THRICE welcome to thy sisters of the East,
  To the strong tillers of a rugged home,
  With spray-wet locks to Northern winds
    released,
      And hardy feet o'erswept by ocean's
        foam ;

And to the young nymphs of the golden
    West,
  Whose harvest mantles, fringed with
    prairie bloom,
Trail in the sunset, — O redeemed and
    blest,
  To the warm welcome of thy sisters
    come !
Broad Pennsylvania, down her sail-white
    bay
  Shall give thee joy, and Jersey from
    her plains,
And the great lakes, where echo, free
    alway,
  Moaned never shoreward with the
    clank of chains,
Shall weave new sun-bows in their toss
    ing spray,
And all their waves keep grateful holiday.
And, smiling on thee through her moun-
    tain rains,
  Vermont shall bless thee ; and the
    Granite peaks,
And vast Katahdin o'er his woods, shall
    wear
Their snow-crowns brighter in the cold
    keen air ;
  And Massachusetts, with her rugged
    cheeks
O'errun with grateful tears, shall turn
    to thee,
  When, at thy bidding, the electric wire
Shall tremble northward with its words
    of fire ;
Glory and praise to God ! another State
    is free !

WORSHIP.

" Pure religion, and undefiled, before God and the Father is this : To visit the widows and the fatherless in their affliction, and to keep himself unspotted from the world." — *James* i. 27.

THE Pagan's myths through marble lips
    are spoken,
  And ghosts of old Beliefs still flit and
    moan
Round fane and altar overthrown and
    broken,
  O'er tree-grown barrow and gray ring
    of stone.

Blind Faith had martyrs in those old
    high places,
  The Syrian hill grove and the Druid's
    wood,

With mother's offering, to the Fiend's
    embraces,
      Bone of their bone, and blood of their
        own blood.

Red altars, kindling through that night
    of error,
      Smoked with warm blood beneath the
        cruel eye
Of lawless Power and sanguinary Terror,
    Throned on the circle of a pitiless sky;

Beneath whose baleful shadow, overcast-
    ing
      All heaven above, and blighting earth
        below,
The scourge grew red, the lip grew pale
    with fasting,
      And man's oblation was his fear and
        woe !

Then through great temples swelled the
    dismal moaning
      Of dirge-like music and sepulchral
        prayer ;
Pale wizard priests, o'er occult symbols
    droning,
      Swung their white censers in the bur-
        dened air :

As if the pomp of rituals, and the savor
    Of gums and spices could the Unseen
      One please ;
As if his ear could bend, with childish
    favor,
      To the poor flattery of the organ keys !

Feet red from war-fields trod the church
    aisles holy,
      With trembling reverence : and the
        oppressor there,
Kneeling before his priest, abased and
    lowly,
      Crushed human hearts beneath his
        knee of prayer.

Not such the service the benignant Father
    Requireth at his earthly children's
      hands :
Not the poor offering of vain rites, but
    rather
      The simple duty man from man de-
        mands.

For Earth he asks it : the full joy of
    Heaven
      Knoweth no change of waning or in-
        crease ;

The great heart of the Infinite beats even,
    Untroubled flows the river of his peace.

He asks no taper lights, on high sur-
    rounding
      The priestly altar and the saintly grave,
No dolorous chant nor organ music sound-
    ing,
      Nor incense clouding up the twilight
        nave.

For he whom Jesus loved hath truly
    spoken :
      The holier worship which he deigns to
        bless
Restores the lost, and binds the spirit
    broken,
      And feeds the widow and the fatherless !

Types of our human weakness and our
    sorrow !
      Who lives unhaunted by his loved ones
        dead ?
Who, with vain longing, seeketh not to
    borrow
      From stranger eyes the home lights
        which have fled ?

O brother man ! fold to thy heart thy
    brother ;
      Where pity dwells, the peace of God
        is there ;
To worship rightly is to love each other,
      Each smile a hymn, each kindly deed
        a prayer.

Follow with reverent steps the great ex-
    ample
      Of Him whose holy work was "doing
        good" ;
So shall the wide earth seem our Father's
    temple,
      Each loving life a psalm of gratitude.

Then shall all shackles fall ; the stormy
    clangor
      Of wild war music o'er the earth shall
        cease ;
Love shall tread out the baleful fire of
    anger,
      And in its ashes plant the tree of peace !

THE DEMON OF THE STUDY.

THE Brownie sits in the Scotchman's
    room,
      And eats his meat and drinks his ale,

And beats the maid with her unused
broom,
And the lazy lout with his idle flail,
But he sweeps the floor and threshes the
corn,
And hies him away ere the break of
dawn.

The shade of Denmark fled from the sun,
And the Cocklane ghost from the barn-
loft cheer,
The fiend of Faust was a faithful one,
Agrippa's demon wrought in fear,
And the devil of Martin Luther sat
By the stout monk's side in social chat.

The Old Man of the Sea, on the neck of
him
Who seven times crossed the deep,
Twined closely each lean and withered
limb,
Like the nightmare in one's sleep.
But he drank of the wine, and Sindbad cast
The evil weight from his back at last.

But the demon that cometh day by day
To my quiet room and fireside nook,
Where the casement light falls dim and
gray
On faded painting and ancient book,
Is a sorrier one than any whose names
Are chronicled well by good King James.

No bearer of burdens like Caliban,
No runner of errands like Ariel,
He comes in the shape of a fat old man,
Without rap of knuckle or pull of bell;
And whence he comes, or whither he goes,
I know as I do of the wind which blows.

A stout old man with a greasy hat
Slouched heavily down to his dark,
red nose,
And two gray eyes enveloped in fat,
Looking through glasses with iron
bows.
Read ye, and heed ye, and ye who can,
Guard well your doors from that old
man!

He comes with a careless "How d' ye do?"
And seats himself in my elbow-chair;
And my morning paper and pamphlet new
Fall forthwith under his special care
And he wipes his glasses and clears his
throat,
And, button by button, unfolds his coat.

And then he reads from paper and book,
In a low and husky asthmatic tone,
With the stolid sameness of posture and
look
Of one who reads to himself alone;
And hour after hour on my senses come
That husky wheeze and that dolorous
hum.

The price of stocks, the auction sales,
The poet's song and the lover's glee,
The horrible murders, the seaboard gales,
The marriage list, and the *jeu d'esprit*,
All reach my ear in the self-same tone, —
I shudder at each, but the fiend reads on!

O, sweet as the lapse of water at noon
O'er the mossy roots of some forest tree,
The sigh of the wind in the woods of June,
Or sound of flutes o'er a moonlight sea,
Or the low soft music, perchance, which
seems
To float through the slumbering singer's
dreams,

So sweet, so dear is the silvery tone,
Of her in whose features I sometimes
look,
As I sit at eve by her side alone,
And we read by turns from the self-
same book, —
Some tale perhaps of the olden time,
Some lover's romance or quaint old rhyme.

Then when the story is one of woe, —
Some prisoner's plaint through his dun-
geon-bar,
Her blue eye glistens with tears, and low
Her voice sinks down like a moan afar;
And I seem to hear that prisoner's wail,
And his face looks on me worn and pale.

And when she reads some merrier song,
Her voice is glad as an April bird's,
And when the tale is of war and wrong,
A trumpet's summons is in her words,
And the rush of the hosts I seem to hear,
And see the tossing of plume and spear! —

O, pity me then, when, day by day,
The stout fiend darkens my parlor door;
And reads me perchance the self-same lay
Which melted in music, the night be-
fore,
From lips as the lips of Hylas sweet,
And moved like twin roses which zephyrs
meet!

I cross my floor with a nervous tread,
   I whistle and laugh and sing and shout,
I flourish my cane above his head,
   And stir up the fire to roast him out ;
I topple the chairs, and drum on the pane,
And press my hands on my ears, in vain !

I 've studied Glanville and James the wise,
   And wizard black-letter tomes which
      treat
Of demons of every name and size,
   Which a Christian man is presumed to
      meet,
But never a hint and never a line
Can I find of a reading fiend like mine.

I 've crossed the Psalter with Brady and
      Tate,
   And laid the Primer above them all,
I 've nailed a horseshoe over the grate,
   And hung a wig to my parlor wall
Once worn by a learned Judge, they
      say,
At Salem court in the witchcraft day !

" *Conjuro te, sceleratissime,*
   Abire ad tuum locum !" — still
Like a visible nightmare he sits by me, —
   The exorcism has lost its skill ;
And I hear again in my haunted room
The husky wheeze and the dolorous hum !

Ah ! — commend me to Mary Magdalen
   With her sevenfold plagues, — to the
      wandering Jew,
To the terrors which haunted Orestes
      when
   The furies his midnight curtains drew,
But charm him off, ye who charm him
      can,
That reading demon, that fat old man !

THE PUMPKIN.

O, GREENLY and fair in the lands of the
      sun,
The vines of the gourd and the rich
      melon run,
And the rock and the tree and the cot-
      tage enfold,
With broad leaves all greenness and
      blossoms all gold,
Like that which o'er Nineveh's prophet
      once grew,
While he waited to know that his warn-
      ing was true,

And longed for the storm-cloud, and
      listened in vain
For the rush of the whirlwind and red
      fire-rain.

On the banks of the Xenil the dark
      Spanish maiden
Comes up with the fruit of the tangled
      vine laden ;
And the Creole of Cuba laughs out to
      behold
Through orange-leaves shining the broad
      spheres of gold ;
Yet with dearer delight from his home
      in the North,
On the fields of his harvest the Yankee
      looks forth,
Where crook-necks are coiling and yel-
      low fruit shines,
And the sun of September melts down
      on his vines.

Ah ! on Thanksgiving day, when from
      East and from West,
From North and from South come the
      pilgrim and guest,
When the gray-haired New-Englander
      sees round his board
The old broken links of affection re-
      stored,
When the care-wearied man seeks his
      mother once more,
And the worn matron smiles where the
      girl smiled before,
What moistens the lip and what bright-
      ens the eye ?
What calls back the past, like the rich
      Pumpkin pie ?

O, — fruit loved of boyhood ! — the old
      days recalling,
When wood-grapes were purpling and
      brown nuts were falling !
When wild, ugly faces we carved in its
      skin,
Glaring out through the dark with a
      candle within !
When we laughed round the corn-heap,
      with hearts all in tune,
Our chair a broad pumpkin, — our lan-
      tern the moon,
Telling tales of the fairy who travelled
      like steam,
In a pumpkin-shell coach, with two rats
      for her team !

Then thanks for thy present ! — none
   sweeter or better
E'er smoked from an oven or circled a
   platter !
Fairer hands never wrought at a pastry
   more fine,
Brighter eyes never watched o'er its
   baking, than thine !
And the prayer, which my mouth is too
   full to express,
Swells my heart that thy shadow may
   never be less,
That the days of thy lot may be length-
   ened below,
And the fame of thy worth like a pump-
   kin-vine grow,
And thy life be as sweet, and its last
   sunset sky
Golden-tinted and fair as thy own
   Pumpkin pie !

EXTRACT FROM " A NEW ENG-
LAND LEGEND."

How has New England's romance fled,
   Even as a vision of the morning !
Its rites foredone, — its guardians dead, —
Its priestesses, bereft of dread,
   Waking the veriest urchin's scorning !
Gone like the Indian wizard's yell
   And fire-dance round the magic rock,
Forgotten like the Druid's spell
   At moonrise by his holy oak !
No more along the shadowy glen,
Glide the dim ghosts of murdered men ;
No more the unquiet churchyard dead
Glimpse upward from their turfy bed,
   Startling the traveller, late and lone ;
As, on some night of starless weather,
They silently commune together,
   Each sitting on his own head-stone !
The roofless house, decayed, deserted,
Its living tenants all departed,
No longer rings with midnight revel
Of witch, or ghost, or goblin evil ;
No pale blue flame sends out its flashes
Through creviced roof and shattered
      sashes ! —
The witch-grass round the hazel spring
May sharply to the night-air sing,
But there no more shall withered hags
Refresh at ease their broomstick nags,
Or taste those hazel-shadowed waters
As beverage meet for Satan's daughters ;
No more their mimic tones be heard, —
The mew of cat, — the chirp of bird, —

Shrill blending with the hoarser laughter
Of the fell demon following after !
The cautious goodman nails no more
A horseshoe on his outer door,
Lest some unseemly hag should fit
To his own mouth her bridle-bit, —
The goodwife's churn no more refuses
Its wonted culinary uses
Until, with heated needle burned,
The witch has to her place returned !
Our witches are no longer old
And wrinkled beldames, Satan-sold,
But young and gay and laughing crea-
    tures,
With the heart's sunshine on their fea-
    tures, —
Their sorcery — the light which dances
Where the raised lid unveils its glances;
Or that low-breathed and gentle tone,
   The music of Love's twilight hours,
Soft, dream-like, as a fairy's moan
   Above her nightly closing flowers,
Sweeter than that which sighed of yore
Along the charmed Ausonian shore !
Even she, our own weird heroine,
Sole Pythoness of ancient Lynn,
   Sleeps calmly where the living laid her
And the wide realm of sorcery,
Left by its latest mistress free,
   Hath found no gray and skilled in-
    vader :
So perished Albion's "glammarye,"
   With him in Melrose Abbey sleeping,
His charmed torch beside his knee,
That even the dead himself might see
   The magic scroll within his keeping.
And now our modern Yankee sees
Nor omens, spells, nor mysteries ;
And naught above, below, around,
Of life or death, of sight or sound,
   Whate'er its nature, form, or look,
Excites his terror or surprise, —
All seeming to his knowing eyes
Familiar as his " catechize,"
   Or " Webster's Spelling-Book."

HAMPTON BEACH.

THE sunlight glitters keen and bright,
   Where, miles away,
Lies stretching to my dazzled sight
A luminous belt, a misty light,
Beyond the dark pine bluffs and waste
   of sandy gray.

The tremulous shadow of the Sea !
   Against its ground

Of silvery light, rock, hill, and tree,
Still as a picture, clear and free,
With varying outline mark the coast for
    miles around.

On — on — we tread with loose-flung
    rein
    Our seaward way,
Through dark-green fields and blos-
    soming grain,
Where the wild brier-rose skirts the
    lane,
And bends above our heads the flowering
    locust spray.

Ha ! like a kind hand on my brow
    Comes this fresh breeze,
Cooling its dull and feverish glow,
While through my being seems to flow
The breath of a new life, — the healing
    of the seas !

Now rest we, where this grassy mound
    His feet hath set
In the great waters, which have bound
His granite ankles greenly round
With long and tangled moss, and weeds
    with cool spray wet.

Good by to pain and care ! I take
    Mine ease to-day :
Here where these sunny waters break,
And ripples this keen breeze, I shake
All burdens from the heart, all weary
    thoughts away.

I draw a freer breath — I seem
    Like all I see —
Waves in the sun — the white-winged
    gleam
Of sea-birds in the slanting beam —
And far-off sails which flit before the
    south-wind free.

So when Time's veil shall fall asunder,
    The soul may know
No fearful change, nor sudden wonder,
Nor sink the weight of mystery under,
But with the upward rise, and with the
    vastness grow.

And all we shrink from now may seem
    No new revealing ;
Familiar as our childhood's stream,
Or pleasant memory of a dream
The loved and cherished Past upon the
    new life stealing.

Serene and mild the untried light
    May have its dawning ;
And, as in summer's northern night
The evening and the dawn unite,
The sunset hues of Time blend with the
    soul's new morning.

I sit alone ; in foam and spray
    Wave after wave
Breaks on the rocks which, stern and
    gray,
Shoulder the broken tide away,
Or murmurs hoarse and strong through
    mossy cleft and cave.

What heed I of the dusty land
    And noisy town ?
I see the mighty deep expand
From its white line of glimmering sand
To where the blue of heaven on bluer
    waves shuts down !

In listless quietude of mind,
    I yield to all
The change of cloud and wave and
    wind
And passive on the flood reclined,
I wander with the waves, and with them
    rise and fall.

But look, thou dreamer ! — wave and
    shore
    In shadow lie ;
The night-wind warns me back once
    more
To where, my native hill-tops o'er,
Bends like an arch of fire the glowing
    sunset sky.

So then, beach, bluff, and wave, fare-
    well !
    I bear with me
No token stone nor glittering shell,
But long and oft shall Memory tell
Of this brief thoughtful hour of musing
    by the Sea.

LINES,

WRITTEN ON HEARING OF THE DEATH
OF SILAS WRIGHT OF NEW YORK.

As they who, tossing midst the storm at
    night,
    While turning shoreward, where a
    beacon shone,

Meet the walled blackness of the
    heaven alone,
So, on the turbulent waves of party tossed,
In gloom and tempest, men have seen
    thy light
Quenched in the darkness. At thy
    hour of noon,
While life was pleasant to thy undimmed
    sight,
And, day by day, within thy spirit grew
A holier hope than young Ambition knew,
As through thy rural quiet, not in vain,
Pierced the sharp thrill of Freedom's cry
    of pain,
    Man of the millions, thou art lost too
        soon !
Portents at which the bravest stand
    aghast, —
The birth-throes of a Future, strange
    and vast,
    Alarm the land ; yet thou, so wise
        and strong,
Suddenly summoned to the burial bed,
    Lapped in its slumbers deep and ever
        long,
Hear'st not the tumult surging overhead.
Who now shall rally Freedom's scatter-
    ing host ?
Who wear the mantle of the leader lost ?
Who stay the march of slavery ? He
    whose voice
    Hath called thee from thy task-field
        shall not lack
    Yet bolder champions, to beat bravely
        back
The wrong which, through his poor ones,
    reaches Him :
Yet firmer hands shall Freedom's torch-
    lights trim,
    And wave them high across the abys-
        mal black,
Till bound, dumb millions there shall
    see them and rejoice.

10th mo., 1847.

LINES,

ACCOMPANYING MANUSCRIPTS PRESENT-
ED TO A FRIEND.

'T is said that in the Holy Land
    The angels of the place have blessed
The pilgrim's bed of desert sand,
    Like Jacob's stone of rest.

That down the hush of Syrian skies
    Some sweet-voiced saint at twilight
        sings

The song whose holy symphonies
    Are beat by unseen wings ;

Till starting from his sandy bed,
    The wayworn wanderer looks to see
The halo of an angel's head
    Shine through the tamarisk-tree.

So through the shadows of my way
    Thy smile hath fallen soft and clear,
So at the weary close of day
    Hath seemed thy voice of cheer.

That pilgrim pressing to his goal
    May pause not for the vision's sake,
Yet all fair things within his soul
    The thought of it shall wake :

The graceful palm-tree by the well,
    Seen on the far horizon's rim ;
The dark eyes of the fleet gazelle,
    Bent timidly on him ;

Each pictured saint, whose golden hair
    Streams sunlike through the convent's
        gloom ;
Pale shrines of martyrs young and fair,
    And loving Mary's tomb ;

And thus each tint or shade which falls,
    From sunset cloud or waving tree,
Along my pilgrim path, recalls
    The pleasant thought of thee.

Of one in sun and shade the same,
    In weal and woe my steady friend,
Whatever by that holy name
    The angels comprehend.

Not blind to faults and follies, thou
    Hast never failed the good to see,
Nor judged by one unseemly bough
    The upward-struggling tree.

These light leaves at thy feet I lay, —
    Poor common thoughts on common
        things,
Which time is shaking, day by day,
    Like feathers from his wings, —

Chance shootings from a frail life-tree,
    To nurturing care but little known,
Their good was partly learned of thee,
    Their folly is my own.

That tree still clasps the kindly mould,
    Its leaves still drink the twilight dew,

And weaving its pale green with gold,
   Still shines the sunlight through.

There still the morning zephyrs play,
   And there at times the spring bird
      sings,
And mossy trunk and fading spray
   Are flowered with glossy wings.

Yet, even in genial sun and rain,
   Root, branch, and leaflet fail and fade ;
The wanderer on its lonely plain
   Erelong shall miss its shade.

O friend beloved, whose curious skill
   Keeps bright the last year's leaves
      and flowers,
With warm, glad summer thoughts to
      fill
   The cold, dark, winter hours !

Pressed on thy heart, the leaves I bring
   May well defy the wintry cold,
Until, in Heaven's eternal spring,
   Life's fairer ones unfold.

THE REWARD.

Who, looking backward from his man-
      hood's prime,
Sees not the spectre of his misspent time ?
   And, through the shade
Of funeral cypress planted thick behind,
Hears no reproachful whisper on the
      wind
   From his loved dead ?

Who bears no trace of passion's evil
      force ?
Who shuns thy sting, O terrible Re-
      morse ? —
   Who does not cast
On the thronged pages of his memory's
      book,
At times, a sad and half-reluctant look,
   Regretful of the past ?

Alas ! — the evil which we fain would
      shun
We do, and leave the wished-for good
      undone :
   Our strength to-day
Is but to-morrow's weakness, prone to
      fall ;
Poor, blind, unprofitable servants all
   Are we alway.

Yet who, thus looking backward o'er
      his years,
Feels not his eyelids wet with grateful
      tears,
   If he hath been
Permitted, weak and sinful as he was,
To cheer and aid, in some ennobling
      cause,
   His fellow-men ?

If he hath hidden the outcast, or let in
A ray of sunshine to the cell of sin, —
   If he hath lent
Strength to the weak, and, in an hour of
      need,
Over the suffering, mindless of his creed
   Or home, hath bent,

He has not lived in vain, and while he
      gives
The praise to Him, in whom he moves
      and lives,
   With thankful heart ;
He gazes backward, and with hope
      before,
Knowing that from his works he never-
      more
   Can henceforth part.

RAPHAEL.

I shall not soon forget that sight :
   The glow of autumn's westering day,
A hazy warmth, a dreamy light,
   On Raphael's picture lay.

It was a simple print I saw,
   The fair face of a musing boy ;
Yet, while I gazed, a sense of awe
   Seemed blending with my joy.

A simple print : — the graceful flow
   Of boyhood's soft and wavy hair,
And fresh young lip and cheek, and
      brow
   Unmarked and clear, were there.

Yet through its sweet and calm repose
   I saw the inward spirit shine ;
It was as if before me rose
   The white veil of a shrine.

As if, as Gothland's sage has told,
   The hidden life, the man within,
Dissevered from its frame and mould,
   By mortal eye were seen.

Was it the lifting of that eye,
　The waving of that pictured hand ?
Loose as a cloud-wreath on the sky,
　I saw the walls expand.

The narrow room had vanished, — space,
　Broad, luminous, remained alone,
Through which all hues and shapes of
　　grace
　And beauty looked or shone.

Around the mighty master came
　The marvels which his pencil wrought,
Those miracles of power whose fame
　Is wide as human thought.

There drooped thy more than mortal
　　face,
　O Mother, beautiful and mild !
Enfolding in one dear embrace
　Thy Saviour and thy Child !

The rapt brow of the Desert John ;
　The awful glory of that day
When all the Father's brightness shone
　Through manhood's veil of clay.

And, midst gray prophet forms, and
　　wild
Dark visions of the days of old,
How sweetly woman's beauty smiled
　Through locks of brown and gold !

There Fornarina's fair young face
　Once more upon her lover shone,
Whose model of an angel's grace
　He borrowed from her own.

Slow passed that vision from my view,
　But not the lesson which it taught ;
The soft, calm shadows which it threw
　Still rested on my thought :

The truth, that painter, bard, and sage,
　Even in Earth's cold and changeful
　　clime,
Plant for their deathless heritage
　The fruits and flowers of time.

We shape ourselves the joy or fear
　Of which the coming life is made,
And fill our Future's atmosphere
　With sunshine or with shade.

The tissue of the Life to be
　We weave with colors all our own,

And in the field of Destiny
　We reap as we have sown.

Still shall the soul around it call
　The shadows which it gathered here,
And, painted on the eternal wall,
　The Past shall reappear.

Think ye the notes of holy song
　On Milton's tuneful ear have died ?
Think ye that Raphael's angel throng
　Has vanished from his side ?

O no ! — We live our life again ;
　Or warmly touched, or coldly dim,
The pictures of the Past remain, —
　Man's works shall follow him !

LUCY HOOPER.[43]

THEY tell me, Lucy, thou art dead, —
　　That all of thee we loved and cher
　　　ished
　　　Has with thy summer roses per
　　　　ished ;
　And left, as its young beauty fled,
　　An ashen memory in its stead, —
The twilight of a parted day
　　Whose fading light is cold and vain
　　The heart's faint echo of a strain
　Of low, sweet music passed away.
That true and loving heart, — that gift
　Of a mind, earnest, clear, profound,
Bestowing, with a glad unthrift,
　Its sunny light on all around,
Affinities which only could
Cleave to the pure, the true, and good ;
　And sympathies which found no rest,
　Save with the loveliest and best.
Of them — of thee — remains there
　　naught
　But sorrow in the mourner's breast ? —
A shadow in the land of thought ?
No ! — Even _my_ weak and trembling
　　faith
　Can lift for thee the veil which doubt
　And human fear have drawn about
The all-awaiting scene of death.

Even as thou wast I see thee still ;
And, save the absence of all ill
And pain and weariness, which here
Summoned the sigh or wrung the tear,
The same as when, two summers back,
Beside our childhood's Merrimack,
I saw thy dark eye wander o'er

Stream, sunny upland, rocky shore,
And heard thy low, soft voice alone
Midst lapse of waters, and the tone
Of pine-leaves by the west-wind blown,
There 's not a charm of soul or brow, —
　Of all we knew and loved in thee, —
But lives in holier beauty now,
　Baptized in immortality !
Not mine the sad and freezing dream
　Of souls that, with their earthly mould,
　Cast off the loves and joys of old, —
Unbodied, — like a pale moonbeam,
　As pure, as passionless, and cold ;
Nor mine the hope of Indra's son,
　Of slumbering in oblivion's rest,
Life's myriads blending into one, —
　In blank annihilation blest ;
Dust-atoms of the infinite, —
Sparks scattered from the central light,
And winning back through mortal pain
Their old unconsciousness again.
No ! — I have FRIENDS in Spirit Land, —
Not shadows in a shadowy band,
　Not *others*, but *themselves* are they.
And still I think of them the same
As when the Master's summons came ;
Their change, — the holy morn-light
　breaking
Upon the dream-worn sleeper, waking,—
　A change from twilight into day.

They 've laid thee midst the household
　graves,
　Where father, brother, sister lie ;
Below thee sweep the dark blue waves,
　Above thee bends the summer sky.
Thy own loved church in sadness read
Her solemn ritual o'er thy head,
And blessed and hallowed with her
　prayer
The turf laid lightly o'er thee there.
That church, whose rites and liturgy,
Sublime and old, were truth to thee,
Undoubted to thy bosom taken,
As symbols of a faith unshaken.
Even I, of simpler views, could feel
The beauty of thy trust and zeal ;
And, owning not thy creed, could see
How deep a truth it seemed to thee,
And how thy fervent heart had thrown
O er all, a coloring of its own,
And kindled up, intense and warm,
A life in every rite and form,
As, when on Chebar's banks of old,
The Hebrew's gorgeous vision rolled,
A spirit filled the vast machine, —
A life " within the wheels " was seen.

Farewell !   A little time, and we
　Who knew thee well, and loved thee
　　here,
One after one shall follow thee
　As pilgrims through the gate of fear,
Which opens on eternity.
Yet shall we cherish not the less
　All that is left our hearts meanwhile ;
The memory of thy loveliness
　Shall round our weary pathway smile,
Like moonlight when the sun has set, —
A sweet and tender radiance yet.
Thoughts of thy clear-eyed sense of
　duty,
　Thy generous scorn of all things
　　wrong, —
The truth, the strength, the graceful
　beauty
　Which blended in thy song.
All lovely things, by thee beloved,
　Shall whisper to our hearts of thee ;
These green hills, where thy childhood
　roved, —
Yon river winding to the sea, —
The sunset light of autumn eves
　Reflecting on the deep, still floods,
Cloud, crimson sky, and trembling
　leaves
　Of rainbow-tinted woods, —
These, in our view, shall henceforth take
A tenderer meaning for thy sake ;
And all thou lovedst of earth and sky,
Seem sacred to thy memory.

CHANNING.[44]

Not vainly did old poets tell,
　Nor vainly did old genius paint
God's great and crowning miracle, —
　The hero and the saint !

For even in a faithless day
　Can we our sainted ones discern ;
And feel, while with them on the way,
　Our hearts within us burn.

And thus the common tongue and pen
　Which, world-wide, echo CHANNING's
　　fame,
As one of Heaven's anointed men,
　Have sanctified his name.

In vain shall Rome her portals bar,
　And shut from him her saintly prize,
Whom, in the world's great calendar,
　All men shall canonize.

By Narragansett's sunny bay,
  Beneath his green embowering wood,
To me it seems but yesterday
  Since at his side I stood.

The slopes lay green with summer rains,
  The western wind blew fresh and
    free,
And glimmered down the orchard lanes
  The white surf of the sea.

With us was one, who, calm and true,
  Life's highest purpose understood,
And, like his blessed Master, knew
  The joy of doing good.

Unlearned, unknown to lettered fame,
  Yet on the lips of England's poor
And toiling millions dwelt his name,
  With blessings evermore.

Unknown to power or place, yet where
  The sun looks o'er the Carib sea,
It blended with the freeman's prayer
  And song of jubilee.

He told of England's sin and wrong, —
  The ills her suffering children know, —
The squalor of the city's throng, —
  The green field's want and woe.

O'er Channing's face the tenderness
  Of sympathetic sorrow stole,
Like a still shadow, passionless, —
  The sorrow of the soul.

But when the generous Briton told
  How hearts were answering to his
    own,
And Freedom's rising murmur rolled
  Up to the dull-eared throne,

I saw, methought, a glad surprise
  Thrill through that frail and pain-
    worn frame,
And, kindling in those deep, calm eyes,
  A still and earnest flame.

His few, brief words were such as move
  The human heart, — the Faith-sown
    seeds
Which ripen in the soil of love
  To high heroic deeds.

No bars of sect or clime were felt, —
  The Babel strife of tongues had
    ceased, —

And at one common altar knelt
  The Quaker and the priest.

And not in vain : with strength renewed,
  And zeal refreshed, and hope less dim,
For that brief meeting, each pursued
  The path allotted him.

How echoes yet each Western hill
  And vale with Channing's dying
    word !
How are the hearts of freemen still
  By that great warning stirred !

The stranger treads his native soil,
  And pleads, with zeal unfelt before
The honest right of British toil,
  The claim of England's poor.

Before him time-wrought barriers fall,
  Old fears subside, old hatreds melt,
And, stretching o'er the sea's blue wall,
  The Saxon greets the Celt.

The yeoman on the Scottish lines,
  The Sheffield grinder, worn and grim,
The delver in the Cornwall mines,
  Look up with hope to him.

Swart smiters of the glowing steel,
  Dark feeders of the forge's flame,
Pale watchers at the loom and wheel,
  Repeat his honored name.

And thus the influence of that hour
  Of converse on Rhode Island's strand
Lives in the calm, resistless power
  Which moves our father-land.

God blesses still the generous thought.
  And still the fitting word He speeds
And Truth, at his requiring taught,
  He quickens into deeds.

Where is the victory of the grave ?
  What dust upon the spirit lies ?
God keeps the sacred life he gave, —
  The prophet never dies !

TO THE MEMORY OF

CHARLES B. STORRS,

LATE PRESIDENT OF WESTERN RESERVE
COLLEGE.

Thou hast fallen in thine armor,
  Thou martyr of the Lord !

With thy last breath crying, — "On-
      ward ! "
  And thy hand upon the sword.
The haughty heart derideth,
  And the sinful lip reviles,
But the blessing of the perishing
  Around thy pillow smiles !

When to our cup of trembling
  The added drop is given,
And the long-suspended thunder
  Falls terribly from Heaven, —
When a new and fearful freedom
  Is proffered of the Lord
To the slow-consuming Famine, —
  The Pestilence and Sword ! —

When the refuges of Falsehood
  Shall be swept away in wrath,
And the temple shall be shaken,
  With its idol, to the earth, —
Shall not thy words of warning
  Be all remembered then ?
And thy now unheeded message
  Burn in the hearts of men ?

Oppression's hand may scatter
  Its nettles on thy tomb,
And even Christian bosoms
  Deny thy memory room ;
For lying lips shall torture
  Thy mercy into crime,
And the slanderer shall flourish
  As the bay-tree for a time.

But where the south-wind lingers
  On Carolina's pines,
Or falls the careless sunbeam
  Down Georgia's golden mines, —
Where now beneath his burthen
  The toiling slave is driven, —
Where now a tyrant's mockery
  Is offered unto Heaven, —

Where Mammon hath its altars
  Wet o'er with human blood,
And pride and lust debases
  The workmanship of God, —
There shall thy praise be spoken,
  Redeemed from Falsehood's ban,
When the fetters shall be broken,
  And the *slave* shall be a *man !*

Joy to thy spirit, brother !
  A thousand hearts are warm, —
A thousand kindred bosoms
  Are baring to the storm.

What though red-handed Violence
  With secret Fraud combine ?
The wall of fire is round us, —
  Our Present Help was thine.

Lo, — the waking up of nations,
  From Slavery's fatal sleep, —
The murmur of a Universe, —
  Deep calling unto Deep !
Joy to thy spirit, brother !
  On every wind of heaven
The onward cheer and summons
  Of FREEDOM'S VOICE is given !

Glory to God forever !
  Beyond the despot's will
The soul of Freedom liveth
  Imperishable still.
The words which thou hast uttered
  Are of that soul a part,
And the good seed thou hast scattered
  Is springing from the heart.

In the evil days before us,
  And the trials yet to come, —
In the shadow of the prison,
  Or the cruel martyrdom, —
We will think of thee, O brother !
  And thy sainted name shall be
In the blessing of the captive,
  And the anthem of the free.
1834.

LINES,

ON THE DEATH OF S. O. TORREY.

GONE before us, O our brother,
  To the spirit-land !
Vainly look we for another
  In thy place to stand.
Who shall offer youth and beauty
  On the wasting shrine
Of a stern and lofty duty,
  With a faith like thine ?

O, thy gentle smile of greeting
  Who again shall see ?
Who amidst the solemn meeting
  Gaze again on thee ? —
Who, when peril gathers o'er us,
  Wear so calm a brow ?
Who, with evil men before us,
  So serene as thou ?

Early hath the spoiler found thee,
  Brother of our love !

Autumn's faded earth around thee,
  And its storms above !
Evermore that turf lie lightly,
  And, with future showers,
O'er thy slumbers fresh and brightly
  Blow the summer flowers !

In the locks thy forehead gracing,
  Not a silvery streak ;
Nor a line of sorrow's tracing
  On thy fair young cheek ;
Eyes of light and lips of roses,
  Such as Hylas wore, —
Over all that curtain closes,
  Which shall rise no more !

Will the vigil Love is keeping
  Round that grave of thine,
Mournfully, like Jazer weeping
  Over Sibmah's vine,[45] —
Will the pleasant memories, swelling
  Gentle hearts, of thee,
In the spirit's distant dwelling
  All unheeded be ?

If the spirit ever gazes,
  From its journeyings, back ;
If the immortal ever traces
  O'er its mortal track ;
Wilt thou not, O brother, meet us
  Sometimes on our way,
And, in hours of sadness, greet us
  As a spirit may ?

Peace be with thee, O our brother,
  In the spirit-land !
Vainly look we for another
  In thy place to stand.
Unto Truth and Freedom giving
  All thy early powers,
Be thy virtues with the living,
  And thy spirit ours !

A LAMENT.

          " The parted spirit,
Knoweth it not our sorrow ? Answereth not
Its blessing to our tears ? "

THE circle is broken, — one seat is for-
    saken, —
One bud from the tree of our friendship
    is shaken, —
One heart from among us no longer
    shall thrill
With joy in our gladness, or grief in our
    ill,

Weep ! — lonely and lowly are slumber-
    ing now
The light of her glances, the pride of her
    brow,
Weep ! — sadly and long shall we listen
    in vain
To hear the soft tones of her welcome
    again.

Give our tears to the dead ! For human-
    ity's claim
From its silence and darkness is ever the
    same ;
The hope of that World whose existence
    is bliss
May not stifle the tears of the mourners
    of this.

For, oh ! if one glance the freed spirit
    can throw
On the scene of its troubled probation
    below,
Than the pride of the marble, the pomp
    of the dead,
To that glance will be dearer the tears
    which we shed.

O, who can forget the mild light of her
    smile,
Over lips moved with music and feeling
    the while —
The eye's deep enchantment, dark,
    dream-like, and clear,
In the glow of its gladness, the shade of
    its tear.

And the charm of her features, while
    over the whole
Played the hues of the heart and the
    sunshine of soul, —
And the tones of her voice, like the mu-
    sic which seems
Murmured low in our ears by the Angel
    of dreams !

But holier and dearer our memories hold
Those treasures of feeling, more precious
    than gold, —
The love and the kindness and pity
    which gave
Fresh flowers for the bridal, green
    wreaths for the grave !

The heart ever open to Charity's claim,
Unmoved from its purpose by censure
    and blame,

While vainly alike on her eye and her
    ear
Fell the scorn of the heartless, the jest-
    ing and jeer.

How true to our hearts was that beauti-
    ful sleeper !
With smiles for the joyful, with tears
    for the weeper ! —
Yet, evermore prompt, whether mourn-
    ful or gay,
With warnings in love to the passing
    astray.

For, though spotless herself, she could
    sorrow for them
Who sullied with evil the spirit's pure
    gem ;
And a sigh or a tear could the erring re-
    prove,
And the sting of reproof was still tem-
    pered by love.

As a cloud of the sunset, slow melting
    in heaven,
As a star that is lost when the daylight
    is given,
As a glad dream of slumber, which
    wakens in bliss,
She hath passed to the world of the
    holy from this.

DANIEL WHEELER.

[DANIEL WHEELER, a minister of the Society of
Friends, and who had labored in the cause of his
Divine Master in Great Britain, Russia, and the
islands of the Pacific, died in New York in the
spring of 1840, while on a religious visit to this
country.]

O DEARLY loved !
And worthy of our love ! — No more
Thy aged form shall rise before
The hushed and waiting worshipper,
In meek obedience utterance giving
To words of truth, so fresh and living,
That, even to the inward sense,
They bore unquestioned evidence
Of an anointed Messenger !
Or, bowing down thy silver hair
In reverent awfulness of prayer, —
    The world, its time and sense, shut
      out, —
The brightness of Faith's holy trance
Gathered upon thy countenance,
    As if each lingering cloud of doubt, —
The cold, dark shadows resting here

In Time's unluminous atmosphere, —
    Were lifted by an angel's hand,
And through them on thy spiritual eye
Shone down the blessedness on high,
    The glory of the Better Land !

    The oak has fallen !
While, meet for no good work, the vine
May yet its worthless branches twine.
Who knoweth not that with thee fell
A great man in our Israel ?
Fallen, while thy loins were girded still,
    Thy feet with Zion's dews still wet,
    And in thy hand retaining yet
The pilgrim's staff and scallop-shell !
Unharmed and safe, where, wild and
    free,
    Across the Neva's cold morass
The breezes from the Frozen Sea
    With winter's arrowy keenness pass ;
Or where the unwarning tropic gale
Smote to the waves thy tattered sail,
Or where the noon-hour's fervid heat
Against Tahiti's mountains beat ;
    The same mysterious Hand which
      gave
    Deliverance upon land and wave,
Tempered for thee the blasts which
    blew
    Ladaga's frozen surface o'er,
And blessed for thee the baleful dew
    Of evening upon Eimeo's shore,
Beneath this sunny heaven of ours,
Midst our soft airs and opening flowers
    Hath given thee a grave !

    His will be done,
Who seeth not as man, whose way
    Is not as ours ! — 'T is well with
      thee !
Nor anxious doubt nor dark dismay
Disquieted thy closing day,
But, evermore, thy soul could say,
    " My Father careth still for me ! "
Called from thy hearth and home, —
    from her,
    The last bud on thy household tree,
    The last dear one to minister
    In duty and in love to thee,
From all which nature holdeth dear,
    Feeble with years and worn with
      pain,
    To seek our distant land again,
Bound in the spirit, yet unknowing
    The things which should befall thee
      here,
    Whether for labor or for death.

In childlike trust serenely going
  To that last trial of thy faith !

    O, far away,
Where never shines our Northern star
  On that dark waste which Balboa saw
From Darien's mountains stretching far,
So strange, heaven-broad, and lone, that
    there,
With forehead to its damp wind bare,
  He bent his mailed knee in awe ;
In many an isle whose coral feet
  The surges of that ocean beat,
In thy palm shadows, Oahu,
  And Honolulu's silver bay,
Amidst Owyhee's hills of blue,
  And taro-plains of Tooboonai,
Are gentle hearts, which long shall be
Sad as our own at thought of thee, —
Worn sowers of Truth's holy seed,
Whose souls in weariness and need
  Were strengthened and refreshed by
    thine.
For blessed by our Father's hand
  Was thy deep love and tender care,
  Thy ministry and fervent prayer, —
Grateful as Eschol's clustered vine
To Israel in a weary land !

    And they who drew
By thousands round thee, in the hour
  Of prayerful waiting, hushed and
    deep,
  That He who bade the islands keep
Silence before him, might renew
  Their strength with his unslumbering
    power,
They too shall mourn that thou art gone,
  That nevermore thy aged lip
Shall soothe the weak, the erring warn,
Of those who first, rejoicing, heard
Through thee the Gospel's glorious
    word, —
  Seals of thy true apostleship.
And, if the brightest diadem,
  Whose gems of glory purely burn
  Around the ransomed ones in bliss,
Be evermore reserved for them
  Who here, through toil and sorrow,
    turn
  Many to righteousness, —
May we not think of thee as wearing
That star-like crown of light, and bear-
    ing,
Amidst Heaven's white and blissful
    band,
The fadeless palm-branch in thy hand ;

And joining with a seraph's tongue
In that new song the elders sung,
Ascribing to its blessed Giver
Thanksgiving, love, and praise forever !

    Farewell !
And though the ways of Zion mourn
When her strong ones are called away,
Who like thyself have calmly borne
The heat and burden of the day,
Yet He who slumbereth not nor sleep-
    eth
His ancient watch around us keepeth ;
Still, sent from his creating hand,
New witnesses for Truth shall stand, —
New instruments to sound abroad
The Gospel of a risen Lord ;
  To gather to the fold once more
The desolate and gone astray,
The scattered of a cloudy day,
  And Zion's broken walls restore ;
And, through the travail and the toil
  Of true obedience, minister
Beauty for ashes, and the oil
  Of joy for mourning, unto her !
So shall her holy bounds increase
With walls of praise and gates of peace :
So shall the Vine, which martyr tears
And blood sustained in other years,
  With fresher life be clothed upon ;
And to the world in beauty show
Like the rose-plant of Jericho,
  And glorious as Lebanon !

DANIEL NEALL.

I.

FRIEND of the Slave, and yet the friend
  of all ;
  Lover of peace, yet ever foremost when
  The need of battling Freedom called
    for men
To plant the banner on the outer wall ;
Gentle and kindly, ever at distress
Melted to more than woman's tender-
    ness,
Yet firm and steadfast, at his duty's post
Fronting the violence of a maddened
    host,
Like some gray rock from which the
    waves are tossed !
Knowing his deeds of love, men ques-
    tioned not
  The faith of one whose walk and word
    were right, —

Who tranquilly in Life's great task-
 field wrought,
And, side by side with evil, scarcely
 caught
 A stain upon his pilgrim garb of white :
Prompt to redress another's wrong, his
 own
Leaving to Time and Truth and Penitence alone.

II.

Such was our friend. Formed on the
 good old plan,
A true and brave and downright honest
 man ! —
He blew no trumpet in the market-place,
Nor in the church with hypocritic face
Supplied with cant the lack of Christian
 grace ;
Loathing pretence, he did with cheerful
 will
What others talked of while their hands
 were still ;
And, while " Lord, Lord ! " the pious
 tyrants cried,
Who, in the poor, their Master crucified,
His daily prayer, far better understood
In acts than words, was simply DOING
 GOOD.
So calm, so constant was his rectitude,
That by his loss alone we know its
 worth,
And feel how true a man has walked with
 us on earth.

6th 6th month, 1846.

TO MY FRIEND ON THE DEATH OF HIS SISTER.[46]

THINE is a grief, the depth of which
 another
  May never know ;
Yet, o'er the waters, O my stricken
 brother !
  To thee I go.

I lean my heart unto thee, sadly folding
  Thy hand in mine ;
With even the weakness of my soul up-
 holding
  The strength of thine.

I never knew, like thee, the dear departed ;
  I stood not by

When, in calm trust, the pure and tran-
 quil-hearted
  Lay down to die.

And on thy ears my words of weak con-
 doling
  Must vainly fall :
The funeral bell which in thy heart is
 tolling,
  Sounds over all !

I will not mock thee with the poor
 world's common
  And heartless phrase,
Nor wrong the memory of a sainted
 woman
  With idle praise.

With silence only as their benediction,
  God's angels come
Where, in the shadow of a great afflic-
 tion,
  The soul sits dumb !

Yet, would I say what thy own heart
 approveth :
  Our Father's will,
Calling to Him the dear one whom He
 loveth,
  Is mercy still.

Not upon thee or thine the solemn an-
 gel
  Hath evil wrought :
Her funeral anthem is a glad evangel, —
  The good die not !

God calls our loved ones, but we lose
 not wholly
  What He hath given ;
They live on earth, in thought and
 deed, as truly
  As in his heaven.

And she is with thee ; in thy path of
 trial
  She walketh yet ;
Still with the baptism of thy self-denial
  Her locks are wet.

Up, then, my brother ! Lo, the fields
 of harvest
  Lie white in view !
She lives and loves thee, and the God
 thou servest
  To both is true.

Thrust in thy sickle ! — England's toil-
worn peasants
Thy call abide ;
And she thou mourn'st, a pure and holy
presence,
Shall glean beside !

GONE.

ANOTHER hand is beckoning us,
Another call is given ;
And glows once more with Angel-steps
The path which reaches Heaven.

Our young and gentle friend, whose
smile
Made brighter summer hours,
Amid the frosts of autumn time
Has left us with the flowers.

No paling of the cheek of bloom
Forewarned us of decay ;
No shadow from the Silent Land
Fell round our sister's way.

The light of her young life went down,
As sinks behind the hill
The glory of a setting star, —
Clear, suddenly, and still.

As pure and sweet, her fair brow seemed
Eternal as the sky ;
And like the brook's low song, her
voice, —
A sound which could not die.

And half we deemed she needed not
The changing of her sphere,
To give to Heaven a Shining One,
Who walked an Angel here.

The blessing of her quiet life
Fell on us like the dew ;
And good thoughts, where her footsteps
pressed
Like fairy blossoms grew.

Sweet promptings unto kindest deeds
Were in her very look ;
We read her face, as one who reads
A true and holy book:

The measure of a blessed hymn,
To which our hearts could move ;
The breathing of an inward psalm ;
A canticle of love.

We miss her in the place of prayer,
And by the hearth-fire's light ;
We pause beside her door to hear
Once more her sweet " Good-night !"

There seems a shadow on the day,
Her smile no longer cheers ;
A dimness on the stars of night,
Like eyes that look through tears.

Alone unto our Father's will
One thought hath reconciled ;
That He whose love exceedeth ours
Hath taken home his child.

Fold her, O Father ! in thine arms,
And let her henceforth be
A messenger of love between
Our human hearts and thee.

Still let her mild rebuking stand
Between us and the wrong,
And her dear memory serve to make
Our faith in Goodness strong.

And grant that she who, trembling, here
Distrusted all her powers,
May welcome to her holier home
The well-beloved of ours.

THE LAKE-SIDE.

THE shadows round the inland sea
Are deepening into night ;
Slow up the slopes of Ossipee
They chase the lessening light.
Tired of the long day's blinding heat,
I rest my languid eye,
Lake of the Hills ! where, cool and
sweet,
Thy sunset waters lie !

Along the sky, in wavy lines,
O'er isle and reach and bay,
Green-belted with eternal pines,
The mountains stretch away.
Below, the maple masses sleep
Where shore with water blends,
While midway on the tranquil deep
The evening light descends.

So seemed it when yon hill's red crown,
Of old, the Indian trod,
And, through the sunset air, looked
down
Upon the Smile of God.[47]

To him of light and shade the laws
  No forest sceptic taught ;
Their living and eternal Cause
  His truer instinct sought.

He saw these mountains in the light
  Which now across them shines ;
This lake, in summer sunset bright,
  Walled round with sombering pines.
God near him seemed ; from earth and
    skies
  His loving voice he heard,
As, face to face, in Paradise,
  Man stood before the Lord.

Thanks, O our Father ! that, like him,
  Thy tender love I see,
In radiant hill and woodland dim,
  And tinted sunset sea.
For not in mockery dost thou fill
  Our earth with light and grace ;
Thou hid'st no dark and cruel will
  Behind thy smiling face !

THE HILL-TOP.

THE burly driver at my side,
  We slowly climbed the hill,
Whose summit, in the hot noontide,
  Seemed rising, rising still.
At last, our short noon-shadows hid
  The top-stone, bare and brown,
From whence, like Gizeh's pyramid,
  The rough mass slanted down.

I felt the cool breath of the North ;
  Between me and the sun,
O'er deep, still lake, and ridgy earth,
  I saw the cloud-shades run.
Before me, stretched for glistening miles,
  Lay mountain-girdled Squam ;
Like green-winged birds, the leafy isles
  Upon its bosom swam.

And, glimmering through the sun-haze
    warm,
  Far as the eye could roam,
Dark billows of an earthquake storm
  Beflecked with clouds like foam,
Their vales in misty shadow deep,
  Their rugged peaks in shine,
I saw the mountain ranges sweep
  The horizon's northern line.

There towered Chocorua's peak ; and
    west,
  Moosehillock's woods were seen,

With many a nameless slide-scarred
    crest
  And pine-dark gorge between.
Beyond them, like a sun-rimmed cloud,
  The great Notch mountains shone,
Watched over by the solemn-browed
  And awful face of stone !

" A good look-off ! " the driver spake :
  " About this time, last year,
I drove a party to the Lake,
  And stopped, at evening, here.
'T was duskish down below ; but all
  These hills stood in the sun,
Till, dipped behind yon purple wall,
  He left them, one by one.

" A lady, who, from Thornton hill,
  Had held her place outside,
And, as a pleasant woman will,
  Had cheered the long, dull ride,
Besought me, with so sweet a smile,
  That — though I hate delays —
I could not choose but rest awhile, —
  (These women have such ways !)

" On yonder mossy ledge she sat,
  Her sketch upon her knees,
A stray brown lock beneath her hat
  Unrolling in the breeze ;
Her sweet face, in the sunset light
  Upraised and glorified, —
I never saw a prettier sight
  In all my mountain ride.

" As good as fair ; it seemed her joy
  To comfort and to give ;
My poor, sick wife, and cripple boy,
  Will bless her while they live ! "
The tremor in the driver's tone
  His manhood did not shame :
"I dare say, sir, you may have known—"
  He named a well-known name.

Then sank the pyramidal mounds,
  The blue lake fled away ;
For mountain-scope a parlor's bounds,
  A lighted hearth for day !
From lonely years and weary miles
  The shadows fell apart ;
Kind   voices cheered, sweet human
    smiles
  Shone warm into my heart.

We journeyed on ; but earth and sky
  Had power to charm no more ;
Still dreamed my inward-turning eye
  The dream of memory o'er.

Ah ! human kindness, human love, —
  To few who seek denied, —
Too late we learn to prize above
  The whole round world beside !

ON RECEIVING AN EAGLE'S QUILL FROM LAKE SUPERIOR.

ALL day the darkness and the cold
  Upon my heart have lain,
Like shadows on the winter sky,
  Like frost upon the pane ;

But now my torpid fancy wakes,
  And, on thy Eagle's plume,
Rides forth, like Sindbad on his bird,
  Or witch upon her broom !

Below me roar the rocking pines,
  Before me spreads the lake
Whose long and solemn-sounding waves
  Against the sunset break.

I hear the wild Rice-Eater thresh
  The grain he has not sown ;
I see, with flashing scythe of fire,
  The prairie harvest mown !

I hear the far-off voyager's horn ;
  I see the Yankee's trail, —
His foot on every mountain-pass,
  On every stream his sail.

By forest, lake, and waterfall,
  I see his pedler show ;
The mighty mingling with the mean,
  The lofty with the low.

He 's whittling by St. Mary's Falls,
  Upon his loaded wain ;
He 's measuring o'er the Pictured Rocks,
  With eager eyes of gain.

I hear the mattock in the mine,
  The axe-stroke in the dell,
The clamor from the Indian lodge,
  The Jesuit chapel bell !

I see the swarthy trappers come
  From Mississippi's springs ;
And war-chiefs with their painted brows,
  And crests of eagle wings.

Behind the scared squaw's birch canoe,
  The steamer smokes and raves ;
And city lots are staked for sale
  Above old Indian graves.

I hear the tread of pioneers
  Of nations yet to be ;
The first low wash of waves, where soon
  Shall roll a human sea.

The rudiments of empire here
  Are plastic yet and warm ;
The chaos of a mighty world
  Is rounding into form !

Each rude and jostling fragment soon
  Its fitting place shall find, —
The raw material of a State,
  Its muscle and its mind !

And, westering still, the star which leads
  The New World in its train
Has tipped with fire the icy spears
  Of many a mountain chain.

The snowy cones of Oregon
  Are kindling on its way ;
And California's golden sands
  Gleam brighter in its ray !

Then blessings on thy eagle quill,
  As, wandering far and wide,
I thank thee for this twilight dream
  And Fancy's airy ride !

Yet, welcomer than regal plumes,
  Which Western trappers find,
Thy free and pleasant thoughts, chance
    sown,
  Like feathers on the wind.

Thy symbol be the mountain-bird,
  Whose glistening quill I hold ;
Thy home the ample air of hope,
  And memory's sunset gold !

In thee, let joy with duty join,
  And strength unite with love,
The eagle's pinions folding round
  The warm heart of the dove !

So, when in darkness sleeps the vale
  Where still the blind bird clings,
The sunshine of the upper sky
  Shall glitter on thy wings !

MEMORIES.

A BEAUTIFUL and happy girl,
  With step as light as summer air,
Eyes glad with smiles, and brow of pearl,
Shadowed by many a careless curl
  Of unconfined and flowing hair ;

A seeming child in everything,
 Save thoughtful brow and ripening
  charms,
As Nature wears the smile of Spring
 When sinking into Summer's arms.

A mind rejoicing in the light
 Which melted through its graceful
  bower,
Leaf after leaf, dew-moist and bright,
And stainless in its holy white,
 Unfolding like a morning flower :
A heart, which, like a fine-toned lute,
 With every breath of feeling woke,
And, even when the tongue was mute,
 From eye and lip in music spoke.

How thrills once more the lengthening
  chain
Of memory, at the thought of thee !
Old hopes which long in dust have lain
Old dreams, come thronging back again,
 And boyhood lives again in me ;
I feel its glow upon my cheek,
 Its fulness of the heart is mine,
As when I leaned to hear thee speak,
 Or raised my doubtful eye to thine.

I hear again thy low replies,
 I feel thy arm within my own,
And timidly again uprise
The fringéd lids of hazel eyes,
 With soft brown tresses overblown.
Ah ! memories of sweet summer eves,
 Of moonlit wave and willowy way,
Of stars and flowers, and dewy leaves,
 And smiles and tones more dear than
  they !

Ere this, thy quiet eye hath smiled
 My picture of thy youth to see,
When, half a woman, half a child,
 Thy very artlessness beguiled,
 And folly's self seemed wise in thee ;
I too can smile, when o'er that hour
 The lights of memory backward stream,
Yet feel the while that manhood's power
 Is vainer than my boyhood's dream.

Years have passed on, and left their trace,
 Of graver care and deeper thought ;
And unto me the calm, cold face
Of manhood, and to thee the grace
Of woman's pensive beauty brought.
More wide, perchance, for blame than
  praise,
 The school-boy's humble name has
  flown ;

Thine, in the green and quiet ways
 Of unobtrusive goodness known.

And wider yet in thought and deed
 Diverge our pathways, one in youth;
Thine the Genevan's sternest creed,
While answers to my spirit's need
 The Derby dalesman's simple truth.
For thee, the priestly rite and prayer,
 And holy day, and solemn psalm;
For me, the silent reverence where
 My brethren gather, slow and calm.

Yet hath thy spirit left on me
 An impress Time has worn not out,
And something of myself in thee,
A shadow from the past, I see,
 Lingering, even yet, thy way about ;
Not wholly can the heart unlearn
 That lesson of its better hours,
Not yet has Time's dull footstep worn
 To common dust that path of flowers.

Thus, while at times before our eyes
 The shadows melt, and fall apart,
And, smiling through them, round us
  lies
The warm light of our morning skies, —
 The Indian Summer of the heart ! —
In secret sympathies of mind,
 In founts of feeling which retain
Their pure, fresh flow, we yet may
  find
 Our early dreams not wholly vain !

THE LEGEND OF ST. MARK.[48]

The day is closing dark and cold,
 With roaring blast and sleety showers ;
And through the dusk the lilacs wear
 The bloom of snow, instead of flowers.

I turn me from the gloom without,
 To ponder o'er a tale of old,
A legend of the age of Faith,
 By dreaming monk or abbess told.

On Tintoretto's canvas lives
 That fancy of a loving heart,
In graceful lines and shapes of power,
 And hues immortal as his art.

In Provence (so the story runs)
 There lived a lord, to whom, as slave,
A peasant-boy of tender years
 The chance of trade or conquest gave.

Forth-looking from the castle tower,
  Beyond the hills with almonds dark,
The straining eye could scarce discern
  The chapel of the good St. Mark.

And there, when bitter word or fare
  The service of the youth repaid,
By stealth, before that holy shrine,
  For grace to bear his wrong, he prayed.

The steed stamped at the castle gate,
  The boar-hunt sounded on the hill;
Why stayed the Baron from the chase,
  With looks so stern, and words so
      ill ?

" Go, bind yon slave ! and let him learn,
  By scath of fire and strain of cord,
How ill they speed who give dead saints
  The homage due their living lord ! "

They bound him on the fearful rack,
  When, through the dungeon's vaulted
      dark,
He saw the light of shining robes,
  And knew the face of good St. Mark.

Then sank the iron rack apart,
  The cords released their cruel clasp,
The pincers, with their teeth of fire,
  Fell broken from the torturer's grasp.

And lo ! before the Youth and Saint,
  Barred door and wall of stone gave way ;
And up from bondage and the night
  They passed to freedom and the
      day !

O dreaming monk ! thy tale is true ; —
  O painter ! true thy pencil's art ;
In tones of hope and prophecy,
  Ye whisper to my listening heart !

Unheard no burdened heart's appeal
  Moans up to God's inclining ear ;
Unheeded by his tender eye,
  Falls to the earth no sufferer's tear.

For still the Lord alone is God !
  The pomp and power of tyrant man
Are scattered at his lightest breath,
  Like chaff before the winnower's fan.

Not always shall the slave uplift
  His heavy hands to Heaven in vain.
God's angel, like the good St. Mark,
  Comes shining down to break his chain !

O weary ones ! ye may not see
  Your helpers in their downward flight ;
Nor hear the sound of silver wings
  Slow beating through the hush of night !

But not the less gray Dothan shone,
  With sunbright watchers bending low,
That Fear's dim eye beheld alone
  The spear-heads of the Syrian foe.

There are, who, like the Seer of old,
  Can see the helpers God has sent,
And how life's rugged mountain-side
  Is white with many an angel tent !

They hear the heralds whom our Lord
  Sends down his pathway to prepare ;
And light, from others hidden, shines
  On their high place of faith and prayer.

Let such, for earth's despairing ones,
  Hopeless, yet longing to be free,
Breathe once again the Prophet's prayer :
  " Lord, ope their eyes, that they may
      see ! "

THE WELL OF LOCH MAREE.[49]

CALM on the breast of Loch Maree
  A little isle reposes ;
A shadow woven of the oak
  And willow o'er it closes.

Within, a Druid's mound is seen,
  Set round with stony warders ;
A fountain, gushing through the turf,
  Flows o'er its grassy borders.

And whoso bathes therein his brow,
  With care or madness burning,
Feels once again his healthful thought
  And sense of peace returning.

O restless heart and fevered brain,
  Unquiet and unstable,
That holy well of Loch Maree
  Is more than idle fable !

Life's changes vex, its discords stun,
  Its glaring sunshine blindeth,
And blest is he who on his way
  That fount of healing findeth !

The shadows of a humbled will
  And contrite heart are o'er it ;
Go read its legend — " TRUST IN GOD "
  On Faith's white stones before it.

TO MY SISTER;

WITH A COPY OF " SUPERNATURALISM
OF NEW ENGLAND."

DEAR SISTER ! — while the wise and sage
Turn coldly from my playful page,
And count it strange that ripened age
  Should stoop to boyhood's folly ;
I know that thou wilt judge aright
Of all which makes the heart more light,
Or lends one star-gleam to the night
  Of clouded Melancholy.

Away with weary cares and themes ! —
Swing wide the moonlit gate of dreams !
Leave free once more the land which teems
  With wonders and romances !
Where thou, with clear discerning eyes,
Shalt rightly read the truth which lies
Beneath the quaintly masking guise
  Of wild and wizard fancies.

Lo ! once again our feet we set
On still green wood-paths, twilight wet,
By lonely brooks, whose waters fret
  The roots of spectral beeches ;
Again the hearth-fire glimmers o'er
Home's whitewashed wall and painted
  floor,
And young eyes widening to the lore
  Of faery-folks and witches.

Dear heart ! — the legend is not vain
Which lights that holy hearth again,
And calling back from care and pain,
  And death's funereal sadness,
Draws round its old familiar blaze
The clustering groups of happier days,
And lends to sober manhood's gaze
  A glimpse of childish gladness.

And, knowing how my life hath been
A weary work of tongue and pen,
A long, harsh strife with strong-willed
  men,
  Thou wilt not chide my turning
To con, at times, an idle rhyme,
To pluck a flower from childhood's clime,
Or listen, at Life's noonday chime,
  For the sweet bells of Morning !

AUTUMN THOUGHTS.

FROM " MARGARET SMITH'S JOURNAL."

GONE hath the Spring, with all its flowers,
  And gone the Summer's pomp and show,

And Autumn, in his leafless bowers,
  Is waiting for the Winter's snow.

I said to Earth, so cold and gray,
  " An emblem of myself thou art " ;
" Not so," the Earth did seem to say,
  " For Spring shall warm my frozen
    heart."

I soothe my wintry sleep with dreams
  Of warmer sun and softer rain,
And wait to hear the sound of streams
  And songs of merry birds again.

But thou, from whom the Spring hath
  gone,
  For whom the flowers no longer blow,
Who standest blighted and forlorn,
  Like Autumn waiting for the snow :

No hope is thine of sunnier hours,
  Thy Winter shall no more depart ;
No Spring revive thy wasted flowers,
  Nor Summer warm thy frozen heart.

CALEF IN BOSTON.

1692.

IN the solemn days of old,
  Two men met in Boston town,
One a tradesman frank and bold,
  One a preacher of renown.

Cried the last, in bitter tone, —
  " Poisoner of the wells of truth !
Satan's hireling, thou hast sown
  With his tares the heart of youth ! "

Spake the simple tradesman then, —
  " God be judge 'twixt thou and I ;
All thou knowest of truth hath been
  Unto men like thee a lie.

" Falsehoods which we spurn to-day
  Were the truths of long ago ;
Let the dead boughs fall away,
  Fresher shall the living grow.

" God is good and God is light,
  In this faith I rest secure ;
Evil can but serve the right,
  Over all shall love endure.

" Of your spectral puppet play
  I have traced the cunning wires ;

Come what will, I needs must say,
  God is true, and ye are liars."

When the thought of man is free,
  Error fears its lightest tones ;
So the priest cried, " Sadducee !"
  And the people took up stones.

In the ancient burying-ground,
  Side by side the twain now lie, —
One with humble grassy mound,
  One with marbles pale and high.

But the Lord hath blest the seed
  Which that tradesman scattered then,
And the preacher's spectral creed
  Chills no more the blood of men.

Let us trust, to one is known
  Perfect love which casts out fear,
While the other's joys atone
  For the wrong he suffered here.

TO PIUS IX.[50]

THE cannon's brazen lips are cold ;
  No red shell blazes down the air ;
And street and tower, and temple old,
  Are silent as despair.

The Lombard stands no more at bay, —
  Rome's fresh young life has bled in
    vain ;
The ravens scattered by the day
  Come back with night again.

Now, while the fratricides of France
  Are treading on the neck of Rome,
Hider at Gaeta, — seize thy chance !
  Coward and cruel, come !

Creep now from Naples' bloody skirt ;
  Thy mummer's part was acted well,
While Rome, with steel and fire begirt,
  Before thy crusade fell !

Her death-groans answered to thy prayer ;
  Thy chant, the drum and bugle-
    call ;
Thy lights, the burning villa's glare ;
  Thy beads, the shell and ball !

Let Austria clear thy way, with hands
  Foul from Ancona's cruel sack,
And Naples, with his dastard bands
  Of murderers, lead thee back !

Rome's lips are dumb ; the orphan's wail,
  The mother's shriek, thou mayst not
    hear
Above the faithless Frenchman's hail,
  The unsexed shaveling's cheer !

Go, bind on Rome her cast-off weight,
  The double curse of crook and crown,
Though woman's scorn and manhood's
    hate
From wall and roof flash down !

Nor heed those blood-stains on the wall,
  Not Tiber's flood can wash away,
Where, in thy stately Quirinal,
  Thy mangled victims lay !

Let the world murmur ; let its cry
  Of horror and disgust be heard ; —
Truth stands alone ; thy coward lie
  Is backed by lance and sword !

The cannon of St. Angelo,
  And chanting priest and clanging bell,
And beat of drum and bugle blow,
  Shall greet thy coming well !

Let lips of iron and tongues of slaves
  Fit welcome give thee ; — for her part,
Rome, frowning o'er her new-made
    graves,
Shall curse thee from her heart !

No wreaths of sad Campagna's flowers
  Shall childhood in thy pathway fling ;
No garlands from their ravaged bowers
  Shall Terni's maidens bring ;

But, hateful as that tyrant old,
  The mocking witness of his crime,
In thee shall loathing eyes behold
  The Nero of our time !

Stand where Rome's blood was freest shed,
  Mock Heaven with impious thanks,
    and call
Its curses on the patriot dead,
  Its blessings on the Gaul !

Or sit upon thy throne of lies,
  A poor, mean idol, blood-besmeared,
Whom even its worshippers despise, —
  Unhonored, unrevered !

Yet, Scandal of the World ! from thee
  One needful truth mankind shall
    learn, —

10

That kings and priests to Liberty
  And God are false in turn.

Earth wearies of them ; and the long
  Meek sufferance of the Heavens doth
    fail ;
Woe for weak tyrants, when the strong
  Wake, struggle, and prevail !

Not vainly Roman hearts have bled
  To feed the Crozier and the Crown,
If, roused thereby, the world shall tread
  The twin-born vampires down !

ELLIOTT.[51]

Hands off ! thou tithe-fat plunderer !
    play
  No trick of priestcraft here !
Back, puny lordling ! darest thou lay
  A hand on Elliott's bier ?
Alive, your rank and pomp, as dust,
  Beneath his feet he trod :
He knew the locust swarm that cursed
  The harvest-fields of God.

On these pale lips, the smothered
    thought
  Which England's millions feel,
A fierce and fearful splendor caught,
  As from his forge the steel.
Strong-armed as Thor,— a shower of fire
  His smitten anvil flung ;
God's curse, Earth's wrong, dumb Hun-
    ger's ire, —
  He gave them all a tongue !

Then let the poor man's horny hands
  Bear up the mighty dead,
And labor's swart and stalwart bands
  Behind as mourners tread.
Leave cant and craft their baptized
    bounds,
  Leave rank its minster floor ;
Give England's green and daisied
    grounds
  The poet of the poor !

Lay down upon his Sheaf's green verge
  That brave old heart of oak,
With fitting dirge from sounding forge,
  And pall of furnace smoke !
Where whirls the stone its dizzy rounds,
  And axe and sledge are swung,
And, timing to their stormy sounds,
  His stormy lays are sung.

There let the peasant's step be heard,
  The grinder chant his rhyme ;
Nor patron's praise nor dainty word
  Befits the man or time.
No soft lament nor dreamer's sigh
  For him whose words were bread, —
The Runic rhyme and spell whereby
  The foodless poor were fed !

Pile up thy tombs of rank and pride,
  O England, as thou wilt !
With pomp to nameless worth denied,
  Emblazon titled guilt !
No part or lot in these we claim ;
  But, o'er the sounding wave,
A common right to Elliott's name,
  A freehold in his grave !

ICHABOD !

So fallen ! so lost ! the light with-
    drawn
  Which once he wore !
The glory from his gray hairs gone
  Forevermore !

Revile him not, — the Tempter hath
  A snare for all ;
And pitying tears, not scorn and wrath,
  Befit his fall !

O, dumb be passion's stormy rage,
  When he who might
Have lighted up and led his age,
  Falls back in night.

Scorn ! would the angels laugh, to
    mark
  A bright soul driven,
Fiend-goaded, down the endless dark,
  From hope and heaven !

Let not the land once proud of him
  Insult him now,
Nor brand with deeper shame his dim,
  Dishonored brow.

But let its humbled sons, instead,
  From sea to lake,
A long lament, as for the dead,
  In sadness make.

Of all we loved and honored, naught
  Save power remains, —
A fallen angel's pride of thought,
  Still strong in chains.

All else is gone ; from those great eyes
    The soul has fled :
When faith is lost, when honor dies,
    The man is dead !

Then, pay the reverence of old days
    To his dead fame ;
Walk backward, with averted gaze,
    And hide the shame !

THE CHRISTIAN TOURISTS.[52]

No aimless wanderers, by the fiend
    Unrest
Goaded from shore to shore ;
No schoolmen, turning, in their classic
    quest,
    The leaves of empire o'er.
Simple of faith, and bearing in their
    hearts
    The love of man and God,
Isles of old song, the Moslem's ancient
    marts,
    And Scythia's steppes, they trod.

Where the long shadows of the fir and pine
    In the night sun are cast,
And the deep heart of many a Norland
    mine
    Quakes at each riving blast ;
Where, in barbaric grandeur, Moskwa
    stands,
    A baptized Scythian queen,
With Europe's arts and Asia's jewelled
    hands,
    The North and East between !

Where still, through vales of Grecian
    fable, stray
    The classic forms of yore,
And beauty smiles, new risen from the
    spray,
    And Dian weeps once more ;
Where every tongue in Smyrna's mart
    resounds ;
    And Stamboul from the sea
Lifts her tall minarets over burial-
    grounds
    Black with the cypress-tree !

From Malta's temples to the gates of
    Rome,
    Following the track of Paul,
And where the Alps gird round the
    Switzer's home
    Their vast, eternal wall ;

They paused not by the ruins of old
    time,
    They scanned no pictures rare,
Nor lingered where the snow-locked
    mountains climb
    The cold abyss of air !

But unto prisons, where men lay in
    chains,
    To haunts where Hunger pined,
To kings and courts forgetful of the
    pains
    And wants of human-kind,
Scattering sweet words, and quiet deeds
    of good,
    Along their way, like flowers,
Or pleading, as Christ's freemen only
    could,
    With princes and with powers ;

Their single aim the purpose to ful-
    fil
    Of Truth, from day to day,
Simply obedient to its guiding will,
    They held their pilgrim way.
Yet dream not, hence, the beautiful and
    old
    Were wasted on their sight,
Who in the school of Christ had learned
    to hold
    All outward things aright.

Not less to them the breath of vineyards
    blown
    From off the Cyprian shore,
Not less for them the Alps in sunset
    shone,
    That man they valued more.
A life of beauty lends to all it sees
    The beauty of its thought ;
And fairest forms and sweetest harmo-
    nies
    Make glad its way, unsought.

In sweet accordancy of praise and
    love,
    The singing waters run ;
And sunset mountains wear in light
    above
    The smile of duty done ;
Sure stands the promise, — ever to the
    meek
    A heritage is given ;
Nor lose they Earth who, single-hearted,
    seek
    The righteousness of Heaven !

THE MEN OF OLD.

WELL speed thy mission, bold Icono-
    clast !
    Yet all unworthy of its trust thou
        art,
    If, with dry eye, and cold, unloving
        heart,
Thou tread'st the solemn Pantheon of
        the Past,
    By the great Future's dazzling hope
        made blind
    To all the beauty, power, and truth
        behind.
Not without reverent awe shouldst thou
        put by
    The cypress branches and the ama-
        ranth blooms,
    Where, with clasped hands of prayer,
        upon their tombs
The effigies of old confessors lie,
God's witnesses ; the voices of his will,
Heard in the slow march of the cen-
        turies still !
Such were the men at whose rebuking
        frown,
Dark with God's wrath, the tyrant's
        knee went down ;
Such from the terrors of the guilty drew
The vassal's freedom and the poor man's
        due.

St. Anselm (may he rest forevermore
    In Heaven's sweet peace !) forbade,
        of old, the sale
    Of men as slaves, and from the sacred
        pale
Hurled the Northumbrian buyers of the
        poor.
To ransom souls from bonds and evil
        fate
St. Ambrose melted down the sacred
        plate, —
Image of saint, the chalice, and the pix,
Crosses of gold, and silver candlesticks.
"MAN IS WORTH MORE THAN TEM-
        PLES !" he replied
To such as came his holy work to chide.
And brave Cesarius, stripping altars bare,
    And coining from the Abbey's golden
        hoard
The captive's freedom, answered to the
        prayer
    Or threat of those whose fierce zeal for
        the Lord
Stifled their love of man, — "An earth-
        en dish

The last sad supper of the Master bore.
Most miserable sinners ! do ye wish
    More than your Lord, and grudge his
        dying poor
What your own pride and not his need
        requires ?
    Souls, than these shining gauds, He
        values more ;
Mercy, not sacrifice, his heart desires ! "
O faithful worthies ! resting far behind
In your dark ages, since ye fell asleep,
Much has been done for truth and hu-
        man-kind, —
Shadows are scattered wherein ye groped
        blind ;
Man claims his birthright, freer pulses
        leap
Through peoples driven in your day like
        sheep ;
Yet, like your own, our age's sphere of
        light,
Though widening still, is walled around
        by night ;
With slow, reluctant eye, the Church has
        read,
Sceptic at heart, the lessons of its Head ;
Counting, too oft, its living members
        less
Than the wall's garnish and the pulpit's
        dress ;
World-moving zeal, with power to bless
        and feed
Life's fainting pilgrims, to their utter
        need,
Instead of bread, holds out the stone of
        creed ;
Sect builds and worships where its
        wealth and pride
And vanity stand shrined and deified,
Careless that in the shadow of its walls
God's living temple into ruin falls.
We need, methinks, the prophet-hero
        still,
Saints true of life, and martyrs strong of
        will,
To tread the land, even now, as Xavier
        trod
    The streets of Goa, barefoot, with his
        bell,
Proclaiming freedom in the name of God,
    And startling tyrants with the fear of
        hell !
    Soft words, smooth prophecies, are
        doubtless well ;
But to rebuke the age's popular crime,
We need the souls of fire, the hearts of
        that old time !

THE PEACE CONVENTION AT BRUSSELS.

STILL in thy streets, O Paris ! doth the stain
Of blood defy the cleansing autumn rain;
Still breaks the smoke Messina's ruins through,
And Naples mourns that new Bartholomew,
When squalid beggary, for a dole of bread,
At a crowned murderer's beck of license, fed
The yawning trenches with her noble dead ;
Still, doomed Vienna, through thy stately halls
The shell goes crashing and the red shot falls,
And, leagued to crush thee, on the Danube's side,
The bearded Croat and Bosniak spearman ride ;
Still in that vale where Himalaya's snow
Melts round the cornfields and the vines below,
The Sikh's hot cannon, answering ball for ball,
Flames in the breach of Moultan's shattered wall ;
On Chenab's side the vulture seeks the slain,
And Sutlej paints with blood its banks again.
" What folly, then," the faithless critic cries,
With sneering lip, and wise world-knowing eyes,
" While fort to fort, and post to post, repeat
The ceaseless challenge of the war-drum's beat,
And round the green earth, to the church-bell's chime,
The morning drum-roll of the camp keeps time,
To dream of peace amidst a world in arms,
Of swords to ploughshares changed by Scriptural charms,
Of nations, drunken with the wine of blood,
Staggering to take the Pledge of Brotherhood,
Like tipplers answering Father Mathew's call, —
The sullen Spaniard, and the mad-cap Gaul,

The bull-dog Briton, yielding but with life,
The Yankee swaggering with his bowie-knife,
The Russ, from banquets with the vulture shared,
The blood still dripping from his amber beard,
Quitting their mad Berserker dance to hear
The dull, meek droning of a drab-coat seer ;
Leaving the sport of Presidents and Kings,
Where men for dice each titled gambler flings,
To meet alternate on the Seine and Thames,
For tea and gossip, like old country dames !
No ! let the cravens plead the weakling's cant,
Let Cobden cipher, and let Vincent rant,
Let Sturge preach peace to democratic throngs,
And Burritt, stammering through his hundred tongues,
Repeat, in all, his ghostly lessons o'er,
Timed to the pauses of the battery's roar;
Check Ban or Kaiser with the barricade
Of "Olive-leaves" and Resolutions made,
Spike guns with pointed Scripture-texts, and hope
To capsize navies with a windy trope ;
Still shall the glory and the pomp of War
Along their train the shouting millions draw ;
Still dusty Labor to the passing Brave
His cap shall doff, and Beauty's kerchief wave ;
Still shall the bard to Valor tune his song,
Still Hero-worship kneel before the Strong ;
Rosy and sleek, the sable-gowned divine,
O'er his third bottle of suggestive wine,
To plumed and sworded auditors, shall prove
Their trade accordant with the Law of Love ;
And Church for State, and State for Church, shall fight,
And both agree, that Might alone is Right ! "
Despite of sneers like these, O faithful few,
Who dare to hold God's word and witness true,

Whose clear-eyed faith transcends our
    evil time,
And o'er the present wilderness of crime
Sees the calm future, with its robes of
    green,
Its fleece-flecked mountains, and soft
    streams between, —
Still keep the path which duty bids ye
    tread,
Though worldly wisdom shake the cau-
    tious head ;
No truth from Heaven descends upon
    our sphere,
Without the greeting of the sceptic's
    sneer ;
Denied and mocked at, till its blessings
    fall,
Common as dew and sunshine, over all.

Then, o'er Earth's war-field, till the
    strife shall cease,
Like Morven's harpers, sing your song
    of peace ;
As in old fable rang the Thracian's lyre,
Midst howl of fiends and roar of penal fire,
Till the fierce din to pleasing murmurs
    fell,
And love subdued the maddened heart
    of hell.

Lend, once again, that holy song a
    tongue,
Which the glad angels of the Advent
    sung,
Their cradle-anthem for the Saviour's
    birth,
Glory to God, and peace unto the earth !
Through the mad discord send that
    calming word
Which wind and wave on wild Genesa-
    reth heard,
Lift in Christ's name his Cross against
    the Sword !
Not vain the vision which the prophets
    saw,
Skirting with green the fiery waste of war,
Through the hot sand-gleam, looming
    soft and calm
On the sky's rim, the fountain-shading
    palm.
Still lives for Earth, which fiends so long
    have trod,
The great hope resting on the truth of
    God, —
Evil shall cease and Violence pass away,
And the tired world breathe free through
    a long Sabbath day.

    11th mo., 1848.

THE WISH OF TO-DAY.

I ASK not now for gold to gild
    With mocking shine a weary frame ;
The yearning of the mind is stilled, —
    I ask not now for Fame.

A rose-cloud, dimly seen above,
    Melting in heaven's blue depths
        away, —
O, sweet, fond dream of human Love !
    For thee I may not pray.

But, bowed in lowliness of mind,
    I make my humble wishes known, —
I only ask a will resigned,
    O Father, to thine own !

To-day, beneath thy chastening eye
    I crave alone for peace and rest,
Submissive in thy hand to lie,
    And feel that it is best.

A marvel seems the Universe,
    A miracle our Life and Death ;
A mystery which I cannot pierce,
    Around, above, beneath.

In vain I task my aching brain,
    In vain the sage's thought I scan,
I only feel how weak and vain,
    How poor and blind, is man.

And now my spirit sighs for home,
    And longs for light whereby to see,
And, like a weary child, would come,
    O Father, unto thee !

Though oft, like letters traced on sand,
    My weak resolves have passed away,
In mercy lend thy helping hand
    Unto my prayer to-day !

OUR STATE.

THE South-land boasts its teeming cane,
The prairied West its heavy grain,
And sunset's radiant gates unfold
On rising marts and sands of gold !

Rough, bleak, and hard, our little State
Is scant of soil, of limits strait ;
Her yellow sands are sands alone,
Her only mines are ice and stone !

From Autumn frost to April rain,
Too long her winter woods complain ;
From budding flower to falling leaf,
Her summer time is all too brief.

Yet, on her rocks, and on her sands,
And wintry hills, the school-house stands,
And what her rugged soil denies,
The harvest of the mind supplies.

The riches of the Commonwealth
Are free, strong minds, and hearts of
        health ;
And more to her than gold or grain,
The cunning hand and cultured brain.

For well she keeps her ancient stock,
The stubborn strength of Pilgrim Rock ;
And still maintains, with milder laws,
And clearer light, the Good Old Cause !

Nor heeds the sceptic's puny hands,
While near her school the church-spire
        stands ;
Nor fears the blinded bigot's rule,
While near her church-spire stands the
        school.

ALL'S WELL.

THE clouds, which rise with thunder,
        slake
    Our thirsty souls with rain ;
The blow most dreaded falls to break
    From off our limbs a chain ;
And wrongs of man to man but make
    The love of God more plain.
As through the shadowy lens of even
The eye looks farthest into heaven
On gleams of star and depths of blue
The glaring sunshine never knew !

SEED–TIME AND HARVEST.

As o'er his furrowed fields which lie
Beneath a coldly-dropping sky,
Yet chill with winter's melted snow,
The husbandman goes forth to sow,

Thus, Freedom, on the bitter blast
The ventures of thy seed we cast,
And trust to warmer sun and rain
To swell the germs and fill the grain.

Who calls thy glorious service hard ?
Who deems it not its own reward ?

Who, for its trials, counts it less
A cause of praise and thankfulness?

It may not be our lot to wield
The sickle in the ripened field ;
Nor ours to hear, on summer eves,
The reaper's song among the sheaves.

Yet where our duty's task is wrought
In unison with God's great thought,
The near and future blend in one,
And whatsoe'er is willed, is done !

And ours the grateful service whence
Comes, day by day, the recompense ;
The hope, the trust, the purpose stayed,
The fountain and the noonday shade.

And were this life the utmost span,
The only end and aim of man,
Better the toil of fields like these
Than waking dream and slothful ease.

But life, though falling like our grain,
Like that revives and springs again ;
And, early called, how blest are they
Who wait in heaven their harvest-day !

TO A. K.

ON RECEIVING A BASKET OF SEA-MOSSES.

    THANKS for thy gift
        Of ocean flowers,
    Born where the golden drift
    Of the slant sunshine falls
    Down the green, tremulous walls
Of water, to the cool still coral bowers,
    Where, under rainbows of perpetual
            showers,
        God's gardens of the deep
        His patient angels keep ;
    Gladdening the dim, strange solitude
        With fairest forms and hues, and
            thus
        Forever teaching us
The lesson which the many-colored skies,
The flowers, and leaves, and painted
            butterflies,
The deer's branched antlers, the gay
            bird that flings
The tropic sunshine from its golden
            wings,
The brightness of the human counte-
            nance,
Its play of smiles, the magic of a glance,

Forevermore repeat,
In varied tones and sweet,
That beauty, in and of itself, is good.

O kind and generous friend, o'er whom
The sunset hues of Time are cast,
Painting, upon the overpast
And scattered clouds of noonday
sorrow
The promise of a fairer morrow,
An earnest of the better life to come ;
The binding of the spirit broken,
The warning to the erring spoken,
The comfort of the sad,
The eye to see, the hand to cull
Of common things the beautiful,
The absent heart made glad
By simple gift or graceful token
Of love it needs as daily food,
All own one Source, and all are good !
Hence, tracking sunny cove and
reach,
Where spent waves glimmer up the
beach,
And toss their gifts of weed and shell
From foamy curve and combing swell,
No unbefitting task was thine
To weave these flowers so soft and
fair
In unison with His design
Who loveth beauty everywhere ;
And makes in every zone and clime,
In ocean and in upper air,
" All things beautiful in their time."

For not alone in tones of awe and
power
He speaks to man ;
The cloudy horror of the thunder-
shower
His rainbows span ;

And where the caravan
Winds o'er the desert, leaving, as in
air
The crane-flock leaves, no trace of pas-
sage there,
He gives the weary eye
The palm-leaf shadow for the hot noon
hours,
And on its branches dry
Calls out the acacia's flowers ;
And where the dark shaft pierces
down
Beneath the mountain roots,
Seen by the miner's lamp alone,
The star-like crystal shoots ;
So, where, the winds and waves
below,
The coral-branchéd gardens grow,
His climbing weeds and mosses
show,
Like foliage, on each stony bough,
Of varied hues more strangely gay
Than forest leaves in autumn's
day ; —
Thus evermore,
On sky, and wave, and shore,
An all-pervading beauty seems to
say :
God's love and power are one ; and
they,
Who, like the thunder of a sultry
day,
Smite to restore,
And they, who, like the gentle wind,
uplift
The petals of the dew-wet flowers, and
drift
Their perfume on the air,
Alike may serve Him, each, with their
own gift,
Making their lives a prayer !

THE CHAPEL OF THE HERMITS,

AND OTHER POEMS.

THE CHAPEL OF THE HERMITS.

"I DO believe, and yet, in grief,
I pray for help to unbelief;
For needful strength aside to lay
The daily cumberings of my way.

"I 'm sick at heart of craft and cant,
Sick of the crazed enthusiast's rant,
Profession's smooth hypocrisies,
And creeds of iron, and lives of ease.

"I ponder o'er the sacred word,
I read the record of our Lord;
And, weak and troubled, envy them
Who touched his seamless garment's
    hem; —

"Who saw the tears of love he wept
Above the grave where Lazarus slept;
And heard, amidst the shadows dim
Of Olivet, his evening hymn.

"How blessed the swineherd's low
    estate,
The beggar crouching at the gate,
The leper loathly and abhorred,
Whose eyes of flesh beheld the Lord!

"O sacred soil his sandals pressed!
Sweet fountains of his noonday rest!
O light and air of Palestine,
Impregnate with his life divine!

"O, bear me thither! Let me look
On Siloa's pool, and Kedron's brook, —
Kneel at Gethsemane, and by
Gennesaret walk, before I die!

"Methinks this cold and northern night
Would melt before that Orient light;
And, wet by Hermon's dew and rain,
My childhood's faith revive again!"

So spake my friend, one autumn day,
Where the still river slid away
Beneath us, and above the brown
Red curtains of the woods shut down.

Then said I, — for I could not brook
The mute appealing of his look, —
"I, too, am weak, and faith is small,
And blindness happeneth unto all.

"Yet, sometimes glimpses on my sight,
Through present wrong, the eternal
    right;
And, step by step, since time began,
I see the steady gain of man;

"That all of good the past hath had
Remains to make our own time glad, —
Our common daily life divine,
And every land a Palestine.

"Thou weariest of thy present state;
What gain to thee time's holiest date?
The doubter now perchance had been
As High Priest or as Pilate then!

"What thought Chorazin's scribes'
    What faith
In Him had Nain and Nazareth?
Of the few followers whom He led
One sold him, — all forsook and fled.

"O friend! we need nor rock nor sand,
Nor storied stream of Morning-Land;
The heavens are glassed in Merri-
    mack, —
What more could Jordan render back?

"We lack but open eye and ear
To find the Orient's marvels here; —
The still small voice in autumn's hush,
Yon maple wood the burning bush.

"For still the new transcends the old,
In signs and tokens manifold; —
Slaves rise up men; the olive waves,
With roots deep set in battle graves!

"Through the harsh noises of our day
A low, sweet prelude finds its way;
Through clouds of doubt, and creeds of
    fear,
A light is breaking, calm and clear.

"That song of Love, now low and far,
Erelong shall swell from star to star !
That light, the breaking day, which tips
The golden-spired Apocalypse !"

Then, when my good friend shook his head,
And, sighing, sadly smiled, I said :
"Thou mind'st me of a story told
In rare Bernardin's leaves of gold." [53]

And while the slanted sunbeams wove
The shadows of the frost-stained grove,
And, picturing all, the river ran
O'er cloud and wood, I thus began :

In Mount Valerien's chestnut wood
The Chapel of the Hermits stood ;
And thither, at the close of day,
Came two old pilgrims, worn and gray.

One, whose impetuous youth defied
The storms of Baikal's wintry side,
And mused and dreamed where tropic day
Flamed o'er his lost Virginia's bay.

His simple tale of love and woe
All hearts had melted, high or low ; —
A blissful pain, a sweet distress,
Immortal in its tenderness.

Yet, while above his charméd page
Beat quick the young heart of his age,
He walked amidst the crowd unknown,
A sorrowing old man, strange and lone.

A homeless, troubled age, — the gray
Pale setting of a weary day ;
Too dull his ear for voice of praise,
Too sadly worn his brow for bays.

Pride, lust of power and glory, slept ;
Yet still his heart its young dream kept,
And, wandering like the deluge-dove,
Still sought the resting-place of love.

And, mateless, childless, envied more
The peasant's welcome from his door
By smiling eyes at eventide,
Than kingly gifts or lettered pride.

Until, in place of wife and child,
All-pitying Nature on him smiled,
And gave to him the golden keys
To all her inmost sanctities.

Mild Druid of her wood-paths dim !
She laid her great heart bare to him,
Its loves and sweet accords ; — he saw
The beauty of her perfect law.

The language of her signs he knew,
What notes her cloudy clarion blew ;
The rhythm of autumn's forest dyes,
The hymn of sunset's painted skies.

And thus he seemed to hear the song
Which swept, of old, the stars along ;
And to his eyes the earth once more
Its fresh and primal beauty wore.

Who sought with him, from summer air,
And field and wood, a balm for care ;
And bathed in light of sunset skies
His tortured nerves and weary eyes ?

His fame on all the winds had flown ;
His words had shaken crypt and throne ;
Like fire, on camp and court and cell
They dropped, and kindled as they fell.

Beneath the pomps of state, below
The mitred juggler's masque and show,
A prophecy — a vague hope — ran
His burning thought from man to man.

For peace or rest too well he saw
The fraud of priests, the wrong of law,
And felt how hard, between the two,
Their breath of pain the millions drew.

A prophet-utterance, strong and wild,
The weakness of an unweaned child,
A sun-bright hope for human-kind,
And self-despair, in him combined.

He loathed the false, yet lived not true
To half the glorious truths he knew ;
The doubt, the discord, and the sin,
He mourned without, he felt within.

Untrod by him the path he showed,
Sweet pictures on his easel glowed
Of simple faith, and loves of home,
And virtue's golden days to come.

But weakness, shame, and folly made
The foil to all his pen portrayed ;
Still, where his dreamy splendors shone,
The shadow of himself was thrown.

Lord, what is man, whose thought, at times,
Up to thy sevenfold brightness climbs,
While still his grosser instinct clings
To earth, like other creeping things !

So rich in words, in acts so mean ;
So high, so low ; chance-swung between
The foulness of the penal pit
And Truth's clear sky, millennium-
    lit !

Vain pride of star-lent genius ! — vain
Quick fancy and creative brain,
Unblest by prayerful sacrifice,
Absurdly great, or weakly wise !

Midst yearnings for a truer life,
Without were fears, within was strife ;
And still his wayward act denied
The perfect good for which he sighed.

The love he sent forth void returned ;
The fame that crowned him scorched
    and burned,
Burning, yet cold and drear and lone, —
A fire-mount in a frozen zone !

Like that the gray-haired sea-king
    passed,[54]
Seen southward from his sleety mast,
About whose brows of changeless frost
A wreath of flame the wild winds tossed.

Far round the mournful beauty played
Of lambent light and purple shade,
Lost on the fixed and dumb despair
Of frozen earth and sea and air !

A man apart, unknown, unloved
By those whose wrongs his soul had
    moved,
He bore the ban of Church and State,
The good man's fear, the bigot's hate !

Forth from the city's noise and throng,
Its pomp and shame, its sin and wrong,
The twain that summer day had strayed
To Mount Valerien's chestnut shade.

To them the green fields and the wood
Lent something of their quietude,
And golden-tinted sunset seemed
Prophetical of all they dreamed.

The hermits from their simple cares
The bell was calling home to prayers,

And, listening to its sound, the twain
Seemed lapped in childhood's trust
    again.

Wide open stood the chapel door ;
A sweet old music, swelling o'er
Low prayerful murmurs, issued thence, —
The Litanies of Providence !

Then Rousseau spake : "Where two or'
    three
In His name meet, He there will be !"
And then, in silence, on their knees
They sank beneath the chestnut-trees.

As to the blind returning light,
As daybreak to the Arctic night,
Old faith revived : the doubts of years
Dissolved in reverential tears.

That gush of feeling overpast,
"Ah me !" Bernardin sighed at last,
"I would thy bitterest foes could see
Thy heart as it is seen of me !

"No church of God hast thou denied ;
Thou hast but spurned in scorn aside
A base and hollow counterfeit,
Profaning the pure name of it !

"With dry dead moss and marish weeds
His fire the western herdsman feeds,
And greener from the ashen plain
The sweet spring grasses rise again.

"Nor thunder-peal nor mighty wind
Disturb the solid sky behind ;
And through the cloud the red bolt rends
The calm, still smile of Heaven descends !

"Thus through the world, like bolt and
    blast,
And scourging fire, thy words have
    passed.
Clouds break, — the steadfast heavens
    remain ;
Weeds burn, — the ashes feed the grain !

"But whoso strives with wrong may find
Its touch pollute, its darkness blind ;
And learn, as latent fraud is shown
In others' faith, to doubt his own.

"With dream and falsehood, simple trust
And pious hope we tread in dust ;
Lost the calm faith in goodness, — lost
The baptism of the Pentecost !

" Alas ! — the blows for error meant
Too oft on truth itself are spent,
As through the false and vile and base
Looks forth her sad, rebuking face.

" Not ours the Theban's charméd life ;
We come not scathless from the strife !
The Python's coil about us clings,
The trampled Hydra bites and stings !

" Meanwhile, the sport of seeming
    chance,
The plastic shapes of circumstance,
What might have been we fondly guess,
If earlier born, or tempted less.

" And thou, in these wild, troubled
    days,
Misjudged alike in blame and praise,
Unsought and undeserved the same
The sceptic's praise, the bigot's blame ; —

" I cannot doubt, if thou hadst been
Among the highly favored men
Who walked on earth with Fenelon,
He would have owned thee as his son ;

" And, bright with wings of cherubim
Visibly waving over him,
Seen through his life, the Church had
    seemed
All that its old confessors dreamed.

" I would have been," Jean Jaques re-
    plied,
" The humblest servant at his side,
Obscure, unknown, content to see
How beautiful man's life may be !

" O, more than thrice-blest relic, more
Than solemn rite or sacred lore,
The holy life of one who trod
The foot-marks of the Christ of God !

" Amidst a blinded world he saw
The oneness of the Dual law ;
That Heaven's sweet peace on Earth
    began,
And God was loved through love of
    man.

" He lived the Truth which reconciled
The strong man Reason, Faith the child :
In him belief and act were one,
The homilies of duty done !"

So speaking, through the twilight gray
The two old pilgrims went their way.

What seeds of life that day were sown,
The heavenly watchers knew alone.

Time passed, and Autumn came to fold
Green Summer in her brown and gold ;
Time passed, and Winter's tears of snow
Dropped on the grave-mound of Rous-
    seau.

" The tree remaineth where it fell,
The pained on earth is pained in hell ! "
So priestcraft from its altars cursed
The mournful doubts its falsehood
    nursed.

Ah ! well of old the Psalmist prayed,
" Thy hand, not man's, on me be laid ! "
Earth frowns below, Heaven weeps above,
And man is hate, but God is love !

No Hermits now the wanderer sees,
Nor chapel with its chestnut-trees ;
A morning dream, a tale that 's told,
The wave of change o'er all has rolled.

Yet lives the lesson of that day ;
And from its twilight cool and gray
Comes up a low, sad whisper, " Make
The truth thine own, for truth's own
    sake.

" Why wait to see in thy brief span
Its perfect flower and fruit in man ?
No saintly touch can save ; no balm
Of healing hath the martyr's palm.

" Midst soulless forms, and false pre-
    tence
Of spiritual pride and pampered sense,
A voice saith, ' What is that to thee ?
Be true thyself, and follow Me ! '

" In days when throne and altar heard
The wanton's wish, the bigot's word,
And pomp of state and ritual show
Scarce hid the loathsome death be-
    low, —

" Midst fawning priests and courtiers
    foul,
The losel swarm of crown and cowl,
White-robed walked François Fenelon,
Stainless as Uriel in the sun !

" Yet in his time the stake blazed red,
The poor were eaten up like bread :
Men knew him not: his garment's hem
No healing virtue had for them.

"Alas ! no present saint we find ;
The white cymar gleams far behind,
Revealed in outline vague, sublime,
Through telescopic mists of time !

"Trust not in man with passing breath,
But in the Lord, old Scripture saith ;
The truth which saves thou mayst not
    blend
With false professor, faithless friend.

"Search thine own heart.   What pain-
    eth thee
In others in thyself may be ;
All dust is frail, all flesh is weak ;
Be thou the true man thou dost seek !

"Where now with pain thou treadest, trod
The whitest of the saints of God !
To show thee where their feet were set,
The light which led them shineth yet.

"The footprints of the life divine,
Which marked their path, remain in
    thine ;
And that great Life, transfused in theirs,
Awaits thy faith, thy love, thy prayers !"

A lesson which I well may heed,
A word of fitness to my need ;
So from that twilight cool and gray
Still saith a voice, or seems to say.

We rose, and slowly homeward turned,
While down the west the sunset burned;
And, in its light, hill, wood, and tide,
And human forms seemed glorified.

The village homes transfigured stood,
And purple bluffs, whose belting wood
Across the waters leaned to hold
The yellow leaves like lamps of gold.

Then spake my friend : "Thy words are
    true ;
Forever old, forever new,
These home-seen splendors are the same
Which over Eden's sunsets came.

"To these bowed heavens let wood and
    hill
Lift voiceless praise and anthem still ;
Fall, warm with blessing, over them,
Light of the New Jerusalem !

"Flow on, sweet river, like the stream
Of John's Apocalyptic dream !
This mapled ridge shall Horeb be,
Yon green-banked lake our Galilee !

"Henceforth my heart shall sigh no
    more
For olden time and holier shore ;
God's love and blessing, then and there,
Are now and here and everywhere."

MISCELLANEOUS.

QUESTIONS OF LIFE.

And the angel that was sent unto me, whose
name was Uriel, gave me an answer and said,
    "Thy heart hath gone too far in this world,
and thinkest thou to comprehend the way of the
Most High ? "
    Then said I, " Yea, my Lord."
    Then said he unto me, " Go thy way, weigh me
the weight of the fire or measure me the blast
of the wind, or call me again the day that is
past." — 2 *Esdras*, chap. iv.

A BENDING staff I would not break,
A feeble faith I would not shake,
Nor even rashly pluck away
The error which some truth may stay,
Whose loss might leave the soul without
A shield against the shafts of doubt.

And yet, at times, when over all
A darker mystery seems to fall,
(May God forgive the child of dust,
Who seeks to *know*, where Faith should
    trust !)
I raise the questions, old and dark,
Of Uzdom's tempted patriarch,
And, speech-confounded, build again
The baffled tower of Shinar's plain.

I am : how little more I know !
Whence came I ?   Whither do I go ?
A centred self, which feels and is ;
A cry between the silences ;
A shadow-birth of clouds at strife
With sunshine on the hills of life ;

A shaft from Nature's quiver cast
Into the Future from the Past ;
Between the cradle and the shroud,
A meteor's flight from cloud to cloud.

Thorough the vastness, arching all,
I see the great stars rise and fall,
The rounding seasons come and go,
The tided oceans ebb and flow ;
The tokens of a central force,
Whose circles, in their widening course,
O'erlap and move the universe ;
The workings of the law whence springs
The rhythmic harmony of things,
Which shapes in earth the darkling spar,
And orbs in heaven the morning star.
Of all I see, in earth and sky, —
Star, flower, beast, bird, — what part have I ?
This conscious life, — is it the same
Which thrills the universal frame,
Whereby the caverned crystal shoots,
And mounts the sap from forest roots,
Whereby the exiled wood-bird tells
When Spring makes green her native dells?
How feels the stone the pang of birth,
Which brings its sparkling prism forth ?
The forest-tree the throb which gives
The life-blood to its new-born leaves ?
Do bird and blossom feel, like me,
Life's many-folded mystery, —
The wonder which it is TO BE ?
Or stand I severed and distinct,
From Nature's chain of life unlinked ?
Allied to all, yet not the less
Prisoned in separate consciousness,
Alone o'erburdened with a sense
Of life, and cause, and consequence ?

In vain to me the Sphinx propounds
The riddle of her sights and sounds ;
Back still the vaulted mystery gives
The echoed question it receives.
What sings the brook ?　What oracle
Is in the pine-tree's organ swell ?
What may the wind's low burden be ?
The meaning of the moaning sea ?
The hieroglyphics of the stars ?
Or clouded sunset's crimson bars ?
I vainly ask, for mocks my skill
The trick of Nature's cipher still.

I turn from Nature unto men,
I ask the stylus and the pen ;

What sang the bards of old ?　What meant
The prophets of the Orient ?
The rolls of buried Egypt, hid
In painted tomb and pyramid ?
What mean Idúmea's arrowy lines,
Or dusk Elora's monstrous signs ?
How speaks the primal thought of man
From the grim carvings of Copan ?
Where rests the secret ?　Where the keys
Of the old death-bolted mysteries ?
Alas ! the dead retain their trust ;
Dust hath no answer from the dust.

The great enigma still unguessed,
Unanswered the eternal quest ;
I gather up the scattered rays
Of wisdom in the early days,
Faint gleams and broken, like the light
Of meteors in a northern night,
Betraying to the darkling earth
The unseen sun which gave them birth ;
I listen to the sibyl's chant,
The voice of priest and hierophant ;
I know what Indian Kreeshna saith,
And what of life and what of death
The demon taught to Socrates ;
And what, beneath his garden-trees
Slow pacing, with a dream-like tread,
The solemn-thoughted Plato said ;
Nor lack I tokens, great or small,
Of God's clear light in each and all,
While holding with more dear regard
The scroll of Hebrew seer and bard,
The starry pages promise-lit
With Christ's Evangel over-writ,
Thy miracle of life and death,
O holy one of Nazareth !

On Aztec ruins, gray and lone,
The circling serpent coils in stone, —
Type of the endless and unknown ;
Whereof we seek the clew to find,
With groping fingers of the blind !
Forever sought, and never found,
We trace that serpent-symbol round
Our resting-place, our starting bound !
O thriftlessness of dream and guess !
O wisdom which is foolishness !
Why idly seek from outward things
The answer inward silence brings ;
Why stretch beyond our proper sphere
And age, for that which lies so near ?
Why climb the far-off hills with pain,
A nearer view of heaven to gain ?
In lowliest depths of bosky dells
The hermit Contemplation dwells.

A fountain's pine-hung slope his seat,
And lotus-twined his silent feet,
Whence, piercing heaven, with screenéd
  sight,
He sees at noon the stars, whose light
Shall glorify the coming night.

Here let me pause, my quest forego;
Enough for me to feel and know
That He in whom the cause and end,
The past and future, meet and blend,—
Who, girt with his immensities,
Our vast and star-hung system sees,
Small as the clustered Pleiades,—
Moves not alone the heavenly quires,
But waves the spring-time's grassy
  spires,
Guards not archangel feet alone,
But deigns to guide and keep my own;
Speaks not alone the words of fate
Which worlds destroy, and worlds
  create,
But whispers in my spirit's ear,
In tones of love, or warning fear,
A language none beside may hear.

To Him, from wanderings long and
  wild,
I come, an over-wearied child,
In cool and shade his peace to find,
Like dew-fall settling on my mind.
Assured that all I know is best,
And humbly trusting for the rest,
I turn from Fancy's cloud-built scheme,
Dark creed, and mournful eastern dream
Of power, impersonal and cold,
Controlling all, itself controlled,
Maker and slave of iron laws,
Alike the subject and the cause;
From vain philosophies, that try
The sevenfold gates of mystery,
And, baffled ever, babble still,
Word-prodigal of fate and will;
From Nature, and her mockery, Art,
And book and speech of men apart,
To the still witness in my heart;
With reverence waiting to behold
His Avatár of love untold,
The Eternal Beauty new and old!

THE PRISONERS OF NAPLES.

I HAVE been thinking of the victims
  bound
In Naples, dying for the lack of air

And sunshine, in their close, damp
  cells of pain,
Where hope is not, and innocence in
  vain
Appeals against the torture and the
  chain!
Unfortunates! whose crime it was to
  share
Our common love of freedom, and to
  dare,
In its behalf, Rome's harlot triple-
  crowned,
And her base pander, the most hateful
  thing
Who upon Christian or on Pagan
  ground
Makes vile the old heroic name of king.
O God most merciful! Father just and
  kind!
Whom man hath bound let thy right
  hand unbind.
Or, if thy purposes of good behind
Their ills lie hidden, let the sufferers
  find
Strong consolations; leave them not to
  doubt
Thy providential care, nor yet without
The hope which all thy attributes in-
  spire,
That not in vain the martyr's robe of
  fire
Is worn, nor the sad prisoner's fretting
  chain;
Since all who suffer for thy truth send
  forth,
Electrical, with every throb of pain,
Unquenchable sparks, thy own bap-
  tismal rain
Of fire and spirit over all the earth,
Making the dead in slavery live again.
Let this great hope be with them, as
  they lie
Shut from the light, the greenness, and
  the sky,—
From the cool waters and the pleasant
  breeze,
The smell of flowers, and shade of sum-
  mer trees;
Bound with the felon lepers, whom
  disease
And sins abhorred make loathsome;
  let them share
Pellico's faith, Foresti's strength to bear
Years of unutterable torment, stern and
  still,
As the chained Titan victor through his
  will!

Comfort them with thy future ; let them
　　see
The day-dawn of Italian liberty ;
For that, with all good things, is hid
　　with Thee,
And, perfect in thy thought, awaits its
　　time to be !

I, who have spoken for freedom at the cost
Of some weak friendships, or some pal-
　　try prize
Of name or place, and more than I have
　　lost
Have gained in wider reach of sym-
　　pathies,
And free communion with the good and
　　wise, —
May God forbid that I should ever
　　boast
Such easy self-denial, or repine
That the strong pulse of health no more
　　is mine ;
That, overworn at noonday, I must
　　yield
To other hands the gleaning of the
　　field, —
A tired on-looker through the day's
　　decline.
For blest beyond deserving still, and
　　knowing
That kindly Providence its care is
　　showing
In the withdrawal as in the bestowing,
Scarcely I dare for more or less to pray.
Beautiful yet for me this autumn day
Melts on its sunset hills ; and, far away,
For me the Ocean lifts its solemn psalm,
To me the pine-woods whisper ; and
　　for me
Yon river, winding through its vales of
　　calm,
By greenest banks, with asters purple-
　　starred,
And gentian bloom and golden-rod
　　made gay,
Flows down in silent gladness to the sea,
Like a pure spirit to its great reward !

Nor lack I friends, long-tried and near
　　and dear,
Whose love is round me like this atmos-
　　phere,
Warm, soft, and golden. For such gifts
　　to me
What shall I render, O my God, to thee ?
Let me not dwell upon my lighter share
Of pain and ill that human life must bear ;

Save me from selfish pining ; let my heart,
Drawn from itself in sympathy, forget
The bitter longings of a vain regret,
The anguish of its own peculiar smart.
Remembering others, as I have to-day,
In their great sorrows, let me live alway
Not for myself alone, but have a part,
Such as a frail and erring spirit may,
In love which is of Thee, and which in-
　　deed Thou art !

MOLOCH IN STATE STREET.

THE moon has set : while yet the dawn
　　Breaks cold and gray,
Between the midnight and the morn
　　Bear off your prey !

On, swift and still ! — the conscious street
　　Is panged and stirred ;
Tread light ! — that fall of serried feet
　　The dead have heard !

The first drawn blood of Freedom's veins
　　Gushed where ye tread ;
Lo ! through the dusk the martyr-stains
　　Blush darkly red !

Beneath the slowly waning stars
　　And whitening day,
What stern and awful presence bars
　　That sacred way ?

What faces frown upon ye, dark
　　With shame and pain ?
Come these from Plymouth's Pilgrim
　　bark ?
　　　Is that young Vane ?

Who, dimly beckoning, speed ye on
　　With mocking cheer ?
Lo ! spectral Andros, Hutchinson,
　　And Gage are here !

For ready mart or favoring blast
　　Through Moloch's fire
Flesh of his flesh, unsparing, passed
　　The Tyrian sire.

Ye make that ancient sacrifice
　　Of Man to Gain,
Your traffic thrives, where Freedom dies,
　　Beneath the chain.

Ye sow to-day, your harvest, scorn
　　And hate, is near ;

How think ye freemen, mountain-born,
    The tale will hear ?

Thank God ! our mother State can yet
    Her fame retrieve ;
To you and to your children let
    The scandal cleave.

Chain Hall and Pulpit, Court and Press,
    Make gods of gold ;
Let honor, truth, and manliness
    Like wares be sold.

Your hoards are great, your walls are
    strong,
    But God is just ;
The gilded chambers built by wrong
    Invite the rust.

What ! know ye not the gains of Crime
    Are dust and dross ;
Its ventures on the waves of time
    Foredoomed to loss !

And still the Pilgrim State remains
    What she hath been ;
Her inland hills, her seaward plains,
    Still nurture men !

Nor wholly lost the fallen mart, —
    Her olden blood
Through many a free and generous heart
    Still pours its flood.

That brave old blood, quick-flowing yet,
    Shall know no check,
Till a free people's foot is set
    On Slavery's neck.

Even now, the peal of bell and gun,
    And hills aflame,
Tell of the first great triumph won
    In Freedom's name.[55]

The long night dies : the welcome gray
    Of dawn we see ;
Speed up the heavens thy perfect day,
    God of the free !
1851.

THE PEACE OF EUROPE.

1852.

" GREAT peace in Europe ! Order reigns
From Tiber's hills to Danube's plains !"
So say her kings and priests ; so say
The lying prophets of our day.

Go lay to earth a listening ear ;
The tramp of measured marches hear, —
The rolling of the cannon's wheel,
The shotted musket's murderous peal,
The night alarm, the sentry's call,
The quick-eared spy in hut and
    hall !
From Polar sea and tropic fen
The dying-groans of exiled men !
The bolted cell, the galley's chains,
The scaffold smoking with its stains !
Order, — the hush of brooding slaves !
Peace, — in the dungeon-vaults and
    graves !

O Fisher ! of the world-wide net,
With meshes in all waters set,
Whose fabled keys of heaven and
    hell
Bolt hard the patriot's prison-cell,
And open wide the banquet-hall,
Where kings and priests hold carni-
    val !
Weak vassal tricked in royal guise,
Boy Kaiser with thy lip of lies ;
Base gambler for Napoleon's crown,
Barnacle on his dead renown !
Thou, Bourbon Neapolitan,
Crowned scandal, loathed of God and
    man ;
And thou, fell Spider of the North !
Stretching thy giant feelers forth,
Within whose web the freedom dies
Of nations eaten up like flies !
Speak, Prince and Kaiser, Priest and
    Czar !
If this be Peace, pray what is War ?

White Angel of the Lord ! unmeet
That soil accursed for thy pure feet.
Never in Slavery's desert flows
The fountain of thy charmed repose ;
No tyrant's hand thy chaplet weaves
Of lilies and of olive-leaves ;
Not with the wicked shalt thou dwell,
Thus saith the Eternal Oracle ;
Thy home is with the pure and free !
Stern herald of thy better day,
Before thee, to prepare thy way,
The Baptist Shade of Liberty,
Gray, scarred and hairy-robed, must
    press
With bleeding feet the wilderness !
O that its voice might pierce the ear
Of princes, trembling while they hear
A cry as of the Hebrew seer :
Repent ! God's kingdom draweth near !

11

WORDSWORTH.

WRITTEN ON A BLANK LEAF OF HIS
MEMOIRS.

DEAR friends, who read the world aright,
    And in its common forms discern
A beauty and a harmony
    The many never learn !

Kindred in soul of him who found
    In simple flower and leaf and stone
The impulse of the sweetest lays
    Our Saxon tongue has known, —

Accept this record of a life
    As sweet and pure, as calm and good,
As a long day of blandest June
    In green field and in wood.

How welcome to our ears, long pained
    By strife of sect and party noise,
The brook-like murmur of his song
    Of nature's simple joys !

The violet by its mossy stone,
    The primrose by the river's brim,
And chance-sown daffodil, have found
    Immortal life through him.

The sunrise on his breezy lake,
    The rosy tints his sunset brought,
World-seen, are gladdening all the vales
    And mountain-peaks of thought.

Art builds on sand ; the works of pride
    And human passion change and fall ;
But that which shares the life of God
    With him surviveth all.

TO ———.

LINES WRITTEN AFTER A SUMMER
DAY'S EXCURSION.

FAIR Nature's priestesses ! to whom,
    In hieroglyph of bud and bloom,
        Her mysteries are told ;
Who, wise in lore of wood and mead,
The seasons' pictured scrolls can read,
        In lessons manifold !

Thanks for the courtesy, and gay
Good-humor, which on Washing Day
    Our ill-timed visit bore ;
Thanks for your graceful oars, which broke
The morning dreams of Artichoke,
    Along his wooded shore !

Varied as varying Nature's ways,
Sprites of the river, woodland fays,
    Or mountain nymphs, ye seem ;
Free-limbed Dianas on the green,
Loch Katrine's Ellen, or Undine,
    Upon your favorite stream.

The forms of which the poets told,
The fair benignities of old,
    Were doubtless such as you ;
What more than Artichoke the rill
Of Helicon ?   Than Pipe-stave hill
    Arcadia's mountain-view ?

No sweeter bowers the bee delayed,
In wild Hymettus' scented shade,
    Than those you dwell among ;
Snow-flowered azalias, intertwined
With roses, over banks inclined
    With trembling harebells hung !

A charmèd life unknown to death,
Immortal freshness Nature hath ;
    Her fabled fount and glen
Are now and here : Dodona's shrine
Still murmurs in the wind-swept pine, —
    All is that e'er hath been.

The Beauty which old Greece or Rome
Sung, painted, wrought, lies close at
        home ;
    We need but eye and ear
In all our daily walks to trace
The outlines of incarnate grace,
    The hymns of gods to hear !

IN PEACE.

A TRACK of moonlight on a quiet lake,
    Whose small waves on a silver-sanded
        shore
Whisper of peace, and with the low winds
        make
Such harmonies as keep the woods awake,
And listening all night long for their sweet
        sake ;
    A green-waved slope of meadow, hov-
        ered o'er
By angel-troops of lilies, swaying light
On viewless stems, with folded wings of
        white ;
A slumberous stretch of mountain-land,
        far seen
Where the low westering day, with gold
        and green,
Purple and amber, softly blended, fills

WORDSWORTH'S GRAVE. Page 162

The wooded vales, and melts among the hills;
A vine-fringed river, winding to its rest
On the calm bosom of a stormless sea,
Bearing alike upon its placid breast,
With earthly flowers and heavenly stars impressed,
The hues of time and of eternity:
Such are the pictures which the thought of thee,
O friend, awakeneth, — charming the keen pain
Of thy departure, and our sense of loss
Requiting with the fulness of thy gain.
Lo! on the quiet grave thy life-borne cross,
Dropped only at its side, methinks doth shine,
Of thy beatitude the radiant sign!
No sob of grief, no wild lament be there,
To break the Sabbath of the holy air;
But, in their stead, the silent-breathing prayer
Of hearts still waiting for a rest like thine.
O spirit redeemed! Forgive us, if henceforth,
With sweet and pure similitudes of earth,
We keep thy pleasant memory freshly green,
Of love's inheritance a priceless part,
Which Fancy's self, in reverent awe, is seen
To paint, forgetful of the tricks of art,
With pencil dipped alone in colors of the heart.

BENEDICITE.

GOD's love and peace be with thee, where
Soe'er this soft autumnal air
Lifts the dark tresses of thy hair!

Whether through city casements comes
Its kiss to thee, in crowded rooms,
Or, out among the woodland blooms,

It freshens o'er thy thoughtful face,
Imparting, in its glad embrace,
Beauty to beauty, grace to grace!

Fair Nature's book together read,
The old wood-paths that knew our tread,
The maple shadows overhead, —

The hills we climbed, the river seen
By gleams along its deep ravine, —
All keep thy memory fresh and green.

Where'er I look, where'er I stray,
Thy thought goes with me on my way,
And hence the prayer I breathe to-day;

O'er lapse of time and change of scene,
The weary waste which lies between
Thyself and me, my heart I lean.

Thou lack'st not Friendship's spell-word, nor
The half-unconscious power to draw
All hearts to thine by Love's sweet law.

With these good gifts of God is cast
Thy lot, and many a charm thou hast
To hold the blessed angels fast.

If, then, a fervent wish for thee
The gracious heavens will heed from me,
What should, dear heart, its burden be?

The sighing of a shaken reed, —
What can I more than meekly plead
The greatness of our common need?

God's love, — unchanging, pure, and true, —
The Paraclete white-shining through
His peace, — the fall of Hermon's dew!

With such a prayer, on this sweet day,
As thou mayst hear and I may say,
I greet thee, dearest, far away!

PICTURES

I.

LIGHT, warmth, and sprouting greenness, and o'er all
Blue, stainless, steel-bright ether, raining down
Tranquillity upon the deep-hushed town,
The freshening meadows, and the hillsides brown;
Voice of the west-wind from the hills of pine,
And the brimmed river from its distant fall,
Low hum of bees, and joyous interlude
Of bird-songs in the streamlet-skirting wood, —
Heralds and prophecies of sound and sight,
Blessed forerunners of the warmth and light,

Attendant angels to the house of prayer,
  With reverent footsteps keeping pace
    with mine, —   .
Once more, through God's great love, with
    you I share
A morn of resurrection sweet and fair
  As that which saw, of old, in Pales-
    tine,
  Immortal Love uprising in fresh bloom
From the dark night and winter of
    the tomb !

5th mo., 2d, 1852.

II.

White with its sun-bleached dust, the
    pathway winds
  Before me ; dust is on the shrunken
    grass,
  And on the trees beneath whose
    boughs I pass ;
Frail screen against the Hunter of the
    sky,
Who, glaring on me with his lidless eye,
  While mounting with his dog-star
    high and higher
Ambushed in light intolerable, unbinds
  The burnished quiver of his shafts
    of fire.
Between me and the hot fields of his
    South
A tremulous glow, as from a furnace-
    mouth,
  Glimmers and swims before my daz-
    zled sight,
  As if the burning arrows of his ire
Broke as they fell, and shattered into
    light ;
Yet on my cheek I feel the western wind,
  And hear it telling to the orchard
    trees,
  And to the faint and flower-forsaken
    bees,
  Tales of fair meadows, green with con-
    stant streams,
And mountains rising blue and cool
    behind,
  Where in moist dells the purple or-
    chis gleams,
And starred with white the virgin's
    bower is twined.
So the o'erwearied pilgrim, as he fares
  Along life's summer waste, at times is
    fanned,
Even at noontide, by the cool, sweet airs
  Of a serener and a holier land,
    Fresh as the morn, and as the dew-
      fall bland.

Breath of the blessed Heaven for which
    we pray,
Blow from the eternal hills ! — make
    glad our earthly way !

8th mo., 1852.

DERNE.[56]

NIGHT on the city of the Moor !
On mosque and tomb, and white-walled
    shore,
On sea-waves, to whose ceaseless knock
The narrow harbor-gates unlock,
On corsair's galley, carack tall,
And plundered Christian caraval !
The sounds of Moslem life are still ;
No mule-bell tinkles down the hill ;
Stretched in the broad court of the
    khan,
The dusty Bornou caravan
Lies heaped in slumber, beast and man ;
The Sheik is dreaming in his tent,
His noisy Arab tongue o'erspent ;
The kiosk's glimmering lights are gone,
The merchant with his wares with-
    drawn ;
Rough pillowed on some pirate breast,
The dancing-girl has sunk to rest ;
And, save where measured footsteps
    fall
Along the Bashaw's guarded wall,
Or where, like some bad dream, the
    Jew
Creeps stealthily his quarter through,
Or counts with fear his golden heaps,
The City of the Corsair sleeps !

But where yon prison long and low
Stands black against the pale star-glow,
Chafed by the ceaseless wash of waves,
There watch and pine the Christian
    slaves ; —
Rough-bearded men, whose far-off wives
Wear out with grief their lonely lives ; /
And youth, still flashing from his eyes
The clear blue of New England skies,
A treasured lock of whose soft hair
Now wakes some sorrowing mother's
    prayer ;
Or, worn upon some maiden breast,
Stirs with the loving heart's unrest !

A bitter cup each life must drain,
The groaning earth is cursed with pain,
And, like the scroll the angel bore
The shuddering Hebrew seer before,

O'erwrit alike, without, within,
With all the woes which follow sin ;
But, bitterest of the ills beneath
Whose load man totters down to death,
Is that which plucks the regal crown
Of Freedom from his forehead down,
And snatches from his powerless hand
The sceptred sign of self-command,
Effacing with the chain and rod
The image and the seal of God ;
Till from his nature, day by day,
The manly virtues fall away,
And leave him naked, blind and mute,
The godlike merging in the brute !

Why mourn the quiet ones who die
Beneath affection's tender eye,
Unto their household and their kin
Like ripened corn-sheaves gathered in ?
O weeper, from that tranquil sod,
That holy harvest-home of God,
Turn to the quick and suffering, — shed
Thy tears upon the living dead !
Thank God above thy dear ones' graves,
They sleep with Him, — they are not
    slaves.

What dark mass, down the mountain-
    sides
Swift-pouring, like a stream divides ? —
A long, loose, straggling caravan,
Camel and horse and arméd man.
The moon's low crescent, glimmering
    o'er
Its grave of waters to the shore,
Lights up that mountain cavalcade,
And glints from gun and spear and
    blade
Near and more near ! — now o'er them
    falls
The shadow of the city walls.
Hark to the sentry's challenge, drowned
In the fierce trumpet's charging
    sound ! —
The rush of men, the musket's peal,
The short, sharp clang of meeting steel !

Vain, Moslem, vain thy lifeblood poured
So freely on thy foeman's sword !
Not to the swift nor to the strong
The battles of the right belong ;
For he who strikes for Freedom wears
The armor of the captive's prayers,
And Nature proffers to his cause
The strength of her eternal laws ;
While he whose arm essays to bind
And herd with common brutes his kind

Strives evermore at fearful odds
With Nature and the jealous gods,
And dares the dread recoil which late
Or soon their right shall vindicate.

'T is done, — the hornéd crescent falls !
The star-flag flouts the broken walls !
Joy to the captive husband ! joy
To thy sick heart, O brown-locked boy !
In sullen wrath the conquered Moor
Wide open flings your dungeon-door,
And leaves ye free from cell and chain,
The owners of yourselves again.
Dark as his allies desert-born,
Soiled with the battle's stain, and worn
With the long marches of his band
Through hottest wastes of rock and
    sand, —
Scorched by the sun and furnace-breath
Of the red desert's wind of death,
With welcome words and grasping
    hands,
The victor and deliverer stands !

The tale is one of distant skies ;
The dust of half a century lies
Upon it ; yet its hero's name
Still lingers on the lips of Fame.
Men speak the praise of him who gave
Deliverance to the Moorman's slave,
Yet dare to brand with shame and crime
The heroes of our land and time, —
The self-forgetful ones, who stake
Home, name, and life for Freedom's
    sake.
God mend his heart who cannot feel
The impulse of a holy zeal,
And sees not, with his sordid eyes,
The beauty of self-sacrifice !
Though in the sacred place he stands,
Uplifting consecrated hands,
Unworthy are his lips to tell
Of Jesus' martyr-miracle,
Or name aright that dread embrace
Of suffering for a fallen race !

ASTRÆA.

" Jove means to settle
Astræa in her seat again,
And let down from his golden chain
    An age of better metal."
        Ben Jonson, 1615

O poet rare and old !
    Thy words are prophecies ;
Forward the age of gold,
    The new Saturnian lies.

The universal prayer
And hope are not in vain ;
Rise, brothers ! and prepare
The way for Saturn's reign.

Perish shall all which takes
From labor's board and can ;
Perish shall all which makes
A spaniel of the man !

Free from its bonds the mind,
The body from the rod ;
Broken all chains that bind
The image of our God.

Just men no longer pine
Behind their prison-bars ;
Through the rent dungeon shine
The free sun and the stars.

Earth own, at last, untrod
By sect, or caste, or clan,
The fatherhood of God,
The brotherhood of man !

Fraud fail, craft perish, forth
The money-changers driven,
And God's will done on earth,
As now in heaven !

INVOCATION.

THROUGH thy clear spaces, Lord, of
    old,
Formless and void the dead earth rolled ;
Deaf to thy heaven's sweet music, blind
To the great lights which o'er it shined ;
No sound, no ray, no warmth, no
    breath, —
A dumb despair, a wandering death.

To that dark, weltering horror came
Thy spirit, like a subtle flame, —
A breath of life electrical,
Awakening and transforming all,
Till beat and thrilled in every part
The pulses of a living heart.

Then knew their bounds the land and
    sea :
Then smiled the bloom of mead and
    tree ;
From flower to moth, from beast to man,
The quick creative impulse ran ;
And earth, with life from thee renewed,
Was in thy holy eyesight good.

As lost and void, as dark and cold
And formless as that earth of old, —
A wandering waste of storm and night,
Midst spheres of song and realms of
    light, —
A blot upon thy holy sky,
Untouched, unwarned of thee, am I.

O thou who movest on the deep
Of spirits, wake my own from sleep !
Its darkness melt, its coldness warm,
The lost restore, the ill transform,
That flower and fruit henceforth may be
Its grateful offering, worthy thee.

THE CROSS.

ON THE DEATH OF RICHARD DILLING-
HAM, IN THE NASHVILLE PENITEN-
TIARY.

"THE cross, if rightly borne, shall be
No burden, but support to thee" ;*
So, moved of old time for our sake,
The holy monk of Kempen spake.

Thou brave and true one ! upon whom
Was laid the cross of martyrdom,
How didst thou, in thy generous youth,
Bear witness to this blessed truth !

Thy cross of suffering and of shame
A staff within thy hands became,
In paths where faith alone could see
The Master's steps supporting thee.

Thine was the seed-time ; God alone
Beholds the end of what is sown ;
Beyond our vision, weak and dim,
The harvest-time is hid with Him.

Yet, unforgotten where it lies,
That seed of generous sacrifice,
Though seeming on the desert cast,
Shall rise with bloom and fruit at last.

EVA.

DRY the tears for holy Eva,
With the blessed angels leave her ;
Of the form so soft and fair
Give to earth the tender care.

For the golden locks of Eva
Let the sunny south-land give her

* Thomas à Kempis. Imit. Christ.

Flowery pillow of repose,—
Orange-bloom and budding rose.

In the better home of Eva
Let the shining ones receive her,
With the welcome-voicéd psalm,
Harp of gold and waving palm !

All is light and peace with Eva ;
There the darkness cometh never ;
Tears are wiped, and fetters fall,
And the Lord is all in all.

Weep no more for happy Eva,
- Wrong and sin no more shall grieve
    her ;
Care and pain and weariness
Lost in love so measureless.

Gentle Eva, loving Eva,
Child confessor, true believer,
Listener at the Master's knee,
"Suffer such to come to me."

O, for faith like thine, sweet Eva,
Lighting all the solemn river,
And the blessings of the poor
Wafting to the heavenly shore !

TO FREDRIKA BREMER.[57]

SEERESS of the misty Norland,
    Daughter of the Vikings bold,
Welcome to the sunny Vineland,
    Which thy fathers sought of old !

Soft as flow of Silja's waters,
    When the moon of summer shines,
Strong as Winter from his mountains
    Roaring through the sleeted pines.

Heart and ear, we long have listened
    To thy saga, rune, and song,
As a household joy and presence
    We have known and loved thee long.

By the mansion's marble mantel,
    Round the log-walled cabin's hearth,
Thy sweet thoughts and northern fancies
    Meet and mingle with our mirth.

And o'er weary spirits keeping
    Sorrow's night-watch, long and chill,
Shine they like thy sun of summer
    Over midnight vale and hill.

We alone to thee are strangers,
    Thou our friend and teacher art ;
Come, and know us as we know thee ;
    Let us meet thee heart to heart !

To our homes and household altars
    We, in turn, thy steps would lead
As thy loving hand has led us
    O'er the threshold of the Swede.

APRIL.

" The spring comes slowly up this way."
Christabel.

'T IS the noon of the spring-time, yet
    never a bird
In the wind-shaken elm or the maple is
    heard ;
For green meadow-grasses wide levels of
    snow,
And blowing of drifts where the crocus
    should blow :
Where wind-flower and violet, amber
    and white,
On south-sloping brooksides should
    smile in the light,
O'er the cold winter-beds of their late-
    waking roots
The frosty flake eddies, the ice-crystal
    shoots ;
And, longing for light, under wind-
    driven heaps,
Round the boles of the pine-wood the
    ground-laurel creeps,
Unkissed of the sunshine, unbaptized of
    showers,
With buds scarcely swelled, which
    should burst into flowers !
We wait for thy coming, sweet wind of
    the south !
For the touch of thy light wings, the
    kiss of thy mouth ;
For the yearly evangel thou bearest from
    God,
Resurrection and life to the graves of the
    sod !
Up our long river-valley, for days, have
    not ceased
The wail and the shriek of the bitter
    northeast, —
Raw and chill, as if winnowed through
    ices and snow,
All the way from the land of the wild
    Esquimau, —
Until all our dreams of the land of the
    blest,

Like that red hunter's, turn to the sunny
        southwest.
O soul of the spring-time, its light and
        its breath,
Bring warmth to this coldness, bring
        life to this death ;
Renew the great miracle ; let us behold
The stone from the mouth of the sepul-
        chre rolled,
And Nature, like Lazarus, rise, as of
        old !
Let our faith, which in darkness and
        coldness has lain,
Revive with the warmth and the bright-
        ness again,
And in blooming of flower and budding
        of tree
The symbols and types of our destiny
        see ;
The life of the spring-time, the life of
        the whole,
And, as sun to the sleeping earth, love
        to the soul !

STANZAS FOR THE TIMES.

1850.

THE evil days have come, — the poor
        Are made a prey ;
Bar up the hospitable door,
Put out the fire-lights, point no more
        The wanderer's way.

For Pity now is crime ; the chain
        Which binds our States
Is melted at her hearth in twain,
Is rusted by her tears' soft rain :
        Close up her gates.

Our Union, like a glacier stirred
        By voice below,
Or bell of kine, or wing of bird,
A beggar's crust, a kindly word
        May overthrow !

Poor, whispering tremblers ! — yet we
        boast
        Our blood and name ;
Bursting its century-bolted frost,
Each gray cairn on the Northman's
        coast
        Cries out for shame !

O for the open firmament,
        The prairie free,

The desert hillside, cavern-rent,
The Pawnee's lodge, the Arab's tent,
        The Bushman's tree !

Than web of Persian loom most rare,
        Or soft divan,
Better the rough rock, bleak and bare,
Or hollow tree, which man may share
        With suffering man.

I hear a voice : "Thus saith the Law,
        Let Love be dumb ;
Clasping her liberal hands in awe,
Let sweet-lipped Charity withdraw
        From hearth and home."

I hear another voice : "The poor
        Are thine to feed ;
Turn not the outcast from thy door,
Nor give to bonds and wrong once more
        Whom God hath freed."

Dear Lord ! between that law and thee
        No choice remains ;
Yet not untrue to man's decree,
Though spurning its rewards, is he
        Who bears its pains.

Not mine Sedition's trumpet-blast
        And threatening word ;
I read the lesson of the Past,
That firm endurance wins at last
        More than the sword.

O clear-eyed Faith, and Patience, thou
        So calm and strong !
Lend strength to weakness, teach us how
The sleepless eyes of God look through
        This night of wrong !

A SABBATH SCENE.

SCARCE had the solemn Sabbath-bell
        Ceased quivering in the steeple,
Scarce had the parson to his desk
        Walked stately through his people,

When down the summer-shaded street
        A wasted female figure,
With dusky brow and naked feet,
        Came rushing wild and eager.

She saw the white spire through the
        trees,
        She heard the sweet hymn swelling :
O pitying Christ ! a refuge give
        That poor one in thy dwelling !

Like a scared fawn before the hounds,
  Right up the aisle she glided,
While close behind her, whip in hand,
  A lank-haired hunter strided.

She raised a keen and bitter cry,
  To Heaven and Earth appealing ; —
Were manhood's generous pulses dead ?
  Had woman's heart no feeling ?

A score of stout hands rose between
  The hunter and the flying :
Age clenched his staff, and maiden eyes
  Flashed tearful, yet defying.

"Who dares profane this house and
    day ? "
) Cried out the angry pastor.
" Why, bless your soul, the wench 's a
    slave,
  And I 'm her lord and master ! "

" I 've law and gospel on my side,
  And who shall dare refuse me ? "
Down came the parson, bowing low,
  " My good sir, pray excuse me !

" Of course I know your right divine
  To own and work and whip her ;
Quick, deacon, throw that Polyglott
  Before the wench, and trip her ! "

Plump dropped the holy tome, and
    o'er
  Its sacred pages stumbling,
Bound hand and foot, a slave once more,
  The hapless wretch lay trembling.

I saw the parson tie the knots,
  The while his flock addressing,
The Scriptural claims of slavery
  With text on text impressing.

"Although," said he, " on Sabbath day
  All secular occupations
Are deadly sins, we must fulfil
  Our moral obligations :

" And this commends itself as one
  To every conscience tender ;
As Paul sent back Onesimus,
  My Christian friends, we send her !'

Shriek rose on shriek, — the Sabbath air
  Her wild cries tore asunder ;
I listened, with hushed breath, to hear
  God answering with his thunder !

All still ! — the very altar's cloth
  Had smothered down her shrieking,
And, dumb, she turned from face to
    face,
  For human pity seeking !

I saw her dragged along the aisle,
  Her shackles harshly clanking ;
I heard the parson, over all,
  The Lord devoutly thanking !

My brain took fire : " Is this," I cried,
  " The end of prayer and preach-
    ing ?
Then down with pulpit, down with
    priest,
  And give us Nature's teaching !

" Foul shame and scorn be on ye all
  Who turn the good to evil,
And steal the Bible from the Lord,
  To give it to the Devil !

" Than garbled text or parchment law
  I own a statute higher ;
And God is true, though every book
  And every man's a liar ! "

Just then I felt the deacon's hand
  In wrath my coat-tail seize on ;
I heard the priest cry, " Infidel ! "
  The lawyer mutter, " Treason ! "

I started up, — where now were church
  Slave, master, priest, and people ?
I only heard the supper-bell,
  Instead of clanging steeple.

But, on the open window's sill,
  O'er which the white blooms drifted,
The pages of a good old Book
  The wind of summer lifted,

And flower and vine, like angel wings
  Around the Holy Mother,
Waved softly there, as if God's truth
  And Mercy kissed each other.

And freely from the cherry-bough
  Above the casement swinging,
With golden bosom to the sun,
  The oriole was singing.

As bird and flower made plain of old
  The lesson of the Teacher,
So now I heard the written Word
  Interpreted by Nature !

For to my ear methought the breeze
  Bore Freedom's blessed word on ;
THUS SAITH THE LORD : BREAK EVERY
    YOKE,
  UNDO THE HEAVY BURDEN !

REMEMBRANCE.

WITH COPIES OF THE AUTHOR'S WRIT-
INGS.

FRIEND of mine ! whose lot was cast
With me in the distant past, —
Where, like shadows flitting fast,

Fact and fancy, thought and theme,
Word and work, begin to seem
Like a half-remembered dream !

Touched by change have all things
    been,
Yet I think of thee as when
We had speech of lip and pen.

For the calm thy kindness lent
To a path of discontent,
Rough with trial and dissent ;

Gentle words where such were few,
Softening blame where blame was
    true,
Praising where small praise was due ;

For a waking dream made good,
For an ideal understood,
For thy Christian womanhood ;

For thy marvellous gift to cull
From our common life and dull
Whatsoe'er is beautiful ;

Thoughts and fancies, Hybla's bees
Dropping sweetness ; true heart's-ease
Of congenial sympathies ; —

Still for these I own my debt ;
Memory, with her eyelids wet,
Fain would thank thee even yet !

And as one who scatters flowers
Where the Queen of May's sweet hours
Sits, o'ertwined with blossomed bowers,

In superfluous zeal bestowing
Gifts where gifts are overflowing,
So I pay the debt I'm owing.

To thy full thoughts, gay or sad,
Sunny-hued or sober clad,
Something of my own I add ;

Well assured that thou wilt take
Even the offering which I make
Kindly for the giver's sake.

THE POOR VOTER ON ELEC-TION DAY.

THE proudest now is but my peer,
  The highest not more high ;
To-day, of all the weary year,
  A king of men am I.
To-day, alike are great and small,
  The nameless and the known ;
My palace is the people's hall,
  The ballot-box my throne !

Who serves to-day upon the list
  Beside the served shall stand ;
Alike the brown and wrinkled fist,
  The gloved and dainty hand !
The rich is level with the poor,
  The weak is strong to-day ;
And sleekest broadcloth counts no more
  Than homespun frock of gray.

To-day let pomp and vain pretence
  My stubborn right abide ;
I set a plain man's common sense
  Against the pedant's pride.
To-day shall simple manhood try
  The strength of gold and land ;
The wide world has not wealth to buy
  The power in my right hand !

While there's a grief to seek redress,
  Or balance to adjust,
Where weighs our living manhood less
  Than Mammon's vilest dust, —
While there's a right to need my vote,
  A wrong to sweep away,
Up ! clouted knee and ragged coat !
  A man's a man to-day !

TRUST.

THE same old baffling questions ! O my
    friend,
I cannot answer them. In vain I send
My soul into the dark, where never burn
  The lamps of science, nor the natural
    light

Or Reason's sun and stars ! I cannot
 learn
Their great and solemn meanings, nor
 discern
The awful secrets of the eyes which turn
 Evermore on us through the day and
 night
 With silent challenge and a dumb
 demand,
Proffering the riddles of the dread un-
 known,
Like the calm Sphinxes, with their eyes
 of stone,
 Questioning the centuries from their
 veils of sand !
I have no answer for myself or thee,
Save that I learned beside my mother's
 knee ;
" All is of God that is, and is to be ;
 And God is good." Let this suffice
 us still,
 Resting in childlike trust upon his
 will
Who moves to his great ends unthwarted
 by the ill.

KATHLEEN.[58]

O NORAH, lay your basket down,
 And rest your weary hand,
And come and hear me sing a song
 Of our old Ireland.

There was a lord of Galaway,
 A mighty lord was he ;
And he did wed a second wife,
 A maid of low degree.

But he was old, and she was young,
 And so, in evil spite,
She baked the black bread for his kin,
 And fed her own with white.

She whipped the maids and starved the
 kern,
 And drove away the poor ;
" Ah, woe is me ! " the old lord said,
 " I rue my bargain sore ! "

This lord he had a daughter fair,
 Beloved of old and young,
And nightly round the shealing-fires
 Of her the gleeman sung.

" As sweet and good is young Kathleen
 As Eve before her fall " ;

So sang the harper at the fair,
 So harped he in the hall.

" O come to me, my daughter dear !
 Come sit upon my knee,
For looking in your face, Kathleen,
 Your mother's own I see ! "

He smoothed and smoothed her hair away,
 He kissed her forehead fair ;
" It is my darling Mary's brow,
 It is my darling's hair ! "

O, then spake up the angry dame,
 " Get up, get up," quoth she,
" I 'll sell ye over Ireland,
 I 'll sell ye o'er the sea ! "

She clipped her glossy hair away,
 That none her rank might know,
She took away her gown of silk,
 And gave her one of tow,

And sent her down to Limerick town
 And to a seaman sold
This daughter of an Irish lord
 For ten good pounds in gold.

The lord he smote upon his breast,
 And tore his beard so gray ;
But he was old, and she was young,
 And so she had her way.

Sure that same night the Banshee howled
 To fright the evil dame,
And fairy folks, who loved Kathleen,
 With funeral torches came.

She watched them glancing through the
 trees,
 And glimmering down the hill ;
They crept before the dead-vault door,
 And there they all stood still !

" Get up, old man ! the wake-lights
 shine ! "
 " Ye murthering witch," quoth he,
" So I 'm rid of your tongue, I little care
 If they shine for you or me."

" O, whoso brings my daughter back,
 My gold and land shall have ! "
O, then spake up his handsome page,
 " No gold nor land I crave !

" But give to me your daughter dear,
 Give sweet Kathleen to me,

Be she on sea or be she on land,
  I 'll bring her back to thee."

" My daughter is a lady born,
  And you of low degree,
But she shall be your bride the day
  You bring her back to me."

He sailed east, he sailed west,
  And far and long sailed he,
Until he came to Boston town,
  Across the great salt sea.

" O, have ye seen the young Kathleen,
  The flower of Ireland ?
Ye 'll know her by her eyes so blue,
  And by her snow-white hand ! "

Out spake an ancient man, " I know
  The maiden whom ye mean ;
I bought her of a Limerick man,
  And she is called Kathleen.

" No skill hath she in household work,
  Her hands are soft and white,
Yet well by loving looks and ways
  She doth her cost requite."

So up they walked through Boston town,
  And met a maiden fair,
A little basket on her arm
  So snowy-white and bare.

" Come hither, child, and say hast thou
  This young man ever seen ? "
They wept within each other's arms,
  The page and young Kathleen.

" O give to me this darling child,
  And take my purse of gold."
" Nay, not by me," her master said,
  " Shall sweet Kathleen be sold.

" We loved her in the place of one
  The Lord hath early ta'en ;
But, since her heart 's in Ireland,
  We give her back again ! "

O, for that same the saints in heaven
  For his poor soul shall pray,
And Mary Mother wash with tears
  His heresies away.

Sure now they dwell in Ireland,
  As you go up Claremore
Ye 'll see their castle looking down
  The pleasant Galway shore.

And the old lord's wife is dead and gone,
  And a happy man is he,
For he sits beside his own Kathleen,
  With her darling on his knee.

FIRST–DAY THOUGHTS.

In calm and cool and silence, once again
  I find my old accustomed place among
  My brethren, where, perchance, no human tongue
    Shall utter words ; where never hymn is sung,
  Nor deep-toned organ blown, nor censer swung,
Nor dim light falling through the pictured pane !
There, syllabled by silence, let me hear
The still small voice which reached the prophet's ear ;
Read in my heart a still diviner law
Than Israel's leader on his tables saw !
There let me strive with each besetting sin,
  Recall my wandering fancies, and restrain
  The sore disquiet of a restless brain ;
  And, as the path of duty is made plain,
May grace be given that I may walk therein,
  Not like the hireling, for his selfish gain,
With backward glances and reluctant tread,
Making a merit of his coward dread, —
  But, cheerful, in the light around me thrown,
  Walking as one to pleasant service led ;
  Doing God's will as if it were my own,
Yet trusting not in mine, but in his strength alone !

KOSSUTH.[59]

Type of two mighty continents ! — combining
  The strength of Europe with the warmth and glow
Of Asian song and prophecy, — the shining
  Of Orient splendors over Northern snow !
Who shall receive him ? Who, unblushing, speak

Welcome to him, who, while he strove
to break
The Austrian yoke from Magyar necks,
smote off
At the same blow the fetters of the
serf, —
Rearing the altar of his Father-land
  On the firm base of freedom, and
  thereby
Lifting to Heaven a patriot's stainless
hand,
  Mocked not the God of Justice with a
  lie !
Who shall be Freedom's mouth-piece ?
Who shall give
Her welcoming cheer to the great fugi-
tive ?
Not he who, all her sacred trusts betray-
ing,
  Is scourging back to slavery's hell of
  pain
  The swarthy Kossuths of our land
  again !
Not he whose utterance now from lips
designed
The bugle-march of Liberty to wind,
And call her hosts beneath the breaking
light, —
The keen reveille of her morn of fight, —
  Is but the hoarse note of the blood-
  hound's baying,
The wolf's long howl behind the bond-
man's flight !
O for the tongue of him who lies at rest
  In Quincy's shade of patrimonial
  trees, —
Last of the Puritan tribunes and the
best, —
  To lend a voice to Freedom's sympa-
  thies,
And hail the coming of the noblest guest
The Old World's wrong has given the
New World of the West !

TO MY OLD SCHOOLMASTER.

AN EPISTLE NOT AFTER THE MANNER
OF HORACE.

OLD friend, kind friend ! lightly down
Drop time's snow-flakes on thy crown !
Never be thy shadow less,
Never fail thy cheerfulness ;
Care, that kills the cat, may plough
Wrinkles in the miser's brow,
Deepen envy's spiteful frown,

Draw the mouths of bigots down,
Plague ambition's dream, and sit
Heavy on the hypocrite,
Haunt the rich man's door, and ride
In the gilded coach of pride ; —
Let the fiend pass ! — what can he
Find to do with such as thee ?
Seldom comes that evil guest
Where the conscience lies at rest,
And brown health and quiet wit
Smiling on the threshold sit.

I, the urchin unto whom,
In that smoked and dingy room,
Where the district gave thee rule
O'er its ragged winter school,
Thou didst teach the mysteries
Of those weary A B C's, —
Where, to fill the every pause
Of thy wise and learned saws,
Through the cracked and crazy wall
Came the cradle-rock and squall,
And the goodman's voice, at strife
With his shrill and tipsy wife, —
Luring us by stories old,
With a comic unction told,
More than by the eloquence
Of terse birchen arguments
(Doubtful gain, I fear), to look
With complacence on a book ! —
Where the genial pedagogue
Half forgot his rogues to flog,
Citing tale or apologue,
Wise and merry in its drift
As old Phædrus' twofold gift,
Had the little rebels known it,
Risum et prudentiam monet !
I, — the man of middle years,
In whose sable locks appears
Many a warning fleck of gray, —
Looking back to that far day,
And thy primal lessons, feel
Grateful smiles my lips unseal,
As, remembering thee, I blend
Olden teacher, present friend,
Wise with antiquarian search,
In the scrolls of State and Church :
Named on history's title-page,
Parish-clerk and justice sage ;
For the ferule's wholesome awe
Wielding now the sword of law.

Threshing Time's neglected sheaves,
Gathering up the scattered leaves
Which the wrinkled sibyl cast
Careless from her as she passed, —
Twofold citizen art thou,

Freeman of the past and now.
He who bore thy name of old
Midway in the heavens did hold
Over Gibeon moōn and sun ;
Thou hast bidden them backward run ;
Of to-day the present ray
Flinging over yesterday !

Let the busy ones deride
What I deem of right thy pride :
Let the fools their tread-mills grind,
Look not forward nor behind,
Shuffle in and wriggle out,
Veer with every breeze about,
Turning like a windmill sail,
Or a dog that seeks his tail ;
Let them laugh to see thee fast
Tabernacled in the Past,
Working out with eye and lip,
Riddles of old penmanship,
Patient as Belzoni there
Sorting out, with loving care,
Mummies of dead questions stripped
From their sevenfold manuscript !

Dabbling, in their noisy way,
In the puddles of to-day,
Little know they of that vast
Solemn ocean of the past,
On whose margin, wreck-bespread,
Thou art walking with the dead,
Questioning the stranded years,
Waking smiles, by turns, and tears,
As thou callest up again
Shapes the dust has long o'erlain, —
Fair-haired woman, bearded man,
Cavalier and Puritan ;
In an age whose eager view
Seeks but present things, and new,
Mad for party, sect and gold,
Teaching reverence for the old.

On that shore, with fowler's tact,
Coolly bagging fact on fact,
Naught amiss to thee can float,
Tale, or song, or anecdote ;
Village gossip, centuries old,
Scandals by our grandams told,
What the pilgrim's table spread,
Where he lived, and whom he wed,
Long-drawn bill of wine and beer
For his ordination cheer,
Or the flip that wellnigh made
Glad his funeral cavalcade ;
Weary prose, and poet's lines,
Flavored by their age, like wines,
Eulogistic of some quaint,

Doubtful, puritanic saint ;
Lays that quickened husking jigs,
Jests that shook grave periwigs,
When the parson had his jokes
And his glass, like other folks ;
Sermons that, for mortal hours,
Taxed our fathers' vital powers,
As the long nineteenthlies poured
Downward from the sounding-board,
And, for fire of Pentecost,
Touched their beards December's frost.

Time is hastening on, and we
What our father's are shall be, —
Shadow-shapes of memory !
Joined to that vast multitude
Where the great are but the good,
And the mind of strength shall prove
Weaker than the heart of love ;
Pride of graybeard wisdom less
Than the infant's guilelessness,
And his song of sorrow more
Than the crown the Psalmist wore !
Who shall then, with pious zeal,
At our moss-grown thresholds kneel,
From a stained and stony page
Reading to a careless age,
With a patient eye like thine,
Prosing tale and limping line,
Names and words the hoary rime
Of the Past has made sublime ?
Who shall work for us as well
The antiquarian's miracle ?
Who to seeming life recall
Teacher grave and pupil small ?
Who shall give to thee and me
Freeholds in futurity ?

Well, whatever lot be mine,
Long and happy days be thine,
Ere thy full and honored age
Dates of time its latest page !
Squire for master, State for school,
Wisely lenient, live and rule ;
Over grown-up knave and rogue
Play the watchful pedagogue ;
Or, while pleasure smiles on duty,
At the call of youth and beauty,
Speak for them the spell of law
Which shall bar and bolt withdraw,
And the flaming sword remove
From the Paradise of Love.
Still, with undimmed eyesight, pore
Ancient tome and record o'er ;
Still thy week-day lyrics croon,
Pitch in church the Sunday tune,
Showing something, in thy part,

Of the old Puritanic art,
Singer after Sternhold's heart!
In thy pew, for many a year,
Homilies from Oldbug hear,[60]
Who to wit like that of South,
And the Syrian's golden mouth,
Doth the homely pathos add
Which the pilgrim preachers had;
Breaking, like a child at play,
Gilded idols of the day,
Cant of knave and pomp of fool
Tossing with his ridicule,

Yet, in earnest or in jest,
Ever keeping truth abreast.
And, when thou art called, at last,
To thy townsmen of the past,
Not as stranger shalt thou come;
Thou shalt find thyself at home!
With the little and the big,
Woollen cap and periwig,
Madam in her high-laced ruff,
Goody in her home-made stuff, —
Wise and simple, rich and poor,
Thou hast known them all before!

THE PANORAMA,

AND OTHER POEMS.

THE PANORAMA.

"A! fredome is a nobill thing!
Fredome mayse man to haif liking.
Fredome all solace to man giffis;
He levys at ese that frely levys!
A nobil hart may haif nane ese
Na ellys nocht that may him plese
Gyff Fredome failythe."
ARCHDEACON BARBOUR.

THROUGH the long hall the shuttered windows shed
A dubious light on every upturned head, —
On locks like those of Absalom the fair,
On the bald apex ringed with scanty hair,
On blank indifference and on curious stare;
On the pale Showman reading from his stage
The hieroglyphics of that facial page;
Half sad, half scornful, listening to the bruit
Of restless cane-tap and impatient foot,
And the shrill call, across the general din,
"Roll up your curtain! Let the show begin!"

At length a murmur like the winds that break
Into green waves the prairie's grassy lake,

Deepened and swelled to music clear and loud,
And, as the west-wind lifts a summer cloud,
The curtain rose, disclosing wide and far
A green land stretching to the evening star,
Fair rivers, skirted by primeval trees
And flowers hummed over by the desert bees,
Marked by tall bluffs whose slopes of greenness show
Fantastic outcrops of the rock below, —
The slow result of patient Nature's pains,
And plastic fingering of her sun and rains, —
Arch, tower, and gate, grotesquely windowed hall,
And long escarpment of half-crumbled wall,
Huger than those which, from steep hills of vine,
Stare through their loopholes on the travelled Rhine;
Suggesting vaguely to the gazer's mind
A fancy, idle as the prairie wind,
Of the land's dwellers in an age unguessed, —
The unsung Jotuns of the mystic West.

Beyond, the prairie's sea-like swells surpass
The Tartar's marvels of his Land of Grass,

Vast as the sky against whose sunset
  shores
Wave after wave the billowy greenness
  pours ;
And, onward still, like islands in that
  main
Loom the rough peaks of many a moun-
  tain chain,
Whence east and west a thousand waters
  run
From winter lingering under summer's
  sun.
And, still beyond, long lines of foam
  and sand
Tell where Pacific rolls his waves a-
  land,
From many a wide-lapped port and
  land-locked bay,
Opening with thunderous pomp the
  world's highway
To Indian isles of spice, and marts of far
  Cathay.

  "Such," said the Showman, as the
    curtain fell,
" Is the new Canaan of our Israel, —
The land of promise to the swarming
  North,
Which, hive-like, sends its annual sur-
  plus forth,
To the poor Southron on his worn-out
  soil,
Scathed by the curses of unnatural toil ;
To Europe's exiles seeking home and
  rest,
And the lank nomads of the wandering
  West,
Who, asking neither, in their love of
  change
And the free bison's amplitude of range,
Rear the log-hut, for present shelter
  meant,
Not future comfort, like an Arab's tent."

  Then spake a shrewd on-looker, " Sir,"
    said he,
" I like your picture, but I fain would
  see
A sketch of what your promised land
  will be
When, with electric nerve, and fiery-
  brained,
With Nature's forces to its chariot
  chained,
The future grasping, by the past obeyed,
The twentieth century rounds a new
  decade."

Then said the Showman, sadly : " He
  who grieves
Over the scattering of the sibyl's leaves
Unwisely mourns. Suffice it, that we
  know
What needs must ripen from the seed
  we sow ;
That present time is but the mould
  wherein
We cast the shapes of holiness and sin.
A painful watcher of the passing hour,
Its lust of gold, its strife for place and
  power ;
Its lack of manhood, honor, reverence,
  truth,
Wise-thoughted age, and generous-
  hearted youth ;
Nor yet unmindful of each better sign, —
The low, far lights, which on th' horizon
  shine,
Like those which sometimes tremble on
  the rim
Of clouded skies when day is closing
  dim,
Flashing athwart the purple spears of
  rain
The hope of sunshine on the hills
  again : —
I need no prophet's word, nor shapes
  that pass
Like clouding shadows o'er a magic
  glass ;
For now, as ever, passionless and cold,
Doth the dread angel of the future hold
Evil and good before us, with no voice
Or warning look to guide us in our
  choice ;
With spectral hands outreaching through
  the gloom
The shadowy contrasts of the coming
  doom.
Transferred from these, it now remains
  to give
The sun and shade of Fate's alternative."

  Then, with a burst of music, touching
    all
The keys of thrifty life, — the mill-
  stream's fall,
The engine's pant along its quivering
  rails,
The anvil's ring, the measured beat of
  flails,
The sweep of scythes, the reaper's
  whistled tune,
Answering the summons of the bells of
  noon,

The woodman's hail along the river
  shores,
The steamboat's signal, and the dip of
  oars, —
Slowly the curtain rose from off a land
Fair as God's garden. Broad on either
  hand
The golden wheat-fields glimmered in
  the sun,
And the tall maize its yellow tassels
  spun.
Smooth highways set with hedge-rows
  living green,
With steepled towns through shaded
  vistas seen,
The school-house murmuring with its
  hive-like swarm,
The brook-bank whitening in the grist-
  mill's storm,
The painted farm-house shining through
  the leaves
Of fruited orchards bending at its eaves,
Where live again, around the Western
  hearth,
The homely old-time virtues of the
  North ;
Where the blithe housewife rises with
  the day,
And well-paid labor counts his task a
  play.
And, grateful tokens of a Bible free,
And the free Gospel of Humanity,
Of diverse sects and differing names the
  shrines,
One in their faith, whate'er their out-
  ward signs,
Like varying strophes of the same sweet
  hymn
From many a prairie's swell and river's
  brim,
A thousand church-spires sanctify the
  air
Of the calm Sabbath, with their sign of
  prayer.

  Like sudden nightfall over bloom and
    green
The curtain dropped : and, momently,
    between
The clank of fetter and the crack of
    thong,
Half sob, half laughter, music swept
    along, —
A strange refrain, whose idle words and
    low,
Like drunken mourners, kept the time
    of woe ;

As if the revellers at a masquerade
Heard in the distance funeral marches
  played.
Such music, dashing all his smiles with
  tears,
The thoughtful voyager on Ponchartrain
  hears,
Where, through the noonday dusk of
  wooded shores
The negro boatman, singing to his oars,
With a wild pathos borrowed of his
  wrong
Redeems the jargon of his senseless song.
"Look," said the Showman, sternly,
  as he rolled
His curtain upward ; "Fate's reverse
  behold !"

  A village straggling in loose disarray
Of vulgar newness, premature decay ;
A tavern, crazy with its whiskey brawls,
With "*Slaves at Auction !*" garnishing
  its walls.
Without, surrounded by a motley crowd,
The shrewd-eyed salesman, garrulous
  and loud,
A squire or colonel in his pride of place,
Known at free fights, the caucus, and
  the race,
Prompt to proclaim his honor without
  blot,
And silence doubters with a ten-pace
  shot,
Mingling the negro-driving bully's rant
With pious phrase and democratic cant,
Yet never scrupling, with a filthy jest,
To sell the infant from its mother's
  breast,
Break through all ties of wedlock, home,
  and kin,
Yield shrinking girlhood up to gray-
  beard sin ;
Sell all the virtues with his human stock,
The Christian graces on his auction-
  block,
And coolly count on shrewdest bargains
  driven
In hearts regenerate, and in souls for-
  given !

  Look once again ! The moving can-
    vas shows
A slave plantation's slovenly repose,
Where, in rude cabins rotting midst
    their weeds,
The human chattel eats, and sleeps, and
    breeds ;

15

And, held a brute, in practice, as in law,
Becomes in fact the thing he 's taken for.
There, early summoned to the hemp and
corn,
The nursing mother leaves her child
new-born ;
There haggard sickness, weak and
deathly faint,
Crawls to his task, and fears to make
complaint ;
And sad-eyed Rachels, childless in de-
cay,
Weep for their lost ones sold and torn
away !
Of ampler size the master's dwelling
stands,
In shabby keeping with his half-tilled
lands, —
The gates unhinged, the yard with weeds
unclean,
The cracked veranda with a tipsy lean.
Without, loose-scattered like a wreck
adrift,
Signs of misrule and tokens of unthrift ;
Within, profusion to discomfort joined,
The listless body and the vacant mind ;
The fear, the hate, the theft and false-
hood, born
In menial hearts of toil, and stripes, and
scorn !
There, all the vices, which, like birds
obscene,
Batten on slavery loathsome and un-
clean,
From the foul kitchen to the parlor rise,
Pollute the nursery where the child-heir
lies,
Taint infant lips beyond all after cure,
With the fell poison of a breast impure ;
Touch boyhood's passions with the
breath of flame,
From girlhood's instincts steal the blush
of shame.
So swells, from low to high, from weak
to strong,
The tragic chorus of the baleful wrong ;
Guilty or guiltless, all within its range
Feel the blind justice of its sure revenge.

Still scenes like these the moving
chart reveals.
Up the long western steppes the blight-
ing steals ;
Down the Pacific slope the evil Fate
Glides like a shadow to the Golden Gate :
From sea to sea the drear eclipse is
thrown,
From sea to sea the *Mauvaises Terres*
have grown,
A belt of curses on the New World's
zone !

The curtain fell. All drew a freer
breath,
As men are wont to do when mournful
death
Is covered from their sight. The Show-
man stood
With drooping brow in sorrow's attitude
One moment, then with sudden gesture
shook
His loose hair back, and with the air
and look
Of one who felt, beyond the narrow stage
And listening group, the presence of the
age,
And heard the footsteps of the things to
be,
Poured out his soul in earnest words and
free.

"O friends !" he said, "in this poor
trick of paint
You see the semblance, incomplete and
faint,
Of the two-fronted Future, which, to-
day,
Stands dim and silent, waiting in your
way.
To-day, your servant, subject to your
will ;
To-morrow, master, or for good or ill.
If the dark face of Slavery on you turns,
If the mad curse its paper barrier spurns,
If the world granary of the West is made
The last foul market of the slaver's trade,
Why rail at fate ? The mischief is your
own.
Why hate your neighbor ? Blame your-
selves alone !

"Men of the North ! The South you
charge with wrong
Is weak and poor, while you are rich
and strong.
If questions, — idle and absurd as those
The old-time monks and Paduan doctors
chose, —
Mere ghosts of questions, tariffs, and
dead banks,
And scarecrow pontiffs, never broke
your ranks,
Your thews united could, at once, roll
back

The jostled nation to its primal track.
Nay, were you simply steadfast, manly,
   just,
True to the faith your fathers left in trust,
If stainless honor outweighed in your
   scale
A codfish quintal or a factory bale,
Full many a noble heart, (and such remain
In all the South, like Lot in Siddim's
   plain,
Who watch and wait, and from the
   wrong's control
Keep white and pure their chastity of
   soul,)
Now sick to loathing of your weak com-
   plaints,
Your tricks as sinners, and your prayers
   as saints,
Would half-way meet the frankness of
   your tone,
And feel their pulses beating with your
   own.

   "The North! the South! no geo-
      graphic line
Can fix the boundary or the point define,
Since each with each so closely inter-
   blends,
Where Slavery rises, and where Freedom
   ends.
Beneath your rocks the roots, far-reach-
   ing, hide
Of the fell Upas on the Southern side;
The tree whose branches in your north-
   winds wave
Dropped its young blossoms on Mount
   Vernon's grave;
The nursling growth of Monticello's crest
Is now the glory of the free Northwest;
To the wise maxims of her olden school
Virginia listened from thy lips, Rantoul;
Seward's words of power, and Sumner's
   fresh renown,
Flow from the pen that Jefferson laid
   down!
And when, at length, her years of mad-
   ness o'er,
Like the crowned grazer on Euphrates'
   shore,
From her long lapse to savagery, her
   mouth
Bitter with baneful herbage, turns the
   South,
Resumes her old attire, and seeks to
   smooth
Her unkempt tresses at the glass of truth,
Her early faith shall find a tongue again,

New Wythes and Pinckneys swell that
   old refrain,
Her sons with yours renew the ancient
   pact,
The myth of Union prove at last a fact!
Then, if one murmur mars the wide con-
   tent,
Some Northern lip will drawl the last
   dissent,
Some Union-saving patriot of your own
Lament to find his occupation gone.

   "Grant that the North's insulted,
      scorned, betrayed,
O'erreached in bargains with her neigh-
   bor made,
When selfish thrift and party held the
   scales
For peddling dicker, not for honest
   sales, —
Whom shall we strike? Who most de-
   serves our blame?
The braggart Southron, open in his
   aim,
And bold as wicked, crashing straight
   through all
That bars his purpose, like a cannon-ball?
Or the mean traitor, breathing northern
   air,
With nasal speech and puritanic hair,
Whose cant the loss of principle survives,
As the mud-turtle e'en its head outlives;
Who, caught, chin-buried in some foul
   offence,
Puts on a look of injured innocence,
And consecrates his baseness to the cause
Of constitution, union, and the laws?

   "Praise to the place-man who can hold
      aloof
His still unpurchased manhood, office-
   proof;
Who on his round of duty walks erect,
And leaves it only rich in self-respect, —
As MORE maintained his virtue's lofty
   port
In the Eighth Henry's base and bloody
   court.
But, if exceptions here and there are
   found,
Who tread thus safely on enchanted
   ground,
The normal type, the fitting symbol still
Of those who fatten at the public mill,
Is the chained dog beside his master's
   door,
Or CIRCE's victim, feeding on all four!

"Give me the heroes who, at tuck of
    drum,
Salute thy staff, immortal Quattlebum !
Or they who, doubly armed with vote
    and gun,
Following thy lead, illustrious Atchison,
Their drunken franchise shift from scene
    to scene.
As tile-beard Jourdan did his guillo-
    tine ! —
Rather than him who, born beneath our
    skies,
To Slavery's hand its supplest tool sup-
    plies, —
The party felon whose unblushing face
Looks from the pillory of his bribe of
    place,
And coolly makes a merit of disgrace, —
Points to the footmarks of indignant
    scorn,
Shows the deep scars of satire's tossing
    horn ;
And passes to his credit side the sum
Of all that makes a scoundrel's martyr-
    dom !

"Bane of the North, its canker and
    its moth ! —
These modern Esaus, bartering rights for
    broth !
Taxing our justice, with their double
    claim,
As fools for pity, and as knaves for
    blame ;
Who, urged by party, sect, or trade,
    within
The fell embrace of Slavery's sphere of
    sin,
Part at the outset with their moral sense,
The watchful angel set for Truth's de-
    fence ;
Confound all contrasts, good and ill ;
    reverse
The poles of life, its blessing and its
    curse ;
And lose thenceforth from their perverted
    sight
The eternal difference 'twixt the wrong
    and right ;
To them the Law is but the iron span
That girds the ankles of imbruted man ;
To them the Gospel has no higher aim
Than simple sanction of the master's
    claim,
Dragged in the slime of Slavery's loath-
    some trail,
Like Chalier's Bible at his ass's tail !

"Such are the men who, with instinc-
    tive dread,
Whenever Freedom lifts her drooping
    head,
Make prophet-tripods of their office-
    stools,
And scare the nurseries and the village
    schools
With dire presage of ruin grim and great,
A broken Union and a foundered State !
Such are the patriots, self-bound to the
    stake
Of office, martyrs for their country's sake :
Who fill themselves the hungry jaws of
    Fate,
And by their loss of manhood save the
    State.
In the wide gulf themselves like Curtius
    throw,
And test the virtues of cohesive dough ;
As tropic monkeys, linking heads and
    tails,
Bridge o'er some torrent of Ecuador's
    vales !

"Such are the men who in your church-
    es rave
To swearing-point, at mention of the
    slave !
When some poor parson, haply unawares,
Stammers of freedom in his timid prayers ;
Who, if some foot-sore negro through the
    town
Steals northward, volunteer to hunt him
    down.
Or, if some neighbor, flying from disease,
Courts the mild balsam of the Southern
    breeze,
With hue and cry pursue him on his
    track,
And write Free-soiler on the poor man's
    back.
Such are the men who leave the pedler's
    cart,
While faring South, to learn the driver's
    art,
Or, in white neckcloth, soothe with pious
    aim
The graceful sorrows of some languid
    dame,
Who, from the wreck of her bereavement,
    saves
The double charm of widowhood and
    slaves ! —
Pliant and apt, they lose no chance to
    show
To what base depths apostasy can go ;

Outdo the natives in their readiness
To roast a negro, or to mob a press ;
Poise a tarred schoolmate on the lynch-
    er's rail,
Or make a bonfire of their birthplace
    mail !

"So some poor wretch, whose lips no
    longer bear
The sacred burden of his mother's prayer,
By fear impelled, or lust of gold enticed,
Turns to the Crescent from the Cross of
    Christ,
And, over-acting in superfluous zeal,
Crawls prostrate where the faithful only
    kneel,
Out-howls the Dervish, hugs his rags to
    court
The squalid Santon's sanctity of dirt ;
And, when beneath the city gateway's
    span
Files slow and long the Meccan caravan,
And through its midst, pursued by Islam's
    prayers,
The prophet's Word some favored camel
    bears,
The marked apostate has his place as-
    signed
The Koran-bearer's sacred rump behind,
With brush and pitcher following, grave
    and mute,
In meek attendance on the holy brute !

"Men of the North ! beneath your
    very eyes,
By hearth and home, your real danger
    lies.
Still day by day some hold of freedom
    falls,
Through home-bred traitors fed within
    its walls. —
Men whom yourselves with vote and
    purse sustain,
At posts of honor, influence, and gain ;
The right of Slavery to your sons to
    teach,
And " South-side " Gospels in your pul-
    pits preach,
Transfix the Law to ancient freedom dear
On the sharp point of her subverted spear,
And imitate upon her cushion plump
The mad Missourian lynching from his
    stump ;
Or, in your name, upon the Senate's floor
Yield up to Slavery all it asks, and more ;
And, ere your dull eyes open to the
    cheat,

Sell your old homestead underneath your
    feet !
While such as these your loftiest outlooks
    hold,
While truth and conscience with your
    wares are sold,
While grave-browed merchants band
    themselves to aid
An annual man-hunt for their Southern
    trade,
What moral power within your grasp
    remains
To stay the mischief on Nebraska's
    plains ? —
High as the tides of generous impulse
    flow,
As far rolls back the selfish undertow ;
And all your brave resolves, though
    aimed as true
As the horse-pistol Balmawhapple drew,
To Slavery's bastions lend as slight a
    shock
As the poor trooper's shot to Stirling
    rock !

" Yet, while the need of Freedom's
    cause demands
The earnest efforts of your hearts and
    hands,
Urged by all motives that can prompt
    the heart
To prayer and toil and manhood's man-
    liest part ;
Though to the soul's deep tocsin Nature
    joins
The warning whisper of her Orphic pines,
The north-wind's anger, and the south-
    wind's sigh,
The midnight sword-dance of the north-
    ern sky,
And, to the ear that bends above the
    sod
Of the green grave-mounds in the Fields
    of God,
In low, deep murmurs of rebuke or cheer,
The land's dead fathers speak their hope
    or fear,
Yet let not Passion wrest from Reason's
    hand
The guiding rein and symbol of com-
    mand.
Blame not the caution proffering to your
    zeal
A well-meant drag upon its hurrying
    wheel ;
Nor chide the man whose honest doubt
    extends

To the means only, not the righteous
    ends ;
Nor fail to weigh the scruples and the
    fears
Of milder natures and serener years.
In the long strife with evil which began
With the first lapse of new-created man,
Wisely and well has Providence assigned
To each his part, — some forward, some
    behind ;
And they, too, serve who temper and
    restrain
The o'erwarm heart that sets on fire the
    brain.
True to yourselves, feed Freedom's altar-
    flame
With what you have ; let others do the
    same.
Spare timid doubters ; set like flint your
    face
Against the self-sold knaves of gain and
    place :
Pity the weak ; but with unsparing hand
Cast out the traitors who infest the
    land, —
From bar, press, pulpit, cast them every-
    where,
By dint of fasting, if you fail by prayer.
And in their place bring men of antique
    mould,
Like the grave fathers of your Age of
    Gold, —
Statesmen like those who sought the
    primal fount
Of righteous law, the Sermon on the
    Mount ;
Lawyers who prize, like Quincy, (to our
    day
Still spared, Heaven bless him !) honor
    more than pay,
And Christian jurists, starry-pure, like
    Jay ;
Preachers like Woolman, or like them
    who bore
The faith of Wesley to our Western shore,
And held no convert genuine till he broke
Alike his servants' and the Devil's yoke ;
And priests like him who Newport's mar-
    ket trod,
And o'er its slave-ships shook the bolts
    of God !
So shall your power, with a wise prudence
    used,
Strong but forbearing, firm but not
    abused,
In kindly keeping with the good of all,
The nobler maxims of the past recall,

Her natural home-born right to Freedom
    give,
And leave her foe his robber-right, — to
    live.
Live, as the snake does in his noisome
    fen !
Live, as the wolf does in his bone-strewn
    den !
Live, clothed with cursing like a robe of
    flame,
The focal point of million-fingered
    shame !
Live, till the Southron, who, with all his
    faults,
Has manly instincts, in his pride re-
    volts,
Dashes from off him, midst the glad
    world's cheers,
The hideous nightmare of his dream of
    years,
And lifts, self-prompted, with his own
    right hand,
The vile encumbrance from his glorious
    land !

  " So, wheresoe'er our destiny sends
    forth
Its widening circles to the South or
    North,
Where'er our banner flaunts beneath
    the stars
Its mimic splendors and its cloudlike
    bars,
There shall Free Labor's hardy children
    stand
The equal sovereigns of a slaveless land.
And when at last the hunted bison tires,
And dies o'ertaken by the squatter's
    fires ;
And westward, wave on wave, the living
    flood
Breaks on the snow-line of majestic
    Hood ;
And lonely Shasta listening hears the
    tread
Of Europe's fair-haired children, Hes-
    per-led ;
And, gazing downward through his
    hoar-locks, sees
The tawny Asian climb his giant knees,
The Eastern sea shall hush his waves to
    hear
Pacific's surf-beat answer Freedom's
    cheer,
And one long rolling fire of triumph
    run
Between the sunrise and the sunset gun !"

My task is done.   The Showman and
    his show,
Themselves but shadows, into shadows
    go ;
And, if no song of idlesse I have sung,
Nor tints of beauty on the canvas
    flung, —
If the harsh numbers grate on tender
    ears,
And the rough picture overwrought ap-
    pears, —
With deeper coloring, with a sterner
    blast,
Before my soul a voice and vision passed,
Such as might Milton's jarring trump
    require,
Or glooms of Dante fringed with lurid
    fire.
O, not of choice, for themes of public
    wrong
I leave the green and pleasant paths of
    song, —
The mild, sweet words which soften and
    adorn,
For griding taunt and bitter laugh of
    scorn,
More dear to me some song of private
    worth,

Some homely idyl of my native North,
Some summer pastoral of her inland
    vales
Or, grim and weird, her winter fireside
    tales
Haunted by ghosts of unreturning
    sails, —
Lost barks at parting hung from stem
    to helm
With prayers of love like dreams on
    Virgil's elm.
Nor private grief nor malice holds my
    pen ;
I owe but kindness to my fellow-men ;
And, South or North, wherever hearts
    of prayer
Their woes and weakness to our Father
    bear,
Wherever fruits of Christian love are
    found
In holy lives, to me is holy ground.
But the time passes. It were vain to
    crave
A late indulgence. What I had I
    gave.
Forget the poet, but his warning heed,
And shame his poor word with your
    nobler deed.

MISCELLANEOUS.

SUMMER BY THE LAKESIDE.

I. NOON.

WHITE clouds, whose shadows haunt
    the deep,
Light mists, whose soft embraces keep
The sunshine on the hills asleep !

O isles of calm ! — O dark, still wood !
And stiller skies that overbrood
Your rest with deeper quietude !

O shapes and hues, dim beckoning,
    through
Yon mountain gaps, my longing view
Beyond the purple and the blue,

To stiller sea and greener land,
And softer lights and airs more bland,
And skies, — the hollow of God's hand !

Transfused through you, O mountain
    friends !
With mine your solemn spirit blends,
And life no more hath separate ends.

I read each misty mountain sign,
I know the voice of wave and pine,
And I am yours, and ye are mine.

Life's burdens fall, its discords cease,
I lapse into the glad release
Of Nature's own exceeding peace.

O, welcome calm of heart and mind !
As falls yon fir-tree's loosened rind
To leave a tenderer growth behind,

So fall the weary years away ;
A child again, my head I lay
Upon the lap of this sweet day.

This western wind hath Lethean powers,
Yon noonday cloud nepenthe showers,
The lake is white with lotus-flowers !

Even Duty's voice is faint and low,
And slumberous Conscience, waking
    slow,
Forgets her blotted scroll to show.

The Shadow which pursues us all,
Whose ever-nearing steps appall,
Whose voice we hear behind us call, —

That Shadow blends with mountain
    gray,
It speaks but what the light waves say, —
Death walks apart from Fear to-day !

Rocked on her breast, these pines and I
Alike on Nature's love rely ;
And equal seems to live or die.

Assured that He whose presence fills
With light the spaces of these hills
No evil to his creatures wills,

The simple faith remains, that He
Will do, whatever that may be,
The best alike for man and tree.

What mosses over one shall grow,
What light and life the other know,
Unanxious, leaving Him to show.

II. EVENING.

Yon mountain's side is black with night,
    While, broad-orbed, o'er its gleaming
      crown
The moon, slow-rounding into sight,
    On the hushed inland sea looks down.

How start to light the clustering isles,
    Each silver-hemmed ! How sharply
      show
The shadows of their rocky piles,
    And tree-tops in the wave below !

How far and strange the mountains
    seem,
    Dim-looming through the pale, still
      light !
The vague, vast grouping of a dream,
    They stretch into the solemn night.

Beneath, lake, wood, and peopled vale,
    Hushed by that presence grand and
      grave,

Are silent, save the cricket's wail,
    And low response of leaf and wave.

Fair scenes ! whereto the Day and Night
    Make rival love, I leave ye soon,
What time before the eastern 'light
    The pale ghost of the setting moon

Shall hide behind yon rocky spines,
    And the young archer, Morn, shall
      break
His arrows on the mountain pines,
    And, golden-sandalled, walk the lake !

Farewell ! around this smiling bay
    Gay-hearted Health, and Life in
      bloom,
With lighter steps than mine, may stray
    In radiant summers yet to come.

But none shall more regretful leave
    These waters and these hills than I :
Or, distant, fonder dream how eve
    Or dawn is painting wave and sky ;

How rising moons shine sad and mild
    On wooded isle and silvering bay,
Or setting suns beyond the piled
    And purple mountains lead the day ;

Nor laughing girl, nor bearding boy,
    Nor full-pulsed manhood, lingering
      here,
Shall add, to life's abounding joy,
    The charmed repose to suffering dear.

Still waits kind Nature to impart
    Her choicest gifts to such as gain
An entrance to her loving heart
    Through the sharp discipline of pain.

Forever from the Hand that takes
    One blessing from us others fall ;
And, soon or late, our Father makes
    His perfect recompense to all !

O, watched by Silence and the Night,
    And folded in the strong embrace
Of the great mountains, with the light
    Of the sweet heavens upon thy face,

Lake of the Northland ! keep thy dower
    Of beauty still, and while above
Thy solemn mountains speak of power,
    Be thou the mirror of God's love.

THE HERMIT OF THE THEBAID.

O STRONG, upwelling prayers of faith,
  From inmost founts of life ye start, —
The spirit's pulse, the vital breath
  Of soul and heart !

From pastoral toil, from traffic's din,
  Alone, in crowds, at home, abroad,
Unheard of man, ye enter in
  The ear of God.

Ye brook no forced and measured tasks,
  Nor weary rote, nor formal chains ;
The simple heart, that freely asks
  In love, obtains.

For man the living temple is :
  The mercy-seat and cherubim,
And all the holy mysteries,
  He bears with him.

And most avails the prayer of love,
  Which, wordless, shapes itself in
    deeds,
And wearies Heaven for naught above
  Our common needs.

Which brings to God's all-perfect will
  That trust of his undoubting child
Whereby all seeming good and ill
  Are reconciled.

And, seeking not for special signs
  Of favor, is content to fall
Within the providence which shines
  And rains on all.

Alone, the Thebaid hermit leaned
  At noontime o'er the sacred word.
Was it an angel or a fiend
  Whose voice he heard ?

It broke the desert's hush of awe,
  A human utterance, sweet and mild ;
And, looking up, the hermit saw
  A little child.

A child, with wonder-widened eyes,
  O'erawed and troubled by the sight
Of hot, red sands, and brazen skies,
  And anchorite.

"What dost thou here, poor man ? No
    shade
  Of cool, green doums, nor grass, nor
    well,

Nor corn, nor vines."   The hermit
    said :
  "With God I dwell.

"Alone with Him in this great calm,
  I live not by the outward sense ;
My Nile his love, my sheltering palm
  His providence."

The child gazed round him.   "Does
    God live
  Here only ? — where the desert's rim
Is green with corn, at morn and eve,
  We pray to Him.

"My brother tills beside the Nile
  His little field : beneath the leaves
My sisters sit and spin the while,
  My mother weaves.

"And when the millet's ripe heads fall,
  And all the bean-field hangs in pod,
My mother smiles, and says that all
  Are gifts from God.

"And when to share our evening meal,
  She calls the stranger at the door,
She says God fills the hands that deal
  Food to the poor."

Adown the hermit's wasted cheeks
  Glistened the flow of human tears ;
"Dear Lord !" he said, "thy angel
    speaks,
  Thy servant hears."

Within his arms the child he took,
  And thought of home and life with
    men ;
And all his pilgrim feet forsook
  Returned again.

The palmy shadows cool and long,
  The eyes that smiled through lavish
    locks,
Home's cradle-hymn and harvest-song,
  And bleat of flocks.

"O child !" he said, "thou teachest me
  There is no place where God is not ;
That love will make, where'er it be,
  A holy spot."

He rose from off the desert sand,
  And, leaning on his staff of thorn,
Went, with the young child, hand-in
    hand,
  Like night with morn.

They crossed the desert's burning line,
   And heard the palm-tree's rustling
      fan,
The Nile-bird's cry, the low of kine,
   And voice of man.

Unquestioning, his childish guide
He followed as the small hand led
To where a woman, gentle-eyed,
   Her distaff fed.

She rose, she clasped her truant boy,
   She thanked the stranger with her
      eyes.
The hermit gazed in doubt and joy
   And dumb surprise.

And lo ! — with sudden warmth and
      light
A tender memory thrilled his frame ;
New-born, the world-lost anchorite
   A man became.

"O sister of El Zara's race,
   Behold me ! — had we not one moth-
      er ?"
She gazed into the stranger's face ; —
   "Thou art my brother ?"

"O kin of blood ! — Thy life of use
   And patient trust is more than mine ;
And wiser than the gray recluse
   This child of thine.

"For, taught of him whom God hath
      sent,
   That toil is praise, and love is prayer,
I come, life's cares and pains content
   With thee to share."

Even as his foot the threshold crossed,
   The hermit's better life began ;
Its holiest saint the Thebaid lost,
   And found a man !

BURNS.

ON RECEIVING A SPRIG OF HEATHER
IN BLOSSOM.

No more these simple flowers belong
   To Scottish maid and lover ;
Sown in the common soil of song,
   They bloom the wide world over.

In smiles and tears, in sun and showers,
   The minstrel and the heather,

The deathless singer and the flowers
   He sang of live together.

Wild heather-bells and Robert Burns !
   The moorland flower and peasant !
How, at their mention, memory turns
   Her pages old and pleasant !

The gray sky wears again its gold
   And purple of adorning,
And manhood's noonday shadows hold
   The dews of boyhood's morning.

The dews that washed the dust and
      soil
   From off the wings of pleasure,
The sky, that flecked the ground of
      toil
   With golden threads of leisure.

I call to mind the summer day,
   The early harvest mowing,
The sky with sun and clouds at play,
   And flowers with breezes blowing.

I hear the blackbird in the corn,
   The locust in the haying ;
And, like the fabled hunter's horn,
   Old tunes my heart is playing.

How oft that day, with fond delay,
   I sought the maple's shadow,
And sang with Burns the hours away,
   Forgetful of the meadow !

Bees hummed, birds twittered, over-
      head
   I heard the squirrels leaping,
The good dog listened while I read,
   And wagged his tail in keeping.

I watched him while in sportive mood
   I read " *The Twa Dogs'* " story,
And half believed he understood
   The poet's allegory.

Sweet day, sweet songs ! — The golden
      hours
   Grew brighter for that singing,
From brook and bird and meadow
      flowers
   A dearer welcome bringing.

New light on home-seen Nature beamed,
   New glory over Woman ;
And daily life and duty seemed
   No longer poor and common.

I woke to find the simple truth
  Of fact and feeling better
Than all the dreams that held my youth
  A still repining debtor:

That Nature gives her handmaid, Art,
  The themes of sweet discoursing;
The tender idyls of the heart
  In every tongue rehearsing.

Why dream of lands of gold and pearl,
  Of loving knight and lady,
When farmer boy and barefoot girl
  Were wandering there already?

I saw through all familiar things
  The romance underlying;
The joys and griefs that plume the wings
  Of Fancy skyward flying.

I saw the same blithe day return,
  The same sweet fall of even,
That rose on wooded Craigie-burn,
  And sank on crystal Devon.

I matched with Scotland's heathery hills
  The sweetbrier and the clover;
With Ayr and Doon, my native rills,
  Their wood-hymns chanting over.

O'er rank and pomp, as he had seen,
  I saw the Man uprising;
No longer common or unclean,
  The child of God's baptizing!

With clearer eyes I saw the worth
  Of life among the lowly;
The Bible at his Cotter's hearth
  Had made my own more holy.

And if at times an evil strain,
  To lawless love appealing,
Broke in upon the sweet refrain
  Of pure and healthful feeling,

It died upon the eye and ear,
  No inward answer gaining;
No heart had I to see or hear
  The discord and the staining.

Let those who never erred forget
  His worth, in vain bewailings;
Sweet Soul of Song! — I own my debt
  Uncancelled by his failings!

Lament who will the ribald line
  Which tells his lapse from duty.

How kissed the maddening lips of wine
  Or wanton ones of beauty;

But think, while falls that shade be-
    tween
  The erring one and Heaven,
That he who loved like Magdalen,
  Like her may be forgiven.

Not his the song whose thunderous
    chime
  Eternal echoes render, —
The mournful Tuscan's haunted rhyme,
  And Milton's starry splendor!

But who his human heart has laid
  To Nature's bosom nearer?
Who sweetened toil like him, or paid
  To love a tribute dearer?

Through all his tuneful art, how strong
  The human feeling gushes!
The very moonlight of his song
  Is warm with smiles and blushes!

Give lettered pomp to teeth of Time,
  So "Bonnie Doon" but tarry;
Blot out the Epic's stately rhyme,
  But spare his Highland Mary!

WILLIAM FORSTER.[61]

THE years are many since his hand
  Was laid upon my head,
Too weak and young to understand
  The serious words he said.

Yet often now the good man's look
  Before me seems to swim,
As if some inward feeling took
  The outward guise of him.

As if, in passion's heated war,
  Or near temptation's charm,
Through him the low-voiced monitor
  Forewarned me of the harm.

Stranger and pilgrim! — from that day
  Of meeting, first and last,
Wherever Duty's pathway lay,
  His reverent steps have passed.

The poor to feed, the lost to seek,
  To proffer life to death,
Hope to the erring, — to the weak
  The strength of his own faith.

To plead the captive's right ; remove
  The sting of hate from Law ;
And soften in the fire of love
  The hardened steel of War.

He walked the dark world, in the mild,
  Still guidance of the Light ;
In tearful tenderness a child,
  A strong man in the right.

From what great perils, on his way,
  He found, in prayer, release ;
Through what abysmal shadows lay
  His pathway unto peace,

God knoweth : we could only see
  The tranquil strength he gained ;
The bondage lost in liberty,
  The fear in love unfeigned.

And I, — my youthful fancies grown
  The habit of the man,
Whose field of life by angels sown
  The wilding vines o'erran, —

Low bowed in silent gratitude,
  My manhood's heart enjoys
That reverence for the pure and good
  Which blessed the dreaming boy's.

Still shines the light of holy lives
  Like star-beams over doubt ;
Each sainted memory, Christlike, drives
  Some dark possession out.

O friend ! O brother ! not in vain
  Thy life so calm and true,
The silver dropping of the rain,
  The fall of summer dew !

How many burdened hearts have prayed
  Their lives like thine might be !
But more shall pray henceforth for aid
  To lay them down like thee.

With weary hand, yet steadfast will,
  In old age as in youth,
Thy Master found thee sowing still
  The good seed of his truth.

As on thy task-field closed the day
  In golden-skied decline,
His angel met thee on the way,
  And lent his arm to thine.

Thy latest care for man, — thy last
  Of earthly thought a prayer, —

O, who thy mantle, backward cast,
  Is worthy now to wear ?

Methinks the mound which marks thy
    bed
  Might bless our land and save,
As rose, of old, to life the dead
  Who touched the prophet's grave !

RANTOUL.[62]

ONE day, along the electric wire
  His manly word for Freedom sped ;
We came next morn : that tongue of fire
  Said only, " He who spake is dead ! '

Dead ! while his voice was living yet,
  In echoes round the pillared dome !
Dead ! while his blotted page lay wet
  With themes of state and loves of
    home !

Dead ! in that crowning grace of time,
  That triumph of life's zenith hour !
Dead ! while we watched his manhood's
    prime
  Break from the slow bud into flower !

Dead ! he so great, and strong, and wise,
  While the mean thousands yet drew
    breath ;
How deepened, through that dread sur-
    prise,
  The mystery and the awe of death !

From the high place whereon our votes
  Had borne him, clear, calm, earnest
    fell
His first words, like the prelude notes
  Of some great anthem yet to swell.

We seemed to see our flag unfurled,
  Our champion waiting in his place
For the last battle of the world, —
  The Armageddon of the race.

Through him we hoped to speak the
    word
  Which wins the freedom of a land ;
And lift, for human right, the sword
  Which dropped from Hampden's dy
    ing hand.

For he had sat at Sidney's feet,
  And walked with Pym and Vane
    apart ;

And, through the centuries, felt the beat
  Of Freedom's march in Cromwell's
    heart.

He knew the paths the worthies held,
  Where England's best and wisest trod ;
And, lingering, drank the springs that
    welled
  Beneath the touch of Milton's rod.

No wild enthusiast of the right,
  Self-poised and clear, he showed alway
The coolness of his northern night,
  The ripe repose of autumn's day.

His steps were slow, yet forward still
  He pressed where others paused or
    failed ;
The calm star clomb with constant will, —
  The restless meteor flashed and paled !

Skilled in its subtlest wile, he knew
  And owned the higher ends of Law ;
Still rose majestic on his view
  The awful Shape the schoolman saw.

Her home the heart of God ; her voice
  The choral harmonies whereby
The stars, through all their spheres, re-
    joice,
  The rhythmic rule of earth and sky !

We saw his great powers misapplied
  To poor ambitions ; yet, through all,
We saw him take the weaker side,
  And right the wronged, and free the
    thrall.

Now, looking o'er the frozen North,
  For one like him in word and act,
To call her old, free spirit forth,
  And give her faith the life of
    fact, —

To break her party bonds of shame,
  And labor with the zeal of him
To make the Democratic name
  Of Liberty the synonyme, —

We sweep the land from hill to strand,
  We seek the strong, the wise, the
    brave,
And, sad of heart, return to stand
  In silence by a new-made grave !

There, where his breezy hills of home
Look out upon his sail-white seas,

The sounds of winds and waters come,
  And shape themselves to words like
    these :

" Why, murmuring, mourn that he,
    whose power
  Was lent to Party over-long,
Heard the still whisper at the hour
  He set his foot on Party wrong ?

" The human life that closed so well
  No lapse of folly now can stain :
The lips whence Freedom's protest fell
  No meaner thought can now profane.

" Mightier than living voice his grave
  That lofty protest utters o'er ;
Through roaring wind and smiting wave
  It speaks his hate of wrong once
    more.

" Men of the North ! your weak regret
  Is wasted here ; arise and pay
To freedom and to him your debt,
  By following where he led the way !"

THE DREAM OF PIO NONO.

It chanced, that while the pious
    troops of France
Fought in the crusade Pio Nono
    preached,
What time the holy Bourbons stayed
    his hands
(The Hur and Aaron meet for such a
    Moses),
Stretched forth from Naples towards
    rebellious Rome
To bless the ministry of Oudinot,
And sanctify his iron homilies
And sharp persuasions of the bayonet,
That the great pontiff fell asleep, and
    dreamed.

He stood by Lake Tiberias, in the
    sun
Of the bright Orient ; and beheld the
    lame,
The sick, and blind, kneel at the Mas-
    ter's feet,
And rise up whole. And, sweetly over
    all,
Dropping the ladder of their hymn of
    praise
From heaven to earth, in silver rounds
    of song,

He heard the blessed angels sing of
  peace,
Good-will to man, and glory to the
  Lord.

Then one, with feet unshod, and
  leathern face
Hardened and darkened by fierce sum-
  mer suns
And hot winds of the desert, closer drew
His fisher's haick, and girded up his
  loins,
Ard spake, as one who had authority :
" Come thou with me."

        Lakeside and eastern sky
And the sweet song of angels passed
  away,
And, with a dream's alacrity of change,
The priest, and the swart fisher by his
  side,
Beheld the Eternal City lift its domes
And solemn fanes and monumental
  pomp
Above the waste Campagna. On the
  hills
The blaze of burning villas rose and
  fell,
And momently the mortar's iron throat
Roared from the trenches ; and, within
  the walls,
Sharp crash of shells, low groans of hu-
  man pain,
Shout, drum beat, and the clanging
  larum-bell,
And tramp of hosts, sent up a mingled
  sound,
Half wail and half defiance. As they
  passed
The gate of Sàn Pancrazio, human blood
Flowed ankle-high about them, and
  dead men
Choked the long street with gashed and
  gory piles, —
A ghastly barricade of mangled flesh,
From which, at times, quivered a living
  hand,
And white lips moved and moaned. A
  father tore
His gray hairs, by the body of his son,
In frenzy ; and his fair young daughter
  wept
On his old bosom. Suddenly a flash
Clove the thick sulphurous air, and
  man and maid
Sank, crushed and mangled by the
  shattering shell.

Then spake the Galilean : "Thou hast
  seen
The blessed Master and his works of
  love ;
Look now on thine ! Hear'st thou the
  angels sing
Above this open hell ? *Thou* God's
  high-priest !
Thou the Vicegerent of the Prince of
  Peace !
Thou the successor of his chosen ones !
I, Peter, fisherman of Galilee,
In the dear Master's name, and for the
  love
Of his true Church, proclaim thee Anti-
  christ,
Alien and separate from his holy faith,
Wide as the difference between death
  and life,
The hate of man and the great love of
  God !
Hence, and repent !"

        Thereat the pontiff woke,
Trembling, and muttering o'er his fear-
  ful dream.
"What means he ?" cried the Bourbon.
  " Nothing more
Than that your majesty hath all too
  well
Catered for your poor guests, and that,
  in sooth,
The Holy Father's supper troubleth
  him,"
Said Cardinal Antonelli, with a smile.

TAULER.

Tauler, the preacher, walked, one
  autumn day,
Without the walls of Strasburg, by the
  Rhine,
Pondering the solemn Miracle of Life ;
As one who, wandering in a starless
  night,
Feels, momently, the jar of unseen
  waves,
And hears the thunder of an unknown
  sea,
Breaking along an unimagined shore.

And as he walked he prayed. Even
  the same
Old prayer with which, for half a score
  of years,

Morning, and noon, and evening, lip and heart
Had groaned : "Have pity upon me, Lord !
Thou seest, while teaching others, I am blind.
Send me a man who can direct my steps ! "

Then, as he mused, he heard along his path
A sound as of an old man's staff among
The dry, dead linden-leaves ; and, looking up,
He saw a stranger, weak, and poor, and old.

"Peace be unto thee, father ! " Tauler said,
"God give thee a good day ! " The old man raised
Slowly his calm blue eyes. "I thank thee, son ;
But *all* my days are good, and none are ill."

Wondering thereat, the preacher spake again,
"God give thee happy life." The old man smiled,
"I never am unhappy."

Tauler laid
His hand upon the stranger's coarse gray sleeve :
"Tell me, O father, what thy strange words mean.
Surely man's days are evil, and his life
Sad as the grave it leads to." "Nay, my son,
Our times are in God's hands, and all our days
Are as our needs : for shadow as for sun,
For cold as heat, for want as wealth, alike
Our thanks are due, since that is best which is ;
And that which is not, sharing not his life,
Is evil only as devoid of good.
And for the happiness of which I spake,
I find it in submission to his will,
And calm trust in the holy Trinity
Of Knowledge, Goodness, and Almighty Power."

Silently wondering, for a little space,
Stood the great preacher ; then he spake as one
Who, suddenly grappling with a haunting thought
Which long has followed, whispering through the dark
Strange terrors, drags it, shrieking, into light :
"What if God's will consign thee hence to Hell ? "

"Then," said the stranger, cheerily, "be it so.
What Hell may be I know not ; this I know, —
I cannot lose the presence of the Lord :
One arm, Humility, takes hold upon
His dear Humanity ; the other, Love,
Clasps his Divinity. So where I go
He goes ; and better fire-walled Hell with Him
Than golden-gated Paradise without."

Tears sprang in Tauler's eyes. A sudden light,
Like the first ray which fell on chaos, clove
Apart the shadow wherein he had walked
Darkly at noon. And, as the strange old man
Went his slow way, until his silver hair
Set like the white moon where the hills of vine
Slope to the Rhine, he bowed his head and said :
"My prayer is answered. God hath sent the man
Long sought, to teach me, by his simple trust,
Wisdom the weary schoolmen never knew."

So, entering with a changed and cheerful step
The city gates, he saw, far down the street,
A mighty shadow break the light of noon,
Which tracing backward till its airy lines
Hardened to stony plinths, he raised his eyes
O'er broad façade and lofty pediment,
O'er architrave and frieze and sainted niche,

Up the stone lace-work chiselled by the
        wise
Erwin of Steinbach, dizzily up to where
In the noon-brightness the great Min-
        ster's tower,
Jewelled with sunbeams on its mural
        crown,
Rose like a visible prayer. "Behold!"
        he said,
"The stranger's faith made plain be-
        fore mine eyes.
As yonder tower outstretches to the
        earth
The dark triangle of its shade alone
When the clear day is shining on its
        top,
So, darkness in the pathway of Man's
        life
Is but the shadow of God's providence,
By the great Sun of Wisdom cast there-
        on ;
And what is dark below is light in
        Heaven."

LINES,

SUGGESTED BY READING A STATE PA-
PER, WHEREIN THE HIGHER LAW IS
INVOKED TO SUSTAIN THE LOWER
ONE.

A PIOUS magistrate ! sound his praise
        throughout
The wondering churches.   Who shall
        henceforth doubt
    That the long-wished millennium
        draweth nigh ?
Sin in high places has become devout,
    Tithes mint, goes painful-faced, and
        prays its lie
    Straight up to Heaven, and calls it
        piety !

The pirate, watching from his bloody
        deck
    The weltering galleon, heavy with the
        gold
Of Acapulco, holding death in check
    While prayers are said, brows crossed,
        and beads are told, —
The robber, kneeling where the wayside
        cross
On dark Abruzzo tells of life's dread loss
From his own carbine, glancing still
        abroad
For some new victim. offering thanks to
        God ! —

Rome, listening at her altars to the
        cry
Of midnight Murder, while her hounds
        of hell
Scour France, from baptized cannon and
        holy bell
    And thousand-throated priesthood,
        loud and high,
    Pealing Te Deums to the shuddering
        sky,
    "Thanks to the Lord, who giveth
        victory !"
What prove these, but that crime was
        ne'er so black
As ghostly cheer and pious thanks to
        lack ?
Satan is modest.   At Heaven's door he
        lays
His evil offspring, and, in Scriptural
        phrase
And saintly posture, gives to God the
        praise
And honor of the monstrous progeny.
What marvel, then, in our own time to
        see
His old devices, smoothly acted o'er, —
Official piety, locking fast the door
Of Hope against three million souls of
        men, —
Brothers, God's children, Christ's re-
        deemed, — and then,
With uprolled eyeballs and on bended
        knee,
Whining a prayer for help to hide the
        key !

THE VOICES.

"WHY urge the long, unequal fight,
    Since Truth has fallen in the street,
Or lift anew the trampled light,
    Quenched by the heedless million's
        feet ?

"Give o'er the thankless task ; forsake
    The fools who know not ill from good ;
Eat, drink, enjoy thy own, and take
    Thine ease among the multitude.

"Live out thyself ; with others share
    Thy proper life no more ; assume
The unconcern of sun and air,
    For life or death, or blight or bloom.

"The mountain pine looks calmly on
    The fires that scourge the plains below,

Nor heeds the eagle in the sun
　The small birds piping in the snow !

"The world is God's, not thine ; let him
　Work out a change, if change must be :
The hand that planted best can trim
　And nurse the old unfruitful tree."

So spake the Tempter, when the light
　Of sun and stars had left the sky,
I listened, through the cloud and night,
　And heard, methought, a voice reply :

"Thy task may well seem over-hard,
　Who scatterest in a thankless soil
Thy life as seed, with no reward
　Save that which Duty gives to Toil.

"Not wholly is thy heart resigned
　To Heaven's benign and just decree,
Which, linking thee with all thy kind,
　Transmits their joys and griefs to
　　　thee.

"Break off that sacred chain, and turn
　Back on thyself thy love and care ;
Be thou thine own mean idol, burn
　Faith, Hope, and Trust, thy children,
　　　there.

"Released from that fraternal law
　Which shares the common bale and
　　　bliss,
No sadder lot could Folly draw,
　Or Sin provoke from Fate, than this.

"The meal unshared is food unblest :
　Thou hoard'st in vain what love
　　　should spend ;
Self-ease is pain ; thy only rest
　Is labor for a worthy end.

"A toil that gains with what it yields,
　And scatters to its own increase,
And hears, while sowing outward fields,
　The harvest-song of inward peace.

"Free-lipped the liberal streamlets run,
　Free shines for all the healthful ray ;
The still pool stagnates in the sun,
　The lurid earth-fire haunts decay !

'What is it that the crowd requite
　Thy love with hate, thy truth with
　　　lies ?
And but to faith, and not to sight,
　The walls of Freedom's temple rise ?

13

"Yet do thy work ; it shall succeed
　In thine or in another's day ;
And, if denied the victor's meed,
　Thou shalt not lack the toiler's pay.

"Faith shares the future's promise ;
　　　Love's
　Self-offering is a triumph won ;
And each good thought or action moves
　The dark world nearer to the sun.

"Then faint not, falter not, nor plead
　Thy weakness ; truth itself is strong ,
The lion's strength, the eagle's speed,
　Are not alone vouchsafed to wrong.

"Thy nature, which, through fire and
　　　flood,
　To place or gain finds out its way,
Hath power to seek the highest good,
　And duty's holiest call obey !

"Strivest thou in darkness ? — Foes
　　　without
　In league with traitor thoughts with-
　　　in ;
Thy night-watch kept with trembling
　　　Doubt
　And pale Remorse the ghost of
　　　Sin ? —

"Hast thou not, on some week of storm,
　Seen the sweet Sabbath breaking fair,
And cloud and shadow, sunlit, form
　The curtains of its tent of prayer ?

"So, haply, when thy task shall end,
　The wrong shall lose itself in right,
And all thy week-day darkness blend
　With the long Sabbath of the light ! "

THE HERO.

"O FOR a knight like Bayard,
　Without reproach or fear ;
My light glove on his casque of steel,
　My love-knot on his spear !

"O for the white plume floating
　Sad Zutphen's field above, —
The lion heart in battle,
　The woman's heart in love !

"O that man once more were manly,
　Woman's pride, and not her scorn :
That once more the pale young mother
　Dared to boast ' a man is born ' !

" But, now life's slumberous current
    No sun-bowed cascade wakes ;
No tall, heroic manhood
    The level dulness breaks.

" O for a knight like Bayard,
    Without reproach or fear !
My light glove on his casque of steel,
    My love-knot on his spear ! "

Then I said, my own heart throbbing
    To the time her proud pulse beat,
" Life hath its regal natures yet, —
    True, tender, brave, and sweet !

" Smile not, fair unbeliever !
    One man, at least, I know,
Who might wear the crest of Bayard
    Or Sidney's plume of snow.

" Once, when over purple mountains
    Died away the Grecian sun,
And the far Cyllenian ranges
    Paled and darkened, one by one, —

" Fell the Turk, a bolt of thunder,
    Cleaving all the quiet sky,
And against his sharp steel lightnings
    Stood the Suliote but to die.

" Woe for the weak and halting !
    The crescent blazed behind
A curving line of sabres,
    Like fire before the wind !

" Last to fly, and first to rally,
    Rode he of whom I speak,
When, groaning in his bridle-path,
    Sank down a wounded Greek.

" With the rich Albanian costume
    Wet with many a ghastly stain,
Gazing on earth and sky as one
    Who might not gaze again !

" He looked forward to the mountains,
    Back on foes that never spare,
Then flung him from his saddle,
    And placed the stranger there.

" ' Allah ! hu ! ' Through flashing sa-
    bres,
    Through a stormy hail of lead,
The good Thessalian charger
    Up the slopes of olives sped.

" Hot spurred the turbaned riders ,
    He almost felt their breath,
Where a mountain stream rolled darkly
    down
    Between the hills and death.

" One brave and manful struggle, —
    He gained the solid land,
And the cover of the mountains,
    And the carbines of his band ! "

" It was very great and noble,"
    Said the moist-eyed listener then,
" But one brave deed makes no hero ;
    Tell me what he since hath been ! "

" Still a brave and generous manhood,
    Still an honor without stain,
In the prison of the Kaiser,
    By the barricades of Seine.

" But dream not helm and harness
    The sign of valor true ;
Peace hath higher tests of manhood
    Than battle ever knew.

" Wouldst know him now ?   Behold
    him,
The Cadmus of the blind,
Giving the dumb lip language,
    The idiot clay a mind.

" Walking his round of duty
    Serenely day by day,
With the strong man's hand of labor
    And childhood's heart of play.

" True as the knights of story,
    Sir Lancelot and his peers,
Brave in his calm endurance
    As they in tilt of spears.

" As waves in stillest waters,
    As stars in noonday skies,
All that wakes to noble action
    In his noon of calmness lies.

' Wherever outraged Nature
    Asks word or action brave,
Wherever struggles labor,
    Wherever groans a slave, —

" Wherever rise the peoples,
    Wherever sinks a throne,
The throbbing heart of Freedom finds
    An answer in his own

"Knight of a better era,
    Without reproach or fear !
Said I not well that Bayards
    And Sidneys still are here ? "

MY DREAM.

In my dream, methought I trod,
Yesternight, a mountain road ;
Narrow as Al Sirat's span,
High as eagle's flight, it ran.

Overhead, a roof of cloud
With its weight of thunder bowed ;
Underneath, to left and right,
Blankness and abysmal night.

Here and there a wild-flower blushed,
Now and then a bird-song gushed ;
Now and then, through rifts of shade,
Stars shone out, and sunbeams played.

But the goodly company,
Walking in that path with me,
One by one the brink o'erslid,
One by one the darkness hid.

Some with wailing and lament,
Some with cheerful courage went ;
But, of all who smiled or mourned,
Never one to us returned.

Anxiously, with eye and ear,
Questioning that shadow drear,
Never hand in token stirred,
Never answering voice I heard !

Steeper, darker ! — lo ! I felt
From my feet the pathway melt,
Swallowed by the black despair,
And the hungry jaws of air,

Past the stony-throated caves,
Strangled by the wash of waves,
Past the splintered crags, I sank
On a green and flowery bank, —

Soft as fall of thistle-down,
Lightly as a cloud is blown,
Soothingly as childhood pressed
To the bosom of its rest.

Of the sharp-horned rocks instead,
Green the grassy meadows spread,
Bright with waters singing by
Trees that propped a golden sky.

Painless, trustful, sorrow-free,
Old lost faces welcomed me,
With whose sweetness of content
Still expectant hope was blent.

Waking while the dawning gray
Slowly brightened into day,
Pondering that vision fled,
Thus unto myself I said : —

" Steep, and hung with clouds of strife
Is our narrow path of life ;
And our death the dreaded fall
Through the dark, awaiting all.

" So, with painful steps we climb
Up the dizzy ways of time,
Ever in the shadow shed
By the forecast of our dread.

" Dread of mystery solved alone,
Of the untried and unknown ;
Yet the end thereof may seem
Like the falling of my dream.

" And this heart-consuming care,
All our fears of here or there,
Change and absence, loss and death,
Prove but simple lack of faith."

Thou, O Most Compassionate !
Who didst stoop to our estate,
Drinking of the cup we drain,
Treading in our path of pain, —

Through the doubt and mystery,
Grant to us thy steps to see,
And the grace to draw from thence
Larger hope and confidence.

Show thy vacant tomb, and let,
As of old, the angels sit,
Whispering, by its open door :
" Fear not !   He hath gone before ! "

THE BAREFOOT BOY.

Blessings on thee, little man,
Barefoot boy, with cheek of tan !
With thy turned-up pantaloons,
And thy merry whistled tunes ;
With thy red lip, redder still
Kissed by strawberries on the hill ;
With the sunshine on thy face,
Through thy torn brim's jaunty grace ;
From my heart I give thee joy, —

I was once a barefoot boy !
Prince thou art, — the grown-up man
Only is republican.
Let the million-dollared ride !
Barefoot, trudging at his side,
Thou hast more than he can buy
In the reach of ear and eye, —
Outward sunshine, inward joy :
Blessings on thee, barefoot boy !

O for boyhood's painless play,
Sleep that wakes in laughing day,
Health that mocks the doctor's rules,
Knowledge never learned of schools,
Of the wild bee's morning chase,
Of the wild-flower's time and place,
Flight of fowl and habitude
Of the tenants of the wood ;
How the tortoise bears his shell,
How the woodchuck digs his cell,
And the ground-mole sinks his well ;
How the robin feeds her young,
How the oriole's nest is hung ;
Where the whitest lilies blow,
Where the freshest berries grow,
Where the groundnut trails its vine,
Where the wood-grape's clusters shine ;
Of the black wasp's cunning way,
Mason of his walls of clay,
And the architectural plans
Of gray hornet artisans ! —
For, eschewing books and tasks,
Nature answers all he asks ;
Hand in hand with her he walks,
Face to face with her he talks,
Part and parcel of her joy, —
Blessings on the barefoot boy !

O for boyhood's time of June,
Crowding years in one brief moon,
When all things I heard or saw,
Me, their master, waited for.
I was rich in flowers and trees,
Humming-birds and honey-bees ;
For my sport the squirrel played,
Plied the snouted mole his spade ;
For my taste the blackberry cone
Purpled over hedge and stone ;
Laughed the brook for my delight
Through the day and through the night,
Whispering at the garden wall,
Talked with me from fall to fall ;
Mine the sand-rimmed pickerel pond,
Mine the walnut slopes beyond,
Mine, on bending orchard trees,
Apples of Hesperides !
Still as my horizon grew,

Larger grew my riches too ;
All the world I saw or knew
Seemed a complex Chinese toy,
Fashioned for a barefoot boy !

O for festal dainties spread,
Like my bowl of milk and bread, —
Pewter spoon and bowl of wood,
On the door-stone, gray and rude !
O'er me, like a regal tent,
Cloudy-ribbed, the sunset bent,
Purple-curtained, fringed with gold,
Looped in many a wind-swung fold ;
While for music came the play
Of the pied frogs' orchestra ;
And, to light the noisy choir,
Lit the fly his lamp of fire.
I was monarch : pomp and joy
Waited on the barefoot boy !

Cheerily, then, my little man,
Live and laugh, as boyhood can !
Though the flinty slopes be hard,
Stubble-speared the new-mown sward,
Every morn shall lead thee through
Fresh baptisms of the dew ;
Every evening from thy feet
Shall the cool wind kiss the heat :
All too soon these feet must hide
In the prison cells of pride,
Lose the freedom of the sod,
Like a colt's for work be shod,
Made to tread the mills of toil,
Up and down in ceaseless moil :
Happy if their track be found
Never on forbidden ground ;
Happy if they sink not in
Quick and treacherous sands of sin.
Ah ! that thou couldst know thy joy,
Ere it passes, barefoot boy !

FLOWERS IN WINTER.

PAINTED UPON A PORTE LIVRE.

How strange to greet, this frosty morn,
  In graceful counterfeit of flowers,
These children of the meadows, born
  Of sunshine and of showers !

How well the conscious wood retains
  The pictures of its flower - sown
      home, —
The lights and snades, the purple
      stains,
  And golden hues of bloom !

It was a happy thought to bring
  To the dark season's frost and rime
This painted memory of spring,
  This dream of summer-time.

Our hearts are lighter for its sake,
  Our fancy's age renews its youth,
And dim-remembered fictions take
  The guise of present truth.

A wizard of the Merrimack, —
  So old ancestral legends say, —
Could call green leaf and blossom back
  To frosted stem and spray.

The dry logs of the cottage wall,
  Beneath his touch, put out their
    leaves ;
The clay-bound swallow, at his call,
  Played round the icy eaves.

The settler saw his oaken flail
  Take bud, and bloom before his eyes ;
From frozen pools he saw the pale,
  Sweet summer lilies rise.

To their old homes, by man profaned,
  Came the sad dryads, exiled long,
And through their leafy tongues com-
    plained
  Of household use and wrong.

The beechen platter sprouted wild,
  The pipkin wore its old-time green ;
The cradle o'er the sleeping child
  Became a leafy screen.

Haply our gentle friend hath met,
  While wandering in her sylvan quest,
Haunting his native woodlands yet,
  That Druid of the West ; —

And, while the dew on leaf and flower
  Glistened in moonlight clear and
    still,
Learned the dusk wizard's spell of
    power,
  And caught his trick of skill.

But welcome, be it new or old,
  The gift which makes the day more
    bright,
And paints, upon the ground of cold
  And darkness, warmth and light !

Without is neither gold nor green ;
  Within, for birds, the birch-logs sing ;

Yet, summer-like, we sit between
  The autumn and the spring.

The one, with bridal blush of rose,
  And sweetest breath of woodland
    balm,
And one whose matron lips unclose
  In smiles of saintly calm.

Fill soft and deep, O winter snow !
  The sweet azalia's oaken dells,
And hide the bank where roses blow,
  And swing the azure bells !

O'erlay the amber violet's leaves,
  The purple aster's brookside home,
Guard all the flowers her pencil gives
  A life beyond their bloom.

And she, when spring comes round again,
  By greening slope and singing flood
Shall wander, seeking, not in vain,
  Her darlings of the wood.

THE RENDITION.

I HEARD the train's shrill whistle call,
  I saw an earnest look beseech,
  And rather by that look than speech
My neighbor told me all.

And, as I thought of Liberty
  Marched   handcuffed   down   that
    sworded street,
  The solid earth beneath my feet
Reeled fluid as the sea.

I felt a sense of bitter loss, —
  Shame, tearless grief, and stifling
    wrath,
  And loathing fear, as if my path
A serpent stretched across.

All love of home, all pride of place,
  All generous confidence and trust,
  Sank smothering in that deep disgust
And anguish of disgrace.

Down on my native hills of June,
  And home's green quiet, hiding all
  Fell sudden darkness like the fall
Of midnight upon noon !

And Law, an unloosed maniac, strong,
  Blood-drunken, through the blackness
    trod,

Hoarse-shouting in the ear of God
The blasphemy of wrong.

" O Mother, from thy memories proud,
    Thy old renown, dear Commonwealth,
    Lend this dead air a breeze of health,
And smite with stars this cloud.

" Mother of Freedom, wise and brave,
    Rise awful in thy strength," I said ;
    Ah me ! I spake but to the dead ;
I stood upon her grave !
    6th mo., 1854.

The vision of a Christian man,
    In virtue as in stature great,
    Embodied in a Christian State.

And thou, amidst thy sisterhood
    Forbearing long, yet standing fast,
    Shalt win their grateful thanks at last;

When North and South shall strive no
        more,
    And all their feuds and fears be lost
    In Freedom's holy Pentecost.
    6th mo., 1855.

LINES,

ON THE PASSAGE OF THE BILL TO PRO-
TECT THE RIGHTS AND LIBERTIES OF
THE PEOPLE OF THE STATE AGAINST
THE FUGITIVE SLAVE ACT.

I SAID I stood upon thy grave,
    My Mother State, when last the moon
    Of blossoms clomb the skies of June.

And, scattering ashes on my head,
    I wore, undreaming of relief,
    The sackcloth of thy shame and grief.

Again that moon of blossoms shines
    On leaf and flower and folded wing,
    And thou hast risen with the spring !

Once more thy strong maternal arms
    Are round about thy children flung,—
    A lioness that guards her young !

No threat is on thy closéd lips,
    But in thine eye a power to smite
    The mad wolf backward from its light.

Southward the baffled robber's track
    Henceforth runs only ; hereaway,
    The fell lycanthrope finds no prey.

Henceforth, within thy sacred gates,
    His first low howl shall downward draw
    The thunder of thy righteous law.

Not mindless of thy trade and gain,
    But, acting on the wiser plan,
    Thou 'rt grown conservative of man.

So shalt thou clothe with life the hope,
    Dream-painted on the sightless eyes
    Of him who sang of Paradise, —

THE FRUIT-GIFT.

LAST night, just as the tints of autumn's
        sky
    Of sunset faded from our hills and
        streams,
    I sat, vague listening, lapped in twi-
        light dreams,
To the leaf's rustle, and the cricket's cry.
Then, like that basket, flush with sum-
        mer fruit,
    Dropped by the angels at the Prophet's
        foot,
Came, unannounced, a gift of clustered
        sweetness,
    Full-orbed, and glowing with the
        prisoned beams
Of summery suns, and rounded to com-
        pleteness
By kisses of the south-wind and the
        dew.
Thrilled with a glad surprise, methought
        I knew
The pleasure of the homeward-turning
        Jew,
When Eschol's clusters on his shoulders
        lay,
Dropping their sweetness on his desert
        way.

I said, " This fruit beseems no world of
        sin.
    Its parent vine, rooted in Paradise,
    O'ercrept the wall, and never paid the
        price
    Of the great mischief, — an ambrosial
        tree,
Eden's exotic, somehow smuggled in,
    To keep the thorns and thistles com-
        pany."
Perchance our frail, sad mother plucked
        in haste

A single vine-slip as she passed the
    gate,
Where the dread sword alternate paled
    and burned,
And the stern angel, pitying her fate,
Forgave the lovely trespasser, and turned
Aside his face of fire ; and thus the waste
And fallen world hath yet its annual
    taste
Of primal good, to prove of sin the cost,
And show by one gleaned ear the
    mighty harvest lost.

A MEMORY.

HERE, while the loom of Winter weaves
    The shroud of flowers and fountains,
I think of thee and summer eves
    Among the Northern mountains.

When thunder tolled the twilight's close,
    And winds the lake were rude on,
And thou wert singing, *Ca' the Yowes*,
    The bonny yowes of Cluden !

When, close and closer, hushing breath,
    Our circle narrowed round thee,
And smiles and tears made up the wreath
    Wherewith our silence crowned thee ;

And, strangers all, we felt the ties
    Of sisters and of brothers ;
Ah ! whose of all those kindly eyes
    Now smile upon another's ?

The sport of Time, who still apart
    The waifs of life is flinging ;
O, nevermore shall heart to heart
    Draw nearer for that singing !

Yet when the panes are frosty-starred,
    And twilight's fire is gleaming,
I hear the songs of Scotland's bard
    Sound softly through my dreaming !

A song that lends to winter snows
    The glow of summer weather, —
Again I hear thee ca' the yowes
    To Cluden's hills of heather !

TO C. S.

IF I have seemed more prompt to cen-
    sure wrong
    Than praise the right ; if seldom to
      thine ear

My voice hath mingled with the ex-
    ultant cheer
Borne upon all our Northern winds
    along ;
If I have failed to join the fickle throng
In wide-eyed wonder, that thou standest
    strong
In victory, surprised in thee to find
Brougham's scathing power with Can-
    ning's grace combined ;
That he, for whom the ninefold Muses
    sang,
From their twined arms a giant athlete
    sprang,
Barbing the arrows of his native tongue
With the spent shafts Latona's archer
    flung,
To smite the Python of our land and
    time,
Fell as the monster born of Crissa's slime,
Like the blind bard who in Castalian
    springs
Tempered the steel that clove the crest
    of kings,
And on the shrine of England's freedom
    laid
The gifts of Cumæ and of Delphi's
    shade, —
Small need hast thou of words of praise
    from me.
    Thou knowest my heart, dear friend,
      and well canst guess
    That, even though silent, I have not
      the less
Rejoiced to see thy actual life agree
With the large future which I shaped for
    thee,
When, years ago, beside the summer sea,
White in the moon, we saw the long
    waves fall
Baffled and broken from the rocky wall,
That, to the menace of the brawling flood,
Opposed alone its massive quietude,
Calm as a fate ; with not a leaf nor
    vine
Nor birch-spray trembling in the still
    moonshine,
Crowning it like God's peace. I some-
    times think
    That night-scene by the sea prophet-
      ical, —
(For Nature speaks in symbols and in
    signs,
And through her pictures human fate
    divines), —
That rock, wherefrom we saw the billows
    sink

In murmuring rout, uprising clear and
    tall
In the white light of heaven, the type
    of one
Who, momently by Error's host assailed,
Stands strong as Truth, in greaves of
    granite mailed ;
    And, tranquil-fronted, listening over
        all
The tumult, hears the angels say, Well
    done !

THE KANSAS EMIGRANTS.

WE cross the prairie as of old
    The pilgrims crossed the sea,
To make the West, as they the East,
    The homestead of the free !

We go to rear a wall of men
    On Freedom's southern line,
And plant beside the cotton-tree
    The rugged Northern pine !

We 're flowing from our native hills
    As our free rivers flow ;
The blessing of our Mother-land
    Is on us as we go.

We go to plant her common school
    On distant prairie swells,
And give the Sabbaths of the wild
    The music of her bells.

Upbearing, like the Ark of old,
    The Bible in our van,
We go to test the truth of God
    Against the fraud of man.

No pause, nor rest, save where the
    streams
    That feed the Kansas run,
Save where our Pilgrim gonfalon
    Shall flout the setting sun !

We 'll tread the prairie as of old
    Our fathers sailed the sea,
And make the West, as they the East,
    The homestead of the free !

SONG OF SLAVES IN THE DESERT.[63]

WHERE are we going ? where are we go-
    ing,
    Where are we going, Rubee ?

Lord of peoples, lord of lands,
Look across these shining sands,
Through the furnace of the noon,
Through the white light of the moon,
Strong the Ghiblee wind is blowing,
Strange and large the world is growing
Speak and tell us where we are going,
    Where are we going, Rubee ?

Bornou land was rich and good,
Wells of water, fields of food,
Dourra fields, and bloom of bean,
And the palm-tree cool and green :
Bornou land we see no longer,
Here we thirst and here we hunger,
Here the Moor-man smites in anger :
    Where are we going, Rubee ?

When we went from Bornou land,
We were like the leaves and sand,
We were many, we are few ;
Life has one, and death has two :
Whitened bones our path are showing,
Thou All-seeing, thou All-knowing !
Hear us, tell us, where are we going,
    Where are we going, Rubee ?

Moons of marches from our eyes
Bornou land behind us lies ;
Stranger round us day by day
Bends the desert circle gray ;
Wild the waves of sand are flowing,
Hot the winds above them blowing, —
Lord of all things ! — where are we go-
        ing ?
    Where are we going, Rubee ?

We are weak, but Thou art strong ;
Short our lives, but Thine is long ;
We are blind, but Thou hast eyes ;
We are fools, but Thou art wise !

Thou, our morrow's pathway knowing
Through the strange world round us
        growing,
Hear us, tell us where are we going,
    Where are we going, Rubee ?

LINES,

INSCRIBED TO FRIENDS UNDER ARREST
    FOR TREASON AGAINST THE SLAVE
    POWER.

THE age is dull and mean.   Men creep,
    Not walk ; with blood too pale and
    tame

To pay the debt they owe to shame ;
Buy cheap, sell dear ; eat, drink, and
sleep
Down-pillowed, deaf to moaning want;
Pay tithes for soul-insurance ; keep
Six days to Mammon, one to Cant.

In such a time, give thanks to God,
That somewhat of the holy rage
With which the prophets in their
age
On all its decent seemings trod,
Has set your feet upon the lie,
That man and ox and soul and clod
Are market stock to sell and buy !

The hot words from your lips, my own,
To caution trained, might not repeat ;
But if some tares among the wheat
Of generous thought and deed were
sown, ·
No common wrong provoked your
zeal ;
The silken gauntlet that is thrown
In such a quarrel rings like steel.

The brave old strife the fathers saw
For Freedom calls for men again
Like those who battled not in vain
For England's Charter, Alfred's law ;
And right of speech and trial just
Wage in your name their ancient war
With venal courts and perjured trust.

God's ways seem dark, but, soon or late,
They touch the shining hills of day ;
The evil cannot brook delay,
The good can well afford to wait.
Give ermined knaves their hour of
crime ;
Ye have the future grand and great,
The safe appeal of Truth to Time !

THE NEW EXODUS.[64]

By fire and cloud, across the desert
sand,
And through the parted waves,
From their long bondage, with an out-
stretched hand,
God led the Hebrew slaves !

Dead as the letter of the Pentateuch,
As Egypt's statues cold,
In the adytum of the sacred book
Now stands that marvel old.

" Lo, God *is* great !" the simple Mos-
lem says.
We seek the ancient date,
Turn the dry scroll, and make that liv-
ing phrase
A dead one : " God *was* great !"

And, like the Coptic monks by Mousa's
wells,
We dream of wonders past,
Vague as the tales the wandering Arab
tells,
Each drowsier than the last.

O fools and blind ! Above the Pyramids
Stretches once more that hand,
And tran\céd Egypt, from her stony lids,
Flings back her veil of sand.

And morning-smitten Memnon, singing,
wakes ;
And, listening by his Nile,
O'er Ammon's grave and awful visage
breaks
A sweet and human smile.

Not, as before, with hail and fire, and
call
Of death for midnight graves,
But in the stillness of the noonday,
fall
The fetters of the slaves.

No longer through the Red Sea, as of
old,
The bondmen walk dry shod ;
Through human hearts, by love of Him
controlled,
Runs now that path of God !

THE HASCHISH.

Of all that Orient lands can vaunt
Of marvels with our own competing,
The strangest is the Haschish plant,
And what will follow on its eating.

What pictures to the taster rise,
Of Dervish or of Almeh dances !
Of Eblis, or of Paradise,
Set all aglow with Houri glances !

The poppy visions of Cathay,
The heavy beer-trance of the Suabian;
The wizard lights and demon play
Of nights Walpurgis and Arabian !

The Mollah and the Christian dog
    Change place in mad metempsycho-
      sis ;
The Muezzin climbs the synagogue,
    The Rabbi shakes his beard at Moses !

The Arab by his desert well
    Sits choosing from some Caliph's
      daughters,
And hears his single camel's bell
    Sound welcome to his regal quarters.

The Koran's reader makes complaint
    Of Shitan dancing on and off it ;
The robber offers alms, the saint
    Drinks Tokay and blasphemes the
      Prophet.

Such scenes that Eastern plant awakes ;
    But we have one ordained to beat it,
The Haschish of the West, which makes
    Or fools or knaves of all who eat it.

The preacher eats, and straight appears
    His Bible in a new translation ;

Its angels negro overseers,
    And Heaven itself a snug planta-
      tion !

The man of peace, about whose dreams
    The sweet millennial angels cluster,
Tastes the mad weed, and plots and
      schemes,
    A raving Cuban filibuster !

The noisiest Democrat, with ease,
    It turns to Slavery's parish beadle ;
The shrewdest statesman eats and sees
    Due southward point the polar needle.

The Judge partakes, and sits erelong
    Upon his bench a railing blackguard ;
Decides off-hand that right is wrong,
    And reads the ten commandments
      backward.

O potent plant ! so rare a taste
    Has never Turk or Gentoo gotten ;
The hempen Haschish of the East
    Is powerless to our Western Cotton !

BALLADS.

MARY GARVIN.

FROM the heart of Waumbek Methna,
    from the lake that never fails,
Falls the Saco in the green lap of Con-
    way's intervales ;
There, in wild and virgin freshness, its
    waters foam and flow,
As when Darby Field first saw them,
    two hundred years ago.

But, vexed in all its seaward course with
    bridges, dams, and mills,
How changed is Saco's stream, how lost
    its freedom of the hills,
Since travelled Jocelyn, factor Vines,
    and stately Champernoon
Heard on its banks the gray wolf's howl,
    the trumpet of the loon !

With smoking axle hot with speed, with
    steeds of fire and steam,
Wide-waked To-day leaves Yesterday
    behind him like a dream.

Still, from the hurrying train of Life,
    fly backward far and fast
The milestones of the fathers, the land-
    marks of the past.

But human hearts remain unchanged :
    the sorrow and the sin,
The loves and hopes and fears of old, are
    to our own akin ;
And if, in tales our fathers told, the
    songs our mothers sung,
Tradition wears a snowy beard, Romance
    is always young.

O sharp-lined man of traffic, on Saco's
    banks to-day !
O mill-girl watching late and long the
    shuttle's restless play !
Let, for the once, a listening ear the
    working hand beguile,
And lend my old Provincial tale, as
    suits, a tear or smile !

The evening gun had sounded from gray
 Fort Mary's walls ;
Through the forest, like a wild beast,
 roared and plunged the Saco's falls.

And westward on the sea-wind, that
 damp and gusty grew,
Over cedars darkening inland the smokes
 of Spurwink blew.

On the hearth of Farmer Garvin blazed
 the crackling walnut log ;
Right and left sat dame and goodman,
 and between them lay the dog,

Head on paws, and tail slow wagging,
 and beside him on her mat,
Sitting drowsy in the fire-light, winked
 and purred the mottled cat.

" Twenty years ! " said Goodman Garvin, speaking sadly, under breath,
And his gray head slowly shaking, as
 one who speaks of death.

The goodwife dropped her needles : " It
 is twenty years to-day,
Since the Indians fell on Saco, and stole
 our child away."

Then they sank into the silence, for
 each knew the other's thought,
Of a great and common sorrow, and
 words were needed not.

" Who knocks ? " cried Goodman Garvin.
 The door was open thrown ;
On two strangers, man and maiden, cloaked
 and furred, the fire-light shone.

One with courteous gesture lifted the
 bear-skin from his head ;
" Lives here Elkanah Garvin ? " " I
 am he," the goodman said.

" Sit ye down, and dry and warm ye,
 for the night is chill with rain."
And the goodwife drew the settle, and
 stirred the fire amain.

The maid unclasped her cloak-hood, the
 fire-light glistened fair
In her large, moist eyes, and over soft
 folds of dark brown hair.

Dame Garvin looked upon her : " It is
 Mary's self I see !

Dear heart ! " she cried, " now tell me,
 has my child come back to me ? "

" My name indeed is Mary," said the
 stranger, sobbing wild ;
" Will you be to me a mother ? I am
 Mary Garvin's child !

" She sleeps by wooded Simcoe, but on
 her dying day
She bade my father take me to her kins-
 folk far away.

" And when the priest besought her to
 do me no such wrong,
She said, ' May God forgive me ! I have
 closed my heart too long.

" ' When I hid me from my father, and
 shut out my mother's call,
I sinned against those dear ones, and
 the Father of us all.

" ' Christ's love rebukes no home-love,
 breaks no tie of kin apart ;
Better heresy in doctrine, than heresy
 of heart.

" 'Tell me not the Church must censure :
 she who wept the Cross beside
Never made her own flesh strangers, nor
 the claims of blood denied ;

" ' And if she who wronged her parents,
 with her child atones to them,
Earthly daughter, Heavenly mother !
 thou at least wilt not condemn ! '

" So, upon her death-bed lying, my
 blessed mother spake ;
As we come to do her bidding, so receive
 us for her sake."

" God be praised ! " said Goodwife Garvin, " He taketh, and he gives ;
He woundeth, but he healeth ; in her
 child our daughter lives ! "

" Amen ! " the old man answered, as he
 brushed a tear away,
And, kneeling by his hearthstone, said,
 with reverence, " Let us pray."

All its Oriental symbols, and its Hebrew
 paraphrase,
Warm with earnest life and feeling, rose
 his prayer of love and praise.

But he started at beholding, as he rose
    from off his knee,
The stranger cross his forehead with the
    sign of Papistrie.

"What is this?" cried Farmer Garvin.
    "Is an English Christian's home
A chapel or a mass-house, that you make
    the sign of Rome?"

Then the young girl knelt beside him,
    kissed his trembling hand, and
    cried:
"O, forbear to chide my father; in that
    faith my mother died!

"On her wooden cross at Simcoe the
    dews and sunshine fall,
As they fall on Spurwink's graveyard;
    and the dear God watches all!"

The old man stroked the fair head that
    rested on his knee;
"Your words, dear child," he answered,
    "are God's rebuke to me.

"Creed and rite perchance may differ,
    yet our faith and hope be one.
Let me be your father's father, let him
    be to me a son."

When the horn, on Sabbath morning,
    through the still and frosty air,
From Spurwink, Pool, and Black Point,
    called to sermon and to prayer,

To the goodly house of worship, where,
    in order due and fit,
As by public vote directed, classed and
    ranked the people sit;

Mistress first and goodwife after, clerkly
    squire before the clown,
From the brave coat, lace-embroidered,
    to the gray frock, shading down;

From the pulpit read the preacher, —
    "Goodman Garvin and his wife
Fain would thank the Lord, whose kind-
    ness has followed them through
    life,

"For the great and crowning mercy,
    that their daughter, from the
    wild,
Where she rests (they hope in God's
    peace), has sent to them her child;

"And the prayers of all God's people
    they ask, that they may prove
Not unworthy, through their weakness,
    of such special proof of love."

As the preacher prayed, uprising, the
    aged couple stood,
And the fair Canadian also, in her mod-
    est maidenhood.

Thought the elders, grave and doubting,
    "She is Papist born and bred";
Thought the young men, "'T is an
    angel in Mary Garvin's stead!"

MAUD MULLER.

MAUD MULLER, on a summer's day,
Raked the meadow sweet with hay.

Beneath her torn hat glowed the wealth
Of simple beauty and rustic health.

Singing, she wrought, and her merry glee
The mock-bird echoed from his tree.

But when she glanced to the far-off
    town,
White from its hill-slope looking down,

The sweet song died, and a vague unrest
And a nameless longing filled her
    breast, —

A wish, that she hardly dared to own,
For something better than she had
    known.

The Judge rode slowly down the lane,
Smoothing his horse's chestnut mane.

He drew his bridle in the shade
Of the apple-trees, to greet the maid,

And asked a draught from the spring that
    flowed
Through the meadow across the road.

She stooped where the cool spring bub-
    bled up,
And filled for him her small tin cup,

And blushed as she gave it, looking
    down
On her feet so bare, and her tattered
    gown.

"Thanks !" said the Judge ; "a sweeter
draught
From a fairer hand was never quaffed."

He spoke of the grass and flowers and
trees,
Of the singing birds and the humming
bees ;

Then talked of the haying, and wondered whether
The cloud in the west would bring foul
weather.

And Maud forgot her brier-torn gown,
And her graceful ankles bare and brown ;

And listened, while a pleased surprise
Looked from her long-lashed hazel eyes.

At last, like one who for delay
Seeks a vain excuse, he rode away.

Maud Muller looked and sighed : "Ah
me !
That I the Judge's bride might be !

"He would dress me up in silks so fine,
And praise and toast me at his wine.

"My father should wear a broadcloth
coat ;
My brother should sail a painted boat.

"I 'd dress my mother so grand and
gay,
And the baby should have a new toy
each day.

"And I'd feed the hungry and clothe
the poor,
And all should bless me who left our
door."

The Judge looked back as he climbed
the hill,
And saw Maud Muller standing still.

"A form more fair, a face more sweet,
Ne'er hath it been my lot to meet.

"And her modest answer and graceful
air
Show her wise and good as she is fair.

"Would she were mine, and I to-day,
Like her, a harvester of hay :

"No doubtful balance of rights and
wrongs,
Nor weary lawyers with endless tongues,

"But low of cattle and song of birds,
And health and quiet and loving words."

But he thought of his sisters proud and
cold,
And his mother vain of her rank and
gold.

So, closing his heart, the Judge rode
on,
And Maud was left in the field alone.

But the lawyers smiled that afternoon,
When he hummed in court an old love-
tune ;

And the young girl mused beside the
well
Till the rain on the unraked clover fell.

He wedded a wife of richest dower,
Who lived for fashion, as he for power.

Yet oft, in his marble hearth's bright
glow,
He watched a picture come and go ;

And sweet Maud Muller's hazel eyes
Looked out in their innocent surprise.

Oft, when the wine in his glass was
red,
He longed for the wayside well instead ;

And closed his eyes on his garnished
rooms
To dream of meadows and clover-blooms.

And the proud man sighed, with a secret pain,
"Ah, that I were free again !

"Free as when I rode that day,
Where the barefoot maiden raked her
hay."

She wedded a man unlearned and poor,
And many children played round her
door.

But care and sorrow, and childbirth
pain,
Left their traces on heart and brain.

And oft, when the summer sun shone hot
On the new-mown hay in the meadow
lot,

And she heard the little spring brook fall
Over the roadside, through the wall,

In the shade of the apple-tree again
She saw a rider draw his rein.

And, gazing down with timid grace,
She felt his pleased eyes read her face.

Sometimes her narrow kitchen walls
Stretched away into stately halls ;

The weary wheel to a spinnet turned,
The tallow candle an astral burned,

And for him who sat by the chimney
lug,
Dozing and grumbling o'er pipe and
mug,

A manly form at her side she saw,
And joy was duty and love was law.

Then she took up her burden of life
again,
Saying only, " It might have been."

Alas for maiden, alas for Judge,
For rich repiner and household drudge !

God pity them both ! and pity us all,
Who vainly the dreams of youth recall.

For of all sad words of tongue or pen,
The saddest are these : " It might have
been ! "

Ah, well ! for us all some sweet hope
lies
Deeply buried from human eyes ;

And, in the hereafter, angels may
Roll the stone from its grave away !

THE RANGER.

ROBERT RAWLIN ! — Frosts were falling
When the ranger's horn was calling
    Through the woods to Canada.
Gone the winter's sleet and snowing,
Gone the spring-time's bud and blowing,
Gone the summer's harvest mowing,

And again the fields are gray.
    Yet away, he 's away !
Faint and fainter hope is growing
    In the hearts that mourn his stay.

Where the lion, crouching high on
Abraham's rock with teeth of iron,
    Glares o'er wood and wave away,
Faintly thence, as pines far sighing,
Or as thunder spent and dying,
Come the challenge and replying,
    Come the sounds of flight and fray.
        Well-a-day ! Hope and pray !
Some are living, some are lying
    In their red graves far away.

Straggling rangers, worn with dangers,
Homeward faring, weary strangers
    Pass the farm-gate on their way ;
Tidings of the dead and living,
Forest march and ambush, giving,
Till the maidens leave their weaving,
    And the lads forget their play.
        " Still away, still away ! "
Sighs a sad one, sick with grieving,
    " Why does Robert still delay ! "

Nowhere fairer, sweeter, rarer,
Does the golden-locked fruit-bearer
    Through his painted woodlands stray,
Than where hillside oaks and beeches
Overlook the long, blue reaches,
Silver coves and pebbled beaches,
    And green isles of Casco Bay ;
        Nowhere day, for delay,
With a tenderer look beseeches,
    "Let me with my charmed earth
        stay."

On the grain-lands of the mainlands
Stands the serried corn like train-bands,
    Plume and pennon rustling gay ;
Out at sea, the islands wooded,
Silver birches, golden-hooded,
Set with maples, crimson-blooded,
    White sea-foam and sand-hills gray,
        Stretch away, far away.
Dim and dreamy, over-brooded
    By the hazy autumn day.

Gayly chattering to the clattering
Of the brown nuts downward pattering,
    Leap the squirrels, red and gray.
On the grass-land, on the fallow,
Drop the apples, red and yellow ;
Drop the russet pears and mellow,
    Drop the red leaves all the day.
        And away, swift away,

Sun and cloud, o'er hill and hollow
  Chasing, weave their web of play.

"Martha Mason, Martha Mason,
Prithee tell us of the reason
  Why you mope at home to-day :
Surely smiling is not sinning ;
Leave your quilling, leave your spinning ;
What is all your store of linen,
  If your heart is never gay ?
  Come away, come away !
Never yet did sad beginning
  Make the task of life a play."

Overbending, till she's blending
With the flaxen skein she's tending
  Pale brown tresses smoothed away
From her face of patient sorrow,
Sits she, seeking but to borrow,
From the trembling hope of morrow,
  Solace for the weary day.
  "Go your way, laugh and play ;
Unto Him who heeds the sparrow
  And the lily, let me pray."

"With our rally, rings the valley, —
Join us !" cried the blue-eyed Nelly ;
  "Join us !" cried the laughing
    May,
"To the beach we all are going,
And, to save the task of rowing,
West by north the wind is blowing,
  Blowing briskly down the bay !
  Come away, come away !
Time and tide are swiftly flowing,
  Let us take them while we may !

"Never tell us that you'll fail us,
Where the purple beach-plum mellows
  On the bluffs so wild and gray.
Hasten, for the oars are falling ;
Hark, our merry mates are calling :
Time it is that we were all in,
  Singing tideward down the bay !"
  "Nay, nay, let me stay ;
Sore and sad for Robert Rawlin
  Is my heart," she said, "to-day."

"Vain your calling for Rob Rawlin !
Some red squaw his moose-meat's broil-
  ing,
  Or some French lass, singing gay ;
Just forget as he's forgetting ;
What avails a life of fretting ?
If some stars must needs be setting,
  Others rise as good as they."
  "Cease, I pray ; go your way !"

Martha cries, her eyelids wetting ;
  "Foul and false the words you say !"

"Martha Mason, hear to reason !
Prithee, put a kinder face on !"
  "Cease to vex me," did she say ;
"Better at his side be lying,
With the mournful pine-trees sighing,
And the wild birds o'er us crying,
  Than to doubt like mine a prey ;
  While away, far away,
Turns my heart, forever trying
  Some new hope for each new day.

"When the shadows veil the meadows,
And the sunset's golden ladders
  Sink from twilight's walls of gray, —
From the window of my dreaming,
I can see his sickle gleaming,
Cheery-voiced, can hear him teaming
  Down the locust-shaded way ;
  But away, swift away,
Fades the fond, delusive seeming,
  And I kneel again to pray.

"When the growing dawn is showing,
And the barn-yard cock is crowing,
  And the horned moon pales away :
From a dream of him awaking,
Every sound my heart is making
Seems a footstep of his taking ;
  Then I hush the thought, and say,
  'Nay, nay, he's away !'
Ah ! my heart, my heart is breaking
  For the dear one far away."

Look up, Martha ! worn and swarthy,
Glows a face of manhood worthy :
  "Robert !" "Martha !" all they say
O'er went wheel and reel together,
Little cared the owner whither ;
Heart of lead is heart of feather,
  Noon of night is noon of day !
  Come away, come away !
When such lovers meet each other,
  Why should prying idlers stay ?

Quench the timber's fallen embers,
Quench the red leaves in December's
  Hoary rime and chilly spray.
But the hearth shall kindle clearer,
Household welcomes sound sincerer,
Heart to loving heart draw nearer,
  When the bridal bells shall say :
"Hope and pray, trust alway ;
Life is sweeter, love is dearer,
  For the trial and delay !"

LATER POEMS.

THE LAST WALK IN AUTUMN.

I.

O'er the bare woods, whose out-
  stretched hands
  Plead with the leaden heavens in
    vain,
I see, beyond the valley lands,
  The sea's long level dim with rain.
Around me all things, stark and dumb,
Seem praying for the snows to come,
And, for the summer bloom and green-
    ness gone,
With winter's sunset lights and dazzling
    morn atone.

II.

Along the river's summer walk,
  The withered tufts of asters nod ;
And trembles on its arid stalk
  The hoar plume of the golden-rod.
And on a ground of sombre fir,
And azure-studded juniper,
The silver birch its buds of purple shows,
And scarlet berries tell where bloomed
    the sweet wild-rose !

III.

With mingled sound of horns and bells,
  A far-heard clang, the wild geese
    fly,
Storm-sent, from Arctic moors and
    fells,
  Like a great arrow through the sky,
Two dusky lines converged in one,
Chasing the southward-flying sun ;
While the brave snow-bird and the hardy
    jay
Call to them from the pines, as if to bid
    them stay.

IV.

I passed this way a year ago :
  The wind blew south ; the noon of
    day
Was warm as June's ; and save that
    snow
  Flecked the low mountains far away,

And that the vernal-seeming breeze
  Mocked faded grass and leafless trees,
I might have dreamed of summer as I lay,
Watching the fallen leaves with the soft
    wind at play.

V.

Since then, the winter blasts have piled
  The white pagodas of the snow
On these rough slopes, and, strong and
    wild,
    Yon river, in its overflow
Of spring-time rain and sun, set free,
Crashed with its ices to the sea ;
And over these gray fields, then green
    and gold,
The summer corn has waved, the thun-
    der's organ rolled.

VI.

Rich gift of God ! A year of time !
  What pomp of rise and shut of day,
What hues wherewith our Northern
    clime
    Makes autumn's dropping woodlands
      gay,
What airs outblown from ferny dells,
And clover - bloom and sweetbrier
    smells,
What songs of brooks and birds, what
    fruits and flowers,
Green woods and moonlit snows, have in
    its round been ours !

VII.

I know not how, in other lands,
  The changing seasons come and go ;
What splendors fall on Syrian sands,
  What purple lights on Alpine snow !
Nor how the pomp of sunrise waits
On Venice at her watery gates ;
A dream alone to me is Arno's vale,
And the Alhambra's halls are but a trav-
    eller's tale.

VIII.

Yet, on life's current, he who drifts
  Is one with him who rows or sails ;

THE LAST WALK IN AUTUMN.   Page 208,

And he who wanders widest lifts
   No more of beauty's jealous veils
Than he who from his doorway sees
   The miracle of flowers and trees,
Feels the warm Orient in the noonday air,
And from cloud minarets hears the sun-
   set call to prayer !

IX.

The eye may well be glad, that looks
   Where Pharpar's fountains rise and
      fall ;
But he who sees his native brooks
   Laugh in the sun, has seen them all.
The marble palaces of Ind
Rise round him in the snow and wind ;
From his lone sweetbrier Persian Hafiz
   smiles,
And Rome's cathedral awe is in his
   woodland aisles.

X.

And thus it is my fancy blends
   The near at hand and far and rare ;
And while the same horizon bends
   Above the silver-sprinkled hair
Which flashed the light of morning
   skies
On childhood's wonder-lifted eyes,
Within its round of sea and sky and field,
Earth wheels with all her zones, the
   Kosmos stands revealed.

XI.

And thus the sick man on his bed,
   The toiler to his task-work bound,
Behold their prison-walls outspread,
   Their clipped horizon widen round !
While freedom-giving fancy waits,
Like Peter's angel at the gates,
The power is theirs to baffle care and pain,
To bring the lost world back, and make
   it theirs again !

XII.

What lack of goodly company,
   When masters of the ancient lyre
Obey my call, and trace for me
   Their words of mingled tears and
      fire !
I talk with Bacon, grave and wise,
I read the world with Pascal's eyes ;
And priest and sage, with solemn brows
   austere,
And poets, garland-bound, the Lords of
   Thought, draw near.

14

XIII.

Methinks, O friend, I hear thee say,
   " In vain the human heart we mock ;
Bring living guests who love the day,
   Not ghosts who fly at crow of cock !
The herbs we share with flesh and blood,
Are better than ambrosial food,
With laurelled shades." I grant it,
   nothing loath,
But doubly blest is he who can partake
   of both.

XIV.

He who might Plato's banquet grace,
   Have I not seen before me sit,
And watched his puritanic face,
   With more than Eastern wisdom lit ?
Shrewd mystic ! who, upon the back
Of his Poor Richard's Almanack,
Writing the Sufi's song, the Gentoo's
   dream,
Links Menu's age of thought to Fulton's
   age of steam !

XV.

Here too, of answering love secure,
   Have I not welcomed to my hearth
The gentle pilgrim troubadour,
   Whose songs have girdled half the
      earth ;
Whose pages, like the magic mat
Whereon the Eastern lover sat,
Have borne me over Rhine-land's purple
   vines,
And Nubia's tawny sands, and Phrygia's
   mountain pines !

XVI.

And he, who to the lettered wealth
   Of ages adds the lore unpriced,
The wisdom and the moral health,
   The ethics of the school of Christ ;
The statesman to his holy trust,
As the Athenian archon, just,
Struck down, exiled like him for truth
   alone,
Has he not graced my home with beauty
   all his own ?

XVII.

What greetings smile, what farewells
   wave,
   What loved ones enter and depart !
The good, the beautiful, the brave,
   The Heaven-lent treasures of the
      heart !

How conscious seems the frozen sod
   And beechen slope whereon they trod !
The oak-leaves rustle, and the dry grass
   bends
Beneath the shadowy feet of lost or ab-
   sent friends.

XVIII.

Then ask not why to these bleak hills
   I cling, as clings the tufted moss,
To bear the winter's lingering chills,
   The mocking spring's perpetual loss.
I dream of lands where summer smiles,
   And soft winds blow from spicy isles,
But scarce would Ceylon's breath of
   flowers be sweet,
Could I not feel thy soil, New England,
   at my feet !

XIX.

At times I long for gentler skies,
   And bathe in dreams of softer air,
But homesick tears would fill the eyes
   That saw the Cross without the Bear.
The pine must whisper to the palm,
   The north-wind break the tropic calm ;
And with the dreamy languor of the Line,
The North's keen virtue blend, and
    strength to beauty join.

XX.

Better to stem with heart and hand
   The roaring tide of life, than lie,
Unmindful, on its flowery strand,
   Of God's occasions drifting by !
Better with naked nerve to bear
The needles of this goading air,
Than, in the lap of sensual ease, forego
The godlike power to do, the godlike
    aim to know.

XXI.

Home of my heart ! to me more fair
   Than gay Versailles or Windsor's
   halls,
The painted, shingly town-house where
   The freeman's vote for Freedom falls !
The simple roof where prayer is made,
Than Gothic groin and colonnade ;
The living temple of the heart of man,
Than Rome's sky-mocking vault, or
   many-spired Milan !

XXII.

More dear thy equal village schools,
   Where rich and poor the Bible read,

Than classic halls where Priestcraft
   rules,
   And Learning wears the chains of
   Creed ;
Thy glad Thanksgiving, gathering in
   The scattered sheaves of home and kin,
Than the mad license following Lenten
   pains,
Or holidays of slaves who laugh and
   dance in chains.

XXIII.

And sweet homes nestle in these dales,
   And perch along these wooded
   swells ;
And, blest beyond Arcadian vales,
   They hear the sound of Sabbath
   bells !
Here dwells no perfect man sublime,
Nor woman winged before her time,
But with the faults and follies of the
   race,
Old home-bred virtues hold their not
   unhonored place.

XXIV.

Here manhood struggles for the sake
   Of mother, sister, daughter, wife,
The graces and the loves which make
   The music of the march of life ;
And woman, in her daily round
Of duty, walks on holy ground.
No unpaid menial tills the soil, nor here
Is the bad lesson learned at human rights
   to sneer.

XXV.

Then let the icy north-wind blow
   The trumpets of the coming storm,
To arrowy sleet and blinding snow
   Yon slanting lines of rain transform.
Young hearts shall hail the drifted
   cold,
   As gayly as I did of old ;
And I, who watch them through the
   frosty pane,
Unenvious, live in them my boyhood
   o'er again.

XXVI.

And I will trust that He who heeds
   The life that hides in mead and
   wold,
Who hangs yon alder's crimson beads,
   And stains these mosses green and
   gold,

Will still, as He hath done, incline
His gracious care to me and mine ;
Grant what we ask aright, from wrong
    debar,
And, as the earth grows dark, make
    brighter every star !

XXVII.

I have not seen, I may not see,
    My hopes for man take form in
        fact,
But God will give the victory
    In due time ; in that faith I act.
And he who sees the future sure,
The baffling present may endure,
And bless, meanwhile, the unseen Hand
    that leads
The heart's desires beyond the halting
    step of deeds.

XXVIII.

And thou, my song, I send thee forth,
    Where harsher songs of mine have
        flown ;
Go, find a place at home and hearth
    Where'er thy singer's name is known ;
Revive for him the kindly thought
Of friends ; and they who love him
    not,
Touched by some strain of thine, per-
    chance may take
The hand he proffers all, and thank him
    for thy sake.

THE MAYFLOWERS.

The trailing arbutus, or mayflower, grows
abundantly in the vicinity of Plymouth, and
was the first flower that greeted the Pilgrims
after their fearful winter.

SAD Mayflower ! watched by winter stars,
    And nursed by winter gales,
With petals of the sleeted spars,
    And leaves of frozen sails !

What had she in those dreary hours,
    Within her ice-rimmed bay,
In common with the wild-wood flowers,
    The first sweet smiles of May ?

Yet, " God be praised ! " the Pilgrim
    said,
    Who saw the blossoms peer
Above the brown leaves, dry and dead,
    " Behold our Mayflower here ! "

" God wills it : here our rest shall be,
    Our years of wandering o'er,
For us the Mayflower of the sea
    Shall spread her sails no more."

O sacred flowers of faith and hope,
    As sweetly now as then
Ye bloom on many a birchen slope,
    In many a pine-dark glen.

Behind the sea-wall's rugged length,
    Unchanged, your leaves unfold,
Like love behind the manly strength
    Of the brave hearts of old.

So live the fathers in their sons,
    Their sturdy faith be ours,
And ours the love that overruns
    Its rocky strength with flowers.

The Pilgrim's wild and wintry day
    Its shadow round us draws ;
The Mayflower of his stormy bay,
    Our Freedom's struggling cause.

But warmer suns erelong shall bring
    To life the frozen sod ;
And, through dead leaves of hope, shall
        spring
    Afresh the flowers of God !

BURIAL OF BARBOUR.

BEAR him, comrades, to his grave ;
Never over one more brave
    Shall the prairie grasses weep,
    In the ages yet to come,
When the millions in our room,
    What we sow in tears, shall reap.

Bear him up the icy hill,
With the Kansas, frozen still
    As his noble heart, below,
And the land he came to till
With a freeman's thews and will,
    And his poor hut roofed with snow !

One more look of that dead face,
Of his murder's ghastly trace !
    One more kiss, O widowed one !
Lay your left hands on his brow,
Lift your right hands up, and vow
    That his work shall yet be done.

Patience, friends ! The eye of God
Every path by Murder trod

Watches, lidless, day and night;
And the dead man in his shroud,
And his widow weeping loud,
    And our hearts, are in his sight.

Every deadly threat that swells
With the roar of gambling hells,
    Every brutal jest and jeer,
Every wicked thought and plan
Of the cruel heart of man,
    Though but whispered, He can hear!

We in suffering, they in crime,
Wait the just award of time,
    Wait the vengeance that is due;
Not in vain a heart shall break,
Not a tear for Freedom's sake
    Fall unheeded: God is true.

While the flag with stars bedecked
Threatens where it should protect,
    And the Law shakes hands with
        Crime,
What is left us but to wait,
Match our patience to our fate,
    And abide the better time?

Patience, friends! The human heart
Everywhere shall take our part,
    Everywhere for us shall pray;
On our side are nature's laws,
And God's life is in the cause
    That we suffer for to-day.

Well to suffer is divine;
Pass the watchword down the line,
    Pass the countersign: "ENDURE."
Not to him who rashly dares,
But to him who nobly bears,
    Is the victor's garland sure.

Frozen earth to frozen breast,
Lay our slain one down to rest;
    Lay him down in hope and faith,
And above the broken sod,
Once again, to Freedom's God,
    Pledge ourselves for life or death,

That the State whose walls we lay,
In our blood and tears, to-day,
    Shall be free from bonds of shame
And our goodly land untrod
By the feet of Slavery, shod
    With cursing as with flame!

Plant the Buckeye on his grave,
For the hunter of the slave

In its shadow cannot rest;
And let martyr mound and tree
Be our pledge and guaranty
    Of the freedom of the West!

TO PENNSYLVANIA.

O STATE prayer-founded! never hung
Such choice upon a people's tongue,
    Such power to bless or ban,
As that which makes thy whisper Fate,
For which on thee the centuries wait,
    And destinies of man!

Across thy Alleghanian chain,
With groanings from a land in pain,
    The west-wind finds its way:
Wild-wailing from Missouri's flood
The crying of thy children's blood
    Is in thy ears to-day!

And unto thee in Freedom's hour
Of sorest need God gives the power
    To ruin or to save;
To wound or heal, to blight or bless
With fertile field or wilderness,
    A free home or a grave!

Then let thy virtue match the crime,
Rise to a level with the time;
    And, if a son of thine
Betray or tempt thee, Brutus-like
For Fatherland and Freedom strike
    As Justice gives the sign.

Wake, sleeper, from thy dream of ease,
The great occasion's forelock seize;
    And, let the north-wind strong,
And golden leaves of autumn, be
Thy coronal of Victory
    And thy triumphal song.
10th mo., 1856.

THE PASS OF THE SIERRA.

ALL night above their rocky bed
    They saw the stars march slow;
The wild Sierra overhead,
    The desert's death below.

The Indian from his lodge of bark,
    The gray bear from his den,
Beyond their camp-fire's wall of dark
    Glared on the mountain men.

Still upward turned, with anxious strain,
　　Their leader's sleepless eye,
Where splinters of the mountain chain
　　Stood black against the sky.

The night waned slow : at last, a glow,
　　A gleam of sudden fire,
Shot up behind the walls of snow,
　　And tipped each icy spire.

"Up, men !" he cried, "yon rocky
　　cone,
To-day, please God, we 'll pass,
And look from Winter's frozen throne
　　On Summer's flowers and grass !"

They set their faces to the blast,
　　They trod the eternal snow,
And faint, worn, bleeding, hailed at last
　　The promised land below.

Behind, they saw the snow-cloud tossed
　　By many an icy horn ;
Before, warm valleys, wood-embossed,
　　And green with vines and corn.

They left the Winter at their backs
　　To flap his baffled wing,
And downward, with the cataracts,
　　Leaped to the lap of Spring.

Strong leader of that mountain band,
　　Another task remains,
To break from Slavery's desert land
　　A path to Freedom's plains.

The winds are wild, the way is drear,
　　Yet, flashing through the night,
Lo ! icy ridge and rocky spear
　　Blaze out in morning light !

Rise up, FREMONT ! and go before ;
　　The Hour must have its Man ;
Put on the hunting-shirt once more,
　　And lead in Freedom's van !
8th mo., 1856.

THE CONQUEST OF FINLAND.[65]

Across the frozen marshes
　　The winds of autumn blow,
And the fen-lands of the Wetter
　　Are white with early snow.

But where the low, gray headlands
　　Look o'er the Baltic brine,
A bark is sailing in the track
　　Of England's battle-line.

No wares hath she to barter
　　For Bothnia's fish and grain ;
She saileth not for pleasure,
　　She saileth not for gain.

But still by isle or mainland
　　She drops her anchor down,
Where'er the British cannon
　　Rained fire on tower and town.

Outspake the ancient Amtman,
　　At the gate of Helsingfors :
"Why comes this ship a-spying
　　In the track of England's wars ?"

"God bless her," said the coast-guard,—
　　"God bless the ship, I say.
The holy angels trim the sails
　　That speed her on her way !

"Where'er she drops her anchor,
　　The peasant's heart is glad ;
Where'er she spreads her parting sail,
　　The peasant's heart is sad.

"Each wasted town and hamlet
　　She visits to restore ;
To roof the shattered cabin,
　　And feed the starving poor.

"The sunken boats of fishers,
　　The foraged beeves and grain,
The spoil of flake and storehouse,
　　The good ship brings again.

"And so to Finland's sorrow
　　The sweet amend is made,
As if the healing hand of Christ
　　Upon her wounds were laid !"

Then said the gray old Amtman,
　　"The will of God be done !
The battle lost by England's hate,
　　By England's love is won !

"We braved the iron tempest
　　That thundered on our shore ;
But when did kindness fail to find
　　The key to Finland's door ?

"No more from Aland's ramparts
　　Shall warning signal come,
Nor startled Sweaborg hear again
　　The roll of midnight drum.

" Beside our fierce Black Eagle
  The Dove of Peace shall rest ;
And in the mouths of cannon
  The sea-bird make her nest.

" For Finland, looking seaward,
  No coming foe shall scan ;
And the holy bells of Abo
  Shall ring, ' Good-will to man !'

"Then row thy boat, O fisher !
  In peace on lake and bay ;
And thou, young maiden, dance again
  Around the poles of May !

" Sit down, old men, together,
  Old wives, in quiet spin ;
Henceforth the Anglo-Saxon
  Is the brother of the Finn ! "

A LAY OF OLD TIME.

WRITTEN FOR THE ESSEX COUNTY
AGRICULTURAL FAIR.

ONE morning of the first sad Fall,
  Poor Adam and his bride
Sat in the shade of Eden's wall —
  But on the outer side.

She, blushing in her fig-leaf suit
  For the chaste garb of old ;
He, sighing o'er his bitter fruit
  For Eden's drupes of gold.

Behind them, smiling in the morn,
  Their forfeit garden lay,
Before them, wild with rock and thorn,
  The desert stretched away.

They heard the air above them fanned,
  A light step on the sward,
And lo ! they saw before them stand
  The angel of the Lord !

" Arise," he said, " why look behind,
  When hope is all before,
And patient hand and willing mind,
  Your loss may yet restore ?

" I leave with you a spell whose power
  Can make the desert glad,
And call around you fruit and flower
  As fair as Eden had.

" I clothe your hands with power to lift
  The curse from off your soil ;

Your very doom shall seem a gift,
  Your loss a gain through Toil.

" Go, cheerful as yon humming-bees,
  To labor as to play."
White glimmering over Eden's trees
  The angel passed away.

The pilgrims of the world went forth
  Obedient to the word,
And found where'er they tilled the earth
  A garden of the Lord !

The thorn-tree cast its evil fruit
  And blushed with plum and pear,
And seeded grass and trodden root
  Grew sweet beneath their care.

We share our primal parents' fate,
  And in our turn and day,
Look back on Eden's sworded gate
  As sad and lost as they.

But still for us his native skies
  The pitying Angel leaves,
And leads through Toil to Paradise
  New Adams and new Eves !

WHAT OF THE DAY ?

A SOUND of tumult troubles all the air,
  Like the low thunders of a sultry sky
Far-rolling ere the downright lightnings
    glare ;
  The hills blaze red with warnings ;
    foes draw nigh,
  Treading the dark with challenge and
    reply.
Behold the burden of the prophet's
    vision, —
The gathering hosts, — the Valley of
    Decision,
  Dusk with the wings of eagles wheel-
    ing o'er.
Day of the Lord, of darkness and not
    light !
  It breaks in thunder and the whirl-
    wind's roar !
Even so, Father ! Let thy will be
    done, —
Turn and o'erturn, end what thou hast
    begun
In judgment or in mercy : as for me,
If but the least and frailest, let me be
Evermore numbered with the truly free
Who find thy service perfect liberty !

I fain would thank Thee that my mor-
tal life
  Has reached the hour (albeit through
  care and pain)
When Good and Evil, as for final strife,
  Close dim and vast on Armageddon's
  plain ;
And Michael and his angels once again
  Drive howling back the Spirits of the
  Night.
O for the faith to read the signs aright
And, from the angle of thy perfect sight,
  See Truth's white banner floating on
  before ;
  And the Good Cause, despite of venal
  friends,
  And base expedients, move to noble
  ends ;
  See Peace with Freedom make to Time
  amends,
And, through its cloud of dust, the
  threshing-floor,
  Flailed by the thunder, heaped with
  chaffless grain !
1857.

THE FIRST FLOWERS.

FOR ages on our river borders,
  These tassels in their tawny bloom,
And willowy studs of downy silver,
  Have prophesied of Spring to come.

For ages have the unbound waters
  Smiled on them from their pebbly hem,
And the clear carol of the robin
  And song of bluebird welcomed them.

But never yet from smiling river,
  Or song of early bird, have they
Been greeted with a gladder welcome
  Than whispers from my heart to-day.

They break the spell of cold and dark-
  ness,
  The weary watch of sleepless pain ;
And from my heart, as from the river,
  The ice of winter melts again.

Thanks, Mary ! for this wild-wood token
  Of Freya's footsteps drawing near ;
Almost, as in the rune of Asgard,
  The growing of the grass I hear.

It is as if the pine-trees called me
  From ceiled room and silent books,

To see the dance of woodland shadows,
  And hear the song of April brooks !

As in the old Teutonic ballad
  Live singing bird and flowering tree,
Together live in bloom and music,
  I blend in song thy flowers and thee.

Earth's rocky tablets bear forever
  The dint of rain and small bird's track :
Who knows but that my idle verses
  May leave some trace by Merrimack !

The bird that trod the mellow layers
  Of the young earth is sought in vain ;
The cloud is gone that wove the sand-
  stone,
  From God's design, with threads of
  rain !

So, when this fluid age we live in
  Shall stiffen round my careless rhyme,
Who made the vagrant tracks may puzzle
  The savans of the coming time :

And, following out their dim suggestions,
  Some idly-curious hand may draw
My doubtful portraiture, as Cuvier
  Drew fish and bird from fin and claw.

And maidens in the far-off twilights,
  Singing my words to breeze and stream,
Shall wonder if the old-time Mary
  Were real, or the rhymer's dream !
1st 3d mo., 1857.

MY NAMESAKE.

YOU scarcely need my tardy thanks,
  Who, self-rewarded, nurse and tend —
A green leaf on your own Green Banks —
  The memory of your friend.

For me, no wreath, bloom-woven, hides
  The sobered brow and lessening hair :
For aught I know, the myrtled sides
  Of Helicon are bare.

Their scallop-shells so many bring
  The fabled founts of song to try,
They've drained, for aught I know, the
  spring
  Of Aganippe dry.

Ah well ! — The wreath the Muses braid
  Proves often Folly's cap and bell ;

Methinks, my ample beaver's shade
  May serve my turn as well.

Let Love's and Friendship's tender debt
  Be paid by those I love in life.
Why should the unborn critic whet
  For me his scalping-knife?

Why should the stranger peer and pry
  One's vacant house of life about,
And drag for curious ear and eye
  His faults and follies out? —

Why stuff, for fools to gaze upon,
  With chaff of words, the garb he wore,
As corn-husks when the ear is gone
  Are rustled all the more?

Let kindly Silence close again,
  The picture vanish from the eye,
And on the dim and misty main
  Let the small ripple die.

Yet not the less I own your claim
  To grateful thanks, dear friends of
    mine.
Hang, if it please you so, my name
  Upon your household line.

Let Fame from brazen lips blow wide
  Her chosen names, I envy none:
A mother's love, a father's pride,
  Shall keep alive my own!

Still shall that name as now recall
  The young leaf wet with morning
    dew,
The glory where the sunbeams fall
  The breezy woodlands through.

That name shall be a household word,
  A spell to waken smile or sigh;
In many an evening prayer be heard
  And cradle lullaby.

And thou, dear child, in riper days
  When asked the reason of thy name,
Shalt answer: "One 't were vain to
    praise
  Or censure bore the same.

"Some blamed him, some believed him
    good, —
  The truth lay doubtless 'twixt the
    two, —
He reconciled as best he could
  Old faith and fancies new.

"In him the grave and playful mixed,
  And wisdom held with folly truce,
And Nature compromised betwixt
  Good fellow and recluse.

"He loved his friends, forgave his foes;
  And, if his words were harsh at times,
He spared his fellow-men, — his blows
  Fell only on their crimes.

"He loved the good and wise, but found
  His human heart to all akin
Who met him on the common ground
  Of suffering and of sin.

"Whate'er his neighbors might endure
  Of pain or grief his own became;
For all the ills he could not cure
  He held himself to blame.

"His good was mainly an intent,
  His evil not of forethought done;
The work he wrought was rarely meant
  Or finished as begun.

"Ill served his tides of feeling strong
  To turn the common mills of use;
And, over restless wings of song,
  His birthright garb hung loose!

"His eye was beauty's powerless slave,
  And his the ear which discord pains·
Few guessed beneath his aspect grave
  What passions strove in chains.

"He had his share of care and pain,
  No holiday was life to him;
Still in the heirloom cup we drain
  The bitter drop will swim.

"Yet Heaven was kind, and here a bird
  And there a flower beguiled his way;
And, cool, in summer noons, he heard
  The fountains plash and play.

"On all his sad or restless moods
  The patient peace of Nature stole;
The quiet of the fields and woods
  Sank deep into his soul.

"He worshipped as his fathers did,
  And kept the faith of childish days,
And, howsoe'er he strayed or slid,
  He loved the good old ways.

"The simple tastes, the kindly traits,
  The tranquil air, and gentle speech,

The silence of the soul that waits
  For more than man to teach.

"The cant of party, school, and sect,
  Provoked at times his honest scorn,
And Folly, in its gray respect,
  He tossed on satire's horn.

"But still his heart was full of awe
  And reverence for all sacred things ;
And, brooding over form and law,
  He saw the Spirit's wings !

"Life's mystery wrapt him like a cloud ;
  He heard far voices mock his own,
The sweep of wings unseen, the loud,
  Long roll of waves unknown.

"The arrows of his straining sight
  Fell quenched in darkness ; priest and
    sage,
Like lost guides calling left and right,
  Perplexed his doubtful age.

"Like childhood, listening for the sound
  Of its dropped pebbles in the well,
All vainly down the dark profound
  His brief-lined plummet fell.

"So, scattering flowers with pious pains
  On old beliefs, of later creeds,
Which claimed a place in Truth's do-
    mains,
  He asked the title-deeds.

"He saw the old-time's groves and
    shrines
In the long distance fair and dim ;
And heard, like sound of far-off pines,
  The century-mellowed hymn !

"He dared not mock the Dervish whirl,
  The Brahmin's rite, the Lama's spell ;
God knew the heart ; Devotion's pearl
  Might sanctify the shell.

"While others trod the altar stairs
  He faltered like the publican ;

And, while they praised as saints, his
    prayers
  Were those of sinful man.

"For, awed by Sinai's Mount of Law,
  The trembling faith alone sufficed,
That, through its cloud and flame, he
    saw
  The sweet, sad face of Christ ! —

"And listening, with his forehead bowed,
  Heard the Divine compassion fill
The pauses of the trump and cloud
  With whispers small and still.

"The words he spake, the thoughts he
    penned,
  Are mortal as his hand and brain,
But, if they served the Master's end,
  He has not lived in vain ! "

Heaven make thee better than thy
    name,
  Child of my friends ! — For thee I
    crave
What riches never bought, nor fame
  To mortal longing gave.

I pray the prayer of Plato old :
  God make thee beautiful within,
And let thine eyes the good behold
  In everything save sin!

Imagination held in check
  To serve, not rule, thy poised mind;
Thy Reason, at the frown or beck
  Of Conscience, loose or bind.

No dreamer thou, but real all, —
  Strong manhood crowning vigorous
    youth ;
Life made by duty epical
  And rhythmic with the truth.

So shall that life the fruitage yield
  Which trees of healing only give,
And green-leafed in the Eternal field
  Of God, forever live !

HOME BALLADS.

I CALL the old time back : I bring these
    lays
To thee, in memory of the summer
    days
When, by our native streams and forest
    ways,

We dreamed them over ; while the rivu-
    lets made
Songs of their own, and the great pine-
    trees laid
On warm noon-lights the masses of their
    shade.

And *she* was with us, living o'er again
Her life in ours, despite of years and
    pain, —
The autumn's brightness after latter
    rain.

Beautiful in her holy peace as one
Who stands, at evening, when the work
    is done,
Glorified in the setting of the sun !

Her memory makes our common land-
    scape seem
Fairer than any of which painters
    dream,
Lights the brown hills and sings in
    every stream ;

For she whose speech was always truth's
    pure gold
Heard, not unpleased, its simple legends
    told,
And loved with us the beautiful and
    old.

THE WITCH'S DAUGHTER.

IT was the pleasant harvest time,
    When cellar-bins are closely stowed,
    And garrets bend beneath their load,

And the old swallow-haunted barns —
    Brown-gabled, long, and full of seams
    Through which the moted sunlight
        streams,

And winds blow freshly in, to shake
    The red plumes of the roosted cocks,
    And the loose hay-mow's scented
        locks —

Are filled with summer's ripened stores,
    Its odorous grass and barley sheaves,
    From their low scaffolds to their eaves.

On Esek Harden's oaken floor,
    With many an autumn threshing
        worn,
    Lay the heaped ears of unhusked corn.

And thither came young men and maids,
    Beneath a moon that, large and low,
    Lit that sweet eve of long ago.

They took their places ; some by chance,
    And others by a merry voice
    Or sweet smile guided to their choice.

How pleasantly the rising moon,
    Between the shadow of the mows,
    Looked on them through the great
        elm-boughs ! —

On sturdy boyhood sun-embrowned,
    On girlhood with its solid curves
    Of healthful strength and painless
        nerves !

And jests went round, and laughs that
        made
    The house-dog answer with his howl,
    And kept astir the barn-yard fowl ;

And quaint old songs their fathers
        sung,
    In Derby dales and Yorkshire moors,
    Ere Norman William trod their
        shores ;

And tales, whose merry license shook
    The fat sides of the Saxon thane,
    Forgetful of the hovering Dane !

But still the sweetest voice was mute
    That river-valley ever heard
    From lip of maid or throat of bird ;

For Mabel Martin sat apart,
And let the hay-mow's shadow fall
Upon the loveliest face of all.

She sat apart, as one forbid,
Who knew that none would conde-
scend
To own the Witch-wife's child a
friend.

The seasons scarce had gone their round,
Since curious thousands thronged to
see
Her mother on the gallows-tree ;

And mocked the palsied limbs of age,
That faltered on the fatal stairs,
And wan lip trembling with its
prayers !

Few questioned of the sorrowing child,
Or, when they saw the mother die,
Dreamed of the daughter's agony.

They went up to their homes that day,
As men and Christians justified :
God willed it, and the wretch had
died !

Dear God and Father of us all,
Forgive our faith in cruel lies, —
Forgive the blindness that denies !

Forgive thy creature when he takes,
For the all-perfect love thou art,
Some grim creation of his heart.

Cast down our idols, overturn
Our bloody altars ; let us see
Thyself in thy humanity !

Poor Mabel from her mother's grave
Crept to her desolate hearth-stone,
And wrestled with her fate alone ;

With love, and anger, and despair,
The phantoms of disordered sense,
The awful doubts of Providence !

The school-boys jeered her as they
passed,
And, when she sought the house of
prayer,
Her mother's curse pursued her there.

And still o'er many a neighboring door
She saw the horseshoe's curvéd charm,
To guard against her mother's harm ; —

That mother, poor, **and** sick, and
lame,
Who daily, by the old arm-chair,
Folded her withered hands in prayer ; —

Who turned, in Salem's dreary jail,
Her worn old Bible o'er and o'er,
When her dim eyes could read **no**
more !

Sore tried and pained, the poor girl
kept
Her faith, and trusted that her
way,
So dark, would somewhere meet the
day.

And still her weary wheel went round
Day after day, with no relief ;
Small leisure have the poor for grief.

So in the shadow Mabel sits ;
Untouched by mirth she sees and
hears,
Her smile is sadder than her tears.

But cruel eyes have found her out,
And cruel lips repeat her name,
And taunt her with her mother's
shame.

She answered not with railing words,
But drew her apron o'er her face,
And, sobbing, glided from the place.

And only pausing at the door,
Her sad eyes met the troubled gaze
Of one who, in her better days,

Had been her warm and steady friend,
Ere yet her mother's doom had made
Even Esek Harden half afraid.

He felt that mute appeal of tears,
And, starting, with an angry frown
Hushed all the wicked murmurs
down.

"Good neighbors mine," he sternly
said,
"This passes harmless mirth or jest ;
I brook no insult to my guest.

"She is indeed her mother's child :
But God's sweet pity ministers
Unto no whiter soul than hers.

"Let Goody Martin rest in peace ;
　I never knew her harm a fly,
　And witch or not, God knows, — not I.

"I know who swore her life away ;
　And, as God lives, I'd not condemn
　An Indian dog on word of them."

The broadest lands in all the town,
　The skill to guide, the power to awe,
　Were Harden's ; and his word was
　　law.

None dared withstand him to his face,
　But one sly maiden spake aside :
　"The little witch is evil-eyed !

"Her mother only killed a cow,
　Or witched a churn or dairy-pan ;
　But she, forsooth, must charm a
　　man !"

Poor Mabel, in her lonely home,
　Sat by the window's narrow pane,
　White in the moonlight's silver rain.

The river, on its pebbled rim,
　Made music such as childhood knew ;
　The door-yard tree was whispered
　　through

By voices such as childhood's ear
　Had heard in moonlights long ago ;
　And through the willow-boughs below

She saw the rippled waters shine ;
　Beyond, in waves of shade and light
　The hills rolled off into the night.

Sweet sounds and pictures mocking so
　The sadness of her human lot,
　She saw and heard, but heeded not.

She strove to drown her sense of wrong,
　And, in her old and simple way,
　To teach her bitter heart to pray.

Poor child ! the prayer, begun in faith,
　Grew to a low, despairing cry
　Of utter misery : "Let me die !

"Oh ! take me from the scornful eyes,
　And hide me where the cruel speech
　And mocking finger may not reach !

"I dare not breathe my mother's name :
　A daughter's right I dare not crave
　To weep above her unblest grave !

"Let me not live until my heart,
　With few to pity, and with none
　To love me, hardens into stone.

'O God ! have mercy on thy child,
　Whose faith in thee grows weak and
　　small,
　And take me ere I lose it all !"

A shadow on the moonlight fell,
　And murmuring wind and wave be-
　　came
　A voice whose burden was her name.

Had then God heard her ? Had he
　　sent
　His angel down ? In flesh and blood,
　Before her Esek Harden stood !

He laid his hand upon her arm :
　"Dear Mabel, this no more shall
　　be ;
　Who scoffs at you, must scoff at
　　me.

"You know rough Esek Harden well ;
　And if he seems no suitor gay,
　And if his hair is touched with gray,

"The maiden grown shall never find
　His heart less warm than when she
　　smiled,
　Upon his knees, a little child !"

Her tears of grief were tears of joy,
　As, folded in his strong embrace,
　She looked in Esek Harden's face.

"O truest friend of all !" she said,
　"God bless you for your kindly
　　thought,
　And make me worthy of my lot !"

He led her through his dewy fields,
　To where the swinging lanterns
　　glowed,
　And through the doors the huskers
　　showed.

"Good friends and neighbors !" Esek
　　said,
　"I'm weary of this lonely life ;
　In Mabel see my chosen wife !

"She greets you kindly, one and all ;
　The past is past, and all offence
　Falls harmless from her innocence.

" Henceforth she stands no more alone ;
  You know what Esek Harden is : —
  He brooks no wrong to him or his."

Now let the merriest tales be told,
  And let the sweetest songs be sung
That ever made the old heart young !

For now the lost has found a home ;
  And a lone hearth shall brighter burn,
As all the household joys return !

O, pleasantly the harvest-moon,
  Between the shadow of the mows,
Looked on them through the great
    elm-boughs !

On Mabel's curls of golden hair,
  On Esek's shaggy strength it fell ;
  And the wind whispered, " It is
    well ! "

THE GARRISON OF CAPE ANN.

FROM the hills of home forth looking,
    far beneath the tent-like span
Of the sky, I see the white gleam of the
    headland of Cape Ann.
Well I know its coves and beaches to the
    ebb-tide glimmering down,
And the white-walled hamlet children of
    its ancient fishing-town.

Long has passed the summer morning,
    and its memory waxes old,
When along yon breezy headlands with
    a pleasant friend I strolled.
Ah ! the autumn sun is shining, and the
    ocean wind blows cool,
And the golden-rod and aster bloom
    around thy grave, Rantoul !

With the memory of that morning by the
    summer sea I blend
A wild and wondrous story, by the
    younger Mather penned,
In that quaint *Magnalia Christi*, with
    all strange and marvellous things,
Heaped up huge and undigested, like
    the chaos Ovid sings.

Dear to me these far, faint glimpses of
    the dual life of old,
Inward, grand with awe and reverence ;
    outward, mean and coarse and
    cold ;

Gleams of mystic beauty playing over
    dull and vulgar clay,
Golden-threaded fancies weaving in a
    web of hodden gray.

The great eventful Present hides the
    Past ; but through the din
Of its loud life hints and echoes from
    the life behind steal in ;
And the lore of home and fireside, and
    the legendary rhyme,
Make the task of duty lighter which the
    true man owes his time.

So, with something of the feeling which
    the Covenanter knew,
When with pious chisel wandering Scot-
    land's   moorland   graveyards
    through,
From the graves of old traditions I part
    the blackberry-vines,
Wipe the moss from off the headstones,
    and retouch the faded lines.

Where the sea-waves back and forward,
    hoarse with rolling pebbles, ran,
The garrison-house stood watching on
    the gray rocks of Cape Ann ;
On its windy site uplifting gabled roof
    and palisade,
And rough walls of unhewn timber with
    the moonlight overlaid.

On his slow round walked the sentry,
    south and eastward looking forth
O'er a rude and broken coast-line, white
    with breakers stretching north, —
Wood and rock and gleaming sand-drift,
    jagged capes, with bush and tree,
Leaning inland from the smiting of the
    wild and gusty sea.

Before the deep-mouthed chimney, dim-
    ly lit by dying brands,
Twenty soldiers sat and waited, with
    their muskets in their hands ;
On the rough-hewn oaken table the veni-
    son haunch was shared,
And the pewter tankard circled slowly
    round from beard to beard.

Long they sat and talked together, —
    talked of wizards Satan-sold ;
Of all ghostly sights and noises, — signs
    and wonders manifold ;

Of the spectre-ship of Salem, with the
    dead men in her shrouds,
Sailing sheer above the water, in the
    loom of morning clouds ;

Of the marvellous valley hidden in the
    depths of Gloucester woods,
Full of plants that love the summer, —
    blooms of warmer latitudes ;
Where the Arctic birch is braided by
    the tropic's flowery vines,
And the white magnolia-blossoms star
    the twilight of the pines !

But their voices sank yet lower, sank to
    husky tones of fear,
As they spake of present tokens of the
    powers of evil near ;
Of a spectral host, defying stroke of steel
    and aim of gun ;
Never yet was ball to slay them in the
    mould of mortals run !

Thrice, with plumes and flowing scalp-
    locks, from the midnight wood
    they came, —
Thrice around the block-house marching,
    met, unharmed, its volleyed flame ;
Then, with mocking laugh and gesture,
    sunk in earth or lost in air,
All the ghostly wonder vanished, and
    the moonlit sands lay bare.

Midnight came ; from out the forest
    moved a dusky mass that soon
Grew to warriors, plumed and painted,
    grimly marching in the moon.
" Ghosts or witches," said the captain,
    " thus I foil the Evil One ! "
And he rammed a silver button, from
    his doublet, down his gun.

Once again the spectral horror moved
    the guarded wall about ;
Once again the levelled muskets through
    the palisades flashed out,
With that deadly aim the squirrel on his
    tree-top might not shun,
Nor the beach-bird seaward flying with
    his slant wing to the sun.

Like the idle rain of summer sped the
    harmless shower of lead.
With a laugh of fierce derision, once
    again the phantoms fled ;

Once again, without a shadow on the
    sands the moonlight lay,
And the white smoke curling through it
    drifted slowly down the bay !

" God preserve us ! " said the captain ;
    " never mortal foes were there ;
They have vanished with their leader,
    Prince and Power of the air !
Lay aside your useless weapons ; skill
    and prowess naught avail ;
They who do the Devil's service wear
    their master's coat of mail ! "

So the night grew near to cock-crow,
    when again a warning call
Roused the score of weary soldiers watch-
    ing round the dusky hall :
And they looked to flint and priming,
    and they longed for break of day ;
But the captain closed his Bible : " Let
    us cease from man, and pray ! "

To the men who went before us, all the
    unseen powers seemed near,
And their steadfast strength of courage
    struck its roots in holy fear.
Every hand forsook the musket, every
    head was bowed and bare,
Every stout knee pressed the flag-stones,
    as the captain led in prayer.

Ceased thereat the mystic marching of
    the spectres round the wall,
But a sound abhorred, unearthly, smote
    the ears and hearts of all, —
Howls of rage and shrieks of anguish !
    Never after mortal man
Saw the ghostly leaguers marching round
    the block-house of Cape Ann.

So to us who walk in summer through
    the cool and sea-blown town,
From the childhood of its people comes
    the solemn legend down.
Not in vain the ancient fiction, in whose
    moral lives the youth
And the fitness and the freshness of an
    undecaying truth.

Soon or late to all our dwellings come
    the spectres of the mind,
Doubts and fears and dread forebodings,
    In the darkness undefined ;
Round us throng the grim projections
    of the heart and of the brain,
And our pride of strength is weakness,
    and the cunning hand is vain.

In the dark we cry like children ; and
  no answer from on high
Breaks the crystal spheres of silence, and
  no white wings downward fly ;
But the heavenly help we pray for comes
  to faith, and not to sight,
And our prayers themselves drive backward all the spirits of the night !

THE PROPHECY OF SAMUEL
SEWALL.

1697.

Up and down the village streets
Strange are the forms my fancy meets,
For the thoughts and things of to-day
  are hid,
And through the veil of a closéd lid
The ancient worthies I see again :
I hear the tap of the elder's cane,
And his awful periwig I see,
And the silver buckles of shoe and knee.
Stately and slow, with thoughtful air,
His black cap hiding his whitened hair,
Walks the Judge of the great Assize,
Samuel Sewall the good and wise.
His face with lines of firmness wrought,
He wears the look of a man unbought,
Who swears to his hurt and changes
  not ;
Yet, touched and softened nevertheless
With the grace of Christian gentleness,
The face that a child would climb to
  kiss !
True and tender and brave and just,
That man might honor and woman trust.

Touching and sad, a tale is told,
Like a penitent hymn of the Psalmist
  old,
Of the fast which the good man lifelong
  kept
With a haunting sorrow that never slept,
As the circling year brought round the
  time
Of an error that left the sting of crime,
When he sat on the bench of the witch-
  craft courts,
With the laws of Moses and Hale's Re-
  ports,
And spake, in the name of both, the
  word
That gave the witch's neck to the
  cord,
And piled the oaken planks that pressed
The feeble life from the warlock's breast !

All the day long, from dawn to dawn,
His door was bolted, his curtain drawn ;
No foot on his silent threshold trod,
No eye looked on him save that of God,
As he baffled the ghosts of the dead with
  charms
Of penitent tears, and prayers, and
  psalms,
And, with precious proofs from the sacred
  word
Of the boundless pity and love of the
  Lord,
His faith confirmed and his trust re-
  newed
That the sin of his ignorance, sorely
  rued,
Might be washed away in the mingled
  flood
Of his human sorrow and Christ's dear
  blood !

  Green forever the memory be
Of the Judge of the old Theocracy,
Whom even his errors glorified,
Like a far-seen, sunlit mountain-side
By the cloudy shadows which o'er it
  glide !
Honor and praise to the Puritan
Who the halting step of his age outran,
And, seeing the infinite worth of man
In the priceless gift the Father gave,
In the infinite love that stooped to save,
Dared not brand his brother a slave !
" Who doth such wrong," he was wont
  to say,
In his own quaint, picture-loving way,
" Flings up to Heaven a hand-grenade
Which God shall cast down upon his
  head ! "

  Widely as heaven and hell, contrast
That brave old jurist of the past
And the cunning trickster and knave of
  courts
Who the holy features of Truth dis-
  torts, —
Ruling as right the will of the strong,
Poverty, crime, and weakness wrong ;
Wide-eared to power, to the wronged
  and weak
Deaf as Egypt's gods of leek ;
Scoffing aside at party's nod
Order of nature and law of God ;
For whose dabbled ermine respect were
  waste,
Reverence folly, and awe misplaced ;
Justice of whom 't were vain to seek

As from Koordish robber or Syrian
    Sheik !
O, leave the wretch to his bribes and
    sins ;
Let him rot in the web of lies he spins !
To the saintly soul of the early day,
To the Christian judge, let us turn and
    say :
" Praise and thanks for an honest
    man ! —
Glory to God for the Puritan ! "

I see, far southward, this quiet day,
The hills of Newbury rolling away,
With the many tints of the season gay,
Dreamily blending in autumn mist
Crimson, and gold, and amethyst.
Long and low, with dwarf trees crowned,
Plum Island lies, like a whale aground,
A stone's toss over the narrow sound.
Inland, as far as the eye can go,
The hills curve round like a bended
    bow ;
A silver arrow from out them sprung,
I see the shine of the Quasycung ;
And, round and round, over valley and
    hill,
Old roads winding, as old roads will,
Here to a ferry, and there to a mill ;
And glimpses of chimneys and gabled
    eaves,
Through green elm arches and maple
    leaves, —
Old homesteads sacred to all that can
Gladden or sadden the heart of man, —
Over whose thresholds of oak and stone
Life and Death have come and gone !
There pictured tiles in the fireplace
    show,
Great beams sag from the ceiling low,
The dresser glitters with polished wares,
The long clock ticks on the foot-worn
    stairs,
And the low, broad chimney shows the
    crack
By the earthquake made a century
    back.
Up from their midst springs the village
    spire
With the crest of its cock in the sun
    afire ;
Beyond are orchards and planting lands,
And great salt marshes and glimmering
    sands,
And, where north and south the coast-
    lines run,
The blink of the sea in breeze and sun !

I see it all like a chart unrolled,
But my thoughts are full of the past
    and old,
I hear the tales of my boyhood told ;
And the shadows and shapes of early
    days
Flit dimly by in the veiling haze,
With measured movement and rhythmic
    chime
Weaving like shuttles my web of rhyme.
I think of the old man wise and good
Who once on yon misty hillsides stood,
(A poet who never measured rhyme,
A seer unknown to his dull-eared time,)
And, propped on his staff of age, looked
    down,
With his boyhood's love, on his native
    town,
Where, written, as if on its hills and
    plains,
His burden of prophecy yet remains,
For the voices of wood, and wave, and
    wind
To read in the ear of the musing mind : —

" As long as Plum Island, to guard
    the coast
As God appointed, shall keep its post ;
As long as a salmon shall haunt the deep
Of Merrimack River, or sturgeon leap ;
As long as pickerel swift and slim,
Or red-backed perch, in Crane Pond swim ;
As long as the annual sea-fowl know
Their time to come and their time to go ;
As long as cattle shall roam at will
The green, grass meadows by Turkey Hill ;
As long as sheep shall look from the side
Of Oldtown Hill on marishes wide,
And Parker River, and salt-sea tide ;
As long as a wandering pigeon shall search
The fields below from his white-oak perch,
When the barley-harvest is ripe and
    shorn,
And the dry husks fall from the stand
    ing corn ;
As long as Nature shall not grow old,
Nor drop her work from her doting hold,
And her care for the Indian corn forget,
And the yellow rows in pairs to set ; —
So long shall Christians here be born,
Grow up and ripen as God's sweet corn ! —
By the beak of bird, by the breath of
    frost,
Shall never a holy ear be lost,
But, husked by Death in the Planter's
    sight,
Be sown again in the fields of light ! "

The Island still is purple with plums,
Up the river the salmon comes,
The sturgeon leaps, and the wild-fowl
    feeds
On hillside berries and marish seeds, —
All the beautiful signs remain,
From spring-time sowing to autumn rain
The good man's vision returns again!
And let us hope, as well we can,
That the Silent Angel who garners man
May find some grain as of old he found
In the human cornfield ripe and sound,
And the Lord of the Harvest deign to
    own
The precious seed by the fathers sown!

SKIPPER IRESON'S RIDE.

Of all the rides since the birth of time,
Told in story or sung in rhyme, —
On Apuleius's Golden Ass,
Or one-eyed Calendar's horse of brass,
Witch astride of a human back,
Islam's prophet on Al-Borák, —
The strangest ride that ever was sped
Was Ireson's, out from Marblehead!
    Old Floyd Ireson, for his hard heart,
    Tarred and feathered and carried in a
        cart
        By the women of Marblehead!

Body of turkey, head of owl,
Wings a-droop like a rained-on fowl,
Feathered and ruffled in every part,
Skipper Ireson stood in the cart.
Scores of women, old and young,
Strong of muscle, and glib of tongue,
Pushed and pulled up the rocky lane,
Shouting and singing the shrill refrain :
    "Here's Flud Oirson, fur his horrd
        horrt,
    Torr'd an' futherr'd an' corr'd in a
        corrt
        By the women o' Morble'ead !"

Wrinkled scolds with hands on hips,
Girls in bloom of cheek and lips,
Wild-eyed, free-limbed, such as chase
Bacchus round some antique vase,
Brief of skirt, with ankles bare,
Loose of kerchief and loose of hair,
With conch-shells blowing and fish-
    horns' twang,
Over and over the Mænads sang :
    "Here's Flud Oirson, fur his horrd
        horrt,

15

    Torr'd an' futherr'd an' corr'd in a
        corrt
        By the women o' Morble'ead !"

Small pity for him ! — He sailed away
From a leaking ship, in Chaleur Bay, —
Sailed away from a sinking wreck,
With his own town's-people on her deck !
"Lay by ! lay by !" they called to him.
Back he answered, "Sink or swim !
Brag of your catch of fish again !"
And off he sailed through the fog and
    rain !
    Old Floyd Ireson, for his hard heart,
    Tarred and feathered and carried in a
        cart
        By the women of Marblehead !

Fathoms deep in dark Chaleur
That wreck shall lie forevermore.
Mother and sister, wife and maid,
Looked from the rocks of Marblehead
Over the moaning and rainy sea, —
Looked for the coming that might not
    be !
What did the winds and the sea-birds
    say
Of the cruel captain who sailed away ? —
    Old Floyd Ireson, for his hard heart,
    Tarred and feathered and carried in a
        cart
        By the women of Marblehead !

Through the street, on either side,
Up flew windows, doors swung wide ;
Sharp-tongued spinsters, old wives gray,
Treble lent the fish-horn's bray.
Sea-worn grandsires, cripple-bound,
Hulks of old sailors run aground,
Shook head, and fist, and hat, and cane,
And cracked with curses the hoarse re-
    frain :
    "Here's Flud Oirson, fur his horrd
        horrt,
    Torr'd an' futherr'd an' corr'd in a
        corrt
        By the women o' Morble'ead !"

Sweetly along the Salem road
Bloom of orchard and lilac showed.
Little the wicked skipper knew
Of the fields so green and the sky so
    blue.
Riding there in his sorry trim,
Like an Indian idol glum and grim,
Scarcely he seemed the sound to hear
Of voices shouting, far and near :

"Here's Flud Oirson, fur his horrd
    horrt,
Torr'd an' futherr'd an' corr'd in a
    corrt
By the women o' Morble'ead!"

"Hear me, neighbors!" at last he
    cried, —
"What to me is this noisy ride?
What is the shame that clothes the skin
To the nameless horror that lives within?
Waking or sleeping, I see a wreck,
And hear a cry from a reeling deck!
Hate me and curse me, — I only dread
The hand of God and the face of the
    dead!"
    Said old Floyd Ireson, for his hard
        heart,
    Tarred and feathered and carried in a
        cart
    By the women of Marblehead!

Then the wife of the skipper lost at sea
Said, "God has touched him! — why
    should we?"
Said an old wife mourning her only son,
"Cut the rogue's tether and let him
    run!"
So with soft relentings and rude excuse,
Half scorn, half pity, they cut him loose,
And gave him a cloak to hide him in,
And left him alone with his shame and
    sin.
    Poor Floyd Ireson, for his hard heart,
    Tarred and feathered and carried in a
        cart
    By the women of Marblehead!

TELLING THE BEES.[66]

HERE is the place; right over the hill
Runs the path I took;
You can see the gap in the old wall still,
    And the stepping-stones in the shal-
        low brook.

There is the house, with the gate red-
        barred,
    And the poplars tall;
And the barn's brown length, and the
        cattle-yard,
    And the white horns tossing above the
        wall.

There are the beehives ranged in the sun;
    And down by the brink

Of the brook are her poor flowers, weed-
        o'errun,
    Pansy and daffodil, rose and pink.

A year has gone, as the tortoise goes,
    Heavy and slow;
And the same rose blows, and the same
        sun glows,
    And the same brook sings of a year
        ago.

There's the same sweet clover-smell in
        the breeze;
    And the June sun warm
Tangles his wings of fire in the trees,
    Setting, as then, over Fernside farm.

I mind me how with a lover's care
    From my Sunday coat
I brushed off the burrs, and smooth_d
        my hair,
    And cooled at the brookside my brow
        and throat.

Since we parted, a month had passed, —
    To love, a year;
Down through the beeches I looked at
        last
    On the little red gate and the well-
        sweep near.

I can see it all now, — the slantwise rain
    Of light through the leaves,
The sundown's blaze on her window-
        pane,
    The bloom of her roses under the eaves.

Just the same as a month before, —
    The house and the trees,
The barn's brown gable, the vine by the
        door, —
    Nothing changed but the hives of bees.

Before them, under the garden wall,
    Forward and back,
Went drearily singing the chore-girl
        small,
    Draping each hive with a shred of
        black.

Trembling, I listened: the summer sun
    Had the chill of snow;
For I knew she was telling the bees of
        one
    Gone on the journey we all must go!

Then I said to myself, "My Mary weeps
    For the dead to-day:

Haply her blind old grandsire sleeps
   The fret and the pain of his age away."

But her dog whined low; on the door-
      way sill,
   With his cane to his chin,
The old man sat; and the chore-girl still
   Sung to the bees stealing out and in.

And the song she was singing ever since
   In my ear sounds on:—
"Stay at home, pretty bees, fly not
      hence!
   Mistress Mary is dead and gone!"

THE SYCAMORES.

IN the outskirts of the village,
   On the river's winding shores,
Stand the Occidental plane-trees,
   Stand the ancient sycamores.

One long century hath been numbered,
   And another half-way told,
Since the rustic Irish gleeman
   Broke for them the virgin mould.

Deftly set to Celtic music,
   At his violin's sound they grew,
Through the moonlit eves of summer,
   Making Amphion's fable true.

Rise again, thou poor Hugh Tallant!
   Pass in jerkin green along,
With thy eyes brimful of laughter,
   And thy mouth as full of song.

Pioneer of Erin's outcasts,
   With his fiddle and his pack;
Little dreamed the village Saxons
   Of the myriads at his back.

How he wrought with spade and fiddle,
   Delved by day and sang by night,
With a hand that never wearied,
   And a heart forever light,—

Still the gay tradition mingles
   With a record grave and drear,
Like the rolic air of Cluny,
   With the solemn march of Mear.

When the box-tree, white with blossoms,
   Made the sweet May woodlands glad,
And the Aronia by the river
   Lighted up the swarming shad,

And the bulging nets swept shoreward,
   With their silver-sided haul,
Midst the shouts of dripping fishers,
   He was merriest of them all.

When, among the jovial huskers,
   Love stole in at Labor's side
With the lusty airs of England,
   Soft his Celtic measures vied.

Songs of love and wailing lyke-wake,
   And the merry fair's carouse;
Of the wild Red Fox of Erin
   And the Woman of Three Cows,

By the blazing hearths of winter,
   Pleasant seemed his simple tales,
Midst the grimmer Yorkshire legends
   And the mountain myths of Wales.

How the souls in Purgatory
   Scrambled up from fate forlorn,
On St. Keven's sackcloth ladder,
   Slyly hitched to Satan's horn.

Of the fiddler who at Tara
   Played all night to ghosts of kings;
Of the brown dwarfs, and the fairies
   Dancing in their moorland rings!

Jolliest of our birds of singing,
   Best he loved the Bob-o-link.
"Hush!" he'd say, "the tipsy fairies!
   Hear the little folks in drink!"

Merry-faced, with spade and fiddle,
   Singing through the ancient town,
Only this, of poor Hugh Tallant,
   Hath Tradition handed down.

Not a stone his grave discloses;
   But if yet his spirit walks,
'T is beneath the trees he planted,
   And when Bob-o-Lincoln talks;

Green memorials of the gleeman!
   Linking still the river-shores,
With their shadows cast by sunset,
   Stand Hugh Tallant's sycamores!

When the Father of his Country
   Through the north-land riding came,
And the roofs were starred with banners,
   And the steeples rang acclaim,—

When each war-scarred Continental,
   Leaving smithy, mill, and farm,

Waved his rusted sword in welcome,
  And shot off his old king's arm, —

Slowly passed that august Presence
  Down the thronged and shouting street ;
Village girls as white as angels,
  Scattering flowers around his feet.

Midway, where the plane-tree's shadow
  Deepest fell, his rein he drew :
On his stately head, uncovered,
  Cool and soft the west-wind blew.

And he stood up in his stirrups,
  Looking up and looking down
On the hills of Gold and Silver
  Rimming round the little town, —

On the river, full of sunshine,
  To the lap of greenest vales
Winding down from wooded headlands,
  Willow-skirted, white with sails.

And he said, the landscape sweeping
  Slowly with his ungloved hand,
"I have seen no prospect fairer
  In this goodly Eastern land."

Then the bugles of his escort
  Stirred to life the cavalcade :
And that head, so bare and stately,
  Vanished down the depths of shade.

Ever since, in town and farm-house,
  Life has had its ebb and flow ;
Thrice hath passed the human harvest
  To its garner green and low.

But the trees the gleeman planted,
  Through the changes, changeless stand ;
As the marble calm of Tadmor
  Marks the desert's shifting sand.

Still the level moon at rising
  Silvers o'er each stately shaft ;
Still beneath them, half in shadow,
  Singing, glides the pleasure craft.

Still beneath them, arm-enfolded,
  Love and Youth together stray ;
While, as heart to heart beats faster,
  More and more their feet delay.

Where the ancient cobbler, Keezar,
  On the open hillside wrought,

Singing, as he drew his stitches,
  Songs his German masters taught,

Singing, with his gray hair floating
  Round his rosy ample face, —
Now a thousand Saxon craftsmen
  Stitch and hammer in his place.

All the pastoral lanes so grassy
  Now are Traffic's dusty streets ;
From the village, grown a city,
  Fast the rural grace retreats.

But, still green, and tall, and stately,
  On the river's winding shores,
Stand the Occidental plane-trees,
  Stand Hugh Tallant's sycamores.

THE DOUBLE–HEADED SNAKE OF NEWBURY.

"Concerning yᵉ Amphisbæna, as soon as I received your commands, I made diligent inquiry : . . . . he assures me yᵗ it had really two heads, one at each end ; two mouths, two stings or tongues." — REV. CHRISTOPHER TOPPAN to COTTON MATHER.

FAR away in the twilight time
Of every people, in every clime,
Dragons and griffins and monsters dire,
Born of water, and air, and fire,
Or nursed, like the Python, in the mud
And ooze of the old Deucalion flood,
Crawl and wriggle and foam with rage,
Through dusk tradition and ballad age.
So from the childhood of Newbury town
And its time of fable the tale comes down
Of a terror which haunted bush and brake,
The Amphisbæna, the Double Snake !

Thou who makest the tale thy mirth,
Consider that strip of Christian earth
On the desolate shore of a sailless sea,
Full of terror and mystery,
Half redeemed from the evil hold
Of the wood so dreary, and dark, and old,
Which drank with its lips of leaves the dew
When Time was young, and the world was new,
And wove its shadows with sun and moon,
Ere the stones of Cheops were squared and hewn,
Think of the sea's dread monotone,

Of the mournful wail from the pine-wood
   blown,
Of the strange, vast splendors that lit
   the North,
Of the troubled throes of the quaking
   earth,
And the dismal tales the Indian told,
Till the settler's heart at his hearth
   grew cold,
And he shrank from the tawny wizard's
   boasts,
And the hovering shadows seemed full of
   ghosts,
And above, below, and on every side,
The fear of his creed seemed verified ; —
And think, if his lot were now thine
   own,
To grope with terrors nor named nor
   known,
How laxer muscle and weaker nerve
And a feebler faith thy need might
   serve ;
And own to thyself the wonder more
That the snake had two heads, and not
   a score !

Whether he lurked in the Oldtown fen
Or the gray earth-flax of the Devil's Den,
Or swam in the wooded Artichoke,
Or coiled by the Northman's Written
   Rock,
Nothing on record is left to show ;
Only the fact that he lived, we know,
And left the cast of a double head
In the scaly mask which he yearly shed.
For he carried a head where his tail
   should be,
And the two, of course, could never
   agree,
But wriggled about with main and might,
Now to the left and now to the right ;
Pulling and twisting this way and that,
Neither knew what the other was at.

A snake with two heads, lurking so
   near ! —
Judge of the wonder, guess at the fear !
Think what ancient gossips might say,
Shaking their heads in their dreary way,
Between the meetings on Sabbath-day !
How urchins, searching at day's decline
The Common Pasture for sheep or kine,
The terrible double-ganger heard
In leafy rustle or whir of bird !
Think what a zest it gave to the sport,
In berry-time, of the younger sort,
As over pastures blackberry-twined,

Reuben and Dorothy lagged behind,
And closer and closer, for fear of harm,
The maiden clung to her lover's arm ;
And how the spark, who was forced to
   stay,
By his sweetheart's fears, till the break of
   day,
Thanked the snake for the fond delay !

Far and wide the tale was told,
Like a snowball growing while it rolled.
The nurse hushed with it the baby's
   cry ;
And it served, in the worthy minister's
   eye,
To paint the primitive serpent by.
Cotton Mather came galloping down
All the way to Newbury town,
With his eyes agog and his ears set
   wide,
And his marvellous inkhorn at his side ;
Stirring the while in the shallow pool
Of his brains for the lore he learned at
   school,
To garnish the story, with here a
   streak
Of Latin, and there another of Greek :
And the tales he heard and the notes he
   took,
Behold ! are they not in his Wonder-
   Book ?

Stories, like dragons, are hard to kill.
If the snake does not, the tale runs
   still
In Byfield Meadows, on Pipestave Hill.
And still, whenever husband and wife
Publish the shame of their daily strife,
And, with mad cross-purpose, tug and
   strain
At either end of the marriage-chain,
The gossips say, with a knowing shake
Of their gray heads, " Look at the
   Double Snake !
One in body and two in will,
The Amphisbæna is living still ! "

THE SWAN SONG OF PARSON
AVERY.

WHEN the reaper's task was ended, and
   the summer wearing late,
Parson Avery sailed from Newbury, with
   his wife and children eight,
Dropping down the river-harbor in the
   shallop " Watch and Wait."

Pleasantly lay the clearings in the mellow summer-morn,
With the newly planted orchards dropping their fruits first-born,
And the homesteads like green islands amid a sea of corn.

Broad meadows reached out seaward the tided creeks between,
And hills rolled wave-like inland, with oaks and walnuts green ; —
A fairer home, a goodlier land, his eyes had never seen.

Yet away sailed Parson Avery, away where duty led,
And the voice of God seemed calling, to break the living bread
To the souls of fishers starving on the rocks of Marblehead.

All day they sailed : at nightfall the pleasant land-breeze died,
The blackening sky, at midnight, its starry lights denied,
And far and low the thunder of tempest prophesied !

Blotted out were all the coast-lines, gone were rock, and wood, and sand ;
Grimly anxious stood the skipper with the rudder in his hand,
And questioned of the darkness what was sea and what was land.

And the preacher heard his dear ones, nestled round him, weeping sore :
" Never heed, my little children ! Christ is walking on before
To the pleasant land of heaven, where the sea shall be no more."

All at once the great cloud parted, like a curtain drawn aside,
To let down the torch of lightning on the terror far and wide ;
And the thunder and the whirlwind together smote the tide.

There was wailing in the shallop, woman's wail and man's despair,
A crash of breaking timbers on the rocks so sharp and bare,
And, through it all, the murmur of Father Avery's prayer.

From his struggle in the darkness with the wild waves and the blast,
On a rock, where every billow broke above him as it passed,
Alone, of all his household, the man of God was cast.

There a comrade heard him praying, in the pause of wave and wind :
" All my own have gone before me, and I linger just behind ;
Not for life I ask, but only for the rest thy ransomed find !

" In this night of death I challenge the promise of thy word ! —
Let me see the great salvation of which mine ears have heard ! —
Let me pass from hence forgiven, through the grace of Christ, our Lord !

" In the baptism of these waters wash white my every sin,
And let me follow up to thee my household and my kin !
Open the sea-gate of thy heaven, and let me enter in !"

When the Christian sings his death-song, all the listening heavens draw near,
And the angels, leaning over the walls of crystal, hear
How the notes so faint and broken swell to music in God's ear.

The ear of God was open to his servant's last request ;
As the strong wave swept him downward the sweet hymn upward pressed,
And the soul of Father Avery went, singing, to its rest.

There was wailing on the mainland, from the rocks of Marblehead ;
In the stricken church of Newbury the notes of prayer were read ;
And long, by board and hearthstone, the living mourned the dead.

And still the fishers outbound, or scudding from the squall,
With grave and reverent faces, the ancient tale recall,
When they see the white waves breaking on the Rock of Avery's Fall !

THE TRUCE OF PISCATAQUA.

1675.

RAZE these long blocks of brick and
        stone,
These huge mill-monsters overgrown ;
Blot out the humbler piles as well,
Where, moved like living shuttles,
        dwell
The weaving genii of the bell ;
Tear from the wild Cocheco's track
The dams that hold its torrents back ;
And let the loud-rejoicing fall
Plunge, roaring, down its rocky wall ;
And let the Indian's paddle play
On the unbridged Piscataqua !
Wide over hill and valley spread
Once more the forest, dusk and dread,
With here and there a clearing cut
From the walled shadows round it shut ;
Each with its farm-house builded rude,
By English yeoman squared and hewed,
And the grim, flankered block-house
        bound
With bristling palisades around.
So, haply shall before thine eyes
The dusty veil of centuries rise,
The old, strange scenery overlay
The tamer pictures of to-day,
While, like the actors in a play,
Pass in their ancient guise along
The figures of my border song :
What time beside Cocheco's flood
The white man and the red man stood,
With words of peace and brotherhood ;
When passed the sacred calumet
From lip to lip with fire-draught wet,
And, puffed in scorn, the peace-pipe's
        smoke
Through the gray beard of Waldron broke,
And Squando's voice, in suppliant plea
For mercy, struck the haughty key
Of one who held, in any fate,
His native pride inviolate !

"Let your ears be opened wide !
He who speaks has never lied.
Waldron of Piscataqua,
Hear what Squando has to say !

"Squando shuts his eyes and sees,
Far off, Saco's hemlock-trees.
In his wigwam, still as stone,
Sits a woman all alone,

"Wampum beads and birchen strands
Dropping from her careless hands,

Listening ever for the fleet
Patter of a dead child's feet !

"When the moon a year ago
Told the flowers the time to blow,
In that lonely wigwam smiled
Menewee, our little child.

"Ere that moon grew thin and old,
He was lying still and cold ;
Sent before us, weak and small,
When the Master did not call !

"On his little grave I lay ;
Three times went and came the day ;
Thrice above me blazed the noon,
Thrice upon me wept the moon.

"In the third night-watch I heard,
Far and low, a spirit-bird ;
Very mournful, very wild,
Sang the totem of my child.

"'Menewee, poor Menewee,
Walks a path he cannot see :
Let the white man's wigwam light
With its blaze his steps aright.

"'All-uncalled, he dares not show
Empty hands to Manito :
Better gifts he cannot bear
Than the scalps his slayers wear.'

"All the while the totem sang,
Lightning blazed and thunder rang ;
And a black cloud, reaching high,
Pulled the white moon from the sky.

"I, the medicine-man, whose ear
All that spirits hear can hear, —
I, whose eyes are wide to see
All the things that are to be, —

"Well I knew the dreadful signs
In the whispers of the pines,
In the river roaring loud,
In the mutter of the cloud.

"At the breaking of the day,
From the grave I passed away ;
Flowers bloomed round me, birds sang
        glad,
But my heart was hot and mad.

"There is rust on Squando's knife,
From the warm, red springs of life ;

On the funeral hemlock-trees
Many a scalp the totem sees.

"Blood for blood ! But evermore
Squando's heart is sad and sore ;
And his poor squaw waits at home
For the feet that never come !

"Waldron of Cocheco, hear !
Squando speaks, who laughs at fear ;
Take the captives he has ta'en ;
Let the land have peace again !"

As the words died on his tongue,
Wide apart his warriors swung ;
Parted, at the sign he gave,
Right and left, like Egypt's wave.

And, like Israel passing free
Through the prophet-charméd sea,
Captive mother, wife, and child
Through the dusky terror filed.

One alone, a little maid,
Middleway her steps delayed,
Glancing, with quick, troubled sight,
Round about from red to white.

Then his hand the Indian laid
On the little maiden's head,
Lightly from her forehead fair
Smoothing back her yellow hair.

"Gift or favor ask I none ;
What I have is all my own :
Never yet the birds have sung,
'Squando hath a beggar's tongue.'

"Yet for her who waits at home,
For the dead who cannot come,
Let the little Gold-hair be
In the place of Menewee !

"Mishanock, my little star !
Come to Saco's pines afar ;
Where the sad one waits at home,
Wequashim, my moonlight, come !"

"What !" quoth Waldron, "leave a
                                   child
Christian-born to heathens wild ?
As God lives, from Satan's hand
I will pluck her as a brand !"

"Hear me, white man !" Squando
                                   cried ;
"Let the little one decide.

Wequashim, my moonlight, say,
Wilt thou go with me, or stay ?"

Slowly, sadly, half afraid,
Half regretfully, the maid
Owned the ties of blood and race, —
Turned from Squando's pleading face.

Not a word the Indian spoke,
But his wampum chain he broke,
And the beaded wonder hung
On that neck so fair and young.

Silence-shod, as phantoms seem
In the marches of a dream,
Single-filed, the grim array
Through the pine-trees wound away.

Doubting, trembling, sore amazed,
Through her tears the young child gazed,
"God preserve her !" Waldron said ;
"Satan hath bewitched the maid !"

Years went and came. At close of day
Singing came a child from play,
Tossing from her loose-locked head
Gold in sunshine, brown in shade.

Pride was in the mother's look,
But her head she gravely shook,
And with lips that fondly smiled
Feigned to chide her truant child.

Unabashed, the maid began :
"Up and down the brook I ran,
Where, beneath the bank so steep,
Lie the spotted trout asleep.

"'Chip !' went squirrel on the wall,
After me I heard him call,
And the cat-bird on the tree
Tried his best to mimic me.

"Where the hemlocks grew so dark
That I stopped to look and hark,
On a log, with feather-hat,
By the path, an Indian sat.

"Then I cried, and ran away ;
But he called, and bade me stay ;
And his voice was good and mild
As my mother's to her child.

"And he took my wampum chain,
Looked and looked it o'er again ;
Gave me berries, and, beside,
On my neck a plaything tied."

Straight the mother stooped to see
What the Indian's gift might be.
On the braid of wampum hung,
Lo ! a cross of silver swung.

Well she knew its graven sign,
Squando's bird and totem pine ;
And, a mirage of the brain,
Flowed her childhood back again.

Flashed the roof the sunshine through,
Into space the walls outgrew ;
On the Indian's wigwam-mat,
Blossom-crowned, again she sat.

Cool she felt the west-wind blow,
In her ear the pines sang low,
And, like links from out a chain,
Dropped the years of care and pain.

From the outward toil and din,
From the griefs that gnaw within,
To the freedom of the woods
Called the birds, and winds, and floods.

Well, O painful minister !
Watch thy flock, but blame not her,
If her ear grew sharp to hear
All their voices whispering near.

Blame her not, as to her soul
All the desert's glamour stole,
That a tear for childhood's loss
Dropped upon the Indian's cross.

When, that night, the Book was read,
And she bowed her widowed head,
And a prayer for each loved name
Rose like incense from a flame,

To the listening ear of Heaven,
Lo ! another name was given :
" Father, give the Indian rest !
Bless him ! for his love has blest ! "

MY PLAYMATE.

THE pines were dark on Ramoth hill,
Their song was soft and low ;
The blossoms in the sweet May wind
Were falling like the snow.

The blossoms drifted at our feet,
The orchard birds sang clear ;
The sweetest and the saddest day
It seemed of all the year.

For, more to me than birds or flowers,
My playmate left her home,
And took with her the laughing spring,
The music and the bloom.

She kissed the lips of kith and kin,
She laid her hand in mine :
What more could ask the bashful boy
Who fed her father's kine ?

She left us in the bloom of May :
The constant years told o'er
Their seasons with as sweet May morns,
But she came back no more.

I walk, with noiseless feet, the round
Of uneventful years ;
Still o'er and o'er I sow the spring
And reap the autumn ears.

She lives where all the golden year
Her summer roses blow ;
The dusky children of the sun
Before her come and go.

There haply with her jewelled hands
She smooths her silken gown, —
No more the homespun lap wherein
I shook the walnuts down.

The wild grapes wait us by the brook,
The brown nuts on the hill,
And still the May-day flowers make
        sweet
The woods of Follymill.

The lilies blossom in the pond,
The bird builds in the tree,
The dark pines sing on Ramoth hill
The slow song of the sea.

I wonder if she thinks of them,
And how the old time seems, —
If ever the pines of Ramoth wood
Are sounding in her dreams.

I see her face, I hear her voice :
Does she remember mine ?
And what to her is now the boy
Who fed her father's kine ?

What cares she that the orioles build
For other eyes than ours, —
That other hands with nuts are filled,
And other laps with flowers ?

O playmate in the golden time !
  Our mossy seat is green,
Its fringing violets blossom yet,
  The old trees o'er it lean.

The winds so sweet with birch and fern
  A sweeter memory blow ;

And there in spring the veeries sing
  The song of long ago.

And still the pines of Ramoth wood
  Are moaning like the sea, —
The moaning of the sea of change
  Between myself and thee !

POEMS AND LYRICS.

THE SHADOW AND THE LIGHT.

"And I sought, whence is Evil: I set before the eye of my spirit the whole creation; whatsoever we see therein, — sea, earth, air, stars, trees, moral creatures, — yea, whatsoever there is we do not see, — angels and spiritual powers. Where is evil, and whence comes it, since God the Good hath created all things? Why made He anything at all of evil, and not rather by His Almightiness cause it not to be? These thoughts I turned in my miserable heart, overcharged with most gnawing cares." "And, admonished to return to myself, I entered even into my inmost soul, Thou being my guide, and beheld even beyond my soul and mind the Light unchangeable. He who knows the Truth knows what that Light is, and he that knows it knows Eternity! O Truth, who art Eternity! Love, who art Truth! Eternity, who art Love! And I beheld that Thou madest all things good, and to Thee is nothing whatsoever evil. From the angel to the worm, from the first motion to the last, Thou settest each in its place, and everything is good in its kind. Woe is me! — how high art Thou in the highest, how deep in the deepest! and Thou never departest from us and we scarcely return to Thee." —*Augustine's Soliloquies*, Book VII.

THE fourteen centuries fall away
  Between us and the Afric saint,
And at his side we urge, to-day,
The immemorial quest and old complaint.

No outward sign to us is given, —
  From sea or earth comes no reply ;
Hushed as the warm Numidian heaven
He vainly questioned bends our frozen
    sky.

No victory comes of all our strife, —
  From all we grasp the meaning slips ;
The Sphinx sits at the gate of life,
With the old question on her awful lips.

In paths unknown we hear the feet
  Of fear before, and guilt behind ;
We pluck the wayside fruit, and eat
Ashes and dust beneath its golden rind.

From age to age descends unchecked
  The sad bequest of sire to son,
The body's taint, the mind's defect, —
Through every web of life the dark
    threads run.

O, why and whither ? — God knows
    all ;
  I only know that he is good,
And that whatever may befall
Or here or there, must be the best that
    could.

Between the dreadful cherubim
  A Father's face I still discern,
As Moses looked of old on him,
And saw his glory into goodness turn !

For he is merciful as just;
  And so, by faith correcting sight,
I bow before his will, and trust
Howe'er they seem he doeth all things
    right.

And dare to hope that he will
    make
  The rugged smooth, the doubtful
    plain ;
His mercy never quite forsake ;
His healing visit every realm of pain ;

That suffering is not his revenge
  Upon his creatures weak and frail,
Sent on a pathway new and strange
With feet that wander and with eyes
    that fail ;

That, o'er the crucible of pain,
  Watches the tender eye of Love
The slow transmuting of the chain
Whose links are iron below to gold
    above !

Ah me ! we doubt the shining skies,
  Seen through our shadows of offence,
And drown with our poor childish
  cries
The cradle-hymn of kindly Providence.

And still we love the evil cause,
  And of the just effect complain:
We tread upon life's broken laws,
And murmur at our self-inflicted pain ;

We turn us from the light, and find
  Our spectral shapes before us
  thrown,
As they who leave the sun behind
Walk in the shadows of themselves
  alone.

And scarce by will or strength of ours
  We set our faces to the day ;
Weak, wavering, blind, the Eternal
  Powers
Alone can turn us from ourselves away.

Our weakness is the strength of sin,
  But love must needs be stronger far,
Outreaching all and gathering in
The erring spirit and the wandering star.

A Voice grows with the growing years ;
  Earth, hushing down her bitter cry,
Looks upward from her graves, and
  hears,
" The Resurrection and the Life am I."

O Love Divine ! — whose constant
  beam
  Shines on the eyes that will not see,
And waits to bless us, while we dream
Thou leavest us because we turn from
  thee !

All souls that struggle and aspire,
  All hearts of prayer by thee are lit ;
And, dim or clear, thy tongues of fire
On dusky tribes and twilight centuries
  sit.

Nor bounds, nor clime, nor creed thou
  know'st,
  Wide as our need thy favors fall ;
The white wings of the Holy Ghost
Stoop, seen or unseen, o'er the heads of
  all.

O Beauty, old yet ever new ! [67]
  Eternal Voice, and Inward Word,

The Logos of the Greek and Jew,
The old sphere-music which the Samian
  heard !

Truth which the sage and prophet
  saw,
  Long sought without, but found
  within,
The Law of Love beyond all law,
The Life o'erflooding mortal death and
  sin !

Shine on us with the light which
  glowed
  Upon the trance-bound shepherd's
  way,
Who saw the Darkness overflowed
And drowned by tides of everlasting
  Day. [68]

Shine, light of God ! — make broad
  thy scope
  To all who sin and suffer ; more
And better than we dare to hope
With Heaven's compassion make our
  longings poor !

THE GIFT OF TRITEMIUS.

Tritemius of Herbipolis, one day,
While kneeling at the altar's foot to
  pray,
Alone with God, as was his pious choice,
Heard from without a miserable voice,
A sound which seemed of all sad things
  to tell,
As of a lost soul crying out of hell.

Thereat the Abbot paused ; the chain
  whereby
His thoughts went upward broken by
  that cry ;
And, looking from the casement, saw
  below
A wretched woman, with gray hair a-flow,
And withered hands held up to him,
  who cried
For alms as one who might not be
  denied.

She cried, " For the dear love of Him
  who gave
His life for ours, my child from bondage
  save, —
My beautiful, brave first-born, chained
  with slaves

In the Moor's galley, where the sun-smit
 waves
Lap the white walls of Tunis !" —
  " What I can
I give," Tritemius said : " my prayers."
 —" O man
Of God !" she cried, for grief had made
 her bold,
" Mock me not thus ; I ask not prayers,
 but gold.
Words will not serve me, alms alone
 suffice ;
Even while I speak perchance my first-
 born dies."

" Woman ! " Tritemius answered, " from
 our door
None go unfed ; hence are we always
 poor,
A single soldo is our only store.
Thou hast our prayers ; — what can we
 give thee more ?"—

" Give me," she said, " the silver can-
 dlesticks
On either side of the great crucifix.
God well may spare them on his errands
 sped,
Or he can give you golden ones instead."

Then spake Tritemius, " Even as thy
 word,
Woman, so be it ! (Our most gracious
 Lord,
Who loveth mercy more than sacrifice,
Pardon me if a human soul I prize
Above the gifts upon his altar piled !)
Take what thou askest, and redeem thy
 child."

But his hand trembled as the holy
 alms
He placed within the beggar's eager
 palms ;
And as she vanished down the linden
 shade,
He bowed his head and for forgiveness
 prayed.

So the day passed, and when the twi-
 light came
He woke to find the chapel all aflame,
And, dumb with grateful wonder, to be-
 hold
Upon the altar candlesticks of gold !

THE EVE OF ELECTION.

FROM gold to gray
 Our mild sweet day
Of Indian Summer fades too soon ;
 But tenderly
 Above the sea
Hangs, white and calm, the hunter's
 moon.

 In its pale fire,
 The village spire
Shows like the zodiac's spectral lance ;
 The painted walls
 Whereon it falls
Transfigured stand in marble trance !

 O'er fallen leaves
 The west-wind grieves,
Yet comes a seed-time round again ;
 And morn shall see
 The State sown free
With baleful tares or healthful grain.

 Along the street
 The shadows meet
Of Destiny, whose hands conceal
 The moulds of fate
 That shape the State,
And make or mar the common weal.

 Around I see
 The powers that be ;
I stand by Empire's primal springs ;
 And princes meet,
 In every street,
And hear the tread of uncrowned kings !

 Hark ! through the crowd
 The laugh runs loud,
Beneath the sad, rebuking moon.
 God save the land
 A careless hand
May shake or swerve ere morrow's noon !

 No jest is this ;
 One cast amiss
May blast the hope of Freedom's year.
 O, take me where
 Are hearts of prayer,
And foreheads bowed in reverent fear !

 Not lightly fall
 Beyond recall
The written scrolls a breath can float ;
 The crowning fact
 The kingliest act
Of Freedom is the freeman's vote !

For pearls that gem
A diadem
The diver in the deep sea dies ;
The regal right
We boast to-night
Is ours through costlier sacrifice ;

The blood of Vane,
His prison pain
Who traced the path the Pilgrim trod,
And hers whose faith
Drew strength from death,
And prayed her Russell up to God !

Our hearts grow cold,
We lightly hold
A right which brave men died to gain ;
The stake, the cord,
The axe, the sword,
Grim nurses at its birth of pain.

The shadow rend,
And o'er us bend,
O martyrs, with your crowns and
    palms, —
Breathe through these throngs
Your battle songs,
Your scaffold prayers, and dungeon
    psalms !

Look from the sky,
Like God's great eye,
Thou solemn noon, with searching beam,
Till in the sight
Of thy pure light
Our mean self-seekings meaner seem.

Shame from our hearts
Unworthy arts,
The fraud designed, the purpose dark ;
And smite away
The hands we lay
Profanely on the sacred ark.

To party claims
And private aims,
Reveal that august face of Truth,
Whereto are given
The age of heaven,
The beauty of immortal youth.

So shall our voice
Of sovereign choice
Swell the deep bass of duty done,
And strike the key
Of time to be,
When God and man shall speak as one !

THE OVER-HEART.

" For of Him, and through Him, and to Him
are all things, to whom be glory forever ! " — PAUL

ABOVE, below, in sky and sod,
    In leaf and spar, in star and man,
    Well might the wise Athenian scan
The geometric signs of God,
    The measured order of his plan.

And India's mystics sang aright
    Of the One Life pervading all,—
    One Being's tidal rise and fall
In soul and form, in sound and sight, —
    Eternal outflow and recall.

God is : and man in guilt and fear
    The central fact of Nature owns ; —
    Kneels, trembling, by his altar-stones,
And darkly dreams the ghastly smear
    Of blood appeases and atones.

Guilt shapes the Terror : deep within
    The human heart the secret lies
    Of all the hideous deities ;
And, painted on a ground of sin,
    The fabled gods of torment rise !

And what is He ? — The ripe grain nods,
    The sweet dews fall, the sweet flowers
        blow ;
    But darker signs his presence show :
The earthquake and the storm are God's,
    And good and evil interflow.

O hearts of love ! O souls that turn
    Like sunflowers to the pure and best !
    To you the truth is manifest :
For they the mind of Christ discern
    Who lean like John upon his breast !

In him of whom the sibyl told,
    For whom the prophet's harp was
        toned,
    Whose need the sage and magian
        owned,
The loving heart of God behold,
    The hope for which the ages groaned !

Fade, pomp of dreadful imagery
    Wherewith mankind have deified
    Their hate, and selfishness, and pride !
Let the scared dreamer wake to see
    The Christ of Nazareth at his side !

What doth that holy Guide require ? —
    No rite of pain, nor gift of blood,
    But man a kindly brotherhood,

Looking, where duty is desire,
To him, the beautiful and good.

Gone be the faithlessness of fear,
And let the pitying heaven's sweet
rain
Wash out the altar's bloody stain ;
The law of Hatred disappear,
The law of Love alone remain.

How fall the idols false and grim ! —
And lo ! their hideous wreck above
The emblems of the Lamb and Dove !
Man turns from God, not God from
him ;
And guilt, in suffering, whispers
Love !

The world sits at the feet of Christ,
Unknowing, blind, and unconsoled ;
It yet shall touch his garment's fold,
And feel the heavenly Alchemist
Transform its very dust to gold.

The theme befitting angel tongues
Beyond a mortal's scope has grown.
O heart of mine ! with reverence own
The fulness which to it belongs,
And trust the unknown for the known.

IN REMEMBRANCE OF JOSEPH
STURGE.

IN the fair land o'erwatched by Ischia's
mountains,
Across the charméd bay
Whose blue waves keep with Capri's sil-
ver fountains
Perpetual holiday,

A king lies dead, his wafer duly eaten,
His gold-bought masses given ;
And Rome's great altar smokes with
gums to sweeten
Her foulest gift to Heaven.

And while all Naples thrills with mute
thanksgiving,
The court of England's queen
For the dead monster so abhorred while
living
In mourning garb is seen.

With a true sorrow God rebukes that
feigning ;
By lone Edgbaston's side

Stands a great city in the sky's sad
raining,
Bareheaded and wet-eyed !

Silent for once the restless hive of labor,
Save the low funeral tread,
Or voice of craftsman whispering to his
neighbor
The good deeds of the dead.

For him no minster's chant of the im-
mortals
Rose from the lips of sin ;
No mitred priest swung back the heav-
enly portals
To let the white soul in.

But Age and Sickness framed their tear-
ful faces
In the low hovel's door,
And prayers went up from all the dark
by-places
And Ghettos of the poor.

The pallid toiler and the negro chattel,
The vagrant of the street,
The human dice wherewith in games of
battle
The lords of earth compete,

Touched with a grief that needs no out-
ward draping,
All swelled the long lament,
Of grateful hearts, instead of marble,
shaping
His viewless monument !

For never yet, with ritual pomp and
splendor,
In the long heretofore,
A heart more loyal, warm, and true,
and tender,
Has England's turf closed o'er.

And if there fell from out her grand old
steeples
No crash of brazen wail,
The   murmurous   woe   of   kindreds,
tongues, and peoples
Swept in on every gale.

It came from Holstein's birchen-belted
meadows,
And from the tropic calms
Of Indian islands in the sun-smit shad-
ows
Of Occidental palms ;

From the locked roadsteads of the
  Bothnian peasants,
    And harbors of the Finn,
Where war's worn victims saw his gentle
  presence
    Come sailing, Christ-like, in,

To seek the lost, to build the old waste
  places,
    To link the hostile shores
Of severing seas, and sow with England's daisies
    The moss of Finland's moors.

Thanks for the good man's beautiful
  example,
    Who in the vilest saw
Some sacred crypt or altar of a temple
    Still vocal with God's law ;

And heard with tender ear the spirit
  sighing
    As from its prison cell,
Praying for pity, like the mournful crying
    Of Jonah out of hell.

Not his the golden pen's or lip's persuasion,
    But a fine sense of right,
And Truth's directness, meeting each
  occasion
    Straight as a line of light.

His faith and works, like streams that
  intermingle,
    In the same channel ran :
The crystal clearness of an eye kept
  single
    Shamed all the frauds of man.

The very gentlest of all human natures
    He joined to courage strong,
And love outreaching unto all God's
  creatures
    With sturdy hate of wrong.

Tender as woman ; manliness and
  meekness
    In him were so allied
That they who judged him by his
  strength or weakness
    Saw but a single side.

Men failed, betrayed him, but his zeal
  seemed nourished
    By failure and by fall ;

Still a large faith in human-kind he
  cherished,
    And in God's love for all.

And now he rests : his greatness and his
  sweetness
    No more shall seem at strife ;
And death has moulded into calm completeness
    The statue of his life.

Where the dews glisten and the song-
  birds warble,
    His dust to dust is laid,
In Nature's keeping, with no pomp of
  marble
    To shame his modest shade.

The forges glow, the hammers all are
  ringing ;
    Beneath its smoky vale,
Hard by, the city of his love is swinging
    Its clamorous iron flail.

But round his grave are quietude and
  beauty,
    And the sweet heaven above, —
The fitting symbols of a life of duty
    Transfigured into love !

TRINITAS.

At morn I prayed, " I fain would see
How Three are One, and One is Three ;
Read the dark riddle unto me."

I wandered forth, the sun and air
I saw bestowed with equal care
On good and evil, foul and fair.

No partial favor dropped the rain ; —
Alike the righteous and profane
Rejoiced above their heading grain.

And my heart murmured, " Is it meet
That blindfold Nature thus should treat
With equal hand the tares and wheat ?"

A presence melted through my mood, —
A warmth, a light, a sense of good,
Like sunshine through a winter wood.

I saw that presence, mailed complete
In her white innocence, pause to greet
A fallen sister of the street.

Upon her bosom snowy pure
The lost one clung, as if secure
From inward guilt or outward lure.

"Beware !" I said ; "in this I see
No gain to her, but loss to thee :
Who touches pitch defiled must be."

I passed the haunts of shame and sin,
And a voice whispered, "Who therein
Shall these lost souls to Heaven's peace
        win ?

"Who there shall hope and health dis-
        pense,
And lift the ladder up from thence
Whose rounds are prayers of penitence ?"

I said, "No higher life they know ;
These earth-worms love to have it so.
Who stoops to raise them sinks as low."

That night with painful care I read
What Hippo's saint and Calvin said, —
The living seeking to the dead !

In vain I turned, in weary quest,
Old pages, where (God give them rest !)
The poor creed-mongers dreamed and
        guessed.

And still I prayed, "Lord, let me see
How Three are One, and One is Three ;
Read the dark riddle unto me !"

Then something whispered, "Dost thou
        pray
For what thou hast ? This very day
The Holy Three have crossed thy way.

"Did not the gifts of sun and air
To good and ill alike declare
The all-compassionate Father's care ?

"In the white soul that stooped to
        raise
The lost one from her evil ways,
Thou saw'st the Christ, whom angels
        praise !

"A bodiless Divinity,
The still small Voice that spake to thee
Was the Holy Spirit's mystery !

"O blind of sight, of faith how small !
Father, and Son, and Holy Call ; —
This day thou hast denied them all !

"Revealed in love and sacrifice,
The Holiest passed before thine eyes,
One and the same, in threefold guise.

"The equal Father in rain and sun,
His Christ in the good to evil done,
His Voice in thy soul ; — and the Three
        are One !"

I shut my grave Aquinas fast ;
The monkish gloss of ages past,
The schoolman's creed aside I cast.

And my heart answered, "Lord, I see
How Three are One, and One is Three ;
Thy riddle hath been read to me !"

THE OLD BURYING-GROUND.

OUR vales are sweet with fern and
        rose,
    Our hills are maple-crowned ;
But not from them our fathers chose
    The village burying-ground.

The dreariest spot in all the land
    To Death they set apart ;
With scanty grace from Nature's hand,
    And none from that of Art.

A winding wall of mossy stone,
    Frost-flung and broken, lines
A lonesome acre thinly grown
    With grass and wandering vines.

Without the wall a birch-tree shows
    Its drooped and tasselled head ;
Within, a stag-horned sumach grows,
    Fern-leafed, with spikes of red.

There, sheep that graze the neighboring
        plain
    Like white ghosts come and go,
The farm-horse drags his fetlock chain,
    The cow-bell tinkles slow.

Low moans the river from its bed,
    The distant pines reply ;
Like mourners shrinking from the dead,
    They stand apart and sigh.

Unshaded smites the summer sun,
    Unchecked the winter blast ;
The school-girl learns the place to
        shun,
    With glances backward cast.

For thus our fathers testified, —
  That he might read who ran, —
The emptiness of human pride,
  The nothingness of man.

They dared not plant the grave with
    flowers,
  Nor dress the funeral sod,
Where, with a love as deep as ours,
  They left their dead with God.

The hard and thorny path they kept
  From beauty turned aside ;
Nor missed they over those who slept
  The grace to life denied.

Yet still the wilding flowers would
    blow,
  The golden leaves would fall,
The seasons come, the seasons go,
  And God be good to all.

Above the graves the blackberry hung
  In bloom and green its wreath,
And harebells swung as if they rung
  The chimes of peace beneath.

The beauty Nature loves to share,
  The gifts she hath for all,
The common light, the common air,
  O'ercrept the graveyard's wall.

It knew the glow of eventide,
  The sunrise and the noon,
And glorified and sanctified
  It slept beneath the moon.

With flowers or snow-flakes for its sod,
  Around the seasons ran,
And evermore the love of God
  Rebuked the fear of man.

We dwell with fears on either hand,
  Within a daily strife,
And spectral problems waiting stand
  Before the gates of life.

The doubts we vainly seek to solve,
  The truths we know, are one ;
The known and nameless stars revolve
  Around the Central Sun.

And if we reap as we have sown,
  And take the dole we deal,
The law of pain is love alone,
  The wounding is to heal.

16

Unharmed from change to change we
    glide,
  We fall as in our dreams ;
The far-off terror at our side
  A smiling angel seems.

Secure on God's all-tender heart
  Alike rest great and small ;
Why fear to lose our little part,
  When he is pledged for all ?

O fearful heart and troubled brain !
  Take hope and strength from this, —
That Nature never hints in vain,
  Nor prophesies amiss.

Her wild birds sing the same sweet stave,
  Her lights and airs are given
Alike to playground and the grave :
  And over both is Heaven.

THE PIPES AT LUCKNOW.

PIPES of the misty moorlands,
  Voice of the glens and hills ;
The droning of the torrents,
  The treble of the rills !
Not the braes of broom and heather,
  Nor the mountains dark with rain,
Nor maiden bower, nor border tower,
  Have heard your sweetest strain !

Dear to the Lowland reaper,
  And plaided mountaineer, —
To the cottage and the castle
  The Scottish pipes are dear ; —
Sweet sounds the ancient pibroch
  O'er mountain, loch, and glade ;
But the sweetest of all music
  The pipes at Lucknow played.

Day by day the Indian tiger
  Louder yelled, and nearer crept ;
Round and round the jungle-serpent
  Near and nearer circles swept.
" Pray for rescue, wives and mothers, —
  Pray to-day ! " the soldier said ;
" To-morrow, death 's between us
  And the wrong and shame we dread.'

O, they listened, looked, and waited,
  Till their hope became despair ;
And the sobs of low bewailing
  Filled the pauses of their prayer.
Then up spake a Scottish maiden,
  With her ear unto the ground :

"Dinna ye hear it ? — dinna ye hear it ?
  The pipes o' Havelock sound ! "

Hushed the wounded man his groaning ;
  Hushed the wife her little ones ;
Alone they heard the drum-roll
  And the roar of Sepoy guns.
But to sounds of home and childhood
  The Highland ear was true ; —
As her mother's cradle-crooning
  The mountain pipes she knew.

Like the march of soundless music
  Through the vision of the seer,
More of feeling than of hearing,
  Of the heart than of the ear,
She knew the droning pibroch,
  She knew the Campbell's call :
"Hark ! hear ye no' MacGregor's, —
  The grandest o' them all ! "

O, they listened, dumb and breathless,
  And they caught the sound at last ;
Faint and far beyond the Goomtee
  Rose and fell the piper's blast !
Then a burst of wild thanksgiving
  Mingled woman's voice and man's ;
"God be praised ! — the march of Have-
    lock !
  The piping of the clans ! "

Louder, nearer, fierce as vengeance,
  Sharp and shrill as swords at strife,
Came the wild MacGregor's clan-call,
  Stinging all the air to life.
But when the far-off dust-cloud
  To plaided legions grew,
Full tenderly and blithesomely
  The pipes of rescue blew !

Round the silver domes of Lucknow,
  Moslem mosque and Pagan shrine,
Breathed the air to Britons dearest,
  The air of Auld Lang Syne.
O'er the cruel roll of war-drums
  Rose that sweet and homelike strain ;
And the tartan clove the turban,
  As the Goomtee cleaves the plain.

Dear to the corn-land reaper
  And plaided mountaineer, —
To the cottage and the castle
  The piper's song is dear.
Sweet sounds the Gaelic pibroch
  O'er mountain, glen, and glade ;
But the sweetest of all music
  The Pipes at Lucknow played !

MY PSALM.

I MOURN no more my vanished years :
    Beneath a tender rain,
An April rain of smiles and tears,
    My heart is young again.

The west-winds blow, and, singing low,
    I hear the glad streams run ;
The windows of my soul I throw
    Wide open to the sun.

No longer forward nor behind
    I look in hope or fear ;
But, grateful, take the good I find,
    The best of now and here.

I plough no more a desert land,
    To harvest weed and tare ;
The manna dropping from God's hand
    Rebukes my painful care.

I break my pilgrim staff, — I lay
    Aside the toiling oar ;
The angel sought so far away
    I welcome at my door.

The airs of spring may never play
    Among the ripening corn,
Nor freshness of the flowers of May
    Blow through the autumn morn ;

Yet shall the blue-eyed gentian look
    Through fringéd lids to heaven,
And the pale aster in the brook
    Shall see its image given ; —

The woods shall wear their robes of
      praise,
    The south-wind softly sigh,
And sweet, calm days in golden haze
    Melt down the amber sky.

Not less shall manly deed and word
    Rebuke an age of wrong ;
The graven flowers that wreathe the
      sword
    Make not the blade less strong.

But smiting hands shall learn to heal,—
    To build as to destroy ;
Nor less my heart for others feel
    That I the more enjoy.

All as God wills, who wisely heeds
    To give or to withhold,

And knoweth more of all my needs
  Than all my prayers have told !

Enough that blessings undeserved
  Have marked my erring track ; —
That wheresoe'er my feet have swerved,
  His chastening turned me back ; —

That more and more a Providence
  Of love is understood,
Making the springs of time and sense
  Sweet with eternal good ; —

That death seems but a covered way
  Which opens into light,
Wherein no blinded child can stray
  Beyond the Father's sight ; —

That care and trial seem at last,
  Through Memory's sunset air,
Like mountain-ranges overpast,
  In purple distance fair ; —

That all the jarring notes of life
  Seem blending in a psalm,
And all the angles of its strife
  Slow rounding into calm.

And so the shadows fall apart,
  And so the west-winds play ;
And all the windows of my heart
  I open to the day.

LE MARAIS DU CYGNE.[69]

A BLUSH as of roses
  Where rose never grew !
Great drops on the bunch-grass,
  But not of the dew !
A taint in the sweet air
  For wild bees to shun !
A stain that shall never
  Bleach out in the sun !

Back, steed of the prairies !
  Sweet song-bird, fly back !
Wheel hither, bald vulture !
  Gray wolf, call thy pack !
The foul human vultures
  Have feasted and fled ;
The wolves of the Border
  Have crept from the dead.

From the hearths of their cabins,
  The fields of their corn,

Unwarned and unweaponed,
  The victims were torn, —
By the whirlwind of murder
  Swooped up and swept on
To the low, reedy fen-lands,
  The Marsh of the Swan.

With a vain plea for mercy
  No stout knee was crooked ;
In the mouths of the rifles
  Right manly they looked.
How paled the May sunshine,
  O Marais du Cygne !
On death for the strong life,
  On red grass for green !

In the homes of their rearing,
  Yet warm with their lives,
Ye wait the dead only,
  Poor children and wives !
Put out the red forge-fire,
  The smith shall not come ;
Unyoke the brown oxen,
  The ploughman lies dumb.

Wind slow from the Swan's Marsh,
  O dreary death-train,
With pressed lips as bloodless
  As lips of the slain !
Kiss down the young eyelids,
  Smooth down the gray hairs ;
Let tears quench the curses
  That burn through your prayers

Strong man of the prairies,
  Mourn bitter and wild !
Wail, desolate woman !
  Weep, fatherless child !
But the grain of God springs up
  From ashes beneath,
And the crown of his harvest
  Is life out of death.

Not in vain on the dial
  The shade moves along,
To point the great contrasts
  Of right and of wrong :
Free homes and free altars,
  Free prairie and flood, —
The reeds of the Swan's Marsh,
  Whose bloom is of blood !

On the lintels of Kansas
  That blood shall not dry ;
Henceforth the Bad Angel
  Shall harmless go by ;

Henceforth to the sunset,
  Unchecked on her way,
Shall Liberty follow
  The march of the day.

"THE ROCK" IN EL GHOR.

DEAD Petra in her hill-tomb sleeps,
  Her stones of emptiness remain ;
Around her sculptured mystery sweeps
  The lonely waste of Edom's plain.

From the doomed dwellers in the cleft
  The bow of vengeance turns not back ;
Of all her myriads none are left
  Along the Wady Mousa's track.

Clear in the hot Arabian day
  Her arches spring, her statues climb ;
Unchanged, the graven wonders pay
  No tribute to the spoiler, Time !

Unchanged the awful lithograph
  Of power and glory undertrod, —
Of nations scattered like the chaff
  Blown from the threshing-floor of God.

Yet shall the thoughtful stranger turn
  From Petra's gates, with deeper awe
To mark afar the burial urn
  Of Aaron on the cliffs of Hor ;

And where upon its ancient guard
  Thy Rock, El Ghor, is standing yet,—
Looks from its turrets desertward,
  And keeps the watch that God has
    set.

The same as when in thunders loud
  It heard the voice of God to man, —
As when it saw in fire and cloud
  The angels walk in Israel's van !

Or when from Ezion-Geber's way
  It saw the long procession file,
And heard the Hebrew timbrèls play
  The music of the lordly Nile ;

Or saw the tabernacle pause,
  Cloud-bound, by Kadesh Barnea's
    wells,
While Moses graved the sacred laws,
  And Aaron swung his golden bells.

Rock of the desert, prophet-sung !
  How grew its shadowing pile at length,

A symbol, in the Hebrew tongue,
  Of God's eternal love and strength.

On lip of bard and scroll of seer,
  From age to age went down the name,
Until the Shiloh's promised year,
  And Christ, the Rock of Ages, came !

The path of life we walk to-day
  Is strange as that the Hebrews trod ;
We need the shadowing rock, as they,—
  We need, like them, the guides of God.

God send his angels, Cloud and Fire,
  To lead us o'er the desert sand !
God give our hearts their long desire,
  His shadow in a weary land !

ON A PRAYER-BOOK,

WITH ITS FRONTISPIECE, ARY SCHEF-
FER'S "CHRISTUS CONSOLATOR,"
AMERICANIZED BY THE OMISSION OF
THE BLACK MAN.

O ARY SCHEFFER ! when beneath thine
    eye,
  Touched with the light that cometh
    from above,
  Grew the sweet picture of the dear
    Lord's love,
No dream hadst thou that Christian
    hands would tear
Therefrom the token of his equal care,
  And make thy symbol of his truth a
    lie !
The poor, dumb slave whose shackles
    fall away
  In his compassionate gaze, grubbed
    smoothly out,
  To mar no more the exercise devout
Of sleek oppression kneeling down to
    pray
Where the great oriel stains the Sabbath
    day !
Let whoso can before such praying-books
  Kneel on his velvet cushion ; I, for
    one,
  Would sooner bow, a Parsee, to the
    sun,
Or tend a prayer-wheel in Thibetan
    brooks,
  Or beat a drum on Yedo's temple-
    floor.
No falser idol man has bowed before,
In Indian groves or islands of the sea,

Than that which through the quaint-
carved Gothic door
Looks forth, — a Church without hu-
manity !
Patron of pride, and prejudice, and
wrong, —
The rich man's charm and fetish of
the strong,
The Eternal Fulness meted, clipped, and
shorn,
The seamless robe of equal mercy torn,
The dear Christ hidden from his kindred
flesh,
And, in his poor ones, crucified afresh !
Better the simple Lama scattering wide,
Where sweeps the storm Alechan's
steppes along,
His paper horses for the lost to ride,
And wearying Buddha with his prayers
to make
The figures living for the traveller's sake,
Than he who hopes with cheap praise to
beguile
The ear of God, dishonoring man the
while ;
Who dreams the pearl gate's hinges,
rusty grown,
Are moved by flattery's oil of tongue
alone ;
That in the scale Eternal Justice bears
The generous deed weighs less than self-
ish prayers,
And words intoned with graceful unction
move
The Eternal Goodness more than lives
of truth and love.
Alas, the Church ! — The reverend head
of Jay,
Enhaloed with its saintly silvered hair,
Adorns no more the places of her
prayer ;
And brave young Tyng, too early called
away,
Troubles the Haman of her courts no
more
Like the just Hebrew at the Assyrian's
door ;
And her sweet ritual, beautiful but
dead
As the dry husk from which the grain
is shed,
And holy hymns from which the life
devout
Of saints and martyrs has wellnigh
gone out,
Like candles dying in exhausted
air,

For Sabbath use in measured grists are
ground ;
And, ever while the spiritual mill goes
round,
Between the upper and the nether
stones,
Unseen, unheard, the wretched bondman groans,
And urges his vain plea, prayer-smoth-
ered, anthem-drowned !

O heart of mine, keep patience ! — Look-
ing forth,
As from the Mount of Vision, I behold,
Pure, just, and free, the Church of Christ
on earth, —
The martyr's dream, the golden age
foretold !
And found, at last, the mystic Graal I
see,
Brimmed with His blessing, pass from
lip to lip
In sacred pledge of human fellowship ;
And over all the songs of angels hear, —
Songs of the love that casteth out all
fear, —
Songs of the Gospel of Humanity !
Lo ! in the midst, with the same look
he wore,
Healing and blessing on Genesaret's
shore,
Folding together, with the all-tender
might
Of his great love, the dark hands and
the white,
Stands the Consoler, soothing every
pain,
Making all burdens light, and breaking
every chain.

TO J. T. F.

ON A BLANK LEAF OF "POEMS PRINT-
ED, NOT PUBLISHED."

WELL thought ! who would not rather
hear
The songs to Love and Friendship sung
Than those which move the stranger's
tongue,
And feed his unselected ear ?

Our social joys are more than fame ·
Life withers in the public look.
Why mount the pillory of a book,
Or barter comfort for a name ?

Who in a house of glass would dwell,
With curious eyes at every pane ?
To ring him in and out again,
Who wants the public crier's bell ?

To see the angel in one's way,
Who wants to play the ass's part, —
Bear on his back the wizard Art,
And in his service speak or bray ?

And who his manly locks would shave,
And quench the eyes of common sense,
To share the noisy recompense
That mocked the shorn and blinded
          slave ?

The heart has needs beyond the head,
And, starving in the plenitude
Of strange gifts, craves its common
          food, —
Our human nature's daily bread.

We are but men : no gods are we,
To sit in mid-heaven, cold and bleak,
Each separate, on his painful peak,
Thin-cloaked in self-complacency !

Better his lot whose axe is swung
In Wartburg woods, or that poor girl's
Who by the Ilm her spindle whirls
And sings the songs that Luther sung,

Than his who, old, and cold, and vain,
At Weimar sat, a demigod,
And bowed with Jove's imperial nod
His votaries in and out again !

Ply, Vanity, thy wingéd feet !
Ambition, hew thy rocky stair !
Who envies him who feeds on air
The icy splendor of his seat ?

I see your Alps, above me, cut
The dark, cold sky ; and dim and lone
I see ye sitting, — stone on stone, —
With human senses dulled and shut.

I could not reach you, if I would,
Nor sit among your cloudy shapes ;
And (spare the fable of the grapes
And fox) I would not if I could.

Keep to your lofty pedestals !
The safer plain below I choose :
Who never wins can rarely lose,
Who never climbs as rarely falls.

Let such as love the eagle's scream
Divide with him his home of ice :
For me shall gentler notes suffice, —
The valley-song of bird and stream ;

The pastoral bleat, the drone of bees,
The flail-beat chiming far away,
The cattle-low, at shut of day,
The voice of God in leaf and breeze !

Then lend thy hand, my wiser friend,
And help me to the vales below,
(In truth, I have not far to go,)
Where sweet with flowers the fields ex-
          tend.

THE PALM-TREE.

Is it the palm, the cocoa-palm,
On the Indian Sea, by the isles of balm !
Or is it a ship in the breezeless calm ?

A ship whose keel is of palm beneath,
Whose ribs of palm have a palm-bark
          sheath,
And a rudder of palm it steereth with.

Branches of palm are its spars and rails,
Fibres of palm are its woven sails,
And the rope is of palm that idly trails !

What does the good ship bearso well ?
The cocoa-nut with its stony shell,
And the milky sap of its inner cell.

What are its jars, so smooth and fine,
But hollowed nuts, filled with oil and
          wine,
And the cabbage that ripens under the
          Line ?

Who smokes his nargileh, cool and calm ?
The master, whose cunning and skill
          could charm
Cargo and ship from the bounteous palm.

In the cabin he sits on a palm-mat soft,
From a beaker of palm his drink is
          quaffed,
And a palm-thatch shields from the sun
          aloft !

His dress is woven of palmy strands,
And he holds a palm-leaf scroll in his
          hands,
Traced with the Prophet's wise com-
          mands !

The turban folded about his head
Was daintily wrought of the palm-leaf
        braid,
And the fan that cools him of palm was
        made.

Of threads of palm was the carpet spun
Whereon he kneels when the day is done,
And the foreheads of Islam are bowed as
        one !

To him the palm is a gift divine,
Wherein all uses of man combine, —
House, and raiment, and food, and wine !

And, in the hour of his great release,
His need of the palm shall only cease
With the shroud wherein he lieth in
        peace.

" Allah il Allah ! " he sings his psalm,
On the Indian Sea, by the isles of balm ;
" Thanks to Allah who gives the palm ! "

LINES,

READ AT THE BOSTON CELEBRATION OF
THE HUNDREDTH ANNIVERSARY OF
THE BIRTH OF ROBERT BURNS, 25TH
1ST MO., 1859.

How sweetly come the holy psalms
    From saints and martyrs down,
The waving of triumphal palms
    Above the thorny crown !
The choral praise, the chanted prayers
    From harps by angels strung,
The hunted Cameron's mountain airs,
    The hymns that Luther sung !

Yet, jarring not the heavenly notes,
    The sounds of earth are heard,
As through the open minster floats
    The song of breeze and bird !
Not less the wonder of the sky
    That daisies bloom below ;
The brook sings on, though loud and
        high
    The cloudy organs blow !

And, if the tender ear be jarred
    That, haply, hears by turns
The saintly harp of Olney's bard,
    The pastoral pipe of Burns,
No discord mars His perfect plan
    Who gave them both a tongue;

For he who sings the love of man
    The love of God hath sung !

To-day be every fault forgiven
    Of him in whom we joy !
We take, with thanks, the gold of Heaven
    And leave the earth's alloy.
Be ours his music as of spring,
    His sweetness as of flowers,
The songs the bard himself might sing
    In holier ears than ours.

Sweet airs of love and home, the hum
    Of household melodies,
Come singing, as the robins come
    To sing in door-yard trees.
And, heart to heart, two nations lean,
    No rival wreaths to twine,
But blending in eternal green
    The holly and the pine !

THE RED RIVER VOYAGEUR.

OUT and in the river is winding
    The links of its long, red chain
Through belts of dusky pine-land
    And gusty leagues of plain.

Only, at times, a smoke-wreath
    With the drifting cloud-rack joins, —
The smoke of the hunting-lodges
    Of the wild Assiniboins !

Drearily blows the north-wind
    From the land of ice and snow ;
The eyes that look are weary,
    And heavy the hands that row.

And with one foot on the water,
    And one upon the shore,
The Angel of Shadow gives warning
    That day shall be no more.

Is it the clang of wild-geese ?
    Is it the Indian's yell,
That lends to the voice of the north
        wind
    The tones of a far-off bell ?

The voyageur smiles as he listens
    To the sound that grows apace ;
Well he knows the vesper ringing
    Of the bells of St. Boniface.

The bells of the Roman Mission,
    That call from their turrets twain,

To the boatman on the river,
　To the hunter on the plain !

Even so in our mortal journey
　The bitter north-winds blow,
And thus upon life's Red River
　Our hearts, as oarsmen, row.

And when the Angel of Shadow
　Rests his feet on wave and shore,
And our eyes grow dim with watching
　And our hearts faint at the oar,

Happy is he who heareth
　· The signal of his release
In the bells of the Holy City,
　The chimes of eternal peace !

KENOZA LAKE.

As Adam did in Paradise,
　To-day the primal right we claim :
Fair mirror of the woods and skies,
　We give to thee a name.

Lake of the pickerel ! — let no more
　The echoes answer back, "Great Pond,"
But sweet Kenoza, from thy shore
　And watching hills beyond,

Let Indian ghosts, if such there be
　Who ply unseen their shadowy lines,
Call back the ancient name to thee,
　As with the voice of pines.

The shores we trod as barefoot boys,
　The nutted woods we wandered
　　through,
To friendship, love, and social joys
　We consecrate anew.

Here shall the tender song be sung,
　And memory's dirges soft and low,
And wit shall sparkle on the tongue,
　And mirth shall overflow,

Harmless as summer lightning plays
　From a low, hidden cloud by night,
A light to set the hills ablaze,
　But not a bolt to smite.

In sunny South and prairied West
　Are exiled hearts remembering still,

As bees their hive, as birds their nest,
　The homes of Haverhill.

They join us in our rites to-day ;
　And, listening, we may hear, ere
　　long,
From inland lake and ocean bay,
　The echoes of our song.

Kenoza ! o'er no sweeter lake
　Shall morning break or noon-cloud
　　sail, —
No fairer face than thine shall take
　The sunset's golden veil.

Long be it ere the tide of trade
　Shall break with harsh-resounding
　　din
The quiet of thy banks of shade,
　And hills that fold thee in.

Still let thy woodlands hide the hare,
　The shy loon sound his trumpet-note,
Wing-weary from his fields of air,
　The wild-goose on thee float.

Thy peace rebuke our feverish stir,
　Thy beauty our deforming strife ;
Thy woods and waters minister
　The healing of their life.

And sinless Mirth, from care released,
　Behold, unawed, thy mirrored sky,
Smiling as smiled on Cana's feast
　The Master's loving eye.

And when the summer day grows dim,
　And light mists walk thy mimic sea,
Revive in us the thought of Him
　Who walked on Galilee !

TO G. B. C.

So spake Esaias : so, in words of flame,
Tekoa's prophet-herdsman smote with
　　blame
The traffickers in men, and put to shame,
　All earth and heaven before,
The sacerdotal robbers of the poor.

All the dread Scripture lives for thee
　　again,
To smite like lightning on the hands
　　profane
Lifted to bless the slave-whip and the
　　chain.

Once more the old Hebrew tongue
Bends with the shafts of God a bow
    new-strung !

Take up the mantle which the prophets
    wore ;
Warn with their warnings, — show the
    Christ once more
Bound, scourged, and crucified in his
    blameless poor ;
    And shake above our land
The unquenched bolts that blazed in
    Hosea's hand !

Not vainly shalt thou cast upon our
    years
The solemn burdens of the Orient seers,
And smite with truth a guilty nation's
    ears.
    Mightier was Luther's word
Than Seckingen's mailed arm or Hut-
    ton's sword !

THE SISTERS.

A PICTURE BY BARRY.

THE shade for me, but over thee
    The lingering sunshine still ;
As, smiling, to the silent stream
    Comes down the singing rill.

So come to me, my little one, —
    My years with thee I share,
And mingle with a sister's love
    A mother's tender care.

But keep the smile upon thy lip,
    The trust upon thy brow ;
Since for the dear one God hath called
    We have an angel now.

Our mother from the fields of heaven
    Shall still her ear incline ;
Nor need we fear her human love
    Is less for love divine.

The songs are sweet they sing beneath
    The trees of life so fair,
But sweetest of the songs of heaven
    Shall be her children's prayer.

Then, darling, rest upon my breast,
    And teach my heart to lean
With thy sweet trust upon the arm
    Which folds us both unseen !

LINES,

FOR THE AGRICULTURAL AND HORTI-
CULTURAL EXHIBITION AT AMESBURY
AND SALISBURY, SEPT. 28, 1858.

THIS day, two hundred years ago,
    The wild grape by the river's side,
And tasteless groundnut trailing low,
    The table of the woods supplied.

Unknown the apple's red and gold,
    The blushing tint of peach and pear ;
The mirror of the Powow told
    No tale of orchards ripe and rare.

Wild as the fruits he scorned to till,
    These vales the idle Indian trod ;
Nor knew the glad, creative skill, —
    The joy of him who toils with God.

O Painter of the fruits and flowers !
    We thank thee for thy wise design
Whereby these human hands of ours
    In Nature's garden work with thine.

And thanks that from our daily need
    The joy of simple faith is born ;
That he who smites the summer weed,
    May trust thee for the autumn corn.

Give fools their gold, and knaves their
    power ;
    Let fortune's bubbles rise and fall ;
Who sows a field, or trains a flower,
    Or plants a tree, is more than all.

For he who blesses most is blest ;
    And God and man shall own his worth
Who toils to leave as his bequest
    An added beauty to the earth.

And, soon or late, to all that sow,
    The time of harvest shall be given ;
The flower shall bloom, the fruit shall
    grow,
    If not on earth, at last in heaven

THE PREACHER.

ITS windows flashing to the sky,
    Beneath a thousand roofs of brown,
Far down the vale, my friend and I
    Beheld the old and quiet town ;
The ghostly sails that out at sea
Flapped their white wings of mystery

The beaches glimmering in the sun,
And the low wooded capes that run
Into the sea-mist north and south ;
The sand-bluffs at the river's mouth ;
The swinging chain-bridge, and, afar,
The foam-line of the harbor-bar.

Over the woods and meadow-lands
   A crimson-tinted shadow lay
   Of clouds through which the setting
      day
   Flung a slant glory far away.
It glittered on the wet sea-sands,
   It flamed upon the city's panes,
Smote the white sails of ships that wore
Outward or in, and glided o'er
   The steeples with their veering vanes !

Awhile my friend with rapid search
   O'erran the landscape. "Yonder spire
   Over gray roofs, a shaft of fire ;
What is it, pray ?" — "The Whitefield
      Church !
Walled about by its basement stones,
There rest the marvellous prophet's
   bones."
Then as our homeward way we walked,
Of the great preacher's life we talked ;
And through the mystery of our theme
The outward glory seemed to stream,
And Nature's self interpreted
The doubtful record of the dead ;
And every level beam that smote
The sails upon the dark afloat
   A symbol of the light became
   Which touched the shadows of our
      blame
   With tongues of Pentecostal flame.

Over the roofs of the pioneers
Gathers the moss of a hundred years ;
On man and his works has passed the
   change
Which needs must be in a century's
   range.
The land lies open and warm in the sun,
Anvils clamor and mill-wheels run, —
Flocks on the hillsides, herds on the
   plain,
The wilderness gladdened with fruit and
   grain !
But the living faith of the settlers old
A dead profession their children hold ;
To the lust of office and greed of trade
A stepping-stone is the altar made.
The Church, to place and power the
   door,

Rebukes the sin of the world no more,
Nor sees its Lord in the homeless poor.
Everywhere is the grasping hand,
And eager adding of land to land ;
And earth, which seemed to the fathers
   meant
But as a pilgrim's wayside tent, —
A nightly shelter to fold away
When the Lord should call at the break
   of day, —
Solid and steadfast seems to be,
And Time has forgotten Eternity !

But fresh and green from the rotting
   roots
Of primal forests the young growth
   shoots ;
From the death of the old the new pro-
   ceeds,
And the life of truth from the rot of
   creeds :
On the ladder of God, which upward leads,
The steps of progress are human needs.
For his judgments still are a mighty
   deep,
And the eyes of his providence never
   sleep :
When the night is darkest he gives the
   morn ;
When the famine is sorest, the wine
   and corn !

In the church of the wilderness Edwards
   wrought,
Shaping his creed at the forge of
   thought ;
And with Thor's own hammer welded
   and bent
The iron links of his argument,
Which strove to grasp in its mighty span
The purpose of God and the fate of man !
Yet faithful still, in his daily round
To the weak, and the poor, and sin-sick
   found,
The schoolman's lore and the casuist's art
Drew warmth and life from his fervent
   heart.
Had he not seen in the solitudes
Of his deep and dark Northampton
   woods
A vision of love about him fall ?
Not the blinding splendor which fell on
   Saul,
But the tenderer glory that rests on them
Who walk in the New Jerusalem,
Where never the sun nor moon are
   known,

But the Lord and his love are the light
alone !
And watching the sweet, still countenance
Of the wife of his bosom rapt in trance,
Had he not treasured each broken word
Of the mystical wonder seen and heard ;
And loved the beautiful dreamer more
That thus to the desert of earth she bore
Clusters of Eschol from Canaan's shore ?

As the barley-winnower, holding with
pain
Aloft in waiting his chaff and grain,
Joyfully welcomes the far-off breeze
Sounding the pine-tree's slender keys,
So he who had waited long to hear
The sound of the Spirit drawing near,
Like that which the son of Iddo heard
When the feet of angels the myrtles
stirred,
Felt the answer of prayer, at last,
As over his church the afflatus passed,
Breaking its sleep as breezes break
To sun-bright ripples a stagnant lake.

At first a tremor of silent fear,
The creep of the flesh at danger near,
A vague foreboding and discontent,
Over the hearts of the people went.
All nature warned in sounds and signs :
The wind in the tops of the forest pines
In the name of the Highest called to
prayer,
As the muezzin calls from the minaret
stair.

Through ceiled chambers of secret sin
Sudden and strong the light shone in ;
A guilty sense of his neighbor's needs
Startled the man of title-deeds ;
The trembling hand of the worldling
shook
The dust of years from the Holy Book ;
And the psalms of David, forgotten long,
Took the place of the scoffer's song.

The impulse spread like the outward
course
Of waters moved by a central force :
The tide of spiritual life rolled down
From inland mountains to seaboard
town.

Prepared and ready the altar stands
Waiting the prophet's outstretched
hands
And prayer availing, to downward call
The fiery answer in view of all.

Hearts are like wax in the furnace, who
Shall mould, and shape, and cast them
anew ?
Lo ! by the Merrimack WHITEFIELD
stands
In the temple that never was made by
hands, —
Curtains of azure, and crystal wall,
And dome of the sunshine over all ! —
A homeless pilgrim, with dubious name
Blown about on the winds of fame ;
Now as an angel of blessing classed,
And now as a mad enthusiast.
Called in his youth to sound and gauge
The moral lapse of his race and age,
And, sharp as truth, the contrast draw
Of human frailty and perfect law ;
Possessed by the one dread thought that
lent
Its goad to his fiery temperament,
Up and down the world he went,
A John the Baptist crying, —Repent !

No perfect whole can our nature make ;
Here or there the circle will break ;
The orb of life as it takes the light
On one side leaves the other in night.
Never was saint so good and great
As to give no chance at St. Peter's gate
For the plea of the Devil's advocate.
So, incomplete by his being's law,
The marvellous preacher had his flaw :
With step unequal, and lame with faults,
His shade on the path of History halts.

Wisely and well said the Eastern bard :
Fear is easy, but love is hard, —
Easy to glow with the Santon's rage,
And walk on the Meccan pilgrimage ;
But he is greatest and best who can
Worship Allah by loving man.

Thus he, — to whom, in the painful
stress
Of zeal on fire from its own excess,
Heaven seemed so vast and earth so small
That man was nothing, since God was
all, —
Forgot, as the best at times have done,
That the love of the Lord and of man
are one.

Little to him whose feet unshod
The thorny path of the desert trod,
Careless of pain, so it led to God,
Seemed the hunger-pang and the poor
man's wrong,

The weak ones trodden beneath the
     strong.
Should the worm be chooser ? — the
     clay withstand
The shaping will of the potter's hand ?

In the Indian fable Arjoon hears
The scorn of a god rebuke his fears :
"Spare thy pity !" Krishna saith ;
"Not in thy sword is the power of
     death !
All is illusion, — loss but seems ;
Pleasure and pain are only dreams ;
Who deems he slayeth doth not kill ;
Who counts as slain is living still.
Strike, nor fear thy blow is crime ;
Nothing dies but the cheats of time ;
Slain or slayer, small the odds
To each, immortal as Indra's gods !"

So by Savannah's banks of shade,
The stones of his mission the preacher
     laid
On the heart of the negro crushed and
     rent,
And made of his blood the wall's cement ;
Bade the slave-ship speed from coast to
     coast
Fanned by the wings of the Holy Ghost ;
And begged, for the love of Christ, the
     gold
Coined from the hearts in its groaning
     hold.
What could it matter, more or less
Of stripes, and hunger, and weariness ?
Living or dying, bond or free,
What was time to eternity ?

Alas for the preacher's cherished schemes !
Mission and church are now but dreams ;
Nor prayer nor fasting availed the plan
To honor God through the wrong of
     man.
Of all his labors no trace remains
Save the bondman lifting his hands in
     chains.
The woof he wove in the righteous warp
Of freedom-loving Oglethorpe,
Clothes with curses the goodly land,
Changes its greenness and bloom to sand ;
And a century's lapse reveals once more
The slave-ship stealing to Georgia's
     shore.
Father of Light ! how blind is he
Who sprinkles the altar he rears to Thee
With the blood and tears of human-
     ity !

He erred : Shall we count his gifts as
     naught ?
Was the work of God in him unwrought ?
The servant may through his deafness
     err,
And blind may be God's messenger ;
But the errand is sure they go upon, —
The word is spoken, the deed is done.
Was the Hebrew temple less fair and
     good
That Solomon bowed to gods of wood ?
For his tempted heart and wandering
     feet,
Were the songs of David less pure and
     sweet ?
So in light and shadow the preacher
     went,
God's erring and human instrument ;
And the hearts of the people where he
     passed
Swayed as the reeds sway in the blast,
Under the spell of a voice which took
In its compass the flow of Siloa's brook,
And the mystical chime of the bells of
     gold
On the ephod's hem of the priest of old, —
Now the roll of thunder, and now the awe
Of the trumpet heard in the Mount of
     Law.

A solemn fear on the listening crowd
Fell like the shadow of a cloud.
The sailor reeling from out the ships
Whose masts stood thick in the river-
     slips
Felt the jest and the curse die on his
     lips.
Listened the fisherman rude and hard,
The calker rough from the builder's
     yard,
The man of the market left his load,
The teamster leaned on his bending goad,
The maiden, and youth beside her, felt
Their hearts in a closer union melt,
And saw the flowers of their love in
     bloom
Down the endless vistas of life to come.
Old age sat feebly brushing away
From his ears the scanty locks of gray ;
And careless boyhood, living the free
Unconscious life of bird and tree,
Suddenly wakened to a sense
Of sin and its guilty consequence.
It was as if an angel's voice
Called the listeners up for their final
     choice ;
As if a strong hand rent apart

The veils of sense from soul and heart,
Showing in light ineffable
The joys of heaven and woes of hell !
All about in the misty air
The hills seemed kneeling in silent
    prayer ;
The rustle of leaves, the moaning sedge,
The water's lap on its gravelled edge,
The wailing pines, and, far and faint,
The wood-dove's note of sad com-
    plaint, —
To the solemn voice of the preacher
    lent
An undertone as of low lament ;
And the rote of the sea from its sandy
    coast,
On the easterly wind, now heard, now
    lost,
Seemed the murmurous sound of the
    judgment host.

Yet wise men doubted, and good men
    wept,
As that storm of passion above them
    swept,
And, comet-like, adding flame to flame,
The priests of the new Evangel came, —
Davenport, flashing upon the crowd,
Charged like summer's electric cloud,
Now holding the listener still as death
With terrible warnings under breath,
Now shouting for joy, as if he viewed
The vision of Heaven's beatitude !
And Celtic Tennant, his long coat
    bound
Like a monk's with leathern girdle
    round,
Wild with the toss of unshorn hair,
And wringing of hands, and eyes aglare,
Groaning under the world's despair !
Grave pastors, grieving their flocks to
    lose,
Prophesied to the empty pews
That gourds would wither, and mush-
    rooms die,
And noisiest fountains run soonest dry,
Like the spring that gushed in New-
    bury Street,
Under the tramp of the earthquake's
    feet,
A silver shaft in the air and light,
For a single day, then lost in night,
Leaving only, its place to tell,
Sandy fissure and sulphurous smell.
With zeal wing-clipped and white-heat
    cool,
Moved by the spirit in grooves of rule,

No longer harried, and cropped, and
    fleeced,
Flogged by sheriff and cursed by priest,
But by wiser counsels left at ease
To settle quietly on his lees,
And, self-concentred, to count as done
The work which his fathers scarce begun,
In silent protest of letting alone,
The Quaker kept the way of his own, —
A non-conductor among the wires,
With coat of asbestos proof to fires.
And quite unable to mend his pace
To catch the falling manna of grace,
He hugged the closer his little store
Of faith, and silently prayed for more.
And vague of creed and barren of rite,
But holding, as in his Master's sight,
Act and thought to the inner light,
The round of his simple duties walked,
And strove to live what the others talked.

And who shall marvel if evil went
Step by step with the good intent,
And with love and meekness, side by
    side,
Lust of the flesh and spiritual pride ? —
That passionate longings and fancies
    vain
Set the heart on fire and crazed the
    brain ? —
That over the holy oracles
Folly sported with cap and bells ?—
That goodly women and learned men
Marvelling told with tongue and pen
How unweaned children chirped like
    birds
Texts of Scripture and solemn words,
Like the infant seers of the rocky glens
In the Puy de Dome of wild Cevennes :
Or baby Lamas who pray and preach
From Tartar cradles in Buddha's
    speech ?

In the war which Truth or Freedom
    wages
With impious fraud and the wrong of
    ages,
Hate and malice and self-love mar
The notes of triumph with painful jar,
And the helping angels turn aside
Their sorrowing faces the shame to hide.
Never on custom's oiled grooves
The world to a higher level moves,
But grates and grinds with friction hard
On granite boulder and flinty shard.
The heart must bleed before it feels,
The pool be troubled before it heals ;

Ever by losses the right must gain,
Every good have its birth of pain ;
The active Virtues blush to find
The Vices wearing their badge behind,
And Graces and Charities feel the fire
Wherein the sins of the age expire :
The fiend still rends as of old he rent
The tortured body from which he went.

But Time tests all. In the over-drift
And flow of the Nile, with its annual
　　gift,
Who cares for the Hadji's relics sunk ?
Who thinks of the drowned-out Coptic
　　monk ?
The tide that loosens the temple's
　　stones,
And scatters the sacred ibis-bones,
Drives away from the valley-land
That Arab robber, the wandering sand,
Moistens the fields that know no rain,
Fringes the desert with belts of grain,
And bread to the sower brings again.
So the flood of emotion deep and strong
Troubled the land as it swept along,
But left a result of holier lives,
Tenderer mothers and worthier wives.
The husband and father whose children
　　fled
And sad wife wept when his drunken
　　tread
Frightened peace from his roof-tree's
　　shade,
And a rock of offence his hearthstone
　　made,
In a strength that was not his own, be-
　　gan
To rise from the brute's to the plane of
　　man.
Old friends embraced, long held apart
By evil counsel and pride of heart ;
And penitence saw through misty tears,
In the bow of hope on its cloud of fears,
The promise of Heaven's eternal
　　years, —
The peace of God for the world's an-
　　noy, —
Beauty for ashes, and oil of joy !

Under the church of Federal Street,
Under the tread of its Sabbath feet,
Walled about by its basement stones,
Lie the marvellous preacher's bones.
No saintly honors to them are shown,
No sign nor miracle have they known ;
But he who passes the ancient church
Stops in the shade of its belfry-porch,

And ponders the wonderful life of him
Who lies at rest in that charnel dim.
Long shall the traveller strain his eye
From the railroad car, as it plunges by,
And the vanishing town behind him
　　search
For the slender spire of the Whitefield
　　Church ;
And feel for one moment the ghosts of
　　trade,
And fashion, and folly, and pleasure
　　laid,
By the thought of that life of pure in-
　　tent,
That voice of warning yet eloquent,
Of one on the errands of angels sent.
And if where he labored the flood of sin
Like a tide from the harbor-bar sets in,
And over a life of time and sense
The church-spires lift their vain de-
　　fence,
As if to scatter the bolts of God
With the points of Calvin's thunder-
　　rod, —
Still, as the gem of its civic crown,
Precious beyond the world's renown,
His memory hallows the ancient town !

THE QUAKER ALUMNI.[70]

FROM the well-springs of Hudson, the
　　sea-cliffs of Maine,
Grave men, sober matrons, you gather
　　again ;
And, with hearts warmer grown as
　　your heads grow more cool,
Play over the old game of going to
　　school.

All your strifes and vexations, your
　　whims and complaints,
(You were not saints yourselves, if the
　　children of saints !)
All your petty self-seekings and rival-
　　ries done,
Round the dear Alma Mater your hearts
　　beat as one !

How widely soe'er you have strayed
　　from the fold,
Though your " thee " has grown " you,"
　　and your drab blue and gold,
To the old friendly speech and the
　　garb's sober form,
Like the heart of Argyle to the tartan,
　　you warm.

But, the first greetings over, you glance
   round the hall ;
Your hearts call the roll, but they answer not all :
Through the turf green above them the
   dead cannot hear ;
Name by name, in the silence, falls sad
   as a tear !

In love, let us trust, they were summoned so soon
From the morning of life, while we toil
   through its noon ;
They were frail like ourselves, they had
   needs like our own,
And they rest as we rest in God's mercy
   alone.

Unchanged by our changes of spirit and
   frame,
Past, now, and henceforward the Lord
   is the same ;
Though we sink in the darkness, his
   arms break our fall,
And in death as in life, he is Father of
   all !

We are older : our footsteps, so light in
   the play
Of the far-away school-time, move slower
   to-day ; —
Here a beard touched with frost, there a
   bald, shining crown,
And beneath the cap's border gray mingles with brown.

But faith should be cheerful, and trust
   should be glad,
And our follies and sins, not our years,
   make us sad.
Should the heart closer shut as the
   bonnet grows prim,
And the face grow in length as the hat
   grows in brim ?

Life is brief, duty grave ; but, with rain-
   folded wings,
Of yesterday's sunshine the grateful
   heart sings ;
And we, of all others, have reason to
   pay
The tribute of thanks, and rejoice on
   our way ;

For the counsels that turned from the
   follies of youth ;
For the beauty of patience, the whiteness of truth ;

For the wounds of rebuke, when love
   tempered its edge ;
For the household's restraint, and the
   discipline's hedge ;

For the lessons of kindness vouchsafed
   to the least
Of the creatures of God, whether human
   or beast,
Bringing hope to the poor, lending
   strength to the frail,
In the lanes of the city, the slave-hut,
   and jail ;

For a womanhood higher and holier, by
   all
Her knowledge of good, than was Eve
   ere her fall, —
Whose task-work of duty moves lightly
   as play,
Serene as the moonlight and warm as
   the day ;

And, yet more, for the faith which embraces the whole,
Of the creeds of the ages the life and the
   soul,
Wherein letter and spirit the same
   channel run,
And man has not severed what God has
   made one !

For a sense of the Goodness revealed
   everywhere,
As sunshine impartial, and free as th
   air ;
For a trust in humanity, Heathen or
   Jew,
And a hope for all darkness The Light
   shineth through.

Who scoffs at our birthright ? — the
   words of the seers,
And the songs of the bards in the twilight of years,
All the foregleams of wisdom in santon
   and sage,
In prophet and priest, are our true
   heritage.

The Word which the reason of Plato
   discerned ;
The truth, as whose symbol the Mithra-
   fire burned ;
The soul of the world which the Stoic
   but guessed,
In the Light Universal the Quaker confessed !

No honors of war to our worthies be-
     long ;
Their plain stem of life never flowered
     into song ;
But the fountains they opened still gush
     by the way,
And the world for their healing is better
     to-day.

He who lies where the minster's groined
     arches curve down
To the tomb-crowded transept of Eng-
     land's renown,
The glorious essayist, by genius en-
     throned,
Whose pen as a sceptre the Muses all
     owned, —

Who through the world's pantheon
     walked in his pride,
Setting new statues up, thrusting old
     ones aside,
And in fiction the pencils of history
     dipped,
To gild o'er or blacken each saint in his
     crypt, —

How vainly he labored to sully with
     blame
The white bust of Penn, in the niche of
     his fame !
Self-will is self-wounding, perversity
     blind :
On himself fell the stain for the Quaker
     designed !

For the sake of his true-hearted father
     before him ;
For the sake of the dear Quaker mother
     that bore him ;
For the sake of his gifts, and the works
     that outlive him,
And his brave words for freedom, we
     freely forgive him !

There are those who take note that our
     numbers are small, —
New Gibbons who write our decline and
     our fall ;
But the Lord of the seed-field takes care
     of his own,
And the world shall yet reap what our
     sowers have sown.

The last of the sect to his fathers may go,
Leaving only his coat for some Barnum
     to show ;

But the truth will outlive him, and
     broaden with years,
Till the false dies away, and the wrong
     disappears.

Nothing fails of its end. Out of sight
     sinks the stone,
In the deep sea of time, but the circles
     sweep on,
Till the low-rippled murmurs along the
     shores run,
And the dark and dead waters leap glad
     in the sun.

Meanwhile shall we learn, in our ease,
     to forget
To the martyrs of Truth and of Freedom
     our debt ? —
Hide their words out of sight, like the
     garb that they wore,
And for Barclay's Apology offer one
     more ?

Shall we fawn round the priestcraft that
     glutted the shears,
And festooned the stocks with our grand-
     fathers' ears ? —
Talk of Woolman's unsoundness ? — count
     Penn heterodox ?
And take Cotton Mather in place of
     George Fox ? —

Make our preachers war-chaplains ? —
     quote Scripture to take
The hunted slave back, for Onesimus'
     sake ? —
Go to burning church-candles, and chant-
     ing in choir,
And on the old meeting-house stick up
     a spire ?

No ! the old paths we 'll keep until bet-
   · ter are shown,
Credit good where we find it, abroad or
     our own ;
And while " Lo here " and " Lo there "
     the multitude call,
Be true to ourselves, and do justice to
     all.

The good round about us we need not
     refuse,
Nor talk of our Zion as if we were Jews ;
But why shirk the badge which our
     fathers have worn,
Or beg the world's pardon for having
     been born ?

We need not pray over the Pharisee's
  prayer,
Nor claim that our wisdom is Benjamin's
  share.
Truth to us and to others is equal and
  one :
Shall we bottle the free air, or hoard up
  the sun ?

Well know we our birthright may serve
  but to show
How the meanest of weeds in the richest
  soil grow ;
But we need not disparage the good
  which we hold ;
Though the vessels be earthen, the treasure is gold !

Enough and too much of the sect and
  the name.
What matters our label, so truth be our
  aim ?
The creed may be wrong, but the life
  may be true,
And hearts beat the same under drab
  coats or blue.

So the man be a man, let him worship,
  at will,
In Jerusalem's courts, or on Gerizim's
  hill.
When she makes up her jewels, what
  cares yon good town
For the Baptist of WAYLAND, the Quaker
  of BROWN ?

And this green, favored island, so fresh
  and sea-blown,
When she counts up the worthies her
  annals have known,
Never waits for the pitiful gaugers of
  sect
To measure her love, and mete out her
  respect.

Three shades at this moment seem walking her strand,
Each with head halo-crowned, and with
  palms in his hand, —
Wise Berkeley, grave Hopkins, and, smiling serene
On prelate and puritan, Channing is
  seen.

One holy name bearing, no longer they
  need
Credentials of party, and pass-words of
  creed :

The new song they sing hath a threefold
  accord,
And they own one baptism, one faith,
  and one Lord !

But the golden sands run out : occasions
  like these
Glide swift into shadow, like sails on
  the seas :
While we sport with the mosses and
  pebbles ashore,
They lessen and fade, and we see them
  no more.

Forgive me, dear friends, if my vagrant
  thoughts seem
Like a school-boy's who idles and plays
  with his theme.
Forgive the light measure whose changes
  display
The sunshine and rain of our brief April
  day.

There are moments in life when the lip
  and the eye
Try the question of whether to smile or
  to cry ;
And scenes and reunions that prompt
  like our own
The tender in feeling, the playful in
  tone.

I, who never sat down with the boys and
  the girls
At the feet of your Slocums, and Cart-
  lands, and Earles, —
By courtesy only permitted to lay
On your festival's altar my poor gift, for
  day, —

I would joy in your joy : let me have a
  friend's part
In the warmth of your welcome of hand
  and of heart, —
On your play-ground of boyhood unbend
  the brow's care,
And shift the old burdens our shoulders
  must bear.

Long live the good School ! giving out
  year by year
Recruits to true manhood and womanhood dear :
Brave boys, modest maidens, in beauty
  sent forth,
The living epistles and proof of its worth !

17

In and out let the young life as steadily
flow
As in broad Narragansett the tides come
and go ;
And its sons and its daughters in prairie
and town
Remember its honor, and guard its renown.

Not vainly the gift of its founder was
made ;
Not prayerless the stones of its corner
were laid :
The blessing of Him whom in secret they
sought
Has owned the good work which the
fathers have wrought.

To Him be the glory forever ! — We bear
To the Lord of the Harvest our wheat
with the tare.
What we lack in our work may He find
in our will,
And winnow in mercy our good from the
ill !

BROWN OF OSSAWATOMIE.

JOHN BROWN OF OSSAWATOMIE spake
on his dying day :
" I will not have to shrive my soul a
priest in Slavery's pay.
But let some poor slave-mother whom I
have striven to free,
With her children, from the gallows-
stair put up a prayer for me ! "

John Brown of Ossawatomie, they led
him out to die ;
And lo ! a poor slave-mother with her
little child pressed nigh.
Then the bold, blue eye grew tender,
and the old harsh face grew mild,
As he stooped between the jeering ranks
and kissed the negro's child !

The shadows of his stormy life that moment fell apart ;
And they who blamed the bloody hand
forgave the loving heart.
That kiss from all its guilty means redeemed the good intent,
And round the grisly fighter's hair the
martyr's aureole bent !

Perish with him the folly that seeks
through evil good !
Long live the generous purpose unstained
with human blood !
Not the raid of midnight terror, but the
thought which underlies ;
Not the borderer's pride of daring, but
the Christian's sacrifice.

Nevermore may yon Blue Ridges the
Northern rifle hear,
Nor see the light of blazing homes flash
on the negro's spear.
But let the free-winged angel Truth
their guarded passes scale,
To teach that right is more than might,
and justice more than mail !

So vainly shall Virginia set her battle
in array ;
In vain her trampling squadrons knead
the winter snow with clay.
She may strike the pouncing eagle, but
she dares not harm the dove ;
And every gate she bars to Hate shall
open wide to Love !

FROM PERUGIA.

" The thing which has the most disservered the
people from the Pope, — the *unforgivable* thing,
— the breaking point between him and them, —
has been the encouragement and promotion he
gave to the officer under whom were executed
the slaughters of Perugia. *That* made the breaking point in many honest hearts that had clung
to him before." — *Harriet Beecher Stowe's "Letters from Italy."*

THE tall, sallow guardsmen their horse-
tails have spread,
Flaming out in their violet, yellow, and
red ;
And behind go the lackeys in crimson
and buff,
And the chamberlains gorgeous in velvet
and ruff ;
Next, in red-legged pomp, come the
cardinals forth,
Each a lord of the church and a prince
of the earth.

What 's this squeak of the fife, and this
batter of drum ?
Lo ! the Swiss of the Church from Perugia come, —
The militant angels, whose sabres drive
home
To the hearts of the malcontents, cursed
and abhorred,

The good Father's missives, and "Thus
    saith the Lord!"
And lend to his logic the point of the
    sword!

O maids of Etruria, gazing forlorn
O'er dark Thrasymenus, dishevelled and
    torn!
O fathers, who pluck at your gray beards
    for shame!
O mothers, struck dumb by a woe with-
    out name!
Well ye know how the Holy Church
    hireling behaves,
And his tender compassion of prisons
    and graves!

There they stand, the hired stabbers,
    the blood-stains yet fresh,
That splashed like red wine from the
    vintage of flesh, —
Grim instruments, careless as pincers
    and rack
How the joints tear apart, and the
    strained sinews crack;
But the hate that glares on them is
    sharp as their swords,
And the sneer and the scowl print the
    air with fierce words!

Off with hats, down with knees, shout
    your vivas like mad!
Here's the Pope in his holiday right-
    eousness clad,
From shorn crown to toe-nail, kiss-worn
    to the quick,
Of sainthood in purple the pattern and
    pick,
Who the *rôle* of the priest and the sol-
    dier unites,
And, praying like Aaron, like Joshua
    fights!

Is this Pio Nono the gracious, for whom
We sang our hosannas and lighted all
    Rome;
With whose advent we dreamed the new
    era began
When the priest should be human, the
    monk be a man?
Ah, the wolf 's with the sheep, and the
    fox with the fowl,
When freedom we trust to the crozier
    and cowl!

Stand aside, men of Rome! Here's a
    hangman-faced Swiss —

(A blessing for him surely can't go
    amiss) —
Would kneel down the sanctified slipper
    to kiss.
Short shrift will suffice him, — he 's
    blest beyond doubt;
But there 's blood on his hands which
    would scarcely wash out,
Though Peter himself held the baptismal
    spout!

Make way for the next! Here 's another
    sweet son!
What 's this mastiff-jawed rascal in epau-
    lets done?
He did, whispers rumor, (its truth God
    forbid!)
At Perugia what Herod at Bethlehem did.
And the mothers? — Don't name them!
    — these humors of war
They who keep him in service must par-
    don him for.

Hist! here 's the arch-knave in a car-
    dinal's hat,
With the heart of a wolf, and the stealth
    of a cat
(As if Judas and Herod together were
    rolled),
Who keeps, all as one, the Pope's con-
    science and gold,
Mounts guard on the altar, and pilfers
    from thence,
And flatters St. Peter while stealing his
    pence!

Who doubts Antonelli? Have miracles
    ceased
When robbers say mass, and Barabbas is
    priest?
When the Church eats and drinks, at its
    mystical board,
The true flesh and blood carved and
    shed by its sword,
When its martyr, unsinged, claps the
    crown on his head,
And roasts, as his proxy, his neighbor
    instead!

There! the bells jow and jangle the
    same blessed way
That they did when they rang for Bar-
    tholomew's day.
Hark! the tallow-faced monsters, nor
    women nor boys,
Vex the air with a shrill, sexless horror
    of noise.

Te Deum laudamus ! — All round without stint
The incense-pot swings with a taint of blood in 't !

And now for the blessing ! Of little account,
You know, is the old one they heard on the Mount.
Its giver was landless, his raiment was poor,
No jewelled tiara his fishermen wore ;
No incense, no lackeys, no riches, no home,
No Swiss guards ! — We order things better at Rome.

So bless us the strong hand, and curse us the weak ;
Let Austria's vulture have food for her beak ;
Let the wolf-whelp of Naples play Bomba again,
With his death-cap of silence, and halter, and chain ;
Put reason, and justice, and truth under ban ;
For the sin unforgiven is freedom for man !

FOR AN AUTUMN FESTIVAL.

The Persian's flowery gifts, the shrine
Of fruitful Ceres, charm no more ;
The woven wreaths of oak and pine
Are dust along the Isthmian shore.

But beauty hath its homage still,
And nature holds us still in debt ;
And woman's grace and household skill,
And manhood's toil, are honored yet.

And we, to-day, amidst our flowers
And fruits, have come to own again
The blessings of the summer hours,
The early and the latter rain ;

To see our Father's hand once more
Reverse for us the plenteous horn
Of autumn, filled and running o'er
With fruit, and flower, and golden corn !

Once more the liberal year laughs out
O'er richer stores than gems or gold ;
Once more with harvest-song and shout
Is Nature's bloodless triumph told.

Our common mother rests and sings,
Like Ruth, among her garnered sheaves ;
Her lap is full of goodly things,
Her brow is bright with autumn leaves.

O favors every year made new !
O gifts with rain and sunshine sent !
The bounty overruns our due,
The fulness shames our discontent.

We shut our eyes, the flowers bloom on ;
We murmur, but the corn-ears fill ;
We choose the shadow, but the sun
That casts it shines behind us still.

God gives us with our rugged soil
The power to make it Eden-fair,
And richer fruits to crown our toil
Than summer-wedded islands bear.

Who murmurs at his lot to-day ?
Who scorns his native fruit and bloom ?
Or sighs for dainties far away,
Beside the bounteous board of home ?

Thank Heaven, instead, that Freedom's arm
Can change a rocky soil to gold, —
That brave and generous lives can warm
A clime with northern ices cold.

And let these altars, wreathed with flowers
And piled with fruits, awake again
Thanksgivings for the golden hours,
The early and the latter rain !

IN WAR TIME.

TO SAMUEL E. SEWALL

AND

HARRIET W. SEWALL,

OF MELROSE.

OLOR ISCANUS queries: "Why should we
Vex at the land's ridiculous miserie?"
So on his Usk banks, in the blood-red dawn
Of England's civil strife, did careless Vaughan
Bemock his times. O friends of many years!
Though faith and trust are stronger than our fears,
And the signs promise peace with liberty,
Not thus we trifle with our country's tears
And sweat of agony. The future's gain
Is certain as God's truth ; but, meanwhile, pain
Is bitter and tears are salt : our voices take
A sober tone ; our very household songs
Are heavy with a nation's griefs and wrongs ;
And innocent mirth is chastened for the sake
Of the brave hearts that nevermore shall beat,
The eyes that smile no more, the unreturning feet !

THY WILL BE DONE.

WE see not, know not ; all our way
Is night, — with Thee alone is day :
From out the torrent's troubled drift,
Above the storm our prayers we lift,
    Thy will be done !

The flesh may fail, the heart may faint,
But who are we to make complaint,
Or dare to plead, in times like these,
The weakness of our love of ease ?
    Thy will be done !

We take with solemn thankfulness
Our burden up, nor ask it less,
And count it joy that even we
May suffer, serve, or wait for Thee,
    Whose will be done !

Though dim as yet in tint and line,
We trace Thy picture's wise design,
And thank Thee that our age supplies
Its dark relief of sacrifice.
    Thy will be done !

And if, in our unworthiness,
Thy sacrificial wine we press ;
If from Thy ordeal's heated bars
Our feet are seamed with crimson scars,
    Thy will be done !

If, for the age to come, this hour
Of trial hath vicarious power,
And, blest by Thee, our present pain,
Be Liberty's eternal gain,
    Thy will be done !

Strike, Thou the Master, we Thy keys,
The anthem of the destinies !
The minor of Thy loftier s train,
Our hearts shall breathe the old refrain,
    Thy will be done !

A WORD FOR THE HOUR.

THE firmament breaks up. In black eclipse
Light after light goes out. One evil star,
Luridly glaring through the smoke of war,
As in the dream of the Apocalypse,
Drags others down. Let us not weakly weep
Nor rashly threaten. Give us grace to keep
Our faith and patience ; wherefore should we leap
On one hand into fratricidal fight,
Or, on the other, yield eternal right,
Frame lies of law, and good and ill confound ?

What fear we ?   Safe on freedom's van-
    tage-ground
Our feet are planted : let us there remain
In unrevengeful calm, no means untried
Which truth can sanction, no just claim
    denied,
The sad spectators of a suicide !
They break the links of Union : shall
    we light
The fires of hell to weld anew the chain
On that red anvil where each blow is
    pain ?
Draw we not even now a freer breath,
As from our shoulders falls a load of
    death
Loathsome as that the Tuscan's victim
    bore
When keen with life to a dead horror
    bound ?
Why take we up the accursed thing
    again ?
Pity, forgive, but urge them back no
    more
Who, drunk with passion, flaunt dis-
    union's rag
With its vile reptile-blazon. Let us press
The golden cluster on our brave old flag
In closer union, and, if numbering less,
Brighter shall shine the stars which still
    remain.

16*th* 1*st mo.*, 1861.

"EIN FESTE BURG IST UNSER GOTT."

(LUTHER'S HYMN.)

WE wait beneath the furnace-blast
    The pangs of transformation ;
Not painlessly doth God recast
    And mould anew the nation.
      Hot burns the fire
      Where wrongs expire ;
      Nor spares the hand
      That from the land
Uproots the ancient evil.

The hand-breadth cloud the sages feared
    Its bloody rain is dropping ;
The poison plant the fathers spared
    All else is overtopping.
      East, West, South, North,
      It curses the earth ;
      All justice dies,
      And fraud and lies
Live only in its shadow.

What gives the wheat-field blades of
    steel ?
What points the rebel cannon ?
What sets the roaring rabble's heel
    On the old star-spangled pennon ?
      What breaks the oath
      Of the men o' the South ?
      What whets the knife
      For the Union's life ? —
Hark to the answer : Slavery !

Then waste no blows on lesser foes
    In strife unworthy freemen.
God lifts to-day the veil, and shows
    The features of the demon !
      O North and South,
      Its victims both,
      Can ye not cry,
      "Let slavery die !"
And union find in freedom ?

What though the cast-out spirit tear
    The nation in his going ?
We who have shared the guilt must
    share
    The pang of his o'erthrowing !
      Whate'er the loss,
      Whate'er the cross,
      Shall they complain
      Of present pain
Who trust in God's hereafter ?

For who that leans on His right arm
    Was ever yet forsaken ?
What righteous cause can suffer harm
    If He its part has taken ?
      Though wild and loud,
      And dark the cloud,
      Behind its folds
      His hand upholds
The calm sky of to-morrow !

Above the maddening cry for blood,
    Above the wild war-drumming,
Let Freedom's voice be heard, with
    good
    The evil overcoming.
      Give prayer and purse
      To stay the Curse
      Whose wrong we share,
      Whose shame we bear,
Whose end shall gladden Heaven !

In vain the bells of war shall ring
    Of triumphs and revenges,

While still is spared the evil thing
  That severs and estranges.
    But blest the ear
    That yet shall hear
    The jubilant bell
    That rings the knell
  Of Slavery forever !

Then let the selfish lip be dumb,
  And hushed the breath of sighing ;
Before the joy of peace must come
  The pains of purifying.
    God give us grace
    Each in his place
    To bear his lot,
    And, murmuring not,
  Endure and wait and labor !

TO JOHN C. FREMONT.

THY error, Fremont, simply was to act
A brave man's part, without the states-
    man's tact,
And, taking counsel but of common
    sense,
To strike at cause as well as consequence.
O, never yet since Roland wound his
    horn
At Roncesvalles, has a blast been blown
Far-heard, wide-echoed, startling as
    thine own,
Heard from the van of freedom's hope
    forlorn !
It had been safer, doubtless, for the time,
To flatter treason, and avoid offence
To that Dark Power whose underlying
    crime
Heaves upward its perpetual turbulence.
But if thine be the fate of all who break
The ground for truth's seed, or forerun
    their years
Till lost in distance, or with stout hearts
    make
A lane for freedom through the level
    spears,
Still take thou courage ! God has spoken
    through thee,
Irrevocable, the mighty words, Be free !
The land shakes with them, and the
    slave's dull ear
Turns from the rice-swamp stealthily to
    hear.
Who would recall them now must first
    arrest
The winds that blow down from the free
    Northwest,

Ruffling the Gulf ; or like a scroll roll
    back
The Mississippi to its upper springs.
Such words fulfil their prophecy, and
    lack
But the full time to harden into things.

THE WATCHERS.

BESIDE a stricken field I stood ;
On the torn turf, on grass and wood
Hung heavily the dew of blood.

Still in their fresh mounds lay the
    slain,
But all the air was quick with pain
And gusty sighs and tearful rain.

Two angels, each with drooping head
And folded wings and noiseless tread,
Watched by that valley of the dead.

The one, with forehead saintly bland
And lips of blessing, not command,
Leaned, weeping, on her olive wand. .

The other's brows were scarred and knit,
His restless eyes were watch-fires lit,
His hands for battle-gauntlets fit.

" How long ! " — I knew the voice of
    Peace, —
" Is there no respite ? — no release ? —
When shall the hopeless quarrel cease ?

" O Lord, how long ! — One human soul
Is more than any parchment scroll,
Or any flag thy winds unroll.

" What price was Ellsworth's, young
    and brave ?
How weigh the gift that Lyon gave,
Or count the cost of Winthrop's grave ?

" O brother ! if thine eye can see,
Tell how and when the end shall be,
What hope remains for thee and me."

Then Freedom sternly said : " I shun
No strife nor pang beneath the sun,
When human rights are staked and
    won.

" I knelt with Ziska's hunted flock,
I watched in Toussaint's cell of rock,
I walked with Sidney to the block.

"The moor of Marston felt my tread,
Through Jersey snows the march I led,
My voice Magenta's charges sped.

"But now, through weary day and night,
I watch a vague and aimless fight
For leave to strike one blow aright.

"On either side my foe they own :
One guards through love his ghastly
    throne,
And one through fear to reverence
    grown.

"Why wait we longer, mocked, be-
    trayed,
By open foes, or those afraid
To speed thy coming through my aid?

"Why watch to see who win or fall ? —
I shake the dust against them all,
I leave them to their senseless brawl."

"Nay," Peace implored : "yet longer
    wait ;
The doom is near, the stake is great :
God knoweth if it be too late.

"Still wait and watch ; the way prepare
Where I with folded wings of prayer
May follow, weaponless and bare."

"Too late !" the stern, sad voice re-
    plied,
"Too late !" its mournful echo sighed,
In low lament the answer died.

A rustling as of wings in flight,
An upward gleam of lessening white,
So passed the vision, sound and sight.

But round me, like a silver bell
Rung down the listening sky to tell
Of holy help, a sweet voice fell.

"Still hope and trust," it sang ; "the
    rod
Must fall, the wine-press must be trod,
But all is possible with God !"

TO ENGLISHMEN.

You flung your taunt across the wave ;
    We bore it as became us,
Well knowing that the fettered slave
Left friendly lips no option save
    To pity or to blame us.

You scoffed our plea. "Mere lack of
    will,
    Not lack of power," you told us :
We showed our free-state records ; still
You mocked, confounding good and ill,
    Slave-haters and slaveholders.

We struck at Slavery ; to the verge
    Of power and means we checked it ;
Lo ! — presto, change ! its claims you
    urge,
Send greetings to it o'er the surge,
    And comfort and protect it.

But yesterday you scarce could shake,
    In slave-abhorring rigor,
Our Northern palms for conscience' sake :
To-day you clasp the hands that ache
    With "walloping the nigger !" [71]

O Englishmen ! — in hope and creed,
    In blood and tongue our brothers !
We too are heirs of Runnymede ;
And Shakespeare's fame and Cromwell's
    deed
    Are not alone our mother's.

"Thicker than water," in one rill
    Through centuries of story
Our Saxon blood has flowed, and still
We share with you its good and ill,
    The shadow and the glory.

Joint heirs and kinfolk, leagues of wave
    Nor length of years can part us :
Your right is ours to shrine and grave,
The common freehold of the brave,
    The gift of saints and martyrs.

Our very sins and follies teach
    Our kindred frail and human :
We carp at faults with bitter speech,
The while, for one unshared by each,
    We have a score in common.

We bowed the heart, if not the knee,
    To England's Queen, God bless her !
We praised you when your slaves went
    free :
We seek to unchain ours. Will ye
    Join hands with the oppressor ?

And is it Christian England cheers
    The bruiser, not the bruiséd ?
And must she run, despite the tears
And prayers of eighteen hundred years,
    Amuck in Slavery's crusade ?

O black disgrace ! O shame and loss
Too deep for tongue to phrase on !
Tear from your flag its holy cross,
And in your van of battle toss
The pirate's skull-bone blazon !

ASTRÆA AT THE CAPITOL.

ABOLITION OF SLAVERY IN THE DIS-
TRICT OF COLUMBIA, 1862.

WHEN first I saw our banner wave
Above the nation's council-hall,
I heard beneath its marble wall
The clanking fetters of the slave !

In the foul market-place I stood,
And saw the Christian mother sold,
And childhood with its locks of gold,
Blue-eyed and fair with Saxon blood.

I shut my eyes, I held my breath,
And, smothering down the wrath and
shame
That set my Northern blood aflame,
Stood silent, — where to speak was
death.

Beside me gloomed the prison-cell
Where wasted one in slow decline
For uttering simple words of mine,
And loving freedom all too well.

The flag that floated from the dome
Flapped menace in the morning air;
I stood a perilled stranger where
The human broker made his home.

For crime was virtue : Gown and Sword
And Law their threefold sanction gave,
And to the quarry of the slave
Went hawking with our symbol-bird.

On the oppressor's side was power ;
And yet I knew that every wrong,
However old, however strong,
But waited God's avenging hour.

I knew that truth would crush the lie,—
Somehow, some time, the end would
be ;
Yet scarcely dared I hope to see
The triumph with my mortal eye.

But now I see it ! In the sun
A free flag floats from yonder dome,
And at the nation's hearth and home
The justice long delayed is done.

Not as we hoped, in calm of prayer,
The message of deliverance comes,
But heralded by roll of drums
On waves of battle-troubled air ! —

Midst sounds that madden and appall,
The song that Bethlehem's shepherds
knew !
The harp of David melting through
The demon-agonies of Saul !

Not as we hoped ; — but what are we ?
Above our broken dreams and plans
God lays, with wiser hand than man's,
The corner-stones of liberty.

I cavil not with Him : the voice
That freedom's blessed gospel tells
Is sweet to me as silver bells,
Rejoicing ! — yea, I will rejoice !

Dear friends still toiling in the sun, —
Ye dearer ones who, gone before,
Are watching from the eternal shore
The slow work by your hands begun, —

Rejoice with me ! The chastening rod
Blossoms with love ; the furnace heat
Grows cool beneath His blessed feet
Whose form is as the Son of God !

Rejoice ! Our Marah's bitter springs
Are sweetened ; on our ground of grief
Rise day by day in strong relief
The prophecies of better things.

Rejoice in hope ! The day and night
Are one with God, and one with them
Who see by faith the cloudy hem
Of Judgment fringed with Mercy's light !

THE BATTLE AUTUMN OF 1862.

THE flags of war like storm-birds fly,
The charging trumpets blow ;
Yet rolls no thunder in the sky,
No earthquake strives below.

And, calm and patient, Nature keeps
Her ancient promise well,
Though o'er her bloom and greenness
sweeps
The battle's breath of hell.

And still she walks in golden hours
  Through harvest-happy farms,
And still she wears her fruits and flowers
  Like jewels on her arms.

What mean the gladness of the plain,
  This joy of eve and morn,
The mirth that shakes the beard of grain
  And yellow locks of corn ?

Ah ! eyes may well be full of tears,
  And hearts with hate are hot ;
But even-paced come round the years,
  And Nature changes not.

She meets with smiles our bitter grief,
  With songs our groans of pain ;
She mocks with tint of flower and leaf
  The war-field's crimson stain.

Still, in the cannon's pause, we hear
  Her sweet thanksgiving-psalm ;
Too near to God for doubt or fear,
  She shares the eternal calm.

She knows the seed lies safe below
  The fires that blast and burn ;
For all the tears of blood we sow
  She waits the rich return.

She sees with clearer eye than ours
  The good of suffering born, —
The hearts that blossom like her flowers,
  And ripen like her corn.

O, give to us, in times like these,
  The vision of her eyes ;
And make her fields and fruited trees
  Our golden prophecies !

O, give to us her finer ear !
  Above this stormy din,
We too would hear the bells of cheer
  Ring peace and freedom in.

MITHRIDATES AT CHIOS.[72]

KNOW'ST thou, O slave-cursed land !
How, when the Chian's cup of guilt
  Was full to overflow, there came
God's justice in the sword of flame
That, red with slaughter to its hilt,
Blazed in the Cappadocian victor's hand ?

  The heavens are still and far ;
But, not unheard of awful Jove,

The sighing of the island slave
  Was answered, when the Ægean
    wave
The keels of Mithridates clove,
And the vines shrivelled in the breath of
  war.

  " Robbers of Chios ! hark,"
The victor cried, " to Heaven's de-
    cree !
  Pluck your last cluster from the
    vine,
  Drain your last cup of Chian wine .
Slaves of your slaves, your doom shall
    be,
In Colchian mines by Phasis rolling
    dark."

  Then rose the long lament
From the hoar sea-god's dusky caves:
  The priestess rent her hair and
    cried,
  " Woe ! woe ! The gods are sleep-
    less-eyed ! "
And, chained and scourged, the slaves
    of slaves,
The lords of Chios into exile went.

  " The gods at last pay well,"
So Hellas sang her taunting song,
  " The fisher in his net is caught,
  The Chian hath his master bought" ;
And isle from isle, with laughter long,
Took up and sped the mocking parable.

  Once more the slow, dumb years
Bring their avenging cycle round,
  And, more than Hellas taught of old,
  Our wiser lesson shall be told,
Of slaves uprising, freedom-crowned,
To break, not wield, the scourge wet
    with their blood and tears.

THE PROCLAMATION.

SAINT PATRICK, slave to Milcho of the
    herds
Of Ballymena, wakened with these
    words :
  " Arise, and flee
Out from the land of bondage, and be
    free ! "

Glad as a soul in pain, who hears from
    heaven
The angels singing of his sins forgiven,

And, wondering, sees
His prison opening to their golden keys,

He rose a man who laid him down a
    slave,
Shook from his locks the ashes of the
    grave,
        And outward trod
Into the glorious liberty of God.

He cast the symbols of his shame away ;
And, passing where the sleeping Milcho
    lay,
        Though back and limb
Smarted with wrong, he prayed, " God
    pardon him ! "

So went he forth ; but in God's time he
    came
To light on Uilline's hills a holy flame ;
        And, dying, gave
The land a saint that lost him as a
    slave.

O dark, sad millions, patiently and dumb
Waiting for God, your hour, at last, has
    come,
        And freedom's song
Breaks the long silence of your night of
    wrong !

Arise and flee ! shake off the vile re-
    straint
Of ages ; but, like Ballymena's saint,
        The oppressor spare,
Heap only on his head the coals of
    prayer.

Go forth, like him ! like him return
    again,
To bless the land whereon in bitter pain
        Ye toiled at first,
And heal with freedom what your slav-
    ery cursed.

ANNIVERSARY POEM.

[Read before the Alumni of the Friends' Yearly
Meeting School, at the Annual Meeting at Newport, R. I., 15th 6th mo., 1863.]

ONCE more, dear friends, you meet be-
    neath
        A clouded sky :
Not yet the sword has found its sheath,
And on the sweet spring airs the breath
        Of war floats by.

Yet trouble springs not from the ground,
        Nor pain from chance ;
The Eternal orders circles round,
And wave and storm find mete and
    bound
        In Providence.

Full long our feet the flowery ways
        Of peace have trod,
Content with creed and garb and phrase
A harder path in earlier days
        Led up to God.

Too cheaply truths, once purchased dear,
        Are made our own ;
Too long the world has smiled to hear
Our boast of full corn in the ear
        By others sown ;

To see us stir the martyr fires
        Of long ago,
And wrap our satisfied desires
In the singed mantles that our sires
        Have dropped below.

But now the cross our worthies bore
        On us is laid ;
Profession's quiet sleep is o'er,
And in the scale of truth once more
        Our faith is weighed.

The cry of innocent blood at last
        Is calling down
An answer in the whirlwind-blast,
The thunder and the shadow cast
        From Heaven's dark frown.

The land is red with judgments.   Who
        Stands guiltless forth ?
Have *we* been faithful as we knew,
To God and to our brother true,
        To Heaven and Earth ?

How faint, through din of merchandise
        And count of gain,
Have seemed to us the captive's cries !
How far away the tears and sighs
        Of souls in pain !

This day the fearful reckoning comes
        To each and all ;
We hear amidst our peaceful homes
The summons of the conscript drums,
        The bugle's call.

Our path is plain ; the war-net draws
        Round us in vain,

While, faithful to the Higher Cause,
We keep our fealty to the laws
   Through patient pain.

The levelled gun, the battle-brand,
   We may not take :
But, calmly loyal, we can stand
And suffer with our suffering land
   For conscience' sake.

Why ask for ease where all is pain ?
   Shall *we* alone
Be left to add our gain to gain,
When over Armageddon's plain
   The trump is blown ?

To suffer well is well to serve ;
   Safe in our Lord
The rigid lines of law shall curve
To spare us ; from our heads shall swerve
   Its smiting sword.

And light is mingled with the gloom,
   And joy with grief ;
Divinest compensations come,
Through thorns of judgment mercies
    bloom
   In sweet relief.

Thanks for our privilege to bless,
   By word and deed,
The widow in her keen distress,
The childless and the fatherless,
   The hearts that bleed !

For fields of duty, opening wide,
   Where all our powers
Are tasked the eager steps to guide
Of millions on a path untried :
   THE SLAVE IS OURS !

Ours by traditions dear and old,
   Which make the race
Our wards to cherish and uphold,
And cast their freedom in the mould
   Of Christian grace.

And we may tread the sick-bed floors
   Where strong men pine,
And, down the groaning corridors,
Pour freely from our liberal stores
   The oil and wine.

Who murmurs that in these dark days
   His lot is cast ?
God's hand within the shadow lays
The stones whereon His gates of praise
   Shall rise at last.

Turn and o'erturn, O outstretched Hand!
   Nor stint, nor stay ;
The years have never dropped their
    sand
On mortal issue vast and grand
   As ours to-day.

Already, on the sable ground
   Of man's despair
Is Freedom's glorious picture found,
With all its dusky hands unbound
   Upraised in prayer.

O, small shall seem all sacrifice
   And pain and loss,
When God shall wipe the weeping eyes
For suffering give the victor's prize,
   The crown for cross !

AT PORT ROYAL.

THE tent-lights glimmer on the land,
   The ship-lights on the sea ;
The night-wind smooths with drifting
    sand
   Our track on lone Tybee.

At last our grating keels outslide,
   Our good boats forward swing ;
And while we ride the land-locked tide,
   Our negroes row and sing.

For dear the bondman holds his gifts
   Of music and of song :
The gold that kindly Nature sifts
   Among his sands of wrong ;

The power to make his toiling days
   And poor home-comforts please ;
The quaint relief of mirth that plays
   With sorrow's minor keys.

Another glow than sunset's fire
   Has filled the West with light,
Where field and garner, barn and byre,
   Are blazing through the night.

The land is wild with fear and hate,
   The rout runs mad and fast ;
From hand to hand, from gate to gate
   The flaming brand is passed.

The lurid glow falls strong across
   Dark faces broad with smiles :
Not theirs the terror, hate, and loss
   That fire yon blazing piles.

With oar-strokes timing to their song,
  They weave in simple lays
The pathos of remembered wrong,
  The hope of better days, —

The triumph-note that Miriam sung,
  The joy of uncaged birds :
Softening with Afric's mellow tongue
  Their broken Saxon words.

SONG OF THE NEGRO BOATMEN.

O, praise an' tanks ! De Lord he come
  To set de people free ;
An' massa tink it day ob doom,
  An' we ob jubilee.
De Lord dat heap de Red Sea waves
  He jus' as 'trong as den ;
He say de word : we las' night slaves ;
  To-day, de Lord's freemen.
    De yam will grow, de cotton blow,
      We'll hab de rice an' corn ;
    O nebber you fear, if nebber you
        hear
      De driver blow his horn !

Ole massa on he trabbels gone ;
  He leaf de land behind :
De Lord's breff blow him furder on,
  Like corn-shuck in de wind.
We own de hoe, we own de plough,
  We own de hands dat hold ;
We sell de pig, we sell de cow,
  But nebber chile be sold.
    De yam will grow, de cotton blow,
      We'll hab de rice an' corn ;
    O nebber you fear, if nebber you
      . hear
      De driver blow his horn !

We pray de Lord : he gib us signs
  Dat some day we be free ;
De norf-wind tell it to de pines,
  De wild-duck to de sea ;
We tink it when de church-bell ring,
  We dream it in de dream ;
De rice-bird mean it when he sing,
  De eagle when he scream.
    De yam will grow, de cotton blow,
      We'll hab de rice an' corn :
    O nebber you fear, if nebber you
        hear
      De driver blow his horn !

We know de promise nebber fail,
  An' nebber lie de word ;

So like de 'postles in de jail,
  We waited for de Lord :
An' now he open ebery door,
  An' trow away de key ;
He tink we lub him so before,
  We lub him better free.
    De yam will grow, de cotton blow,
      He'll gib de rice an' corn ;
    O nebber you fear, if nebber you
        hear
      De driver blow his horn !

So sing our dusky gondoliers ;
  And with a secret pain,
And smiles that seem akin to tears,
  We hear the wild refrain.

We dare not share the negro's trust,
  Nor yet his hope deny ;
We only know that God is just,
  And every wrong shall die.

Rude seems the song ; each swarthy face,
  Flame-lighted, ruder still :
We start to think that hapless race
  Must shape our good or ill ;

That laws of changeless justice bind
  Oppressor with oppressed ;
And, close as sin and suffering joined,
  We march to Fate abreast.

Sing on, poor hearts ! your chant shall
      be
  Our sign of blight or bloom, —
The Vala-song of Liberty,
  Or death-rune of our doom !

BARBARA FRIETCHIE.

UP from the meadows rich with corn,
Clear in the cool September morn,

The clustered spires of Frederick stand
Green-walled by the hills of Maryland.

Round about them orchards sweep,
Apple and peach tree fruited deep,

Fair as the garden of the Lord
To the eyes of the famished rebel horde,

On that pleasant morn of the early fall
When Lee marched over the mountain-
      wall, —

Over the mountains winding down,
Horse and foot, into Frederick town.

Forty flags with their silver stars,
Forty flags with their crimson bars,

Flapped in the morning wind : the sun
Of noon looked down, and saw not one.

Up rose old Barbara Frietchie then,
Bowed with her fourscore years and ten ;

Bravest of all in Frederick town,
She took up the flag the men hauled
    down ;

In her attic window the staff she set,
To show that one heart was loyal yet.

Up the street came the rebel tread,
Stonewall Jackson riding ahead.

Under his slouched hat left and right
He glanced : the old flag met his sight.

"Halt !"—the dust-brown ranks stood
    fast.
"Fire !"—out blazed the rifle-blast.

It shivered the window, pane and sash ;
It rent the banner with seam and gash.

Quick, as it fell, from the broken staff
Dame Barbara snatched the silken scarf.

She leaned far out on the window-sill,
And shook it forth with a royal will.

"Shoot, if you must, this old gray head,
But spare your country's flag," she said.

A shade of sadness, a blush of shame,
Over the face of the leader came ;

The nobler nature within him stirred
To life at that woman's deed and word:

"Who touches a hair of yon gray head
Dies like a dog !   March on !" he said.

All day long through Frederick street
Sounded the tread of marching feet :

All day long that free flag tost
Over the heads of the rebel host.

Ever its torn folds rose and fell
On the loyal winds that loved it well ;

And through the hill-gaps sunset light
Shone over it with a warm good-night.

Barbara Frietchie's work is o'er,
And the Rebel rides on his raids no
    more.

Honor to her ! and let a tear
Fall, for her sake, on Stonewall's bier.

Over Barbara Frietchie's grave,
Flag of Freedom and Union, wave !

Peace and order and beauty draw
Round thy symbol of light and law ;

And ever the stars above look down
On thy stars below in Frederick town !

BALLADS.

COBBLER KEEZAR'S VISION.[73]

THE beaver cut his timber
  With patient teeth that day,
The minks were fish-wards, and the
    crows
  Surveyors of highway, —

When Keezar sat on the hillside
  Upon his cobbler's form,
With a pan of coals on either hand
  To keep his waxed-ends warm.

And there, in the golden weather,
  He stitched and hammered and sung ;
In the brook he moistened his leather,
  In the pewter mug his tongue.

Well knew the tough old Teuton
  Who brewed the stoutest ale,
And he paid the goodwife's reckoning
  In the coin of song and tale.

The songs they still are singing
  Who dress the hills of vine,

The tales that haunt the Brocken
　And whisper down the Rhine.

Woodsy and wild and lonesome,
　The swift stream wound away,
Through birches and scarlet maples
　Flashing in foam and spray, —

Down on the sharp-horned ledges
　Plunging in steep cascade,
Tossing its white-maned waters
　Against the hemlock's shade.

Woodsy and wild and lonesome,
　East and west and north and south ;
Only the village of fishers
　Down at the river's mouth ;

Only here and there a clearing,
　With its farm-house rude and new,
And tree-stumps, swart as Indians,
　Where the scanty harvest grew.

No shout of home-bound reapers,
　No vintage-song he heard,
And on the green no dancing feet
　The merry violin stirred.

" Why should folk be glum," said Kee-
　zar,
　" When Nature herself is glad,
And the painted woods are laughing
　At the faces so sour and sad ? "

Small heed had the careless cobbler
　What sorrow of heart was theirs
Who travailed in pain with the births
　of God,
And planted a state with prayers, —

Hunting of witches and warlocks,
　Smiting the heathen horde, —
One hand on the mason's trowel,
　And one on the soldier's sword !

But give him his ale and cider,
　Give him his pipe and song,
Little he cared for Church or State,
　Or the balance of right and wrong.

" 'T is work, work, work," he mut-
　tered, —
　" And for rest a snuffle of psalms ! "
He smote on his leathern apron
　With his brown and waxen palms.

" O for the purple harvests
　Of the days when I was young !

For the merry grape-stained maidens,
　And the pleasant songs they sung !

" O for the breath of vineyards,
　Of apples and nuts and wine !
For an oar to row and a breeze to blow
　Down the grand old river Rhine ! "

A tear in his blue eye glistened,
　And dropped on his beard so gray.
" Old, old am I," said Keezar,
　" And the Rhine flows far away ! "

But a cunning man was the cobbler ;
　He could call the birds from the trees,
Charm the black snake out of the ledges,
　And bring back the swarming bees.

All the virtues of herbs and metals,
　All the lore of the woods, he knew,
And the arts of the Old World mingled
　With the marvels of the New.

Well he knew the tricks of magic,
　And the lapstone on his knee
Had the gift of the Mormon's goggles
　Or the stone of Doctor Dee.

For the mighty master Agrippa
　Wrought it with spell and rhyme
From a fragment of mystic moonstone
　In the tower of Nettesheim.

To a cobbler Minnesinger
　The marvellous stone gave he, —
And he gave it, in turn, to Keezar,
　Who brought it over the sea.

He held up that mystic lapstone,
　He held it up like a lens,
And he counted the long years coming
　By twenties and by tens.

" One hundred years," quoth Keezar,
　" And fifty have I told :
Now open the new before me,
　And shut me out the old ! "

Like a cloud of mist, the blackness
　Rolled from the magic stone,
And a marvellous picture mingled
　The unknown and the known.

Still ran the stream to the river,
　And river and ocean joined ;
And there were the bluffs and the blue
　sea-line,
　And cold north hills behind.

But the mighty forest was broken
    By many a steepled town,
By many a white-walled farm-house,
    And many a garner brown.

Turning a score of mill-wheels,
    The stream no more ran free ;
White sails on the winding river,
    White sails on the far-off sea.

Below in the noisy village
    The flags were floating gay,
And shone on a thousand faces
    The light of a holiday.

Swiftly the rival ploughmen
    Turned the brown earth from their
        shares ;
Here were the farmer's treasures,
    There were the craftsman's wares.

Golden the goodwife's butter,
    Ruby her currant-wine ;
Grand were the strutting turkeys,
    Fat were the beeves and swine.

Yellow and red were the apples,
    And the ripe pears russet-brown,
And the peaches had stolen blushes
    From the girls who shook them
        down.

And with blooms of hill and wild-
        wood,
    That shame the toil of art,
Mingled the gorgeous blossoms
    Of the garden's tropic heart.

"What is it I see ? " said Keezar :
    " Am I here, or am I there ?
Is it a fête at Bingen ?
    Do I look on Frankfort fair ?

"But where are the clowns and pup-
        pets,
    And imps with horns and tail ?
And where are the Rhenish flagons ?
    And where is the foaming ale ?

"Strange things, I know, will hap-
        pen, —
Strange things the Lord permits ;
But that droughty folk should be jolly
    Puzzles my poor old wits.

" Here are smiling manly faces,
    And the maiden's step is gay ;

Nor sad by thinking, nor mad by drink
        ing,
    Nor mopes, nor fools, are they.

" Here 's pleasure without regretting,
    And good without abuse,
The holiday and the bridal
    Of beauty and of use.

" Here 's a priest and there is a Qua-
        ker, —
    Do the cat and dog agree ?
Have they burned the stocks for oven-
        wood ?
    Have they cut down the gallows-tree ?

" Would the old folk know their chil-
        dren ?
    Would they own the graceless town,
With never a ranter to worry
    And never a witch to drown ? "

Loud laughed the cobbler Keezar,
    Laughed like a school-boy gay ;
Tossing his arms above him,
    The lapstone rolled away.

It rolled down the rugged hillside,
    It spun like a wheel bewitched,
It plunged through the leaning willows,
    And into the river pitched.

There, in the deep, dark water,
    The magic stone lies still,
Under the leaning willows
    In the shadow of the hill.

But oft the idle fisher
    Sits on the shadowy bank,
And his dreams make marvellous pic-
        tures
    Where the wizard's lapstone sank.

And still, in the summer twilights,
    When the river seems to run
Out from the inner glory,
    Warm with the melted sun,

The weary mill-girl lingers
    Beside the charmèd stream,
And the sky and the golden water
    Shape and color her dream.

Fair wave the sunset gardens,
    The rosy signals fly ;
Her homestead beckons from the cloud,
    And love goes sailing by.

AMY WENTWORTH.

TO W. B.

As they who watch by sick-beds find
  relief
Unwittingly from the great stress of
  grief
And anxious care in fantasies out-
  wrought
From the hearth's embers flickering low,
  or caught
From whispering wind, or tread of pass-
  ing feet,
Or vagrant memory calling up some
  sweet
Snatch of old song or romance, whence
  or why
They scarcely know or ask, — so, thou
  and I,
Nursed in the faith that Truth alone is
  strong
In the endurance which outwearies
  Wrong,
With meek persistence baffling brutal
  force,
And trusting God against the universe, —
We, doomed to watch a strife we may
  not share
With other weapons than the patriot's
  prayer,
Yet owning, with full hearts and moist-
  ened eyes,
The awful beauty of self-sacrifice,
And wrung by keenest sympathy for all
Who give their loved ones for the living
  wall
'Twixt law and treason, — in this evil
  day
May haply find, through automatic play
Of pen and pencil, solace to our pain,
And hearten others with the strength we
  gain.
I know it has been said our times re-
  quire
No play of art, nor dalliance with the
  lyre,
No weak essay with Fancy's chloroform
To calm the hot, mad pulses of the
  storm,
But the stern war-blast rather, such as
  sets
The battle's teeth of serried bayonets,
And pictures grim as Vernet's.   Yet
  with these
Some softer tints may blend, and milder
  keys

Relieve the storm-stunned ear.   Let us
  keep sweet,
If so we may, our hearts, even while we
  eat
The bitter harvest of our own device
And half a century's moral cowardice.
As Nürnberg sang while Wittenberg
  defied,
And Kranach painted by his Luther's
  side,
And through the war-march of the Pu-
  ritan
The silver stream of Marvell's music
  ran,
So let the household melodies be sung,
The pleasant pictures on the wall be
  hung, —
So let us hold against the hosts of night
And slavery all our vantage-ground of
  light.
Let Treason boast its savagery, and
  shake
From its flag-folds its symbol rattle-
  snake,
Nurse its fine arts, lay human skins in
  tan,
And carve its pipe-bowls from the bones
  of man,
And make the tale of Fijian banquets
  dull
By drinking whiskey from a loyal
  skull, —
But let us guard, till this sad war shall
  cease,
(God grant it soon !) the graceful arts
  of peace :
No foes are conquered who the victors
  teach
Their vandal manners and barbaric
  speech.

And while, with hearts of thankfulness,
  we bear
Of the great common burden our full
  share,
Let none upbraid us that the waves
  entice
Thy sea-dipped pencil, or some quaint
  device,
Rhythmic and sweet, beguiles my pen
  away
From the sharp strifes and sorrows of
  to-day.
Thus, while the east-wind keen from
  Labrador
Sings in the leafless elms, and from the
  shore

18

Of the great sea comes the monotonous
    roar
Of the long-breaking surf, and all the
    sky
Is gray with cloud, home-bound and
    dull, I try
To time a simple legend to the sounds
Of winds in the woods, and waves on
    pebbled bounds, —
A song for oars to chime with, such as
    might
Be sung by tired sea-painters, who at
    night
Look from their hemlock camps, by
    quiet cove
Or beach, moon-lighted, on the waves
    they love.
(So hast thou looked, when level sunset
    lay
On the calm bosom of some Eastern
    bay,
And all the spray-moist rocks and waves
    that rolled
Up the white sand-slopes flashed with
    ruddy gold.)
Something it has — a flavor of the
    sea,
And the sea's freedom — which reminds
    of thee.
Its faded picture, dimly smiling down
From the blurred fresco of the ancient
    town,
I have not touched with warmer tints in
    vain,
If, in this dark, sad year, it steals one
    thought from pain.

HER fingers shame the ivory keys
    They dance so light along ;
The bloom upon her parted lips
    Is sweeter than the song.

O perfumed suitor, spare thy smiles !
    Her thoughts are not of thee ;
She better loves the salted wind,
    The voices of the sea.

Her heart is like an outbound ship
    That at its anchor swings ;
The murmur of the stranded shell
    Is in the song she sings.

She sings, and, smiling, hears her praise,
    But dreams the while of one
Who watches from his sea-blown deck
    The icebergs in the sun.

She questions all the winds that blow,
    And every fog-wreath dim,
And bids the sea-birds flying north
    Bear messages to him.

She speeds them with the thanks of men
    He perilled life to save,
And grateful prayers like holy oil
    To smooth for him the wave.

Brown Viking of the fishing-smack !
    Fair toast of all the town ! —
The skipper's jerkin ill beseems
    The lady's silken gown !

But ne'er shall Amy Wentworth wear
    For him the blush of shame
Who dares to set his manly gifts
    Against her ancient name.

The stream is brightest at its spring,
    And blood is not like wine ;
Nor honored less than he who heirs
    Is he who founds a line.

Full lightly shall the prize be won,
    If love be Fortune's spur ;
And never maiden stoops to him
    Who lifts himself to her.

Her home is brave in Jaffrey Street,
    With stately stairways worn
By feet of old Colonial knights
    And ladies gentle-born.

Still green about its ample porch
    The English ivy twines,
Trained back to show in English oak
    The herald's carven signs.

And on her, from the wainscot old,
    Ancestral faces frown, —
And this has worn the soldier's sword,
    And that the judge's gown.

But, strong of will and proud as they,
    She walks the gallery floor
As if she trod her sailor's deck
    By stormy Labrador !

The sweetbrier blooms on Kittery-side,
    And green are Elliot's bowers ;
Her garden is the pebbled beach,
    The mosses are her flowers.

She looks across the harbor-bar
    To see the white gulls fly ;

His greeting from the Northern sea
Is in their clanging cry.

She hums a song, and dreams that he,
As in its romance old,
Shall homeward ride with silken sails
And masts of beaten gold !

O, rank is good, and gold is fair,
And high and low mate ill ;
But love has never known a law
Beyond its own sweet will !

THE COUNTESS.

TO E. W.

I KNOW not, Time and Space so inter-
vene,
Whether, still waiting with a trust serene,
Thou bearest up thy fourscore years and
ten,
Or, called at last, art now Heaven's citizen ;
But, here or there, a pleasant thought
of thee,
Like an old friend, all day has been
with me.
The shy, still boy, for whom thy kindly
hand
Smoothed his hard pathway to the won-
der-land
Of thought and fancy, in gray manhood
yet
Keeps green the memory of his early
debt.
To-day, when truth and falsehood speak
their words
Through hot-lipped cannon and the teeth
of swords,
Listening with quickened heart and ear
intent
To each sharp clause of that stern argu-
ment,
I still can hear at times a softer note
Of the old pastoral music round me float,
While through the hot gleam of our
civil strife
Looms the green mirage of a simpler
life.
As, at his alien post, the sentinel
Drops the old bucket in the homestead
well,
And hears old voices in the winds that
toss

Above his head the live-oak's beard of
moss,
So, in our trial-time, and under skies
Shadowed by swords like Islam's paradise,
I wait and watch, and let my fancy
stray
To milder scenes and youth's Arcadian
day ;
And howsoe'er the pencil dipped in
dreams
Shades the brown woods or tints the
sunset streams,
The country doctor in the foreground
seems,
Whose ancient sulky down the village
lanes
Dragged, like a war-car, captive ills and
pains.
I could not paint the scenery of my
song,
Mindless of one who looked thereon so
long ;
Who, night and day, on duty's lonely
round,
Made friends o' the woods and rocks,
and knew the sound
Of each small brook, and what the hill-
side trees
Said to the winds that touched their
leafy keys ;
Who saw so keenly and so well could
paint
The village-folk, with all their humors
quaint, —
The parson ambling on his wall-eyed
roan,
Grave and erect, with white hair back-
ward blown ;
The tough old boatman, half amphibious
grown ;
The muttering witch-wife of the gossip's
tale,
And the loud straggler levying his black-
mail, —
Old customs, habits, superstitions, fears,
All that lies buried under fifty years.
To thee, as is most fit, I bring my
lay,
And, grateful, own the debt I cannot
pay.

Over the wooded northern ridge,
Between its houses brown,
To the dark tunnel of the bridge
The street comes straggling down.

You catch a glimpse, through birch and
　　pine,
　Of gable, roof, and porch,
The tavern with its swinging sign,
　The sharp horn of the church.

The river's steel-blue crescent curves
　To meet, in ebb and flow,
The single broken wharf that serves
　For sloop and gundelow.

With salt sea-scents along its shores
　The heavy hay-boats crawl,
The long antennæ of their oars
　In lazy rise and fall.

Along the gray abutment's wall
　The idle shad-net dries;
The toll-man in his cobbler's stall
　Sits smoking with closed eyes.

You hear the pier's low undertone
　Of waves that chafe and gnaw ;
You start, — a skipper's horn is blown
　To raise the creaking draw.

At times a blacksmith's anvil sounds
　With slow and sluggard beat,
Or stage-coach on its dusty rounds
　Wakes up the staring street.

A place for idle eyes and ears,
　A cobwebbed nook of dreams ;
Left by the stream whose waves are
　　years
　The stranded village seems.

And there, like other moss and rust,
　The native dweller clings,
And keeps, in uninquiring trust,
　The old, dull round of things.

The fisher drops his patient lines,
　The farmer sows his grain,
Content to hear the murmuring pines
　Instead of railroad-train.

Go where, along the tangled steep
　That slopes against the west,
The hamlet's buried idlers sleep
　In still profounder rest.

Throw back the locust's flowery plume,
　The birch's pale-green scarf,
And break the web of brier and bloom
　From name and epitaph.

A simple muster-roll of death,
　Of pomp and romance shorn,
The dry, old names that common breath
　Has cheapened and outworn.

Yet pause by one low mound, and part
　The wild vines o'er it laced,
And read the words by rustic art
　Upon its headstone traced.

Haply yon white-haired villager
　Of fourscore years can say
What means the noble name of her
　Who sleeps with common clay

An exile from the Gascon land
　Found refuge here and rest,
And loved, of all the village band,
　Its fairest and its best.

He knelt with her on Sabbath morns,
　He worshipped through her eyes,
And on the pride that doubts and scorns
　Stole in her faith's surprise.

Her simple daily life he saw
　By homeliest duties tried,　.
In all things by an untaught law
　Of fitness justified.

For her his rank aside he laid ;
　He took the hue and tone
Of lowly life and toil, and made
　Her simple ways his own.

Yet still, in gay and careless ease,
　To harvest-field or dance
He brought the gentle courtesies,
　The nameless grace of France.

And she who taught him love not less
　From him she loved in turn
Caught in her sweet unconsciousness
　What love is quick to learn.

Each grew to each in pleased accord,
　Nor knew the gazing town
If she looked upward to her lord
　Or he to her looked down.

How sweet, when summer's day was o'er,
　His violin's mirth and wail,
The walk on pleasant Newbury's shore,
　The river's moonlit sail !

Ah ! life is brief, though love be long ;
　The altar and the bier,
The burial hymn and bridal song,
　Were both in one short year !

Her rest is quiet on the hill,
 Beneath the locust's bloom :
Far off her lover sleeps as still
 Within his scutcheoned tomb.

The Gascon lord, the village maid,
 In death still clasp their hands ;
The love that levels rank and grade
 Unites their severed lands.

What matter whose the hillside grave,
 Or whose the blazoned stone ?
Forever to her western wave
 Shall whisper blue Garonne !

O Love ! — so hallowing every soil
 That gives thy sweet flower room,
Wherever, nursed by ease or toil,
 The human heart takes bloom ! —

Plant of lost Eden, from the sod
 Of sinful earth unriven,
White blossom of the trees of God
 Dropped down to us from heaven ! —

This tangled waste of mound and stone
 Is holy for thy sake ;
A sweetness which is all thy own
 Breathes out from fern and brake.

And while ancestral pride shall twine
 The Gascon's tomb with flowers,
Fall sweetly here, O song of mine,
 With summer's bloom and showers !

And let the lines that severed seem
 Unite again in thee,
As western wave and Gallic stream
 Are mingled in one sea !

OCCASIONAL POEMS

NAPLES.

1860.

INSCRIBED TO ROBERT C. WATERSTON,
OF BOSTON.

I GIVE thee joy ! — I know to thee
 The dearest spot on earth must
 be
Where sleeps thy loved one by the summer sea ;

Where, near her sweetest poet's
 tomb,
 The land of Virgil gave thee room
To lay thy flower with her perpetual
 bloom.

I know that when the sky shut
 down
Behind thee on the gleaming town,
On Baiæ's baths and Posilippo's crown ;

And, through thy tears, the mocking day
 Burned Ischia's mountain lines
 away,
And Capri melted in its sunny bay, —

Through thy great farewell sorrow
 shot
The sharp pang of a bitter thought
That slaves must tread around that holy
 spot.

Thou knewest not the land was
 blest
In giving thy beloved rest,
Holding the fond hope closer to her
 breast

That every sweet and saintly grave
 Was freedom's prophecy, and gave
The pledge of Heaven to sanctify and
 save.

That pledge is answered. To thy ear
 The unchained city sends its cheer,
And, turned to joy, the muffled bells of
 fear

Ring Victor in. The land sits free
 And happy by the summer sea,
And Bourbon Naples now is Italy !

She smiles above her broken chain
 The languid smile that follows pain,
Stretching her cramped limbs to the sun
 again.

O, joy for all, who hear her call
   From gray Camaldoli's convent-wall
And Elmo's towers to freedom's carni-
   val!

A new life breathes among her vines
   And olives, like the breath of pines
Blown downward from the breezy Apen-
   nines.

   Lean, O, my friend, to meet that
      breath,
   Rejoice as one who witnesseth
Beauty from ashes rise, and life from
   death!

Thy sorrow shall no more be pain,
   Its tears shall fall in sunlit rain,
Writing the grave with flowers : " Arisen
   again!"

THE SUMMONS.

MY ear is full of summer sounds,
   Of summer sights my languid eye ;
Beyond the dusty village bounds
I loiter in my daily rounds,
   And in the noon-time shadows lie.

I hear the wild bee wind his horn,
   The bird swings on the ripened wheat,
The long green lances of the corn
Are tilting in the winds of morn,
   The locust shrills his song of heat.

Another sound my spirit hears,
   A deeper sound that drowns them
      all, —
A voice of pleading choked with tears,
The call of human hopes and fears,
   The Macedonian cry to Paul!

The storm-bell rings, the trumpet blows ;
   I know the word and countersign ;
Wherever Freedom's vanguard goes,
Where stand or fall her friends or foes,
   I know the place that should be mine.

Shamed be the hands that idly fold,
   And lips that woo the reed's accord,
When laggard Time the hour has tolled
For true with false and new with old
   To fight the battles of the Lord!

O brothers! blest by partial Fate
   With power to match the will and
      deed,

To him your summons comes too late
Who sinks beneath his armor's weight,
   And has no answer but God-speed!

THE WAITING.

I WAIT and watch : before my eyes
   Methinks the night grows thin and
      gray ;
I wait and watch the eastern skies
To see the golden spears uprise
   Beneath the oriflamme of day!

Like one whose limbs are bound in
      trance
   I hear the day-sounds swell and grow,
And see across the twilight glance,
Troop after troop, in swift advance,
   The shining ones with plumes of
      snow !

I know the errand of their feet,
   I know what mighty work is theirs ;
I can but lift up hands unmeet,
The threshing-floors of God to beat,
   And speed them with unworthy
      prayers.

I will not dream in vain despair
   The steps of progress wait for me :
The puny leverage of a hair
The planet's impulse well may spare,
   A drop of dew the tided sea.

The loss, if loss there be, is mine,
   And yet not mine if understood ;
For one shall grasp and one resign,
One drink life's rue, and one its wine,
   And God shall make the balance
      good.

O power to do ! O baffled will !
   O prayer and action ! ye are one.
Who may not strive, may yet fulfil
The harder task of standing still,
   And good but wished with God is
      done !

MOUNTAIN PICTURES.

I.

FRANCONIA FROM THE PEMIGEWASSET.

ONCE more, O Mountains of the North,
    unveil
   Your brows, and lay your cloudy
    mantles by !

And once more, ere the eyes that seek
  ye fail,
Uplift against the blue walls of the sky
Your mighty shapes, and let the sun-
  shine weave
  Its golden net-work in your belting
    woods,
  Smile down in rainbows from your
    falling floods,
And on your kingly brows at morn and eve
  Set crowns of fire ! So shall my soul
    receive
Haply the secret of your calm and
  strength,
  Your unforgotten beauty interfuse
  My common life, your glorious shapes
    and hues
  And sun-dropped splendors at my
    bidding come,
  Loom vast through dreams, and
    stretch in billowy length
From the sea-level of my lowland home !

They rise before me ! Last night's
  thunder-gust
Roared not in vain : for where its
  lightnings thrust
Their tongues of fire, the great peaks
  seem so near,
Burned clean of mist, so starkly bold
  and clear,
I almost pause the wind in the pines to
  hear,
The loose rock's fall, the steps of brows-
  ing deer.
The clouds that shattered on yon slide-
  worn walls
  And splintered on the rocks their
    spears of rain
Have set in play a thousand waterfalls,
Making the dusk and silence of the woods
Glad with the laughter of the chasing
  floods,
And luminous with blown spray and
  silver gleams,
While, in the vales below, the dry-
  lipped streams
  Sing to the freshened meadow-lands
    again.
So, let me hope, the battle-storm that
  beats
  The land with hail and fire may pass
    away
  With its spent thunders at the break of
    day,
Like last night's clouds, and leave, as it
  retreats,

A greener earth and fairer sky be-
  hind,
Blown crystal-clear by Freedom's
  Northern wind !

II.

MONADNOCK FROM WACHUSET.

I WOULD I were a painter, for the sake
  Of a sweet picture, and of her who led,
  A fitting guide, with reverential tread,
Into that mountain mystery. First a
  lake
  Tinted with sunset ; next the wavy
    lines
    Of far receding hills ; and yet more
    far,
  Monadnock lifting from his night of
    pines
    His rosy forehead to the evening star.
Beside us, purple-zoned, Wachuset laid
  His head against the West, whose
    warm light made
    His aureole ; and o'er him, sharp
    and clear,
Like a shaft of lightning in mid-launch-
  ing stayed,
  A single level cloud-line, shone upon
    By the fierce glances of the sunken sun,
    Menaced the darkness with its gold-
    en spear !

So twilight deepened round us. Still
  and black
The great woods climbed the mountain
  at our back ;
And on their skirts, where yet the linger-
  ing day
On the shorn greenness of the clearing lay,
  The brown old farm-house like a
    bird's-nest hung.
With home-life sounds the desert air was
  stirred :
The bleat of sheep along the hill we
  heard,
The bucket plashing in the cool, sweet
  well,
The pasture-bars that clattered as they
  fell ;
Dogs barked, fowls fluttered, cattle
  lowed ; the gate
Of the barn-yard creaked beneath the
  merry weight
  Of sun-brown children, listening,
    while they swung,

The welcome sound of supper-call
    to hear ;
And down the shadowy lane, in
    tinklings clear,
The pastoral curfew of the cow-bell
    rung.
Thus soothed and pleased, our backward
    path we took,
Praising the farmer's home. He only
    spake,
Looking into the sunset o'er the lake,
    Like one to whom the far-off is
    most near :
"Yes, most folks think it has a pleasant
    look ;
I love it for my good old mother's sake,
    Who lived and died here in the
    peace of God ! "
The lesson of his words we pondered
    o'er,
As silently we turned the eastern flank
Of the mountain, where its shadow
    deepest sank,
Doubling the night along our rugged
    road :
We felt that man was more than his
    abode, —
    The inward life than Nature's rai-
    ment more ;
And the warm sky, the sundown-tinted
    hill,
    The forest and the lake, seemed
    dwarfed and dim
Before the saintly soul, whose human
    will
    Meekly in the Eternal footsteps
    trod,
Making her homely toil and household
    ways
An earthly echo of the song of praise
    Swelling from angel lips and harps of
    seraphim.

OUR RIVER.

FOR A SUMMER FESTIVAL AT "THE
    LAURELS" ON THE MERRIMACK.

ONCE more on yonder laurelled height
    The summer flowers have budded ;
Once more with summer's golden light
    The vales of home are flooded ;
And once more, by the grace of Him
    Of every good the Giver,
We sing upon its wooded rim
    The praises of our river:

Its pines above, its waves below,
    The west-wind down it blowing,
As fair as when the young Brissot
    Beheld it seaward flowing, —
And bore its memory o'er the deep,
    To soothe a martyr's sadness,
And fresco, in his troubled sleep,
    His prison-walls with gladness.

We know the world is rich with streams
    Renowned in song and story,
Whose music murmurs through our
    dreams
    Of human love and glory :
We know that Arno's banks are fair,
    And Rhine has castled shadows,
And, poet-tuned, the Doon and Ayr
    Go singing down their meadows.

But while, unpictured and unsung
    By painter or by poet,
Our river waits the tuneful tongue
    And cunning hand to show it, —
We only know the fond skies lean
    Above it, warm with blessing,
And the sweet soul of our Undine
    Awakes to our caressing.

No fickle sun-god holds the flocks
    That graze its shores in keeping ;
No icy kiss of Dian mocks
    The youth beside it sleeping :
Our Christian river loveth most
    The beautiful and human ;
The heathen streams of Naiads boast,
    But ours of man and woman.

The miner in his cabin hears
    The ripple we are hearing ;
It whispers soft to homesick ears
    Around the settler's clearing :
In Sacramento's vales of corn,
    Or Santee's bloom of cotton,
Our river by its valley-born
    Was never yet forgotten.

The drum rolls loud, — the bugle fills
    The summer air with clangor ;
The war-storm shakes the solid hills
    Beneath its tread of anger ;
Young eyes that last year smiled in
    ours
    Now point the rifle's barrel,
And hands then stained with fruits and
    flowers
    Bear redder stains of quarrel.

But blue skies smile, and flowers bloom
 on,
 And rivers still keep flowing, —
The dear God still his rain and sun
 On good and ill bestowing.
His pine-trees whisper, "Trust and
 wait!"
His flowers are prophesying
That all we dread of change or fall
 His love is underlying.

And thou, O Mountain-born! — no more
 We ask the wise Allotter
Than for the firmness of thy shore,
 The calmness of thy water,
The cheerful lights that overlay
 Thy rugged slopes with beauty,
To match our spirits to our day
 And make a joy of duty.

ANDREW RYKMAN'S PRAYER.

ANDREW RYKMAN'S dead and gone;
 You can see his leaning slate
In the graveyard, and thereon
 Read his name and date.

" *Trust is truer than our fears,*"
 Runs the legend through the moss,
" *Gain is not in added years,*
 Nor in death is loss."

Still the feet that thither trod,
 All the friendly eyes are dim;
Only Nature, now, and God
 Have a care for him.

There the dews of quiet fall,
 Singing birds and soft winds stray;
Shall the tender Heart of all
 Be less kind than they?

What he was and what he is
 They who ask may haply find,
If they read this prayer of his
 Which he left behind.

Pardon, Lord, the lips that dare
Shape in words a mortal's prayer!
Prayer, that, when my day is done,
And I see its setting sun,
Shorn and beamless, cold and dim,
Sink beneath the horizon's rim, —
When this ball of rock and clay
Crumbles from my feet away,

And the solid shores of sense
Melt into the vague immense,
Father! I may come to Thee
Even with the beggar's plea,
As the poorest of Thy poor,
With my needs, and nothing more.

Not as one who seeks his home
With a step assured I come;
Still behind the tread I hear
Of my life-companion, Fear;
Still a shadow deep and vast
From my westering feet is cast,
Wavering, doubtful, undefined,
Never shapen nor outlined:
From myself the fear has grown,
And the shadow is my own.
Yet, O Lord, through all a sense
Of Thy tender providence
Stays my failing heart on Thee,
And confirms the feeble knee;
And, at times, my worn feet press
Spaces of cool quietness,
Lilied whiteness shone upon
Not by light of moon or sun.
Hours there be of inmost calm,
Broken but by grateful psalm,
When I love Thee more than fear Thee,
And Thy blessed Christ seems near me,
With forgiving look, as when
He beheld the Magdalen.
Well I know that all things move
To the spheral rhythm of love, —
That to Thee, O Lord of all!
Nothing can of chance befall:
Child and seraph, mote and star,
Well Thou knowest what we are;
Through Thy vast creative plan
Looking, from the worm to man,
There is pity in Thine eyes,
But no hatred nor surprise.
Not in blind caprice of will,
Not in cunning sleight of skill,
Not for show of power, was wrought
Nature's marvel in Thy thought.
Never careless hand and vain
Smites these chords of joy and pain:
No immortal selfishness
Plays the game of curse and bless:
Heaven and earth are witnesses
That Thy glory goodness is.
Not for sport of mind and force
Hast Thou made Thy universe,
But as atmosphere and zone
Of Thy loving heart alone.
Man, who walketh in a show,
Sees before him, to and fro,

Shadow and illusion go ;
All things flow and fluctuate,
Now contract and now dilate.
In the welter of this sea,
Nothing stable is but Thee;
In this whirl of swooning trance,
Thou alone art permanence ;
All without Thee only seems,
All beside is choice of dreams.
Never yet in darkest mood
Doubted I that Thou wast good,
Nor mistook my will for fate,
Pain of sin for heavenly hate, —
Never dreamed the gates of pearl
Rise from out the burning marl,
Or that good can only live
Of the bad conservative,
And through counterpoise of hell
Heaven alone be possible.
For myself alone I doubt ;
All is well, I know, without ;
I alone the beauty mar,
I alone the music jar.
Yet, with hands by evil stained,
And an ear by discord pained,
I am groping for the keys
Of the heavenly harmonies ;
Still within my heart I bear
Love for all things good and fair.
Hands of want or souls in pain
Have not sought my door in vain ;
I have kept my fealty good
To the human brotherhood ;
Scarcely have I asked in prayer
That which others might not share.
I, who hear with secret shame
Praise that paineth more than blame,
Rich alone in favors lent,
Virtuous by accident,
Doubtful where I fain would rest,
Frailest where I seem the best,
Only strong for lack of test, —
What am I, that I should press
Special pleas of selfishness,
Coolly mounting into heaven
On my neighbor unforgiven ?
Ne'er to me, howe'er disguised,
Comes a saint unrecognized ;
Never fails my heart to greet
Noble deed with warmer beat ;
Halt and maimed, I own not less
All the grace of holiness ;
Nor, through shame or self-distrust,
Less I love the pure and just.
Lord, forgive these words of mine :
What have I that is not Thine ? —
Whatsoe'er I fain would boast

Needs Thy pitying pardon most.
Thou, O Elder Brother ! who
In Thy flesh our trial knew,
Thou, who hast been touched by these
Our most sad infirmities,
Thou alone the gulf canst span
In the dual heart of man,
And between the soul and sense
Reconcile all difference,
Change the dream of me and mine
For the truth of Thee and Thine,
And, through chaos, doubt, and strife,
Interfuse Thy calm of life.
Haply, thus by Thee renewed,
In Thy borrowed goodness good,
Some sweet morning yet in God's
Dim, æonian periods,
Joyful I shall wake to see
Those I love who rest in Thee,
And to them in Thee allied
Shall my soul be satisfied.

Scarcely Hope hath shaped for me
What the future life may be.
Other lips may well be bold ;
Like the publican of old,
I can only urge the plea,
" Lord, be merciful to me ! "
Nothing of desert I claim,
Unto me belongeth shame.
Not for me the crowns of gold,
Palms, and harpings manifold ;
Not for erring eye and feet
Jasper wall and golden street.
What thou wilt, O Father, give !
All is gain that I receive.
If my voice I may not raise
In the elders' song of praise,
If I may not, sin-defiled,
Claim my birthright as a child,
Suffer it that I to Thee
As an hired servant be ;
Let the lowliest task be mine,
Grateful, so the work be Thine ;
Let me find the humblest place
In the shadow of Thy grace :
Blest to me were any spot
Where temptation whispers not.
If there be some weaker one,
Give me strength to help him on ;
If a blinder soul there be,
Let me guide him nearer Thee.
Make my mortal dreams come true
With the work I fain would do ;
Clothe with life the weak intent,
Let me be the thing I meant ;
Let me find in Thy employ

Peace that dearer is than joy;
Out of self to love be led
And to heaven acclimated,
Until all things sweet and good
Seem my natural habitude.

So we read the prayer of him
Who, with John of Labadie,
Trod, of old, the oozy rim
Of the Zuyder Zee.

Thus did Andrew Rykman pray.
Are we wiser, better grown,
That we may not, in our day,
Make his prayer our own?

THE CRY OF A LOST SOUL.[74]

IN that black forest, where, when day is
  done,
With a snake's stillness glides the
  Amazon
Darkly from sunset to the rising sun,

A cry, as of the pained heart of the wood,
The long, despairing moan of solitude
And darkness and the absence of all good,

Startles the traveller, with a sound so
  drear,
So full of hopeless agony and fear,
His heart stands still and listens like
  his ear.

The guide, as if he heard a dead-bell toll,
Starts, drops his oar against the gun-
  wale's thole,
Crosses himself, and whispers, "A lost
  soul!"

"No, Señor, not a bird. I know it well,—
It is the pained soul of some infidel
Or cursèd heretic that cries from hell.

"Poor fool! with hope still mocking
  his despair,
He wanders, shrieking on the midnight
  air
For human pity and for Christian prayer.

"Saints strike him dumb! Our Holy
  Mother hath
No prayer for him who, sinning unto
  death,
Burns always in the furnace of God's
  wrath!"

Thus to the baptized pagan's cruel lie,
Lending new horror to that mournful
  cry,
The voyager listens, making no reply.

Dim burns the boat-lamp: shadows
  deepen round,
From giant trees with snake-like creep-
  ers wound,
And the black water glides without a
  sound.

But in the traveller's heart a secret sense
Of nature plastic to benign intents,
And an eternal good in Providence,

Lifts to the starry calm of heaven his
  eyes;
And lo! rebuking all earth's ominous
  cries,
The Cross of pardon lights the tropic
  skies!

"Father of all!" he urges his strong
  plea,
"Thou lovest all: thy erring child may
  be
Lost to himself, but never lost to Thee!

"All souls are Thine; the wings of
  morning bear
None from that Presence which is everywhere,
Nor hell itself can hide, for Thou art
  there.

"Through sins of sense, perversities of
  will,
Through doubt and pain, through guilt
  and shame and ill,
Thy pitying eye is on Thy creature
  still.

"Wilt thou not make, Eternal Source
  and Goal!
In thy long years, life's broken circle
  whole,
And change to praise the cry of a lost
  soul?"

ITALY.

ACROSS the sea I heard the groans
  Of nations in the intervals
Of wind and wave. Their blood and
  bones
Cried out in torture, crushed by thrones,
  And sucked by priestly cannibals.

I dreamed of Freedom slowly gained
  By martyr meekness, patience, faith,
And lo ! an athlete grimly stained,
With corded muscles battle-strained,
  Shouting it from the fields of death !

I turn me, awe-struck, from the sight,
  Among the clamoring thousands mute,
I only know that God is right,
And that the children of the light
  Shall tread the darkness under foot.

I know the pent fire heaves its crust,
  That sultry skies the bolt will form
To smite them clear ; that Nature must
The balance of her powers adjust,
  Though with the earthquake and the
    storm.

God reigns, and let the earth rejoice !
  I bow before His sterner plan.
Dumb are the organs of my choice ;
He speaks in battle's stormy voice,
  His praise is in the wrath of man!

Yet, surely as He lives, the day
  Of peace He promised shall be ours,
To fold the flags of war, and lay
Its sword and spear to rust away,
  And sow its ghastly fields with flowers !

THE RIVER PATH.

No bird-song floated down the hill,
The tangled bank below was still ;

No rustle from the birchen stem,
No ripple from the water's hem.

The dusk of twilight round us grew,
We felt the falling of the dew ;

For, from us, ere the day was done,
The wooded hills shut out the sun.

But on the river's farther side
We saw the hill-tops glorified, —

A tender glow, exceeding fair,
A dream of day without its glare.

With us the damp, the chill, the gloom :
With them the sunset's rosy bloom ;

While dark, through willowy vistas seen,
The river rolled in shade between.

From out the darkness where we trod,
We gazed upon those hills of God,

Whose light seemed not of moon or
    sun.
We spake not, but our thought was one.

We paused, as if from that bright shore
Beckoned our dear ones gone before ;

And stilled our beating hearts to hear
The voices lost to mortal ear !

Sudden our pathway turned from night ;
The hills swung open to the light ;

Through their green gates the sunshine
    showed,
A long, slant splendor downward flowed.

Down glade and glen and bank it rolled ;
It bridged the shaded stream with gold ;

And, borne on piers of mist, allied
The shadowy with the sunlit side !

" So," prayed we, " when our feet draw
    near
The river dark, with mortal fear,

" And the night cometh chill with dew,
O Father ! let thy light break through !

" So let the hills of doubt divide,
So bridge with faith the sunless tide !

" So let the eyes that fail on earth
On thy eternal hills look forth ;

" And in thy beckoning angels know
The dear ones whom we loved below ! "

A MEMORIAL.

M. A. C.

O, THICKER, deeper, darker growing,
  The solemn vista to the tomb
Must know henceforth another shadow,
  And give another cypress room.

In love surpassing that of brothers,
  We walked, O friend, from childhood's
    day ;
And, looking back o'er fifty summers,
  Our footprints track a common way.

One in our faith, and one our longing
  To make the world within our reach
Somewhat the better for our living,
  And gladder for our human speech.

Thou heard'st with me the far-off voices,
  The old beguiling song of fame,
But life to thee was warm and present,
  And love was better than a name.

To homely joys and loves and friendships
  Thy genial nature fondly clung;
And so the shadow on the dial
  Ran back and left thee always young.

And who could blame the generous
    weakness
  Which, only to thyself unjust,
So overprized the worth of others,
  And dwarfed thy own with self-dis-
    trust?

All hearts grew warmer in the presence
  Of one who, seeking not his own,
Gave freely for the love of giving,
  Nor reaped for self the harvest sown.

Thy greeting smile was pledge and prel-
    ude
  Of generous deeds and kindly words;
In thy large heart were fair guest-cham-
    bers,
  Open to sunrise and the birds!

The task was thine to mould and fashion
  Life's plastic newness into grace:
To make the boyish heart heroic,
  And light with thought the maiden's
    face.

O'er all the land, in town and prairie,
  With bended heads of mourning,
    stand
The living forms that owe their beauty
  And fitness to thy shaping hand.

Thy call has come in ripened manhood,
  The noonday calm of heart and mind,
While I, who dreamed of thy remaining
  To mourn me, linger still behind:

Live on, to own, with self-upbraiding,
  A debt of love still due from me, —
The vain remembrance of occasions,
  Forever lost, of serving thee.

It was not mine among thy kindred
  To join the silent funeral prayers,

But all that long sad day of summer
  My tears of mourning dropped with
    theirs.

All day the sea-waves sobbed with sor-
    row,
  The birds forgot their merry trills:
All day I heard the pines lamenting
  With thine upon thy homestead hill

Green be those hillside pines forever,
  And green the meadowy lowlands be,
And green the old memorial beeches,
  Name-carven in the woods of Lee!

Still let them greet thy life companions
  Who thither turn their pilgrim feet,
In every mossy line recalling
  A tender memory sadly sweet.

O friend! if thought and sense avail not
  To know thee henceforth as thou art,
That all is well with thee forever
  I trust the instincts of my heart.

Thine be the quiet habitations,
  Thine the green pastures, blossom-
    sown,
And smiles of saintly recognition,
  As sweet and tender as thy own.

Thou com'st not from the hush and
    shadow
  To meet us, but to thee we come;
With thee we never can be strangers,
  And where thou art must still be home.

HYMN,

SUNG AT CHRISTMAS BY THE SCHOL-
ARS OF ST. HELENA'S ISLAND, S. C.

O NONE in all the world before
  Were ever glad as we!
We 're free on Carolina's shore,
  We 're all at home and free.

Thou Friend and Helper of the poor,
  Who suffered for our sake,
To open every prison door,
  And every yoke to break!

Bend low thy pitying face and mild,
  And help us sing and pray;
The hand that blessed the little child,
  Upon our foreheads lay.

We hear no more the driver's horn,
  No more the whip we fear,
This holy day that saw thee born
  Was never half so dear.

The very oaks are greener clad,
  The waters brighter smile ;
O never shone a day so glad
  On sweet St. Helen's Isle.

We praise thee in our songs to-day,
  To thee in prayer we call,
Make swift the feet and straight the way
  Of freedom unto all.

Come once again, O blessed Lord !
  Come walking on the sea !
And let the mainlands hear the word
  That sets the islands free !

SNOW-BOUND.

A WINTER IDYL.

Thompson's Seasons
"Cotter's Saturday Night"

TO THE MEMORY

OF

THE HOUSEHOLD IT DESCRIBES,

THIS POEM IS DEDICATED BY THE AUTHOR.

" As the Spirits of Darkness be stronger in the dark, so Good Spirits which be Angels of Light are augmented not only by the Divine light of the Sun, but also by our common VVood Fire : and as the Celestial Fire drives away dark spirits, so also this our Fire of VVood doth the same."
— COR. AGRIPPA, *Occult Philosophy*, Book I. ch. v.

" Announced by all the trumpets of the sky,
Arrives the snow ; and, driving o'er the fields,
Seems nowhere to alight ; the whited air
Hides hills and woods, the river and the heaven
And veils the farm-house at the garden's end.
The sled and traveller stopped, the courier's feet
Delayed, all friends shut out, the housemates sit
Around the radiant fireplace, enclosed
In a tumultuous privacy of storm."
                                    EMERSON.

THE sun that brief December day
Rose cheerless over hills of gray,
And, darkly circled, gave at noon
A sadder light than waning moon.
Slow tracing down the thickening sky
Its mute and ominous prophecy,
A portent seeming less than threat,
It sank from sight before it set.

A chill no coat, however stout,
Of homespun stuff could quite shut out,
A hard, dull bitterness of cold,
  That checked, mid-vein, the circling race
Of life-blood in the sharpened face,
The coming of the snow-storm told.
The wind blew east ; we heard the roar
Of Ocean on his wintry shore,
And felt the strong pulse throbbing there
Beat with low rhythm our inland air.

Meanwhile we did our nightly chores,—
Brought in the wood from out of doors,
Littered the stalls, and from the mows
Raked down the herd's-grass for the cows :
Heard the horse whinnying for his corn ;
And, sharply clashing horn on horn,
Impatient down the stanchion rows
The cattle shake their walnut bows ;
While, peering from his early perch
Upon the scaffold's pole of birch,
The cock his crested helmet bent
And down his querulous challenge sent

"SNOW-BOUND." Page 286.

Unwarmed by any sunset light
The gray day darkened into night,
A night made hoary with the swarm,
And whirl-dance of the blinding storm,
As zigzag wavering to and fro
Crossed and recrossed the wingéd snow :
And ere the early bedtime came
The white drift piled the window-frame,
And through the glass the clothes-line
    posts
Looked in like tall and sheeted ghosts.

So all night long the storm roared on :
The morning broke without a sun ;
In tiny spherule traced with lines
Of Nature's geometric signs,
In starry flake, and pellicle,
All day the hoary meteor fell ;
And, when the second morning shone,
We looked upon a world unknown,
On nothing we could call our own.
Around the glistening wonder bent
The blue walls of the firmament,
No cloud above, no earth below, —
A universe of sky and snow!
The old familiar sights of ours
Took marvellous shapes ; strange domes
    and towers
Rose up where sty or corn-crib stood,
Or garden-wall, or belt of wood ;
A smooth white mound the brush-pile
    showed,
A fenceless drift what once was road ;
The bridle-post an old man sat
With loose-flung coat and high cocked
    hat ;
The well-curb had a Chinese roof ;
And even the long sweep, high aloof,
In its slant splendor, seemed to tell
Of Pisa's leaning miracle.

A prompt, decisive man, no breath
Our father wasted : " Boys, a path ! "
Well pleased, (for when did farmer boy
Count such a summons less than joy ?)
Our buskins on our feet we drew ;
    With mittened hands, and caps drawn
        low,
    To guard our necks and ears from
        snow,
We cut the solid whiteness through.
And, where the drift was deepest, made
A tunnel walled and overlaid
With dazzling crystal : we had read
Of rare Aladdin's wondrous cave,
And to our own his name we gave,
With many a wish the luck were ours

To test his lamp's supernal powers.
We reached the barn with merry din,
And roused the prisoned brutes within.
The old horse thrust his long head out,
And grave with wonder gazed about ;
The cock his lusty greeting said,
And forth his speckled harem led ;
The oxen lashed their tails, and hooked,
And mild reproach of hunger looked ;
The hornéd patriarch of the sheep,
Like Egypt's Amun roused from sleep,
Shook his sage head with gesture mute,
And emphasized with stamp of foot.

All day the gusty north-wind bore
The loosening drift its breath before ;
Low circling round its southern zone,
The sun through dazzling snow-mist
    shone.
No church-bell lent its Christian tone
To the savage air, no social smoke
Curled over woods of snow-hung oak.
A solitude made more intense
By dreary-voicéd elements,
The shrieking of the mindless wind,
The moaning tree-boughs swaying blind,
And on the glass the unmeaning beat
Of ghostly finger-tips of sleet.
Beyond the circle of our hearth
No welcome sound of toil or mirth
Unbound the spell, and testified
Of human life and thought outside.
We minded that the sharpest ear
The buried brooklet could not hear,
The music of whose liquid lip
Had been to us companionship,
And, in our lonely life, had grown
To have an almost human tone.

As night drew on, and, from the crest
Of wooded knolls that ridged the west,
The sun, a snow-blown traveller, sank
From sight beneath the smothering
    bank,
We piled, with care, our nightly stack
Of wood against the chimney-back, —
The oaken log, green, huge, and thick,
And on its top the stout back-stick ;
The knotty forestick laid apart,
And filled between with curious art
The ragged brush ; then, hovering near,
We watched the first red blaze appear,
Heard the sharp crackle, caught the
    gleam
On whitewashed wall and sagging beam,
Until the old, rude-furnished room
Burst, flower-like, into rosy bloom ;

While radiant with a mimic flame
Outside the sparkling drift became,
And through the bare-boughed lilac-tree
Our own warm hearth seemed blazing
    free.
The crane and pendent trammels showed,
The Turks' heads on the andirons glowed;
While childish fancy, prompt to tell
The meaning of the miracle,
Whispered the old rhyme : " *Under the*
    tree,
When fire outdoors burns merrily,
There the witches are making tea."

The moon above the eastern wood
Shone at its full; the hill-range stood
Transfigured in the silver flood,
Its blown snows flashing cold and keen,
Dead white, save where some sharp
    ravine
Took shadow, or the sombre green
Of hemlocks turned to pitchy black
Against the whiteness at their back.
For such a world and such a night
Most fitting that unwarming light,
Which only seemed where'er it fell
To make the coldness visible.

Shut in from all the world without,
We sat the clean-winged hearth about,
Content to let the north-wind roar
In baffled rage at pane and door,
While the red logs before us beat
The frost-line back with tropic heat ;
And ever, when a louder blast
Shook beam and rafter as it passed,
The merrier up its roaring draught
The great throat of the chimney laughed,
The house-dog on his paws outspread
Laid to the fire his drowsy head,
The cat's dark silhouette on the wall
A couchant tiger's seemed to fall ;
And, for the winter fireside meet,
Between the andirons' straddling feet,
The mug of cider simmered slow,
The apples sputtered in a row,
And, close et hand, the basket stood
With nuts from brown October's wood.

What matter how the night behaved ?
What matter how the north-wind raved ?
Blow high, blow low, not all its snow
Could quench our hearth-fire's ruddy
    glow.
O Time and Change ! — with hair as
    gray
As was my sire's that winter day,

How strange it seems, with so much
    gone
Of life and love, to still live on !
Ah, brother ! only I and thou
Are left of all that circle now, —
The dear home faces whereupon
That fitful firelight paled and shone.
Henceforward, listen as we will,
The voices of that hearth are still ;
Look where we may, the wide earth o'er
Those lighted faces smile no more.
We tread the paths their feet have worn,
    We sit beneath their orchard trees,
    We hear, like them, the hum of bees
And rustle of the bladed corn ;
We turn the pages that they read,
    Their written words we linger o'er,
But in the sun they cast no shade,
No voice is heard, no sign is made,
    No step is on the conscious floor !
Yet Love will dream, and Faith will
    trust,
(Since He who knows our need is just,)
That somehow, somewhere, meet we
    must.
Alas for him who never sees
The stars shine through his cypress-
    trees !
Who, hopeless, lays his dead away,
Nor looks to see the breaking day
Across the mournful marbles play !
Who hath not learned, in hours of faith,
    The truth to flesh and sense unknown,
That Life is ever lord of Death,
    And Love can never lose its own !

We sped the time with stories old,
Wrought puzzles out, and riddles told,
Or stammered from our school-book lore
" The Chief of Gambia's golden shore."
How often since, when all the land
Was clay in Slavery's shaping hand,
As if a trumpet called, I 've heard
Dame Mercy Warren's rousing word :
" *Does not the voice of reason cry,*
    Claim the first right which Nature gave,
From the red scourge of bondage fly,
    Nor deign to live a burdened slave !"
Our father rode again his ride
On Memphremagog's wooded side ;
Sat down again to moose and samp
In trapper's hut and Indian camp ;
Lived o'er the old idyllic ease
Beneath St. François' hemlock-trees ;
Again for him the moonlight shone
On Norman cap and bodiced zone ;
Again he heard the violin play

Which led the village dance away,
And mingled in its merry whirl
The grandam and the laughing girl.
Or, nearer home, our steps he led
Where Salisbury's level marshes spread
    Mile-wide as flies the laden bee ;
Where merry mowers, hale and strong,
Swept, scythe on scythe, their swaths
        along
    The low green prairies of the sea.
We shared the fishing off Boar's Head,
    And round the rocky Isles of Shoals
    The hake-broil on the drift-wood
            coals ;
The chowder on the sand-beach made,
Dipped by the hungry, steaming hot,
With spoons of clam-shell from the
        pot.
We heard the tales of witchcraft old,
And dream and sign and marvel told
To sleepy listeners as they lay
Stretched idly on the salted hay,
Adrift along the winding shores,
When favoring breezes deigned to blow
The square sail of the gundelow
And idle lay the useless oars.

Our mother, while she turned her wheel
Or run the new-knit stocking-heel,
Told how the Indian hordes came down
At midnight on Cochecho town,
And how her own great-uncle bore
His cruel scalp-mark to fourscore.
Recalling, in her fitting phrase,
    So rich and picturesque and free,
    (The common unrhymed poetry
Of simple life and country ways,)
The story of her early days, —
She made us welcome to her home ;
Old hearths grew wide to give us room ;
We stole with her a frightened look
At the gray wizard's conjuring-book,
The fame whereof went far and wide
Through all the simple country side ;
We heard the hawks at twilight play,
The boat-horn on Piscataqua,
The loon's weird laughter far away ;
We fished her little trout-brook, knew
What flowers in wood and meadow grew,
What sunny hillsides autumn-brown
She climbed to shake the ripe nuts
        down,
Saw where in sheltered cove and bay
The ducks' black squadron anchored
        lay,
And heard the wild geese calling loud
Beneath the gray November cloud.

Then, haply, with a look more grave,
And soberer tone, some tale she gave
From painful Sewell's ancient tome,
Beloved in every Quaker home,
Of faith fire-winged by martyrdom,
Or Chalkley's Journal, old and quaint, —
Gentlest of skippers, rare sea-saint ! —
Who, when the dreary calms prevailed,
And water-butt and bread-cask failed,
And cruel, hungry eyes pursued
His portly presence mad for food,
With dark hints muttered under breath
Of casting lots for life or death,
Offered, if Heaven withheld supplies,
To be himself the sacrifice.
Then, suddenly, as if to save
The good man from his living grave,
A ripple on the water grew,
A school of porpoise flashed in view.
"Take, eat," he said, "and be content;
These fishes in my stead are sent
By Him who gave the tangled ram
To spare the child of Abraham."

Our uncle, innocent of books,
Was rich in lore of fields and brooks,
The ancient teachers never dumb
Of Nature's unhoused lyceum.
In moons and tides and weather wise,
He read the clouds as prophecies,
And foul or fair could well divine,
By many an occult hint and sign,
Holding the cunning-warded keys
To all the woodcraft mysteries ;
Himself to Nature's heart so near
That all her voices in his ear
Of beast or bird had meanings clear,
Like Apollonius of old,
Who knew the tales the sparrows told,
Or Hermes who interpreted
What the sage cranes of Nilus said ;
A simple, guileless, childlike man,
Content to live where life began ;
Strong only on his native grounds,
The little world of sights and sounds
Whose girdle was the parish bounds,
Whereof his fondly partial pride
The common features magnified,
As Surrey hills to mountains grew
In White of Selborne's loving view, —
He told how teal and loon he shot,
And how the eagle's eggs he got,
The feats on pond and river done,
The prodigies of rod and gun ;
Till, warming with the tales he told,
Forgotten was the outside cold,
The bitter wind unheeded blew,

From ripening corn the pigeons flew,
The partridge drummed i' the wood, the
    mink
Went fishing down the river-brink.
In fields with bean or clover gay,
The woodchuck, like a hermit gray,
    Peered from the doorway of his cell;
The muskrat plied the mason's trade,
And tier by tier his mud-walls laid;
And from the shagbark overhead
    The grizzled squirrel dropped his shell.

Next, the dear aunt, whose smile of
    cheer
And voice in dreams I see and hear, —
The sweetest woman ever Fate
Perverse denied a household mate,
Who, lonely, homeless, not the less
Found peace in love's unselfishness,
And welcome wheresoe'er she went,
A calm and gracious element,
Whose presence seemed the sweet in-
    come
And womanly atmosphere of home, —
Called up her girlhood memories,
The huskings and the apple-bees,
The sleigh-rides and the summer sails,
Weaving through all the poor details
And homespun warp of circumstance
A golden woof-thread of romance.
For well she kept her genial mood
And simple faith of maidenhood;
Before her still a cloud-land lay,
The mirage loomed across her way;
The morning dew, that dries so soon
With others, glistened at her noon;
Through years of toil and soil and care,
From glossy tress to thin gray hair,
All unprofaned she held apart
The virgin fancies of the heart.
Be shame to him of woman born
Who hath for such but thought of scorn.

There, too, our elder sister plied
Her evening task the stand beside;
A full, rich nature, free to trust,
Truthful and almost sternly just,
Impulsive, earnest, prompt to act,
And make her generous thought a
    fact,
Keeping with many a light disguise
The secret of self-sacrifice.
O heart sore-tried! thou hast the best
That Heaven itself could give thee, —
    rest,
Rest from all bitter thoughts and things!
How many a poor one's blessing went

With thee beneath the low green
    tent
Whose curtain never outward swings!

As one who held herself a part
Of all she saw, and let her heart
    Against the household bosom lean,
Upon the motley-braided mat
Our youngest and our dearest sat,
Lifting her large, sweet, asking eyes,
    Now bathed within the fadeless green
And holy peace of Paradise.
O, looking from some heavenly hill,
    Or from the shade of saintly palms,
    Or silver reach of river calms,
Do those large eyes behold me still?
With me one little year ago: —
The chill weight of the winter snow
    For months upon her grave has lain;
And now, when summer south-winds
    blow
    And brier and harebell bloom again,
I tread the pleasant paths we trod,
I see the violet-sprinkled sod
Whereon she leaned, too frail and weak
The hillside flowers she loved to seek,
Yet following me where'er I went
With dark eyes full of love's content.
The birds are glad; the brier-rose fills
The air with sweetness; all the hills
Stretch green to June's unclouded
    sky;
But still I wait with ear and eye
For something gone which should be
    nigh,
A loss in all familiar things,
In flower that blooms, and bird that
    sings.
And yet, dear heart! remembering thee,
    Am I not richer than of old?
Safe in thy immortality,
    What change can reach the wealth I
    hold?
    What chance can mar the pearl and
    gold
Thy love hath left in trust with me?
And while in life's late afternoon,
    Where cool and long the shadows
    grow,
I walk to meet the night that soon
    Shall shape and shadow overflow,
I cannot feel that thou art far,
Since near at need the angels are;
And when the sunset gates unbar,
    Shall I not see thee waiting stand,
And, white against the evening star,
    The welcome of thy beckoning hand?

Brisk wielder of the birch and rule,
The master of the district school
Held at the fire his favored place,
Its warm glow lit a laughing face
Fresh-hued and fair, where scarce ap-
peared
The uncertain prophecy of beard.
He teased the mitten-blinded cat,
Played cross-pins on my uncle's hat,
Sang songs, and told us what befalls
In classic Dartmouth's college halls.
Born the wild Northern hills among,
From whence his yeoman father wrung
By patient toil subsistence scant,
Not competence and yet not want,
He early gained the power to pay
His cheerful, self-reliant way ;
Could doff at ease his scholar's gown
To peddle wares from town to town ;
Or through the long vacation's reach
In lonely lowland districts teach,
Where all the droll experience found
At stranger hearths in boarding round,
The moonlit skater's keen delight,
The sleigh - drive through the frosty
night,
The rustic party, with its rough
Accompaniment of blind-man's-buff,
And whirling plate, and forfeits paid,
His winter task a pastime made.
Happy the snow-locked homes wherein
He tuned his merry violin,
Or played the athlete in the barn,
Or held the good dame's winding-yarn,
Or mirth-provoking versions told
Of classic legends rare and old,
Wherein the scenes of Greece and Rome
Had all the commonplace of home,
And little seemed at best the odds
'Twixt Yankee pedlers and old gods ;
Where Pindus-born Araxes took
The guise of any grist-mill brook,
And dread Olympus at his will
Became a huckleberry hill.

A careless boy that night he seemed ;
But at his desk he had the look
And air of one who wisely schemed,
And hostage from the future took
In trainéd thought and lore of book.
Large-brained, clear-eyed, — of such as
he
Shall Freedom's young apostles be,
Who, following in War's bloody trail,
Shall every lingering wrong assail ;
All chains from limb and spirit strike,
Uplift the black and white alike ;

Scatter before their swift advance
The darkness and the ignorance,
The pride, the lust, the squalid sloth,
Which nurtured Treason's monstrous
growth,
Made murder pastime, and the hell
Of prison-torture possible ;
The cruel lie of caste refute,
Old forms remould, and substitute
For Slavery's lash the freeman's will,
For blind routine, wise-handed skill ;
A school-house plant on every hill,
Stretching in radiate nerve-lines thence
The quick wires of intelligence ;
Till North and South together brought
Shall own the same electric thought,
In peace a common flag salute,
And, side by side in labor's free
And unresentful rivalry,
Harvest the fields wherein they fought.

Another guest that winter night
Flashed back from lustrous eyes the
light.
Unmarked by time, and yet not young,
The honeyed music of her tongue
And words of meekness scarcely told
A nature passionate and bold,
Strong, self-concentred, spurning guide,
Its milder features dwarfed beside
Her unbent will's majestic pride.
She sat among us, at the best,
A not unfeared, half-welcome guest,
Rebuking with her cultured phrase
Our homeliness of words and ways.
A certain pard-like, treacherous grace
Swayed the lithe limbs and dropped
the lash,
Lent the white teeth their dazzling
flash ;
And under low brows, black with
night,
Rayed out at times a dangerous light;
The sharp heat-lightnings of her face
Presaging ill to him whom Fate
Condemned to share her love or hate.
A woman tropical, intense
In thought and act, in soul and sense,
She blended in a like degree
The vixen and the devotee,
Revealing with each freak or feint
The temper of Petruchio's Kate,
The raptures of Siena's saint.
Her tapering hand and rounded wrist
Had facile power to form a fist ;
The warm, dark languish of her eyes
Was never safe from wrath's surprise.

Brows saintly calm and lips devout
Knew every change of scowl and pout ;
And the sweet voice had notes more
    high
And shrill for social battle-cry.
Since then what old cathedral town
Has missed her pilgrim staff and gown,
What convent-gate has held its lock
Against the challenge of her knock !
Through Smyrna's plague-hushed thor-
    oughfares,
Up sea-set Malta's rocky stairs,
Gray olive slopes of hills that hem
Thy tombs and shrines, Jerusalem,
Or startling on her desert throne
The crazy Queen of Lebanon
With claims fantastic as her own,
Her tireless feet have held their way ;
And still, unrestful, bowed, and gray,
She watches under Eastern skies,
    With hope each day renewed and
        fresh,
    The Lord's quick coming in the flesh,
Whereof she dreams and prophesies !

Where'er her troubled path may be,
    The Lord's sweet pity with her go !
The outward wayward life we see,
    The hidden springs we may not know.
Nor is it given us to discern
    What threads the fatal sisters spun,
    Through what ancestral years has
        run
The sorrow with the woman born,
What forged her cruel chain of moods,
What set her feet in solitudes,
    And held the love within her mute,
What mingled madness in the blood,
    A life-long discord and annoy,
    Water of tears with oil of joy,
And hid within the folded bud
    Perversities of flower and fruit.
It is not ours to separate
The tangled skein of will and fate,
To show what metes and bounds should
        stand
Upon the soul's debatable land,
And between choice and Providence
Divide the circle of events ;
    But He who knows our frame is just,
    Merciful and compassionate,
    And full of sweet assurances
And hope for all the language is,
    That He remembereth we are dust !

At last the great logs, crumbling low,
Sent out a dull and duller glow,

The bull's-eye watch that hung in view,
Ticking its weary circuit through,
Pointed with mutely warning sign
Its black hand to the hour of nine.
That sign the pleasant circle broke :
My uncle ceased his pipe to smoke,
Knocked from its bowl the refuse gray,
And laid it tenderly away,
Then roused himself to safely cover
The dull red brands with ashes over.
And while, with care, our mother laid
The work aside, her steps she stayed
One moment, seeking to express
Her grateful sense of happiness
For food and shelter, warmth and
        health,
And love's contentment more than
        wealth,
With simple wishes (not the weak,
Vain prayers which no fulfilment seek,
But such as warm the generous heart,
O'er-prompt to do with Heaven its part)
That none might lack, that bitter night,
For bread and clothing, warmth and
        light.

Within our beds awhile we heard
The wind that round the gables roared,
With now and then a ruder shock,
Which made our very bedsteads rock.
We heard the loosened clapboards tost,
The board-nails snapping in the frost ;
And on us, through the unplastered
        wall,
Felt the light sifted snow-flakes fall.
But sleep stole on, as sleep will do
When hearts are light and life is new ;
Faint and more faint the murmurs grew,
Till in the summer-land of dreams
They softened to the sound of streams,
Low stir of leaves, and dip of oars,
And lapsing waves on quiet shores.

Next morn we wakened with the shout
Of merry voices high and clear ;
And saw the teamsters drawing near
To break the drifted highways out.
Down the long hillside treading slow
We saw the half-buried oxen go,
Shaking the snow from heads uptost,
Their straining nostrils white with frost.
Before our door the straggling train
Drew up, an added team to gain.
The elders threshed their hands a-cold,
    Passed, with the cider-mug, their
        jokes
    From lip to lip ; the younger folks

Down the loose snow-banks, wrestling,
    rolled,
Then toiled again the cavalcade
    O'er windy hill, through clogged ra-
        vine,
    And woodland paths that wound be-
        tween
Low drooping pine - boughs winter-
    weighed.
From every barn a team afoot,
At every house a new recruit,
Where, drawn by Nature's subtlest law
Haply the watchful young men saw
Sweet doorway pictures of the curls
And curious eyes of merry girls,
Lifting their hands in mock defence
Against the snow-ball's compliments,
And reading in each missive tost
The charm with Eden never lost.

We heard once more the sleigh-bells'
    sound ;
    And, following where the teamsters
        led,
The wise old Doctor went his round,
Just pausing at our door to say,
In the brief autocratic way
Of one who, prompt at Duty's call,
Was free to urge her claim on all,
    That some poor neighbor sick abed
At night our mother's aid would need.
For, one in generous thought and deed,
    What mattered in the sufferer's sight
    The Quaker matron's inward light,
The Doctor's mail of Calvin's creed ?
All hearts confess the saints elect
    Who, twain in faith, in love agree,
And melt not in an acid sect
    The Christian pearl of charity !

So days went on : a week had passed
Since the great world was heard from
    last.
The Almanac we studied o'er,
Read and reread our little store,
Of books and pamphlets, scarce a score ;
One harmless novel, mostly hid
From younger eyes, a book forbid,
And poetry, (or good or bad,
A single book was all we had,)
Where Ellwood's meek, drab-skirted
    Muse,
    A stranger to the heathen Nine,
    Sang, with a somewhat nasal whine,
The wars of David and the Jews.
At last the floundering carrier bore
The village paper to our door.

Lo ! broadening outward as we read,
To warmer zones the horizon spread ;
In panoramic length unrolled
We saw the marvels that it told.
Before us passed the painted Creeks,
    And daft McGregor on his raids
    In Costa Rica's everglades.
And up Taygetos winding slow
Rode Ypsilanti's Mainote Greeks,
A Turk's head at each saddle-bow !
Welcome to us its week-old news,
Its corner for the rustic Muse,
    Its monthly gauge of snow and rain,
Its record, mingling in a breath
The wedding knell and dirge of death ;
Jest, anecdote, and love-lorn tale,
The latest culprit sent to jail ;
Its hue and cry of stolen and lost,
Its vendue sales and goods at cost,
    And traffic calling loud for gain.
We felt the stir of hall and street,
The pulse of life that round us beat ;
The chill embargo of the snow
Was melted in the genial glow ;
Wide swung again our ice-locked door,
And all the world was ours once more !

Clasp, Angel of the backward look
    And folded wings of ashen gray
    And voice of echoes far away,
The brazen covers of thy book ;
The weird palimpsest old and vast,
Wherein thou hid'st the spectral past ;
Where, closely mingling, pale and glow
The characters of joy and woe ;
The monographs of outlived years,
Or smile-illumed or dim with tears,
    Green hills of life that slope to death,
And haunts of home, whose vistaed trees
Shade off to mournful cypresses
    With the white amaranths underneath.
Even while I look, I can but heed
    The restless sands' incessant fall,
Importunate hours that hours succeed,
Each clamorous with its own sharp
    need,
    And duty keeping pace with all.
Shut down and clasp the heavy lids ;
I hear again the voice that bids
The dreamer leave his dream midway
For larger hopes and graver fears :
Life greatens in these later years,
The century's aloe flowers to-day !

Yet, haply, in some lull of life,
Some Truce of God which breaks its
    strife,

The worldling's eyes shall gather dew,
  Dreaming in throngful city ways
Of winter joys his boyhood knew ;
And dear and early friends — the few
Who yet remain — shall pause to view
These Flemish pictures of old days ;
Sit with me by the homestead hearth,
And stretch the hands of memory forth
  To warm them at the wood-fire's blaze !

And thanks untraced to lips unknown
Shall greet me like the odors blown
From unseen meadows newly mown,
Or lilies floating in some pond,
Wood-fringed, the wayside gaze beyond;
The traveller owns the grateful sense
Of sweetness near, he knows not whence,
And, pausing, takes with forehead bare
The benediction of the air.

THE TENT ON THE BEACH,

AND OTHER POEMS.

I WOULD not sin, in this half-playful
      strain, —
  Too light perhaps for serious years,
      though born
Of the enforced leisure of slow pain, —
  Against the pure ideal which has
      drawn
My feet to follow its far-shining gleam.
A simple plot is mine : legends and
      runes
Of credulous days, old fancies that have
      lain
Silent from boyhood taking voice again,
Warmed into life once more, even as the
      tunes
That, frozen in the fabled hunting-horn,
Thawed into sound : — a winter fireside
      dream
Of dawns and sunsets by the summer
      sea,
Whose sands are traversed by a silent
      throng
Of voyagers from that vaster mystery
Of which it is an emblem ; — and the
      dear
Memory of one who might have tuned
      my song
To sweeter music by her delicate ear.
  1st mo., 1867.

THE TENT ON THE BEACH.

WHEN heats as of a tropic clime
  Burned all our inland valleys
      through,

Three friends, the guests of summer
      time,
  Pitched their white tent where sea
      winds blew.
Behind them, marshes, seamed and
      crossed
  With narrow creeks, and flower-em-
      bossed,
Stretched to the dark oak wood, whose
      leafy arms
Screened from the stormy East the
      pleasant inland farms.

At full of tide their bolder shore
  Of sun-bleached sand the waters
      beat ;
  At ebb, a smooth and glistening
      floor
  They touched with light, receding
      feet.
Northward a green bluff broke the
      chain
  Of sand-hills ; southward stretched a
      plain
Of salt grass, with a river winding
      down,
Sail-whitened, and beyond the steeples
  of the town,

  Whence sometimes, when the wind
      was light
  And dull the thunder of the beach,
  They heard the bells of morn and
      night
  Swing, miles away, their silver
      speech.

Above low scarp and turf-grown
    wall
They saw the fort-flag rise and fall ;
And, the first star to signal twilight's
    hour,
The lamp-fire glimmer down from the
    tall lighthouse tower.

They rested there, escaped awhile
    From cares that wear the life away,
To eat the lotus of the Nile
    And drink the poppies of Cathay, —
To fling their loads of custom down,
Like drift-weed, on the sand-slopes
    brown,
And in the sea waves drown the restless
    pack
Of duties, claims, and needs that barked
    upon their track.

One, with his beard scarce silvered,
    bore
    A ready credence in his looks,
A lettered magnate, lording o'er
    An ever-widening realm of books.
In him brain - currents, near and
    far,
Converged as in a Leyden jar ;
The old, dead authors thronged him
    round about,
And Elzevir's gray ghosts from leathern
    graves looked out.

He knew each living pundit well,
    Could weigh the gifts of .him or
    her,
And well the market value tell
    Of poet and philosopher.
But if he lost, the scenes behind,
Somewhat of reverence vague and
    blind,
Finding the actors human at the best,
No readier lips than his the good he
    saw confessed.

His boyhood fancies not outgrown,
    He loved himself the singer's art ;
Tenderly, gently, by his own
    He knew and judged an author's
    heart.
No Rhadamanthine brow of doom
Bowed the dazed pedant from his
    room ;
And bards, whose name is legion, if
    denied,
Bore off alike intact their verses and
    their pride.

Pleasant it was to roam about
    The lettered world as he had done,
And see the lords of song without
    Their singing robes and garlands
    on.
With Wordsworth paddle Rydal
    mere,
Taste rugged Elliott's home-brewed
    beer,
And with the ears of Rogers, at four-
    score,
Hear Garrick's buskined tread and
    Walpole's wit once more.

And one there was, a dreamer born,
    Who, with a mission to fulfil,
Had left the Muses' haunts to turn
    The crank of an opinion-mill,
Making his rustic reed of song
A weapon in the war with wrong,
Yoking his fancy to the breaking-plough
That beam-deep turned the soil for truth
    to spring and grow.

Too quiet seemed the man to ride
    The winged Hippogriff Reform ;
Was his a voice from side to side
    To pierce the tumult of the storm ?
A silent, shy, peace-loving man,
He seemed no fiery partisan
To hold his way against the public
    frown,
The ban of Church and State, the fierce
    mob's hounding down.

For while he wrought with strenuous
    will
    The work his hands had found to
    do,
He heard the fitful music still
    Of winds that out of dream-land
    blew.
The din about him could not drown
What the strange voices whispered
    down ;
Along his task-field weird processions
    swept,
The visionary pomp of stately phantoms
    stepped.

The common air was thick with
    dreams, —
    He told them to the toiling crowd ;
Such music as the woods and streams
    Sang in his ear he sang aloud ;
In still, shut bays, on windy capes,
He heard the call of beckoning shapes,

And, as the gray old shadows prompted
    him,
To homely moulds of rhyme he shaped
    their legends grim.

He rested now his weary hands,
    And lightly moralized and laughed,
As, tracing on the shifting sands
    A burlesque of his paper-craft,
He saw the careless waves o'errun
His words, as time before had done,
Each day's tide-water washing clean
    away,
Like letters from the sand, the work of
    yesterday.

And one, whose Arab face was tanned
    By tropic sun and boreal frost,
So travelled there was scarce a land
    Or people left him to exhaust,
In idling mood had from him hurled
The poor squeezed orange of the
    world,
And in the tent-shade, as beneath a
    palm,
Smoked, cross-legged like a Turk, in
    Oriental calm.

The very waves that washed the
    sand
    Below him, he had seen before
Whitening the Scandinavian strand
    And sultry Mauritanian shore.
From ice-rimmed isles, from summer
    seas
Palm-fringed, they bore him messages;
He heard the plaintive Nubian songs
    again,
And mule-bells tinkling down the moun-
    tain-paths of Spain.

His memory round the ransacked
    earth
    On Puck's long girdle slid at ease;
And, instant, to the valley's girth
    Of mountains, spice isles of the
    seas,
Faith flowered in minster stones,
    Art's guess
At truth and beauty, found access;
Yet loved the while, that free cosmopo-
    lite,
Old friends, old ways, and kept his boy-
    hood's dreams in sight.

Untouched as yet by wealth and pride,
    That virgin innocence of beach:

No shingly monster, hundred-eyed,
    Stared its gray sand-birds out of
    reach;
Unhoused, save where, at intervals,
The white tents showed their canvas
    walls,
Where brief sojourners, in the cool,
    soft air,
Forgot their inland heats, hard toil, and
    year-long care.

Sometimes along the wheel-deep sand
    A one-horse wagon slowly crawled,
Deep laden with a youthful band,
    Whose look some homestead old
    recalled;
Brother perchance, and sisters twain,
    And one whose blue eyes told, more
    plain
Than the free language of her rosy lip,
Of the still dearer claim of love's rela-
    tionship.

With cheeks of russet-orchard tint,
    The light laugh of their native rills,
The perfume of their garden's mint,
    The breezy freedom of the hills,
They bore, in unrestrained delight,
The motto of the Garter's knight,
Careless as if from every gazing thing
Hid by their innocence, as Gyges by
    his ring.

The clanging sea-fowl came and went,
    The hunter's gun in the marshes
    rang;
At nightfall from a neighboring tent
    A flute-voiced woman sweetly sang.
Loose-haired, barefooted, hand-in-
    hand,
    Young girls went tripping down the
    sand;
And youths and maidens, sitting in the
    moon,
Dreamed o'er the old fond dream from
    which we wake too soon.

At times their fishing-lines they plied,
    With an old Triton at the oar,
Salt as the sea-wind, tough and dried
    As a lean cusk from Labrador.
Strange tales he told of wreck and
    storm, —
Had seen the sea-snake's awful form,
And heard the ghosts on Haley's Isle
    complain,
Speak him off shore, and beg a passage
    to old Spain!

And there, on breezy morns, they saw
The fishing-schooners outward run,
Their low-bent sails in tack and flaw
Turned white or dark to shade and
sun.
Sometimes, in calms of closing day,
They watched the spectral mirage
play,
Saw low, far islands looming tall and
nigh,
And ships, with upturned keels, sail like
a sea the sky.

Sometimes a cloud, with thunder
black,
Stooped low upon the darkening
main,
Piercing the waves along its track
With the slant javelins of rain.
And when west-wind and sunshine
warm
Chased out to sea its wrecks of storm,
They saw the prismy hues in thin spray
showers
Where the green buds of waves burst
into white froth flowers.

And when along the line of shore
The mists crept upward chill and
damp,
Stretched, careless, on their sandy
floor
Beneath the flaring lantern lamp,
They talked of all things old and
new,
Read, slept, and dreamed as idlers
do ;
And in the unquestioned freedom of the
tent,
Body and o'er-taxed mind to healthful
ease unbent.

Once, when the sunset splendors died,
And, trampling up the sloping sand,
In lines outreaching far and wide,
The white-maned billows swept to
land,
Dim seen across the gathering shade,
A vast and ghostly cavalcade,
They sat around their lighted kerosene,
Hearing the deep bass roar their every
pause between.

Then, urged thereto, the Editor
Within his full portfolio dipped,
Feigning excuse while searching for
(With secret pride) his manuscript.

His pale face flushed from eye to
beard,
With nervous cough his throat he
cleared,
And, in a voice so tremulous it betrayed
The anxious fondness of an author's
heart, he read :

THE WRECK OF RIVERMOUTH

RIVERMOUTH Rocks are fair to see,
By dawn or sunset shone across,
When the ebb of the sea has left them
free,
To dry their fringes of gold-green
moss :
For there the river comes winding down
From salt sea-meadows and uplands
brown,
And waves on the outer rocks afoam
Shout to its waters, " Welcome home ! "

And fair are the sunny isles in view
East of the grisly Head of the Boar,
And Agamenticus lifts its blue
Disk of a cloud the woodlands o'er ;
And southerly, when the tide is down,
'Twixt white sea-waves and sand-hills
brown,
The beach-birds dance and the gray
gulls wheel
Over a floor of burnished steel.

Once, in the old Colonial days,
Two hundred years ago and more,
A boat sailed down through the wind-
ing ways
Of Hampton River to that low shore,
Full of a goodly company
Sailing out on the summer sea,
Veering to catch the land-breeze light,
With the Boar to left and the Rocks to
right.

In Hampton meadows, where mowers
laid
Their scythes to the swaths of salted
grass,
" Ah, well-a-day ! our hay must be
made ! "
A young man sighed, who saw them
pass.
Loud laughed his fellows to see him
stand
Whetting his scythe with a listless hand,
Hearing a voice in a far-off song,
Watching a white hand beckoning long.

"Fie on the witch!" cried a merry
    girl,
  As they rounded the point where
    Goody Cole
Sat by her door with her wheel atwirl,
  A bent and blear-eyed poor old soul.
"Oho!" she muttered, "ye 're brave
    to-day!
But I hear the little waves laugh and
    say,
'The broth will be cold that waits at
    home;
For it 's one to go, but another to
    come!'"

"She 's cursed," said the skipper;
    "speak her fair:
I 'm scary always to see her shake
Her wicked head, with its wild gray
    hair,
  And nose like a hawk, and eyes like a
    snake."
But merrily still, with laugh and shout,
From Hampton River the boat sailed
    out,
Till the huts and the flakes on Star
    seemed nigh,
And they lost the scent of the pines of
    Rye.

They dropped their lines in the lazy
    tide,
  Drawing up haddock and mottled
    cod;
They saw not the Shadow that walked
    beside,
  They heard not the feet with silence
    shod.
But thicker and thicker a hot mist
    grew,
Shot by the lightnings through and
    through;
And muffled growls, like the growl of a
    beast,
Ran along the sky from west to east.

Then the skipper looked from the dark-
    ening sea
  Up to the dimmed and wading sun;
But he spake like a brave man cheer-
    ily,
  "Yet there is time for our homeward
    run."
Veering and tacking, they backward
    wore;
And just as a breath from the woods
    ashore

Blew out to whisper of danger past,
The wrath of the storm came down at
    last!

The skipper hauled at the heavy sail:
  "God be our help!" he only cried,
As the roaring gale, like the stroke of a
    flail,
  Smote the boat on its starboard side.
The Shoalsmen looked, but saw alone
Dark films of rain-cloud slantwise blown,
Wild rocks lit up by the lightning's
    glare,
The strife and torment of sea and air.

Goody Cole looked out from her door:
  The Isles of Shoals were drowned and
    gone,
Scarcely she saw the Head of the Boar
  Toss the foam from tusks of stone.
She clasped her hands with a grip of
    pain,
The tear on her cheek was not of rain:
"They are lost," she muttered, "boat
    and crew!
Lord, forgive me! my words were
    true!"

Suddenly seaward swept the squall;
  The low sun smote through cloudy
    rack;
The Shoals stood clear in the light, and
    all
  The trend of the coast lay hard and
    black.
But far and wide as eye could reach,
No life was seen upon wave or beach;
The boat that went out at morning
    never
Sailed back again into Hampton River.

O mower, lean on thy bended snath,
  Look from the meadows green and
    low:
The wind of the sea is a waft of death,
  The waves are singing a song of woe!
By silent river, by moaning sea,
Long and vain shall thy watching be:
Never again shall the sweet voice call,
Never the white hand rise and fall!

O Rivermouth Rocks, how sad a sight
  Ye saw in the light of breaking
    day!
Dead faces looking up cold and white
  From sand and sea-weed where they
    lay.

The mad old witch-wife wailed and
wept,
And cursed the tide as it backward
crept :
" Crawl back, crawl back, blue water-
snake !
Leave your dead for the hearts that
break ! "

Solemn it was in that old day
In Hampton town and its log-built
church,
Where side by side the coffins lay
And the mourners stood in aisle and
porch.
In the singing-seats young eyes were
dim,
The voices faltered that raised the
hymn,
And Father Dalton, grave and stern,
Sobbed through his prayer and wept in
turn.

But his ancient colleague did not pray,
Because of his sin at fourscore years :
He stood apart, with the iron-gray
Of his strong brows knitted to hide
his tears.
And a wretched woman, holding her
breath
In the awful presence of sin and death,
Cowered and shrank, while her neigh-
bors thronged
To look on the dead her shame had
wronged.

Apart with them, like them forbid,
Old Goody Cole looked drearily
round,
As, two by two, with their faces hid,
The mourners walked to the burying-
ground.
She let the staff from her clasped hands
fall :
" Lord, forgive us ! we 're sinners all ! "
And the voice of the old man answered
her :
" Amen ! " said Father Bachiler.

So, as I sat upon Appledore
In the calm of a closing summer day,
And the broken lines of Hampton shore
In purple mist of cloudland lay,
The Rivermouth Rocks their story told ;
And waves aglow with sunset gold,
Rising and breaking in steady chime,
Beat the rhythm and kept the time.

And the sunset paled, and warmed once
more
With a softer, tenderer after-glow ;
In the east was moon-rise, with boats
off-shore
And sails in the distance drifting
slow.
The beacon glimmered from Ports-
mouth bar,
The White Isle kindled its great red
star ;
And life and death in my old-time lay
Mingled in peace like the night and
day !

———

" Well ! " said the Man of Books,
" your story
Is really not ill told in verse.
As the Celt said of purgatory,
One might go farther and fare worse."
The Reader smiled ; and once again
With steadier voice took up his
strain,
While the fair singer from the neighbor-
ing tent
Drew near, and at his side a graceful
listener bent.

THE GRAVE BY THE LAKE.

WHERE the Great Lake's sunny smiles
Dimple round its hundred isles,
And the mountain's granite ledge
Cleaves the water like a wedge,
Ringed about with smooth, gray stones,
Rest the giant's mighty bones.

Close beside, in shade and gleam,
Laughs and ripples Melvin stream ;
Melvin water, mountain-born,
All fair flowers its banks adorn ;
All the woodland's voices meet,
Mingling with its murmurs sweet.

Over lowlands forest-grown,
Over waters island-strown,
Over silver-sanded beach,
Leaf-locked bay and misty reach,
Melvin stream and burial-heap,
Watch and ward the mountains keep.

Who that Titan cromlech fills ?
Forest-kaiser, lord o' the hills ?
Knight who on the birchen tree
Carved his savage heraldry ?

Priest o' the pine-wood temples dim,
Prophet, sage, or wizard grim?

Rugged type of primal man,
Grim utilitarian,
Loving woods for hunt and prowl,
Lake and hill for fish and fowl,
As the brown bear blind and dull
To the grand and beautiful:

Not for him the lesson drawn
From the mountains smit with dawn.
Star-rise, moon-rise, flowers of May,
Sunset's purple bloom of day, —
Took his life no hue from thence,
Poor amid such affluence?

Haply unto hill and tree
All too near akin was he:
Unto him who stands afar
Nature's marvels greatest are;
Who the mountain purple seeks
Must not climb the higher peaks.

Yet who knows in winter tramp,
Or the midnight of the camp,
What revealings faint and far,
Stealing down from moon and star,
Kindled in that human clod
Thought of destiny and God?

Stateliest forest patriarch,
Grand in robes of skin and bark,
What sepulchral mysteries,
What weird funeral-rites, were his?
What sharp wail, what drear lament,
Back scared wolf and eagle sent?

Now, whate'er he may have been,
Low he lies as other men;
On his mound the partridge drums,
There the noisy blue-jay comes;
Rank nor name nor pomp has he
In the grave's democracy.

Part thy blue lips, Northern lake!
Moss-grown rocks, your silence break!
Tell the tale, thou ancient tree!
Thou, too, slide-worn Ossipee!
Speak, and tell us how and when
Lived and died this king of men!

Wordless moans the ancient pine;
Lake and mountain give no sign;
Vain to trace this ring of stones;
Vain the search of crumbling bones:
Deepest of all mysteries,
And the saddest, silence is.

Nameless, noteless, clay with clay
Mingles slowly day by day;
But somewhere, for good or ill,
That dark soul is living still;
Somewhere yet that atom's force
Moves the light-poised universe.

Strange that on his burial-sod
Harebells bloom, and golden-rod,
While the soul's dark horoscope
Holds no starry sign of hope!
Is the Unseen with sight at odds?
Nature's pity more than God's?

Thus I mused by Melvin's side,
While the summer eventide
Made the woods and inland sea
And the mountains mystery;
And the hush of earth and air
Seemed the pause before a prayer, —

Prayer for him, for all who rest,
Mother Earth, upon thy breast, —
Lapped on Christian turf, or hid
In rock-cave or pyramid:
All who sleep, as all who live,
Well may need the prayer, "Forgive!"

Desert-smothered caravan,
Knee-deep dust that once was man,
Battle-trenches ghastly piled,
Ocean-floors with white bones tiled,
Crowded tomb and mounded sod,
Dumbly crave that prayer to God.

O the generations old
Over whom no church-bells tolled,
Christless, lifting up blind eyes
To the silence of the skies!
For the innumerable dead
Is my soul disquieted.

Where be now these silent hosts?
Where the camping-ground of ghosts?
Where the spectral conscripts led
To the white tents of the dead?
What strange shore or chartless sea
Holds the awful mystery?

Then the warm sky stooped to make
Double sunset in the lake;
While above I saw with it,
Range on range, the mountains lit;
And the calm and splendor stole
Like an answer to my soul.

Hear'st thou, O of little faith,
What to thee the mountain saith,

What is whispered by the trees ? —
"Cast on God thy care for these ;
Trust him, if thy sight be dim :
Doubt for them is doubt of Him.

"Blind must be their close-shut eyes
Where like night the sunshine lies,
Fiery-linked the self-forged chain
Binding ever sin to pain,
Strong their prison-house of will,
But without He waiteth still.

"Not with hatred's undertow
Doth the Love Eternal flow ;
Every chain that spirits wear
Crumbles in the breath of prayer ;
And the penitent's desire
Opens every gate of fire.

"Still Thy love, O Christ arisen,
Yearns to reach these souls in prison !
Through all depths of sin and loss
Drops the plummet of Thy cross !
Never yet abyss was found
Deeper than that cross could sound !"

Therefore well may Nature keep
Equal faith with all who sleep,
Set her watch of hills around
Christian grave and heathen mound,
And to cairn and kirkyard send
Summer's flowery dividend.

Keep, O pleasant Melvin stream,
Thy sweet laugh in shade and gleam !
On the Indian's grassy tomb
Swing, O flowers, your bells of bloom !
Deep below, as high above,
Sweeps the circle of God's love.

He paused and questioned with his
    eye
The hearers' verdict on his song.
A low voice asked : Is 't well to pry
    Into the secrets which belong
    Only to God ? — The life to be
Is still the unguessed mystery :
Unscaled, unpierced the cloudy walls
    remain,
We beat with dream and wish the
    soundless doors in vain.

"But faith beyond our sight may go."
He said : "The gracious Fatherhood
Can only know above, below,
    Eternal purposes of good.

From our free heritage of will,
    The bitter springs of pain and ill
Flow only in all worlds. The perfect
    day
Of God is shadowless, and love is love
    alway."

"I know," she said, "the letter kills ;
    That on our arid fields of strife
And heat of clashing texts distils
    The dew of spirit and of life.
But, searching still the written Word,
I fain would find, Thus saith the Lord,
A voucher for the hope I also feel
That sin can give no wound beyond
    love's power to heal."

"Pray," said the Man of Books,
    "give o'er
A theme too vast for time and place.
Go on, Sir Poet, ride once more
    Your hobby at his old free pace.
But let him keep, with step discreet,
The solid earth beneath his feet.
In the great mystery which around us
    lies,
The wisest is a fool, the fool Heaven-
    helped is wise."

The Traveller said : "If songs have
    creeds,
    Their choice of them let singers
    make ;
But Art no other sanction needs
    Than beauty for its own fair sake.
It grinds not in the mill of use,
Nor asks for leave, nor begs excuse ;
It makes the flexile laws it deigns to
    own,
And gives its atmosphere its color and
    its tone.

"Confess, old friend, your austere
    school
    Has left your fancy little chance ;
You square to reason's rigid rule
    The flowing outlines of romance.
With conscience keen from exercise,
    And chronic fear of compromise,
You check the free play of your rhymes,
    to clap
A moral underneath, and spring it like
    a trap."

The sweet voice answered : "Better so
    Than bolder flights that know no
    check ;

Better to use the bit, than throw
  The reins all loose on fancy's neck.
The liberal range of Art should be
  The breadth of Christian liberty,
Restrained alone by challenge and alarm
Where its charmed footsteps tread the
  border land of harm.

" Beyond the poet's sweet dream lives
  The eternal epic of the man.
He wisest is who only gives,
  True to himself, the best he can ;
Who, drifting in the winds of praise,
The inward monitor obeys ;
And, with the boldness that confesses fear,
Takes in the crowded sail, and lets his
  conscience steer.

" Thanks for the fitting word he speaks,
  Nor less for doubtful word unspoken ;
For the false model that he breaks,
  As for the moulded grace unbroken ;
For what is missed and what remains,
For losses which are truest gains,
For reverence conscious of the Eternal
  eye,
And truth too fair to need the garnish
  of a lie."

Laughing, the Critic bowed.   " I
  yield
  The point without another word ;
Who ever yet a case appealed
  Where beauty's judgment had been
  heard ?
And you, my good friend, owe to me
Your warmest thanks for such a plea,
As true withal as sweet.   For my offence
Of cavil, let her words be ample recom-
  pense."

Across the sea one lighthouse star,
  With crimson ray that came and
  went,
Revolving on its tower afar,
  Looked through the doorway of the
  tent.
While outward, over sand-slopes wet,
The lamp flashed down its yellow jet
On the long wash of waves, with red and
  green
Tangles of weltering weed through the
  white foam-wreaths seen.

" ' Sing while we may, — another day
  May bring enough of sorrow ' ; —
  thus

Our Traveller in his own sweet lay,
  His Crimean camp-song, hints to us,"
The lady said.   " So let it be ;
  Sing us a song," exclaimed all three.
She smiled : " I can but marvel at your
  choice
To hear our poet's words through my
  poor borrowed voice."

Her window opens to the bay,
On glistening light or misty gray,
And there at dawn and set of day
  In prayer she kneels :
" Dear Lord ! " she saith, " to many a
  home
From wind and wave the wanderers
  come ;
I only see the tossing foam
  Of stranger keels.

" Blown out and in by summer gales,
The stately ships, with crowded sails,
And sailors leaning o'er their rails,
  Before me glide ;
They come, they go, but nevermore,
Spice-laden from the Indian shore,
I see his swift-winged Isidore
  The waves divide.

" O Thou ! with whom the night is day
And one the near and far away,
Look out on yon gray waste, and say
  Where lingers he.
Alive, perchance, on some lone beach
Or thirsty isle beyond the reach
Of man, he hears the mocking speech
  Of wind and sea.

" O dread and cruel deep, reveal
The secret which thy waves conceal,
And, ye wild sea-birds, hither wheel
  And tell your tale.
Let winds that tossed his raven hair
A message from my lost one bear, —
Some thought of me, a last fond prayer
  Or dying wail !

" Come, with your dreariest truth shut
  out
The fears that haunt me round about ;
O God ! I cannot bear this doubt
  That stifles breath.
The worst is better than the dread ;
Give me but leave to mourn my dead
Asleep in trust and hope, instead
  Of life in death ! "

It might have been the evening breeze
That whispered in the garden trees,
It might have been the sound of seas
    That rose and fell ;
But, with her heart, if not her ear,
The old loved voice she seemed to hear :
" I wait to meet thee : be of cheer,
    For all is well ! "

———

The sweet voice into silence went,
    A silence which was almost pain
As through it rolled the long lament,
    The cadence of the mournful main.
Glancing his written pages o'er,
The Reader tried his part once more ;
Leaving the land of hackmatack and
    pine
For Tuscan valleys glad with olive and
    with vine.

THE BROTHER OF MERCY.

PIERO LUCA, known of all the town
As the gray porter by the Pitti wall
Where the noon shadows of the gardens
    fall,
Sick and in dolor, waited to lay down
His last sad burden, and beside his mat
The barefoot monk of La Certosa sat.

Unseen, in square and blossoming
    garden drifted,
Soft sunset lights through green Val
    d' Arno sifted ;
Unheard, below the living shuttles
    shifted
Backward and forth, and wove, in love
    or strife,
In mirth or pain, the mottled web of
    life :
But when at last came upward from the
    street
Tinkle of bell and tread of measured feet,
The sick man started, strove to rise in
    vain,
Sinking back heavily with a moan of
    pain.
And the monk said, " 'T is but the
    Brotherhood
Of Mercy going on some errand good :
Their black masks by the palace-wall I
    see."
Piero answered faintly, " Woe is me !
This day for the first time in forty
    years

In vain the bell hath sounded in my
    ears,
Calling me with my brethren of the
    mask,
Beggar and prince alike, to some new
    task
Of love or pity, — haply from the street
To bear a wretch plague-stricken, or,
    with feet
Hushed to the quickened ear and fêve
    ish brain,
To tread the crowded lazaretto's floors,
Down the long twilight of the corridors,
Midst tossing arms and faces full of
    pain.
I loved the work : it was its own reward.
I never counted on it to offset
My sins, which are many, or make less
    my debt
To the free grace and mercy of our Lord ;
But somehow, father, it has come to be
In these long years so much a part of me,
I should not know myself, if lacking
    it,
But with the work the worker too would
    die,
And in my place some other self would
    sit
Joyful or sad, — what matters, if not I ?
And now all 's over. Woe is me ! " —
    " My son,"
The monk said soothingly, " thy work
    is done ;
And no more as a servant, but the guest
Of God thou enterest thy eternal rest.
No toil, no tears, no sorrow for the lost,
Shall mar thy perfect bliss. Thou shalt
    sit down
Clad in white robes, and wear a golden
    crown
Forever and forever." — Piero tossed
On his sick-pillow : " Miserable me !
I am too poor for such grand company ;
The crown would be too heavy for this
    gray
Old head ; and God forgive me if I say
It would be hard to sit there night and
    day,
Like an image in the Tribune, doing
    naught
With these hard hands, that all my life
    have wrought,
Not for bread only, but for pity's sake.
I 'm dull at prayers : I could not keep
    awake,
Counting my beads. Mine 's but a crazy
    head,

Scarce worth the saving, if all else be
    dead.
And if one goes to heaven without a
    heart,
God knows he leaves behind his better
    part.
I love my fellow-men : the worst I know
I would do good to. Will death change
    me so
That I shall sit among the lazy saints,
Turning a deaf ear to the sore complaints
Of souls that suffer ? Why, I never yet
Left a poor dog in the *strada* hard beset,
Or ass o'erladen ! Must I rate man less
Than dog or ass, in holy selfishness ?
Methinks (Lord, pardon, if the thought
    be sin !)
The world of pain were better, if therein
One's heart might still be human, and
    desires
Of natural pity drop upon its fires
Some cooling tears."
          Thereat the pale monk crossed
His brow, and, muttering, "Madman !
    thou art lost !"
Took up his pyx and fled ; and, left alone,
The sick man closed his eyes with a
    great groan
That sank into a prayer, "Thy will be
    done !"

Then was he made aware, by soul or
    ear,
Of somewhat pure and holy bending o'er
    him,
And of a voice like that of her who bore
    him,
Tender and most compassionate : "Never
    fear !
For heaven is love, as God himself is
    love ;
Thy work below shall be thy work
    above."
And when he looked, lo ! in the stern
    monk's place
He saw the shining of an angel's face !

———

The Traveller broke the pause. "I've
    seen
    The Brothers down the long street
      steal,
Black, silent, masked, the crowd be-
    tween,
And felt to doff my hat and kneel
With heart, if not with knee, in prayer,
For blessings on their pious care."

The Reader wiped his glasses : "Friends
    of mine,
We'll try our home-brewed next, in-
    stead of foreign wine."

THE CHANGELING.

For the fairest maid in Hampton
    They needed not to search,
Who saw young Anna Favor
    Come walking into church, —

Or bringing from the meadows,
    At set of harvest-day,
The frolic of the blackbirds,
    The sweetness of the hay.

Now the weariest of all mothers,
    The saddest two-years bride,
She scowls in the face of her husband,
    And spurns her child aside.

"Rake out the red coals, goodman, —
    For there the child shall lie,
Till the black witch comes to fetch her
    And both up chimney fly.

"It's never my own little daughter,
    It's never my own," she said ;
"The witches have stolen my Anna,
    And left me an imp instead.

"O, fair and sweet was my baby,
    Blue eyes, and hair of gold ;
But this is ugly and wrinkled,
    Cross, and cunning, and old.

"I hate the touch of her fingers,
    I hate the feel of her skin ;
It's not the milk from my bosom,
    But my blood, that she sucks in.

"My face grows sharp with the torment;
    Look ! my arms are skin and bone ! —
Rake open the red coals, goodman,
    And the witch shall have her own.

"She'll come when she hears it crying,
    In the shape of an owl or bat,
And she'll bring us our darling Anna
    In place of her screeching brat."

Then the goodman, Ezra Dalton,
    Laid his hand upon her head :
"Thy sorrow is great, O woman !
    I sorrow with thee," he said.

"And the cloud of her soul was lifted."   Page 305.

"The paths to trouble are many,
    And never but one sure way
Leads out to the light beyond it:
    My poor wife, let us pray."

Then he said to the great All-Father,
    "Thy daughter is weak and blind;
Let her sight come back, and clothe her
    Once more in her right mind.

"Lead her out of this evil shadow,
    Out of these fancies wild ;
Let the holy love of the mother
    Turn again to her child.

"Make her lips like the lips of Mary
    Kissing her blessed Son ;
Let her hands, like the hands of Jesus,
    Rest on her little one.

"Comfort the soul of thy handmaid,
    Open her prison-door,
And thine shall be all the glory
    And praise forevermore."

Then into the face of its mother
    The baby looked up and smiled ;
And the cloud of her soul was lifted,
    And she knew her little child.

A beam of the slant west sunshine
    Made the wan face almost fair,
Lit the blue eyes' patient wonder,
    And the rings of pale gold hair.

She kissed it on lip and forehead,
    She kissed it on cheek and chin,
And she bared her snow-white bosom
    To the lips so pale and thin.

O, fair on her bridal morning
    Was the maid who blushed and smiled,
But fairer to Ezra Dalton
    Looked the mother of his child.

With more than a lover's fondness
    He stooped to her worn young face,
And the nursing child and the mother
    He folded in one embrace.

"Blessed be God ! " he murmured.
    "Blessed be God ! " she said ;
"For I see, who once was blinded, —
    I live, who once was dead.

"Now mount and ride, my goodman,
    As thou lovest thy own soul !
20

Woe 's me, if my wicked fancies
    Be the death of Goody Cole !'

His horse he saddled and bridled,
    And into the night rode he, —
Now through the great black woodland,
    Now by the white-beached sea.

He rode through the silent clearings,
    He came to the ferry wide,
And thrice he called to the boatman
    Asleep on the other side.

He set his horse to the river,
    He swam to Newbury town,
And he called up Justice Sewall
    In his nightcap and his gown.

And the grave and worshipful justice
    (Upon whose soul be peace !)
Set his name to the jailer's warrant
    For Goodwife Cole's release.

Then through the night the hoof-beats
    Went sounding like a flail ;
And Goody Cole at cockcrow
    Came forth from Ipswich jail.

"Here is a rhyme : — I hardly dare
    To venture on its theme worn out ;
What seems so sweet by Doon and
        Ayr
    Sounds simply silly hereabout ;
And pipes by lips Arcadian blown
Are only tin horns at our own.
Yet still the muse of pastoral walks
        with us,
While Hosea Biglow sings, our new
        Theocritus."

THE MAIDS OF ATTITASH.

IN sky and wave the white clouds swam,
And the blue hills of Nottingham
    Through gaps of leafy green
    Across the lake were seen, —

When, in the shadow of the ash
That dreams its dream in Attitash,
    In the warm summer weather,
    Two maidens sat together.

They sat and watched in idle mood
The gleam and shade of lake and
        wood, —

The beach the keen light smote,
The white sail of a boat, —

Swan flocks of lilies shoreward lying,
In sweetness, not in music, dying, —
　　Hardhack, and virgin's-bower,
　　And white-spiked clethra-flower.

With careless ears they heard the plash
And breezy wash of Attitash,
　　The wood-bird's plaintive cry,
　　The locust's sharp reply.

And teased the while, with playful hand,
The shaggy dog of Newfoundland,
　　Whose uncouth frolic spilled
　　Their baskets berry-filled.

Then one, the beauty of whose eyes
Was evermore a great surprise,
　　Tossed back her queenly head,
　　And, lightly laughing, said, —

" No bridegroom's hand be mine to hold
That is not lined with yellow gold ;
　　I tread no cottage-floor ;
　　I own no lover poor.

" My love must come on silken wings,
With bridal lights of diamond rings, —
　　Not foul with kitchen smirch,
　　With tallow-dip for torch."

The other, on whose modest head
Was lesser dower of beauty shed,
　　With look for home-hearths meet,
　　And voice exceeding sweet,

Answered, — " We will not rivals be ;
Take thou the gold, leave love to me ;
　　Mine be the cottage small,
　　And thine the rich man's hall.

" I know, indeed, that wealth is good ;
But lowly roof and simple food,
　　With love that hath no doubt,
　　Are more than gold without."

Hard by a farmer hale and young
His cradle in the rye-field swung,
　　Tracking the yellow plain
　　With windrows of ripe grain.

And still, whene'er he paused to whet
His scythe, the sidelong glance he met
　　Of large dark eyes, where strove
　　False pride and secret love.

Be strong, young mower of the grain ;
That love shall overmatch disdain,
　　Its instincts soon or late
　　The heart shall vindicate.

In blouse of gray, with fishing-rod,
Half screened by leaves, a stranger trod
　　The margin of the pond,
　　Watching the group beyond.

The supreme hours unnoted come ;
Unfelt the turning tides of doom ;
　　And so the maids laughed on,
　　Nor dreamed what Fate had done, —

Nor knew the step was Destiny's
That rustled in the birchen trees,
　　As, with their lives forecast,
　　Fisher and mower passed.

Erelong by lake and rivulet side
The summer roses paled and died,
　　And Autumn's fingers shed
　　The maple's leaves of red.

Through the long gold-hazed afternoon,
Alone, but for the diving loon,
　　The partridge in the brake,
　　The black duck on the lake,

Beneath the shadow of the ash
Sat man and maid by Attitash ;
　　And earth and air made room
　　For human hearts to bloom.

Soft spread the carpets of the sod,
And scarlet-oak and golden-rod
　　With blushes and with smiles
　　Lit up the forest aisles.

The mellow light the lake aslant,
The pebbled margin's ripple-chant
　　Attempered and low-toned,
　　The tender mystery owned.

And through the dream the lovers
　　　dreamed
Sweet sounds stole in and soft lights
　　　streamed ;
　　The sunshine seemed to bless,
　　The air was a caress.

Not she who lightly laughed is there,
With scornful toss of midnight hair,
　　Her dark, disdainful eyes,
　　And proud lip worldly-wise.

Her haughty vow is still unsaid,
But all she dreamed and coveted
    Wears, half to her surprise,
    The youthful farmer's guise !

With more than all her old-time pride
She walks the rye-field at his side,
    Careless of cot or hall,
    Since love transfigures all.

Rich beyond dreams, the vantage-
        ground
Of life is gained ; her hands have found
    The talisman of old
    That changes all to gold.

While she who could for love dispense
With all its glittering accidents,
    And trust her heart alone,
    Finds love and gold her own.

What wealth can buy or art can build
Awaits her ; but her cup is filled
    Even now unto the brim ;
    Her world is love and him !

⸻

The while he heard, the Book-man
        drew
    A length of make-believing face,
With smothered mischief laughing
        through :
    "Why, you shall sit in Ramsay's
        place,
And, with his Gentle Shepherd, keep
    On Yankee hills immortal sheep,
While lovelorn swains and maids the
        seas beyond
Hold dreamy tryst around your huckle-
        berry-pond."

The Traveller laughed ; " Sir Gala-
        had
    Singing of love the Trouvere's lay !
How should he know the blindfold
        lad
    From one of Vulcan's forge-boys ? "
    — " Nay,
He better sees who stands outside
    Than they who in procession ride,"
The Reader answered : " selectmen and
        squire
Miss, while they make, the show that
        wayside folks admire.

    " Here is a wild tale of the North,
    Our travelled friend will own as
        one

Fit for a Norland Christmas hearth
    And lips of Christian Andersen.
They tell it in the valleys green
    Of the fair island he has seen,
Low lying off the pleasant Swedish
        shore,
Washed by the Baltic Sea, and watched
    by Elsinore."

KALLUNDBORG CHURCH.

"Tie stille, barn min !
    Imorgen kommer Fin,
    Fa'er din,
Og gi'er dig Esbern Snares öine og hjerte at lege
        med ! "
                                Zealand Rhyme.

" BUILD at Kallundborg by the sea
A church as stately as church may be,
And there shalt thou wed my daughter
        fair,"
Said the Lord of Nesvek to Esbern
        Snare.

And the Baron laughed. But Esbern
        said,
" Though I lose my soul, I will Helva
        wed ! "
And off he strode, in his pride of will,
To the Troll who dwelt in Ulshoi hill.

" Build, O Troll, a church for me
At Kallundborg by the mighty sea ;
Build it stately, and build it fair,
Build it quickly," said Esbern Snare.

But the sly Dwarf said, " No work is
        wrought
By Trolls of the Hills, O man, for
        naught.
What wilt thou give for thy church so
        fair ? "
" Set thy own price," quoth Esbern
        Snare.

" When Kallundborg church is builded
        well,
Thou must the name of its builder tell,
Or thy heart and thy eyes must be my
        boon."
" Build," said Esbern, " and build it
        soon."

By night and by day the Troll wrought
        on ;
He hewed the timbers, he piled the
        stone ;

But day by day, as the walls rose fair,
Darker and sadder grew Esbern Snare.

He listened by night, he watched by day,
He sought and thought, but he dared
    not pray ;
In vain he called on the Elle-maids shy,
And the Neck and the Nis gave no
    reply.

Of his evil bargain far and wide
A rumor ran through the country-side ;
And Helva of Nesvek, young and fair,
Prayed for the soul of Esbern Snare.

And now the church was wellnigh done ;
One pillar it lacked, and one alone ;
And the grim Troll muttered, "Fool
    thou art !
To-morrow gives me thy eyes and
    heart !"

By Kallundborg in black despair,
Through wood and meadow, walked
    Esbern Snare,
Till, worn and weary, the strong man
    sank
Under the birches on Ulshoi bank.

At his last day's work he heard the
    Troll
Hammer and delve in the quarry's hole ;
Before him the church stood large and
    fair :
"I have builded my tomb," said Esbern
    Snare.

And he closed his eyes the sight to hide,
When he heard a light step at his side :
"O Esbern Snare !" a sweet voice said,
"Would I might die now in thy stead !"

With a grasp by love and by fear made
    strong,
He held her fast, and he held her long ;
With the beating heart of a bird afeard,
She hid her face in his flame-red beard.

"O love !" he cried, "let me look to-
    day
In thine eyes ere mine are plucked away ;
Let me hold thee close, let me feel thy
    heart
Ere mine by the Troll is torn apart !

"I sinned, O Helva, for love of thee !
Pray that the Lord Christ pardon me !"

But fast as she prayed, and faster still,
Hammered the Troll in Ulshoi hill.

He knew, as he wrought, that a loving
    heart
Was somehow baffling his evil art ;
For more than spell of Elf or Troll
Is a maiden's prayer for her lover's soul.

And Esbern listened, and caught the
    sound
Of a Troll-wife singing underground :
"To-morrow comes Fine, father thine :
Lie still and hush thee, baby mine !

"Lie still, my darling ! next sunrise
Thou 'lt play with Esbern Snare's heart
    and eyes !"
"Ho ! ho !" quoth Esbern, "is that
    your game ?
Thanks to the Troll-wife, I know his
    name !"

The Troll he heard him, and hurried on
To Kallundborg church with the lack-
    ing stone.
"Too late, Gaffer Fine !" cried Esbern
    Snare ;
And Troll and pillar vanished in air !

That night the harvesters heard the
    sound
Of a woman sobbing underground,
And the voice of the Hill-Troll loud
    with blame
Of the careless singer who told his
    name.

Of the Troll of the Church they sing the
    rune
By the Northern Sea in the harvest
    moon ;
And the fishers of Zealand hear him
    still
Scolding his wife in Ulshoi hill.

And seaward over its groves of birch
Still looks the tower of Kallundborg
    church,
Where, first at its altar, a wedded pair,
Stood Helva of Nesvek and Esbern
    Snare !

———

"What," asked the Traveller, "would
    our sires,
    The old Norse story-tellers, say

Of sun-graved pictures, ocean wires,
  And smoking steamboats of to-day ?
And this, O lady, by your leave,
  Recalls your song of yester eve :
?ray, let us have that Cable-hymn once
    more."
" Hear, hear ! " the Book-man cried,
    " the lady has the floor.

  " These noisy waves below perhaps
    To such a strain will lend their ear,
With softer voice and lighter lapse
    Come stealing up the sands to hear,
And what they once refused to do
For old King Knut accord to you.
Nay, even the fishes shall your listeners
    be,
As once, the legend runs, they heard
    St. Anthony."

O lonely bay of Trinity,
  O dreary shores, give ear !
Lean down unto the white-lipped sea
  The voice of God to hear !

From world to world his couriers fly,
  Thought-winged and shod with fire ;
The angel of His stormy sky
  Rides down the sunken wire.

What saith the herald of the Lord ?
  " The world's long strife is done ;
Close wedded by that mystic cord,
  Its continents are one.

" And one in heart, as one in blood,
  Shall all her peoples be ;
The hands of human brotherhood
  Are clasped beneath the sea.

" Through Orient seas, o'er Afric's plain
  And Asian mountains borne,
The vigor of the Northern brain
  Shall nerve the world outworn.

" From clime, to clime, from shore to
    shore,
  Shall thrill the magic thread ;
The new Prometheus steals once more
  The fire that wakes the dead."

Throb on, strong pulse of thunder !
    beat
  From answering beach to beach ;
Fuse nations in thy kindly heat,
  And melt the chains of each !

Wild terror of the sky above,
  Glide tamed and dumb below !
Bear gently, Ocean's carrier-dove,
  Thy errands to and fro.

Weave on, swift shuttle of the Lord,
  Beneath the deep so far,
The bridal robe of earth's accord,
  The funeral shroud of war !

For lo ! the fall of Ocean's wall
  Space mocked and time outrun ;
And round the world the thought of all
  Is as the thought of one !

The poles unite, the zones agree,
  The tongues of striving cease ;
As on the Sea of Galilee
  The Christ is whispering, Peace !

  " Glad prophecy ! to this at last,"
    The Reader said, " shall all things
      come.
Forgotten be the bugle's blast,
  And battle-music of the drum.
A little while the world may run
  Its old mad way, with needle-gun
And iron-clad, but truth, at last, shall
    reign :
The cradle-song of Christ was never sung
    in vain ! "

  Shifting his scattered papers, "Here,"
    He said, as died the faint applause,
  " Is something that I found last year
    Down on the island known as Orr's.
I had it from a fair-haired girl
  Who, oddly, bore the name of Pearl,
(As if by some droll freak of circum-
    stance,)
Classic, or wellnigh so, in Harriet
  Stowe's romance."

THE DEAD SHIP OF HARPS-
WELL.

WHAT flecks the outer gray beyond
  The sundown's golden trail ?
The white flash of a sea-bird's wing,
  Or gleam of slanting sail ?
Let young eyes watch from Neck and
    Point,
  And sea-worn elders pray, —
The ghost of what was once a ship
  Is sailing up the bay !

From gray sea-fog, from icy drift,
    From peril and from pain,
The home-bound fisher greets thy lights,
    O hundred-harbored Maine !
But many a keel shall seaward turn,
    And many a sail outstand,
When, tall and white, the Dead Ship
        looms
    Against the dusk of land.

She rounds the headland's bristling
        pines ;
    She threads the isle-set bay ;
No spur of breeze can speed her on,
    Nor ebb of tide delay.
Old men still walk the Isle of Orr
    Who tell her date and name,
Old shipwrights sit in Freeport yards
    Who hewed her oaken frame.

What weary doom of baffled quest,
    Thou sad sea-ghost, is thine ?
What makes thee in the haunts of
        home
    A wonder and a sign ?
No foot is on thy silent deck,
    Upon thy helm no hand ;
No ripple hath the soundless wind
    That smites thee from the land !

For never comes the ship to port,
    Howe'er the breeze may be ;
Just when she nears the waiting shore
    She drifts again to sea.
No tack of sail, nor turn of helm,
    Nor sheer of veering side ;
Stern-fore she drives to sea and night,
    Against the wind and tide.

In vain o'er Harpswell Neck the star
    Of evening guides her in ;
In vain for her the lamps are lit
    Within thy tower, Seguin !
In vain the harbor-boat shall hail,
    In vain the pilot call ;
No hand shall reef her spectral sail,
    Or let her anchor fall.

Shake, brown old wives, with dreary
        joy,
    Your gray-head hints of ill ;
And, over sick-beds whispering low,
    Your prophecies fulfil.
Some home amid yon birchen trees
    Shall drape its door with woe ;
And slowly where the Dead Ship sails,
    The burial boat shall row !

From Wolf Neck and from Flying Point,
    From island and from main,
From sheltered cove and tided creek,
    Shall glide the funeral train.
The dead-boat with the bearers four,
    The mourners at her stern, —
And one shall go the silent way
    Who shall no more return !

And men shall sigh, and women weep,
    Whose dear ones pale and pine,
And sadly over sunset seas
    Await the ghostly sign.
They know not that its sails are filled
    By pity's tender breath,
Nor see the Angel at the helm
    Who steers the Ship of Death !

———

" Chill as a down-east breeze should
        be,"
    The Book-man said.   " A ghostly
        touch
The legend has.   I 'm glad to see
    Your flying Yankee beat the Dutch."
" Well, here is something of the
        sort
Which one midsummer day I caught
In Narragansett Bay, for lack of fish."
" We wait," the Traveller said ; " serve
    hot or cold your dish."

THE PALATINE.

LEAGUES north, as fly the gull and
        auk,
Point Judith watches with eye of hawk ;
Leagues south, thy beacon flames, Mon-
        tauk !

Lonely and wind-shorn, wood-forsaken,
With never a tree for Spring to waken,
For tryst of lovers or farewells taken,

Circled by waters that never freeze,
Beaten by billow and swept by breeze,
Lieth the island of Manisees,

Set at the mouth of the Sound to hold
The coast lights up on its turret old,
Yellow with moss and sea-fog mould.

Dreary the land when gust and sleet
At its doors and windows howl and
        beat,
And Winter laughs at its fires of peat !

But in summer time, when pool and pond,
Held in the laps of valleys fond,
Are blue as the glimpses of sea beyond ;

When the hills are sweet with the brier-rose,
And, hid in the warm, soft dells, unclose
Flowers the mainland rarely knows ;

When boats to their morning fishing go,
And, held to the wind and slanting low,
Whitening and darkening the small sails show, —

Then is that lonely island fair ;
And the pale health-seeker findeth there
The wine of life in its pleasant air.

No greener valleys the sun invite,
On smoother beaches no sea-birds light,
No blue waves shatter to foam more white !

There, circling ever their narrow range,
Quaint tradition and legend strange
Live on unchallenged, and know no change.

Old wives spinning their webs of tow,
Or rocking weirdly to and fro
In and out of the peat's dull glow,

And old men mending their nets of twine,
Talk together of dream and sign,
Talk of the lost ship Palatine, —

The ship that, a hundred years before,
Freighted deep with its goodly store,
In the gales of the equinox went ashore.

The eager islanders one by one
Counted the shots of her signal gun,
And heard the crash when she drove right on !

Into the teeth of death she sped :
(May God forgive the hands that fed
The false lights over the rocky Head !)

O men and brothers ! what sights were there !
White upturned faces, hands stretched in prayer !
Where waves had pity, could ye not spare ?

Down swooped the wreckers, like birds of prey
Tearing the heart of the ship away,
And the dead had never a word to say.

And then, with ghastly shimmer and shine
Over the rocks and the seething brine,
They burned the wreck of the Palatine.

In their cruel hearts, as they homeward sped,
"The sea and the rocks are dumb," they said :
"There 'll be no reckoning with the dead."

But the year went round, and when once more
Along their foam-white curves of shore
They heard the line-storm rave and roar,

Behold ! again, with shimmer and shine,
Over the rocks and the seething brine,
The flaming wreck of the Palatine !

So, haply in fitter words than these,
Mending their nets on their patient knees
They tell the legend of Manisees.

Nor looks nor tones a doubt betray ;
"It is known to us all," they quietly say ;
"We too have seen it in our day."

Is there, then, no death for a word once spoken ?
Was never a deed but left its token
Written on tables never broken ?

Do the elements subtle reflections give ?
Do pictures of all the ages live
On Nature's infinite negative,

Which, half in sport, in malice half,
She shows at times, with shudder or laugh,
Phantom and shadow in photograph ?

For still, on many a moonless night,
From Kingston Head and from Montauk light
The spectre kindles and burns in sight.

Now low and dim, now clear and higher,
Leaps up the terrible Ghost of Fire,
Then, slowly sinking, the flames expire.

And the wise Sound skippers, though
    skies be fine,
Reef their sails when they see the sign
Of the blazing wreck of the Palatine !

  " A fitter tale to scream than sing,"
    The Book-man said. " Well, fan-
    cy, then,"
  The Reader answered, " on the wing
    The sea - birds shriek it, not for
    men,
But in the ear of wave and breeze ! "
The Traveller mused : " Your Mani-
    sees
Is fairy-land : off Narragansett shore
Who ever saw the isle or heard its name
    before ?

  " 'T is some strange land of Flyaway,
    Whose dreamy shore the ship be-
    guiles,
  St. Brandan's in its sea-mist gray,
    Or sunset loom of Fortunate Isles ! "
  " No ghost, but solid turf and rock
Is the good island known as Block,"
The Reader said. " For beauty and for
    ease
I chose its Indian name, soft-flowing
    Manisees !

  " But let it pass ; here is a bit
    Of unrhymed story, with a hint
Of the old preaching mood in it,
    The sort of sidelong moral squint
Our friend objects to, which has
    grown,
I fear, a habit of my own.
'T was written when the Asian plague
    drew near,
And the land held its breath and paled
    with sudden fear."

ABRAHAM DAVENPORT.

In the old days (a custom laid aside
With breeches and cocked hats) the peo-
    ple sent
Their wisest men to make the public
    laws.
And so, from a brown homestead, where
    the Sound
Drinks the small tribute of the Mianas,
Waved over by the woods of Rippowams,
And hallowed by pure lives and tranquil
    deaths,

Stamford sent up to the councils of the
    State
Wisdom and grace in Abraham Daven-
    port.

'T was on a May-day of the far old
    year
Seventeen hundred eighty, that there
    fell
Over the bloom and sweet life of the
    Spring,
Over the fresh earth and the heaven of
    noon,
A horror of great darkness, like the
    night
In day of which the Norland sagas
    tell, —
The Twilight of the Gods. The low-
    hung sky
Was black with ominous clouds, save
    where its rim
Was fringed with a dull glow, like that
    which climbs
The crater's sides from the red hell be-
    low.
Birds ceased to sing, and all the barn-
    yard fowls
Roosted ; the cattle at the pasture
    bars
Lowed, and looked homeward ; bats on
    leathern wings
Flitted abroad ; the sounds of labor
    died ;
Men prayed, and women wept ; all ears
    grew sharp
To hear the doom-blast of the trumpet
    shatter
The black sky, that the dreadful face of
    Christ
Might look from the rent clouds, not as
    he looked
A loving guest at Bethany, but stern
As Justice and inexorable Law.

Meanwhile in the old State House,
    dim as ghosts,
Sat the lawgivers of Connecticut,
Trembling beneath their legislative
    robes.
" It is the Lord's Great Day ! Let us
    adjourn,"
Some said ; and then, as if with one
    accord,
All eyes were turned to Abraham Daven-
    port.
He rose, slow cleaving with his steady
    voice

The intolerable hush. "This well may
    be
The Day of Judgment which the world
    awaits ;
But be it so or not, I only know
My present duty, and my Lord's com-
    mand
To occupy till he come. So at the post
Where he hath set me in his providence,
I choose, for one, to meet him face to
    face, —
No faithless servant frightened from my
    task,
But ready when the Lord of the harvest
    calls ;
And therefore, with all reverence, I
    would say,
Let God do his work, we will see to
    ours.
Bring in the candles." And they
    brought them in.

Then by the flaring lights the Speaker
    read,
Albeit with husky voice and shaking
    hands,
An act to amend an act to regulate
The shad and alewive fisheries. Where-
    upon
Wisely and well spake Abraham Daven-
    port,
Straight to the question, with no figures
    of speech
Save the ten Arab signs, yet not without
The shrewd dry humor natural to the
    man :
His awe-struck colleagues listening all
    the while,
Between the pauses of his argument,
To hear the thunder of the wrath of
    God
Break from the hollow trumpet of the
    cloud.

And there he stands in memory to
    this day,
Erect, self-poised, a rugged face, half
    seen
Against the background of unnatural
    dark,
A witness to the ages as they pass,
That simple duty hath no place for fear.

He ceased : just then the ocean
    seemed
    To lift a half-faced moon in sight ;

And, shore-ward, o'er the waters
    gleamed,
    From crest to crest, a line of light,
Such as of old, with solemn awe,
    The fishers by Gennesaret saw,
When dry-shod o'er it walked the Son
    of God,
Tracking the waves with light where'er
    his sandals trod.

Silently for a space each eye
    Upon that sudden glory turned :
Cool from the land the breeze blew
    by,
    The tent-ropes flapped, the long
      beach churned
Its waves to foam ; on either hand
Stretched, far as sight, the hills of
    sand ;
With bays of marsh, and capes of bush
    and tree,
The wood's black shore-line loomed be-
    yond the meadowy sea.

The lady rose to leave. "One song,
    Or hymn," they urged, "before we
    part."
And she, with lips to which belong
    Sweet intuitions of all art,
Gave to the winds of night a strain
Which they who heard would hear
    again ;
And to her voice the solemn ocean lent,
Touching its harp of sand, a deep ac-
    companiment.

The harp at Nature's advent strung
    Has never ceased to play ;
The song the stars of morning sung
    Has never died away.

And prayer is made, and praise is given,
    By all things near and far ;
The ocean looketh up to heaven,
    And mirrors every star.

Its waves are kneeling on the strand,
    As kneels the human knee,
Their white locks bowing to the sand,
    The priesthood of the sea !

They pour their glittering treasures
    forth,
    Their gifts of pearl they bring,
And all the listening hills of earth
    Take up the song they sing.

The green earth sends her incense up
  From many a mountain shrine ;
From folded leaf and dewy cup
  She pours her sacred wine.

The mists above the morning rills
  Rise white as wings of prayer ;
The altar-curtains of the hills
  Are sunset's purple air.

The winds with hymns of praise are loud,
  Or low with sobs of pain, —
The thunder-organ of the cloud,
  The dropping tears of rain.

With drooping head and branches crossed
  The twilight forest grieves,
Or speaks with tongues of Pentecost
  From all its sunlit leaves.

The blue sky is the temple's arch,
  Its transept earth and air,
The music of its starry march
  The chorus of a prayer.

So Nature keeps the reverent frame
  With which her years began,

And all her signs and voices shame
  The prayerless heart of man.

———

The singer ceased.   The moon's white
    rays
  Fell on the rapt, still face of her.
" *Allah il Allah!*   He hath praise
  From all things," said the Traveller.
"Oft from the desert's silent nights,
  And mountain hymns of sunset lights,
My heart has felt rebuke, as in his tent
The Moslem's prayer has shamed my
    Christian knee unbent."

He paused, and lo ! far, faint, and slow
  The bells in Newbury's steeples
    tolled
  The twelve dead hours ; the lamp
    burned low ;
  The singer sought her canvas fold.
One sadly said, " At break of day
We strike our tent and go our way."
But one made answer cheerily, "Never
    fear,
We 'll pitch this tent of ours in type
    another year."

———

NATIONAL LYRICS.

THE MANTLE OF ST. JOHN DE MATHA.

A LEGEND OF " THE RED, WHITE, AND
  BLUE," A. D. 1154 – 1864.

A STRONG and mighty Angel,
  Calm, terrible, and bright,
The cross in blended red and blue
  Upon his mantle white !

Two captives by him kneeling,
  Each on his broken chain,
Sang praise to God who raiseth
  The dead to life again !

Dropping his cross-wrought mantle,
  " Wear this," the Angel said ;
'Take thou, O Freedom's priest, its
    sign, —
  The white, the blue, and red."

Then rose up John de Matha
  In the strength the Lord Christ gave,
And begged through all the land of
    France
  The ransom of the slave.

The gates of tower and castle
  Before him open flew,
The drawbridge at his coming fell,
  The door-bolt backward drew.

For all men owned his errand,
  And paid his righteous tax ;
And the hearts of lord and peasant
  Were in his hands as wax.

At last, outbound from Tunis,
  His bark her anchor weighed,
Freighted with seven-score Christian
    souls
  Whose ransom he had paid.

But, torn by Paynim hatred,
  Her sails in tatters hung ;
And on the wild waves, rudderless,
  A shattered hulk she swung.

"God save us !" cried the captain,
  "For naught can man avail ;
O, woe betide the ship that lacks
  Her rudder and her sail !

"Behind us are the Moormen ;
  At sea we sink or strand :
There's death upon the water,
  There's death upon the land !"

Then up spake John de Matha :
  "God's errands never fail !
Take thou the mantle which I wear,
  And make of it a sail."

They raised the cross-wrought mantle,
  The blue, the white, the red ;
And straight before the wind off-shore
  The ship of Freedom sped.

"God help us !" cried the seamen,
  "For vain is mortal skill :
The good ship on a stormy sea
  Is drifting at its will."

Then up spake John de Matha :
  "My mariners, never fear !
The Lord whose breath has filled her sail
  May well our vessel steer !"

So on through storm and darkness
  They drove for weary hours ;
And lo ! the third gray morning shone
  On Ostia's friendly towers.

And on the walls the watchers
  The ship of mercy knew, —
They knew far off its holy cross,
  The red, the white, and blue.

And the bells in all the steeples
  Rang out in glad accord,
To welcome home to Christian soil
  The ransomed of the Lord.

So runs the ancient legend
  By bard and painter told ;
And lo ! the cycle rounds again,
  The new is as the old !

With rudder foully broken,
  And sails by traitors torn,

Our country on a midnight sea
  Is waiting for the morn.

Before her, nameless terror ;
  Behind, the pirate foe ;
The clouds are black above her,
  The sea is white below.

The hope of all who suffer,
  The dread of all who wrong,
She drifts in darkness and in storm,
  How long, O Lord ! how long ?

But courage, O my mariners !
  Ye shall not suffer wreck ;
While up to God the freedman's prayers
  Are rising from your deck.

Is not your sail the banner
  Which God hath blest anew,
The mantle that De Matha wore,
  The red, the white, the blue ?

Its hues are all of heaven, —
  The red of sunset's dye,
The whiteness of the moon-lit cloud,
  The blue of morning's sky.

Wait cheerily, then, O mariners,
  For daylight and for land ;
The breath of God is in your sail,
  Your rudder is His hand.

Sail on, sail on, deep-freighted
  With blessings and with hopes ;
The saints of old with shadowy hands
  Are pulling at your ropes.

Behind ye holy martyrs
  Uplift the palm and crown ;
Before ye unborn ages send
  Their benedictions down.

Take heart from John de Matha ! —
  God's errands never fail !
Sweep on through storm and darkness,
  The thunder and the hail !

Sail on ! The morning cometh,
  The port ye yet shall win ;
And all the bells of God shall ring
  The good ship bravely in !

WHAT THE BIRDS SAID.

THE birds against the April wind
  Flew northward, singing as they flew ;

They sang, " The land we leave behind
  Has swords for corn-blades, blood for
    dew."

" O wild-birds, flying from the South,
  What saw and heard ye, gazing down ?"
" We saw the mortar's upturned mouth,
  The sickened camp, the blazing town !

" Beneath the bivouac's starry lamps,
  We saw your march-worn children
    die ;
In shrouds of moss, in cypress swamps,
  We saw your dead uncoffined lie.

" We heard the starving prisoner's
    sighs,
  And saw, from line and trench, your
    sons
Follow our flight with home-sick eyes
  Beyond the battery's smoking guns."

" And heard and saw ye only wrong
  And pain," I cried, " O wing-worn
    · flocks ?"
" We heard," they sang, " the freed-
    man's song,
  The crash of Slavery's broken locks !

" We saw from new, uprising States
  The treason-nursing mischief spurned,
As, crowding Freedom's ample gates,
  The long-estranged and lost returned.

" O'er dusky faces, seamed and old,
  And hands horn-hard with unpaid
    toil,
With hope in every rustling fold,
  We saw your star-dropt flag uncoil.

" And struggling up through sounds
    accursed,
  A grateful murmur clomb the air ;
A whisper scarcely heard at first,
  It filled the listening heavens with
    prayer.

" And sweet and far, as from a star,
  Replied a voice which shall not cease,
Till, drowning all the noise of war,
  It sings the blessed song of peace !"

So to me, in a doubtful day
  Of chill and slowly greening spring,
Low stooping from the cloudy gray,
  The wild-birds sang or seemed to
    sing.

They vanished in the misty air,
  The song went with them in their
    flight ;
But lo ! they left the sunset fair,
  And in the evening there was light.

LAUS DEO !

ON HEARING THE BELLS RING ON THE
PASSAGE OF THE CONSTITUTIONAL
AMENDMENT ABOLISHING SLAVERY.

IT is done!
  Clang of bell and roar of gun
Send the tidings up and down.
  How the belfries rock and reel !
  How the great guns, peal on peal,
Fling the joy from town to town !

Ring, O bells !
  Every stroke exulting tells
Of the burial hour of crime.
  Loud and long, that all may hear,
  Ring for every listening ear
Of Eternity and Time !

Let us kneel :
  God's own voice is in that peal,
And this spot is holy ground.
  Lord, forgive us ! What are we,
  That our eyes this glory see,
That our ears have heard the sound !

For the Lord
  On the whirlwind is abroad ;
In the earthquake he has spoken ;
  He has smitten with his thunder
  The iron walls asunder,
And the gates of brass are broken !

Loud and long
  Lift the old exulting song ;
Sing with Miriam by the sea
  He has cast the mighty down ;
  Horse and rider sink and drown ;
" He hath triumphed gloriously ! "

Did we dare,
  In our agony of prayer,
Ask for more than He has done ?
  When was ever his right hand
  Over any time or land
Stretched as now beneath the sun ?

How they pale,
  Ancient myth and song and tale,

In this wonder of our days,
  When the cruel rod of war
  Blossoms white with righteous law,
And the wrath of man is praise !

  Blotted out !
All within and all about
Shall a fresher life begin ;
  Freer breathe the universe
  As it rolls its heavy curse
On the dead and buried sin !

  It is done !
In the circuit of the sun
Shall the sound thereof go forth.
  It shall bid the sad rejoice,
  It shall give the dumb a voice,
It shall belt with joy the earth !

  Ring and swing,
Bells of joy ! On morning's wing
Send the song of praise abroad !
  With a sound of broken chains
  Tell the nations that He reigns,
Who alone is Lord and God !

THE PEACE AUTUMN.

WRITTEN FOR THE ESSEX COUNTY
AGRICULTURAL FESTIVAL, 1865.

THANK God for rest, where none molest,
  And none can make afraid, —
For Peace that sits as Plenty's guest
  Beneath the homestead shade !

Bring pike and gun, the sword's red
      scourge,
  The negro's broken chains,
And beat them at the blacksmith's
      forge
  To ploughshares for our plains.

Alike henceforth our hills of snow,
  And vales where cotton flowers ;
All streams that flow, all winds that
      blow,
  Are Freedom's motive-powers.

Henceforth to Labor's chivalry
  Be knightly honors paid ;
For nobler than the sword's shall be
  The sickle's accolade.

Build up an altar to the Lord,
  O grateful hearts of ours !

And shape it of the greenest sward
  That ever drank the showers.

Lay all the bloom of gardens there,
  And there the orchard fruits ;
Bring golden grain from sun and air,
  From earth her goodly roots.

There let our banners droop and flow,
  The stars uprise and fall ;
Our roll of martyrs, sad and slow,
  Let sighing breezes call.

Their names let hands of horn and tan
  And rough-shod feet applaud,
Who died to make the slave a man,
  And link with toil reward.

There let the common heart keep time
  To such an anthem sung
As never swelled on poet's rhyme,
  Or thrilled on singer's tongue.

Song of our burden and relief,
  Of peace and long annoy ;
The passion of our mighty grief
  And our exceeding joy !

A song of praise to Him who filled
  The harvests sown in tears,
And gave each field a double yield
  To feed our battle-years !

A song of faith that trusts the end
  To match the good begun,
Nor doubts the power of Love to blend
  The hearts of men as one !

TO THE THIRTY-NINTH
CONGRESS.

O PEOPLE-CHOSEN ! are ye not
  Likewise the chosen of the Lord,
  To do his will and speak his word ?

From the loud thunder-storm of war
  Not man alone hath called ye forth,
  But he, the God of all the earth !

The torch of vengeance in your hands
  He quenches ; unto Him belongs
  The solemn recompense of wrongs.

Enough of blood the land has seen,
  And not by cell or gallows-stair
  Shall ye the way of God prepare.

Say to the pardon-seekers, — Keep
  Your manhood, bend no suppliant
    knees,
  Nor palter with unworthy pleas.

Above your voices sounds the wail
  Of starving men ; we shut in vain
  Our eyes to Pillow's ghastly stain.

What words can drown that bitter
    cry ?
  What tears wash out that stain of
    death ?
  What oaths confirm your broken faith ?

From you alone the guaranty
  Of union, freedom, peace, we claim ;
  We urge no conqueror's terms of
    shame.

Alas ! no victor's pride is ours ;
  We bend above our triumphs won
  Like David o'er his rebel son.

Be men, not beggars. Cancel all
  By one brave, generous action ; trust
  Your better instincts, and be just !

Make all men peers before the law,
  Take hands from off the negro's throat,
  Give black and white an equal vote.

Keep all your forfeit lives and lands,
  But give the common law's redress
  To labor's utter nakedness.

Revive the old heroic will ;
  Be in the right as brave and strong
  As ye have proved yourselves in wrong.

Defeat shall then be victory,
  Your loss the wealth of full amends,
  And hate be love, and foes be friends.

Then buried be the dreadful past,
  Its common slain be mourned, and let
  All memories soften to regret.

Then shall the Union's mother-heart
  Her lost and wandering ones recall,
  Forgiving and restoring all, —

And Freedom break her marble trance
  Above the Capitolian dome,
  Stretch hands, and bid ye welcome
    home !

OCCASIONAL POEMS.

THE ETERNAL GOODNESS.

O FRIENDS ! with whom my feet have
    trod
  The quiet aisles of prayer,
Glad witness to your zeal for God
  And love of man I bear.

I trace your lines of argument ;
  Your logic linked and strong
I weigh as one who dreads dissent,
  And fears a doubt as wrong.

But still my human hands are weak
  To hold your iron creeds :
Against the words ye bid me speak
  My heart within me pleads.

Who fathoms the Eternal Thought ?
  Who talks of scheme and plan ?

The Lord is God ! He needeth not
  The poor device of man.

I walk with bare, hushed feet the ground
  Ye tread with boldness shod ;
I dare not fix with mete and bound
  The love and power of God.

Ye praise His justice ; even such
  His pitying love I deem :
Ye seek a king ; I fain would touch
  The robe that hath no seam.

Ye see the curse which overbroods
  A world of pain and loss ;
I hear our Lord's beatitudes
  And prayer upon the cross.

More than your schoolmen teach, within
  Myself, alas ! I know :

Too dark ye cannot paint the sin,
  Too small the merit show.

I bow my forehead to the dust,
  I veil mine eyes for shame,
And urge, in trembling self-distrust,
  A prayer without a claim.

I see the wrong that round me lies,
  I feel the guilt within ;
I hear, with groan and travail-cries,
  The world confess its sin.

Yet, in the maddening maze of things,
  And tossed by storm and flood,
To one fixed trust my spirit clings ;
  I know that God is good !

Not mine to look where cherubim
  And seraphs may not see,
But nothing can be good in Him
  Which evil is in me.

The wrong that pains my soul below
  I dare not throne above :
I know not of His hate, — I know
  His goodness and His love.

I dimly guess from blessings known
  Of greater out of sight,
And, with the chastened Psalmist, own
  His judgments too are right.

I long for household voices gone,
  For vanished smiles I long,
But God hath led my dear ones on,
  And He can do no wrong.

I know not what the future hath
  Of marvel or surprise,
Assured alone that life and death
  His mercy underlies.

And if my heart and flesh are weak
  To bear an untried pain,
The bruised reed He will not break,
  But strengthen and sustain.

No offering of my own I have,
  Nor works my faith to prove ;
I can but give the gifts He gave,
  And plead His love for love.

And so beside the Silent Sea
  I wait the muffled oar ;
No harm from Him can come to me
  On ocean or on shore.

I know not where His islands lift
  Their fronded palms in air ;
I only know I cannot drift
  Beyond His love and care.

O brothers ! if my faith is vain,
  If hopes like these betray,
Pray for me that my feet may gain
  The sure and safer way.

And Thou, O Lord ! by whom are seen
  Thy creatures as they be,
Forgive me if too close I lean
  My human heart on Thee !

OUR MASTER.

IMMORTAL Love, forever full,
  Forever flowing free,
Forever shared, forever whole,
  A never-ebbing sea !

Our outward lips confess the name
  All other names above ;
Love only knoweth whence it came,
  And comprehendeth love.

Blow, winds of God, awake and blow
  The mists of earth away !
Shine out, O Light Divine, and show
  How wide and far we stray !

Hush every lip, close every book,
  The strife of tongues forbear ;
Why forward reach, or backward look,
  For love that clasps like air ?

We may not climb the heavenly steeps
  To bring the Lord Christ down :
In vain we search the lowest deeps,
  For him no depths can drown.

Nor holy bread, nor blood of grape,
  The lineaments restore
Of him we know in outward shape
  And in the flesh no more.

He cometh not a king to reign ;
  The world's long hope is dim ;
The weary centuries watch in vain
  The clouds of heaven for him.

Death comes, life goes ; the asking eye
  And ear are answerless ;
The grave is dumb, the hollow sky
  Is sad with silentness.

The letter fails, and systems fall,
  And every symbol wanes ;
The Spirit over-brooding all
  Eternal Love remains.

And not for signs in heaven above
  Or earth below they look,
Who know with John his smile of
    love,
  With Peter his rebuke.

In joy of inward peace, or sense
  Of sorrow over sin,
He is his own best evidence,
  His witness is within.

No fable old, nor mythic lore,
  Nor dream of bards and seers,
No dead fact stranded on the shore
  Of the oblivious years ; —

But warm, sweet, tender, even yet
  A present help is he ;
And faith has still its Olivet,
  And love its Galilee.

The healing of his seamless dress
  Is by our beds of pain ;
We touch him in life's throng and
    press,
  And we are whole again.

Through him the first fond prayers are
    said
  Our lips of childhood frame,
The last low whispers of our dead
  Are burdened with his name.

O Lord and Master of us all !
  Whate'er our name or sign,
We own thy sway, we hear thy call,
  We test our lives by thine.

Thou judgest us ; thy purity
  Doth all our lusts condemn ;
The love that draws us nearer thee
  Is hot with wrath to them.

Our thoughts lie open to thy sight ;
  And, naked to thy glance,
Our secret sins are in the light
  Of thy pure countenance.

Thy healing pains, a keen distress
  Thy tender light shines in ;
Thy sweetness is the bitterness,
  Thy grace the pang of sin.

Yet, weak and blinded though we be,
  Thou dost our service own ;
We bring our varying gifts to thee,
  And thou rejectest none.

To thee our full humanity,
  Its joys and pains, belong ;
The wrong of man to man on thee
  Inflicts a deeper wrong.

Who hates, hates thee, who loves be-
    comes
  Therein to thee allied ;
All sweet accords of hearts and homes
  In thee are multiplied.

Deep strike thy roots, O heavenly Vine,
  Within our earthly sod,
Most human and yet most divine,
  The flower of man and God !

O Love ! O Life ! Our faith and
    sight
  Thy presence maketh one :
As through transfigured clouds of
    white
  We trace the noon-day sun.

So, to our mortal eyes subdued,
  Flesh-veiled, but not concealed,
We know in thee the fatherhood
  And heart of God revealed.

We faintly hear, we dimly see,
  In differing phrase we pray ;
But, dim or clear, we own in thee
  The Light, the Truth, the Way !

The homage that we render thee
  Is still our Father's own ;
Nor jealous claim or rivalry
  Divides the Cross and Throne.

To do thy will is more than praise,
  As words are less than deeds,
And simple trust can find thy ways
  We miss with chart of creeds.

No pride of self thy service hath,
  No place for me and mine ;
Our human strength is weakness, death
  Our life, apart from thine.

Apart from thee all gain is loss,
  All labor vainly done ;
The solemn shadow of thy Cross
  Is better than the sun.

Alone, O Love ineffable!
  Thy saving name is given;
To turn aside from thee is hell,
  To walk with thee is heaven!

How vain, secure in all thou art,
  Our noisy championship! —
The sighing of the contrite heart
  Is more than flattering lip.

Not thine the bigot's partial plea,
  Nor thine the zealot's ban ;
Thou well canst spare a love of thee
  Which ends in hate of man.

Our Friend, our Brother, and our Lord,
  What may thy service be ? —
Nor name, nor form, nor ritual word,
  But simply following thee.

We bring no ghastly holocaust,
  We pile no graven stone;
He serves thee best who loveth most
  His brothers and thy own.

Thy litanies, sweet offices
  Of love and gratitude ;
Thy sacramental liturgies,
  The joy of doing good.

In vain shall waves of incense drift
  The vaulted nave around,
In vain the minster turret lift
  Its brazen weights of sound.

The heart must ring thy Christmas
    bells,
  Thy inward altars raise ;
Its faith and hope thy canticles,
  And its obedience praise !

THE VANISHERS.

Sweetest of all childlike dreams
  In the simple Indian lore
Still to me the legend seems
  Of the shapes who flit before.

Flitting, passing, seen and gone,
  Never reached nor found at rest,
Baffling search, but beckoning on
  To the Sunset of the Blest.

From the clefts of mountain rocks,
  Through the dark of lowland firs,
Flash the eyes and flow the locks
  Of the mystic Vanishers !

And the fisher in his skiff,
  And the hunter on the moss,
Hear their call from cape and cliff,
  See their hands the birch-leaves toss.

Wistful, longing, through the green
  Twilight of the clustered pines,
In their faces rarely seen
  Beauty more than mortal shines.

Fringed with gold their mantles flow
  On the slopes of westering knolls ;
In the wind they whisper low
  Of the Sunset Land of Souls.

Doubt who may, O friend of mine !
  Thou and I have seen them too ;
On before with beck and sign
  Still they glide, and we pursue.

More than clouds of purple trail
  In the gold of setting day ;
More than gleams of wing or sail
  Beckon from the sea-mist gray.

Glimpses of immortal youth,
  Gleams and glories seen and flown,
Far-heard voices sweet with truth,
  Airs from viewless Eden blown, —

Beauty that eludes our grasp,
  Sweetness that transcends our taste,
Loving hands we may not clasp,
  Shining feet that mock our haste, —

Gentle eyes we closed below,
  Tender voices heard once more,
Smile and call us, as they go
  On and onward, still before.

Guided thus, O friend of mine !
  Let us walk our little way,
Knowing by each beckoning sign
  That we are not quite astray.

Chase we still, with baffled feet,
  Smiling eye and waving hand,
Sought and seeker soon shall meet,
  Lost and found, in Sunset Land !

REVISITED.

READ AT THE "LAURELS," ON THE
MERRIMACK, 6TH MONTH, 1865.

The roll of drums and the bugle's wail-
    ing
  Vex the air of our vales no more ;

21

The spear is beaten to hooks of prun-
ing,
  The share is the sword the soldier
    wore!

Sing soft, sing low, our lowland river,
  Under thy banks of laurel bloom ;
Softly and sweet, as the hour beseemeth,
  Sing us the songs of peace and home.

Let all the tenderer voices of nature
  Temper the triumph and chasten
    mirth,
Full of the infinite love and pity
  For fallen martyr and darkened
    hearth.

But to Him who gives us beauty for
    ashes,
  And the oil of joy for mourning long,
Let thy hills give thanks, and all thy
    waters
  Break into jubilant waves of song!

Bring us the airs of hills and forests,
  The sweet aroma of birch and pine,
Give us a waft of the north-wind laden
  With sweetbrier odors and breath of
    kine !

Bring us the purple of mountain sunsets,
  Shadows of clouds that rake the hills,
The green repose of thy Plymouth
    meadows,
  The gleam and ripple of Campton rills.

Lead us away in shadow and sunshine,
  Slaves of fancy, through all thy miles,
The winding ways of Pemigewasset,
  And Winnipesaukee's hundred isles.

Shatter in sunshine over thy ledges,
  Laugh in thy plunges from fall to
    fall ;
Play with thy fringes of elms, and darken
  Under the shade of the mountain wall.

The cradle-song of thy hillside fountains
  Here in thy glory and strength repeat ;
Give us a taste of thy upland music,
  Show us the dance of thy silver feet.

Into thy dutiful life of uses
  Pour the music and weave the flowers ;
With the song of birds and bloom of
    meadows
  Lighten and gladden thy heart and
    ours.

Sing on ! bring down, O lowland river,
  The joy of the hills to the waiting
    sea ;
The wealth of the vales, the pomp of
    mountains,
  The breath of the woodlands, bear
    with thee.

Here, in the calm of thy seaward val-
    ley,
  Mirth and labor shall hold their truce ;
Dance of water and mill of grinding,
  Both are beauty and both are use.

Type of the Northland's strength and
    glory,
  Pride and hope of our home and
    race, —
Freedom lending to rugged labor
  Tints of beauty and lines of grace.

Once again, O beautiful river,
  Hear our greetings and take our
    thanks ;
Hither we come, as Eastern pilgrims
  Throng to the Jordan's sacred banks.

For though by the Master's feet un-
    trodden,
  Though never his word has stilled
    thy waves,
Well for us may thy shores be holy,
  With Christian altars and saintly
    graves.

And well may we own thy hint and
    token
  Of fairer valleys and streams than
    these,
Where the rivers of God are full of water,
  And full of sap are his healing trees !

THE COMMON QUESTION.

BEHIND us at our evening meal
  The gray bird ate his fill,
Swung downward by a single claw,
  And wiped his hookèd bill.

He shook his wings and crimson tail,
  And set his head aslant,
And, in his sharp, impatient way,
  Asked, "What does Charlie want ?"

"Fie, silly bird !" I answered, "tuck
  Your head beneath your wing,

And go to sleep " ; — but o'er and o'er
  He asked the self-same thing.

Then, smiling, to myself I said : —
  How like are men and birds !
We all are saying what he says,
  In action or in words.

The boy with whip and top and drum,
  The girl with hoop and doll,
And men with lands and houses, ask
  The question of Poor Poll.

However full, with something more
  We fain the bag would cram ;
We sigh above our crowded nets
  For fish that never swam.

No bounty of indulgent Heaven
  The vague desire can stay ;
Self-love is still a Tartar mill
  For grinding prayers alway.

The dear God hears and pities all ;
  He knoweth all our wants ;
And what we blindly ask of him
  His love withholds or grants.

And so I sometimes think our prayers
  Might well be merged in one ;
And nest and perch and hearth and church
  Repeat, "Thy will be done."

BRYANT ON HIS BIRTHDAY.

WE praise not now the poet's art,
  The rounded beauty of his song ;
Who weighs him from his life apart
  Must do his nobler nature wrong.

Not for the eye, familiar grown
  With charms to common sight denied, —
The marvellous gift he shares alone
  With him who walked on Rydal-side ;

Not for rapt hymn nor woodland lay,
  Too grave for smiles, too sweet for tears ;
We speak his praise who wears to-day
  The glory of his seventy years.

When Peace brings Freedom in her train,
  Let happy lips his songs rehearse ;

His life is now his noblest strain,
  His manhood better than his verse !

Thank God ! his hand on Nature's keys
  Its cunning keeps at life's full span ;
But, dimmed and dwarfed, in times like these,
  The poet seems beside the man !

So be it ! let the garlands die,
  The singer's wreath, the painter's meed,
Let our names perish, if thereby
  Our country may be saved and freed !

HYMN

FOR THE OPENING OF THOMAS STARR
KING'S HOUSE OF WORSHIP, 1864.

AMIDST these glorious works of thine,
The solemn minarets of the pine,
And awful Shasta's icy shrine, —

Where swell thy hymns from wave and gale,
And organ-thunders never fail,
Behind the cataract's silver veil, —

Our puny walls to Thee we raise,
Our poor reed-music sounds thy praise :
Forgive, O Lord, our childish ways !

For, kneeling on these altar-stairs,
We urge Thee not with selfish prayers,
Nor murmur at our daily cares.

Before Thee, in an evil day,
Our country's bleeding heart we lay,
And dare not ask thy hand to stay ;

But, through the war-cloud, pray to thee
For union, but a union free,
With peace that comes of purity !

That Thou wilt bare thy arm to save
And, smiting through this Red Sea wave,
Make broad a pathway for the slave !

For us, confessing all our need,
We trust nor rite nor word nor deed,
Nor yet the broken staff of creed.

Assured alone that Thou art good
To each, as to the multitude,
Eternal Love and Fatherhood, —

Weak, sinful, blind, to Thee we kneel,
Stretch dumbly forth our hands, and feel
Our weakness is our strong appeal.

So, by these Western gates of Even
We wait to see with thy forgiven
The opening Golden Gate of Heaven!

Suffice it now.   In time to be
Shall holier altars rise to thee, —
Thy Church our broad humanity!

White flowers of love its walls shall
      climb,
Soft bells of peace shall ring its chime,
Its days shall all be holy time.

A sweeter song shall then be heard, —
The music of the world's accord
Confessing Christ, the Inward Word!

That song shall swell from shore to
      shore,
One hope, one faith, one love, restore
The seamless robe that Jesus wore.

THOMAS STARR KING.

THE great work laid upon his twoscore
      years
Is done, and well done.   If we drop our
      tears,
Who loved him as few men were ever
      loved,
We mourn no blighted hope nor bro-
      ken plan
With him whose life stands rounded
      and approved
In the full growth and stature of a man.
Mingle, O bells, along the Western
      slope,
With your deep toll a sound of faith and
      hope!
Wave cheerily still, O banner, half-way
      down,
From thousand-masted bay and stee
      pled town!
Let the strong organ with its loftiest
      swell
Lift the proud sorrow of the land, and
      tell
That the brave sower saw his ripened
      grain.
O East and West! O morn and sunset
      twain
No more forever! — has he lived in
      vain
Who, priest of Freedom, made ye one,
      and told
Your bridal service from his lips of
      gold?

AMONG THE HILLS,

AND OTHER POEMS.

TO ANNIE FIELDS

THIS LITTLE VOLUME,

DESCRIPTIVE OF SCENES WITH WHICH SHE IS FAMILIAR,

IS GRATEFULLY OFFERED.

PRELUDE.

ALONG the roadside, like the flowers of gold
That tawny Incas for their gardens wrought,
Heavy with sunshine droops the golden-rod,
And the red pennons of the cardinal-flowers
Hang motionless upon their upright staves.
The sky is hot and hazy, and the wind,
Wing-weary with its long flight from the south,
Unfelt; yet, closely scanned, yon maple leaf
With faintest motion, as one stirs in dreams,
Confesses it. The locust by the wall
Stabs the noon-silence with his sharp alarm.
A single hay-cart down the dusty road
Creaks slowly, with its driver fast asleep
On the load's top. Against the neighboring hill,
Huddled along the stone wall's shady side,
The sheep show white, as if a snowdrift still
Defied the dog-star. Through the open door
A drowsy smell of flowers — gray heliotrope,
And white sweet clover, and shy mignonette —

Comes faintly in, and silent chorus lends
To the pervading symphony of peace.

No time is this for hands long overworn
To task their strength: and (unto Him be praise
Who giveth quietness!) the stress and strain
Of years that did the work of centuries
Have ceased, and we can draw our breath once more
Freely and full. So, as yon harvesters
Make glad their nooning underneath the elms
With tale and riddle and old snatch of song,
I lay aside grave themes, and idly turn
The leaves of memory's sketch-book, dreaming o'er
Old summer pictures of the quiet hills,
And human life, as quiet, at their feet.

And yet not idly all. A farmer's son,
Proud of field-lore and harvest craft, and feeling
All their fine possibilities, how rich
And restful even poverty and toil
Become when beauty, harmony, and love
Sit at their humble hearth as angels sat
At evening in the patriarch's tent, when man
Makes labor noble, and his farmer's frock
The symbol of a Christian chivalry
Tender and just and generous to her

Who clothes with grace all duty ; still,
  I know
Too well the picture has another side, —
How wearily the grind of toil goes on
Where love is wanting, how the eye and
  ear
And heart are starved amidst the plen-
  itude
Of nature, and how hard and colorless
Is life without an atmosphere. I look
Across the lapse of half a century,
And call to mind old homesteads, where
  no flower
Told that the spring had come, but evil
  weeds,
Nightshade and rough-leaved burdock
  in the place
Of the sweet doorway greeting of the
  rose
And honeysuckle, where the house
  walls seemed
Blistering in sun, without a tree or vine
To cast the tremulous shadow of its
  leaves
Across the curtainless windows from
  whose panes
Fluttered the signal rags of shiftlessness ;
Within, the cluttered kitchen-floor, un-
  washed
(Broom-clean I think they called it) ;
  the best room
Stifling with cellar damp, shut from the
  air
In hot midsummer, bookless, pictureless
Save the inevitable sampler hung
Over the fireplace, or a mourning piece,
A green-haired woman, peony-cheeked,
  beneath
Impossible willows ; the wide-throated
  hearth
Bristling with faded pine-boughs half
  concealing
The piled-up rubbish at the chimney's
  back ;
And, in sad keeping with all things
  about them,
Shrill, querulous women, sour and sullen
  men,
Untidy, loveless, old before their time,
With scarce a human interest save their
  own
Monotonous round of small economies,
Or the poor scandal of the neighborhood ;
Blind to the beauty everywhere re-
  vealed,
Treading the May-flowers with regard-
  less feet ;

For them the song-sparrow and the
  bobolink
Sang not, nor winds made music in the
  leaves ;
For them in vain October's holocaust
Burned, gold and crimson, over all the
  hills,
The sacramental mystery of the woods.
Church-goers, fearful of the unseen
  Powers,
But grumbling over pulpit-tax and pew-
  rent,
Saving, as shrewd economists, their souls
And winter pork with the least possible
  outlay
Of salt and sanctity ; in daily life
Showing as little actual comprehension
Of Christian charity and love and duty,
As if the Sermon on the Mount had been
Outdated like a last year's almanac :
Rich in broad woodlands and in half-
  tilled fields,
And yet so pinched and bare and com-
  fortless,
The veriest straggler limping on his
  rounds,
The sun and air his sole inheritance,
Laughed at a poverty that paid its taxes,
And hugged his rags in self-compla-
  cency !

Not such should be the homesteads of
  a land
Where whoso wisely wills and acts may
  dwell
As king and lawgiver, in broad-acred
  state,
With beauty, art, taste, culture, books,
  to make
His hour of leisure richer than a life
Of fourscore to the barons of old time,
Our yeoman should be equal to his home
Set in the fair, green valleys, purple
  walled,
A man to match his mountains, not to
  creep
Dwarfed and abased below them. I
  would fain
In this light way (of which I needs must
  own
With the knife-grinder of whom Can-
  ning sings,
"Story, God bless you ! I have none to
  tell you !")
Invite the eye to see and heart to feel
The beauty and the joy within their
  reach, —

Home, and home loves, and the beatitudes
Of nature free to all   Happy in years
That wait to take the places of our own,
Heard where some breezy balcony looks down
On happy homes, or where the lake in the moon
Sleeps dreaming of the mountains, fair as Ruth,
In the old Hebrew pastoral, at the feet
Of Boaz, even this simple lay of mine
May seem the burden of a prophecy,
Finding its late fulfilment in a change
Slow as the oak's growth, lifting manhood up
Through broader culture, finer manners, love,
And reverence, to the level of the hills.

O Golden Age, whose light is of the dawn,
And not of sunset, forward, not behind,
Flood the new heavens and earth, and with thee bring
All the old virtues, whatsoever things
Are pure and honest and of good repute,
But add thereto whatever bard has sung
Or seer has told of when in trance and dream
They saw the Happy Isles of prophecy !
Let Justice hold her scale, and Truth divide
Between the right and wrong; but give the heart
The freedom of its fair inheritance ;
Let the poor prisoner, cramped and starved so long,
At Nature's table feast his ear and eye
With joy and wonder ; let all harmonies
Of sound, form, color, motion, wait upon
The princely guest, whether in soft attire
Of leisure clad, or the coarse frock of toil,
And, lending life to the dead form of faith,
Give human nature reverence for the sake
Of One who bore it, making it divine
With the ineffable tenderness of God ;
Let common need, the brotherhood of prayer,
The heirship of an unknown destiny,
The unsolved mystery round about us, make

A man more precious than the gold of Ophir.
Sacred, inviolate, unto whom all things
Should minister, as outward types and signs
Of the eternal beauty which fulfils
The one great purpose of creation, Love,
The sole necessity of Earth and Heaven !

AMONG THE HILLS.

FOR weeks the clouds had raked the hills
And vexed the vales with raining,
And all the woods were sad with mist,
And all the brooks complaining.

At last, a sudden night-storm tore
The mountain veils asunder,
And swept the valleys clean before
The besom of the thunder.

Through Sandwich notch the west-wind sang
Good morrow to the cotter;
And once again Chocorua's horn
Of shadow pierced the water.

Above his broad lake Ossipee,
Once more the sunshine wearing,
Stooped, tracing on that silver shield
His grim armorial bearing.

Clear drawn against the hard blue sky
The peaks had winter's keenness ;
And, close on autumn's frost, the vales
Had more than June's fresh greenness.

Again the sodden forest floors
With golden lights were checkered,
Once more rejoicing leaves in wind
And sunshine danced and flickered.

It was as if the summer's late
Atoning for its sadness
Had borrowed every season's charm
To end its days in gladness.

I call to mind those banded vales
Of shadow and of shining,
Through which, my hostess at my side,
I drove in day's declining.

We held our sideling way above
The river's whitening shallows,

By homesteads old, with wide-flung
  barns
  Swept through and through by swal-
  lows, —

By maple orchards, belts of pine
  And larches climbing darkly
The mountain slopes, and, over all,
  The great peaks rising starkly.

You should have seen that long hill-
  range
  With gaps of brightness riven, —
How through each pass and hollow
  streamed
  The purpling lights of heaven, —

Rivers of gold-mist flowing down
  From far celestial fountains, —
The great sun flaming through the
  rifts
  Beyond the wall of mountains !

We paused at last where home-bound
  cows
  Brought down the pasture's treasure,
And in the barn the rhythmic flails
  Beat out a harvest measure.

We heard the night-hawk's sullen
  plunge,
  The crow his tree-mates calling :
The shadows lengthening down the
  slopes
  About our feet were falling.

And through them smote the level sun
  In broken lines of splendor,
Touched the gray rocks and made the
  green
  Of the shorn grass more tender.

The maples bending o'er the gate,
  Their arch of leaves just tinted
With yellow warmth, the golden glow
  Of coming autumn hinted.

Keen white between the farm-house
  showed,
  And smiled on porch and trellis,
The fair democracy of flowers
  That equals cot and palace.

And weaving garlands for her dog,
  'Twixt chidings and caresses,
A human flower of childhood shook
  The sunshine from her tresses.

On either hand we saw the signs
  Of fancy and of shrewdness,
Where taste had wound its arms of vines
  Round thrift's uncomely rudeness.

The sun-brown farmer in his frock
  Shook hands, and called to Mary :
Bare-armed, as Juno might, she came.
  White-aproned from her dairy.

Her air, her smile, her motions, told
  Of womanly completeness ;
A music as of household songs
  Was in her voice of sweetness.

Not **fair alone in** curve and line,
  But something more and better,
The secret charm eluding art,
  Its spirit, not its letter ; —

An inborn grace that nothing lacked
  Of culture or appliance, —
The warmth of genial courtesy,
  The calm of self-reliance.

Before her queenly womanhood
  How dared our hostess utter
The paltry errand of her need
  To buy her fresh-churned butter ?

She led the way with housewife pride,
  Her goodly store disclosing,
Full tenderly the golden balls
  With practised hands disposing.

Then, while along the western hills
  We watched the changeful glory
Of sunset, on our homeward way,
  I heard her simple story.

The early crickets sang ; the stream
  Plashed through my friend's narra-
  tion :
Her rustic patois of the hills
  Lost in my free translation.

"More wise," she said, "than those
  who swarm
  Our hills in middle summer,
She came, when June's first roses blow,
  To greet the early comer.

"From school and ball and rout she
  came,
  The city's fair, pale daughter,
To drink the wine of mountain air
  Beside the Bearcamp Water.

'Her step grew firmer on the hills
That watch our homesteads over;
On cheek and lip, from summer fields,
She caught the bloom of clover.

"For health comes sparkling in the streams
From cool Chocorua stealing:
There's iron in our Northern winds;
· Our pines are trees of healing.

"She sat beneath the broad-armed elms
That skirt the mowing-meadow,
And watched the gentle west-wind weave
The grass with shine and shadow.

"Beside her, from the summer heat
To share her grateful screening,
With forehead bared, the farmer stood,
Upon his pitchfork leaning.

"Framed in its damp, dark locks, his face
Had nothing mean or common, —
Strong, manly, true, the tenderness
And pride beloved of woman.

"She looked up, glowing with the health
The country air had brought her,
And, laughing, said: 'You lack a wife,
Your mother lacks a daughter.

"'To mend your frock and bake your bread
You do not need a lady:
Be sure among these brown old homes
Is some one waiting ready, —

"'Some fair, sweet girl with skilful hand
And cheerful heart for treasure,
Who never played with ivory keys,
Or danced the polka's measure.'

"He bent his black brows to a frown,
He set his white teeth tightly.
''T is well,' he said, 'for one like you
To choose for me so lightly.

"'You think, because my life is rude
I take no note of sweetness:
I tell you love has naught to do
With meetness or unmeetness.

"'Itself its best excuse, it asks
No leave of pride or fashion
When silken zone or homespun frock
It stirs with throbs of passion.

"'You think me deaf and blind: you bring
Your winning graces hither
As free as if from cradle-time
We two had played together.

"'You tempt me with your laughing eyes,
Your cheek of sundown's blushes,
A motion as of waving grain,
A music as of thrushes.

"'The plaything of your summer sport,
The spells you weave around me
You cannot at your will undo,
Nor leave me as you found me.

"'You go as lightly as you came,
Your life is well without me;
What care you that these hills will close
Like prison-walls about me?

"'No mood is mine to seek a wife,
Or daughter for my mother:
Who loves you loses in that love
All power to love another!

"'I dare your pity or your scorn,
With pride your own exceeding;
I fling my heart into your lap
Without a word of pleading.'

"She looked up in his face of pain
So archly, yet so tender:
'And if I lend you mine,' she said,
'Will you forgive the lender?

"'Nor frock nor tan can hide the man;
And see you not, my farmer,
How weak and fond a woman waits
Behind this silken armor?

"'I love you: on that love alone,
And not my worth, presuming,
Will you not trust for summer fruit
The tree in May-day blooming?'

"Alone the hangbird overhead,
His hair-swung cradle straining,
Looked down to see love's miracle, —
The giving that is gaining.

" And so the farmer found a wife,
  His mother found a daughter :
There looks no happier home than hers
  On pleasant Bearcamp Water.

" Flowers spring to blossom where she
      walks
  The careful ways of duty ;
Our hard, stiff lines of life with her
  Are flowing curves of beauty.

" Our homes are cheerier for her sake,
  Our door-yards brighter blooming,
And all about the social air
  Is sweeter for her coming.

" Unspoken homilies of peace
  Her daily life is preaching ;
The still refreshment of the dew
  Is her unconscious teaching.

" And never tenderer hand than hers
  Unknits the brow of ailing ;
Her garments to the sick man's ear
  Have music in their trailing.

" And when, in pleasant harvest moons,
  The youthful huskers gather,
Or sleigh-drives on the mountain ways
  Defy the winter weather, —

" In sugar-camps, when south and
      warm
  The winds of March are blowing,
And sweetly from its thawing veins
  The maple's blood is flowing, —

" In summer, where some lilied pond
  Its virgin zone is bearing,
Or where the ruddy autumn fire
  Lights up the apple-paring, —

" The coarseness of a ruder time
  Her finer mirth displaces,
A subtler sense of pleasure fills
  Each rustic sport she graces.

" Her presence lends its warmth and
      health
  To all who come before it.
If woman lost us Eden, such
  As she alone restore it.

" For larger life and wiser aims
  The farmer is her debtor ;
Who holds to his another's heart
  Must needs be worse or better.

" Through her his civic service shows
  A purer-toned ambition ;
No double consciousness divides
  The man and politician.

" In party's doubtful ways he trusts
  Her instincts to determine ;
At the loud polls, the thought of
     her
  Recalls Christ's Mountain Sermon.

" He owns her logic of the heart,
  And wisdom of unreason,
Supplying, while he doubts and weighs,
  The needed word in season.

" He sees with pride her richer thought,
  Her fancy's freer ranges ;
And love thus deepened to respect
  Is proof against all changes.

" And if she walks at ease in ways
  His feet are slow to travel,
And if she reads with cultured eyes
  What his may scarce unravel,

" Still clearer, for her keener sight
  Of beauty and of wonder,
He learns the meaning of the hills
  He dwelt from childhood under.

" And higher, warmed with summer
      lights,
  Or winter-crowned and hoary,
The ridged horizon lifts for him
  Its inner veils of glory.

" He has his own free, bookless lore,
  The lessons nature taught him,
The wisdom which the woods and
     hills
  And toiling men have brought him :

" The steady force of will whereby
  Her flexile grace seems sweeter ;
The sturdy counterpoise which makes
  Her woman's life completer :

" A latent fire of soul which lacks
  No breath of love to fan it ;
And wit, that, like his native brooks,
  Plays over solid granite.

" How dwarfed against his manliness
  She sees the poor pretension,
The wants, the aims, the follies, born
  Of fashion and convention !

" How life behind its accidents
  Stands strong and self-sustaining,
The human fact transcending all
  The losing and the gaining.

" And so, in grateful interchange
  Of teacher and of hearer,
Their lives their true distinctness keep
  While daily drawing nearer.

" And if the husband or the wife
  In home's strong light discovers
Such slight defaults as failed to meet
  The blinded eyes of lovers,

" Why need we care to ask ? — who
      dreams
  Without their thorns of roses,
Or wonders that the truest steel
  The readiest spark discloses ?

" For still in mutual sufferance lies
  The secret of true living :
Love scarce is love that never knows
  The sweetness of forgiving.

" We send the Squire to General Court,
  He takes his young wife thither ;
No prouder man election day
  Rides through the sweet June weather.

" He sees with eyes of manly trust
  All hearts to her inclining ;
Not less for him his household light
  That others share its shining."

Thus, while my hostess spake, there
      grew
  Before me, warmer tinted
And outlined with a tenderer grace,
  The picture that she hinted.

The sunset smouldered as we drove
  Beneath the deep hill-shadows.
Below us wreaths of white fog walked
  Like ghosts the haunted meadows.

Sounding the summer night, the stars
  Dropped down their golden plum-
    mets ;
The pale arc of the Northern lights
  Rose o'er the mountain summits, —

Until, at last, beneath its bridge,
  We heard the Bearcamp flowing,
And saw across the mapled lawn
  The welcome home-lights glowing ; —

And, musing on the tale I heard,
  'T were well, thought I, if often
To rugged farm-life came the gift
  To harmonize and soften ; —

If more and more we found the troth
  Of fact and fancy plighted,
And culture's charm and labor's strength
  In rural homes united, —

The simple life, the homely hearth,
  With beauty's sphere surrounding,
And blessing toil where toil abounds
  With graces more abounding.

MISCELLANEOUS POEMS.

THE CLEAR VISION.

I DID but dream. I never knew
  What charms our sternest season
      wore.
Was never yet the sky so blue,
  Was never earth so white before.
Till now I never saw the glow
Of sunset on yon hills of snow,
And never learned the bough's designs
Of beauty in its leafless lines.

Did ever such a morning break
  As that my eastern windows see ?

Did ever such a moonlight take
  Weird photographs of shrub and
      tree ?
Rang ever bells so wild and fleet
The music of the winter street ?
Was ever yet a sound by half
So merry as yon school-boy's laugh ?

O Earth ! with gladness overfraught,
  No added charm thy face hath found ;
Within my heart the change is wrought,
  My footsteps make enchanted ground.
From couch of pain and curtained room
Forth to thy light and air I come,

To find in all that meets my eyes
The freshness of a glad surprise.

Fair seem these winter days, and soon
    Shall blow the warm west-winds of
        spring
To set the unbound rills in tune,
    And hither urge the bluebird's wing.
The vales shall laugh in flowers, the
        woods
Grow misty green with leafing buds,
And violets and wind-flowers sway,
Against the throbbing heart of May.

Break forth, my lips, in praise, and
        own
    The wiser love severely kind ;
Since, richer for its chastening grown,
    I see, whereas I once was blind.
The world, O Father ! hath not wronged
With loss the life by thee prolonged ;
But still, with every added year,
More beautiful thy works appear !

As thou hast made thy world without,
    Make thou more fair my world with-
        in ;
Shine through its lingering clouds of
        doubt ;
    Rebuke its haunting shapes of sin ;
Fill, brief or long, my granted span
Of life with love to thee and man ;
Strike when thou wilt the hour of rest,
But let my last days be my best !

    2d mo., 1868.

THE DOLE OF JARL THORKELL.

THE land was pale with famine
    And racked with fever-pain ;
The frozen fiords were fishless,
    The earth withheld her grain.

Men saw the boding Fylgja
    Before them come and go,
And, through their dreams, the Urdar-
        moon
    From west to east sailed slow !

Jarl Thorkell of Thevera
    At Yule-time made his vow ;
On Rykdal's holy Doom-stone
    He slew to Frey his cow.

To bounteous Frey he slew her ;
    To Skuld, the younger Norn,

Who watches over birth and death,
    He gave her calf unborn.

And his little gold-haired daughter
    Took up the sprinkling-rod,
And smeared with blood the temple
    And the wide lips of the god.

Hoarse below, the winter water
    Ground its ice-blocks o'er and o'er ;
Jets of foam, like ghosts of dead waves,
    Rose and fell along the shore.

The red torch of the Jokul,
    Aloft in icy space,
Shone down on the bloody Horg-stone,
    And the statue's carven face.

And closer round and grimmer
    Beneath its baleful light
The Jotun shapes of mountains
    Came crowding through the night.

The gray-haired Hersir trembled
    As a flame by wind is blown ;
A weird power moved his white lips,
    And their voice was not his own !

"The Æsir thirst !" he muttered ;
    "The gods must have more blood
Before the tun shall blossom
    Or fish shall fill the flood.

"The Æsir thirst and hunger,
    And hence our blight and ban ;
The mouths of the strong gods water
    For the flesh and blood of man !

"Whom shall we give the strong ones ?
    Not warriors, sword on thigh ;
But let the nursling infant
    And bedrid old man die."

"So be it !" cried the young men,
    "There needs nor doubt nor parle" ;
But, knitting hard his red brows,
    In silence stood the Jarl.

A sound of woman's weeping
    At the temple door was heard,
But the old men bowed their white
        heads,
    And answered not a word.

Then the Dream-wife of Thingvalla,
    A Vala young and fair,
Sang softly, stirring with her breath
    The veil of her loose hair.

She sang : "The winds from Alfheim
    Bring never sound of strife ;
The gifts for Frey the meetest
    Are not of death, but life.

"He loves the grass-green meadows,
    The grazing kine's sweet breath ;
He loathes your bloody Horg-stones,
    Your gifts that smell of death.

"No wrong by wrong is righted,
    No pain is cured by pain ;
The blood that smokes from Doom-rings
    Falls back in redder rain.

"The gods are what you make them,
    As earth shall Asgard prove ;
And hate will come of hating,
    And love will come of love.

"Make dole of skyr and black bread
    That old and young may live ;
And look to Frey for favor
    When first like Frey you give.

"Even now o'er Njord's sea-meadows
    The summer dawn begins :
The tun shall have its harvest,
    The fiord its glancing fins."

Then up and swore Jarl Thorkell :
    "By Gimli and by Hel,
O Vala of Thingvalla,
    Thou singest wise and well !

"Too dear the Æsir's favors
    Bought with our children's lives;
Better die than shame in living
    Our mothers and our wives.

"The full shall give his portion
    To him who hath most need ;
Of curdled skyr and black bread,
    Be daily dole decreed."

He broke from off his neck-chain
    Three links of beaten gold ;
And each man, at his bidding,
    Brought gifts for young and old.

Then mothers nursed their children,
    And daughters fed their sires,
And Healtn sat down with Plenty
    Before the next Yule fires.

The Horg-stones stand in Rykdal;
    The Doom-ring still remains ;

But the snows of a thousand winters
    Have washed away the stains.

Christ ruleth now ; the Æsir
    Have found their twilight dim ;
And, wiser than she dreamed, of old
    The Vala sang of Him !

THE TWO RABBIS.

THE Rabbi Nathan, twoscore years and
    ten,
Walked blameless through the evil
    world, and then,
Just as the almond blossomed in his
    hair,
Met a temptation all too strong to bear,
And miserably sinned. So, adding not
Falsehood to guilt, he left his seat, and
    taught
No more among the elders, but went out
From the great congregation girt about
With sackcloth, and with ashes on his
    head,
Making his gray locks grayer. Long he
    prayed,
Smiting his breast ; then, as the Book
    he laid
Open before him for the Bath-Col's
    choice,
Pausing to hear that Daughter of a
    Voice,
Behold the royal preacher's words : "A
    friend
Loveth at all times, yea, unto the end ;
And for the evil day thy brother lives."
Marvelling, he said : "It is the Lord
    who gives
Counsel in need. At Ecbatana dwells
Rabbi Ben Isaac, who all men excels
In righteousness and wisdom, as the
    trees
Of Lebanon the small weeds that the
    bees
Bow with their weight. I will arise,
    and lay
My sins before him."

                    And he went his way
Barefooted, fasting long, with many
    prayers ;
But even as one who, followed una-
    wares,
Suddenly in the darkness feels a hand
Thrill with its touch his own, and his
    cheek fanned

By odors subtly sweet, and whispers near
Of words he loathes, yet cannot choose
    but hear,
So, while the Rabbi journeyed, chanting
    low
The wail of David's penitential woe,
Before him still the old temptation came,
And mocked him with the motion and
    the shame
Of such desires that, shuddering, he ab-
    horred
Himself; and, crying mightily to the
    Lord
To free his soul and cast the demon out,
Smote with his staff the blankness round
    about.

At length, in the low light of a spent
    day,
The towers of Ecbatana far away
Rose on the desert's rim; and Nathan,
    faint
And footsore, pausing where for some
    dead saint
The faith of Islam reared a doméd tomb,
Saw some one kneeling in the shadow,
    whom
He greeted kindly: "May the Holy
    One
Answer thy prayers, O stranger!"
    Whereupon
The shape stood up with a loud cry, and
    then,
Clasped in each other's arms, the two
    gray men
Wept, praising Him whose gracious prov-
    idence
Made their paths one. But straightway,
    as the sense
Of his transgression smote him, Nathan
    tore
Himself away: "O friend beloved, no
    more
Worthy am I to touch thee, for I came,
Foul from my sins, to tell thee all my
    shame.
Haply thy prayers, since naught availeth
    mine,
May purge my soul, and make it white
    like thine.
Pity me, O Ben Isaac, I have sinned!"

Awestruck Ben Isaac stood. The des-
    ert wind
Blew his long mantle backward, laying
    bare
The mournful secret of his shirt of hair.

"I too, O friend, if not in act," he said,
"In thought have verily sinned. Hast
    thou not read,
'Better the eye should see than that de-
    sire
Should wander'? Burning with a hid-
    den fire
That tears and prayers quench not, I
    come to thee
For pity and for help, as thou to me.
Pray for me, O my friend!" But Na-
    than cried,
"Pray thou for me, Ben Isaac!"

                     Side by side
In the low sunshine by the turban stone
They knelt; each made his brother's woe
    his own,
Forgetting, in the agony and stress
Of pitying love, his claim of selfishness;
Peace, for his friend besought, his own
    became;
His prayers were answered in another's
    name;
And, when at last they rose up to em-
    brace,
Each saw God's pardon in his brother's
    face!

Long after, when his headstone gathered
    moss,
Traced on the targum-marge of Onkelos
In Rabbi Nathan's hand these words
    were read:
"*Hope not the cure of sin till Self is
    dead;*
Forget it in love's service, and the debt
*Thou canst not pay the angels shall for-
    get;*
*Heaven's gate is shut to him who comes
    alone;*
*Save thou a soul, and it shall save thy
    own!*"

THE MEETING.

THE elder folks shook hands at last,
Down seat by seat the signal passed.
To simple ways like ours unused,
Half solemnized and half amused,
With long-drawn breath and shrug, my
    guest
His sense of glad relief expressed.
Outside the hills lay warm in sun;
The cattle in the meadow-run
Stood half-leg deep; a single bird

The green repose above us stirred.
"What part or lot have you," he said,
"In these dull rites of drowsy-head?
Is silence worship? Seek it where
It soothes with dreams the summer
    air,
Not in this close and rude-benched hall,
But where soft lights and shadows
    fall,
And all the slow, sleep-walking hours
Glide soundless over grass and flowers!
From time and place and form apart,
Its holy ground the human heart,
Nor ritual-bound nor templeward
Walks the free spirit of the Lord!
Our common Master did not pen
His followers up from other men;
His service liberty indeed,
He built no church, he framed no creed;
But while the saintly Pharisee
Made broader his phylactery,
As from the synagogue was seen
The dusty-sandalled Nazarene
Through ripening cornfields lead the way
Upon the awful Sabbath day,
His sermons were the healthful talk
That shorter made the mountain-walk,
His wayside texts were flowers and birds,
Where mingled with His gracious words
The rustle of the tamarisk-tree
And ripple-wash of Galilee."

"Thy words are well, O friend," I said;
"Unmeasured and unlimited,
With noiseless slide of stone to stone,
The mystic Church of God has grown.
Invisible and silent stands
The temple never made with hands,
Unheard the voices still and small
Of its unseen confessional.
He needs no special place of prayer
Whose hearing ear is everywhere;
He brings not back the childish days
That ringed the earth with stones of
    praise,
Roofed Karnak's hall of gods, and laid
The plinths of Philæ's colonnade.
Still less He owns the selfish good
And sickly growth of solitude, —
The worthless grace that, out of sight,
Flowers in the desert anchorite;
Dissevered from the suffering whole,
Love hath no power to save a soul.
Not out of Self, the origin
And native air and soil of sin,
The living waters spring and flow,
The trees with leaves of healing grow.

"Dream not, O friend, because I seek
This quiet shelter twice a week,
I better deem its pine-laid floor
Than breezy hill or sea-sung shore;
But nature is not solitude:
She crowds us with her thronging wood;
Her many hands reach out to us,
Her many tongues are garrulous;
Perpetual riddles of surprise
She offers to our ears and eyes;
She will not leave our senses still,
But drags them captive at her will:
And, making earth too great for heaven,
She hides the Giver in the given.

"And so, I find it well to come
For deeper rest to this still room,
For here the habit of the soul
Feels less the outer world's control;
The strength of mutual purpose pleads
More earnestly our common needs;
And from the silence multiplied
By these still forms on either side,
The world that time and sense have
    known
Falls off and leaves us God alone.

"Yet rarely through the charmed repose
Unmixed the stream of motive flows,
A flavor of its many springs,
The tints of earth and sky it brings;
In the still waters needs must be
Some shade of human sympathy;
And here, in its accustomed place,
I look on memory's dearest face;
The blind by-sitter guesseth not
What shadow haunts that vacant spot;
No eyes save mine alone can see
The love wherewith it welcomes me!
And still, with those alone my kin,
In doubt and weakness, want and sin,
I bow my head, my heart I bare
As when that face was living there,
And strive (too oft, alas! in vain)
The peace of simple trust to gain,
Fold fancy's restless wings, and lay
The idols of my heart away.

"Welcome the silence all unbroken,
Nor less the words of fitness spoken, —
Such golden words as hers for whom
Our autumn flowers have just made
    room;
Whose hopeful utterance through and
    through
The freshness of the morning blew;
Who loved not less the earth that light

Fell on it from the heavens in sight,
But saw in all fair forms more fair
The Eternal beauty mirrored there.
Whose eighty years but added grace
And saintlier meaning to her face, —
The look of one who bore away
Glad tidings from the hills of day,
While all our hearts went forth to meet
The coming of her beautiful feet !
Or haply hers, whose pilgrim tread
Is in the paths where Jesus led ;
Who dreams her childhood's sabbath
    dream
By Jordan's willow-shaded stream,
And, of the hymns of hope and faith,
Sung by the monks of Nazareth,
Hears pious echoes, in the call
To prayer, from Moslem minarets fall,
Repeating where His works were wrought
The lesson that her Master taught,
Of whom an elder Sibyl gave,
The prophecies of Cumæ's cave !

" I ask no organ's soulless breath
To drone the themes of life and death,
No altar candle-lit by day,
No ornate wordsman's rhetoric-play,
No cool philosophy to teach
Its bland audacities of speech
To double-tasked idolaters
Themselves their gods and worshippers,
No pulpit hammered by the fist
Of loud-asserting dogmatist,
Who borrows from the hand of love
The smoking thunderbolts of Jove.
I know how well the fathers taught,
What   work   the   later   schoolmen
    wrought ;
I reverence old-time faith and men,
But God is near us now as then ;
His force of love is still unspent,
His hate of sin as imminent ;
And still the measure of our needs
Outgrows   the   cramping   bounds   of
    creeds ;
The manna gathered yesterday
Already savors of decay ;
Doubts to the world's child-heart un-
    known
Question us now from star and stone ;
Too little or too much we know,
And sight is swift and faith is slow ;
The power is lost to self-deceive
With shallow forms of make-believe.
We walk at high noon, and the bells
Call to a thousand oracles,
But the sound deafens, and the light

Is stronger than our dazzled sight ;
The letters of the sacred Book
Glimmer and swim beneath our look ;
Still struggles in the Age's breast
With deepening agony of quest
The old entreaty : ' Art thou He,
Or look we for the Christ to be ? '

" God should be most where man is
    least :
So, where is neither church nor priest,
And never rag of form or creed
To clothe the nakedness of need, —
Where farmer-folk in silence meet, —
I turn my bell-unsummoned feet ;
I lay the critic's glass aside,
I tread upon my lettered pride,
And, lowest-seated, testify
To the oneness of humanity ;
Confess the universal want,
And share whatever Heaven may grant.
He findeth not who seeks his own,
The soul is lost that 's saved alone.
Not on one favored forehead fell
Of old the fire-tongued miracle,
But flamed o'er all the thronging host
The baptism of the Holy Ghost ;
Heart answers heart : in one desire
The blending lines of prayer aspire ;
' Where, in my name, meet two or
    three,'
Our Lord hath said, ' I there will be ! '

" So sometimes comes to soul and
    sense
The feeling which is evidence
That very near about us lies
The realm of spiritual mysteries.
The sphere of the supernal powers
Impinges on this world of ours.
The low and dark horizon lifts,
To light the scenic terror shifts ;
The breath of a diviner air
Blows down the answer of a prayer :
That all our sorrow, pain, and doubt
A great compassion clasps about,
And law and goodness, love and force,
Are wedded fast beyond divorce.
Then duty leaves to love its task,
The beggar Self forgets to ask ;
With smile of trust and folded hands,
The passive soul in waiting stands
To feel, as flowers the sun and dew,
The One true Life its own renew.

" So, to the calmly gathered thought
The innermost of truth is taught,

The mystery dimly understood,
That love of God is love of good,
And, chiefly, its divinest trace
In Him of Nazareth's holy face;
That to be saved is only this, —
Salvation from our selfishness,
From more than elemental fire,
The soul's unsanctified desire,
From sin itself, and not the pain
That warns us of its chafing chain;
That worship's deeper meaning lies
In mercy, and not sacrifice,
Not proud humilities of sense
And posturing of penitence,
But love's unforced obedience;
That Book and Church and Day are
      given
For man, not God, — for earth, not
      heaven, —
The blessed means to holiest ends,
Not masters, but benignant friends;
That the dear Christ dwells not afar,
The king of some remoter star,
Listening, at times, with flattered ear
To homage wrung from selfish fear,
But here, amidst the poor and blind,
The bound and suffering of our kind,
In works we do, in prayers we pray,
Life of our life, he lives to-day."

THE ANSWER.

Spare me, dread angel of reproof,
  And let the sunshine weave to-day
Its gold-threads in the warp and woof
  Of life so poor and gray.

Spare me awhile; the flesh is weak.
  These lingering feet, that fain would
      stray
Among the flowers, shall some day seek
  The strait and narrow way.

Take off thy ever-watchful eye,
  The awe of thy rebuking frown;
The dullest slave at times must sigh
  To fling his burdens down;

To drop his galley's straining oar,
  And press, in summer warmth and
      calm,
The lap of some enchanted shore
  Of blossom and of balm.

Grudge not my life its hour of bloom,
  My heart its taste of long desire;
22

This day be mine : be those to come
  As duty shall require.

The deep voice answered to my own,
  Smiting my selfish prayers away;
" To-morrow is with God alone,
  And man hath but to-day.

" Say not, thy fond, vain heart within,
  The Father's arm shall still be wide,
When from these pleasant ways of sin
  Thou turn'st at eventide.

" ' Cast thyself down,' the tempter saith,
  ' And angels shall thy feet upbear.'
He bids thee make a lie of faith,
  And blasphemy of prayer.

"Though God be good and free be
      Heaven,
  No force divine can love compel;
And, though the song of sins forgiven
  May sound through lowest hell,

" The sweet persuasion of His voice
  Respects thy sanctity of will.
He giveth day : thou hast thy choice
  To walk in darkness still;

" As one who, turning from the light,
  Watches his own gray shadow fall,
Doubting, upon his path of night,
  If there be day at all !

" No word of doom may shut thee
      out,
  No wind of wrath may downward
      whirl,
No swords of fire keep watch about
  The open gates of pearl;

" A tenderer light than moon or sun,
  Than song of earth a sweeter hymn,
May shine and sound forever on,
  And thou be deaf and dim.

" Forever round the Mercy-seat
  The guiding lights of Love shall
      burn ;
But what if, habit-bound, thy feet
  Shall lack the will to turn?

" What if thine eye refuse to see,
  Thine ear of Heaven's free welcome
      fail,
And thou a willing captive be,
  Thyself thy own dark jail?

"O doom beyond the saddest guess,
  As the long years of God unroll
To make thy dreary selfishness
  The prison of a soul!

"To doubt the love that fain would
      break
  The fetters from thy self-bound limb;
And dream that God can thee forsake
  As thou forsakest him!"

G. L. S.

HE has done the work of a true man, —
  Crown him, honor him, love him.
Weep over him, tears of woman,
  Stoop manliest brows above him!

O dusky mothers and daughters,
  Vigils of mourning keep for him!
Up in the mountains, and down by the
      waters,
  Lift up your voices and weep for him!

For the warmest of hearts is frozen,
  The freest of hands is still;
And the gap in our picked and chosen
  The long years may not fill.

No dúty could overtask him,
  No need his will outrun;
Or ever our lips could ask him,
  His hands the work had done.

He forgot his own soul for others,
  Himself to his neighbor lending;
He found the Lord in his suffering
      brothers,
  And not in the clouds descending.

So the bed was sweet to die on,
  Whence he saw the doors wide swung
Against whose bolted iron
  The strength of his life was flung.

And he saw ere his eye was darkened
  The sheaves of the harvest-bringing,
And knew while his ear yet hearkened
  The voice of the reapers singing.

Ah, well! — The world is discreet;
  There are plenty to pause and wait;
But here was a man who set his feet
  Sometimes in advance of fate, —

Plucked off the old bark when the inner
  Was slow to renew it,

And put to the Lord's work the sinner
  When saints failed to do it.

Never rode to the wrong's redressing
  A worthier paladin.
Shall he not hear the blessing,
  "Good and faithful, enter in!"

FREEDOM IN BRAZIL.

WITH clearer light, Cross of the South,
      shine forth
  In blue Brazilian skies;
And thou, O river, cleaving half the
      earth
  From sunset to sunrise,
From the great mountains to the At-
      lantic waves
  Thy joy's long anthem pour.
Yet a few days (God make them less!)
      and slaves
  Shall shame thy pride no more.
No fettered feet thy shaded margins
      press;
  But all men shall walk free
Where thou, the high-priest of the wil-
      derness,
  Hast wedded sea to sea.

And thou, great-hearted ruler, through
      whose mouth
  The word of God is said,
Once more, "Let there be light!" —
      Son of the South,
  Lift up thy honored head,
Wear unashamed a crown by thy desert
  More than by birth thy own,
Careless of watch and ward; thou art
      begirt
  By grateful hearts alone.
The moated wall and battle-ship may
      fail,
  But safe shall justice prove;
Stronger than greaves of brass or iron
      mail
  The panoply of love.

Crowned doubly by man's blessing and
      God's grace,
  Thy future is secure;
Who frees a people makes his statue's
      place
  In Time's Valhalla sure.
Lo! from his Neva's banks the Scythian
      Czar
  Stretches to thee his hand,

Who, with the pencil of the Northern
    star,
  Wrote freedom on his land.
And he whose grave is holy by our
    calm
  And prairied Sangamon,
From his gaunt hand shall drop the
    martyr's palm
  To greet thee with "Well done!"

And thou, O Earth, with smiles thy
    face make sweet,
  And let thy wail be stilled,
To hear the Muse of prophecy repeat
  Her promise half fulfilled.
The Voice that spake at Nazareth speaks
    still,
  No sound thereof hath died;
Alike thy hope and Heaven's eternal
    will
  Shall yet be satisfied.
The years are slow, the vision tarrieth
    long,
  And far the end may be;
But, one by one, the fiends of ancient
    wrong
  Go out and leave thee free.

DIVINE COMPASSION.

LONG since, a dream of heaven I had,
  And still the vision haunts me oft;
I see the saints in white robes clad,
  The martyrs with their palms aloft;
But hearing still, in middle song,
  The ceaseless dissonance of wrong;
And shrinking, with hid faces, from the
    strain
Of sad, beseeching eyes, full of remorse
  and pain.

The glad song falters to a wail,
  The harping sinks to low lament;
Before the still uplifted veil
  I see the crownéd foreheads bent,
Making more sweet the heavenly air,
  With breathings of unselfish prayer;
And a Voice saith: "O Pity which is
  pain,
O Love that weeps, fill up my sufferings
  which remain!

"Shall souls redeemed by me refuse
  To share my sorrow in their turn?
Or, sin-forgiven, my gift abuse
  Of peace with selfish unconcern?

Has saintly ease no pitying care?
  Has faith no work, and love no prayer?
While sin remains, and souls in dark-
    ness dwell,
Can heaven itself be heaven, and look
    unmoved on hell?"

Then through the Gates of Pain, I dream,
  A wind of heaven blows coolly in;
Fainter the awful discords seem,
  The smoke of torment grows more thin,
Tears quench the burning soil, and
    thence
  Spring sweet, pale flowers of penitence;
And through the dreary realm of man's
    despair,
Star-crowned an angel walks, and lo!
    God's hope is there!

Is it a dream? Is heaven so high
  That pity cannot breathe its air?
Its happy eyes forever dry,
  Its holy lips without a prayer!
My God! my God! if thither led
  By thy free grace unmerited,
No crown nor palm be mine, but let me
  keep
A heart that still can feel, and eyes that
  still can weep.

LINES ON A FLY-LEAF.

I NEED not ask thee, for my sake,
To read a book which well may make
Its way by native force of wit
Without my manual sign to it.
Its piquant writer needs from me
No gravely masculine guaranty,
And well might laugh her merriest laugh
At broken spears in her behalf;
Yet, spite of all the critics tell,
I frankly own I like her well.
It may be that she wields a pen
Too sharply nibbed for thin-skinned
  men,
That her keen arrows search and try
The armor joints of dignity,
And, though alone for error meant,
Sing through the air irreverent.
I blame her not, the young athlete
Who plants her woman's tiny feet,
And dares the chances of debate
Where bearded men might hesitate,
Who, deeply earnest, seeing well
The ludicrous and laughable,
Mingling in eloquent excess

Her anger and her tenderness,
And, chiding with a half-caress,
Strives, less for her own sex than ours,
With principalities and powers,
And points us upward to the clear
Sunned heights of her new atmosphere.

Heaven mend her faults ! — I will not
      pause
To weigh and doubt and peck at flaws,
Or waste my pity when some fool
Provokes her measureless ridicule.
Strong-minded is she ?   Better so
Than dulness set for sale or show,
A household folly, capped and belled
In fashion's dance of puppets held,
Or poor pretence of womanhood,
Whose formal, flavorless platitude
Is warranted from all offence
Of robust meaning's violence.
Give me the wine of thought whose
      bead
Sparkles along the page I read.
Electric words in which I find
The tonic of the northwest wind, —
The wisdom which itself allies
To sweet and pure humanities,
Where   scorn   of   meanness,   hate   of
      wrong,
Are underlaid by love as strong ;
The genial play of mirth that lights
Grave themes of thought, as, when on
      nights
Of summer-time, the harmless blaze
Of thunderless heat-lightning plays,
And tree and hill-top resting dim
And doubtful on the sky's vague rim,
Touched by that soft and lambent gleam,
Start sharply outlined from their dream.

Talk not to me of woman's sphere,
Nor point with Scripture texts a sneer,
Nor wrong the manliest saint of all
By doubt, if he were here, that Paul
Would own the heroines who have lent
Grace to truth's stern arbitrament,
Foregone the praise to woman sweet,
And cast their crowns at Duty's feet ;
Like her, who by her strong Appeal
Made Fashion weep and Mammon feel,
Who, earliest summoned to withstand
The color-madness of the land,
Counted her life-long losses gain,
And made her own her sisters' pain ;
Or her who, in her greenwood shade,
Heard   the   sharp   call   that   Freedom
      made,

And, answering, struck from Sappho's
      lyre
Of love the Tyrtæan carmen's fire :
Or that young girl, — Domrémy's maid
Revived a nobler cause to aid, —
Shaking from warning finger-tips
The doom of her apocalypse ;
Or her, who world-wide entrance gave
To the log-cabin of the slave,
Made all his want and sorrow known,
And all earth's languages his own.

HYMN

FOR   THE   HOUSE   OF   WORSHIP   AT
GEORGETOWN.

ERECTED IN MEMORY OF A MOTHER.

THOU dwellest not, O Lord of all !
   In temples which thy children raise ;
Our work to thine is mean and small,
   And brief to thy eternal days.

Forgive the weakness and the pride,
   If marred thereby our gift may be,
For love, at least, has sanctified
   The altar that we rear to thee.

The heart and not the hand has wrought
   From sunken base to tower above
The image of a tender thought,
   The memory of a deathless love !

And though should never sound of
      speech
   Or organ echo from its wall,
Its stones would pious lessons teach,
   Its shade in benedictions fall.

Here should the dove of peace be found,
   And blessings and not curses given ;
Nor strife profane, nor hatred wound,
   The mingled loves of earth and heaven.

Thou, who didst soothe with dying
      breath
   The dear one watching by thy cross,
Forgetful of the pains of death
   In sorrow for her mighty loss,

In memory of that tender claim,
   O Mother-born, the offering take,
And make it worthy of thy name,
   And bless it for a mother's sake !

MIRIAM,

AND OTHER POEMS.

TO FREDERICK A. P. BARNARD.

The years are many since, in youth and
    hope,
Under the Charter Oak, our horoscope
We drew thick-studded with all favor-
    ing stars.
Now, with gray beards, and faces seamed
    with scars
From life's hard battle, meeting once
    again,
We smile, half sadly, over dreams so
    vain ;
Knowing, at last, that it is not in man
Who walketh to direct his steps, or plan
His permanent house of life.   Alike we
    loved
The muses' haunts, and all our fancies
    moved
To measures of old song.   How since
    that day
Our feet have parted from the path that
    lay
So fair before us !   Rich, from lifelong
    search
Of truth, within thy Academic porch
Thou sittest now, lord of a realm of fact,
Thy servitors the sciences exact ;
Still listening with thy hand on Na-
    ture's keys,
To hear the Samian's spheral harmonies
And rhythm of law.   I called from
    dream and song,
Thank God ! so early to a strife so long,
That, ere it closed, the black, abundant
    hair
Of boyhood rested silver-sown and spare
On manhood's temples, now at sunset-
    chime
Tread with fond feet the path of morn-
    ing time.
And if perchance too late I linger where
The flowers have ceased to blow, and
    trees are bare,
Thou, wiser in thy choice, wilt scarcely
    blame
The friend who shields his folly with
    thy name.

    Amesbury, 10th mo., 1870.

MIRIAM.

One Sabbath day my friend and I
After the meeting, quietly
Passed from the crowded village lanes,
White with dry dust for lack of rains,
And climbed the neighboring slope,
    with feet
Slackened and heavy from the heat,
Although the day was wellnigh done,
And the low angle of the sun
Along the naked hillside cast
Our shadows as of giants vast.
We reached, at length, the topmost
    swell,
Whence, either way, the green turf
    fell
In terraces of nature down
To fruit-hung orchards, and the town
With white, pretenceless houses, tall
Church-steeples, and, o'ershadowing all,
Huge mills whose windows had the
    look
Of eager eyes that ill could brook
The Sabbath rest.   We traced the track
Of the sea-seeking river back
Glistening for miles above its mouth,
Through the long valley to the south,
And, looking eastward, cool to view,
Stretched the illimitable blue
Of ocean, from its curved coast-line ;
Sombred and still, the warm sunshine
Filled with pale gold-dust all the reach
Of slumberous woods from hill to
    beach, —
Slanted on walls of thronged retreats
From city toil and dusty streets,
On grassy bluff, and dune of sand,
And rocky islands miles from land ;
Touched the far-glancing sails, and
    showed
White lines of foam where long waves
    flowed
Dumb in the distance.   In the north,
Dim through their misty hair, looked
    forth
The space-dwarfed mountains to the
    sea,
From mystery to mystery !

So, sitting on that green hill-slope,
We talked of human life, its hope
And fear, and unsolved doubts, and
      what
It might have been, and yet was not.
And, when at last the evening air
Grew sweeter for the bells of prayer
Ringing in steeples far below,
We watched the people churchward go,
Each to his place, as if thereon
The true shekinah only shone ;
And my friend queried how it came
To pass that they who owned the same
Great Master still could not agree
To worship Him in company.
Then, broadening in his thought, he
      ran
Over the whole vast field of man, —
The varying forms of faith and creed
That somehow served the holders'
      need ;
In which, unquestioned, undenied,
Uncounted millions lived and died ;
The bibles of the ancient folk,
Through which the heart of nations
      spoke ;
The old moralities which lent
To home its sweetness and content,
And rendered possible to bear
The life of peoples everywhere :
And asked if we, who boast of light,
Claim not a too exclusive right
To truths which must for all be meant,
Like rain and sunshine freely sent.
In bondage to the letter still,
We give it power to cramp and kill, —
To tax God's fulness with a scheme
Narrower than Peter's house-top dream,
His wisdom and his love with plans
Poor and inadequate as man's.
It must be that He witnesses
Somehow to all men that He is :
That something of His saving grace
Reaches the lowest of the race,
Who, through strange creed and rite,
      may draw
The hints of a diviner law.
We walk in clearer light ; — but then,
Is He not God ? — are they not men ?
Are His responsibilities
For us alone and not for these ?

And I made answer : " Truth is one ;
And, in all lands beneath the sun,
Whoso hath eyes to see may see
The tokens of its unity.
No scroll of creed its fulness wraps,

We trace it not by school-boy maps,
Free as the sun and air it is
Of latitudes and boundaries.
In Vedic verse, in dull Korán,
Are messages of good to man ;
The angels to our Aryan sires
Talked by the earliest household fires ;
The prophets of the elder day,
The slant-eyed sages of Cathay,
Read not the riddle all amiss
Of higher life evolved from this.

" Nor doth it lessen what He taught,
Or make the gospel Jesus brought
Less precious, that His lips retold
Some portion of that truth of old ;
Denying not the proven seers,
The tested wisdom of the years ;
Confirming with his own impress
The common law of righteousness.
We search the world for truth ; we cull
The good, the pure, the beautiful,
From graven stone and written scroll,
From all old flower-fields of the soul ;
And, weary seekers of the best,
We come back laden from our quest,
To find that all the sages said
Is in the Book our mothers read,
And all our treasure of old thought
In His harmonious fulness wrought
Who gathers in one sheaf complete
The scattered blades of God's sown
      wheat,
The common growth that maketh good
His all-embracing Fatherhood.

"Wherever through the ages rise
The altars of self-sacrifice,
Where love its arms has opened wide,
Or man for man has calmly died,
I see the same white wings outspread
That hovered o'er the Master's head !
Up from undated time they come,
The martyr souls of heathendom,
And to His cross and passion bring
Their fellowship of suffering.
I trace His presence in the blind
Pathetic gropings of my kind, —
In prayers from sin and sorrow wrung,
In cradle-hymns of life they sung,
Each, in its measure, but a part
Of the unmeasured Over-Heart ;
And with a stronger faith confess
The greater that it owns the less.
Good cause it is for thankfulness
That the world-blessing of His life
With the long past is not at strife ;

That the great marvel of His death
To the one order witnesseth,
No doubt of changeless goodness wakes,
No link of cause and sequence breaks,
But, one with nature, rooted is
In the eternal verities ;
Whereby, while differing in degree
As finite from infinity,
The pain and loss for others borne,
Love's crown of suffering meekly worn,
The life man giveth for his friend
Become vicarious in the end ;
Their healing place in nature take,
And make life sweeter for their sake.

"So welcome I from every source
The tokens of that primal Force,
Older than heaven itself, yet new
As the young heart it reaches to,
Beneath whose steady impulse rolls
The tidal wave of human souls ;
Guide, comforter, and inward word,
The eternal spirit of the Lord !
Nor fear I aught that science brings
From searching through material
things ;
Content to let its glasses prove,
Not by the letter's oldness move,
The myriad worlds on worlds that
course
The spaces of the universe ;
Since everywhere the Spirit walks
The garden of the heart, and talks
With man, as under Eden's trees,
In all his varied languages.
Why mourn above some hopeless flaw
In the stone tables of the law,
When scripture every day afresh
Is traced on tablets of the flesh?
By inward sense, by outward signs,
God's presence still the heart divines ;
Through deepest joy of Him we learn,
In sorest grief to Him we turn,
And reason stoops its pride to share
The child-like instinct of a prayer."

And then, as is my wont, I told
A story of the days of old,
Not found in printed books, — in
sooth,
A fancy, with slight hint of truth,
Showing how differing faiths agree
In one sweet law of charity.
Meanwhile the sky had golden grown,
Our faces in its glory shone ;
But shadows down the valley swept,
And gray below the ocean slept,

As time and space I wandered o'er
To tread the Mogul's marble floor,
And see a fairer sunset fall
On Jumna's wave and Agra's wall.

THE good Shah Akbar (peace be his
alway !)
Came forth from the Divan at close of
day
Bowed with the burden of his many
cares,
Worn with the hearing of unnumbered
prayers, —
Wild cries for justice, the importunate
Appeals of greed and jealousy and hate,
And all the strife of sect and creed and
rite,
Santon and Gouroo waging holy fight :
For the wise monarch, claiming not to
be
Allah's avenger, left his people free,
With a faint hope, his Book scarce
justified,
That all the paths of faith, though sev-
ered wide,
O'er which the feet of prayerful rever-
ence passed,
Met at the gate of Paradise at last.

He sought an alcove of his cool
hareem,
Where, far beneath, he heard the
Jumna's stream
Lapse soft and low along his palace
wall,
And all about the cool sound of the fall
Of fountains, and of water circling free
Through marble ducts along the bal-
cony ;
The voice of women in the distance
sweet,
And, sweeter still, of one who, at his
feet,
Soothed his tired ear with songs of a
far land
Where Tagus shatters on the salt sea-
sand
The mirror of its cork-grown hills of
drouth
And vales of vine, at Lisbon's harbor-
mouth.

The date-palms rustled not ; the
peepul laid
Its topmost boughs against the balus-
trade,

Motionless as the mimic leaves and
    vines
That, light and graceful as the shawl-
    designs
Of Delhi or Umritsir, twined in stone ;
And the tired monarch, who aside had
    thrown
The day's hard burden, sat from care
    apart,
And let the quiet steal into his heart
From the still hour. Below him Agra
    slept,
By the long light of sunset overswept :
The river flowing through a level land,
By mango-groves and banks of yellow
    sand,
Skirted with lime and orange, gay
    kiosks,
Fountains at play, tall minarets of
    mosques,
Fair pleasure-gardens, with their flow-
    ering trees
Relieved against the mournful cypresses ;
And, air-poised lightly as the blown
    sea-foam,
The marble wonder of some holy dome
Hung a white moonrise over the still
    wood,
Glassing its beauty in a stiller flood.

Silent the monarch gazed, until the
    night
Swift-falling hid the city from his
    sight,
Then to the woman at his feet he said :
"Tell me, O Miriam, something thou
    hast read
In childhood of the Master of thy faith,
Whom Islam also owns. Our Prophet
    saith :
' He was a true apostle, yea, a Word
And Spirit sent before me from the
    Lord.'
Thus the Book witnesseth ; and well I
    know
By what thou art, O dearest, it is so.
As the lute's tone the maker's hand be-
    trays,
The sweet disciple speaks her Master's
    praise."

Then Miriam, glad of heart, (for in
    some sort
She cherished in the Moslem's liberal
    court
The sweet traditions of a Christian
    child ;

And, through her life of sense, the un-
    defiled
And chaste ideal of the sinless One
Gazed on her with an eye she might not
    shun, —
The sad, reproachful look of pity, born
Of love that hath no part in wrath or
    scorn,)
Began, with low voice and moist eyes,
    to tell
Of the all-loving Christ, and what befell
When the fierce zealots, thirsting for
    her blood,
Dragged to his feet a shame of woman-
    hood.
How, when his searching answer pierced
    within
Each heart, and touched the secret of
    its sin,
And her accusers fled his face before,
He bade the poor one go and sin no
    more.
And Akbar said, after a moment's
    thought,
" Wise is the lesson by thy prophet
    taught ;
Woe unto him who judges and forgets
What hidden evil his own heart besets !
Something of this large charity I find
In all the sects that sever human kind ;
I would to Allah that their lives agreed
More nearly with the lesson of their
    creed !
Those yellow Lamas who at Meerut pray
By wind and water power, and love to
    say :
' He who forgiveth not shall, unfor-
    given,
Fail of the rest of Buddha,' and who
    even
Spare the black gnat that stings them,
    vex my ears
With the poor hates and jealousies and
    fears
Nursed in their human hives. That
    lean, fierce priest
Of thy own people, (be his heart in-
    creased
By Allah's love !) his black robes
    smelling yet
Of Goa's roasted Jews, have I not met
Meek-faced, barefooted, crying in the
    street
The saying of his prophet true and
    sweet, —
' He who is merciful shall mercy
    meet ! ' "

But, next day, so it chanced, as night
    began
To fall, a murmur through the hareem
    ran
That one, recalling in her dusky face
The full-lipped, mild-eyed beauty of a
    race
Known as the blameless Ethiops of
    Greek song,
Plotting to do her royal master wrong,
Watching, reproachful of the lingering
    light,
The evening shadows deepen for her
    flight,
Love-guided, to her home in a far land,
Now waited death at the great Shah's
    command.

Shapely as that dark princess for
    whose smile
A world was bartered, daughter of the
    Nile
Herself, and veiling in her large, soft
    eyes
The passion and the languor of her skies,
The Abyssinian knelt low at the feet
Of her stern lord : "O king, if it be
    meet,
And for thy honor's sake," she said,
    "that I,
Who am the humblest of thy slaves,
    should die,
I will not tax thy mercy to forgive.
Easier it is to die than to outlive
All that life gave me, — him whose
    wrong of thee
Was but the outcome of his love for
    me,
Cherished from childhood, when, be-
    neath the shade
Of templed Axum, side by side we
    played.
Stolen from his arms, my lover followed
    me
Through weary seasons over land and
    sea ;
And two days since, sitting disconso-
    late
Within the shadow of the hareem gate,
Suddenly, as if dropping from the sky,
Down from the lattice of the balcony
Fell the sweet song by Tigre's cow-
    herds sung
In the old music of his native tongue.
He knew my voice, for love is quick of
    ear,
Answering in song.

This night he waited near
To fly with me. The fault was mine
    alone :
He knew thee not, he did but seek his
    own ;
Who, in the very shadow of thy throne,
Sharing thy bounty, knowing all thou
    art,
Greatest and best of men, and in her
    heart
Grateful to tears for favor undeserved,
Turned ever homeward, nor one mo-
    ment swerved
From her young love. He looked into
    my eyes,
He heard my voice, and could not
    otherwise
Than he hath done ; yet, save one wild
    embrace
When first we stood together face to
    face,
And all that fate had done since last we
    met
Seemed but a dream that left us chil-
    dren yet,
He hath not wronged thee nor thy royal
    bed ;
Spare him, O king ! and slay me in his
    stead !"

But over Akbar's brows the frown
    hung black,
And, turning to the eunuch at his back,
"Take them," he said, "and let the
    Jumna's waves
Hide both my shame and these accursed
    slaves !"
His loathly length the unsexed bond-
    man bowed :
"On my head be it !"
                Straightway from a cloud
Of dainty shawls and veils of woven
    mist
The Christian Miriam rose, and, stoop-
    ing, kissed
The monarch's hand. Loose down her
    shoulders bare
Swept all the rippled darkness of her
    hair,
Veiling the bosom that, with high, quick
    swell
Of fear and pity, through it rose and fell.

"Alas !" she cried, "hast thou for-
    gotten quite
The words of Him we spake of yester-
    night ?

Or thy own prophet's, — 'Whoso doth
     endure
And pardon, of eternal life is sure'?
O great and good! be thy revenge
     alone
Felt in thy mercy to the erring shown;
Let thwarted love and youth their par-
     don plead,
Who sinned but in intent, and not in
     deed!"

   One moment the strong frame of Akbar
     shook
With the great storm of passion. Then
     his look
Softened to her uplifted face, that still
Pleaded more strongly than all words,
     until
Its pride and anger seemed like over-
     blown,
Spent clouds of thunder left to tell
     alone
Of strife and overcoming. With bowed
     head,
And smiting on his bosom: "God," he
     said,
"Alone is great, and let His holy name
Be honored, even to His servant's
     shame!
Well spake thy prophet, Miriam, — he
     alone
Who hath not sinned is meet to cast a
     stone
At such as these, who here their doom
     await,
Held like myself in the strong grasp of
     fate.
They sinned through love, as I through
     love forgive;
Take them beyond my realm, but let
     them live!"

   And, like a chorus to the words of
     grace,
The ancient Fakir, sitting in his place,
Motionless as an idol and as grim,
In the pavilion Akbar built for him
Under the court-yard trees, (for he was
     wise,
Knew Menu's laws, and through his
     close-shut eyes
Saw things far off, and as an open book
Into the thoughts of other men could
     look,)
Began, half chant, half howling, to re-
     hearse
The fragment of a holy Vedic verse;

And thus it ran: "He who all things
     forgives
Conquers himself and all things else,
     and lives
Above the reach of wrong or hate or
     fear,
Calm as the gods, to whom he is most
     dear."

   Two leagues from Agra still the trav-
     eller sees
The tomb of Akbar through its cypress-
     trees;
And, near at hand, the marble walls
     that hide
The Christian Begum sleeping at his
     side.
And o'er her vault of burial (who shall
     tell
If it be chance alone or miracle?)
The Mission press with tireless hand
     unrolls
The words of Jesus on its lettered
     scrolls, —
Tells, in all tongues, the tale of mercy
     o'er,
And bids the guilty, "Go and sin no
     more!"

———

   It now was dew-fall; very still
The night lay on the lonely hill,
Down which our homeward steps we
     bent,
And, silent, through great silence
     went,
Save that the tireless crickets played
Their long, monotonous serenade.
A young moon, at its narrowest,
Curved sharp against the darkening
     west;
And, momently, the beacon's star,
Slow wheeling o'er its rock afar,
From out the level darkness shot
One instant and again was not.
And then my friend spake quietly
The thought of both: "Yon crescent
     see!
Like Islam's symbol-moon it gives
Hints of the light whereby it lives:
Somewhat of goodness, something true
From sun and spirit shining through
All faiths, all worlds, as through the
     dark
Of ocean shines the lighthouse spark,
Attests the presence everywhere
Of love and providential care.

The faith the old Norse heart confessed
In one dear name, — the hopefulest
And tenderest heard from mortal lips
In pangs of birth or death, from ships

Ice-bitten in the winter sea,
Or lisped beside a mother's knee, —
The wiser world hath not outgrown,
And the All-Father is our own !

MISCELLANEOUS POEMS.

NOREMBEGA.

[Norembega, or Norimbegue, is the name given by early French fishermen and explorers to a fabulous country south of Cape Breton, first discovered by Verrazzani in 1524. It was supposed to have a magnificent city of the same name on a great river, probably the Penobscot. The site of this barbaric city is laid down on a map published at Antwerp in 1570. In 1604 Champlain sailed in search of the Northern Eldorado, twenty-two leagues up the Penobscot from the Isle Haute. He supposed the river to be that of Norembega, but wisely came to the conclusion that those travellers who told of the great city had never seen it. He saw no evidences of anything like civilization, but mentions the finding of a cross, very old and mossy, in the woods.]

THE winding way the serpent takes
  The mystic water took,
From where, to count its beaded lakes,
  The forest sped its brook.

A narrow space 'twixt shore and shore,
  For sun or stars to fall,
While evermore, behind, before,
  Closed in the forest wall.

The dim wood hiding underneath
  Wan flowers without a name ;
Life tangled with decay and death,
  League after league the same.

Unbroken over swamp and hill
  The rounding shadow lay,
Save where the river cut at will
  A pathway to the day.

Beside that track of air and light,
  Weak as a child unweaned,
At shut of day a Christian knight
  Upon his henchman leaned.

The embers of the sunset's fires
  Along the clouds burned down ;
" I see," he said, " the domes and spires
  Of Norembega town."

" Alack ! the domes, O master mine,
  Are golden clouds on high ;

Yon spire is but the branchless pine
  That cuts the evening sky."

" O hush and hark ! What sounds are these
  But chants and holy hymns ? "
" Thou hear'st the breeze that stirs the trees
  Through all their leafy limbs."

" Is it a chapel bell that fills
  The air with its low tone ? "
" Thou hear'st the tinkle of the rills,
  The insect's vesper drone."

" The Christ be praised ! — He sets for me
  A blessed cross in sight ! "
" Now, nay, 't is but yon blasted tree
  With two gaunt arms outright ! "

" Be it wind so sad or tree so stark,
  It mattereth not, my knave ;
Methinks to funeral hymns I hark,
  The cross is for my grave !

" My life is sped ; I shall not see
  My home-set sails again ;
The sweetest eyes of Normandie
  Shall watch for me in vain.

" Yet onward still to ear and eye
  The baffling marvel calls ;
I fain would look before I die
  On Norembega's walls.

" So, haply, it shall be thy part
  At Christian feet to lay
The mystery of the desert's heart
  My dead hand plucked away.

" Leave me an hour of rest ; go thou
  And look from yonder heights ;
Perchance the valley even now
  Is starred with city lights."

The henchman climbed the nearest hill,
  He saw nor tower nor town,

But, through the drear woods, lone and
    still,
    The river rolling down.

He heard the stealthy feet of things
    Whose shapes he could not see,
A flutter as of evil wings,
    The fall of a dead tree.

The pines stood black against the moon,
    A sword of fire beyond ;
He heard the wolf howl, and the loon
    Laugh from his reedy pond.

He turned him back : " O master dear,
    We are but men misled ;
And thou hast sought a city here
    To find a grave instead.

" As God shall will ! what matters where
    A true man's cross may stand,
So Heaven be o'er it here as there
    In pleasant Norman land ?

" These woods, perchance, no secret
    hide
Of lordly tower and hall ;
Yon river in its wanderings wide
    Has washed no city wall ;

" Yet mirrored in the sullen stream
    The holy stars are given :
Is Norembega, then, a dream
    Whose waking is in Heaven ?

" No builded wonder of these lands
    My weary eyes shall see ;
A city never made with hands
    Alone awaiteth me —

" ' *Urbs Syon mystica* ' ; I see
    Its mansions passing fair,
' *Condita cœlo* ' ; let me be,
    Dear Lord, a dweller there ! "

Above the dying exile hung
    The vision of the bard,
As faltered on his failing tongue
    The song of good Bernard.

The henchman dug at dawn a grave
    Beneath the hemlocks brown,
And to the desert's keeping gave
    The lord of fief and town.

Years after, when the Sieur Champlain
    Sailed up the unknown stream,

And Norembega proved again
    A shadow and a dream,

He found the Norman's nameless grave
    Within the hemlock's shade,
And, stretching wide its arms to save,
    The sign that God had made,

The cross-boughed tree that marked the
    spot
    And made it holy ground :
He needs the earthly city not
    Who hath the heavenly found.

NAUHAUGHT, THE DEACON.

Nauhaught, the Indian deacon, who
    of old
Dwelt, poor but blameless, where his
    narrowing Cape
Stretches its shrunk arm out to all the
    winds
And the relentless smiting of the waves,
Awoke one morning from a pleasant
    dream
Of a good angel dropping in his hand
A fair, broad gold-piece, in the name of
    God.

He rose and went forth with the early
    day
Far inland, where the voices of the
    waves
Mellowed and mingled with the whis-
    pering leaves,
As, through the tangle of the low, thick
    woods,
He searched his traps. Therein nor
    beast nor bird
He found ; though meanwhile in the
    reedy pools
The otter plashed, and underneath the
    pines
The partridge drummed : and as his
    thoughts went back
To the sick wife and little child at
    home,
What marvel that the poor man felt his
    faith
Too weak to bear its burden, — like a
    rope
That, strand by strand uncoiling, breaks
    above
The hand that grasps it. "Even now,
    O Lord !

Send me," he prayed, " the angel of my
  dream !
Nauhaught is very poor; he cannot
  wait."

Even as he spake he heard at his bare
  feet
A low, metallic clink, and, looking
  down,
He saw a dainty purse with disks of
  gold
Crowding its silken net.   Awhile he
  held
The treasure up before his eyes, alone
With his great need, feeling the won-
  drous coins
Slide through his eager fingers, one by
  one.
So then the dream was true.   The angel
  brought
One broad piece only; should he take
  all these?
Who would be wiser, in the blind, dumb
  woods ?
The loser, doubtless rich, would scarcely
  miss
This dropped crumb from a table always
  full.
Still, while he mused, he seemed to hear
  the cry
Of a starved child; the sick face of his
  wife
Tempted him.   Heart and flesh in fierce
  revolt
Urged the wild license of his savage
  youth
Against his later scruples.   Bitter toil,
Prayer, fasting, dread of blame, and pit-
  iless eyes
To watch his halting, — had he lost for
  these
The freedom of the woods ; — the hunt-
  ing-grounds
Of happy spirits for a walled-in heaven
Of everlasting psalms ?   One healed the
  sick
Very far off thousands of moons ago:
Had he not prayed him night and day to
  come
And cure his bed-bound wife?   Was
  there a hell ?
Were all his fathers' people writhing
  there —
Like the poor shell-fish set to boil alive—
Forever, dying never?   If he kept
This gold, so needed, would the dread-
  ful God

Torment him like a Mohawk's captive
  stuck
With slow-consuming splinters?   Would
  the saints
And the white angels dance and laugh
  to see him
Burn like a pitch-pine torch ?   His
  Christian garb
Seemed falling from him ; with the fear
  and shame
Of Adam naked at the cool of day,
He gazed around.   A black snake lay in
  coil
On the hot sand, a crow with sidelong
  eye
Watched from a dead bough.   All his
  Indian lore
Of evil blending with a convert's faith
In the supernal terrors of the Book,
He saw the Tempter in the coiling
  snake
And ominous, black-winged bird ; and
  all the while
The low rebuking of the distant waves
Stole in upon him like the voice of
  God
Among the trees of Eden.   Girding
  up
His soul's loins with a resolute hand, he
  thrust
The base thought from him : "Nau-
  haught, be a man !
Starve, if need be ; but, while you live,
  look out
From honest eyes on all men, un-
  ashamed.
God help me !   I am deacon of the
  church,
A baptized, praying Indian !   Should I
  do
This secret meanness, even the barken
  knots
Of the old trees would turn to eyes to
  see it,
The birds would tell of it, and all the
  leaves
Whisper above me : ' Nauhaught is a
  thief ! '
The sun would know it, and the stars
  that hide
Behind his light would watch me, and
  at night
Follow me with their sharp, accusing
  eyes.
Yea, thou, God, seest me !"   Then
  Nauhaught drew
Closer his belt of leather, dulling thus

The pain of hunger, and walked bravely
    back
To the brown fishing-hamlet by the
    sea ;
And, pausing at the inn-door, cheerily
    asked :
"Who hath lost aught to-day ?"
        "I," said a voice ;
"Ten golden pieces, in a silken purse,
My daughter's handiwork." He looked,
    and lo !
One stood before him in a coat of frieze,
And the glazed hat of a seafaring man,
Shrewd-faced, broad-shouldered, with
    no trace of wings.
Marvelling, he dropped within the
    stranger's hand
The silken web, and turned to go his
    way.
But the man said : "A tithe at least is
    yours ;
Take it in God's name as an honest
    man."
And as the deacon's dusky fingers closed
Over the golden gift, "Yea, in God's
    name
I take it, with a poor man's thanks,"
    he said.

So down the street that, like a river of
    sand,
Ran, white in sunshine, to the summer
    sea,
He sought his home, singing and prais-
    ing God ;
And when his neighbors in their careless
    way
Spoke of the owner of the silken purse —
A Wellfleet skipper, known in every
    port
That the Cape opens in its sandy wall —
He answered, with a wise smile, to him-
    self :
"I saw the angel where they see a man."

IN SCHOOL-DAYS.

STILL sits the school-house by the road,
    A ragged beggar sunning ;
Around it still the sumachs grow,
    And blackberry-vines are running.

Within, the master's desk is seen,
    Deep scarred by raps official ;
The warping floor, the battered seats,
    The jack-knife's carved initial ;

The charcoal frescos on its wall ;
    Its door's worn sill, betraying
The feet that, creeping slow to school,
    Went storming out to playing !

Long years ago a winter sun
    Shone over it at setting ;
Lit up its western window-panes,
    And low eaves' icy fretting.

It touched the tangled golden curls,
    And brown eyes full of grieving,
Of one who still her steps delayed
    When all the school were leaving.

For near her stood the little boy
    Her childish favor singled :
His cap pulled low upon a face
    Where pride and shame were mingled

Pushing with restless feet the snow
    To right and left, he lingered ; —
As restlessly her tiny hands
    The blue-checked apron fingered.

He saw her lift her eyes ; he felt
    The soft hand's light caressing,
And heard the tremble of her voice,
    As if a fault confessing.

"I'm sorry that I spelt the word :
    I hate to go above you,
Because," — the brown eyes lower
    fell, —
    "Because, you see, I love you !"

Still memory to a gray-haired man
    That sweet child-face is showing.
Dear girl ! the grasses on her grave
    Have forty years been growing !

He lives to learn, in life's hard school,
    How few who pass above him
Lament their triumph and his loss,
    Like her, — because they love him.

GARIBALDI.

IN trance and dream of old, God's
    prophet saw
    The casting down of thrones. Thou,
        watching lone
    The hot Sardinian coast-line, hazy-
        hilled,

" On woods that dream of bloom." Page 351.

Where, fringing round Caprera's rocky
    zone
With foam, the slow waves gather and
    withdraw,
    Behold'st the vision of the seer ful-
    filled,
And hear'st the sea-winds burdened
    with a sound
Of falling chains, as, one by one, un-
    bound,
The nations lift their right hands up
    and swear
    Their oath of freedom. From the
    chalk-white wall
Of England, from the black Carpathian
    range,
    Along the Danube and the Theiss,
    through all
The passes of the Spanish Pyrenees,
And from the Seine's thronged banks,
    a murmur strange
And glad floats to thee o'er thy sum-
    mer seas
On the salt wind that stirs thy whiten-
    ing hair, —
    The song of freedom's bloodless
    victories!
Rejoice, O Garibaldi! Though thy
    sword
Failed at Rome's gates, and blood
    seemed vainly poured
Where, in Christ's name, the crownéd
    infidel
Of France wrought murder with the
    arms of hell
    On that sad mountain slope whose
    ghostly dead,
Unmindful of the gray exorcist's ban,
Walk, unappeased, the chambered Vat-
    ican,
    And draw the curtains of Napoleon's
    bed!
God's providence is not blind, but, full
    of eyes,
It searches all the refuges of lies;
And in His time and way, the accursed
    things
    Before whose evil feet thy battle-
    gage
    Has clashed defiance from hot youth
    to age
Shall perish. All men shall be priests
    and kings, —
    One royal brotherhood, one church
    made free
By love, which is the law of liberty!
1869.

AFTER ELECTION.

The day's sharp strife is ended now,
Our work is done, God knoweth how!
As on the thronged, unrestful town
The patience of the moon looks down,
I wait to hear, beside the wire,
The voices of its tongues of fire.

Slow, doubtful, faint, they seem at first:
Be strong, my heart, to know the worst!
Hark! — there the Alleghanies spoke;
That sound from lake and prairie broke,
That sunset-gun of triumph rent
The silence of a continent!

That signal from Nebraska sprung,
This, from Nevada's mountain tongue!
Is that thy answer, strong and free,
O loyal heart of Tennessee?
What strange, glad voice is that which
    calls
From Wagner's grave and Sumter's
    walls?

From Mississippi's fountain-head
A sound as of the bison's tread!
There rustled freedom's Charter Oak!
In that wild burst the Ozarks spoke!
Cheer answers cheer from rise to set
Of sun. We have a country yet!

The praise, O God, be thine alone!
Thou givest not for bread a stone;
Thou hast not led us through the night
To blind us with returning light;
Not through the furnace have we passed,
To perish at its mouth at last.

O night of peace, thy flight restrain!
November's moon, be slow to wane!
Shine on the freedman's cabin floor,
On brows of prayer a blessing pour;
And give, with full assurance blest,
The weary heart of Freedom rest!
1868.

MY TRIUMPH.

The autumn-time has come;
On woods that dream of bloom,
And over purpling vines,
The low sun fainter shines.

The aster-flower is failing,
The hazel's gold is paling;

Yet overhead more near
The eternal stars appear!

And present gratitude
Insures the future's good,
And for the things I see
I trust the things to be;

That in the paths untrod,
And the long days of God,
My feet shall still be led,
My heart be comforted.

O living friends who love me!
O dear ones gone above me!
Careless of other fame,
I leave to you my name.

Hide it from idle praises,
Save it from evil phrases:
Why, when dear lips that spake it
Are dumb, should strangers wake it?

Let the thick curtain fall;
I better know than all
How little I have gained,
How vast the unattained.

Not by the page word-painted
Let life be banned or sainted:
Deeper than written scroll
The colors of the soul.

Sweeter than any sung
My songs that found no tongue;
Nobler than any fact
My wish that failed of act.

Others shall sing the song,
Others shall right the wrong, —
Finish what I begin,
And all I fail of win.

What matter, I or they?
Mine or another's day,
So the right word be said
And life the sweeter made?

Hail to the coming singers!
Hail to the brave light-bringers!
Forward I reach and share
All that they sing and dare.

The airs of heaven blow o'er me;
A glory shines before me
Of what mankind shall be, —
Pure, generous, brave, and free.

A dream of man and woman
Diviner but still human,
Solving the riddle old,
Shaping the Age of Gold!

The love of God and neighbor;
An equal-handed labor;
The richer life, where beauty
Walks hand in hand with duty.

Ring, bells in unreared steeples,
The joy of unborn peoples!
Sound, trumpets far off blown,
Your triumph is my own!

Parcel and part of all,
I keep the festival,
Fore-reach the good to be,
And share the victory.

I feel the earth move sunward,
I join the great march onward,
And take, by faith, while living,
My freehold of thanksgiving.

THE HIVE AT GETTYSBURG.

In the old Hebrew myth the lion's frame,
    So terrible alive,
Bleached by the desert's sun and wind, became
    The wandering wild bees' hive;
And he who, lone and naked-handed, tore
    Those jaws of death apart,
In after time drew forth their honeyed store
    To strengthen his strong heart.

Dead seemed the legend: but it only slept
    To wake beneath our sky;
Just on the spot whence ravening Treason crept
    Back to its lair to die,
Bleeding and torn from Freedom's mountain bounds,
    A stained and shattered drum
Is now the hive where, on their flowery rounds,
    The wild bees go and come.

Unchallenged by a ghostly sentinel,
    They wander wide and far,

Along green hillsides, sown with shot
  and shell,
  Through vales once choked with war.
The low reveille of their battle-drum
  Disturbs no morning prayer;
With deeper peace in summer noons
  their hum
  Fills all the drowsy air.

And Samson's riddle is our own to-
  day,
  Of sweetness from the strong,
Of union, peace, and freedom plucked
  away
  From the rent jaws of wrong.
From Treason's death we draw a purer
  life,
  As, from the beast he slew,
A sweetness sweeter for his bitter strife
  The old-time athlete drew!

HOWARD AT ATLANTA.

RIGHT in the track where Sherman
  Ploughed his red furrow,
Out of the narrow cabin,
  Up from the cellar's burrow,
Gathered the little black people,
  With freedom newly dowered,
Where, beside their Northern teacher,
  Stood the soldier, Howard.

He listened and heard the children
  Of the poor and long-enslavéd
Reading the words of Jesus,
  Singing the songs of David.
Behold! — the dumb lips speaking,
  The blind eyes seeing!
Bones of the Prophet's vision
  Warmed into being!

Transformed he saw them passing
  Their new life's portal!
Almost it seemed the mortal
  Put on the immortal.
No more with the beasts of burden,
  No more with stone and clod,
But crowned with glory and honor
  In the image of God!

There was the human chattel
  Its manhood taking;
There, in each dark, brown statue
  A soul was waking!
The man of many battles,
  With tears his eyelids pressing,

Stretched over those dusky foreheads
  His one-armed blessing.

And he said : "Who hears can never
  Fear for or doubt you;
What shall I tell the children
  Up North about you?"
Then ran round a whisper, a murmur,
  Some answer devising;
And a little boy stood up: "Massa,
  Tell 'em we're rising!"

O black boy of Atlanta!
  But half was spoken :
The slave's chain and the master's
  Alike are broken.
The one curse of the races
  Held both in tether:
They are rising, — all are rising,
  The black and white together!

O brave men and fair women!
  Ill comes of hate and scorning:
Shall the dark faces only
  Be turned to morning? —
Make Time your sole avenger,
  All-healing, all-redressing;
Meet Fate half-way, and make it
  A joy and blessing!

TO LYDIA MARIA CHILD,

ON READING HER POEM IN "THE
          STANDARD."

THE sweet spring day is glad with music,
  But through it sounds a sadder strain ;
The worthiest of our narrowing circle
  Sings Loring's dirges o'er again.

O woman greatly loved! I join thee
  In tender memories of our friend;
With thee across the awful spaces
  The greeting of a soul I send!

What cheer hath he? How is it with
  him?
Where lingers he this weary while?
Over what pleasant fields of Heaven
  Dawns the sweet sunrise of his smile?

Does he not know our feet are treading
  The earth hard down on Slavery's
  grave?
That, in our crowning exultations,
  We miss the charm his presence gave?

Why on this spring air comes no whis-
  per
  From him to tell us all is well ?
Why to our flower-time comes no token
  Of lily and of asphodel ?

I feel the unutterable longing,
  Thy hunger of the heart is mine ;
I reach and grope for hands in darkness,
  My ear grows sharp for voice or sign.

Still on the lips of all we question
  The finger of God's silence lies ;
Will the lost hands in ours be folded ?
  Will the shut eyelids ever rise ?

O friend ! no proof beyond this yearning,
  This outreach of our hearts, we need ;
God will not mock the hope He giveth,
  No love He prompts shall vainly
    plead.

Then let us stretch our hands in dark-
  ness,
  And call our loved ones o'er and o'er ;
Some day their arms shall close about
  us,
  And the old voices speak once more.

No dreary splendors wait our coming
  Where rapt ghost sits from ghost
    apart ;
Homeward we go to Heaven's thanks-
  giving,
  The harvest-gathering of the heart.

THE PRAYER-SEEKER.

Along the aisle where prayer was made
A woman, all in black arrayed,
Close-veiled, between the kneeling host,
With gliding motion of a ghost,
Passed to the desk, and laid thereon
A scroll which bore these words alone,
          Pray for me !

Back from the place of worshipping
She glided like a guilty thing :
The rustle of her draperies, stirred
By hurrying feet, alone was heard ;
While, full of awe, the preacher read,
As out into the dark she sped :
          "Pray for me !"

Back to the night from whence she
  came,
To unimagined grief or shame !
Across the threshold of that door
None knew the burden that she bore ;
Alone she left the written scroll,
The legend of a troubled soul, —
          Pray for me !

Glide on, poor ghost of woe or sin !
Thou leav'st a common need within ;
Each bears, like thee, some nameless
  weight,
Some misery inarticulate,
Some secret sin, some shrouded dread,
Some household sorrow all unsaid.
          Pray for us !

Pass on ! The type of all thou art,
Sad witness to the common heart !
With face in veil and seal on lip,
In mute and strange companionship,
Like thee we wander to and fro,
Dumbly imploring as we go :
          Pray for us !

Ah, who shall pray, since he who
  pleads
Our want perchance hath greater needs ?
Yet they who make their loss the gain
Of others shall not ask in vain,
And Heaven bends low to hear the
  prayer
Of love from lips of self-despair :
          Pray for us !

In vain remorse and fear and hate
Beat with bruised hands against a fate
Whose walls of iron only move
And open to the touch of love.
He only feels his burdens fall
Who, taught by suffering, pities all.
          Pray for us !

He prayeth best who leaves unguessed
The mystery of another's breast.
Why cheeks grow pale, why eyes o'er-
  flow,
Or heads are white, thou need'st not
  know.
Enough to note by many a sign
That every heart hath needs like thine.
          Pray for us !

POEMS FOR PUBLIC OCCASIONS.

A SPIRITUAL MANIFESTATION.

AT THE PRESIDENT'S LEVEE, BROWN
UNIVERSITY, 29TH 6TH MONTH, 1870.

TO-DAY the plant by Williams set
Its summer bloom discloses ;
The wilding sweetbrier of his prayers
Is crowned with cultured roses.

Once more the Island State repeats
The lesson that he taught her,
And binds his pearl of charity
Upon her brown-locked daughter.

Is 't fancy that he watches still
His Providence plantations ?
That still the careful Founder takes
A part on these occasions ?

Methinks I see that reverend form,
Which all of us so well know :
He rises up to speak ; he jogs
The presidential elbow

"Good friends," he says, "you reap a
field
I sowed in self-denial,
For toleration had its griefs
And charity its trial.

"Great grace, as saith Sir Thomas
More,
To him must needs be given
Who heareth heresy and leaves
The heretic to Heaven !

"I hear again the snuffled tones,
I see in dreary vision
Dyspeptic dreamers, spiritual bores,
And prophets with a mission.

"Each zealot thrust before my eyes
His Scripture-garbled label ;
All creeds were shouted in my ears
As with the tongues of Babel.

"Scourged at one cart-tail. each de-
nied
The hope of every other ;
Each martyr shook his branded fist
At the conscience of his brother !

"How cleft the dreary drone of man
The shriller pipe of woman,
As Gorton led his saints elect,
Who held all things in common !

"Their gay robes trailed in ditch and
swamp,
And torn by thorn and thicket,
The dancing-girls of Merry Mount
Came dragging to my wicket.

"Shrill Anabaptists, shorn of ears ;
Gray witch-wives, hobbling slowly ;
And Antinomians, free of law,
Whose very sins were holy.

"Hoarse ranters, crazed Fifth Mon-
archists,
Of stripes and bondage braggarts,
Pale Churchmen, with singed rubrics
snatched
From Puritanic fagots.

"And last, not least, the Quakers came,
With tongues still sore from burning,
The Bay State's dust from off their
feet
Before my threshold spurning ;

"A motley host, the Lord's débris,
Faith's odds and ends together ;
Well might I shrink from guests with
lungs
Tough as their breeches leather :

"If, when the hangman at their heel
Came, rope in hand to catch them,
I took the hunted outcasts in,
I never sent to fetch them.

"I fed, but spared them not a whit ;
I gave to all who walked in,
Not clams and succotash alone,
But stronger meat of doctrine.

"I proved the prophets false, I pricked
The bubble of perfection,
And clapped upon their inner light
The snuffers of election.

"And looking backward on my times,
This credit I am taking ;

I kept each sectary's dish apart,
  No spiritual chowder making.

"Where now the blending signs of sect
  Would puzzle their assorter,
The dry-shod Quaker kept the land,
  The Baptist held the water.

"A common coat now serves for both,
  The hat's no more a fixture ;
And which was wet and which was
      dry,
  Who knows in such a mixture ?

"Well ! He who fashioned Peter's
      dream
  To bless them all is able ;
And bird and beast and creeping thing
  Make clean upon His table !

"I walked by my own light ; but when
  The ways of faith divided,
Was I to force unwilling feet
  To tread the path that I did ?

"I touched the garment-hem of truth,
  Yet saw not all its splendor ;
I knew enough of doubt to feel
  For every conscience tender.

"God left men free of choice, as when
  His Eden-trees were planted ;
Because they chose amiss, should I
  Deny the gift He granted ?

"So, with a common sense of need,
  Our common weakness feeling,
I left them with myself to God
  And His all-gracious dealing !

"I kept His plan whose rain and sun
  To tare and wheat are given ;
And if the ways to hell were free,
  I left them free to heaven !"

Take heart with us, O man of old,
  Soul-freedom's brave confessor,
So love of God and man wax strong,
  Let sect and creed be lesser.

The jarring discords of thy day
  In ours one hymn are swelling ;
The wandering feet, the severed paths,
  All seek our Father's dwelling.

And slowly learns the world the truth
  That makes us all thy debtor, —

That holy life is more than rite,
  And spirit more than letter ;

That they who differ pole-wide serve
  Perchance the common Master,
And other sheep He hath than they
  Who graze one narrow pasture !

For truth's worst foe is he who claims
  To act as God's avenger,
And deems, beyond his sentry-beat,
  The crystal walls in danger !

Who sets for heresy his traps
  Of verbal quirk and quibble,
And weeds the garden of the Lord
  With Satan's borrowed dibble.

To-day our hearts like organ keys
  One Master's touch are feeling ;
The branches of a common Vine
  Have only leaves of healing.

Co-workers, yet from varied fields,
  We share this restful nooning ;
The Quaker with the Baptist here
  Believes in close communing.

Forgive, dear saint, the playful tone,
  Too light for thy deserving ;
Thanks for thy generous faith in man,
  Thy trust in God unswerving.

Still echo in the hearts of men
  The words that thou hast spoken ;
No forge of hell can weld again
  The fetters thou hast broken.

The pilgrim needs a pass no more
  From Roman or Genevan ;
Thought-free, no ghostly tollman keeps
  Henceforth the road to Heaven !

"THE LAURELS."

AT THE TWENTIETH AND LAST ANNI-
  VERSARY.

FROM these wild rocks I look to-day
  O'er leagues of dancing waves, and
      see
The far, low coast-line stretch away
  To where our river meets the sea.

The light wind blowing off the land
  Is burdened with old voices , through

Shut eyes I see how lip and hand
　The greeting of old days renew.

O friends whose hearts still keep their
　　prime,
　Whose bright example warms and
　　cheers,
Ye teach us how to smile at Time,
　And set to music all his years !

I thank you for sweet summer days,
　For pleasant memories lingering long,
For joyful meetings, fond delays,
　And ties of friendship woven strong.

As for the last time, side by side,
　You tread the paths familiar grown,
I reach across the severing tide,
　And blend my farewells with your
　　own.

Make room, O river of our home !
　For other feet in place of ours,
And in the summers yet to come,
　Make glad another Feast of Flowers !

Hold in thy mirror, calm and deep,
　The pleasant pictures thou hast seen ;
Forget thy lovers not, but keep
　Our memory like thy laurels green.

ISLES OF SHOALS, 7th mo., 1870.

HYMN

FOR THE CELEBRATION OF EMANCIPA- TION AT NEWBURYPORT.

NOT unto us who did but seek
The word that burned within to speak,
Not unto us this day belong
The triumph and exultant song.

Upon us fell in early youth
The burden of unwelcome truth,
And left us, weak and frail and few,
The censor's painful work to do.

Thenceforth our life a fight became,
The air we breathed was hot with
　blame ;

For not with gauged and softened tone
We made the bondman's cause our
　own.

We bore, as Freedom's hope forlorn,
The private hate, the public scorn ;
Yet held through all the paths we trod
Our faith in man and trust in God.

We prayed and hoped ; but still, with
　awe,
The coming of the sword we saw ;
We heard the nearing steps of doom,
We saw the shade of things to come

In grief which they alone can feel
Who from a mother's wrong appeal,
With blended lines of fear and hope
We cast our country's horoscope.

For still within her house of life
We marked the lurid sign of strife,
And, poisoning and imbittering all,
We saw the star of Wormwood fall.

Deep as our love for her became
Our hate of all that wrought her shame,
And if, thereby, with tongue and pen
We erred, — we were but mortal men.

We hoped for peace ; our eyes survey
The blood-red dawn of Freedom's day :
We prayed for love to loose the chain ;
'T is shorn by battle's axe in twain !

Nor skill nor strength nor zeal of ours
Has mined and heaved the hostile
　towers ;
Not by our hands is turned the key
That sets the sighing captives free.

A redder sea than Egypt's wave
Is piled and parted for the slave ;
A darker cloud moves on in light ;
A fiercer fire is guide by night !

The praise, O Lord ! is Thine alone,
In Thy own way Thy work is done !
Our poor gifts at Thy feet we cast,
To whom be glory, first and last !
1865.

THE PENNSYLVANIA PILGRIM,

AND OTHER POEMS.

FRANCIS DANIEL PASTORIUS.

THE beginning of German emigration to America may be traced to the personal influence of William Penn, who in 1677 visited the Continent, and made the acquaintance of an intelligent and highly cultivated circle of Pietists, or Mystics, who, reviving in the seventeenth century the spiritual faith and worship of Tauler and the "Friends of God" in the fourteenth, gathered about the pastor Spener, and the young and beautiful Eleonora Johanna Von Merlau. In this circle originated the Frankfort Land Company, which bought of William Penn, the Governor of Pennsylvania, a tract of land near the new city of Philadelphia.

The company's agent in the New World was a rising young lawyer, Francis Daniel Pastorius, son of Judge Pastorius, of Windsheim, who, at the age of seventeen, entered the University of Altorf. He studied law at Strasburg, Basle, and Jena, and at Ratisbon, the seat of the Imperial Government, obtained a practical knowledge of international polity. Successful in all his examinations and disputations, he received the degree of Doctor of Law at Nuremberg in 1676. In 1679 he was a law-lecturer at Frankfort, where he became deeply interested in the teachings of Dr. Spener. In 1680–81 he travelled in France, England, Ireland, and Italy with his friend Herr Von Rodeck. "I was," he says, "glad to enjoy again the company of my Christian friends, rather than be with Von Rodeck feasting and dancing." In 1683, in company with a small number of German Friends, he emigrated to America, settling upon the Frankfort Company's tract between the Schuylkill and the Delaware Rivers. The township was divided into four hamlets, namely, Germantown, Krisheim, Crefield, and Sommerhausen. Soon after his arrival he united himself with the Society of Friends, and became one of its most able and devoted members, as well as the recognized head and lawgiver of the settlement. He married, two years after his arrival, Anneke (Anna), daughter of Dr. Klosterman, of Muhlheim.

In the year 1688 he drew up a memorial against slaveholding, which was adopted by the Germantown Friends and sent up to the Monthly Meeting, and thence to the Yearly Meeting at Philadelphia. It is noteworthy as the first protest made by a religious body against Negro Slavery. The original document was discovered in 1844 by the Philadelphia antiquarian, Nathan Kite, and published in "The Friend" (Vol. XVIII No. 16). It is a bold and direct appeal to the best instincts of the heart. "Have not," he asks, "these negroes as much right to fight for their freedom as you have to keep them slaves?"

Under the wise direction of Pastorius, the Germantown settlement grew and prospered. The inhabitants planted orchards and vineyards, and surrounded themselves with souvenirs of their old home. A large number of them were linen-weavers, as well as small farmers. The Quakers were the principal sect, but men of all religions were tolerated, and lived together in harmony. In 1692 Richard Frame published, in what he called verse, a "Description of Pennsylvania," in which he alludes to the settlement: —

" The German town of which I spoke before,
 Which is at least in length one mile or more,
 Where lives High German people and Low Dutch,
 Whose trade in weaving linen cloth is much, —
 There grows the flax, as also you may know
 That from the same they do divide the tow.
 Their trade suits well their habitation, —
 We find convenience for their occupation."

Pastorius seems to have been on intimate terms with William Penn, Thomas Lloyd, Chief Justice Logan, Thomas Story, and other leading men in the Province belonging to his own religious society, as also with Kelpius, the learned Mystic of the Wissahickon, with the pastor of the Swedes' church, and the leaders of the Mennonites. He wrote a description of Pennsylvania, which was published at Frankfort and Leipsic in 1700 and 1701. His "Lives of the Saints," etc., written in German and dedicated to Prof. Schurmberg, his old teacher, was published in 1690. He left behind him many unpublished manuscripts covering a very wide range of subjects, most of which are now lost. One huge manuscript folio, entitled "Hive Beestock, Melliotropheum Alucar, or Rusca Apium," still remains, containing one thousand pages with about one hundred lines to a page. It is a medley of knowledge and fancy, history, philosophy, and poetry, written in seven languages. A large portion of his poetry is devoted to the pleasures of gardening, the description of flowers, and the care of bees. The following specimen of his punning Latin is addressed to an orchard-pilferer: —

" Quisquis in hæc furtim reptas viridaria nostra
 Tangere fallaci poma caveto manu,
 Si non obsequeris faxit Deus omne quod opto,
 Cum malis nostris ut mala cuncta feras."

Professor Oswald Seidensticker, to whose papers in Der Deutsche Pioneer and that able periodical the "Penn Monthly," of Philadelphia, I am indebted for many of the foregoing facts in regard to the German pilgrims of the New World, thus closes his notice of Pastorius: —

"No tombstone, not even a record of burial, indicates where his remains have found their last resting-place, and the pardonable desire to associate the homage due to this distinguished man with some visible memento cannot be gratified. There is no reason to suppose that he was interred in any other place than the Friends' old burying-ground in Germantown, though the fact is not attested by any definite source of information. After all, this obliteration of the last trace of his earthly existence is but typical of what has overtaken the times which he represents; that Germantown which he founded, which saw him live and move, is at present but a quaint idyl of the past, almost a myth, barely remembered and little cared for by the keener race that has succeeded."

The Pilgrims of Plymouth have not lacked historian and poet. Justice has been done to their faith, courage, and self-sacrifice, and to the mighty influence of their endeavors to establish righteousness on the earth. The Quaker pilgrims of Pennsylvania, seeking the same object by different means, have not been equally fortunate. The power of their testimony for truth and holiness, peace and freedom, enforced only by what Milton calls "the unresistible might of meekness," has been felt through two centuries in the amelioration of penal severities, the abolition of slavery, the reform of the erring, the relief of the poor and suffering, — felt, in brief, in every step of human progress. But of the men themselves, with the single exception of William Penn, scarcely anything is known. Contrasted, from the outset, with the stern, aggressive Puritans of New England, they have come to be regarded as "a feeble folk," with a personality as doubtful as their unrecorded graves. They were not soldiers, like Miles Standish; they had no figure so picturesque as Vane, no leader so rashly brave and haughty as Endicott. No Cotton Mather wrote their Magnalia; they had no awful drama of supernaturalism in which Satan and his angels were actors; and the only witch mentioned in their simple annals was a poor old Swedish woman, who, on complaint of her countrywomen, was tried and acquitted of everything but imbecility and folly. Nothing but commonplace offices of civility came to pass between them and the Indians; indeed, their enemies taunted them with the fact that the savages did not regard them as Christians, but just such men as themselves. Yet it must be apparent to every careful observer of the progress of American civilization that its two principal currents had their sources in the entirely opposite directions of the Puritan and Quaker colonies. To use the words of a late writer : * "The historical forces, with which no others may be compared in their influence on the people, have been those of the Puritan and the Quaker. The strength of the one was in the confession of an invisible Presence, a righteous, eternal Will, which would establish righteousness on earth; and thence arose the conviction of a direct personal responsibility, which could be tempted by no external splendor and could be shaken by no internal agitation, and could not be evaded or transferred. The strength of the other was the witness in the human spirit to an eternal Word, an Inner Voice which spoke to each alone, while yet it spoke to every man; a Light which each was to follow, and which yet was the light of the world; and all other voices were silent before this, and the solitary path whither it led was more sacred than the worn ways of cathedral-aisles."

It will be sufficiently apparent to the reader that, in the poem which follows, I have attempted nothing beyond a study of the life and times of the Pennsylvania colonist, — a simple picture of a noteworthy man and his locality. The colors of my sketch are all very sober, toned down to the quiet and dreamy atmosphere through which its subject is visible. Whether, in the glare and tumult of the present time, such a picture

Mulford's Nation, pp. 267, 268.

will find favor may well be questioned. I only know that it has beguiled for me some hours of weariness, and that, whatever may be its measure of public appreciation, it has been to me its own reward.

J. G. W.

AMESBURY, 5th mo., 1872.

———

Hail to posterity!
Hail, future men of Germanopolis!
   Let the young generations yet to be
   Look kindly upon this.
Think how your fathers left their native
            land, —
   Dear German-land!   O sacred
            hearths and homes ! —
   And, where the wild beast roams,
            In patience planned
New forest-homes beyond the mighty
            sea,
   There undisturbed and free
To live as brothers of one family.
   What pains and cares befell,
      What trials and what fears,
Remember, and wherein we have done
            well
   Follow our footsteps, men of coming
            years !
   Where we have failed to do
      Aright, or wisely live,
Be warned by us, the better way pursue,
And, knowing we were human, even as
            you,
   Pity us and forgive !
   Farewell, Posterity !
   Farewell, dear Germany !
   Forevermore farewell !

From the Latin of FRANCIS DANIEL PASTORIUS
in the Germantown Records. 1688.

———

PRELUDE.

I SING the Pilgrim of a softer clime
   And milder speech than those brave
            men's who brought
To the ice and iron of our winter time
   A will as firm, a creed as stern, and
            wrought
   With one mailed hand, and with the
            other fought.
Simply, as fits my theme, in homely
            rhyme
   I sing the blue-eyed German Spener
            taught,

Through whose veiled, mystic faith the
   Inward Light,
Steady and still, an easy brightness,
   shone,
Transfiguring all things in its radiance
   white.
The garland which his meekness never
   sought
   I bring him ; over fields of harvest
   sown
With seeds of blessing, now to ripe-
   ness grown,
I bid the sower pass before the reapers'
   sight.

THE PENNSYLVANIA PILGRIM.

NEVER in tenderer quiet lapsed the
   day
From Pennsylvania's vales of spring
   away,
Where, forest-walled, the scattered hamlets lay

Along the wedded rivers.   One long
   bar
Of purple cloud, on which the evening
   star
Shone like a jewel on a scimitar,

Held the sky's golden gateway. Through
   the deep
Hush of the woods a murmur seemed to
   creep,
The Schuylkill whispering in a voice of
   sleep.

All else was still.   The oxen from their
   ploughs
Rested at last, and from their long day's
   browse
Came the dun files of Krisheim's home-
   bound cows.

And the young city, round whose virgin
   zone
The rivers like two mighty arms were
   thrown,
Marked by the smoke of evening fires
   alone,

Lay in the distance, lovely even then
With its fair women and its stately
   men
Gracing the forest court of William
   Penn,

Urban yet sylvan; in its rough-hewn
   frames
Of oak and pine the dryads held their
   claims,
And lent its streets their pleasant woodland names.

Anna Pastorius down the leafy lane
Looked city-ward, then stooped to prune
   again
Her vines and simples, with a sigh of pain.

For fast the streaks of ruddy sunset paled
In the oak clearing, and, as daylight
   failed,
Slow, overhead, the dusky night-birds
   sailed.

Again she looked: between green walls
   of shade,
With low-bent head as if with sorrow
   weighed,
Daniel Pastorius slowly came and said,

"God's peace be with thee, Anna!"
   Then he stood
Silent before her, wrestling with the mood
Of one who sees the evil and not good.

What is it, my Pastorius?" As she
   spoke,
A slow, faint smile across his features
   broke,
Sadder than tears.   "Dear heart," he
   said, "our folk

"Are even as others.   Yea, our good-
   liest Friends
Are frail ; our elders have their selfish
   ends,
And few dare trust the Lord to make
   amends

"For duty's loss. So even our feeble word
For the dumb slaves the startled meet-
   ing heard
As if a stone its quiet waters stirred ;

"And, as the clerk ceased reading, there
   began
A ripple of dissent which downward ran
In widening circles, as from man to man.

"Somewhat was said of running before
   sent,
Of tender fear that some their guide out-
   went,
Troublers of Israel.   I was scarce intent

"On hearing, for behind the reverend
 row
Of gallery Friends, in dumb and piteous
 show,
I saw, methought, dark faces full of woe.

" And, in the spirit, I was taken where
They toiled and suffered ; I was made
 aware
Of shame and wrath and anguish and
 despair !

"And while the meeting smothered our
 poor plea
With cautious phrase, a Voice there
 seemed to be,
' As ye have done to these ye do to me !' "

"So it all passed; and the old tithe
 went on
Of anise, mint, and cumin, till the sun
Set, leaving still the weightier work
 undone.

" Help, for the good man faileth ! Who
 is strong,
If these be weak ? Who shall rebuke
 the wrong,
If these consent ? How long, O Lord !
 how long ! ' "

He ceased ; and, bound in spirit with
 the bound,
With folded arms, and eyes that sought
 the ground,
Walked musingly his little garden round.

About him, beaded with the falling dew,
Rare plants of power and herbs of healing
 grew,
Such as Van Helmont and Agrippa knew.

For, by the lore of Gorlitz' gentle sage,
With the mild mystics of his dreamy age
He read the herbal signs of nature's page,

As once he heard in sweet Von Merlau's[75]
 bowers
Fair as herself, in boyhood's happy hours,
The pious Spener read his creed in
 flowers.

" The dear Lord give us patience ! " said
 his wife,
Touching with finger-tip an aloe, rife
With leaves sharp-pointed like an Aztec
 knife

Or Carib spear, a gift to William Penn
From the rare gardens of John Evelyn,
Brought from the Spanish Main by
 merchantmen.

" See this strange plant its steady purpose hold,
And, year by year, its patient leaves
 unfold,
Till the young eyes that watched it first
 are old.

" But some time, thou hast told me,
 there shall come
A sudden beauty, brightness, and perfume,
The century-moulded bud shall burst in
 bloom.

" So may the seed which hath been sown
 to-day
Grow with the years, and, after long
 delay,
Break into bloom, and God's eternal Yea

" Answer at last the patient prayers of
 them
Who now, by faith alone, behold its
 stem
Crowned with the flowers of Freedom's
 diadem.

" Meanwhile, to feel and suffer, work
 and wait,
Remains for us. The wrong indeed is
 great,
But love and patience conquer soon or
 late."

" Well hast thou said, my Anna ! "
 Tenderer
Than youth's caress upon the head of
 her
Pastorius laid his hand. "Shall we demur

" Because the vision tarrieth ? In an
 hour
We dream not of the slow-grown bud
 may flower,
And what was sown in weakness rise in
 power ! "

Then through the vine-draped door whose
 legend read,
" PROCUL ESTE PROPHANI ! " Anna led
To where their child upon his little
 bed

Looked up and smiled. "Dear heart,"
she said, "if we
Must bearers of a heavy burden be,
Our boy, God willing, yet the day shall see

"When, from the gallery to the farthest
seat,
Slave and slave-owner shall no longer
meet,
But all sit equal at the Master's feet."

On the stone hearth the blazing walnut
block
Set the low walls a-glimmer, showed the
cock
Rebuking Peter on the Van Wyck clock,

Shone on old tomes of law and physic,
side
By side with Fox and Behmen, played
at hide
And seek with Anna, midst her household pride

Of flaxen webs, and on the table, bare
Of costly cloth or silver cup, but where,
Tasting the fat shads of the Delaware,

The courtly Penn had praised the goodwife's cheer,
And quoted Horace o'er her home-brewed
beer,
Till even grave Pastorius smiled to hear.

In such a home, beside the Schuylkill's
wave,
He dwelt in peace with God and man,
and gave
Food to the poor and shelter to the slave.

For all too soon the New World's scandal shamed
The righteous code by Penn and Sidney
framed,
And men withheld the human rights
they claimed.

And slowly wealth and station sanction
lent,
And hardened avarice, on its gains intent,
Stifled the inward whisper of dissent.

Yet all the while the burden rested sore
On tender hearts. At last Pastorius bore
Their warning message to the Church's
door

In God's name; and the leaven of the
word
Wrought ever after in the souls who
heard,
And a dead conscience in its grave-
clothes stirred

To troubled life, and urged the vain
excuse
Of Hebrew custom, patriarchal use,
Good in itself if evil in abuse.

Gravely Pastorius listened, not the less
Discerning through the decent fig-leaf
dress
Of the poor plea its shame of selfishness.

One Scripture rule, at least, was unforgot;
He hid the outcast, and bewrayed him
not;
And, when his prey the human hunter
sought,

He scrupled not, while Anna's wise delay
And proffered cheer prolonged the mas-
ter's stay,
To speed the black guest safely on his way.

Yet, who shall guess his bitter grief who
lends
His life to some great cause, and finds
his friends
Shame or betray it for their private ends?

How felt the Master when his chosen
strove
In childish folly for their seats above;
And that fond mother, blinded by her
love,

Besought him that her sons, beside his
throne,
Might sit on either hand? Amidst his
own
A stranger oft, companionless and lone,

God's priest and prophet stands. The
martyr's pain
Is not alone from scourge and cell and
chain;
Sharper the pang when, shouting in his
train,

His weak disciples by their lives deny
The loud hosannas of their daily cry,
And make their echo of his truth a lie.

His forest home no hermit's cell he found,
Guests, motley-minded, drew his hearth
    around,
And held armed truce upon its neutral
    ground.

Their Indian chiefs with battle-bows un-
    strung,
Strong, hero-limbed, like those whom
    Homer sung,
Pastorius fancied, when the world was
    young,

Came with their tawny women, lithe and
    tall,
Like bronzes in his friend Von Rodeck's
    hall,
Comely, if black, and not unpleasing all.

There hungry folk in homespun drab and
    gray
Drew round his board on Monthly Meet-
    ing day,
Genial, half merry in their friendly way.

Or, haply, pilgrims from the Fatherland,
Weak, timid, homesick, slow to under-
    stand
The New World's promise, sought his
    helping hand.

Or painful Kelpius [76] from his hermit den
By Wissahickon, maddest of good men,
Dreamed o'er the Chiliast dreams of
    Petersen.

Deep in the woods, where the small
    river slid
Snake-like in shade, the Helmstadt
    Mystic hid,
Weird as a wizard over arts forbid,

Reading the books of Daniel and of John,
And Behmen's Morning-Redness, through
    the Stone
Of Wisdom, vouchsafed to his eyes alone,

Whereby he read what man ne'er read
    before,
And saw the visions man shall see no
    more,
Till the great angel, striding sea and
    shore,

Shall bid all flesh await, on land or ships,
The warning trump of the Apocalypse,
Shattering the heavens before the dread
    eclipse.

Or meek-eyed Mennonist his bearded chin
Leaned o'er the gate; or Ranter, pure
    within,
Aired his perfection in a world of sin.

Or, talking of old home scenes, Op der
    Graaf
Teased the low back-log with his shod-
    den staff,
Till the red embers broke into a laugh

And dance of flame, as if they fain would
    cheer
The rugged face, half tender, half aus-
    tere,
Touched with the pathos of a homesick
    tear !

Or Sluyter, [77] saintly familist, whose word
As law the Brethren of the Manor heard,
Announced the speedy terrors of the
    Lord,

And turned, like Lot at Sodom, from
    his race,
Above a wrecked world with complacent
    face
Riding secure upon his plank of grace !

Haply, from Finland's birchen groves
    exiled,
Manly in thought, in simple ways a
    child,
His white hair floating round his visage
    mild,

The Swedish pastor sought the Quaker's
    door,
Pleased from his neighbor's lips to hear
    once more
His long-disused and half-forgotten lore.

For both could baffle Babel's lingual
    curse,
And speak in Bion's Doric, and rehearse
Cleanthes' hymn or Virgil's sounding
    verse.

And oft Pastorius and the meek old man
Argued as Quaker and as Lutheran,
Ending in Christian love, as they began.

With lettered Lloyd on pleasant morns
    he strayed
Where Sommerhausen over vales of shade
Looked miles away, by every flower
    delayed,

Or song of bird, happy and free with one
Who loved, like him, to let his memory run
Over old fields of learning, and to sun

Himself in Plato's wise philosophies,
And dream with Philo over mysteries
Whereof the dreamer never finds the keys;

To touch all themes of thought, nor weakly stop
For doubt of truth, but let the buckets drop
Deep down and bring the hidden waters up.[78]

For there was freedom in that wakening time
Of tender souls; to differ was not crime;
The varying bells made up the perfect chime.

On lips unlike was laid the altar's coal,
The white, clear light, tradition-colored, stole
Through the stained oriel of each human soul.

Gathered from many sects, the Quaker brought
His old beliefs, adjusting to the thought
That moved his soul the creed his fathers taught.

One faith alone, so broad that all mankind
Within themselves its secret witness find,
The soul's communion with the Eternal Mind,

The Spirit's law, the Inward Rule and Guide,
Scholar and peasant, lord and serf, allied,
The polished Penn and Cromwell's Ironside.

As still in Hemskerck's Quaker Meeting,[79] face
By face in Flemish detail, we may trace
How loose-mouthed boor and fine ancestral grace

Sat in close contrast, — the clipt-headed churl,
Broad market-dame, and simple serving-girl
By skirt of silk and periwig in curl!

For soul touched soul; the spiritual treasure-trove
Made all men equal, none could rise above
Nor sink below that level of God's love.

So, with his rustic neighbors sitting down,
The homespun frock beside the scholar's gown,
Pastorius to the manners of the town

Added the freedom of the woods, and sought
The bookless wisdom by experience taught,
And learned to love his new-found home, while not

Forgetful of the old; the seasons went
Their rounds, and somewhat to his spirit lent
Of their own calm and measureless content.

Glad even to tears, he heard the robin sing
His song of welcome to the Western spring,
And bluebird borrowing from the sky his wing.

And when the miracle of autumn came,
And all the woods with many-colored flame
Of splendor, making summer's greenness tame,

Burned, unconsumed, a voice without a sound
Spake to him from each kindled bush around,
And made the strange, new landscape holy ground!

And when the bitter north-wind, keen and swift,
Swept the white street and piled the dooryard drift,
He exercised, as Friends might say, his gift

Of verse, Dutch, English, Latin, like the hash
Of corn and beans in Indian succotash;
Dull, doubtless, but with here and there a flash

Of wit and fine conceit, — the good
    man's play
Of quiet fancies, meet to while away
The slow hours measuring off an idle day.

At evening, while his wife put on her
    look
Of love's endurance, from its niche he
    took
The written pages of his ponderous book.

And read, in half the languages of man,
His "Rusca Apium," which with bees
    began,
And through the gamut of creation ran.

Or, now and then, the missive of some
    friend
In gray Altorf or storied Nürnberg
    penned
Dropped in upon him like a guest to
    spend

The night beneath his roof-tree.
    Mystical
The fair Von Merlau spake as waters
    fall
And voices sound in dreams, and yet
    withal

Human and sweet, as if each far, low
    tone,
Over the roses of her gardens blown
Brought the warm sense of beauty all
    her own.

Wise Spener questioned what his friend
    could trace
Of spiritual influx or of saving grace
In the wild natures of the Indian race.

And learned Schurmberg, fain, at times,
    to look
From Talmud, Koran, Veds, and Penta-
    teuch,
Sought out his pupil in his far-off nook,

To query with him of climatic change,
Of bird, beast, reptile, in his forest range,
Of flowers and fruits and simples new
    and strange.

And thus the Old and New World
    reached their hands
Across the water, and the friendly lands
Talked with each other from their
    severed strands.

Pastorius answered all : while seed and
    root
Sent from his new home grew to flower
    and fruit
Along the Rhine and at the Spessart's
    foot;

And, in return, the flowers his boyhood
    knew
Smiled at his door, the same in form
    and hue,
And on his vines the Rhenish clusters
    grew.

No idler he ; whoever else might shirk,
He set his hand to every honest work,—
Farmer and teacher, court and meeting
    clerk.

Still on the town seal his device is found,
Grapes, flax, and thread-spool on a tre-
    foil ground,
With "VINUM, LINUM ET TEXTRINUM"
    wound.

One house sufficed for gospel and for law,
Where Paul and Grotius, Scripture text
    and saw,
Assured the good, and held the rest in awe.

Whatever legal maze he wandered
    through,
He kept the Sermon on the Mount in
    view,
And justice always into mercy grew.

No whipping-post he needed, stocks, nor
    jail,
Nor ducking-stool ; the orchard-thief
    grew pale
At his rebuke, the vixen ceased to rail,

The usurer's grasp released the forfeit
    land ;
The slanderer faltered at the witness-
    stand,
And all men took his counsel for com-
    mand.

Was it caressing air, the brooding love
Of tenderer skies than German land
    knew of,
Green calm below, blue quietness above,

Still flow of water, deep repose of wood
That, with a sense of loving Fatherhood
And childlike trust in the Eternal Good,

Softened all hearts, and dulled the edge
of hate,
Hushed strife, and taught impatient zeal
to wait
The slow assurance of the better state ?

Who knows what goadings in their
sterner way
O'er jagged ice, relieved by granite gray,
Blew round the men of Massachusetts
Bay ?

What hate of heresy the east-wind woke ?
What hints of pitiless power and terror
spoke
In waves that on their iron coast-line
broke ?

Be it as it may : within the Land of Penn
The sectary yielded to the citizen,
And peaceful dwelt the many-creeded
men.

Peace brooded over all. No trumpet
stung
The air to madness, and no steeple flung
Alarums down from bells at midnight
rung.

The land slept well. The Indian from
his face
Washed all his war-paint off, and in the
place
Of battle-marches sped the peaceful
chase,

Or wrought for wages at the white man's
side, —
Giving to kindness what his native pride
And lazy freedom to all else denied.

And well the curious scholar loved the
old
Traditions that his swarthy neighbors
told
By wigwam-fires when nights were growing cold,

Discerned the fact round which their
fancy drew
Its dreams, and held their childish faith
more true
To God and man than half the creeds he
knew.[80]

The desert blossomed round him ; wheat-
fields rolled
Beneath the warm wind waves of green
and gold ;
The planted ear returned its hundred-
fold.

Great clusters ripened in a warmer sun
Than that which by the Rhine stream
shines upon
The purpling hillsides with low vines
o'errun.

About each rustic porch the humming-
bird
Tried with light bill, that scarce a petal
stirred,
The Old World flowers to virgin soil
transferred ;

And the first-fruits of pear and apple,
bending
The young boughs down, their gold and
russet blending,
Made glad his heart, familiar odors lending

To the fresh fragrance of the birch and
pine,
Life-everlasting, bay, and eglantine,
And all the subtle scents the woods combine.

Fair First-Day mornings, steeped in
summer calm
Warm, tender, restful, sweet with woodland balm,
Came to him, like some mother-hallowed
psalm

To the tired grinder at the noisy wheel
Of labor, winding off from memory's reel
A golden thread of music. With no peal

Of bells to call them to the house of
praise,
The scattered settlers through green for-
est-ways
Walked meeting-ward. In reverent
amaze

The Indian trapper saw them, from the
dim
Shade of the alders on the rivulet's rim,
Seek the Great Spirit's house to talk
with Him.

There, through the gathered stillness
multiplied
And made intense by sympathy, outside
The sparrows sang, and the gold-robin
cried,

A-swing upon his elm. A faint perfume
Breathed through the open windows of
the room
From locust-trees, heavy with clustered
bloom.

Thither, perchance, sore-tried confessors
came,
Whose fervor jail nor pillory could tame,
Proud of the cropped ears meant to be
their shame,

Men who had eaten slavery's bitter
bread
In Indian isles; pale women who had
bled
Under the hangman's lash, and bravely
said

God's message through their prison's iron
bars;
And gray old soldier-converts, seamed
with scars
From every stricken field of England's
wars

Lowly before the Unseen Presence knelt
Each waiting heart, till haply some one
felt
On his moved lips the seal of silence
melt.

Or, without spoken words, low breathings stole
Of a diviner life from soul to soul,
Baptizing in one tender thought the
whole.

When shaken hands announced the
meeting o'er,
The friendly group still lingered at the
door,
Greeting, inquiring, sharing all the store

Of weekly tidings. Meanwhile youth
and maid
Down the green vistas of the woodland
strayed,
Whispered and smiled and oft their feet
delayed.

Did the boy's whistle answer back the
thrushes?
Did light girl laughter ripple through
the bushes,
As brooks make merry over roots and
rushes?

Unvexed the sweet air seemed. Without
a wound
The ear of silence heard, and every
sound
Its place in nature's fine accordanc'
found.

And solemn meeting, summer sky and
wood,
Old kindly faces, youth and maidenhood
Seemed, like God's new creation, very
good!

And, greeting all with quiet smile and
word,
Pastorius went his way. The unscared
bird
Sang at his side; scarcely the squirrel
stirred

At his hushed footstep on the mossy sod;
And, wheresoe'er the good man looked
or trod,
He felt the peace of nature and of God.

His social life wore no ascetic form,
He loved all beauty, without fear of
harm,
And in his veins his Teuton blood ran
warm.

Strict to himself, of other men no spy,
He made his own no circuit-judge to try
The freer conscience of his neighbors by.

With love rebuking, by his life alone,
Gracious and sweet, the better way was
shown,
The joy of one, who, seeking not his own,

And faithful to all scruples, finds at last
The thorns and shards of duty overpast,
And daily life, beyond his hope's forecast,

Pleasant and beautiful with sight and
sound,
And flowers upspringing in its narrow
round,
And all his days with quiet gladness
crowned.

He sang not ; but, if sometimes tempted
    strong,
He hummed what seemed like Altorf's
    Burschen-song,
His good wife smiled, and did not count
    it wrong.

For well he loved his boyhood's brother
    band ;
His Memory, while he trod the New
    World's strand,
A double-ganger walked the Fatherland !

If, when on frosty Christmas eves the
    light
Shone on his quiet hearth, he missed
    the sight
Of Yule-log, Tree, and Christ-child all
    in white :

And closed his eyes, and listened to the
    sweet
Old wait-songs sounding down his native
    street,
And watched again the dancers' min-
    gling feet ;

Yet not the less, when once the vision
    passed,
He held the plain and sober maxims fast
Of the dear Friends with whom his lot
    was cast.

Still all attuned to nature's melodies,
He loved the bird's song in his dooryard
    trees,
And the low hum of home-returning
    bees ;

The blossomed flax, the tulip-trees in
    bloom
Down the long street, the beauty and
    perfume
Of apple-boughs, the mingling light and
    gloom

Of Sommerhausen's woodlands, woven
    through
With sun-threads; and the music the
    wind drew,
Mournful and sweet, from leaves it over-
    blew.

And evermore, beneath this outward
    sense,
And through the common sequence of
    events,
He felt the guiding hand of Providence

Reach out of space. A Voice spake in
    his ear,
And lo ! all other voices far and near
Died at that whisper, full of meanings
    clear.

The Light of Life shone round him; one
    by one
The wandering lights, that all-mislead-
    ing run,
Went out like candles paling in the sun.

That Light he followed, step by step,
    where'er
It led, as in the vision of the seer
The wheels moved as the spirit in the
    clear

And terrible crystal moved, with all
    their eyes
Watching the living splendor sink or rise,
Its will their will, knowing no otherwise.

Within himself he found the law of
    right,
He walked by faith and not the letter's
    sight,
And read his Bible by the Inward Light.

And if sometimes the slaves of form and
    rule,
Frozen in their creeds like fish in win-
    ter's pool,
Tried the large tolerance of his liberal
    school,

His door was free to men of every name,
He welcomed all the seeking souls who
    came,
And no man's faith he made a cause of
    blame.

But best he loved in leisure hours to see
His own dear Friends sit by him knee
    to knee,
In social converse, genial, frank, and free.

There sometimes silence (it were hard to
    tell
Who owned it first) upon the circle fell,
Hushed Anna's busy wheel, and laid its
    spell

On the black boy who grimaced by the
    hearth,
To solemnize his shining face of mirth ;
Only the old clock ticked amidst the
    dearth

"A jewelled elm-tree avenue." Page 369.

Of sound ; nor eye was raised nor hand
    was stirred
In that soul-sabbath, till at last some
    word
Of tender counsel or low prayer was
    heard.

Then guests, who lingered but farewell
    to say
And take love's message, went their
    homeward way ;
So passed in peace the guileless Quaker's
    day.

His was the Christian's unsung Age of
    Gold,
A truer idyl than the bards have told
Of Arno's banks or Arcady of old.

Where still the Friends their place of
    burial keep,
And century-rooted mosses o'er it creep,
The Nürnberg scholar and his helpmeet
    sleep.

And Anna's aloe? If it flowered at last
In Bartram's garden, did John Wool-
    man cast
A glance upon it as he meekly passed ?

And did a secret sympathy possess
That tender soul, and for the slave's
    redress
Lend hope, strength, patience ? It were
    vain to guess.

Nay, were the plant itself but mythical,
Set in the fresco of tradition's wall
Like Jotham's bramble, mattereth not
    at all.

Enough to know that, through the
    winter's frost
And summer's heat, no seed of truth is
    lost,
And every duty pays at last its cost.

For, ere Pastorius left the sun and air,
God sent the answer to his life-long
    prayer ;
The child was born beside the Delaware,

Who, in the power a holy purpose
    lends,
Guided his people unto nobler ends,
And left them worthier of the name of
    Friends.

And lo ! the fulness of the time has
    come,
And over all the exile's Western home,
From sea to sea the flowers of freedom
    bloom !

And joy-bells ring, and silver trumpets
    blow ;
But not for thee, Pastorius ! Even
    so
The world forgets, but the wise angels
    know.

MISCELLANEOUS.

THE PAGEANT.

A sound as if from bells of silver,
    Or elfin cymbals smitten clear,
      Through the frost-pictured panes I
      hear.

A brightness which outshines the morn-
    ing,
    A splendor brooking no delay,
    Beckons and tempts my feet away.

I leave the trodden village highway
    For virgin snow-paths glimmering
      through
    A jewelled elm-tree avenue ;

24

Where, keen against the walls of sap-
    phire,
    The gleaming tree-bolls, ice-em-
      bossed,
    Hold up their chandeliers of frost.

I tread in Orient halls enchanted,
    I dream the Saga's dream of caves
    Gem-lit beneath the North Sea
      waves !

I walk the land of Eldorado,
    I touch its mimic garden bowers,
    Its silver leaves and diamond flow-
      ers !

The flora of the mystic mine-world
   Around me lifts on crystal stems
   The petals of its clustered gems!

What miracle of weird transforming
   In this wild work of frost and
      light,
   This glimpse of glory infinite !

This foregleam of the Holy City
   Like that to him of Patmos given,
   The white bride coming down from
      heaven !

How flash the ranked and mail-clad al-
      ders,
   Through what sharp-glancing spears
      of reeds
   The brook its muffled water leads !

Yon maple, like the bush of Horeb,
   Burns unconsumed : a white, cold
      fire
   Rays out from every grassy spire.

Each slender rush and spike of mullein,
   Low laurel shrub and drooping fern,
   Transfigured, blaze where'er I turn.

How yonder Ethiopian hemlock
   Crowned with his glistening circlet
      stands !
   What jewels light his swarthy
      hands !

Here, where the forest opens southward,
   Between its hospitable pines,
   As through a door, the warm sun
      shines.

The jewels loosen on the branches,
   And lightly, as the soft winds
      blow,
   Fall, tinkling, on the ice below.

And through the clashing of their cym-
      bals
   I hear the old familiar fall
   Of water down the rocky wall,

Where, from its wintry prison breaking,
   In dark and silence hidden long,
   The brook repeats its summer song.

One instant flashing in the sunshine,
   Keen as a sabre from its sheath,
   Then lost again the ice beneath.

I hear the rabbit lightly leaping,
   The foolish screaming of the jay,
   The chopper's axe-stroke far away :

The clamor of some neighboring barn-
      yard,
   The lazy cock's belated crow,
   Or cattle-tramp in crispy snow.

And, as in some enchanted forest
   The lost knight hears his comrades
      sing,
   And, near at hand, their bridles
      ring,

So welcome I these sounds and voices,
   These airs from far-off summer
      blown,
   This life that leaves me not alone.

For the white glory overawes me ;
   The crystal terror of the seer
   Of Chebar's vision blinds me here.

Rebuke me not, O sapphire heaven !
   Thou stainless earth, lay not on
      me.
   Thy keen reproach of purity,

If, in this august presence-chamber,
   I sigh for summer's leaf-green
      gloom
   And warm airs thick with odorous
      bloom !

Let the strange frost-work sink and
      crumble,
   And let the loosened tree-boughs
      swing,
   Till all their bells of silver ring.

Shine warmly down, thou sun of noon-
      time,
   On this chill pageant, melt and
      move
   The winter's frozen heart with love.

And, soft and low, thou wind south-
      blowing,
   Breathe through a veil of tenderest
      haze
   Thy prophecy of summer days.

Come with thy green relief of promise,
   And to this dead, cold splendor
      bring
   The living jewels of the spring !

THE SINGER.

YEARS since (but names to me before),
Two sisters sought at eve my door ;
Two song-birds wandering from their
    nest,
A gray old farm-house in the West.

How fresh of life the younger one,
Half smiles, half tears, like rain in
    sun !
Her gravest mood could scarce displace
The dimples of her nut-brown face.

Wit sparkled on her lips not less
For quick and tremulous tenderness ;
And, following close her merriest glance,
Dreamed through her eyes the heart's
    romance.

Timid and still, the elder had
Even then a smile too sweetly sad ;
The crown of pain that all must wear
Too early pressed her midnight hair.

Yet ere the summer eve grew long,
Her modest lips were sweet with song ;
A memory haunted all her words
Of clover-fields and singing birds.

Her dark, dilating eyes expressed
The broad horizons of the west ;
Her speech dropped prairie flowers ; the
    gold
Of harvest wheat about her rolled.

Fore-doomed to song she seemed to
    me :
I queried not with destiny :
I knew the trial and the need,
Yet, all the more, I said, God speed !

What could I other than I did ?
Could I a singing-bird forbid ?
Deny the wind-stirred leaf ? Rebuke
The music of the forest brook ?

She went with morning from my door,
But left me richer than before ;
Thenceforth I knew her voice of cheer,
The welcome of her partial ear.

Years passed : through all the land her
    name
A pleasant household word became :
All felt behind the singer stood
A sweet and gracious womanhood.

Her life was earnest work, not play ;
Her tired feet climbed a weary way ;
And even through her lightest strain
We heard an undertone of pain.

Unseen of her her fair fame grew,
The good she did she rarely knew.
Unguessed of her in life the love
That rained its tears her grave above.

When last I saw her, full of peace,
She waited for her great release ;
And that old friend so sage and bland,
Our later Franklin, held her hand.

For all that patriot bosoms stirs
Had moved that woman's heart of
    hers,
And men who toiled in storm and sun
Found her their meet companion.

Our converse, from her suffering bed
To healthful themes of life she led :
The out-door world of bud and bloom
And light and sweetness filled her
    room.

Yet evermore an underthought
Of loss to come within us wrought,
And all the while we felt the strain
Of the strong will that conquered pain.

God giveth quietness at last !
The common way that all have passed
She went, with mortal yearnings fond,
To fuller life and love beyond.

Fold the rapt soul in your embrace,
My dear ones ! Give the singer place
To you, to her, — I know not where, —
I lift the silence of a prayer.

For only thus our own we find ;
The gone before, the left behind,
All mortal voices die between ;
The unheard reaches the unseen.

Again the blackbirds sing ; the streams
Wake, laughing, from their winter
    dreams,
And tremble in the April showers
The tassels of the maple flowers.

But not for her has spring renewed
The sweet surprises of the wood ;
And bird and flower are lost to her
Who was their best interpreter !

What to shut eyes has God revealed?
What hear the ears that death has sealed?
What undreamed beauty passing show
Requites the loss of all we know?

O silent land, to which we move,
Enough if there alone be love,
And mortal need can ne'er outgrow
What it is waiting to bestow!

O white soul! from that far-off shore
Float some sweet song the waters o'er,
Our faith confirm, our fears dispel,
With the old voice we loved so well!

How instant rose, to take thy part,
The angel in the human heart!

Ah! not in vain the flames that tossed
Above thy dreadful holocaust;
The Christ again has preached through
    thee
The Gospel of Humanity!

Then lift once more thy towers on
    high,
And fret with spires the western sky,
To tell that God is yet with us,
And love is still miraculous!

CHICAGO.

MEN said at vespers: "All is well!"
In one wild night the city fell;
Fell shrines of prayer and marts of gain
Before the fiery hurricane.

On threescore spires had sunset shone,
Where ghastly sunrise looked on none.
Men clasped each other's hands, and said:
"The City of the West is dead!"

Brave hearts who fought, in slow retreat,
The fiends of fire from street to street,
Turned, powerless, to the blinding glare,
The dumb defiance of despair.

A sudden impulse thrilled each wire
That signalled round that sea of fire;
Swift words of cheer, warm heart-throbs
    came;
In tears of pity died the flame!

From East, from West, from South and
    North,
The messages of hope shot forth,
And, underneath the severing wave,
The world, full-handed, reached to save.

Fair seemed the old; but fairer still
The new, the dreary void shall fill
With dearer homes than those o'erthrown,
For love shall lay each corner-stone.

Rise, stricken city! — from thee throw
The ashen sackcloth of thy woe;
And build, as to Amphion's strain,
To songs of cheer thy walls again!

How shrivelled in thy hot distress
The primal sin of selfishness!

MY BIRTHDAY.

BENEATH the moonlight and the snow
Lies dead my latest year;
The winter winds are wailing low
Its dirges in my ear.

I grieve not with the moaning wind
As if a loss befell;
Before me, even as behind,
God is, and all is well!

His light shines on me from above,
His low voice speaks within, —
The patience of immortal love
Outwearying mortal sin.

Not mindless of the growing years
Of care and loss and pain,
My eyes are wet with thankful tears
For blessings which remain.

If dim the gold of life has grown,
I will not count it dross,
Nor turn from treasures still my own
To sigh for lack and loss.

The years no charm from Nature take;
As sweet her voices call,
As beautiful her mornings break,
As fair her evenings fall.

Love watches o'er my quiet ways,
Kind voices speak my name,
And lips that find it hard to praise
Are slow, at least, to blame.

How softly ebb the tides of will!
How fields, once lost or won,
Now lie behind me green and still
Beneath a level sun!

How hushed the hiss of party hate,
　The clamor of the throng !
How old, harsh voices of debate
　Flow into rhythmic song !

Methinks the spirit's temper grows
　Too soft in this still air ;
Somewhat the restful heart foregoes
　Of needed watch and prayer.

The bark by tempest vainly tossed
　May founder in the calm,
And he who braved the polar frost
　Faint by the isles of balm.

Better than self-indulgent years
　The outflung heart of youth,
Than pleasant songs in idle **ears**
　The tumult of the truth.

Rest for the weary hands is good,
　And love for hearts that pine,
But let the manly habitude
　Of upright souls be mine.

Let winds that blow from heaven refresh,
　Dear Lord, the languid air ;
And let the weakness of the flesh
　Thy strength of spirit share.

And, if the eye must fail of light,
　The ear forget to hear,
Make clearer still the spirit's sight,
　More fine the inward ear !

Be near me in mine hours of need
　To soothe, or cheer, or warn,
And down these slopes of sunset lead
　As up the hills of morn !

THE BREWING OF SOMA.

"These libations mixed with milk have been prepared for Indra : offer Soma to the drinker of Soma." — VASHISTA, Trans. by MAX MÜLLER.

THE fagots blazed, the caldron's smoke
　Up through the green wood curled ;
" Bring honey from the hollow oak,
Bring milky sap," the brewers spoke,
　In the childhood of the world.

And brewed they well or brewed they ill,
　The priests thrust in their rods,
First tasted, and then drank their fill,
And shouted, with one voice and will,
　" Behold the drink of gods ! "

They drank, and lo ! in heart and brain
　A new, glad life began ;
The gray of hair grew young again,
The sick man laughed away his pain,
　The cripple leaped and ran.

" Drink, mortals, what the gods have
　　sent,
　Forget your long annoy."
So sang the priests.　From tent to tent
The Soma's sacred madness went,
　A storm of drunken joy.

Then knew each rapt inebriate
　A winged and glorious birth,
Soared upward, with strange joy elate,
Beat, with dazed head, Varuna's gate,
　And, sobered, sank to earth.

The land with Soma's praises rang ;
　On Gihon's banks of shade
Its hymns the dusky maidens sang ;
In joy of life or mortal pang
　All men to Soma prayed.

The morning twilight of the race
　Sends down these matin psalms ;
And still with wondering eyes we trace
The simple prayers to Soma's grace,
　That Vedic verse embalms.

As in that child-world's early year,
　Each after age has striven
By music, incense, vigils drear,
And trance, to bring the skies more near,
　Or lift men up to heaven ! —

Some fever of the blood and brain,
　Some self-exalting spell,
The scourger's keen delight of pain,
The Dervish dance, the Orphic strain,
　The wild-haired Bacchant's yell, —

The desert's hair-grown hermit sunk
　The saner brute below ;
The naked Santon, hashish-drunk,
The cloister madness of the monk,
　The fakir's torture-show !

And yet the past comes round again,
　And new doth old fulfil ;
In sensual transports wild as vain
We brew in many a Christian fane
　The heathen Soma still !

Dear Lord and Father of mankind,
　Forgive our foolish ways !

Reclothe us in our rightful mind,
In purer lives thy service find,
  In deeper reverence, praise.

In simple trust like theirs who heard
  Beside the Syrian sea
The gracious calling of the Lord,
Let us, like them, without a word,
  Rise up and follow thee.

O Sabbath rest by Galilee !
  O calm of hills above,
Where Jesus knelt to share with thee
The silence of eternity
  Interpreted by love !

With that deep hush subduing all
Our words and works that drown
The tender whisper of thy call,
As noiseless let thy blessing fall
  As fell thy manna down.

Drop thy still dews of quietness,
  Till all our strivings cease ;
Take from our souls the strain and stress,
And let our ordered lives confess
  The beauty of thy peace.

Breathe through the heats of our desire
  Thy coolness and thy balm ;
Let sense be dumb, let flesh retire ;
Speak through the earthquake, wind,
    and fire,
  O still, small voice of calm !

A WOMAN.

O, DWARFED and wronged, and stained
    with ill,
Behold ! thou art a woman still !
And, by that sacred name and dear,
I bid thy better self appear.
Still, through thy foul disguise, I see
The rudimental purity,
That, spite of change and loss, makes
    good
Thy birthright-claim of womanhood ;
An inward loathing, deep, intense ;
A shame that is half innocence.
Cast off the grave-clothes of thy sin !
Rise from the dust thou liest in,
As Mary rose at Jesus' word,
Redeemed and white before the Lord !
Reclaim thy lost soul ! In His name,
Rise up, and break thy bonds of
    shame.

Art weak ? He 's strong. Art fearful ?
    Hear
The world's O'ercomer : " Be of cheer !"
What lip shall judge when He approves ?
Who dare to scorn the child he loves ?

DISARMAMENT.

"PUT up the sword ! " The voice of
    Christ once more
Speaks, in the pauses of the cannon's
    roar,
O'er fields of corn by fiery sickles reaped
And left dry ashes ; over trenches heaped
With nameless dead ; o'er cities starving
    slow
Under a rain of fire ; through wards of
    woe
Down which a groaning diapason runs
From tortured brothers, husbands,
    lovers, sons
Of desolate women in their far-off homes,
Waiting to hear the step that never
    comes !
O men and brothers ! let that voice be
    heard.
War fails, try peace ; put up the useless
    sword !

Fear not the end. There is a story told
In Eastern tents, when autumn nights
    grow cold,
And round the fire the Mongol shepherds
    sit
With grave responses listening unto it :
Once, on the errands of his mercy bent,
Buddha, the holy and benevolent,
Met a fell monster, huge and fierce of
    look,
Whose awful voice the hills and forests
    shook.
"O son of peace ! " the giant cried,
    " thy fate
Is sealed at last, and love shall yield to
    hate."
The unarmed Buddha looking, with no
    trace
Of fear or anger, in the monster's face,
In pity said : " Poor fiend, even thee I
    love."
Lo ! as he spake the sky-tall terror sank
To hand-breadth size ; the huge abhor-
    rence shrank
Into the form and fashion of a dove ;
And where the thunder of its rage was
    heard,

Circling above him sweetly sang the
bird :
" Hate hath no harm for love," so ran
the song;
" And peace unweaponed conquers every
wrong ! "

THE ROBIN.

MY old Welch neighbor over the way
Crept slowly out in the sun of spring,
Pushed from her ears the locks of gray,
And listened to hear the robin sing.

Her grandson, playing at marbles,
stopped,
And, cruel in sport as boys will be,
Tossed a stone at the bird, who hopped
From bough to bough in the apple-tree.

" Nay ! " said the grandmother ; " have
you not heard,
My poor, bad boy ! of the fiery pit,
And how, drop by drop, this merciful
bird
Carries the water that quenches it ?

" He brings cool dew in his little bill,
And lets it fall on the souls of sin :
You can see the mark on his red breast
still
Of fires that scorch as he drops it in.

" My poor Bron rhuddyn ! my breast-
burned bird,
Singing so sweetly from limb to limb,
Very dear to the heart of Our Lord
Is he who pities the lost like Him ! "

" Amen ! " I said to the beautiful myth ;
" Sing, bird of God, in my heart as
well :
Each good thought is a drop wherewith
To cool and lessen the fires of hell.

" Prayers of love like rain-drops fall,
Tears of pity are cooling dew,
And dear to the heart of Our Lord are all
Who suffer like Him in the good they
do ! "

THE SISTERS.

ANNIE and Rhoda, sisters twain,
Woke in the night to the sound of rain,

The rush of wind, the ramp and roar
Of great waves climbing a rocky shore.

Annie rose up in her bed-gown white,
And looked out into the storm and night.

" Hush, and hearken ! " she cried in fear,
" Hearest thou nothing, sister dear ? "

" I hear the sea, and the plash of rain,
And roar of the northeast hurricane.

" Get thee back to the bed so warm,
No good comes of watching a storm.

" What is it to thee, I fain would know,
That waves are roaring and wild winds
blow ?

" No lover of thine 's afloat to miss
The harbor-lights on a night like this."

" But I heard a voice cry out my name.
Up from the sea on the wind it came !

" Twice and thrice have I heard it call,
And the voice is the voice of Estwick
Hall ! "

On her pillow the sister tossed her head.
" Hall of the Heron is safe," she said.

" In the tautest schooner that ever swam
He rides at anchor in Anisquam.

" And, if in peril from swamping sea
Or lee shore rocks, would he call on
thee ? "

But the girl heard only the wind and
tide,
And wringing her small white hands she
cried :

" O sister • Rhoda, there 's something
wrong ;
I hear it again, so loud and long.

" ' Annie ! Annie ! ' I hear it call,
And the voice is the voice of Estwick
Hall ! "

Up sprang the elder, with eyes aflame,
" Thou liest ! He never would call thy
name !

" If he did, I would pray the wind and
sea
To keep him forever from thee and me ! "

Then out of the sea blew a dreadful blast;
Like the cry of a dying man it passed.

The young girl hushed on her lips a
    groan,
But through her tears a strange light
    shone, —

The solemn joy of her heart's release
To own and cherish its love in peace.

"Dearest!" she whispered, under breath,
"Life was a lie, but true is death.

"The love I hid from myself away
Shall crown me now in the light of day.

"My ears shall never to wooer list,
Never by lover my lips be kissed.

"Sacred to thee am I henceforth,
Thou in heaven and I on earth!"

She came and stood by her sister's bed:
"Hall of the Heron is dead!" she said.

"The wind and the waves their work
    have done,
We shall see him no more beneath the sun.

"Little will reck that heart of thine,
It loved him not with a love like mine.

"I, for his sake, were he but here,
Could hem and 'broider thy bridal gear,

"Though hands should tremble and eyes
    be wet,
And stitch for stitch in my heart be set.

"But now my soul with his soul I wed;
Thine the living, and mine the dead!"

MARGUERITE.

MASSACHUSETTS BAY, 1760.

THE robins sang in the orchard, the buds
    into blossoms grew;
Little of human sorrow the buds and the
    robins knew!

Sick, in an alien household, the poor
    French neutral lay;
Into her lonesome garret fell the light of
    the April day.

Through the dusty window, curtained
    by the spider's warp and woof,
On the loose-laid floor of hemlock, on
    oaken ribs of roof.

The bedquilt's faded patchwork, the tea-
    cups on the stand,
The wheel with flaxen tangle, as it
    dropped from her sick hand!

What to her was the song of the robin,
    or warm morning light,
As she lay in the trance of the dying,
    heedless of sound or sight?

Done was the work of her hands, she
    had eaten her bitter bread;
The world of the alien people lay behind
    her dim and dead.

But her soul went back to its child-time;
    she saw the sun o'erflow
With gold the basin of Minas, and set
    over Gasperau;

The low, bare flats at ebb-tide, the rush
    of the sea at flood,
Through inlet and creek and river, from
    dike to upland wood;

The gulls in the red of morning, the
    fish-hawk's rise and fall,
The drift of the fog in moonshine, over
    the dark coast-wall.

She saw the face of her mother, she
    heard the song she sang;
And far off, faintly, slowly, the bell for
    vespers rang!

By her bed the hard-faced mistress sat,
    smoothing the wrinkled sheet,
Peering into the face, so helpless, and
    feeling the ice-cold feet.

With a vague remorse atoning for her
    greed and long abuse,
By care no longer heeded and pity too
    late for use.

Up the stairs of the garret softly the son
    of the mistress stepped,
Leaned over the head-board, covering
    his face with his hands, and wept.

Outspake the mother, who watched him
    sharply, with brow a-frown:
"What! love you the Papist, the beg-
    gar, the charge of the town?"

"Be she Papist or beggar who lies here,
    I know and God knows
I love her, and fain would go with her
    wherever she goes !

"O mother ! that sweet face came plead-
    ing, for love so athirst.
You saw but the town-charge ; I knew
    her God's angel at first."

Shaking her gray head, the mistress
    hushed down a bitter cry ;
And awed by the silence and shadow of
    death drawing nigh,

She murmured a psalm of the Bible ; but
    closer the young girl pressed,
With the last of her life in her fingers,
    the cross to her breast.

"My son, come away," cried the mother,
    her voice cruel grown.
"She is joined to her idols, like Eph-
    raim ; let her alone ! "

But he knelt with his hand on her fore-
    head, his lips to her ear,
And he called back the soul that was pass-
    ing : "Marguerite, do you hear ? "

She paused on the threshold of Heaven ;
    love, pity, surprise,
Wistful, tender, lit up for an instant the
    cloud of her eyes.

With his heart on his lips he kissed her,
    but never her cheek grew red,
And the words the living long for he
    spake in the ear of the dead.

And the robins sang in the orchard,
    where buds to blossoms grew ;
Of the folded hands and the still face
    never the robins knew !

KING VOLMER AND ELSIE.

AFTER THE DANISH OF CHRISTIAN
WINTER.

WHERE, over heathen doom-rings and
    gray stones of the Horg,
In its little Christian city stands the
    church of Vordingborg,

In merry mood King Volmer sat, for-
    getful of his power,
As idle as the Goose of Gold that brooded
    on his tower.

Out spake the King to Henrik, his young
    and faithful squire :
"Dar'st trust thy little Elsie, the maid
    of thy desire ? "
"Of all the men in Denmark she loveth
    only me :
As true to me is Elsie as thy Lily is to
    thee." •

Loud laughed the king : " To-morrow
    shall bring another day, *
When I myself will test her ; she will
    not say me nay."
Thereat the lords and gallants, that
    round about him stood,
Wagged all their heads in concert and
    smiled as courtiers should.

The gray lark sings o'er Vordingborg,
    and on the ancient town
From the tall tower of Valdemar the
    Golden Goose looks down :
The yellow grain is waving in the pleas-
    ant wind of morn,
The wood resounds with cry of hounds
    and blare of hunter's horn.

In the garden of her father little Elsie
    sits and spins,
And, singing with the early birds, her
    daily task begins.
Gay tulips bloom and sweet mint curls
    around her garden-bower,
But she is sweeter than the mint and
    fairer than the flower.

About her form her kirtle blue clings
    lovingly, and, white
As snow, her loose sleeves only leave
    her small, round wrists in sight ;
Below the modest petticoat can only half
    conceal
The motion of the lightest foot that ever
    turned a wheel.

The cat sits purring at her side, bees
    hum in sunshine warm ;
But, look ! she starts, she lifts her face,
    she shades it with her arm.

* A common saying of Valdemar; hence his
sobriquet *Alterday*.

And, hark! a train of horsemen, with
    sound of dog and horn,
Come leaping o'er the ditches, come
    trampling down the corn!

Merrily rang the bridle-reins, and scarf
    and plume streamed gay,
As fast beside her father's gate the riders
    held their way;
And one was brave in scarlet cloak, with
    golden spur on heel,
And, as he checked his foaming steed,
    the maiden checked her wheel.

"All hail among thy roses, the fairest
    rose to me!
For weary months in secret my heart
    has longed for thee!"
What noble knight was this? What
    words for modest maiden's ear?
She dropped a lowly courtesy of bashful-
    ness and fear.

She lifted up her spinning-wheel; she
    fain would seek the door,
Trembling in every limb, her cheek with
    blushes crimsoned o'er.
"Nay, fear me not," the rider said, "I
    offer heart and hand,
Bear witness these good Danish knights
    who round about me stand.

"I grant you time to think of this, to
    answer as you may,
For to-morrow, little Elsie, shall bring
    another day."
He spake the old phrase slyly as, glan-
    cing round his train,
He saw his merry followers seek to hide
    their smiles in vain.

"The snow of pearls I'll scatter in your
    curls of golden hair,
I'll line with furs the velvet of the kirtle
    that you wear;
All precious gems shall twine your neck;
    and in a chariot gay
You shall ride, my little Elsie, behind
    four steeds of gray.

"And harps shall sound, and flutes shall
    play, and brazen lamps shall glow;
On marble floors your feet shall weave
    the dances to and fro.
At frosty eventide for us the blazing
    hearth shall shine,
While, at our ease, we play at draughts,
    and drink the blood-red wine."

Then Elsie raised her head and met her
    wooer face to face;
A roguish smile shone in her eye and on
    her lip found place.
Back from her low white forehead the
    curls of gold she threw,
And lifted up her eyes to his steady and
    clear and blue.

"I am a lowly peasant, and you a gal-
    lant knight;
I will not trust a love that soon may
    cool and turn to slight.
If you would wed me henceforth be a
    peasant, not a lord;
I bid you hang upon the wall your tried
    and trusty sword."

"To please you, Elsie, I will lay keen
    Dynadel away,
And in its place will swing the scythe
    and mow your father's hay."
"Nay, but your gallant scarlet cloak
    my eyes can never bear;
A Vadmal coat, so plain and gray, is all
    that you must wear."

"Well, Vadmal will I wear for you,"
    the rider gayly spoke,
"And on the Lord's high altar I'll lay
    my scarlet cloak."
"But mark," she said, "no stately horse
    my peasant love must ride,
A yoke of steers before the plough is all
    that he must guide."

The knight looked down upon his steed:
    "Well, let him wander free:
No other man must ride the horse that
    has been backed by me.
Henceforth I'll tread the furrow and to
    my oxen talk,
If only little Elsie beside my plough will
    walk."

"You must take from out your cellar
    cask of wine and flask and can;
The homely mead I brew you may serve
    a peasant-man."
"Most willingly, fair Elsie, I'll drink
    that mead of thine,
And leave my minstrel's thirsty throat
    to drain my generous wine."

"Now break your shield asunder, and
    shatter sign and boss,
Unmeet for peasant-wedded arms, your
    knightly knee across.

And pull me down your castle from top
 to basement wall,
And let your plough trace furrows in the
 ruins of your hall !"

Then smiled he with a lofty pride;
 right well at last he knew
The maiden of the spinning-wheel was
 to her troth-plight true.
" Ah, roguish little Elsie ! you act your
 part full well :
You know that I must bear my shield
 and in my castle dwell !

"The lions ramping on that shield between the hearts aflame
Keep watch o'er Denmark's honor, and
 guard her ancient name.
For know that I am Volmer ; I dwell in
 yonder towers,
Who ploughs them ploughs up Denmark,
 this goodly home of ours !

"I tempt no more, fair Elsie! your heart
 I know is true ;
Would God that all our maidens were
 good and pure as you !
Well have you pleased your monarch,
 and he shall well repay ;
God's peace ! Farewell ! To-morrow will
 bring another day !"

He lifted up his bridle hand, he spurred
 his good steed then,
And like a whirl-blast swept away with
 all his gallant men.
The steel hoofs beat the rocky path ;
 again on winds of morn
The wood resounds with cry of hounds
 and blare of hunter's horn.

"Thou true and ever faithful !" the
 listening Henrik cried ;
And, leaping o'er the green hedge, he
 stood by Elsie's side.
None saw the fond embracing, save,
 shining from afar,
The Golden Goose that watched them
 from the tower of Valdemar.

O darling girls of Denmark ! of all the
 flowers that throng
Her vales of spring the fairest, I sing for
 you my song.

No praise as yours so bravely rewards
 the singer's skill ;
Thank God ! of maids like Elsie the land
 has plenty still!

THE THREE BELLS.

BENEATH the low-hung night cloud
 That raked her splintering mast
The good ship settled slowly,
 The cruel leak gained fast.

Over the awful ocean
 Her signal guns pealed out.
Dear God ! was that thy answer
 From the horror round about ?

A voice came down the wild wind,
 " Ho ! ship ahoy !" its cry :
" Our stout Three Bells of Glasgow
 Shall lay till daylight by !"

Hour after hour crept slowly,
 Yet on the heaving swells
Tossed up and down the ship-lights,
 The lights of the Three Bells !

And ship to ship made signals,
 Man answered back to man,
While oft, to cheer and hearten,
 The Three Bells nearer ran ;

And the captain from her taffrail
 Sent down his hopeful cry.
" Take heart ! Hold on !" he shouted.
 " The Three Bells shall lay by !"

All night across the waters
 The tossing lights shone clear ;
All night from reeling taffrail
 The Three Bells sent her cheer.

And when the dreary watches
 Of storm and darkness passed,
Just as the wreck lurched under
 All souls were saved at last.

Sail on, Three Bells, forever,
 In grateful memory sail !
Ring on, Three Bells of rescue,
 Above the wave and gale !

Type of the Love eternal,
 Repeat the Master's cry,
As tossing through our darkness
 The lights of God draw nigh !

HAZEL BLOSSOMS.

NOTE. — I have ventured, in compliance with the desire of dear friends of my beloved sister ELIZABETH H. WHITTIER, to add to this little volume the few poetical pieces which she left behind her. As she was very distrustful of her own powers, and altogether without ambition for literary distinction, she shunned everything like publicity, and found far greater happiness in generous appreciation of the gifts of her friends than in the cultivation of her own. Yet it has always seemed to me, that had her health, sense of duty and fitness, and her extreme self-distrust permitted, she might have taken a high place among lyrical singers. These poems, with perhaps two or three exceptions, afford but slight indications of the inward life of the writer, who had an almost morbid dread of spiritual and intellectual egotism, or of her tenderness of sympathy, chastened mirthfulness, and pleasant play of thought and fancy, when her shy, beautiful soul opened like a flower in the warmth of social communion. In the lines on Dr. Kane her friends will see something of her fine individuality, — the rare mingling of delicacy and intensity of feeling which made her dear to them. This little poem reached Cuba while the great explorer lay on his death-bed, and we are told that he listened with grateful tears while it was read to him by his mother.

I am tempted to say more, but I write as under the eye of her who, while with us, shrank with painful deprecation from the praise or mention of performances which seemed so far below her ideal of excellence. To those who best knew her, the beloved circle of her intimate friends, I dedicate this slight memorial.

J. G. W.

AMESBURY, 9th mo., 1874.

THE summer warmth has left the sky,
The summer songs have died away;
And, withered, in the footpaths lie
The fallen leaves, but yesterday
With ruby and with topaz gay.

The grass is browning on the hills;
No pale, belated flowers recall
The astral fringes of the rills,
And drearily the dead vines fall,
Frost-blackened, from the roadside wall.

Yet through the gray and sombre wood,
Against the dusk of fir and pine,
Last of their floral sisterhood,
The hazel's yellow blossoms shine,
The tawny gold of Afric's mine!

Small beauty hath my unsung flower,
For spring to own or summer hail;
But, in the season's saddest hour,
To skies that weep and winds that wail
Its glad surprisals never fail.

O days grown cold! O life grown old!
No rose of June may bloom again;
But, like the hazel's twisted gold,

Through early frost and latter rain
Shall hints of summer-time remain.

And as within the hazel's bough
A gift of mystic virtue dwells,
That points to golden ores below,
And in dry desert places tells
Where flow unseen the cool, sweet wells,

So, in the wise Diviner's hand,
Be mine the hazel's grateful part
To feel, beneath a thirsty land,
The living waters thrill and start,
The beating of the rivulet's heart!

Sufficeth me the gift to light
With latest bloom the dark, cold days;
To call some hidden spring to sight
That, in these dry and dusty ways,
Shall sing its pleasant song of praise.

O Love! the hazel-wand may fail,
But thou canst lend the surer spell,
That, passing over Baca's vale,
Repeats the old-time miracle,
And makes the desert-land a well.

SUMNER.

"I am not one who has disgraced beauty of sentiment by deformity of conduct, or the maxims of a freeman by the actions of a slave ; but, by the grace of God, I have kept my life unsullied."
— MILTON'S *Defence of the People of England.*

O MOTHER STATE ! — the winds of March
  Blew chill o'er Auburn's Field of God,
Where, slow, beneath a leaden arch
  Of sky, thy mourning children trod.

And now, with all thy woods in leaf,
  Thy fields in flower, beside thy dead
Thou sittest, in thy robes of grief,
  A Rachel yet uncomforted !

And once again the organ swells,
  Once more the flag is half-way hung,
And yet again the mournful bells
  In all thy steeple-towers are rung.

And I, obedient to thy will,
  Have come a simple wreath to lay,
.,uperfluous, on a grave that still
  Is sweet with all the flowers of May.

I take, with awe, the task assigned ;
  It may be that my friend might miss,
In his new sphere of heart and mind,
  Some token from my hand in this.

By many a tender memory moved,
  Along the past my thought I send ;
The record of the cause he loved
  Is the best record of its friend.

No trumpet sounded in his ear,
  He saw not Sinai's cloud and flame,
But never yet to Hebrew seer
  A clearer voice of duty came.

God said : "Break thou these yokes ; undo
  These heavy burdens.   I ordain
A work to last thy whole life through,
  A ministry of strife and pain.

" Forego thy dreams of lettered ease,
  Put thou the scholar's promise by,
The rights of man are more than these."
  He heard, and answered : "Here am I !"

He set his face against the blast,
  His feet against the flinty shard,

Till the hard service grew, at last,
  Its own exceeding great reward.

Lifted like Saul's above the crowd,
  Upon his kingly forehead fell
The first, sharp bolt of Slavery's cloud,
  Launched at the truth he urged so well.

Ah ! never yet, at rack or stake,
  Was sorer loss made Freedom's gain,
Than his, who suffered for her sake
  The beak-torn Titan's lingering pain !

The fixed star of his faith, through all
  Loss, doubt, and peril, shone the same ;
As through a night of storm, some tall,
  Strong lighthouse lifts its steady flame.

Beyond the dust and smoke he saw
  The sheaves of freedom's large in-
    crease,
The holy fanes of equal law,
  The New Jerusalem of peace.

The weak might fear, the worldling
    mock,
  The faint and blind of heart regret ;
All knew at last th' eternal rock
  On which his forward feet were set.

The subtlest scheme of compromise
  Was folly to his purpose bold ;
The strongest mesh of party lies
  Weak to the simplest truth he told.

One language held his heart and lip,
  Straight onward to his goal he trod,
And proved the highest statesmanship
  Obedience to the voice of God.

No wail was in his voice, — none heard,
  When treason's storm-cloud blackest
    grew,
The weakness of a doubtful word ;
  His duty, and the end, he knew.

The first to smite, the first to spare ;
  When once the hostile ensigns fell,

He stretched out hands of generous care
　　To lift the foe he fought so well.

For there was nothing base or small
　　Or craven in his soul's broad plan ;
Forgiving all things personal,
　　He hated only wrong to man.

The old traditions of his State,
　　The memories of her great and good,
Took from his life a fresher date,
　　And in himself embodied stood.

How felt the greed of gold and place,
　　The venal crew that schemed and
　　　　planned,
The fine scorn of that haughty face,
　　The spurning of that bribeless hand !

If than Rome's tribunes statelier
　　He wore his senatorial robe,
His lofty port was all for her,
　　The one dear spot on all the globe.

If to the master's plea he gave
　　The vast contempt his manhood felt,
He saw a brother in the slave, —
　　With man as equal man he dealt.

Proud was he ?　If his presence kept
　　Its grandeur wheresoe'er he trod,
As if from Plutarch's gallery stepped
　　The hero and the demigod,

None failed, at least, to reach his ear,
　　Nor want nor woe appealed in vain ;
The homesick soldier knew his cheer,
　　And blessed him from his ward of
　　　　pain.

Safely his dearest friends may own
　　The slight defects he never hid,
The surface-blemish in the stone
　　Of the tall, stately pyramid.

Suffice it that he never brought
　　His conscience to the public mart ;
But lived himself the truth he taught,
　　White-souled, clean-handed, pure of
　　　　heart.

What if he felt the natural pride
　　Of power in noble use, too true
With thin humilities to hide
　　The work he did, the lore he knew ?

Was he not just ?　Was any wronged
　　By that assured self-estimate ?

He took but what to him belonged,
　　Unenvious of another's state.

Well might he heed the words he spake,
　　And scan with care the written page
Through which he still shall warm and
　　　　wake
　　The hearts of men from age to age.

Ah ! who shall blame him now because
　　He solaced thus his hours of pain !
Should not the o'erworn thresher pause,
　　And hold to light his golden grain ?

No sense of humor dropped its oil
　　On the hard ways his purpose went ;
Small play of fancy lightened toil ;
　　He spake alone the thing he meant.

He loved his books, the Art that hints
　　A beauty veiled behind its own,
The graver's line, the pencil's tints,
　　The chisel's shape evoked from stone.

He cherished, void of selfish ends,
　　The social courtesies that bless
And sweeten life, and loved his friends
　　With most unworldly tenderness.

But still his tired eyes rarely learned
　　The glad relief by Nature brought ;
Her mountain ranges never turned
　　His current of persistent thought.

The sea rolled chorus to his speech
　　Three-banked like Latium's tall tri-
　　　　reme,
With laboring oars ; the grove and
　　　　beach
　　Were Forum and the Academe.

The sensuous joy from all things fair
　　His strenuous bent of soul repressed,
And left from youth to silvered hair
　　Few hours for pleasure, none for rest.

For all his life was poor without,
　　O Nature, make the last amends !
Train all thy flowers his grave about,
　　And make thy singing-birds his
　　　　friends !

Revive again, thou summer rain,
　　The broken turf upon his bed !
Breathe, summer wind, thy tenderest
　　　　strain
　　Of low, sweet music overhead !

With calm and beauty symbolize
  The peace which follows long annoy,
And lend our earth-bent, mourning eyes
  Some hint of his diviner joy.

For safe with right and truth he is,
  As God lives he must live alway ;
There is no end for souls like his,
  No night for children of the day !

Nor cant nor poor solicitudes
  Made weak his life's great argument ;
Small leisure his for frames and moods
  Who followed Duty where she went.

The broad, fair fields of God he saw
  Beyond the bigot's narrow bound ;
The truths he moulded into law
  In Christ's beatitudes he found.

His State-craft was the Golden Rule,
  His right of vote a sacred trust ;
Clear, over threat and ridicule,
  All heard his challenge : "Is it just?"

And when the hour supreme had come,
  Not for himself a thought he gave ;
In that last pang of martyrdom,
  His care was for the half-freed slave.

Not vainly dusky hands upbore,
  In prayer, the passing soul to heaven

Whose mercy to His suffering poor
  Was service to the Master given.

Long shall the good State's annals tell,
  Her children's children long be taught,
How, praised or blamed, he guarded well
  The trust he neither shunned nor
      sought.

If for one moment turned thy face,
  O Mother, from thy son, not long
He waited calmly in his place
  The sure remorse which follows wrong.

Forgiven be the State he loved
  The one brief lapse, the single blot ;
Forgotten be the stain removed,
  Her righted record shows it not !

The lifted sword above her shield
  With jealous care shall guard his fame,
The pine-tree on her ancient field
  To all the winds shall speak his name.

The marble image of her son
  Her loving hands shall yearly crown,
And from her pictured Pantheon
  His grand, majestic face look down.

O State so passing rich before,
  Who now shall doubt thy highest claim?
The world that counts thy jewels o'er
  Shall longest pause at SUMNER'S name !

HAZEL BLOSSOMS.

THE PRAYER OF AGASSIZ.

On the isle of Penikese,
Ringed about by sapphire seas,
Fanned by breezes salt and cool,
Stood the Master with his school.
Over sails that not in vain
Wooed the west-wind's steady strain,
Line of coast that low and far
Stretched its undulating bar,
Wings aslant along the rim
Of the waves they stooped to skim,
Rock and isle and glistening bay,
Fell the beautiful white day.
Said the Master to the youth :
"We have come in search of truth,

Trying with uncertain key
Door by door of mystery ;
We are reaching, through His laws,
To the garment-hem of Cause,
Him, the endless, unbegun,
The Unnamable, the One
Light of all our light the Source,
Life of life, and Force of force.
As with fingers of the blind,
We are groping here to find
What the hieroglyphics mean
Of the Unseen in the seen,
What the Thought which underlies
Nature's masking and disguise,
What it is that hides beneath
Blight and bloom and birth and death.

By past efforts unavailing,
Doubt and error, loss and failing,
Of our weakness made aware,
On the threshold of our task
Let us light and guidance ask,
Let us pause in silent prayer!"

Then the Master in his place
Bowed his head a little space,
And the leaves by soft airs stirred,
Lapse of wave and cry of bird
Left the solemn hush unbroken
Of that wordless prayer unspoken,
While its wish, on earth unsaid,
Rose to heaven interpreted.
As, in life's best hours, we hear
By the spirit's finer ear
His low voice within us, thus
The All-Father heareth us;
And his holy ear we pain
With our noisy words and vain.
Not for Him our violence
Storming at the gates of sense,
His the primal language, his
The eternal silences!

Even the careless heart was moved,
And the doubting gave assent,
With a gesture reverent,
To the Master well-beloved.
As thin mists are glorified
By the light they cannot hide,
All who gazed upon him saw,
Through its veil of tender awe,
How his face was still uplit
By the old sweet look of it,
Hopeful, trustful, full of cheer,
And the love that casts out fear.
Who the secret may declare
Of that brief, unuttered prayer?
Did the shade before him come
Of th' inevitable doom,
Of the end of earth so near,
And Eternity's new year?

In the lap of sheltering seas
Rests the isle of Penikese;
But the lord of the domain
Comes not to his own again:
Where the eyes that follow fail,
On a vaster sea his sail
Drifts beyond our beck and hail.
Other lips within its bound
Shall the laws of life expound;
Other eyes from rock and shell
Read the world's old riddles well:
But when breezes light and bland

Blow from Summer's blossomed land,
When the air is glad with wings,
And the blithe song-sparrow sings,
Many an eye with his still face
Shall the living ones displace,
Many an ear the word shall seek
He alone could fitly speak.
And one name forevermore
Shall be uttered o'er and o'er
By the waves that kiss the shore,
By the curlew's whistle sent
Down the cool, sea-scented air;
In all voices known to her,
Nature owns her worshipper,
Half in triumph, half lament.
Thither Love shall tearful turn,
Friendship pause uncovered there,
And the wisest reverence learn
From the Master's silent prayer.

THE FRIEND'S BURIAL.

MY thoughts are all in yonder town,
    Where, wept by many tears,
To-day my mother's friend lays down
    The burden of her years.

True as in life, no poor disguise
    Of death with her is seen,
And on her simple casket lies
    No wreath of bloom and green.

O, not for her the florist's art,
    The mocking weeds of woe,
Dear memories in each mourner's heart
    Like heaven's white lilies blow.

And all about the softening air
    Of new-born sweetness tells,
And the ungathered May-flowers wear
    The tints of ocean shells.

The old, assuring miracle
    Is fresh as heretofore;
And earth takes up its parable
    Of life from death once more.

Here organ-swell and church-bell toll
    Methinks but discord were,—
The prayerful silence of the soul
    Is best befitting her.

No sound should break the quietude
    Alike of earth and sky;—
O wandering wind in Seabrook wood,
    Breathe but a half-heard sigh!

Sing softly, spring-bird, for her sake ;
  And thou not distant sea,
Lapse lightly as if Jesus spake,
  And thou wert Galilee !

For all her quiet life flowed on
  As meadow streamlets flow,
Where fresher green reveals alone
  The noiseless ways they go.

From her loved place of prayer I see
  The plain-robed mourners pass,
With slow feet treading reverently
  The graveyard's springing grass.

Make room, O mourning ones, for me,
  Where, like the friends of Paul,
That you no more her face shall see
  You sorrow most of all.

Her path shall brighten more and more
  Unto the perfect day ;
She cannot fail of peace who bore
  Such peace with her away.

O sweet, calm face that seemed to wear
  The look of sins forgiven !
O voice of prayer that seemed to bear
  Our own needs up to heaven !

How reverent in our midst she stood,
  Or knelt in grateful praise !
What grace of Christian womanhood
  Was in her household ways !

For still her holy living meant
  No duty left undone' ;
The heavenly and the human blent
  Their kindred loves in one.

And if her life small leisure found
  For feasting ear and eye,
And Pleasure, on her daily round,
  She passed unpausing by,

Yet with her went a secret sense
  Of all things sweet and fair,
And Beauty's gracious providence
  Refreshed her unaware.

She kept her line of rectitude
  With love's unconscious ease ;
Her kindly instincts understood
  All gentle courtesies.

An inborn charm of graciousness
  Made sweet her smile and tone,
25.

And glorified her farm-wife dress
  With beauty not its own.

The dear Lord's best interpreters
  Are humble human souls ;
The Gospel of a life like hers
  Is more than books or scrolls.

From scheme and creed the light goes
    out,
  The saintly fact survives ;
The blessed Master none can doubt
  Revealed in holy lives.

JOHN UNDERHILL.

A SCORE of years had come and gone
Since the Pilgrims landed on Plymouth
    stone,
When Captain Underhill, bearing scars
From Indian ambush and Flemish wars,
Left three-hilled Boston and wandered
    down,
East by north, to Cocheco town.

With Vane the younger, in counsel
    sweet
He had sat at Anna Hutchinson's feet,
And, when the bolt of banishment fell
On the head of his saintly oracle,
He had shared her ill as her good report,
And braved the wrath of the General
    Court.

He shook from his feet as he rode away
The dust of the Massachusetts Bay.
The world might bless and the world
    might ban,
What did it matter the perfect man,
To whom the freedom of earth was
    given,
Proof against sin, and sure of heaven ?

He cheered his heart as he rode along
With screed of Scripture and holy song,
Or thought how he rode with his lances
    free
By the Lower Rhine and the Zuyder-
    Zee,
Till his wood-path grew to a trodden
    road,
And Hilton Point in the distance
    showed.

He saw the church with the block-
house nigh,
The two fair rivers, the flakes thereby,
And, tacking to windward, low and
crank,
The little shallop from Strawberry
Bank;
And he rose in his stirrups and looked
abroad
Over land and water, and praised the
Lord.

Goodly and stately and grave to see,
Into the clearing's space rode he,
With the sun on the hilt of his sword
in sheath,
And his silver buckles and spurs be-
neath,
And the settlers welcomed him, one and
all,
From swift Quampeagan to Gonic Fall.

And he said to the elders: "Lo, I come
As the way seemed open to seek a home.
Somewhat the Lord hath wrought by
my hands
In the Narragansett and Netherlands,
And if here ye have work for a Chris-
tian man,
I will tarry, and serve ye as best I can.

"I boast not of gifts, but fain would
own
The wonderful favor God hath shown,
The special mercy vouchsafed one day
On the shore of Narragansett Bay,
As I sat, with my pipe, from the camp
aside,
And mused like Isaac at eventide.

"A sudden sweetness of peace I found,
A garment of gladness wrapped me
round;
I felt from the law of works released,
The strife of the flesh and spirit ceased,
My faith to a full assurance grew,
And all I had hoped for myself I knew.

"Now, as God appointeth, I keep my
way,
I shall not stumble, I shall not stray;
He hath taken away my fig-leaf dress,
I wear the robe of his righteousness;
And the shafts of Satan no more avail
Than Pequot arrows on Christian mail."

"Tarry with us," the settlers cried,
"Thou man of God, as our ruler and
guide."
And Captain Underhill bowed his head.
"The will of the Lord be done!" he said.
And the morrow beheld him sitting down
In the ruler's seat in Cocheco town.

And he judged therein as a just man
should;
His words were wise and his rule was
good;
He coveted not his neighbor's land,
From the holding of bribes he shook his
hand;
And through the camps of the heathen
ran
A wholesome fear of the valiant man.

But the heart is deceitful, the good Book
saith,
And life hath ever a savor of death.
Through hymns of triumph the tempter
calls,
And whoso thinketh he standeth falls.
Alas! ere their round the seasons ran,
There was grief in the soul of the saintly
man.

The tempter's arrows that rarely fail
Had found the joints of his spiritual mail;
And men took note of his gloomy air,
The shame in his eye, the halt in his
prayer,
The signs of a battle lost within,
The pain of a soul in the coils of sin.

Then a whisper of scandal linked his
name
With broken vows and a life of blame;
And the people looked askance on him
As he walked among them sullen and
grim,
Ill at ease, and bitter of word,
And prompt of quarrel with hand or
sword.

None knew how, with prayer and fasting
still,
He strove in the bonds of his evil will;
But he shook himself like Samson at
length,
And girded anew his loins of strength,
And bade the crier go up and down
And call together the wondering town.

Jeer and murmur and shaking of head
Ceased as he rose in his place and said:
"Men, brethren, and fathers, well ye
     know
How I came among you a year ago,
Strong in the faith that my soul was
     freed
From sin of feeling, or thought, or deed.

"I have sinned, I own it with grief and
     shame,
But not with a lie on my lips I came.
In my blindness I verily thought my
     heart
Swept and garnished in every part.
He chargeth His angels with folly; He
     sees
The heavens unclean. Was I more than
     these?

"I urge no plea. At your feet I lay
The trust you gave me, and go my way.
Hate me or pity me, as you will,
The Lord will have mercy on sinners
     still;
And I, who am chiefest, say to all,
Watch and pray, lest ye also fall."

No voice made answer: a sob so low
That only his quickened ear could know
Smote his heart with a bitter pain,
As into the forest he rode again,
And the veil of its oaken leaves shut
     down
On his latest glimpse of Cocheco town.

Crystal-clear on the man of sin
The streams flashed up, and the sky
     shone in;
On his cheek of fever the cool wind blew,
The leaves dropped on him their tears
     of dew,
And angels of God, in the pure, sweet
     guise
Of flowers, looked on him with sad sur-
     prise.

Was his ear at fault that brook and
     breeze
Sang in their saddest of minor keys?
What was it the mournful wood-thrush
     said?
What whispered the pine-trees overhead.
Did he hear the Voice on his lonely way
That Adam heard in the cool of day?

Into the desert alone rode he,
Alone with the Infinite Purity;

And, bowing his soul to its tender rebuke,
As Peter did to the Master's look,
He measured his path with prayers of
     pain
For peace with God and nature again.

And in after years to Cocheco came
The bruit of a once familiar name;
How among the Dutch of New Nether-
     lands,
From wild Danskamer to Haarlem sands,
A penitent soldier preached the Word,
And smote the heathen with Gideon's
     sword!

And the heart of Boston was glad to hear
How he harried the foe on the long
     frontier,
And heaped on the land against him
     barred
The coals of his generous watch and ward.
Frailest and bravest! the Bay State still
Counts with her worthies John Underhill.

IN QUEST.

HAVE I not voyaged, friend beloved,
     with thee
On the great waters of the unsounded
     sea,
Momently listening with suspended oar
For the low rote of waves upon a shore
Changeless as heaven, where never fog-
     cloud drifts
Over its windless woods, nor mirage lifts
The steadfast hills; where never birds
     of doubt
Sing to mislead, and every dream dies
     out,
And the dark riddles which perplex us
     here
In the sharp solvent of its light are clear?
Thou knowest how vain our quest; how,
     soon or late,
The baffling tides and circles of debate
Swept back our bark unto its starting-
     place,
Where, looking forth upon the blank,
     gray space,
And round about us seeing, with sad eyes,
The same old difficult hills and cloud-
     cold skies,
We said: "This outward search availeth
     not

To find Him. He is farther than we
    thought,
Or, haply, nearer. To this very spot
Whereon we wait, this commonplace of
    home,
As to the well of Jacob, He may come
And tell us all things." As I listened
    there,
Through the expectant silences of prayer,
Somewhat I seemed to hear, which hath
    to me
Been hope, strength, comfort, and I give
    it thee.

"The riddle of the world is understood
Only by him who feels that God is good,
As only he can feel who makes his love
The ladder of his faith, and climbs above
On th' rounds of his best instincts;
    draws no line
Between mere human goodness and di-
    vine,
But, judging God by what in him is best,
With a child's trust leans on a Father's
    breast,
And hears unmoved the old creeds bab-
    ble still
Of kingly power and dread caprice of
    will,
Chary of blessing, prodigal of curse,
The pitiless doomsman of the universe.
Can Hatred ask for love? Can Selfish-
    ness
Invite to self-denial? Is He less
Than man in kindly dealing? Can He
    break
His own great law of fatherhood, forsake
And curse His children? Not for earth
    and heaven
Can separate tables of the law be given.
No rule can bind which He himself de-
    nies;
The truths of time are not eternal lies."

So heard I; and the chaos round me
    spread
To light and order grew; and, "Lord,"
    I said,
"Our sins are our tormentors, worst of
    all
Felt in distrustful shame that dares not
    call
Upon Thee as our Father. We have set
A strange god up, but Thou remainest
    yet.
All that I feel of pity Thou hast known
Before I was; my best is all Thy own.

From Thy great heart of goodness mine
    but drew
Wishes and prayers; but Thou, O Lord,
    wilt do,
In Thy own time, by ways I cannot see,
All that I feel when I am nearest Thee!"

A SEA DREAM.

WE saw the slow tides go and come,
    The curving surf-lines lightly drawn,
The gray rocks touched with tender
    bloom
    Beneath the fresh-blown rose of dawn.

We saw in richer sunsets lost
    The sombre pomp of showery noons;
And signalled spectral sails that crossed
    The weird, low light of rising moons.

On stormy eves from cliff and head
    We saw the white spray tossed and
        spurned;
While over all, in gold and red,
    Its face of fire the lighthouse turned.

The rail-car brought its daily crowds,
    Half curious, half indifferent,
Like passing sails or floating clouds,
    We saw them as they came and went.

But, one calm morning, as we lay
    And watched the mirage-lifted wall
Of coast, across the dreamy bay,
    And heard afar the curlew call,

And nearer voices, wild or tame,
    Of airy flock and childish throng,
Up from the water's edge there came
    Faint snatches of familiar song.

Careless we heard the singer's choice
    Of old and common airs; at last
The tender pathos of his voice
    In one low chanson held us fast.

A song that mingled joy and pain,
    And memories old and sadly sweet;
While, timing to its minor strain,
    The waves in lapsing cadence beat.

———

The waves are glad in breeze and sun;
    The rocks are fringed with foam;

I walk once more a haunted shore,
  A stranger, yet at home, —
  A land of dreams I roam.

Is this the wind, the soft sea-wind
  That stirred thy locks of brown?
Are these the rocks whose mosses knew
  The trail of thy light gown,
  Where boy and girl sat down?

I see the gray fort's broken wall,
  The boats that rock below;
And, out at sea, the passing sails
  We saw so long ago
  Rose-red in morning's glow.

The freshness of the early time
  On every breeze is blown;
As glad the sea, as blue the sky, —
  The change is ours alone;
  The saddest is my own.

A stranger now, a world-worn man,
  Is he who bears my name;
But thou, methinks, whose mortal life
  Immortal youth became,
  Art evermore the same.

Thou art not here, thou art not there,
  Thy place I cannot see;
I only know that where thou art
  The blessed angels be,
  And heaven is glad for thee.

Forgive me if the evil years
  Have left on me their sign;
Wash out, O soul so beautiful,
  The many stains of mine
  In tears of love divine!

I could not look on thee and live,
  If thou wert by my side;
The vision of a shining one,
  The white and heavenly bride,
  Is well to me denied.

But turn to me thy dear girl-face
  Without the angel's crown,
The wedded roses of thy lips,
  Thy loose hair rippling down
  In waves of golden brown.

Look forth once more through space and time,
  And let thy sweet shade fall
In tenderest grace of soul and form

On memory's frescoed wall.
  A shadow, and yet all!

Draw near, more near, forever dear!
  Where'er I rest or roam,
Or in the city's crowded streets,
  Or by the blown sea foam,
  The thought of thee is home!

At breakfast hour the singer read
  The city news, with comment wise,
Like one who felt the pulse of trade
  Beneath his finger fall and rise.

His look, his air, his curt speech, told
  The man of action, not of books,
To whom the corners made in gold
  And stocks were more than seaside
    nooks.

Of life beneath the life confessed
  His song had hinted unawares;
Of flowers in traffic's ledgers pressed,
  Of human hearts in bulls and bears.

But eyes in vain were turned to watch
  That face so hard and shrewd and
    strong;
And ears in vain grew sharp to catch
  The meaning of that morning song.

In vain some sweet-voiced querist sought
  To sound him, leaving as she came;
Her baited album only caught
  A common, unromantic name.

No word betrayed the mystery fine,
  That trembled on the singer's tongue;
He came and went, and left no sign
  Behind him save the song he sung.

A MYSTERY.

THE river hemmed with leaning trees
  Wound through its meadows green;
A low, blue line of mountains showed
  The open pines between.

One sharp, tall peak above them all
  Clear into sunlight sprang:
I saw the river of my dreams,
  The mountains that I sang!

No clew of memory led me on,
  But well the ways I knew ;
A feeling of familiar things
  With every footstep grew.

Not otherwise above its crag
  Could lean the blasted pine ;
Not otherwise the maple hold
  Aloft its red ensign.

So up the long and shorn foot-hills
  The mountain road should creep ;
So, green and low, the meadow fold
  Its red-haired kine asleep.

The river wound as it should wind ;
  Their place the mountains took ;
The white torn fringes of their clouds
  Wore no unwonted look.

Yet ne'er before that river's rim
  Was pressed by feet of mine,
Never before mine eyes had crossed
  That broken mountain line.

A presence, strange at once and known,
  Walked with me as my guide ;
The skirts of some forgotten life
  Trailed noiseless at my side.

Was it a dim-remembered dream ?
  Or glimpse through æons old ?
The secret which the mountains kept
  The river never told.

But from the vision ere it passed
  A tender hope I drew,
And, pleasant as a dawn of spring,
  The thought within me grew,

That love would temper every change,
  And soften all surprise,
And, misty with the dreams of earth,
  The hills of Heaven arise.

CONDUCTOR BRADLEY.

Conductor Bradley, (always may his
    name
Be said with reverence !) as the swift
    doom came,
Smitten to death, a crushed and mangled
    frame,

Sank, with the brake he grasped just
    where he stood
To do the utmost that a brave man
    could,
And die, if needful, as a true man should.

Men stooped above him ; women dropped
    their tears
On that poor wreck beyond all hopes or
    fears,
Lost in the strength and glory of his
    years.

What heard they ? Lo ! the ghastly lips
    of pain,
Dead to all thought save duty's, moved
    again :
" Put out the signals for the other
    train ! "

No nobler utterance since the world
    began
From lips of saint or martyr ever ran,
Electric, through the sympathies of man.

Ah me ! how poor and noteless seem to
    this
The sick-bed dramas of self-conscious-
    ness,
Our sensual fears of pain and hopes of
    bliss !

O, grand, supreme endeavor ! Not in
    vain
That last brave act of failing tongue and
    brain !
Freighted with life the downward rush-
    ing train,

Following the wrecked one, as wave fol-
    lows wave,
Obeyed the warning which the dead lips
    gave.
Others he saved, himself he could not
    save.

Nay, the lost life *was* saved. He is not
    dead
Who in his record still the earth shall
    tread
With God's clear aureole shining round
    his head.

We bow as in the dust, with all our pride
Of virtue dwarfed the noble deed beside.
God give us grace to live as Bradley died !

CHILD-SONGS.

STILL linger in our noon of time
  And on our Saxon tongue
The echoes of the home-born hymns
  The Aryan mothers sung.

And childhood had its litanies
  In every age and clime ;
The earliest cradles of the race
  Were rocked to poet's rhyme.

Nor sky, nor wave, nor tree, nor flower,
  Nor green earth's virgin sod,
So moved the singer's heart of old
  As these small ones of God.

The mystery of unfolding life
  Was more than dawning morn,
Than opening flower or crescent moon
  The human soul new-born !

And still to childhood's sweet appeal
  The heart of genius turns,
And more than all the sages teach
  From lisping voices learns, —

The voices loved of him who sang,
  Where Tweed and Teviot glide,
That sound to-day on all the winds
  That blow from Rydal-side, —

Heard in the Teuton's household songs,
  And folk-lore of the Finn,
Where'er to holy Christmas hearths
  The Christ-child enters in !

Before life's sweetest mystery still
  The heart in reverence kneels ;
The wonder of the primal birth
  The latest mother feels.

We need love's tender lessons taught
  As only weakness can ;
God hath his small interpreters ;
  The child must teach the man.

We wander wide through evil years,
  Our eyes of faith grow dim ;
But he is freshest from His hands
  And nearest unto Him !

And haply, pleading long with Him
  For sin-sick hearts and cold,
The angels of our childhood still
  The Father's face behold.

Of such the kingdom ! — Teach thou us,
  O Master most divine,
To feel the deep significance
  Of these wise words of thine !

The haughty eye shall seek in vain
  What innocence beholds ;
No cunning finds the key of heaven,
  No strength its gate unfolds.

Alone to guilelessness and love
  That gate shall open fall ;
The mind of pride is nothingness,
  The childlike heart is all !

THE GOLDEN WEDDING OF LONGWOOD.

WITH fifty years between you and your
  well-kept wedding vow,
The Golden Age, old friends of mine, is
  not a fable now.

And, sweet as has life's vintage been
  through all your pleasant past,
Still, as at Cana's marriage-feast, the
  best wine is the last !

Again before me, with your names, fair
  Chester's landscape comes,
Its meadows, woods, and ample barns,
  and quaint, stone-builded homes.

The smooth-shorn vales, the wheaten
  slopes, the boscage green and soft,
Of which their poet sings so well from
  towered Cedarcroft.

And lo ! from all the country-side come
  neighbors, kith and kin ;
From city, hamlet, farm-house old, the
  wedding guests come in.

And they who, without scrip or purse,
  mob-hunted, travel-worn,
In Freedom's age of martyrs came, as
  victors now return.

Older and slower, yet the same, files in
  the long array,
And hearts are light and eyes are glad,
  though heads are badger-gray.

The fire-tried men of Thirty-eight who
  saw with me the fall,
Midst roaring flames and shouting mob,
  of Pennsylvania Hall ;

And they of Lancaster who turned the
    cheeks of tyrants pale,
Singing of freedom through the grates
    of Moyamensing jail !

And haply with them, all unseen, old
    comrades, gone before,
Pass, silently as shadows pass, within
    your open door, —

The eagle face of Lindley Coates, brave
    Garrett's daring zeal,
The Christian grace of Pennock, the
    steadfast heart of Neal.

Ah me ! beyond all power to name, the
    worthies tried and true,
Grave men, fair women, youth and maid,
    pass by in hushed review.

Of varying faiths, a common cause fused
    all their hearts in one.
God give them now, whate'er their
    names, the peace of duty done !

How gladly would I tread again the old-
    remembered places,
Sit down beside your hearth once more
    and look in the dear old faces !

And thank you for the lessons your fifty
    years are teaching,
For honest lives that louder speak than
    half our noisy preaching ;

For your steady faith and courage in
    that dark and evil time,
When the Golden Rule was treason, and
    to feed the hungry, crime ;

For the poor slave's house of refuge when
    the hounds were on his track,
And saint and sinner, church and state,
    joined hands to send him back.

Blessings upon you ! — What you did
    for each sad, suffering one,
So homeless, faint, and naked, unto our
    Lord was done !

Fair fall on Kennett's pleasant vales and
    Longwood's bowery ways
The mellow sunset of your lives, friends
    of my early days.

May many more of quiet years be added
    to your sum,
And, late at last, in tenderest love, the
    beckoning angel come.

Dear hearts are here, dear hearts are
    there, alike below, above ;
Our friends are now in either world, and
    love is sure of love.

KINSMAN.

DIED AT THE ISLAND OF PANAY (PHI-
LIPPINE GROUP), AGED 19 YEARS.

WHERE ceaseless Spring her garland
    twines,
    As sweetly shall the loved one rest,
As if beneath the whispering pines
    And maple shadows of the West.

Ye mourn, O hearts of home ! for him,
    But, haply, mourn ye not alone;
For him shall far-off eyes be dim,
    And pity speak in tongues unknown.

There needs no graven line to give
    The story of his blameless youth;
All hearts shall throb intuitive,
    And nature guess the simple truth.

The very meaning of his name
    Shall many a tender tribute win ;
The stranger own his sacred claim,
    And all the world shall be his kin.

And there, as here, on main and isle,
    The dews of holy peace shall fall,
The same sweet heavens above him
    smile,
    And God's dear love be over all !

VESTA.

O CHRIST of God ! whose life and death
    Our own have reconciled,
Most quietly, most tenderly
    Take home thy star-named child !

Thy grace is in her patient eyes,
    Thy words are on her tongue ;
The very silence round her seems
    As if the angels sung.

Her smile is as a listening child's
  Who hears its mother call;
The lilies of Thy perfect peace
  About her pillow fall.

She leans from out our clinging arms
  To rest herself in Thine;
Alone to Thee, dear Lord, can we
  Our well-beloved resign!

O, less for her than for ourselves
  We bow our heads and pray;
Her setting star, like Bethlehem's,
  To Thee shall point the way!

THE HEALER.

TO A YOUNG PHYSICIAN, WITH DORÉ'S
  PICTURE OF CHRIST HEALING THE
  SICK.

So stood of old the holy Christ
  Amidst the suffering throng;
With whom his lightest touch sufficed
  To make the weakest strong.

That healing gift he lends to them
  Who use it in his name;
The power that filled his garment's hem
  Is evermore the same.

For lo! in human hearts unseen
  The Healer dwelleth still,
And they who make his temples clean
  The best subserve his will.

The holiest task by Heaven decreed,
  An errand all divine,
The burden of our common need
  To render less is thine.

The paths of pain are thine. Go forth
  With patience, trust, and hope;
The sufferings of a sin-sick earth
  Shall give thee ample scope.

Beside the unveiled mysteries
  Of life and death go stand,
With guarded lips and reverent eyes
  And pure of heart and hand.

So shalt thou be with power endued
  From Him who went about
The Syrian hillsides doing good,
  And casting demons out.

That Good Physician liveth yet
  Thy friend and guide to be;
The Healer by Gennesaret
  Shall walk the rounds with thee.

A CHRISTMAS CARMEN.

I.

SOUND over all waters, reach out from
    all lands,
The chorus of voices, the clasping of
    hands;
Sing hymns that were sung by the stars
    of the morn,
Sing songs of the angels when Jesus was
    born!
    With glad jubilations
    Bring hope to the nations!
The dark night is ending and dawn has
    begun:
Rise, hope of the ages, arise like the sun,
  All speech flow to music, all hearts
    beat as one!

II.

Sing the bridal of nations! with chorals
    of love
Sing out the war-vulture and sing in the
    dove,
Till the hearts of the peoples keep time
    in accord,
And the voice of the world is the voice
    of the Lord!
    Clasp hands of the nations
    In strong gratulations:
The dark night is ending and dawn has
    begun;
Rise, hope of the ages, arise like the sun,
  All speech flow to music, all hearts
    beat as one!

III.

Blow, bugles of battle, the marches of
    peace;
East, west, north, and south let the long
    quarrel cease:
Sing the song of great joy that the
    angels began,
Sing of glory to God and of good-will to
    man!
    Hark! joining in chorus
    The heavens bend o'er us!
The dark night is ending and dawn has
    begun;

Rise, hope of the ages, arise like the
　　sun,
　All speech flow to music, all hearts
　　beat as one!

HYMN

FOR THE OPENING OF PLYMOUTH
CHURCH, ST. PAUL, MINNESOTA.

ALL things are Thine: no gift have we,
Lord of all gifts! to offer Thee;
And hence with grateful hearts to-day,
Thy own before Thy feet we lay.

Thy will was in the builders' thought;
Thy hand unseen amidst us wrought;

Through mortal motive, scheme and plan,
Thy wise eternal purpose ran.

No lack Thy perfect fulness knew;
For human needs and longings grew
This house of prayer, this home of rest,
In the fair garden of the West.

In weakness and in want we call
On Thee for whom the heavens are small;
Thy glory is Thy children's good,
Thy joy Thy tender Fatherhood.

O Father! deign these walls to bless.
Fill with Thy love their emptiness.
And let their door a gateway be
To lead us from ourselves to Thee!

POEMS BY ELIZABETH H. WHITTIER.

THE DREAM OF ARGYLE.

EARTHLY arms no more uphold him
　On his prison's stony floor;
Waiting death in his last slumber,
　Lies the doomed MacCallum More.

And he dreams a dream of boyhood;
　Rise again his heathery hills,
Sound again the hound's long baying,
　Cry of moor-fowl, laugh of rills.

Now he stands amidst his clansmen
　In the low, long banquet-hall,
Over grim, ancestral armor
　Sees the ruddy firelight fall.

Once again, with pulses beating,
　Hears the wandering minstrel tell
How Montrose on Inverary
　Thief-like from his mountains fell.

Down the glen, beyond the castle,
　Where the linn's swift waters shine,
Round the youthful heir of Argyle
　Shy feet glide and white arms twine.

Fairest of the rustic dancers,
　Blue-eyed Effie smiles once more,
Bends to him her snooded tresses,
　Treads with him the grassy floor.

Now he hears the pipes lamenting,
　Harpers for his mother mourn,
Slow, with sable plume and pennon,
　To her cairn of burial borne.

Then anon his dreams are darker,
　Sounds of battle fill his ears,
And the pibroch's mournful wailing
　For his father's fall he hears.

Wild Lochaber's mountain echoes
　Wail in concert for the dead,
And Loch Awe's deep waters murmur
　For the Campbell's glory fled!

Fierce and strong the godless tyrants
　Trample the apostate land,
While her poor and faithful remnant
　Wait for the Avenger's hand.

Once again at Inverary,
　Years of weary exile o'er,
Armed to lead his scattered clansmen,
　Stands the bold MacCallum More.

Once again to battle calling
　Sound the war-pipes through the glen;
And the court-yard of Dunstaffnage
　Rings with tread of arméd men.

All is lost! The godless triumph,
And the faithful ones and true
From the scaffold and the prison
Covenant with God anew.

On the darkness of his dreaming
Great and sudden glory shone;
Over bonds and death victorious
Stands he by the Father's throne!

From the radiant ranks of martyrs
Notes of joy and praise he hears,
Songs of his poor land's deliverance
Sounding from the future years.

Lo, he wakes! but airs celestial
Bathe him in immortal rest,
And he sees with unsealed vision
Scotland's cause with victory blest.

Shining hosts attend and guard him
As he leaves his prison door;
And to death as to a triumph
Walks the great MacCallum More!

LINES

WRITTEN ON THE DEPARTURE OF
JOSEPH STURGE, AFTER HIS VISIT
TO THE ABOLITIONISTS OF THE
UNITED STATES.

FAIR islands of the sunny sea! midst
all rejoicing things,
No more the wailing of the slave a wild
discordance brings;
On the lifted brows of freemen the tropic
breezes blow,
The mildew of the bondman's toil the
land no more shall know.

How swells from those green islands,
where bird and leaf and flower
Are praising in their own sweet way the
dawn of freedom's hour,
The glorious resurrection song from
hearts rejoicing poured,
Thanksgiving for the priceless gift, —
man's regal crown restored!

How beautiful through all the green and
tranquil summer land,
Uplifted, as by miracle, the solemn
churches stand!

The grass is trodden from the paths
where waiting freemen throng,
Athirst and fainting for the cup of life
denied so long.

O, blessed were the feet of him whose
generous errand here
Was to unloose the captive's chain and
dry the mourner's tear;
To lift again the fallen ones a brother's
robber hand
Had left in pain and wretchedness by the
waysides of the land.

The islands of the sea rejoice; the harvest anthems rise;
The sower of the seed must own 't is
marvellous in his eyes;
The old waste places are rebuilt, — the
broken walls restored, —
And the wilderness is blooming like the
garden of the Lord!

Thanksgiving for the holy fruit! should
not the laborer rest,
His earnest faith and works of love have
been so richly blest?
The pride of all fair England shall her
ocean islands be,
And their peasantry with joyful hearts
keep ceaseless jubilee.

Rest, never! while his countrymen have
trampled hearts to bleed,
The stifled murmur of their wrongs his
listening ear shall heed,
Where England's far dependencies her
might, not *mercy*, know,
To all the crushed and suffering there
his pitying love shall flow.

The friend of freedom everywhere, how
mourns he for our land,
The brand of whose hypocrisy burns on
her guilty hand!
Her thrift a theft, the robber's greed and
cunning in her eye,
Her glory shame, her flaunting flag on
all the winds a lie!

For us with steady strength of heart and
zeal forever true,
The champion of the island slave the
conflict doth renew,
His labor here hath been to point the
Pharisaic eye
Away from empty creed and form to
where the wounded lie.

How beautiful to us should seem the
    coming feet of such!
Their garments of self-sacrifice have heal-
    ing in their touch ;
Their gospel mission none may doubt,
    for they heed the Master's call,
Who here walked with the multitude,
    and sat at meat with all !

And so they bear him to his grave in
    the fulness of his years,
True sage and prophet, leaving us in a
    time of many fears.
Nevermore amid the darkness of our
    wild and evil day
Shall his voice be heard to cheer us,
    shall his finger point the way.

JOHN QUINCY ADAMS.

HE rests with the immortals ; his jour-
    ney has been long :
For him no wail of sorrow, but a pæan
    full and strong!
So well and bravely has he done the
    work he found to do,
To justice, freedom, duty, God, and man
    forever true.

Strong to the end, a man of men, from
    out the strife he passed ;
The grandest hour of all his life was that
    of earth the last.
Now midst his snowy hills of home to
    the grave they bear him down,
The glory of his fourscore years resting
    on him like a crown.

The mourning of the many bells, the
    drooping flags, all seem
Like some dim, unreal pageant passing
    onward in a dream ;
And following with the living to his last
    and narrow bed,
Methinks I see a shadowy band, a train
    of noble dead.

'T is a strange and weird procession that
    is slowly moving on,
The phantom patriots gathered to the
    funeral of their son !
In shadowy guise they move along, brave
    Otis with hushed tread,
And Warren walking reverently by the
    father of the dead.

Gliding foremost in the misty band a
    gentle form is there,
In the white robes of the angels and
    their glory round her hair.
She hovers near and bends above her
    world-wide honored child,
And the joy that heaven alone can know
    beams on her features mild.

DR. KANE IN CUBA.

A NOBLE life is in thy care,
    A sacred trust to thee is given ;
Bright Island ! let thy healing air
    Be to him as the breath of Heaven.

The marvel of his daring life —
    The self-forgetting leader bold —
Stirs, like the trumpet's call to strife,
    A million hearts of meaner mould.

Eyes that shall never meet his own
    Look dim with tears across the sea,
Where from the dark and icy zone,
    Sweet Isle of Flowers ! he comes to thee.

Fold him in rest, O pitying clime !
    Give back his wasted strength again ;
Soothe, with thy endless summer time,
    His winter-wearied heart and brain.

Sing soft and low, thou tropic bird,
    From out the fragrant, flowery tree, —
The ear that hears thee now has heard
    The ice-break of the winter sea.

Through his long watch of awful night,
    He saw the Bear in Northern skies ;
Now, to the Southern Cross of light
    He lifts in hope his weary eyes.

Prayers from the hearts that watched in
    fear,
    When the dark North no answer gave,
Rise, trembling, to the Father's ear,
    That still His love may help and save.

LADY FRANKLIN.

FOLD thy hands, thy work is over ;
    Cool thy watching eyes with tears:
Let thy poor heart, over-wearied,
    Rest alike from hopes and fears. —

Hopes, that saw with sleepless vision
  One sad picture fading slow ;
Fears, that followed, vague and name-
    less,
  Lifting back the veils of snow.

For thy brave one, for thy lost one,
  Truest heart of woman, weep !
Owning still the love that granted
  Unto thy beloved sleep.

Not for him that hour of terror
  When, the long ice-battle o'er,
In the sunless day his comrades'
  Deathward trod the Polar shore.

Spared the cruel cold and famine,
  Spared the fainting heart's despair,
What but that could mercy grant him ?
  What but that has been thy prayer ?

Dear to thee that last memorial
  From the cairn beside the sea ;
Evermore the month of roses
  Shall be sacred time to thee.

Sad it is the mournful yew-tree
  O'er his slumbers may not wave ;
Sad it is the English daisy
  May not blossom on his grave.

But his tomb shall storm and winter
  Shape and fashion year by year,
Pile his mighty mausoleum,
  Block by block, and tier on tier.

Guardian of its gleaming portal
  Shall his stainless honor be,
While thy love, a sweet immortal,
  Hovers o'er the winter sea.

NIGHT AND DEATH.

The storm-wind is howling
  Through old pines afar ;
The drear night is falling
  Without moon or star.

The roused sea is lashing
  The bold shore behind,
And the moan of its ebbing
  Keeps time with the wind.

On, on through the darkness,
  A spectre, I pass

Where, like moaning of broken hearts,
  Surges the grass !

I see her lone head-stone, —
  'T is white as a shroud ;
Like a pall, hangs above it
  The low drooping cloud.

Who speaks through the dark night
  And lull of the wind ?
'T is the sound of the pine-leaves
  And sea-waves behind.

The dead girl is silent, —
  I stand by her now ;
And her pulse beats no quicker,
  Nor crimsons her brow.

The small hand that trembled,
  When last in my own,
Lies patient and folded,
  And colder than stone.

Like the white blossoms falling
  To-night in the gale,
So she in her beauty
  Sank mournful and pale.

Yet I loved her ! I utter
  Such words by her grave,
As I would not have spoken
  Her last breath to save.

Of *her* love the angels
  In heaven might tell,
While mine would be whispered
  With shudders in hell !

'T was well that the white ones
  Who bore her to bliss
Shut out from her new life
  The vision of this.

Else, sure as I stand here,
  And speak of my love,
She would leave for my darkness
  Her glory above.

THE MEETING WATERS.

Close beside the meeting waters.
  Long I stood as in a dream,
Watching how the little river
  Fell into the broader stream.

Calm and still the mingled current
  Glided to the waiting sea;
On its breast serenely pictured
  Floating cloud and skirting tree.

And I thought, " O human spirit !
  Strong and deep and pure and blest,
Let the stream of my existence
  Blend with thine, and find its rest !"

I could die as dies the river,
  In that current deep and wide ;
I would live as live its waters,
  Flashing from a stronger tide !

THE WEDDING VEIL.

DEAR Anna, when I brought her veil,
  Her white veil, on her wedding night,
Threw o'er my thin brown hair its folds,
  And, laughing, turned me to the light.

" See, Bessie, see ! you wear at last
  The bridal veil, forsworn for years !"
She saw my face, — her laugh was
    hushed,
  Her happy eyes were filled with tears.

With kindly haste and trembling hand
  She drew away the gauzy mist ;
" Forgive, dear heart !" her sweet voice
    said :
  Her loving lips my forehead kissed.

We passed from out the searching light ;
  The summer night was calm and fair :
I did not see her pitying eyes,
  I felt her soft hand smooth my hair.

Her tender love unlocked my heart ;
  Mid falling tears, at last I said,
" Forsworn indeed to me that veil
  Because I only love the dead !"

She stood one moment statue-still,
  And, musing, spake in undertone,
" The living love may colder grow ;
  The dead is safe with God alone !"

CHARITY.

THE pilgrim and stranger who through
    the day
Holds over the desert his trackless way,
Where the terrible sands no shade have
    known,
No sound of life save his camel's moan,
Hears, at last, through the mercy of
    Allah to all,
From his tent-door at evening the Be-
    douin's call :
" *Whoever thou art whose need is great,*
In the name of God, the Compassionate
And Merciful One, for thee I wait !"

For gifts in His name of food and rest
The tents of Islam of God are blest,
Thou who hast faith in the Christ above,
Shall the Koran teach thee the Law of
    Love ? —
O Christian ! — open thy heart and door,
Cry east and west to the wandering poor :
" *Whoever thou art whose need is great,*
In the name of Christ, the Compassionate
And Merciful One, for thee I wait !"

THE VISION OF ECHARD,

AND OTHER POEMS.

THE VISION OF ECHARD.

THE Benedictine Echard
  Sat, worn by wanderings far,
Where Marsberg sees the bridal
  Of the Moselle and Sarre.

Fair with its sloping vineyards
  And tawny chestnut bloom,
The happy vale Ausonius sung
  For holy Treves made room.

On the shrine Helena builded
  To keep the Christ coat well,
On minster tower and kloster cross,
  The westering sunshine fell.

There, where the rock-hewn circles
  O'erlooked the Roman's game,
The veil of sleep fell on him,
  And his thought a dream became.

He felt the heart of silence
  Throb with a soundless word,
And by the inward ear alone
  A spirit's voice he heard.

And the spoken word seemed written
  On air and wave and sod,
And the bending walls of sapphire
  Blazed with the thought of God:

"What lack I, O my children?
  All things are in my hand;
The vast earth and the awful stars
  I hold as grains of sand.

"Need I your alms? The silver
  And gold are mine alone;
The gifts ye bring before me
  Were evermore my own.

"Heed I the noise of viols,
  Your pomp of masque and show?
Have I not dawns and sunsets?
  Have I not winds that blow?

"Do I smell your gums of incense?
  Is my ear with chantings fed?

"Taste I your wine of worship,
  Or eat your holy bread?

"Of rank and name and honors
  Am I vain as ye are vain?
What can Eternal Fullness
  From your lip-service gain?

"Ye make me not your debtor
  Who serve yourselves alone;
Ye boast to me of homage
  Whose gain is all your own.

"For you I gave the prophets,
  For you the Psalmist's lay:
For you the law's stone tables,
  And holy book and day.

"Ye change to weary burdens
  The helps that should uplift;
Ye lose in form the spirit,
  The Giver in the gift.

"Who called ye to self-torment,
  To fast and penance vain?
Dream ye Eternal Goodness
  Has joy in mortal pain?

"For the death in life of Nitria,
  For your Chartreuse ever dumb,
What better is the neighbor,
  Or happier the home?

"Who counts his brother's welfare
  As sacred as his own,
And loves, forgives, and pities,
  He serveth me alone.

"I note each gracious purpose,
  Each kindly word and deed;
Are ye not all my children?
  Shall not the Father heed?

"No prayer for light and guidance
  Is lost upon mine ear:
The child's cry in the darkness
  Shall not the Father hear?

"I loathe your wrangling councils,
　I tread upon your creeds ;
Who made ye mine avengers,
　Or told ye of my needs ;

"I bless men and ye curse them,
　I love them and ye hate ;
Ye bite and tear each other,
　I suffer long and wait.

"Ye bow to ghastly symbols,
　To cross and scourge and thorn ;
Ye seek his Syrian manger
　Who in the heart is born.

"For the dead Christ, not the living,
　Ye watch his empty grave
Whose life alone within you
　Has power to bless and save.

"O blind ones, outward groping,
　The idle quest forego ;
Who listens to his inward voice
　Alone of him shall know.

"His love all love exceeding
　The heart must needs recall,
Its self-surrendering freedom,
　Its loss that gaineth all.

"Climb not the holy mountains,
　Their eagles know not me ;
Seek not the Blessed Islands,
　I dwell not in the sea.

"The gods are gone for ever
　From Zanskar's glacier sides,
And in the Buddha's footprints
　The Ceylon serpent glides.

"No more from shaded Delphos
　The weird responses come ;
Dodona's oaks are silent,
　The Hebrew Bath-Col dumb !

"No more from rocky Horeb
　The smitten waters gush ;
Fallen is Bethel's ladder,
　Quenched is the burning bush.

"The jewels of the Urim
　And Thummim all are dim ;
The fire has left the altar,
　The sign the teraphim.

"No more in ark or hill grove
　The Holiest abides ;

"Not in the scroll's dead letter
　The eternal secret hides.

"The eye shall fail that searches
　For me the hollow sky ;
The far is even as the near,
　The low is as the high.

"What if the earth is hiding
　Her old faiths, long outworn ?
What is it to the changeless truth
　That yours shall fail in turn ?

"What if the o'erturned altar
　Lays bare the ancient lie ?
What if the dreams and legends
　Of the world's childhood die ?

"Have ye not still my witness
　Within yourselves alway,
My hand that on the keys of life
　For bliss or bale I lay ?

"Still, in perpetual judgment,
　I hold assize within,
With sure reward of holiness,
　And dread rebuke of sin.

"A light, a guide, a warning,
　A presence ever near,
Through the deep silence of the flesh
　I reach the inward ear.

"My Gerizim and Ebal
　Are in each human soul,
The still, small voice of blessing,
　And Sinai's thunder-roll.

"The stern behest of duty,
　The doom-book open thrown,
The heaven ye seek, the hell ye fear,
　Are with yourselves alone."

A gold and purple sunset
　Flowed down the broad Moselle ;
On hills of vine and meadow lands
　The peace of twilight fell.

A slow, cool wind of evening
　Blew over leaf and bloom ;
And, faint and far, the Angelus
　Rang from Saint Matthew's tomb.

Then up rose Master Echard,
　And marvelled : "Can it be

"That here, in dream and vision,
　The Lord hath talked with me?"

He went his way; behind him
　The shrines of saintly dead,
The holy coat and nail of cross,
　He left unvisited.

He sought the vale of Eltzbach
　His burdened soul to free,
Where the foot-hills of the Eifel
　Are glassed in Laachersee.

And, in his Order's kloster,
　He sat, in night-long parle,
With Tauler of the Friends of God,
　And Nicolas of Basle.

And lo! the twain made answer:
　"Yea, brother, even thus
The Voice above all voices
　Hath spoken unto us.

"The world will have its idols,
　And flesh and sense their sign;
But the blinded eyes shall open,
　And the gross ear be fine.

"What if the vision tarry?
　God's time is always best;
The true Light shall be witnessed,
　The Christ within confessed.

"In mercy or in judgment
　He shall turn and overturn,
Till the heart shall be his temple
　Where all of Him shall learn."

THE WITCH OF WENHAM.

I.

ALONG Crane River's sunny slopes,
　Blew warm the winds of May,
And over Naumkeag's ancient oaks
　The green outgrew the gray.

The grass was green on Rial-side,
　The early birds at will
Waked up the violet in its dell,
　The wind-flower on its hill.

"Where go you, in your Sunday coat
　Son Andrew, tell me, pray."

"For strip'd perch in Wenham Lake
　I go to fish to-day."

"Unharmed of thee in Wenham Lake
　The mottled perch shall be:
A blue-eyed witch sits on the bank
　And weaves her net for thee.

"She weaves her golden hair; she sings
　Her spell-song low and faint;
The wickedest witch in Salem jail
　Is to that girl a saint."

"Nay, mother, hold thy cruel tongue;
　God knows," the young man cried,
"He never made a whiter soul
　Than hers by Wenham side.

"She tends her mother sick and blind,
　And every want supplies;
To her above the blessed Book
　She lends her soft blue eyes.

"Her voice is glad with holy songs,
　Her lips are sweet with prayer;
Go where you will, in ten miles round
　Is none more good and fair."

"Son Andrew, for the love of God
　And of thy mother, stay!"
She clasped her hands, she wept aloud,
　But Andrew rode away.

"O reverend sir, my Andrew's soul
　The Wenham witch has caught;
She holds him with the curl'd gold
　Whereof her snare is wrought.

"She charms him with her great blue
　　eyes,
　She binds him with her hair;
Oh, break the spell with holy words,
　Unbind him with a prayer!"

"Take heart," the painful preacher said,
　"This mischief shall not be;
The witch shall perish in her sins
　And Andrew shall go free.

"Our poor Ann Putnam testifies
　She saw her weave a spell,
Bare-armed, loose-haired, at full of moon,
　Around a dried-up well.

"'Spring up, O well!' she softly sang
　The Hebrew's old refrain

(For Satan uses Bible words),
  Till water flowed amain.

" And many a goodwife heard her speak
  By Wenham water words
That made the buttercups take wings
  And turn to yellow birds.

" They say that swarming wild bees seek
  The hive at her command :
And fishes swim to take their food
  From out her dainty hand.

"Meek as she sits in meeting-time,
  The godly minister
Notes well the spell that doth compel
  The young men's eyes to her.

" The mole upon her dimpled chin
  Is Satan's seal and sign ;
Her lips are red with evil bread
  And stain of unblest wine.

" For Tituba, my Indian, saith
  At Quasycung she took
The Black Man's godless sacrament
  And signed his dreadful book.

" Last night my sore-afflicted child
  Against the young witch cried.
To take her Marshal Herrick rides
  Even now to Wenham side."

The marshal in his saddle sat,
  His daughter at his knee ;
" I go to fetch that arrant witch,
  Thy fair playmate," quoth he.

" Her spectre walks the parsonage,
  And haunts both hall and stair ;
They know her by the great blue eyes
  And floating gold of hair."

" They lie, they lie, my father dear !
  No foul old witch is she,
But sweet and good and crystal-pure
  As Wenham waters be."

" I tell thee, child, the Lord hath set
  Before us good and ill,
And woe to all whose carnal loves
  Oppose his righteous will.

" Between Him and the powers of hell
  Choose thou, my child, to-day :
No sparing hand, no pitying eye,
  When God commands to slay ! "

He went his way ; the old wives shook
  With fear as he drew nigh ;
The children in the dooryards held
  Their breath as he passed by.

Too well they knew the gaunt gray horse
  The grim witch-hunter rode —
The pale Apocalyptic beast
  By grisly Death bestrode

II.

Oh, fair the face of Wenham Lake
  Upon the young girl's shone,
Her tender mouth, her dreaming ey
  Her yellow hair outblown.

By happy youth and love attuned
  To natural harmonies,
The singing birds, the whispering wind,
  She sat beneath the trees.

Sat shaping for her bridal dress
  Her mother's wedding gown,
When lo ! the marshal, writ in hand.
  From Alford hill rode down.

His face was hard with cruel fear,
  He grasped the maiden's hands :
" Come with me unto Salem town,
  For so the law commands ! "

" Oh, let me to my mother say
  Farewell before I go ! "
He closer tied her little hands
  Unto his saddle bow.

" Unhand me," cried she piteously,
  " For thy sweet daughter's sake."
" I 'll keep my daughter safe," he said,
  "From the witch of Wenham Lake."

" Oh, leave me for my mother's sake,
  She needs my eyes to see."
" Those eyes, young witch, the crows
    shall peck
  From off the gallows-tree."

He bore her to a farm-house old,
  And up its stairway long,
And closed on her the garret-door
  With iron bolted strong.

The day died out, the night came
    down :
  Her evening prayer she said,

While, through the dark, strange faces
        seemed
    To mock her as she prayed.

The present horror deepened all
    The fears her childhood knew ;
The awe wherewith the air was filled
    With every breath she drew.

And could it be, she trembling asked,
    Some secret thought or sin
Had shut good angels from her heart
    And let the bad ones in ?

Had she in some forgotten dream
    Let go her hold on Heaven,
And sold herself unwittingly
    To spirits unforgiven ?

Oh, weird and still the dark hours
        passed ;
    No human sound she heard,
But up and down the chimney stack
    The swallows moaned and stirred.

And o'er her, with a dread surmise
    Of evil sight and sound,
The blind bats on their leathern wings
    Went wheeling round and round.

Low hanging in the midnight sky
    Looked in a half-faced moon.
Was it a dream, or did she hear
    Her lover's whistled tune ?

She forced the oaken scuttle back ;
    A whisper reached her ear :
" Slide down the roof to me," it said,
    " So softly none may hear."

She slid along the sloping roof
    Till from its eaves she hung,
And felt the loosened shingles yield
    To which her fingers clung.

Below, her lover stretched his hands
    And touched her feet so small ;
" Drop down to me, dear heart," he said,
    " My arms shall break the fall."

He set her on his pillion soft,
    Her arms about him twined ;
And, noiseless as if velvet-shod,
    They left the house behind.

But when they reached the open way
    Full free the rein he cast ;

Oh, never through the mirk midnight
    Rode man and maid more fast.

Along the wild wood-paths they sped,
    The bridgeless streams they swam ;
At set of moon they passed the Bass,
    At sunrise Agawam.

At high noon on the Merrimac
    The ancient ferryman
Forgot, at times, his idle oars,
    So fair a freight to scan.

And when from off his grounded boat
    He saw them mount and ride,
" God keep her from the evil eye,
    And harm of witch ! " he cried.

The maiden laughed, as youth will
        laugh
    At all its fears gone by ;
" He does not know," she whispered low,
    " A little witch am I."

All day he urged his weary horse,
    And, in the red sundown,
Drew rein before a friendly door
    In distant Berwick town.

A fellow-feeling for the wronged
    The Quaker people felt ;
And safe beside their kindly hearths
    The hunted maiden dwelt,

Until from off its breast the land
    The haunting horror threw,
And hatred, born of ghastly dreams,
    To shame and pity grew.

Sad were the year's spring morns, and
        sad
    Its golden summer day,
But blithe and glad its withered fields,
    And skies of ashen gray ;

For spell and charm had power no more,
    The spectres ceased to roam,
And scattered households knelt again
    Around the hearths of home.

And when once more by Beaver Dam
    The meadow-lark outsang,
And once again on all the hills
    The early violets sprang,

And all the windy pasture slopes
    Lay green within the arms

Of creeks that bore the salted sea
  To pleasant inland farms,

The smith filed off the chains he forged,
  The jail-bolts backward fell ;
And youth and hoary age came forth
  Like souls escaped from hell.

SUNSET ON THE BEARCAMP.

A GOLD fringe on the purpling hem
  Of hills the river runs
As down its long, green valley falls
  The last of summer's suns.
Along its tawny gravel-bed
  Broad-flowing, swift, and still,
As if its meadow levels felt
  The hurry of the hill,
Noiseless between its banks of green
  From curve to curve it slips ;
The drowsy maple-shadows rest
  Like fingers on its lips.
A waif from Carroll's wildest hills,
  Unstoried and unknown ;
The ursine legend of its name
  Prowls on its banks alone,
Yet flowers as fair its slopes adorn
  As ever Yarrow knew,
Or, under rainy Irish skies,
  By Spenser's Mulla grew ;
And through the gaps of leaning trees
  Its mountain cradle shows :
The gold against the amethyst,
  The green against the rose.

Touched by a light that hath no name,
  A glory never sung,
Aloft on sky and mountain wall
  Are God's great pictures hung.
How changed the summits vast and old !
  No longer granite-browed,
They melt in rosy mist ; the rock
  Is softer than the cloud ;
The valley holds its breath ; no leaf
  Of all its elms is twirled :
The silence of eternity
  Seems falling on the world.

The pause before the breaking seals
  Of mystery is this ;
Yon miracle-play of night and day
  Makes dumb its witnesses.
What unseen altar crowns the hills
  That reach up stair on stair ?

What eyes look through, what white
    wings fan
  These purple veils of air ?
What Presence from the heavenly
    heights
  To those of earth stoops down ?
Not vainly Hellas dreamed of gods
  On Ida's snowy crown !

Slow fades the vision of the sky,
  The golden water pales,
And over all the valley-land
  A gray-winged vapor sails.
I go the common way of all ;
  The sunset fires will burn,
The flowers will blow, the river flow,
  When I no more return.
No whisper from the mountain pine
  Nor lapsing stream shall tell
The stranger, treading where I tread,
  Of him who loved them well.
But beauty seen is never lost,
  God's colors all are fast ;
The glory of this sunset heaven
  Into my soul has passed, —
A sense of gladness unconfined
  To mortal date or clime ;
As the soul liveth, it shall live
  Beyond the years of time.
Beside the mystic asphodels
  Shall bloom the home-born flowers,
And new horizons flush and glow
  With sunset hues of ours.

Farewell ! these smiling hills must wear
  Too soon their wintry frown,
And snow-cold winds from off them shake
  The maple's red leaves down.
But I shall see a summer sun
  Still setting broad and low ;
The mountain slopes shall blush and
    bloom,
  The golden water flow.
A lover's claim is mine on all
  I see to have and hold, —
The rose-light of perpetual hills,
  And sunsets never cold !

THE SEEKING OF THE WATER-
FALL.

THEY left their home of summer ease
Beneath the lowland's sheltering trees,
To seek, by ways unknown to all,
The promise of the waterfall.

"And still the water sang the sweet
Glad song." Page 405.

Some vague, faint rumor to the vale
Had crept — perchance a hunter's tale —
Of its wild mirth of waters lost
On the dark woods through which it
    tossed.

Somewhere it laughed and sang ; some-
    where
Whirled in mad dance its misty hair ;
But who had raised its veil, or seen
The rainbow skirts of that Undine ?

They sought it where the mountain brook
Its swift way to the valley took ;
Along the rugged slope they clomb,
Their guide a thread of sound and foam.

Height after height they slowly won ;
The fiery javelins of the sun
Smote the bare ledge ; the tangled shade
With rock and vine their steps delayed.

But, through leaf-openings, now and
    then
They saw the cheerful homes of men,
And the great mountains with their wall
Of misty purple girdling all.

The leaves through which the glad winds
    blew
Shared the wild dance the waters knew ;
And where the shadows deepest fell
The wood-thrush rang his silver bell.

Fringing the stream, at every turn
Swung low the waving fronds of fern ;
From stony cleft and mossy sod
Pale asters sprang, and golden-rod.

And still the water sang the sweet,
Glad song that stirred its gliding feet,
And found in rock and root the keys
Of its beguiling melodies.

Beyond, above, its signals flew
Of tossing foam the birch-trees through ;
Now seen, now lost, but baffling still
The weary seekers' slackening will.

Each called to each : " Lo here ! Lo
    there !
Its white scarf flutters in the air ! "
They climbed anew ; the vision fled,
To beckon higher overhead.

So toiled they up the mountain-slope
With faint and ever fainter hope ;

With faint and fainter voice the brook
Still bade them listen, pause, and look.

Meanwhile below the day was done ;
Above the tall peaks saw the sun
Sink, beam-shorn, to its misty set
Behind the hills of violet.

" Here ends our quest ! " the seekers
    cried,
" The brook and rumor both have lied !
The phantom of a waterfall
Has led us at its beck and call."

But one, with years grown wiser, said :
" So, always baffled, not misled,
We follow where before us runs
The vision of the shining ones.

" Not where they seem their signals fly,
Their voices while we listen die ;
We cannot keep, however fleet,
The quick time of their wingèd feet.

" From youth to age unresting stray
These kindly mockers in our way ;
Yet lead they not, the baffling elves,
To something better than themselves ?

" Here, though unreached the goal we
    sought,
Its own reward our toil has brought :
The winding water's sounding rush,
The long note of the hermit thrush,

" The turquoise lakes, the glimpse of
    pond
And river track, and, vast, beyond
Broad meadows belted round with pines,
The grand uplift of mountain lines !

" What matter though we seek with pain
The garden of the gods in vain,
If lured thereby we climb to greet
Some wayside blossom Eden-sweet ?

" To seek is better than to gain,
The fond hope dies as we attain ;
Life's fairest things are those which seem,
The best is that of which we dream.

" Then let us trust our waterfall
Still flashes down its rocky wall,
With rainbow crescent curved across
Its sunlit spray from moss to moss.

"And we, forgetful of our pain,
In thought shall seek it oft again ;
Shall see this aster-blossomed sod,
This sunshine of the golden-rod,

"And haply gain, through parting
      boughs,
Grand glimpses of great mountain brows
Cloud-turbaned, and the sharp steel sheen
Of lakes deep set in valleys green.

"So failure wins ; the consequence
Of loss becomes its recompense ;
And evermore the end shall tell
The unreached ideal guided well.

"Our sweet illusions only die
Fulfilling love's sure prophecy ;
And every wish for better things
An undreamed beauty nearer brings.

"For fate is servitor of love ;
Desire and hope and longing prove
The secret of immortal youth,
And Nature cheats us into truth.

"O kind allurers, wisely sent,
Beguiling with benign intent,
Still move us, through divine unrest,
To seek the loveliest and the best !

"Go with us when our souls go free,
And, in the clear, white light to be,
Add unto Heaven's beatitude
The old delight of seeking good ! "

JUNE ON THE MERRIMAC.

O DWELLERS in the stately towns,
    What come ye out to see ?
This common earth, this common sky,
    This water flowing free ?

As gayly as these kalmia flowers
    Your door-yard blossoms spring ;
As sweetly as these wild wood birds
    Your caged minstrels sing.

You find but common bloom and green,
    The rippling river's rune,
The beauty which is everywhere
    Beneath the skies of June ;

The Hawkswood oaks, the storm-torn
        plumes
    Of old pine-forest kings,

Beneath whose century-woven shade
    Deer Island's mistress sings.

And here are pictured Artichoke,
    And Curson's bowery mill ;
And Pleasant Valley smiles between
    The river and the hill.

You know full well these banks of bloom,
    The upland's wavy line,
And how the sunshine tips with fire
    The needles of the pine.

Yet, like some old remembered psalm,
    Or sweet, familiar face,
Not less because of commonness
    You love the day and place.

And not in vain in this soft air
    Shall hard-strung nerves relax,
Not all in vain the o'erworn brain
    Forego its daily tax.

The lust of power, the greed of gain
    Have all the year their own ;
The haunting demons well may let
    Our one bright day alone.

Unheeded let the newsboy call,
    Aside the ledger lay :
The world will keep its tread-mill step
    Though we fall out to-day.

The truants of life's weary school,
    Without excuse from thrift
We change for once the gains of toil
    For God's unpurchased gift.

From ceilèd rooms, from silent books,
    From crowded car and town,
Dear Mother Earth, upon thy lap,
    We lay our tired heads down.

Cool, summer wind, our heated brows ;
    Blue river, through the green
Of clustering pines, refresh the eyes
    Which all too much have seen.

For us these pleasant woodland ways
    Are thronged with memories old,
Have felt the grasp of friendly hands
    And heard love's story told.

A sacred presence overbroods
    The earth whereon we meet ;
These winding forest-paths are trod
    By more than mortal feet

Old friends called from us by the voice
  Which they alone could hear,
From mystery to mystery,
  From life to life, draw near.

More closely for the sake of them
  Each other's hands we press ;
Our voices take from them a tone
  Of deeper tenderness.

Our joy is theirs, their trust is ours,
  Alike below, above,
Or here or there, about us fold
  The arms of one great love !

We ask to-day no countersign,
  No party names we own ;
Unlabelled, individual,
  We bring ourselves alone.

What cares the unconventioned wood
  For pass-words of the town ?
The sound of fashion's shibboleth
  The laughing waters drown.

Here cant forgets his dreary tone,
  And care his face forlorn ;
The liberal air and sunshine laugh
  The bigot's zeal to scorn.

From manhood's weary shoulder falls
  His load of selfish cares ;
And woman takes her rights as flowers
  And brooks and birds take theirs.

The license of the happy woods,
  The brook's release are ours ;
The freedom of the unshamed wind
  Among the glad-eyed flowers.

Yet here no evil thought finds place,
  Nor foot profane comes in ;
Our grove, like that of Samothrace,
  Is set apart from sin.

We walk on holy ground ; above
  A sky more holy smiles ;
The chant of the beatitudes
  Swells down these leafy aisles.

Thanks to the gracious Providence
  That brings us here once more ;
For memories of the good behind
  And hopes of good before !

And if, unknown to us, sweet days
  Of June like this must come,

Unseen of us these laurels clothe
  The river-banks, with bloom ;

And these green paths must soon be trod
  By other feet than ours,
Full long may annual pilgrims come
  To keep the Feast of Flowers ;

The matron be a girl once more,
  The bearded man a boy,
And we, in heaven's eternal June,
  Be glad for earthly joy !

HYMN OF THE DUNKERS.

KLOSTER KEDAR, EPHRATA, PENNSYL-
VANIA (1738).

SISTER MARIA CHRISTIANA *sings.*

WAKE, sisters, wake ! the day-star shine
Above Ephrata's eastern pines
The dawn is breaking, cool and calm.
Wake, sisters, wake to prayer and psalm

Praised be the Lord for shade and light
For toil by day, for rest by night !
Praised be His name who deigns to bless
Our Kedar of the wilderness ! —

Our refuge when the spoiler's hand
Was heavy on our native land ;
And freedom, to her children due,
The wolf and vulture only knew.

We praised Him when to prison led,
We owned Him when the stake blazed
  red ;
We knew, whatever might befall,
His love and power were over all.

He heard our prayers ; with outstretched
  arm
He led us forth from cruel harm ;
Still, wheresoe'er our steps were bent,
His cloud and fire before us went !

The watch of faith and prayer He set,
We kept it then, we keep it yet.
At midnight, crow of cock, or noon,
He cometh sure, He cometh soon.

He comes to chasten, not destroy,
To purge the earth from sin's alloy.
At last, at last shall all confess
His mercy as His righteousness.

The dead shall live, the sick be whole,
The scarlet sin be white as wool ;
No discord mar below, above,
The music of eternal love !

Sound, welcome trump, the last alarm !
Lord God of hosts, make bare thine arm,
Fulfil this day our long desire,
Make sweet and clean the world with fire !

Sweep, flaming besom, sweep from sight
The lies of time ; be swift to smite,
Sharp sword of God, all idols down,
Genevan creed and Roman crown.

Quake, earth, through all thy zones, till
    all
The fanes of pride and priestcraft fall ;
And lift thou up in place of them
Thy gates of pearl, Jerusalem !

Lo ! rising from baptismal flame,
Transfigured, glorious, yet the same,
Within the heavenly city's bound
Our Kloster Kedar shall be found.

He cometh soon ! at dawn or noon
Or set of sun, He cometh soon.
Our prayers shall meet Him on his way ;
Wake, sisters, wake ! arise and pray !

IN THE " OLD SOUTH."

1677.

SHE came and stood in the Old South
    Church,
    A wonder and a sign,
With a look the old-time sibyls wore,
    Half-crazed and half-divine.

Save the mournful sackcloth about her
    wound
Unclothed as the primal mother,
With limbs that trembled and eyes that
    blazed
With a fire she dared not smother.

Loose on her shoulders fell her hair
    With sprinkled ashes gray,
She stood in the broad aisle strange and
    weird
As a soul at the judgment day.

And the minister paused in his sermon's
    midst,
    And the people held their breath,
For these were the words the maiden
    spoke
    Through lips as pale as death :

" Thus saith the Lord, with equal feet
    All men my courts shall tread,
And priest and ruler no more shall eat
    My people up like bread !

" Repent ! repent ! ere the Lord shall
    speak
    In thunder and breaking seals !
Let all souls worship Him in the way
    His light within reveals."

She shook the dust from her naked feet,
    And her sackcloth closer drew,
And into the porch of the awe-hushed
    church
    She passed like a ghost from view.

They whipped her away at the tail o' the
    cart
    Through half the streets of the town,
But the words she uttered that day nor
    fire
    Could burn nor water drown.

And now the aisles of the ancient church
    By equal feet are trod,
And the bell that swings in its belfry
    rings
    Freedom to worship God !

And now whenever a wrong is done
    It thrills the conscious walls ;
The stone from the basement cries aloud
    And the beam from the timber calls.

There are steeple-houses on every hand,
    And pulpits that bless and ban,
And the Lord will not grudge the single
    church
    That is set apart for man.

For in two commandments are all the law
    And the prophets under the sun,
And the first is last and the last is first.
    And the twain are verily one.

So, long as Boston shall Boston be,
    And her bay-tides rise and fall,
Shall freedom stand in the Old South
    Church
    And plead for the rights of all !

LEXINGTON.

1775.

No Berserk thirst of blood had they,
　No battle-joy was theirs, who set
　Against the alien bayonet
Their homespun breasts in that old day.

Their feet had trodden peaceful ways ;
　They loved not strife, they dreaded
　　pain ;
　They saw not, what to us is plain,
That God would make man's wrath his
　　praise.

No seers were they, but simple men ;
　Its vast results the future hid :
　The meaning of the work they did
Was strange and dark and doubtful then.

Swift as their summons came they left
　The plow mid-furrow standing still,
　The half-ground corn grist in the mill,
The spade in earth, the axe in cleft.

They went where duty seemed to call,
　They scarcely asked the reason why ;
　They only knew they could but die,
And death was not the worst of all !

Of man for man the sacrifice,
　All that was theirs to give, they gave.
　The flowers that blossomed from their
　　grave
Have sown themselves beneath all skies.

Their death-shot shook the feudal tower,
　And shattered slavery's chain as well ;
　On the sky's dome, as on a bell,
Its echo struck the world's great hour.

That fateful echo is not dumb :
　The nations listening to its sound
　Wait, from a century's vantage-ground,
The holier triumphs yet to come, —

The bridal time of Law and Love,
　The gladness of the world's release,
　When, war-sick, at the feet of Peace
The hawk shall nestle with the dove ! —

The golden age of brotherhood
　Unknown to other rivalries
　Than of the mild humanities,
And gracious interchange of good,

When closer strand shall lean to strand,
　Till meet, beneath saluting flags,
　The eagle of our mountain-crags,
The lion of our Motherland !

CENTENNIAL HYMN.

I.

OUR fathers' God ! from out whose hand
The centuries fall like grains of sand,
We meet to-day, united, free,
And loyal to our land and Thee,
To thank Thee for the era done,
And trust Thee for the opening one.

II.

Here, where of old, by Thy design,
The fathers spake that word of Thine
Whose echo is the glad refrain
Of rended bolt and falling chain,
To grace our festal time, from all
The zones of earth our guests we call.

III.

Be with us while the New World greets
The Old World thronging all its streets,
Unveiling all the triumphs won
By art or toil beneath the sun ;
And unto common good ordain
This rivalship of hand and brain.

IV.

Thou, who hast here in concord furled
The war flags of a gathered world,
Beneath our Western skies fulfil
The Orient's mission of good-will,
And, freighted with love's Golden Fleece,
Send back its Argonauts of peace.

V.

For art and labor met in truce,
For beauty made the bride of use,
We thank Thee ; but, withal, we crave
The austere virtues strong to save,
The honor proof to place or gold,
The manhood never bought nor sold !

VI.

Oh make Thou us, through centuries
　long,
In peace secure, in justice strong ;
Around our gift of freedom draw
The safeguards of Thy righteous law :
And, cast in some diviner mould,
Let the new cycle shame the old !

THIERS.

I.

Fate summoned, in gray-bearded age,
  to act
A history stranger than his written fact,
  Him who portrayed the splendor and
  the gloom
Of that great hour when throne and altar
  fell
With long death-groan which still is
  audible.
  He, when around the walls of Paris
  rung
  The Prussian bugle like the blast of
  doom,
And every ill which follows unblest war
Maddened all France from Finistère to
  Var,
  The weight of fourscore from his
  shoulders flung,
And guided Freedom in the path he saw
Lead out of chaos into light and law,
Peace, not imperial, but republican,
And order pledged to all the Rights of
  Man.

II.

Death called him from a need as immi-
  nent
As that from which the Silent William
  went
When powers of evil, like the smiting
  seas
On Holland's dikes, assailed her liberties.
Sadly, while yet in doubtful balance hung
The weal and woe of France, the bells
  were rung
For her lost leader.   Paralyzed of will,
Above his bier the hearts of men stood
  still.
Then, as if set to his dead lips, the horn
Of Roland wound once more to rouse and
  warn,
The old voice filled the air !   His last
  brave word
Not vainly France to all her boundaries
  stirred.
Strong as in life, he still for Freedom
  wrought,
As the dead Cid at red Toloso fought.

FITZ-GREENE HALLECK.

AT THE UNVEILING OF HIS STATUE.

Among their graven shapes to whom
  Thy civic wreaths belong,
O city of his love, make room
  For one whose gift was song.

Not his the soldier's sword to wield,
  Nor his the helm of state,
Nor glory of the stricken field,
  Nor triumph of debate.

In common ways, with common men,
  He served his race and time
As well as if his clerkly pen
  Had never danced to rhyme.

If, in the thronged and noisy mart,
  The Muses found their son,
Could any say his tuneful art
  A duty left undone ?

He toiled and sang; and year by year
  Men found their homes more sweet,
And through a tenderer atmosphere
  Looked down the brick-walled street.

The Greek's wild onset Wall Street
  knew ;
  The Red King walked Broadway ;
And Alnwick Castle's roses blew
  From Palisades to Bay.

Fair City by the Sea ! upraise
  His veil with reverent hands ;
And mingle with thy own the praise
  And pride of other lands.

Let Greece his fiery lyric breathe
  Above her hero-urns ;
And Scotland, with her holly, wreathe
  The flower he culled for Burns.

O, stately stand thy palace walls,
  Thy tall ships ride the seas ;
To-day thy poet's name recalls
  A prouder thought than these.

Not less thy pulse of trade shall beat,
  Nor less thy tall fleets swim,
That shaded square and dusty street
  Are classic ground through him.

Alive, he loved, like all who sing,
  The echoes of his song ;
Too late the tardy meed we bring,
  The praise delayed so long.

Too late, alas ! Of all who knew
  The living man, to-day
Before his unveiled face, how few
  Make bare their locks of gray !

Our lips of praise must soon be dumb,
  Our grateful eyes be dim ;
O brothers of the days to come,
  Take tender charge of him !

New hands the wires of song may sweep,
  New voices challenge fame ;
But let no moss of years o'ercreep
  The lines of Halleck's name.

WILLIAM FRANCIS BARTLETT.

O, WELL may Essex sit forlorn
  Beside her sea-blown shore ;
Her well beloved, her noblest born,
  Is hers in life no more !

No lapse of years can render less
  Her memory's sacred claim ;
No fountain of forgetfulness
  Can wet the lips of Fame.

A grief alike to wound and heal,
  A thought to soothe and pain,
The sad, sweet pride that mothers feel
  To her must still remain.

Good men and true she has not lacked,
  And brave men yet shall be ;
The perfect flower, the crowning fact,
  Of all her years was he !

As Galahad pure, as Merlin sage,
  What worthier knight was found
To grace in Arthur's golden age
  The fabled Table Round ?

A voice, the battle's trumpet-note,
  To welcome and restore ;
A hand, that all unwilling smote,
  To heal and build once more !

A soul of fire, a tender heart
  Too warm for hate, he knew

The generous victor's graceful part
  To sheathe the sword he drew.

When Earth, as if on evil dreams,
  Looks back upon her wars,
And the white light of Christ outstreams
  From the red disk of Mars,

His fame who led the stormy van
  Of battle well may cease,
But never that which crowns the man
  Whose victory was Peace.

Mourn, Essex, on thy sea-blown shore
  Thy beautiful and brave,
Whose failing hand the olive bore,
  Whose dying lips forgave !

Let age lament the youthful chief,
  And tender eyes be dim ;
The tears are more of joy than grief
  That fall for one like him !

THE TWO ANGELS.

GOD called the nearest angels who dwell
  with Him above :
The tenderest one was Pity, the dearest
  one was Love.

" Arise," He said, " my angels ! a wail
  of woe and sin
Steals through the gates of heaven, and
  saddens all within.

" My harps take up the mournful strain
  that from a lost world swells,
The smoke of torment clouds the light
  and blights the asphodels.

" Fly downward to that under world,
  and on its souls of pain
Let Love drop smiles like sunshine, and
  Pity tears like rain ! "

Two faces bowed before the Throne, veiled
  in their golden hair ;
Four white wings lessened swiftly down
  the dark abyss of air.

The way was strange, the flight was
  long ; at last the angels came
Where swung the lost and nether world,
  red-wrapped in rayless flame.

There Pity, shuddering, wept; but Love,
  with faith too strong for fear,
Took heart from God's almightiness and
  smiled a smile of cheer.

And lo ! that tear of Pity quenched the
  flame whereon it fell,
And, with the sunshine of that smile,
  hope entered into hell !

Two unveiled faces full of joy looked up-
  ward to the Throne,
Four white wings folded at the feet of
  Him who sat thereon !

And deeper than the sound of seas, more
  soft than falling flake,
Amidst the hush of wing and song the
  Voice Eternal spake :

"Welcome, my angels ! ye have brought
  a holier joy to heaven ;
Henceforth its sweetest song shall be the
  song of sin forgiven !"

THE LIBRARY.

SUNG AT THE OPENING OF THE HAVER-
HILL LIBRARY.

"LET THERE BE LIGHT !" God spake of
  old,
And over chaos dark and cold,
And, through the dead and formless
  frame
Of nature, life and order came.

Faint was the light at first that shone
On giant fern and mastodon,
On half-formed plant and beast of prey,
And man as rude and wild as they.

Age after age, like waves, o'erran
The earth, uplifting brute and man ;
And mind, at length, in symbols dark
Its meanings traced on stone and bark.

On leaf of palm, on sedge-wrought roll,
On plastic clay and leathern scroll,
Man wrote his thoughts ; the ages passed,
And lo ! the Press was found at last !

Then dead souls woke ; the thoughts of
  men
Whose bones were dust revived again ;

The cloister's silence found a tongue,
Old prophets spake, old poets sung.

And here, to-day, the dead look down
The kings of mind again we crown ;
We hear the voices lost so long,
The sage's word, the sibyl's song.

Here Greek and Roman find themselves
Alive along these crowded shelves ;
And Shakespeare treads again his stage,
And Chaucer paints anew his age.

As if some Pantheon's marbles broke
Their stony trance, and lived and spoke,
Life thrills along the alcoved hall,
The lords of thought await our call !

THE HENCHMAN.

MY lady walks her morning round,
My lady's page her fleet greyhound
My lady's hair the fond winds stir,
And all the birds make songs for her.

Her thrushes sing in Rathburn bowers,
And Rathburn side is gay with flowers ;
But ne'er like hers, in flower or bird,
Was beauty seen or music heard.

The distance of the stars is hers ;
The least of all her worshippers,
The dust beneath her dainty heel,
She knows not that I see or feel.

O proud and calm ! — she cannot know
Where'er she goes with her I go ;
O cold and fair ! — she cannot guess
I kneel to share her hound's caress !

Gay knights beside her hunt and hawk,
I rob their ears of her sweet talk ;
Her suitors come from east and west,
I steal her smiles from every guest.

Unheard of her, in loving words,
I greet her with the song of birds ;
I reach her with her green-armed bowers,
I kiss her with the lips of flowers.

The hound and I are on her trail,
The wind and I uplift her veil ;
As if the calm, cold moon she were,
And I the tide, I follow her.

As unrebuked as they, I share
The license of the sun and air,
And in a common homage hide
My worship from her scorn and pride.

World-wide apart, and yet so near,
I breathe her charmèd atmosphere,
Wherein to her my service brings
The reverence due to holy things.

Wer maiden pride, her haughty name,
My dumb devotion shall not shame ;
The love that no return doth crave
To knightly levels lifts the slave.

No lance have I, in joust or fight,
To splinter in my lady's sight ;
But, at her feet, how blest were I
For any need of hers to die !

KING SOLOMON AND THE ANTS.

OUT from Jerusalem
  The king rode with his great
  War chiefs and lords of state,
And Sheba's queen with them,

Comely, but black withal,
  To whom, perchance, belongs
  That wondrous Song of songs,
Sensuous and mystical,

Whereto devout souls turn
  In fond, ecstatic dream,
  And through its earth-born theme
The Love of loves discern.

Proud in the Syrian sun,
  In gold and purple sheen,
  The dusky Ethiop queen
Smiled on King Solomon.

Wisest of men, he knew
  The languages of all
  The creatures great or small
That trod the earth or flew.

Across an ant-hill led
  The king's path, and he heard
  Its small folk, and their word
He thus interpreted :

"Here comes the king men greet
  As wise and good and just,

To crush us in the dust
Under his heedless feet."

The great king bowed his head,
  And saw the wide surprise
  Of the Queen of Sheba's eyes
As he told her what they said.

"O king !" she whispered sweet,
  "Too happy fate have they
  Who perish in thy way
Beneath thy gracious feet !

"Thou of the God-lent crown,
  Shall these vile creatures dare
  Murmur against thee where
The knees of kings kneel down ?"

"Nay," Solomon replied, .
  "The wise and strong should seek
  The welfare of the weak,"
And turned his horse aside.

His train, with quick alarm,
  Curved with their leader round
  The ant-hill's peopled mound,
And left it free from harm.

The jewelled head bent low ;
  "O king !" she said, "henceforth
  The secret of thy worth
And wisdom well I know.

"Happy must be the State
  Whose ruler heedeth more
  The murmurs of the poor
Than flatteries of the great."

RED RIDING-HOOD.

ON the wide lawn the snow lay deep,
Ridged o'er with many a drifted heap ;
The wind that through the pine-trees
    sung
The naked elm-boughs tossed and
    swung ;
While, through the window, frosty-
    starred,
Against the sunset purple barred,
We saw the sombre crow flap by,
The hawk's gray fleck along the sky,
The crested blue-jay flitting swift,
The squirrel poising on the drift,
Erect, alert, his broad gray tail
Set to the north wind like a sail.

It came to pass, our little lass,
With flattened face against the glass,
And eyes in which the tender dew
Of pity shone, stood gazing through
The narrow space her rosy lips
Had melted from the frost's eclipse :
" Oh, see," she cried, " the poor blue-
        jays !
What is it that the black crow says ?
The squirrel lifts his little legs
Because he has no hands, and begs ;
He 's asking for my nuts, I know :
May I not feed them on the snow ? "

Half lost within her boots, her head
Warm-sheltered in her hood of red,
Her plaid skirt close about her drawn,
She floundered down the wintry lawn ;
Now struggling through the misty veil
Blown round her by the shrieking gale ;
Now sinking in a drift so low
Her scarlet hood could scarcely show
Its dash of color on the snow.

She dropped for bird and beast forlorn
Her little store of nuts and corn,
And thus her timid guests bespoke :
" Come, squirrel, from your hollow
        oak, —
Come, black old crow, — come, poor
        blue-jay,
Before your supper 's blown away !
Don't be afraid, we all are good ;
And I 'm mamma's Red Riding-Hood ! "

O Thou whose care is over all,
Who heedest even the sparrow's fall,
Keep in the little maiden's breast
The pity which is now its guest !
Let not her cultured years make less
The childhood charm of tenderness,
But let her feel as well as know,
Nor harder with her polish grow !
Unmoved by sentimental grief
That wails along some printed leaf,
But, prompt with kindly word and deed
To own the claims of all who need,
Let the grown woman's self make good
The promise of Red Riding-Hood !

THE PRESSED GENTIAN.

THE time of gifts has come again,
And, on my northern window-pane,
Outlined against the day's brief light,

A Christmas token hangs in sight.
The wayside travellers, as they pass,
Mark the gray disk of clouded glass ;
And the dull blankness seems, perchance,
Folly to their wise ignorance.

They cannot from their outlook see
The perfect grace it hath for me ;
For there the flower, whose fringes
        through
The frosty breath of autumn blew,
Turns from without its face of bloom
To the warm tropic of my room,
As fair as when beside its brook
The hue of bending skies it took.

So from the trodden ways of earth,
Seem some sweet souls who veil their
        worth,
And offer to the careless glance
The clouding gray of circumstance.
They blossom best where hearth-fires
        burn,
To loving eyes alone they turn
The flowers of inward grace, that hide
Their beauty from the world outside.

But deeper meanings come to me,
My half-immortal flower, from thee !
Man judges from a partial view,
None ever yet his brother knew ;
The Eternal Eye that sees the whole
May better read the darkened soul,
And find, to outward sense denied,
The flower upon its inmost side !

OVERRULED.

THE threads our hands in blindness spin
No self-determined plan weaves in ;
The shuttle of the unseen powers
Works out a pattern not as ours.

Ah ! small the choice of him who sings
What sound shall leave the smitten
        strings ;
Fate holds and guides the hand of art ;
The singer's is the servant's part.

The wind-harp chooses not the tone
That through its trembling threads is
        blown ;
The patient organ cannot guess
What hand its passive keys shall press.

Through wish, resolve, and act, our will
Is moved by undreamed forces still ;
And no man measures in advance
His strength with untried circumstance.

As streams take hue from shade and sun,
As runs the life the song must run ;
But, glad or sad, to his good end
God grant the varying notes may tend !

HYMN.

SUNG AT THE ANNIVERSARY OF THE
CHILDREN'S MISSION, BOSTON (1878).

THINE are all the gifts, O God !
  Thine the broken bread ;
Let the naked feet be shod,
  And the starving fed.

Let Thy children, by Thy grace,
  Give as they abound,
Till the poor have breathing-space,
  And the lost are found.

Wiser than the miser's hoards
  Is the giver's choice ;
Sweeter than the song of birds
  Is the thankful voice.

Welcome smiles on faces sad
  As the flowers of spring ;
Let the tender hearts be glad
  With the joy they bring.

Happier for their pity's sake
  Make their sports and plays,
And from lips of childhood take
  Thy perfected praise !

GIVING AND TAKING.[1]

WHO gives and hides the giving hand,
  Nor counts on favor, fame, or praise,
  Shall find his smallest gift outweighs
The burden of the sea and land.

Who gives to whom hath naught been
    given,
  His gift in need, though small indeed

[1] I have attempted to put in English verse a
prose translation of a poem by Tinnevaluva, a
Hindoo poet of the third century of our era.

As is the grass-blade's wind-blown seed,
Is large as earth and rich as heaven.

Forget it not, O man, to whom
  A gift shall fall, while yet on earth ;
  Yea, even to thy seven-fold birth
Recall it in the lives to come.

Who broods above a wrong in thought
  Sins much ; but greater sin is his
  Who, fed and clothed with kindnesses,
Shall count the holy alms as nought.

Who dares to curse the hands that bless
  Shall know of sin the deadliest cost ;
  The patience of the heavens is lost
Beholding man's unthankfulness.

For he who breaks all laws may still
  In Sivam's mercy be forgiven ;
  But none can save, in earth or heaven,
The wretch who answers good with ill.

"I WAS A STRANGER, AND YE TOOK ME IN."

'NEATH skies that winter never knew
  The air was full of light and balm,
And warm and soft the Gulf wind blew
    Through orange bloom and groves of
      palm.

A stranger from the frozen North,
  Who sought the fount of health in
    vain,
Sank homeless on the alien earth,
  And breathed the languid air with
    pain.

God's angel came ! The tender shade
  Of pity made her blue eye dim ;
Against her woman's breast she laid
  The drooping, fainting head of him.

She bore him to a pleasant room,
  Flower-sweet and cool with salt sea air,
And watched beside his bed, for whom
  His far-off sisters might not care.

She fanned his feverish brow and
    smoothed
  Its lines of pain with tenderest touch.
With holy hymn and prayer she soothed
  The trembling soul that feared so much.

Through her the peace that passeth sight
  Came to him, as he lapsed away
As one whose troubled dreams of night
  Slide slowly into tranquil day.

The sweetness of the Land of Flowers
  Upon his lonely grave she laid :
The jasmine dropped its golden showers,
  The orange lent its bloom and shade.

And something whispered in her thought,
  More sweet than mortal voices be :
" The service thou for him hast wrought
  O daughter ! hath been done for me."

AT SCHOOL—CLOSE.

BOWDOIN STREET (1877).

THE end has come, as come it must
  To all things ; in these sweet June days
The teacher and the scholar trust
  Their parting feet to separate ways.

They part : but in the years to be
  Shall pleasant memories cling to each,
As shells bear inland from the sea
  The murmur of the rhythmic beach.

One knew the joy the sculptor knows
  When, plastic to his lightest touch,
His clay-wrought model slowly grows
  To that fine grace desired so much.

So daily grew before her eyes
  The living shapes whereon she
    wrought,
Strong, tender, innocently wise,
  The child's heart with the woman's
    thought.

And one shall never quite forget
  The voice that called from dream and
    play,
The firm but kindly hand that set
  Her feet in learning's pleasant way, —

The joy of Undine soul-possessed,
  The wakening sense, the strange de-
    light
That swelled the fabled statue's breast
  And filled its clouded eyes with sight !

O Youth and Beauty, loved of all !
  Ye pass from girlhood's gate of dreams ;

In broader ways your footsteps fall,
  Ye test the truth of all that seems.

Her little realm the teacher leaves,
  She breaks her wand of power apart,
While, for your love and trust, she gives
  The warm thanks of a grateful heart.

Hers is the sober summer noon
  Contrasted with your morn of spring ,
The waning with the waxing moon,
  The folded with the outspread wing.

Across the distance of the years
  She sends her God-speed back to you ;
She has no thought of doubts or fears :
  Be but yourselves, be pure, be true,

And prompt in duty ; heed the deep,
  Low voice of conscience ; through the
    ill
And discord round about you, keep
  Your faith in human nature still.

Be gentle : unto griefs and needs,
  Be pitiful as woman should,
And, spite of all the lies of creeds,
  Hold fast the truth that God is good.

Give and receive ; go forth and bless
  The world that needs the hand and
    heart
Of Martha's helpful carefulness
  No less than Mary's better part.

So shall the stream of time flow by
  And leave each year a richer good,
And matron loveliness outvie
  The nameless charm of maidenhood.

And, when the world shall link your
    names
  With gracious lives and manners fine,
The teacher shall assert her claims,
  And proudly whisper, "These were
    mine ! "

AT EVENTIDE.

POOR and inadequate the shadow-play
  Of gain and loss, of waking and of
    dream,
  Against life's solemn background needs
    must seem
At this late hour.   Yet, not unthank-
  fully,

I call to mind the fountains by the way,
The breath of flowers, the bird-song on
the spray,
Dear friends, sweet human loves, the joy
of giving
And of receiving, the great boon of living
In grand historic years when Liberty
Had need of word and work, quick sym-
pathies
For all who fail and suffer, song's relief,
Nature's uncloying loveliness ; and chief,
The kind restraining hand of Provi-
dence,
The inward witness, the assuring sense
Of an Eternal Good which overlies
The sorrow of the world, Love which out-
lives
All sin and wrong, Compassion which
forgives
To the uttermost, and Justice whose clear
eyes
Through lapse and failure look to the
intent,
And judge our frailty by the life we
meant.

II.

And well for Gain if it ungrudging yields
Labor its just demand ; and well for
Ease
If in the uses of its own, it sees
No wrong to him who tills its pleasant
fields
And spreads the table of its luxuries.
The interests of the rich man and the
poor
Are one and same, inseparable evermore ;
And, when scant wage or labor fail to
give
Food, shelter, raiment, wherewithal to
live,
Need has its rights, necessity its claim.
Yea, even self-wrought misery and shame
Test well the charity suffering long and
kind.
The home-pressed question of the age can
find
No answer in the catch-words of the blind
Leaders of blind.   Solution there is none
Save in the Golden Rule of Christ alone.

THE PROBLEM.

I.

Not without envy Wealth at times must
look
On their brown strength who wield the
reaping-hook
And scythe, or at the forge-fire shape
the plow
Or the steel harness of the steeds of
steam ; —
All who, by skill and patience, anyhow
Make service noble, and the earth redeem
From savageness.   By kingly accolade
Than theirs was never worthier knight-
hood made.
Well for them, if, while demagogues
their vain
And evil counsels proffer, they maintain
Their honest manhood unseduced, and
wage
No war with Labor's right to Labor's gain
Of sweet home-comfort, rest of hand and
brain,
And softer pillow for the head of Age.

RESPONSE.

1877.

Beside that milestone where the level
sun,
Nigh unto setting, sheds his last, low
rays
On word and work irrevocably done,
Life's blending threads of good and ill
outspun,
I hear, O friends ! your words of cheer
and praise,
Half doubtful if myself or otherwise.
Like him who, in the old Arabian joke,
A beggar slept and crowned Caliph
woke.
Thanks not the less.   With not unglad
surprise
I see my life-work through your partial
eyes ;
Assured, in giving to my home-taught
songs
A higher value than of right belongs,
You do but read between the written
lines
The finer grace of unfulfilled designs.

THE KING'S MISSIVE,

AND OTHER POEMS.

THE PRELUDE.

I SPREAD a scanty board too late ;
The old-time guests for whom I wait
   Come few and slow, methinks, to-day.
Ah ! who could hear my messages
Across the dim unsounded seas
   On which so many have sailed away !

Come, then, old friends, who linger yet,
And let us meet, as we have met,
   Once more beneath this low sunshine ;
And grateful for the good we 've known,
The riddles solved, the ills outgrown,
   Shake hands upon the border line.

The favor, asked too oft before,
From your indulgent ears, once more
   I crave, and, if belated lays
To slower, feebler measures move,
The silent sympathy of love
   To me is dearer now than praise.

And ye, O younger friends, for whom
My hearth and heart keep open room,
   Come smiling through the shadows
     long,
Be with me while the sun goes down,
And with your cheerful voices drown
   The minor of my even-song.

For, equal through the day and night,
The wise Eternal oversight
   And love and power and righteous
     will
Remain : the law of destiny
The best for each and all must be,
   And life its promise shall fulfil.

THE KING'S MISSIVE.[81]

1661.

UNDER the great hill sloping bare
   To cove and meadow and Common
     lot,
In his council chamber and oaken chair,
   Sat the worshipful Governor Endi-
     cott.
A grave, strong man, who knew no peer
In the pilgrim land, where he ruled in
     fear
Of God, not man, and for good or ill
Held his trust with an iron will.

He had shorn with his sword the cross
     from out
   The flag, and cloven the May-pole
     down,
Harried the heathen round about,
   And whipped the Quakers from town
     to town.
Earnest and honest, a man at need
To burn like a torch for his own harsh
     creed,
He kept with the flaming brand of his
     zeal
The gate of the holy common weal.

His brow was clouded, his eye was
     stern,
   With a look of mingled sorrow and
     wrath ;
" Woe 's me ! " he murmured : " at every
     turn
   The pestilent Quakers are in my path !
Some we have scourged, and banished
     some,
Some hanged, more doomed, and still
     they come,
Fast as the tide of yon bay sets in,
Sowing their heresy's seed of sin.

" Did we count on this ? Did we leave
     behind
   The graves of our kin, the comfort
     and ease
Of our English hearths and homes, to
     find
   Troublers of Israel such as these ?
Shall I spare ? Shall I pity them ? God
     forbid !
I will do as the prophet to Agag did :

They come to poison the wells of the
    Word,
I will hew them in pieces before the
    Lord ! "

The door swung open, and Rawson the
    clerk
Entered, and whispered under breath,
" There waits below for the hangman's
    work
A fellow banished on pain of death —
Shattuck, of Salem, unhealed of the
    whip,
Brought over in Master Goldsmith's
    ship
At anchor here in a Christian port,
With freight of the devil and all his
    sort ! "

Twice and thrice on the chamber floor
    Striding fiercely from wall to wall,
" The Lord do so to me and more,"
    The Governor cried, " if I hang not
    all !
Bring hither the Quaker." Calm, se-
    date,
With the look of a man at ease with
    fate,
Into that presence grim and dread
Came Samuel Shattuck, with hat on
    head.

" Off with the knave's hat ! " An angry
    hand
    Smote down the offence ; but the
    wearer said,
With a quiet smile, " By the king's com-
    mand
    I bear his message and stand in his
    stead."
In the Governor's hand a missive he laid
With the royal arms on its seal dis-
    played,
And the proud man spake as he gazed
    thereat,
Uncovering, "Give Mr. Shattuck his
    hat."

He turned to the Quaker, bowing low, —
    " The king commandeth your friends'
    release,
Doubt not he shall be obeyed, although
    To his subjects' sorrow and sin's in-
    crease.
What he here enjoineth, John Endi-
    cott,
His loyal servant, questioneth not.

You are free ! God grant the spirit you
    own
May take you from us to parts un-
    known."

So the door of the jail was open cast,
    And, like Daniel, out of the lion's
    den
Tender youth and girlhood passed,
    With age-bowed women and gray-
    locked men.
And the voice of one appointed to die
Was lifted in praise and thanks on high,
And the little maid from New Nether-
    lands
Kissed, in her joy, the doomed man's
    hands.

And one, whose call was to minister
    To the souls in prison, beside him
    went,
An ancient woman, bearing with her
    The linen shroud for his burial meant.
For she, not counting her own life
    dear,
In the strength of a love that cast out
    fear,
Had watched and served where her
    brethren died,
Like those who waited the cross be-
    side.

One moment they paused on their way
    to look
    On the martyr graves by the Common
    side,
And much scourged Wharton of Salem
    took
    His burden of prophecy up and cried :
" Rest, souls of the valiant ! Not in
    vain
Have ye borne the Master's cross of
    pain ;
Ye have fought the fight, ye are victors
    crowned,
With a fourfold chain ye have Satan
    bound ! "

The autumn haze lay soft and still
    On wood and meadow and upland
    farms ;
On the brow of Snow Hill the great
    windmill
    Slowly and lazily swung its arms ;
Broad in the sunshine stretched away,
With its capes and islands, the turquoise
    bay ;

And over water and dusk of pines
Blue hills lifted their faint outlines.

The topaz leaves of the walnut glowed,
  The sumach added its crimson fleck,
And double in air and water showed
 . The tinted maples along the Neck ;
Through frost flower clusters of pale
     star-mist,
And gentian fringes of amethyst,
And royal plumes of golden-rod,
The grazing cattle on Centry trod.

But as they who see not, the Quakers
    saw
  The world about them ; they only
    thought
With deep thanksgiving and pious awe
  On the great deliverance God had
    wrought.
Through lane and alley the gazing town
Noisily followed them up and down ;
Some with scoffing and brutal jeer,
Some with pity and words of cheer.

One brave voice rose above the din.
  Upsall, gray with his length of days,
Cried from the door of his Red Lion
    Inn :
  "Men of Boston, give God the praise !
No more shall innocent blood call down
The bolts of wrath on your guilty town.
The freedom of worship, dear to you,
Is dear to all, and to all is due.

"I see the vision of days to come,
  When your beautiful City of the Bay
Shall be Christian liberty's chosen home,
  And none shall his neighbor's rights
    gainsay.
The varying notes of worship shall blend
And as one great prayer to God ascend,
And hands of mutual charity raise
Walls of salvation and gates of praise."

So passed the Quakers through Boston
    town,
  Whose painful ministers sighed to see
The walls of their sheep-fold falling
    down,
  And wolves of heresy prowling free.
But the years went on, and brought no
    wrong ;
With milder counsels the State grew
    strong,
As outward Letter and inward Light
Kept the balance of truth aright.

The Puritan spirit perishing not,
  To Concord's yeomen the signal sent,
And spake in the voice of the cannon-
    shot
  That severed the chains of a conti-
    nent.
With its gentler mission of peace and
    good-will
The thought of the Quaker is living
    still,
And the freedom of soul he prophesied
Is gospel and law where the martyrs
    died.

ST. MARTIN'S SUMMER.[82]

THOUGH flowers have perished at the
    touch
  Of Frost, the early comer,
I hail the season loved so much,
  The good St. Martin's summer.

O gracious morn, with rose-red dawn,
  And thin moon curving o'er it !
The old year's darling, latest born,
  More loved than all before it !

How flamed the sunrise through the
    pines !
  How stretched the birchen shadows,
Braiding in long, wind-wavered lines
  The westward sloping meadows !

The sweet day, opening as a flower
  Unfolds its petals tender,
Renews for us at noontide's hour
  The summer's tempered splendor.

The birds are hushed ; alone the wind,
  That through the woodland searches,
The red-oak's lingering leaves can find,
  And yellow plumes of larches.

But still the balsam-breathing pine
  Invites no thought of sorrow,
No hint of loss from air like wine
  The earth's content can borrow.

The summer and the winter here
  Midway a truce are holding,
A soft, consenting atmosphere
  Their tents of peace enfolding.

The silent woods, the lonely hills,
  Rise solemn in their gladness ;

The quiet that the valley fills
　Is scarcely joy or sadness.

How strange !　The autumn yesterday
　In winter's grasp seemed dying ;
On whirling winds from skies of gray
　The early snow was flying.

And now, while over Nature's mood
　There steals a soft relenting,
I will not mar the present good,
　Forecasting or lamenting.

My autumn time and Nature's hold
　A dreamy tryst together,
And, both grown old, about us fold
　The golden-tissued weather.

I lean my heart against the day
　To feel its bland caressing ;
I will not let it pass away
　Before it leaves its blessing.

God's angels come not as of old
　The Syrian shepherds knew them ;
In reddening dawns, in sunset gold,
　And warm noon lights I view them.

Nor need there is, in times like this
　When heaven to earth draws nearer,
Of wing or song as witnesses
　To make their presence clearer.

O stream of life, whose swifter flow
　Is of the end forewarning,
Methinks thy sundown afterglow
　Seems less of night than morning !

Old cares grow light ; aside I lay
　The doubts and fears that troubled ;
The quiet of the happy day
　Within my soul is doubled.

That clouds must veil this fair sunshine
　Not less a joy I find it ;
Nor less yon warm horizon line
　That winter lurks behind it.

The mystery of the untried days
　I close my eyes from reading ;
His will be done whose darkest ways
　To light and life are leading !

Less drear the winter night shall be,
　If memory cheer and hearten
Its heavy hours with thoughts of thee,
　Sweet summer of St. Martin !

THE DEAD FEAST OF THE KOL-FOLK.[83]

CHOTA NAGPOOR.

WE have opened the door,
　Once, twice, thrice !
We have swept the floor,
　We have boiled the rice.
Come hither, come hither !
Come from the far lands,
Come from the star lands,
　Come as before !
We lived long together,
We loved one another ;
　Come back to our life.
Come father, come mother,
Come sister and brother,
　Child, husband, and wife,
For you we are sighing.
Come take your old places,
Come look in our faces,
　The dead on the dying,
　　Come home !

We have opened the door,
　Once, twice, thrice !
We have kindled the coals,
　And we boil the rice
For the feast of souls.
　Come hither, come hither !
Think not we fear you,
Whose hearts are so near you.
Come tenderly thought on,
Come all unforgotten,
Come from the shadow-lands,
From the dim meadow-lands
Where the pale grasses bend
　Low to our sighing.
Come father, come mother,
Come sister and brother,
Come husband and friend,
　The dead to the dying,
　　Come home !

We have opened the door
　You entered so oft ;
For the feast of souls
We have kindled the coals,
　And we boil the rice soft.
Come you who are dearest
To us who are nearest,
Come hither, come hither,
From out the wild weather ;
The storm clouds are flying,
The peepul is sighing ;
　Come in from the rain.

Come father, come mother,
Come sister and brother,
Come husband and lover,
Beneath our roof-cover.
  Look on us again,
  The dead on the dying,
    Come home!

We have opened the door!
For the feast of souls
We have kindled the coals
  We may kindle no more!
Snake, fever, and famine,
The curse of the Brahmin,
  The sun and the dew,
They burn us, they bite us,
They waste us and smite us;
  Our days are but few!
In strange lands far yonder
To wonder and wander
  We hasten to you.
List then to our sighing,
  While yet we are here:
Nor seeing nor hearing,
We wait without fearing,
  To feel you draw near.
O dead to the dying
    Come home!

THE LOST OCCASION.

SOME die too late and some too soon,
At early morning, heat of noon,
Or the chill evening twilight. Thou,
Whom the rich heavens did so endow
With eyes of power and Jove's own
  brow,
With all the massive strength that fills
Thy home-horizon's granite hills,
With rarest gifts of heart and head
From manliest stock inherited,
New England's stateliest type of man,
In port and speech Olympian;
Whom no one met, at first, but took
A second awed and wondering look
(As turned, perchance, the eyes of Greece
On Phidias' unveiled masterpiece);
Whose words in simplest home-spun clad,
The Saxon strength of Cædmon's had,
With power reserved at need to reach
The Roman forum's loftiest speech,
Sweet with persuasion, eloquent
In passion, cool in argument,
Or, ponderous, falling on thy foes
As fell the Norse god's hammer blows,
Crushing as if with Talus' flail

Through Error's logic-woven mail,
And failing only when they tried
The adamant of the righteous side, —
Thou, foiled in aim and hope, bereaved
Of old friends, by the new deceived,
Too soon for us, too soon for thee,
Beside thy lonely Northern sea,
Where long and low the marsh-lands
  spread,
Laid wearily down thy august head.

Thou shouldst have lived to feel below
Thy feet Disunion's fierce upthrow, —
The late-sprung mine that underlaid
Thy sad concessions vainly made.
Thou shouldst have seen from Sumter's
  wall
The star-flag of the Union fall,
And armed rebellion pressing on
The broken lines of Washington!
No stronger voice than thine had then
Called out the utmost might of men,
To make the Union's charter free
And strengthen law by liberty.
How had that stern arbitrament
To thy gray age youth's vigor lent,
Shaming ambition's paltry prize
Before thy disillusioned eyes;
Breaking the spell about thee wound
Like the green withes that Samson
  bound;
Redeeming in one effort grand,
Thyself and thy imperilled land!
Ah, cruel fate, that closed to thee,
O sleeper by the Northern sea,
The gates of opportunity!
God fills the gaps of human need,
Each crisis brings its word and deed.
Wise men and strong we did not lack;
But still, with memory turning back,
In the dark hours we thought of thee,
And thy lone grave beside the sea.

Above that grave the east winds blow,
And from the marsh-lands drifting slow
The sea-fog comes, with evermore
The wave-wash of a lonely shore,
And sea-bird's melancholy cry,
As Nature fain would typify
The sadness of a closing scene,
The loss of that which should have been
But, where thy native mountains bare
Their foreheads to diviner air,
Fit emblem of enduring fame,
One lofty summit keeps thy name.
For thee the cosmic forces did
The rearing of that pyramid,

The prescient ages shaping with
Fire, flood, and frost thy monolith.
Sunrise and sunset lay thereon
With hands of light their benison,
The stars of midnight pause to set
Their jewels in its coronet.
And evermore that mountain mass
Seems climbing from the shadowy pass
To light, as if to manifest
Thy nobler self, thy life at best !

THE EMANCIPATION GROUP.

BOSTON, 1879.

AMIDST thy sacred effigies
Of old renown give place,
O city, Freedom-loved ! to his
Whose hand unchained a race.

Take the worn frame, that rested not
Save in a martyr's grave —
The care-lined face, that none forgot,
Bent to the kneeling slave.

Let man be free ! The mighty word
He spake was not his own ;
An impulse from the Highest stirred
These chiselled lips alone.

The cloudy sign, the fiery guide,
Along his pathway ran,
And Nature, through his voice, denied
The ownership of man.

We rest in peace where these sad eyes
Saw peril, strife, and pain ;
His was the nation's sacrifice,
And ours the priceless gain.

O symbol of God's will on earth
As it is done above !
Bear witness to the cost and worth
Of justice and of love.

Stand in thy place and testify
To coming ages long,
That truth is stronger than a lie,
And righteousness than wrong.

THE JUBILEE SINGERS.

VOICE of a people suffering long,
The pathos of their mournful song,
The sorrow of their night of wrong !

Their cry like that which Israel gave,
A prayer for one to guide and save,
Like Moses by the Red Sea's wave !

The stern accord her timbrel lent
To Miriam's note of triumph sent
O'er Egypt's sunken armament !

The tramp that startled camp and town,
And shook the walls of slavery down,
The spectral march of old John Brown !

The storm that swept through battle-
days,
The triumph after long delays,
The bondmen giving God the praise !

Voice of a ransomed race, sing on
Till Freedom's every right is won,
And Slavery's every wrong undone !

WITHIN THE GATE.

L. M. C.

WE sat together, last May-day, and
talked
Of the dear friends who walked
Beside us, sharers of the hopes and fears
Of five and forty years

Since first we met in Freedom's hope
forlorn,
And heard her battle-horn
Sound through the valleys of the sleep-
ing North,
Calling her children forth,

And youth pressed forward with hope-
lighted eyes,
And age, with forecast wise
Of the long strife before the triumph won,
Girded his armor on.

Sadly, as name by name we called the
roll,
We heard the dead-bells toll
For the unanswering many, and we
knew
The living were the few.

And we, who waited our own call before
The inevitable door,
Listened and looked, as all have done,
to win
Some token from within.

No sign we saw, we heard no voices
    call;
    The impenetrable wall
Cast down its shadow, like an awful
    doubt,
    On all who sat without.

Of many a hint of life beyond the veil,
    And many a ghostly tale
Wherewith the ages spanned the gulf
    between
    The seen and the unseen,

Seeking from omen, trance, and dream
    to gain
    Solace to doubtful pain,
And touch, with groping hands, the gar-
    ment hem
    Of truth sufficing them,

We talked; and, turning from the sore
    unrest
    Of an all-baffling quest,
We thought of holy lives that from us
    passed
    Hopeful unto the last,

As if they saw beyond the river of death,
    Like him of Nazareth,
The many mansions of the Eternal days
    Lift up their gates of praise.

And, hushed to silence by a reverent
    awe,
    Methought, O friend, I saw
In thy true life of word, and work, and
    thought
    The proof of all we sought.

Did we not witness in the life of thee
    Immortal prophecy?
And feel, when with thee, that thy foot-
    steps trod
    An everlasting road?

Not for brief days thy generous sympa-
    thies,
    Thy scorn of selfish ease;
Not for the poor prize of an earthly
    goal
    Thy strong uplift of soul.

Than thine was never turned a fonder
    heart
    To nature and to art
In fair-formed Hellas in her golden prime,
    Thy Philothea's time.

Yet, loving beauty, thou couldst pass it
    by,
    And for the poor deny
Thyself, and see thy fresh, sweet flower
    of fame
    Wither in blight and blame.

Sharing His love who holds in His em-
    brace
    The lowliest of our race,
Sure the Divine economy must be
    Conservative of thee!

For truth must live with truth, self-sac-
    rifice
    Seek out its great allies;
Good must find good by gravitation
    sure,
    And love with love endure.

And so, since thou hast passed within
    the gate
    Whereby awhile I wait,
I give blind grief and blinder sense the
    lie:
    Thou hast not lived to die!

THE KHAN'S DEVIL.

THE Khan came from Bokhara town
To Hamza, santon of renown.

"My head is sick, my hands are weak;
Thy help, O holy man, I seek."

In silence marking for a space
The Khan's red eyes and purple face,

Thick voice, and loose, uncertain tread,
"Thou hast a devil!" Hamza said.

"Allah forbid!" exclaimed the Khan.
"Rid me of him at once, O man!"

"Nay," Hamza said, "no spell of
    mine
Can slay that cursed thing of thine.

"Leave feast and wine, go forth and
    drink
Water of healing on the brink

"Where clear and cold from mountain
    snows,
The Nahr el Zeben downward flows.

"Six moons remain, then come to me;
May Allah's pity go with thee!"

Awe-struck, from feast and wine, the Khan
Went forth where Nahr el Zeben ran.

Roots were his food, the desert dust
His bed, the water quenched his thirst,

And when the sixth moon's scimetar
Curved sharp above the evening star,

He sought again the santon's door,
Not weak and trembling as before,

But strong of limb and clear of brain;
"Behold," he said, "the fiend is slain."

"Nay," Hamza answered, "starved and drowned,
The curst one lies in death-like swound.

"But evil breaks the strongest gyves,
And jins like him have charmed lives.

"One beaker of the juice of grape
May call him up in living shape.

"When the red wine of Badakshan
Sparkles for thee, beware, O Khan!

"With water quench the fire within,
And drown each day thy devilkin!"

Thenceforth the great Khan shunned the cup
As Shitan's own, though offered up,

With laughing eyes and jewelled hands,
By Yarkand's maids and Samarcand's.

And, in the lofty vestibule
Of the medress of Kaush Kodul,

The students of the holy law
A golden-lettered tablet saw,

With these words, by a cunning hand,
Graved on it at the Khan's command:

"In Allah's name, to him who hath
A devil, Khan el Hamed saith,

"Wisely our Prophet cursed the vine:
The fiend that loves the breath of wine

"No prayer can slay, no marabout
Nor Meccan dervis can drive out.

"I, Khan el Hamed, know the charm
That robs him of his power to harm.

"Drown him, O Islam's child! the spell
To save thee lies in tank and well!"

ABRAM MORRISON.

'MIDST the men and things which will
Haunt an old man's memory still,
Drollest, quaintest of them all,
With a boy's laugh I recall
        Good old Abram Morrison.

When the Grist and Rolling Mill
Ground and rumbled by Po Hill,
And the old red school-house stood
Midway in the Powow's flood,
        Here dwelt Abram Morrison.

From the Beach to far beyond
Bear-Hill, Lion's Mouth and Pond,
Marvellous to our tough old stock,
Chips o' the Anglo-Saxon block,
        Seemed the Celtic Morrison.

Mudknock, Balmawhistle, all
Only knew the Yankee drawl,
Never brogue was heard till when,
Foremost of his countrymen,
        Hither came Friend Morrison;

Yankee born, of alien blood,
Kin of his had well withstood
Pope and King with pike and ball
Under Derry's leaguered wall,
        As became the Morrisons.

Wandering down from Nutfield woods
With his household and his goods,
Never was it clearly told
How within our quiet fold
        Came to be a Morrison.

Once a soldier, blame him not
That the Quaker he forgot,
When, to think of battles won,
And the red-coats on the run,
        Laughed aloud Friend Morrison.

From gray Lewis over sea
Bore his sires their family tree,

On the rugged boughs of it
Grafting Irish mirth and wit,
　　And the brogue of Morrison.

Half a genius, quick to plan,
Blundering like an Irishman,
But with canny shrewdness lent
By his far-off Scotch descent,
　　Such was Abram Morrison.

Back and forth to daily meals,
Rode his cherished pig on wheels,
And to all who came to see :
"Aisier for the pig an' me,
　　Sure it is," said Morrison.

Simple-hearted, boy o'er-grown,
With a humor quite his own,
Of our sober-stepping ways,
Speech and look and cautious phrase,
　　Slow to learn was Morrison.

Much we loved his stories told
Of a country strange and old,
Where the fairies danced till dawn,
And the goblin Leprecaun
　　Looked, we thought, like Morrison.

Or wild tales of feud and fight,
Witch and troll and second sight
Whispered still where Stornoway
Looks across its stormy bay,
　　Once the home of Morrisons.

First was he to sing the praise
Of the Powow's winding ways ;
And our straggling village took
City grandeur to the look
　　Of its poet Morrison.

All his words have perished.　Shame
On the saddle-bags of Fame,
That they bring not to our time
One poor couplet of the rhyme
　　Made by Abram Morrison !

When, on calm and fair First Days,
Rattled down our one-horse chaise
Through the blossomed apple-boughs
To the old, brown meeting-house,
　　There was Abram Morrison.

Underneath his hat's broad brim
Peered the queer old face of him ;
And with Irish jauntiness
Swung the coat-tails of the dress
　　Worn by Abram Morrison.

Still, in memory, on his feet,
Leaning o'er the elders' seat,
Mingling with a solemn drone,
Celtic accents all his own,
　　Rises Abram Morrison.

" Don't," he 's pleading, " don't ye go,
Dear young friends, to sight and show ;
Don't run after elephants,
Learned pigs and presidents
　　And the likes !" said Morrison.

On his well-worn theme intent,
Simple, child-like, innocent,
Heaven forgive the half-checked smile
Of our careless boyhood, while
　　Listening to Friend Morrison !

We have learned in later days
Truth may speak in simplest phrase ;
That the man is not the less
For quaint ways and home-spun dress,
　　Thanks to Abram Morrison !

Not to pander nor to please
Come the needed homilies,
With no lofty argument
Is the fitting message sent
　　Through such lips as Morrison's

Dead and gone !　But while its track
Powow keeps to Merrimack,
While Po Hill is still on guard,
Looking land and ocean ward.
　　They shall tell of Morrison !

After half a century's lapse,
We are wiser now, perhaps,
But we miss our streets amid
Something which the past has hid,
　　Lost with Abram Morrison.

Gone forever with the queer
Characters of that old year !
Now the many are as one ;
Broken is the mould that run
　　Men like Abram Morrison.

VOYAGE OF THE JETTIE.[86]

A SHALLOW stream, from fountains
Deep in the Sandwich mountains,
　　Ran lakeward Bearcamp River ;
And, between its flood-torn shores,
Sped by sail or urged by oars
　　No keel had vexed it ever.

Alone the dead trees yielding
To the dull axe Time is wielding,
  The shy mink and the otter,
And golden leaves and red,
By countless autumns shed,
  Had floated down its water.

From the gray rocks of Cape Ann,
Came a skilled sea-faring man,
  With his dory, to the right place;
Over hill and plain he brought her,
Where the boatless Bearcamp water
  Comes winding down from White-
    Face.

Quoth the skipper : " Ere she floats forth,
I'm sure my pretty boat's worth,
  At least, a name as pretty."
On her painted side he wrote it,
And the flag that o'er her floated
  Bore aloft the name of Jettie.

On a radiant morn of summer,
Elder guest and latest comer
  Saw her wed the Bearcamp water;
Heard the name the skipper gave her.
And the answer to the favor
  From the Bay State's graceful daugh-
    ter.

Then, a singer, richly gifted,
Her charmèd voice uplifted;
  And the wood-thrush and song-sparrow
Listened, dumb with envious pain,
To the clear and sweet refrain
  Whose notes they could not borrow.

Then the skipper plied his oar,
And from off the shelving shore,
  Glided out the strange explorer;
Floating on, she knew not whither, —
The tawny sands beneath her,
  The great hills watching o'er her.

On, where the stream flows quiet
As the meadows' margins by it,
  Or widens out to borrow a
New life from that wild water,
The mountain giant's daughter,
  The pine-besung Chocorua.

Or, mid the tangling cumber
And pack of mountain lumber
  That spring floods downward force,
Over sunken snag, and bar
Where the grating shallows are,
  The good boat held her course.

Under the pine-dark highlands,
Around the vine-hung islands,
  She ploughed her crooked furrow;
And her rippling and her lurches
Scared the river eels and perches,
  And the musk-rat in his burrow.

Every sober clam below her,
Every sage and grave pearl-grower,
  Shut his rusty valves the tighter;
Crow called to crow complaining,
And old tortoises sat craning
  Their leathern necks to sight her.

So, to where the still lake glasses
The misty mountain masses
  Rising dim and distant northward,
And, with faint-drawn shadow pictures,
Low shores, and dead pine spectres,
  Blends the skyward and the earth-
    ward,

On she glided, overladen,
With merry man and maiden
  Sending back their song and laugh-
    ter, —
While, perchance, a phantom crew,
In a ghostly birch canoe,
  Paddled dumb and swiftly after !

And the bear on Ossipee
Climbed the topmost crag to see
  The strange thing drifting under;
And, through the haze of August,
Passaconaway and Paugus
  Looked down in sleepy wonder.

All the pines that o'er her hung
In mimic sea-tones sung
  The song familiar to her;
And the maples leaned to screen her,
And the meadow-grass seemed greener,
  And the breeze more soft to woo her.

The lone stream mystery-haunted,
To her the freedom granted
  To scan its every feature,
Till new and old were blended,
And round them both extended
  The loving arms of Nature.

Of these hills the little vessel
Henceforth is part and parcel;
  And on Bearcamp shall her log
Be kept, as if by George's
Or Grand Menàn, the surges
  Tossed her skipper through the fog.

And I, who, half in sadness,
Recall the morning gladness
  Of life, at evening time,
By chance, onlooking idly,
Apart from all so widely,
  Have set her voyage to rhyme.

Dies now the gay persistence
Of song and laugh, in distance;
  Alone with me remaining
The stream, the quiet meadow,
The hills in shine and shadow,
  The sombre pines complaining.

And, musing here, I dream
Of voyagers on a stream
  From whence is no returning,
Under sealèd orders going,
Looking forward little knowing,
  Looking back with idle yearning.

And I pray that every venture
The port of peace may enter,
  That, safe from snag and fall
And siren-haunted islet,
And rock, the Unseen Pilot
  May guide us one and all.

OUR AUTOCRAT.

READ AT DR. HOLMES' BREAKFAST.

His laurels fresh from song and lay,
  Romance, art, science, rich in all,
And young of heart, how dare we say
  We keep his seventieth festival ?

No sense is here of loss or lack ;
  Before his sweetness and his light
The dial holds its shadow back,
  The charmèd hours delay their flight.

His still the keen analysis
  Of men and moods, electric wit,
Free play of mirth, and tenderness
  To heal the slightest wound from it.

And his the pathos touching all
  Life's sins and sorrows and regrets,
Its hopes and fears, its final call
  And rest beneath the violets.

His sparkling surface scarce betrays
  The thoughtful tide beneath it rolled,
The wisdom of the latter days,
  And tender memories of the old.

What shapes and fancies, grave or gay,
  Before us at his bidding come !
The Treadmill tramp, the One-Horse
    Shay,
  The dumb despair of Elsie's doom !

The tale of Avis and the Maid,
  The plea for lips that cannot speak,
The holy kiss that Iris laid
  On Little Boston's pallid cheek !

Long may he live to sing for us
  His sweetest songs at evening time,
And, like his Chambered Nautilus,
  To holier heights ot beauty climb !

Though now unnumbered guests sur
    round
  The table that he rules at will,
Its Autocrat, however crowned,
  Is but our friend and comrade still.

The world may keep his honored name
  The wealth of all his varied powers ;
A stronger claim has love than fame,
  And he himself is only ours !

GARRISON.

The storm and peril overpast,
  The hounding hatred shamed and
    still,
Go, soul of freedom ! take at last
  The place which thou alone canst
    fill.

Confirm the lesson taught of old —
  Life saved for self is lost, while they
Who lose it in His service hold
  The lease of God's eternal day.

Not for thyself, but for the slave
  Thy words of thunder shook the world;
No selfish griefs or hatred gave
  The strength wherewith thy bolts were
    hurled.

From lips that Sinai's trumpet blew
  We heard a tender undersong ;
Thy very wrath from pity grew,
  From love of man thy hate of wrong

Now past and present are as one ;
  The life below is life above ;
Thy mortal years have but begun
  The immortality of love.

With somewhat of thy lofty faith
We lay thy outworn garment by,
Give death but what belongs to death,
And life the life that cannot die!

Not for a soul like thine the calm
Of selfish ease and joys of sense;
But duty, more than crown or palm,
Its own exceeding recompense.

Go up and on! thy day well done,
Its morning promise well fulfilled,
Arise to triumphs yet unwon,
To holier tasks that God has willed.

Go, leave behind thee all that mars
The work below of man for man;
With the white legions of the stars
Do service such as angels can.

Wherever wrong shall right deny
Or suffering spirits urge their plea,
Be thine a voice to smite the lie,
A hand to set the captive free!

BAYARD TAYLOR.

I.

"And where now, Bayard, will thy foot-
    steps tend?"
  My sister asked our guest one winter's
    day.
  Smiling he answered in the Friends'
    sweet way
Common to both: "Wherever thou shalt
    send!
What wouldst thou have me see for
    thee?" She laughed,
  Her dark eyes dancing in the wood-
    fire's glow:
  "Loffoden isles, the Kilpis, and the
    low,
Unsetting sun on Finmark's fishing-
    craft."
"All these and more I soon shall see
    for thee!"
  He answered cheerily: and he kept
    his pledge
  On Lapland snows, the North Cape's
    windy wedge,
And Tromso freezing in its winter sea.
  He went and came. But no man knows
    the track
  Of his last journey, and he comes not
    back!

II.

He brought us wonders of the new and
    old;
  We shared all climes with him. The
    Arab's tent
To him its story-telling secret lent.
And, pleased, we listened to the tales he
    told.
His task, beguiled with songs that shall
    endure,
  In manly, honest thoroughness he
    wrought;
  From humble home-lays to the heights
    of thought
Slowly he climbed, but every step was
    sure.
How, with the generous pride that friend-
    ship hath,
  We, who so loved him, saw at last the
    crown
  Of civic honor on his brows pressed
    down,
Rejoiced, and knew not that the gift was
    death.
  And now for him, whose praise in
    deafened ears
  Two nations speak, we answer but
    with tears!

III.

O Vale of Chester! trod by him so
    oft,
  Green as thy June turf keep his mem-
    ory. Let
  Nor wood, nor dell, nor storied stream
    forget,
Nor winds that blow round lonely Cedar-
    croft;
  Let the home voices greet him in the
    far,
  Strange land that holds him; let the
    messages
  Of love pursue him o'er the chartless
    seas
And unmapped vastness of his unknown
    star!
Love's language, heard beyond the loud
    discourse
  Of perishable fame, in every sphere
  Itself interprets; and its utterance
    here
Somewhere in God's unfolding uni-
    verse
  Shall reach our traveller, softening the
    surprise
  Of his rapt gaze on unfamiliar skies!

A NAME.

TO G. W. P.

THE name the Gallic exile bore,
  St. Malo! from thy ancient mart,
Became upon our Western shore
  Greenleaf for Feuillevert.

A name to hear in soft accord
  Of leaves by light winds overrun,
Or read, upon the greening sward
  Of May, in shade and sun.

The name my infant ear first heard
  Breathed softly with a mother's kiss;
His mother's own, no tenderer word
  My father spake than this.

No child have I to bear it on;
  Be thou its keeper; let it take
From gifts well used and duty done
  New beauty for thy sake.

The fair ideals that outran
  My halting footsteps seek and find —
The flawless symmetry of man,
  The poise of heart and mind.

Stand firmly where I felt the sway
  Of every wing that fancy flew,
See clearly where I groped my way,
  Nor real from seeming knew.

And wisely choose, and bravely hold
  Thy faith unswerved by cross or
     crown,
Like the stout Huguenot of old
  Whose name to thee comes down.

As Marot's songs made glad the heart
  Of that lone exile, haply mine
May in life's heavy hours impart
  Some strength and hope to thine.

Yet when did Age transfer to Youth
  The hard-gained lessons of its day?
Each lip must learn the taste of truth,
  Each foot must feel its way.

We cannot hold the hands of choice
  That touch or shun life's fateful keys;
The whisper of the inward voice
  Is more than homilies.

Dear boy! for whom the flowers are born,
  Stars shine, and happy song-birds sing,

What can my evening give to morn,
  My winter to thy spring!

A life not void of pure intent,
  With small desert of praise or blame,
The love I felt, the good I meant,
  I leave thee with my name.

THE MINISTER'S DAUGHTER.

IN the minister's morning sermon
  He had told of the primal fall,
And how thenceforth the wrath of God
  Rested on each and all.

And how, of His will and pleasure,
  All souls, save a chosen few,
Were doomed to the quenchless burn-
    ing,
  And held in the way thereto.

Yet never by faith's unreason
  A saintlier soul was tried,
And never the harsh old lesson
  A tenderer heart belied.

And, after the painful service
  On that pleasant Sabbath day,
He walked with his little daughter
  Through the apple-bloom of May.

Sweet in the fresh green meadows
  Sparrow and blackbird sung;
Above him their tinted petals
  The blossoming orchards hung.

Around on the wonderful glory
  The minister looked and smiled;
"How good is the Lord who gives us
  These gifts from His hand, my child.

"Behold in the bloom of apples
  And the violets in the sward
A hint of the old, lost beauty
  Of the Garden of the Lord!"

Then up spake the little maiden,
  Treading on snow and pink:
"O father! these pretty blossoms
  Are very wicked, I think.

"Had there been no Garden of Eden
  There never had been a fall;
And if never a tree had blossomed
  God would have loved us all."

" Hush, child!" the father answered,
  " By His decree man fell;
His ways are in clouds and darkness,
  But He doeth all things well.

" And whether by His ordaining
  To us cometh good or ill,
Joy or pain, or light or shadow,
  We must fear and love Him still."

" Oh, I fear Him!" said the daugh-
    ter,
  " And I try to love Him, too;
But I wish He was good and gentle,
  Kind and loving as you."

The minister groaned in spirit
  As the tremulous lips of pain
And wide, wet eyes uplifted
  Questioned his own in vain.

Bowing his head he pondered
  The words of the little one;
Had he erred in his life-long teach-
    ing?
  Had he wrong to his Master done?

To what grim and dreadful idol
  Had he lent the holiest name?
Did his own heart, loving and human,
  The God of his worship shame?

And lo! from the bloom and green-
    ness,
  From the tender skies above,
And the face of his little daughter,
  He read a lesson of love.

No more as the cloudy terror
  Of Sinai's mount of law,
But as Christ in the Syrian lilies
  The vision of God he saw.

And, as when, in the clefts of Horeb,
  Of old was His presence known,
The dread Ineffable Glory
  Was Infinite Goodness alone.

Thereafter his hearers noted
  In his prayers a tenderer strain,
And never the gospel of hatred
  Burned on his lips again.

And the scoffing tongue was prayerful,
  And the blinded eyes found sight,
And hearts, as flint aforetime,
  Grew soft in his warmth and light.

MY TRUST.

A PICTURE memory brings to me:
I look across the years and see
Myself beside my mother's knee.

I feel her gentle hand restrain
My selfish moods, and know again
A child's blind sense of wrong and pain

But wiser now, a man gray grown,
My childhood's needs are better known,
My mother's chastening love I own.

Gray grown, but in our Father's sight
A child still groping for the light
To read His works and ways aright.

I wait, in His good time to see
That as my mother dealt with me
So with His children dealeth He.

I bow myself beneath His hand:
That pain itself was wisely planned
I feel, and partly understand.

The joy that comes in sorrow's guise,
The sweet pains of self-sacrifice,
I would not have them otherwise.

And what were life and death if sin
Knew not the dread rebuke within,
The pang of merciful discipline?

Not with thy proud despair of old,
Crowned stoic of Rome's noblest mould!
Pleasure and pain alike I hold.

I suffer with no vain pretence
Of triumph over flesh and sense,
Yet trust the grievous providence,

How dark soe'er it seems, may tend,
By ways I cannot comprehend,
To some unguessed benignant end;

That every loss and lapse may gain
The clear-aired heights by steps of pain,
And never cross is borne in vain.

THE TRAILING ARBUTUS.

I WANDERED lonely where the pine
    trees made
Against the bitter East their barricade,
  And, guided by its sweet

Perfume, I found, within a narrow dell,
The trailing spring flower tinted like a
   shell
   Amid dry leaves and mosses at my
     feet.

From under dead boughs, for whose loss
   the pines
Moaned ceaseless overhead, the blossom-
   ing vines
   Lifted their glad surprise,
While yet the bluebird smoothed in leaf-
   less trees
His feathers ruffled by the chill sea-
   breeze,
   And snow-drifts lingered under April
     skies.

As, pausing, o'er the lonely flower I
   bent,
I thought of lives thus lowly, clogged
   and pent,
   Which yet find room,
Through care and cumber, coldness and
   decay,
To lend a sweetness to the ungenial day
   And make the sad earth happier for
     their bloom.

BY THEIR WORKS.

CALL him not heretic whose works at-
   test
His faith in goodness by no creed con-
   fessed.
Whatever in love's name is truly done
To free the bound and lift the fallen
   one
Is done to Christ. Whoso in deed and
   word
Is not against Him labors for our Lord.
When He, who, sad and weary, longing
   sore
For love's sweet service, sought the sis-
   ters' door,
One saw the heavenly, one the human
   guest,
But who shall say which loved the Mas-
   ter best?

THE WORD.

VOICE of the Holy Spirit, making known
   Man to himself, a witness swift and
     sure,

Warning, approving, true and wise
   and pure,
Counsel and guidance that misleadeth
   none !
By thee the mystery of life is read ;
   The picture-writing of the world's gray
     seers,
   The myths and parables of the primal
     years,
Whose letter kills, by thee interpreted
   Take healthful meanings fitted to our
     needs,
   And in the soul's vernacular express
    The common law of simple righteous-
     ness.
Hatred of cant and doubt of human
   creeds
May well be felt : the unpardonable sin
Is to deny the Word of God within !

THE BOOK.

GALLERY of sacred pictures manifold,
   A minster rich in holy effigies,
   And bearing on entablature and frieze
The hieroglyphic oracles of old.
Along its transept aureoled martyrs sit ;
   And the low chancel side-lights half
     acquaint
   The eye with shrines of prophet, bard,
     and saint,
Their age-dimmed tablets traced in
   doubtful writ !
But only when on form and word obscure
   Falls from above the white supernal
     light
   We read the mystic characters aright,
And life informs the silent portraiture,
Until we pause at last, awe-held, before
The One ineffable Face, love, wonder,
   and adore.

REQUIREMENT.

WE live by Faith ; but Faith is not the
   slave
   Of text and legend. Reason's voice
    and God's,
   Nature's and Duty's, never are at odds.
What asks our Father of His children,
   save
Justice and mercy and humility,
   A reasonable service of good deeds,
   Pure living, tenderness to human
    needs,

Reverence and trust, and prayer for light
    to see
The Master's footprints in our daily
    ways ?
  No knotted scourge nor sacrificial knife,
  But the calm beauty of an ordered life
Whose very breathing is unworded
    praise ! —
A life that stands as all true lives have
    stood,
  Firm-rooted in the faith that God is Good.

HELP.

DREAM not, O Soul, that easy is the
    task
    Thus set before thee. If it proves at
      length,
    As well it may, beyond thy natural
      strength,
Faint not, despair not. As a child may
    ask
A father, pray the Everlasting Good
    For light and guidance midst the subtle
      snares
    Of sin thick planted in life's thorough-
      fares,
For spiritual strength and moral hardi-
    hood ;
Still listening, through the noise of time
    and sense,
    To the still whisper of the Inward
      Word ;
    Bitter in blame, sweet in approval
      heard,
Itself its own confirming evidence :
To health of soul a voice to cheer and
    please,
To guilt the wrath of the Eumenides.

UTTERANCE.

BUT what avail inadequate words to
    reach
    The innermost of Truth ? Who shall
      essay,
    Blinded and weak, to point and lead
      the way,
Or solve its mystery in familiar speech ?
Yet, if it be that something not thy own,
    Some shadow of the Thought to which
      our schemes,
    Creeds, cult, and ritual are at best but
      dreams,
Is even to thy unworthiness made known,
27

Thou mayst not hide what yet thou
    shouldst not dare
  To utter lightly, lest on lips of thine
  The real seem false, the beauty un-
    divine.
So, weighing duty in the scale of prayer,
Give what seems given thee. It may
    prove a seed
Of goodness dropped in fallow-grounds
    of need.

INSCRIPTIONS.

ON A SUN-DIAL.

FOR DR. HENRY I. BOWDITCH.

WITH warning hand I mark Time's
    rapid flight
From life's glad morning to its solemn
    night ;
Yet, through the dear God's love, I also
    show
There 's Light above me by the Shade
    below.

ON A FOUNTAIN.

FOR DOROTHEA L. DIX.

STRANGER and traveller
    Drink freely, and bestow
A kindly thought on her
    Who bade this fountain flow,
Yet hath no other claim
    Than as the minister
Of blessing in God's name.
    Drink, and in His peace go !

ORIENTAL MAXIMS.

PARAPHRASE OF SANSCRIT TRANSLA-TIONS.

THE INWARD JUDGE.

FROM "INSTITUTES OF MANU."

THE soul itself its awful witness is.
Say not in evil doing, "No one sees,"
And so offend the conscious One within,
Whose ear can hear the silences of sin

Ere they find voice, whose eyes unsleep-
    ing see
The secret motions of iniquity.

Nor in thy folly say, " I am alone."
For, seated in thy heart, as on a throne,
The ancient Judge and Witness liveth
    still,
To note thy act and thought ; and as thy
    ill
Or good goes from thee, far beyond thy
    reach,
The solemn Doomsman's seal is set on
    each.

LAYING UP TREASURE.

FROM THE "MAHÀBHÁRATA."

BEFORE the Ender comes, whose char-
    ioteer
Is swift or slow Disease, lay up each
    year

Thy harvests of well-doing, wealth that
    kings
Nor thieves can take away.   When all
    the things
Thou callest thine, goods, pleasures, hon-
    ors fall,
Thou in thy virtue shalt survive them
    all.

CONDUCT.

FROM THE "MAHÀBHÁRATA."

HEED how thou livest. Do no act by
    day
Which from the night shall drive thy
    peace away.
In months of sun so live that months of
    rain
Shall still be happy. Evermore restrain
Evil and cherish good, so shall there
    be
Another and a happier life for thee.

THE BAY OF SEVEN ISLANDS,
AND OTHER POEMS.

TO EDWIN P. WHIPPLE,

ONE OF THE FIRST TO WELCOME MY EARLIEST VOLUME, I OFFER THE
LATEST, AS A TOKEN OF FRIENDSHIP NEVER INTERRUPTED,
AND WHICH YEARS HAVE ONLY STRENGTHENED.

TO H. P. S.

FROM the green Amesbury hill which
    bears the name
Of that half mythic ancestor of mine
Who trod its slopes two hundred years
    ago,
Down the long valley of the Merrimac
Midway between me and the river's
    mouth,
I see thy home, set like an eagle's nest
Among Deer Island's immemorial pines,
Crowning the crag on which the sunset
    breaks

Its last red arrow. Many a tale and
    song,
Which thou hast told or sung, I call to
    mind,
Softening with silvery mist the woods
    and hills,
The out-thrust headlands and inreach-
    ing bays
Of our northeastern coast-line, trending
    where
The Gulf, midsummer, feels the chill
    blockade
Of icebergs stranded at its northern
    gate.

EDWIN P. WHIPPLE.   Page 434.

To thee the echoes of the Island Sound
Answer not vainly, nor in vain the
    moan
Of the South Breaker prophesying
    storm.

And thou hast listened, like myself, to
    men
Sea-periled oft where Anticosti lies
Like a fell spider in its web of fog,
Or where the Grand Bank shallows with
    the wrecks
Of sunken fishers; and to whom strange
    isles
And frost-rimmed bays and trading sta-
    tions seem
Familiar as Great Neck and Kettle
    Cove,
Nubble and Boon, the common names of
    home.

So let me offer thee this lay of mine,
Simple and homely, lacking much thy
    play
Of color and of fancy. If its theme
And treatment seem to thee befitting
    youth
Rather than age, let this be my ex-
    cuse:
It has beguiled some heavy hours and
    called
Some pleasant memories up; and, better
    still,
Occasion lent me for a kindly word
To one who is my neighbor and my
    friend.

THE BAY OF SEVEN ISLANDS.

THE skipper sailed out of the harbor
    mouth,
Leaving the apple-bloom of the South
    For the ice of the Eastern seas,
    In his fishing schooner Breeze.

Handsome and brave and young was
    he,
And the maids of Newbury sighed to
    see
    His lessening white sail fall
    Under the sea's blue wall.

Through the Northern Gulf and the
    misty screen
Of the isles of Mingan and Madeleine,
    St. Paul's and Blanc Sablon,
    The little Breeze sailed on,

Backward and forward, along the shore
Of lorn and desolate Labrador,
    And found at last her way
    To the Seven Islands Bay.

The little hamlet, nestling below
Great hills white with lingering snow,
    With its tin-roofed chapel stood
    Half hid in the dwarf spruce wood:

Green-turfed, flower-sown, the last out-
    post
Of summer upon the dreary coast,
    With its gardens small and spare,
    Sad in the frosty air.

Hard by where the skipper's schooner
    lay,
A fisherman's cottage looked away
    Over isle and bay, and behind
    On mountains dim-defined.

And there twin sisters, fair and young,
Laughed with their stranger guest, and
    sung
    In their native tongue the lays
    Of the old Provençal days.

Alike were they, save the faint out-
    line
Of a scar on Suzette's forehead fine;
    And both, it so befell,
    Loved the heretic stranger well.

Both were pleasant to look upon,
But the heart of the skipper clave to
    one;
    Though less by his eye than heart
    He knew the twain apart.

Despite of alien race and creed,
Well did his wooing of Marguerite
    speed;
    And the mother's wrath was vain
    As the sister's jealous pain.

The shrill-tongued mistress her house
    forbade,
And solemn warning was sternly said
    By the black-robed priest, whose
    word
    As law the hamlet heard.

But half by voice and half by signs
The skipper said, " A warm sun shines
    On the green-banked Merrimac;
    Wait, watch, till I come back.

"And when you see, from my mast
    head,
The signal fly of a kerchief red,
    My boat on the shore shall wait ;
    Come, when the night is late."

Ah! weighed with childhood's haunts
    and friends,
And all that the home sky overbends,
    Did ever young love fail
    To turn the trembling scale ?

Under the night, on the wet sea sands,
Slowly unclasped their plighted hands :
    One to the cottage hearth,
  · And one to his sailor's berth.

What was it the parting lovers heard ?
Nor leaf, nor ripple, nor wing of bird,
    But a listener's stealthy tread
    On the rock-moss, crisp and dead.

He weighed his anchor, and fished once
    more
By the black coast-line of Labrador ;
    And by love and the north wind
        driven,
    Sailed back to the Islands Seven.

In the sunset's glow the sisters twain
Saw the Breeze come sailing in again ;
    Said Suzette, "Mother dear,
    The heretic's sail is here."

"Go, Marguerite, to your room, and
    hide ;
Your door shall be bolted !" the mother
    cried :
    While Suzette, ill at ease,
    Watched the red sign of the Breeze.

At midnight, down to the waiting skiff
She stole in the shadow of the cliff ;
    And out of the Bay's mouth ran
    The schooner with maid and man.

And all night long, on a restless bed,
Her prayers to the Virgin Marguerite
    said ;
    And thought of her lover's pain
    Waiting for her in vain.

Did he pace the sands ? Did he pause
    to hear
The sound of her light step drawing near?
    And, as the slow hours passed,
    Would he doubt her faith at last ?

But when she saw through the misty
    pane,
The morning break on a sea of rain,
    Could even her love avail
    To follow his vanished sail ?

Meantime the Breeze, with favoring
    wind,
Left the rugged Moisic hills behind,
    And heard from an unseen shore
    The falls of Manitou roar.

On the morrow's morn, in the thick,
    gray weather
They sat on the reeling deck together,
    Lover and counterfeit,
    Of hapless Marguerite.

With a lover's hand, from her forehead
    fair
He smoothed away her jet-black hair.
    What was it his fond eyes met ?
    The scar of the false Suzette !

Fiercely he shouted : "Bear away
East by north for Seven Isles Bay !"
    The maiden wept and prayed,
    But the ship her helm obeyed.

Once more the Bay of the Isles they
    found :
They heard the bell of the chapel
    sound,
    And the chant of the dying sung
    In the harsh, wild Indian tongue.

A feeling of mystery, change, and awe
Was in all they heard and all they saw :
    Spell-bound the hamlet lay
    In the hush of its lonely bay.

And when they came to the cottage
    door,
The mother rose up from her weeping
    sore,
    And with angry gestures met
    The scared look of Suzette.

"Here is your daughter," the skipper
    said ;
"Give me the one I love instead."
    But the woman sternly spake ;
    "Go, see if the dead will wake !"

He looked. Her sweet face still and
    white
And strange in the noonday taper light,

She lay on her little bed,
With the cross at her feet and head.

In a passion of grief the strong man bent
Down to her face, and, kissing it, went
    Back to the waiting Breeze,
    Back to the mournful seas.

Never again to the Merrimac
And Newbury's homes that bark came back.
    Whether her fate she met
    On the shores of Carraquette,

Miscou, or Tracadie, who can say ?
But even yet at Seven Isles Bay
    Is told the ghostly tale
    Of a weird, unspoken sail,

In the pale, sad light of the Northern day
Seen by the blanketed Montagnais,
    Or squaw, in her small kyack,
    Crossing the spectre's track.

On the deck a maiden wrings her hands ;
Her likeness kneels on the gray coast sands ;
    One in her wild despair,
    And one in the trance of prayer.

She flits before no earthly blast,
The red sign fluttering from her mast,
    Over the solemn seas,
    The ghost of the schooner Breeze !

HOW THE WOMEN WENT FROM DOVER.

1662.

THE tossing spray of Cocheco's fall
Hardened to ice on its rocky wall,
As through Dover town in the chill, gray dawn,
Three women passed, at the cart-tail drawn ![1]

Bared to the waist, for the north wind's grip
And keener sting of the constable's whip,
The blood that followed each hissing blow
Froze as it sprinkled the winter snow.

Priest and ruler, boy and maid
Followed the dismal cavalcade ;
And from door and window, open thrown,
Looked and wondered gaffer and crone.

" God is our witness," the victims cried,
" We suffer for Him who for all men died ;
The wrong ye do has been done before,
We bear the stripes that the Master bore !

" And thou, O Richard Waldron, for whom
We hear the feet of a coming doom,
On thy cruel heart and thy hand of wrong
Vengeance is sure, though it tarry long.

" In the light of the Lord, a flame we see
Climb and kindle a proud roof-tree ;
And beneath it an old man lying dead,
With stains of blood on his hoary head."

these vagabond Quakers are carried out of this jurisdiction.

You, and every one of you, are required, in the King's Majesty's name, to take these vagabond Quakers, Anne Colman, Mary Tomkins, and Alice Ambrose, and make them fast to the cart's tail, and driving the cart through your several towns, to whip them upon their naked backs not exceeding ten stripes apiece on each of them, in each town ; and so to convey them from constable to constable till they are out of this jurisdiction, as you will answer it at your peril ; and this shall be your warrant.

           RICHARD WALDRON.

Dated at Dover, December 22, 1662.

This warrant was executed only in Dover and Hampton. At Salisbury the constable refused to obey it. He was sustained by the town's people, who were under the influence of Major Robert Pike, the leading man in the lower valley of the Merrimac, who stood far in advance of his time, as an advocate of religious freedom, and an opponent of ecclesiastical authority. He had the moral courage to address an able and manly letter to the court at Salem, remonstrating against the witchcraft trials.

---

[1] The following is a copy of the warrant issued by Major Waldron, of Dover, in 1662. The Quakers, as was their wont, prophesied against him, and saw, as they supposed, the fulfillment of their prophecy when, many years after, he was killed by the Indians.

To the constables of Dover, Hampton, Salisbury, Newbury, Rowley, Ipswich, Wenham Lynn, Boston, Roxbury, Dedham, and until

" Smite, Goodman Hate-Evil ! — harder
    still ! "
The magistrate cried, "lay on with a
    will !
Drive out of their bodies the Father of
    Lies,
Who through them preaches and proph-
    esies ! "

So into the forest they held their way,
By winding river and frost - rimmed
    bay,
Over wind-swept hills that felt the beat
Of the winter sea at their icy feet.

The Indian hunter, searching his traps,
Peered stealthily through the forest
    gaps ;
And the outlying settler shook his
    head, —
" They 're witches going to jail," he said.

At last a meeting-house came in view ;
A blast on his horn the constable blew ;
And the boys of Hampton cried up and
    down,
" The Quakers have come ! " to the
    wondering town.

From barn and woodpile the goodman
    came ;
The goodwife quitted her quilting frame,
With her child at her breast ; and, hob-
    bling slow,
The grandam followed to see the show.

Once more the torturing whip was
    swung,
Once more keen lashes the bare flesh
    stung.
" Oh, spare ! they are bleeding ! " a lit-
    tle maid cried,
And covered her face the sight to hide.

A murmur ran round the crowd : " Good
    folks,"
Quoth the constable, busy counting the
    strokes,
" No pity to wretches like these is due,
They have beaten the gospel black and
    blue ! "

Then a pallid woman, in wild - eyed
    fear,
With her wooden noggin of milk drew
    near.

" Drink, poor hearts ! " a rude hand
    smote
Her draught away from a parching
    throat.

" Take heed," one whispered, " they 'll
    take your cow
For fines, as they took your horse and
    plow,
And the bed from under you." " Even
    so,"
She said. " They are cruel as death, I
    know."

Then on they passed, in the waning
    day,
Through Seabrook woods, a weariful
    way ;
By great salt meadows and sand-hills
    bare,
And glimpses of blue sea here and there.

By the meeting - house in Salisbury
    town,
The sufferers stood, in the red sun-
    down,
Bare for the lash ! O pitying Night,
Drop swift thy curtain and hide the
    sight !

With shame in his eye and wrath on his
    lip
The Salisbury constable dropped his
    whip.
" This warrant means murder foul and
    red ;
Cursed is he who serves it," he said.

" Show me the order, and meanwhile
    strike
A blow at your peril ! " said Justice
    Pike.
Of all the rulers the land possessed,
Wisest and boldest was he and best.

He scoffed at witchcraft; the priest he
    met
As man meets man ; his feet he set
Beyond his dark age, standing up-
    right,
Soul-free, with his face to the morning
    light.

He read the warrant : "*These convey
*From our precincts ; at every town on th
    way*

Give each ten lashes." " God judge the
    brute !
I tread his order under my foot !

" Cut loose these poor ones and let them
    go ;
Come what will of it, all men shall know
No warrant is good, though backed by
    the Crown,
For whipping women in Salisbury
    town ! "

The hearts of the villagers, half re-
    leased
From creed of terror and rule of priest,
By a primal instinct owned the right
Of human pity in law's despite.

For ruth and chivalry only slept,
His Saxon manhood the yeoman kept ;
Quicker or slower, the same blood ran
In the Cavalier and the Puritan.

The Quakers sank on their knees in
    praise
And thanks. A last, low sunset blaze
Flashed out from under a cloud, and
    shed
A golden glory on each bowed head.

The tale is one of an evil time,
When souls were fettered and thought
    was crime,
And heresy's whisper above its breath
Meant shameful scourging and bonds
    and death !

What marvel, that hunted and sorely
    tried,
Even woman rebuked and prophesied,
And soft words rarely answered back
The grim persuasion of whip and rack !

If her cry from the whipping-post and
    jail
Pierced sharp as the Kenite's driven
    nail,
O woman, at ease in these happier days,
Forbear to judge of thy sister's ways !

How much thy beautiful life may owe
To her faith and courage thou canst not
    know,
Nor how from the paths of thy calm re-
    treat
She smoothed the thorns with her bleed-
    ing feet.

A SUMMER PILGRIMAGE.

To kneel before some saintly shrine,
To breathe the health of airs divine,
Or bathe where sacred rivers flow,
The cowled and turbaned pilgrims go.
I too, a palmer, take, as they
With staff and scallop-shell, my way
To feel, from burdening cares and ills,
The strong uplifting of the hills.

The years are many since, at first,
For dreamed-of wonders all athirst,
I saw on Winnepesaukee fall
The shadow of the mountain wall.
Ah ! where are they who sailed with me
The beautiful island-studded sea ?
And am I he whose keen surprise
Flashed out from such unclouded eyes ?

Still, when the sun of summer burns,
My longing for the hills returns ;
And northward, leaving at my back
The warm vale of the Merrimac,
I go to meet the winds of morn,
Blown down the hill - gaps, mountain-
    born,
Breathe scent of pines, and satisfy
The hunger of a lowland eye.

Again I see the day decline
Along a ridged horizon line ;
Touching the hill-tops, as a nun
Her beaded rosary, sinks the sun.
One lake lies golden, which shall soon
Be silver in the rising moon ;
And one, the crimson of the skies
And mountain purple multiplies.

With the untroubled quiet blends
The distance-softened voice of friends ;
The girl's light laugh no discord brings
To the low song the pine-tree sings ;
And, not unwelcome, comes the hail
Of boyhood from his nearing sail.
The human presence breaks no spell,
And sunset still is miracle !

Calm as the hour, methinks I feel
A sense of worship o'er me steal ;
Not that of satyr-charming Pan,
No cult of Nature shaming man,
Not Beauty's self, but that which lives
And shines through all the veils it
    weaves, —
Soul of the mountain, lake, and wood,
Their witness to the Eternal Good !

And if, by fond illusion, here
The earth to heaven seems drawing
      near,
And yon outlying range invites
To other and serener heights,
Scarce hid behind its topmost swell,
The shining Mounts Delectable !
A dream may hint of truth no less
Than the sharp light of wakefulness.

As through her veil of incense smoke
Of old the spell-rapt priestess spoke,
More than her heathen oracle,
May not this trance of sunset tell
That Nature's forms of loveliness
Their heavenly archetypes confess,
Fashioned like Israel's ark alone
From patterns in the Mount made
      known ?

A holier beauty overbroods
These fair and faint similitudes ;
Yet not unblest is he who sees
Shadows of God's realities,
And knows beyond this masquerade
Of shape and color, light and shade,
And dawn and set, and wax and
      wane,
Eternal verities remain.

O gems of sapphire, granite set !
O hills that charmed horizons fret !
I know how fair your morns can break,
In rosy light on isle and lake ;
How over wooded slopes can run
The noonday play of cloud and sun,
And evening droop her oriflamme
Of gold and red in still Asquam.

The summer moons may round again,
And careless feet these hills profane ;
These sunsets waste on vacant eyes
The lavish splendor of the skies ;
Fashion and folly, misplaced here,
Sigh for their natural atmosphere,
And traveled pride the outlook scorn
Of lesser heights than Matterhorn :

But let me dream that hill and sky
Of unseen beauty prophesy ;
And in these tinted lakes behold
The trailing of the raiment fold
Of that which, still eluding gaze,
Allures to upward-tending ways,
Whose footprints make, wherever found,
Our common earth a holy ground.

THE ROCK-TOMB OF BRADORE.

A DREAR and desolate shore !
Where no tree unfolds its leaves,
And never the spring wind weaves
Green grass for the hunter's tread ;
A land forsaken and dead,
Where the ghostly icebergs go
And come with the ebb and flow
      Of the waters of Bradore ?

A wanderer, from a land
By summer breezes fanned,
Looked round him, awed, subdued,
By the dreadful solitude,
Hearing alone the cry
Of sea-birds clanging by,
The crash and grind of the floe,
Wail of wind and wash of tide.
" O wretched land ! " he cried,
" Land of all lands the worst,
God forsaken and curst !
Thy gates of rock should show
      The words the Tuscan seer
Read in the Realm of Woe :
      Hope entereth not here ! "

Lo ! at his feet there stood
A block of smooth larch wood,
Waif of some wandering wave,
Beside a rock-closed cave
By Nature fashioned for a grave,
Safe from the ravening bear
And fierce fowl of the air,
Wherein to rest was laid
A twenty summers' maid,
Whose blood had equal share
Of the lands of vine and snow,
Half French, half Eskimo.
In letters uneffaced,
Upon the block were traced
The grief and hope of man,
And thus the legend ran :
      " We loved her !
Words cannot tell how well !
      We loved her !
      God loved her !
And called her home to peace and rest,
      We love her ! "

The stranger paused and read.
" O winter land ! " he said,
" Thy right to be I own ;
God leaves thee not alone.
And if thy fierce winds blow
Over drear wastes of rock and snow,

And at thy iron gates
The ghostly iceberg waits,
    Thy homes and hearts are dear.
Thy sorrow o'er thy sacred dust
Is sanctified by hope and trust;
    God's love and man's are here.
And love where'er it goes
Makes its own atmosphere;
Its flowers of Paradise
Take root in the eternal ice,
    And bloom through Polar snows! "

STORM ON LAKE ASQUAM.

A CLOUD, like that the old-time Hebrew saw
    On Carmel prophesying rain, began
To lift itself o'er wooded Cardigan,
Growing and blackening. Suddenly, a flaw

Of chill wind menaced; then a strong blast beat
    Down the long valley's murmuring pines, and woke
The noon-dream of the sleeping lake, and broke
Its smooth steel mirror at the mountains' feet.

Thunderous and vast, a fire-veined darkness swept
    Over the rough pine-bearded Asquam range;
A wraith of tempest, wonderful and strange,
From peak to peak the cloudy giant stepped.

One moment, as if challenging the storm,
    Chocorua's tall, defiant sentinel
Looked from his watch-tower; then the shadow fell,
And the wild rain-drift blotted out his form.

And over all the still unhidden sun,
    Weaving its light through slant-blown veils of rain,
    Smiled on the trouble, as hope smiles on pain;
And, when the tumult and the strife were done,

With one foot on the lake and one on land,
    Framing within his crescent's tinted streak
    A far-off picture of the Melvin peak,
Spent broken clouds the rainbow's angel spanned.

THE WISHING BRIDGE.

AMONG the legends sung or said
    Along our rocky shore,
The Wishing Bridge of Marblehead
    May well be sung once more.

An hundred years ago (so ran
    The old-time story) all
Good wishes said above its span
    Would, soon or late, befall.

If pure and earnest, never failed
    The prayers of man or maid
For him who on the deep sea sailed,
    For her at home who stayed.

Once thither came two girls from school,
    And wished in childish glee:
And one would be a queen and rule,
    And one the world would see.

Time passed; with change of hopes and fears,
    And in the self-same place,
Two women, gray with middle years,
    Stood, wondering, face to face.

With wakened memories, as they met,
    They queried what had been:
" A poor man's wife am I, and yet,"
    Said one, " I am a queen.

" My realm a little homestead is,
    Where, lacking crown and throne,
I rule by loving services
    And patient toil alone."

The other said: " The great world lies
    Beyond me as it laid;
O'er love's and duty's boundaries
    My feet have never strayed.

" I see but common sights of home,
    Its common sounds I hear,
My widowed mother's sick-bed room
    Sufficeth for my sphere.

" I read to her some pleasant page
Of travel far and wide,
And in a dreamy pilgrimage
We wander side by side.

" And when, at last, she falls asleep,
My book becomes to me
A magic glass : my watch I keep,
But all the world I see.

" A farm-wife queen your place you fill,
While fancy's privilege
Is mine to walk the earth at will,
Thanks to the Wishing Bridge."

" Nay, leave the legend for the truth,"
The other cried, " and say
God gives the wishes of our youth
But in His own best way ! "

THE MYSTIC'S CHRISTMAS.

"ALL hail ! " the bells of Christmas
rang,
"All hail ! " the monks at Christmas
sang,
The merry monks who kept with cheer
The gladdest day of all their year.

But still apart, unmoved thereat,
A pious elder brother sat
Silent, in his accustomed place,
With God's sweet peace upon his face.

"Why sitt'st thou thus ? " his brethren
cried.
" It is the blessed Christmas-tide ;
The Christmas lights are all aglow,
The sacred lilies bud and blow.

" Above our heads the joy-bells ring,
Without the happy children sing,
And all God's creatures hail the morn
On which the holy Christ was born !

" Rejoice with us ; no more rebuke
Our gladness with thy quiet look."
The gray monk answered : " Keep, I
pray,
Even as ye list, the Lord's birthday.

" Let heathen Yule fires flicker red
Where thronged refectory feasts are
spread ;
With mystery-play and masque and mime
And wait-songs speed the holy time !

" The blindest faith may haply save ;
The Lord accepts the things we have ;
And reverence, howsoe'er it strays,
May find at last the shining ways.

" They needs must grope who cannot
see,
The blade before the ear must be ;
As ye are feeling I have felt,
And where ye dwell I too have dwelt.

" But now, beyond the things of sense,
Beyond occasions and events,
I know, through God's exceeding grace,
Release from form and time and place.

" I listen, from no mortal tongue,
To hear the song the angels sung ;
And wait within myself to know
The Christmas lilies bud and blow.

" The outward symbols disappear
From him whose inward sight is clear ;
And small must be the choice of days
To him who fills them all with praise !

" Keep while you need it, brothers mine,
With honest zeal your Christmas sign,
But judge not him who every morn
Feels in his heart the Lord Christ
born ! "

WHAT THE TRAVELER SAID AT SUNSET.

THE shadows grow and deepen round
me,
I feel the dew-fall in the air ;
The muezzin of the darkening thicket
I hear the night-thrush call to prayer.

The evening wind is sad with farewells,
And loving hands unclasp from mine ;
Alone I go to meet the darkness
Across an awful boundary-line.

As from the lighted hearths behind me
I pass with slow, reluctant feet,
What waits me in the land of strange-
ness ?
What face shall smile, what voice
shall greet ?

What space shall awe, what brightness
blind me ?
What thunder-roll of music stun ?

What vast processions sweep before me
Of shapes unknown beneath the sun ?

I shrink from unaccustomed glory,
I dread the myriad-voicèd strain ;
Give me the unforgotten faces,
And let my lost ones speak again.

He will not chide my mortal yearning
Who is our Brother and our Friend ;
In whose full life, divine and human,
The heavenly and the earthly blend.

Mine be the joy of soul-communion,
The sense of spiritual strength re-
newed,
The reverence for the pure and holy,
The dear delight of doing good.

No fitting ear is mine to listen
An endless anthem's rise and fall ;
No curious eye is mine to measure
The pearl gate and the jasper wall.

For love must needs be more than knowl-
edge :
What matter if I never know
Why Aldebaran's star is ruddy,
Or warmer Sirius white as snow !

Forgive my human words, O Father !
I go Thy larger truth to prove ;
Thy mercy shall transcend my longing :
I seek but love, and Thou art Love !

I go to find my lost and mourned for
Safe in Thy sheltering goodness still,
And all that hope and faith foreshadow
Made perfect in Thy holy will !

A GREETING.

HARRIET BEECHER STOWE'S SEVENTI-
ETH ANNIVERSARY, 1882.

THRICE welcome from the Land of
Flowers
And golden-fruited orange bowers
To this sweet, green - turfed June of
ours !
To her who, in our evil time,
Dragged into light the nation's crime
With strength beyond the strength of
men,
And, mightier than their swords, her
pen !

To her who world-wide entrance gave
To the log-cabin of the slave ;
Made all his wrongs and sorrows known,
And all earth's languages his own, —
North, South, and East and West, made
all
The common air electrical,
Until the o'ercharged bolts of heaven
Blazed down, and every chain was
riven !

Welcome from each and all to her
Whose Wooing of the Minister
Revealed the warm heart of the man
Beneath the creed-bound Puritan,
And taught the kinship of the love
Of man below and God above ;
To her whose vigorous pencil-strokes
Sketched into life her Oldtown Folks, —
Whose fireside stories, grave or gay,
In quaint Sam Lawson's vagrant way,
With old New England's flavor rife,
Waifs from her rude idyllic life,
Are racy as the legends old
By Chaucer or Boccaccio told ;
To her who keeps, through change of
place
And time, her native strength and grace,
Alike where warm Sorrento smiles,
Or where, by birchen-shaded isles,
Whose summer winds have shivered
o'er
The icy drift of Labrador,
She lifts to light the priceless Pearl
Of Harpswell's angel-beckoned girl !
To her at threescore years and ten
Be tributes of the tongue and pen ;
Be honor, praise, and heart-thanks given,
The loves of earth, the hopes of heaven !

Ah, dearer than the praise that stirs
The air to-day, our love is hers !
She needs no guaranty of fame
Whose own is linked with Freedom's
name.
Long ages after ours shall keep
Her memory living while we sleep ;
The waves that wash our gray coast
lines,
The winds that rock the Southern pines,
Shall sing of her ; the unending years
Shall tell her tale in unborn ears.
And when, with sins and follies past,
Are numbered color-hate and caste,
White, black, and red shall own as
one
The noblest work by woman done.

WILSON.[1]

THE lowliest born of all the land,
He wrung from Fate's reluctant hand
    The gifts which happier boyhood
        claims;
And, tasting on a thankless soil
The bitter bread of unpaid toil,
    He fed his soul with noble aims.

And Nature, kindly provident,
To him the future's promise lent;
    The powers that shape man's destinies,
Patience and faith and toil, he knew,
The close horizon round him grew,
    Broad with great possibilities.

By the low hearth-fire's fitful blaze
He read of old heroic days,
    The sage's thought, the patriot's
        speech;
Unhelped, alone, himself he taught,
His school the craft at which he wrought,
    His lore the book within his reach.

He felt his country's need; he knew
The work her children had to do;
    And when, at last, he heard the call
In her behalf to serve and dare,
Beside his senatorial chair
    He stood the unquestioned peer of all.

Beyond the accident of birth
He proved his simple manhood's worth;
    Ancestral pride and classic grace
Confessed the large-brained artisan,
So clear of sight, so wise in plan
    And counsel, equal to his place.

With glance intuitive he saw
Through all disguise of form and law,
    And read men like an open book;
Fearless and firm, he never quailed
Nor turned aside for threats, nor failed
    To do the thing he undertook.

How wise, how brave, he was, how well
He bore himself, let history tell
    While waves our flag o'er land and
        sea,
No black thread in its warp or weft;
He found dissevered States, he left
    A grateful Nation, strong and free!

[1] Read at the Massachusetts Club on the seventieth anniversary of the birthday of Vice-President Wilson.

IN MEMORY.

J. T. F.

As a guest who may not stay
Long and sad farewells to say
Glides with smiling face away,

Of the sweetness and the zest
Of thy happy life possessed
Thou hast left us at thy best.

Warm of heart and clear of brain,
Of thy sun-bright spirit's wane
Thou hast spared us all the pain.

Now that thou hast gone away,
What is left of one to say
Who was open as the day?

What is there to gloss or shun?
Save with kindly voices none
Speak thy name beneath the sun.

Safe thou art on every side,
Friendship nothing finds to hide,
Love's demand is satisfied.

Over manly strength and worth,
At thy desk of toil, or hearth,
Played the lambent light of mirth, —

Mirth that lit, but never burned;
All thy blame to pity turned;
Hatred thou hadst never learned.

Every harsh and vexing thing
At thy home-fire lost its sting;
Where thou wast was always spring.

And thy perfect trust in good,
Faith in man and womanhood,
Chance and change and time with
    stood.

Small respect for cant and whine,
Bigot's zeal and hate malign,
Had that sunny soul of thine.

But to thee was duty's claim
Sacred, and thy lips became
Reverent with one holy Name.

Therefore, on thy unknown way,
Go in God's peace! We who stay
But a little while delay.

Keep for us, O friend, where'er
Thou art waiting, all that here
Made thy earthly presence dear ;

Something of thy pleasant past
On a ground of wonder cast,
In the stiller waters glassed !

Keep the human heart of thee ;
Let the mortal only be
Clothed in immortality.

And when fall our feet as fell
Thine upon the asphodel,
Let thy old smile greet us well ;

Proving in a world of bliss
What we fondly dream in this, —
Love is one with holiness !

THE POET AND THE CHIL-
DREN.

H. W. L.

WITH a glory of winter sunshine
Over his locks of gray,
In the old historic mansion
He sat on his last birthday ;

With his books and his pleasant pic-
tures,
And his household and his kin,
While a sound as of myriads singing
From far and near stole in.

It came from his own fair city,
From the prairie's boundless plain,
From the Golden Gate of sunset,
And the cedarn woods of Maine.

And his heart grew warm within him,
And his moistening eyes grew dim,
For he knew that his country's chil-
dren
Were singing the songs of him :

The lays of his life's glad morning,
The psalms of his evening time,
Whose echoes shall float forever
On the winds of every clime.

All their beautiful consolations,
Sent forth like birds of cheer,
Came flocking back to his windows,
And sang in the Poet's ear.

Grateful, but solemn and tender,
The music rose and fell
With a joy akin to sadness
And a greeting like farewell.

With a sense of awe he listened
To the voices sweet and young ;
The last of earth and the first of heaven
Seemed in the songs they sung.

And waiting a little longer
For the wonderful change to come,
He heard the Summoning Angel,
Who calls God's children home !

And to him in a holier welcome
Was the mystical meaning given
Of the words of the blessed Master :
" Of such is the kingdom of heaven ! "

RABBI ISHMAEL.

THE Rabbi Ishmael, with the woe and sin
Of the world heavy upon him, entering
in
The Holy of Holies, saw an awful Face
With terrible splendor filling all the
place.
" O Ishmael Ben Elisha ! " said a voice,
" What seekest thou ? What blessing
is thy choice ? "
And, knowing that he stood before the
Lord,
Within the shadow of the cherubim,
Wide-winged between the blinding light
and him,
He bowed himself, and uttered not a
word,
But in the silence of his soul was prayer :
" O Thou Eternal ! I am one of all,
And nothing ask that others may not
share.
Thou art almighty ; we are weak and
small,
And yet thy children : let thy mercy
spare ! "
Trembling, he raised his eyes, and in the
place
Of the insufferable glory, lo ! a face
Of more than mortal tenderness, that
bent
Graciously down in token of assent,
And, smiling, vanished ! With strange
joy elate,
The wondering Rabbi sought the tem-
ple's gate.

Radiant as Moses from the Mount, he
   stood
And cried aloud unto the multitude :
"O Israel, hear ! The Lord our God is
   good !
Mine eyes have seen his glory and his
   grace ;
Beyond his judgments shall his love en-
   dure ;
The mercy of the All Merciful is sure ! "

VALUATION.

THE old Squire said, as he stood by his
   gate,
   And his neighbor, the Deacon, went
     by,
"In spite of my bank stock and real
   estate,
   You are better off, Deacon, than I.

"We 're both growing old, and the end 's
   drawing near,
   You have less of this world to resign,
But in Heaven's appraisal your assets, I
   fear,
   Will reckon up greater than mine.

"They say I am rich, but I 'm feeling
   so poor,
   I wish I could swap with you even :
The pounds I have lived for and laid up
   in store
   For the shillings and pence you have
     given."

"Well, Squire," said the Deacon, with
   shrewd common sense,
   While his eye had a twinkle of fun,
"Let your pounds take the way of my
   shillings and pence,
   And the thing can be easily done ! "

WINTER ROSES.[1]

MY garden roses long ago
   Have perished from the leaf-strewn
     walks ;
Their pale, fair sisters smile no more
   Upon the sweet-brier stalks.

[1] In reply to a flower gift from Mrs. Putnam's
school at Jamaica Plain.

Gone with the flower-time of my life,
   Spring's violets, summer's blooming
     pride,
And Nature's winter and my own
   Stand, flowerless, side by side.

So might I yesterday have sung ;
   To-day, in bleak December's noon,
Come sweetest fragrance, shapes, and
    hues,
   The rosy wealth of June !

Bless the young hands that cullęd the
   gift,
   And bless the hearts that prompted it ;
If undeserved it comes, at least
   It seems not all unfit.

Of old my Quaker ancestors
   Had gifts of forty stripes save one ;
To-day as many roses crown
   The gray head of their son.

And with them, to my fancy's eye,
   The fresh-faced givers smiling come,
And nine and thirty happy girls
   Make glad a lonely room.

They bring the atmosphere of youth ;
   The light and warmth of long ago
Are in my heart, and on my cheek
   The airs of morning blow.

O buds of girlhood, yet unblown,
   And fairer than the gift ye chose,
For you may years like leaves unfold
   The heart of Sharon's rose !

HYMN.

(FOR THE AMERICAN HORTICULTURAL
SOCIETY.)

1882.

O PAINTER of the fruits and flowers,
   We own Thy wise design,
Whereby these human hands of ours
   May share the work of Thine !

Apart from Thee we plant in vain
   The root and sow the seed ;
Thy early and Thy later rain,
   Thy sun and dew we need.

Our toil is sweet with thankfulness,
   Our burden is our boon ;

The curse of Earth's gray morning is
  The blessing of its noon.

Why search the wide world everywhere
  For Eden's unknown ground ? —
That garden of the primal pair
  May nevermore be found.

But, blest by Thee, our patient toil
  May right the ancient wrong,
And give to every clime and soil
  The beauty lost so long.

Our homestead flowers and fruited trees
  May Eden's orchard shame ;
We taste the tempting sweets of these
  Like Eve, without her blame.

And, North and South and East and West
  The pride of every zone,
The fairest, rarest, and the best
  May all be made our own.

Its earliest shrines the young world
    sought
  In hill-groves and in bowers,
The fittest offerings thither brought
  Were Thy own fruits and flowers.

And still with reverent hands we cull
  Thy gifts each year renewed ;
The good is always beautiful,
  The beautiful is good.

GODSPEED.

OUTBOUND, your bark awaits you.
    Were I one
  Whose prayer availeth much, my
    wish should be
  Your favoring trade-wind and con-
    senting sea.
By sail or steed was never love outrun,
And, here or there, love follows her in
    whom
  All graces and sweet charities unite,
  The old Greek beauty set in holier
    light ;
And her for whom New England's by-
    ways bloom,
Who walks among us welcome as the
    Spring,
  Calling up blossoms where her light
    feet stray.
God keep you both, make beautiful
  your way,

Comfort, console, and bless ; and safely
    bring,
Ere yet I make upon a vaster sea
The unreturning voyage, my friends to
    me.

AT LAST.

WHEN on my day of life the night is
    falling,
  And, in the winds from unsunned
    spaces blown,
I hear far voices out of darkness calling
  My feet to paths unknown,

Thou who hast made my home of life so
    pleasant,
  Leave not its tenant when its walls
    decay ;
O Love Divine, O Helper ever present,
  Be Thou my strength and stay !

Be near me when all else is from me
    drifting :
  Earth, sky, home's pictures, days of
    shade and shine,
And kindly faces to my own uplifting
  The love which answers mine.

I have but Thee, my Father ! let Thy
    spirit
  Be with me then to comfort and up-
    hold ;
No gate of pearl, no branch of palm I
    merit,
  Nor street of shining gold.

Suffice it if — my good and ill unreck-
    oned,
  And both forgiven through Thy aboun-
    ding grace —
I find myself by hands familiar beck-
    oned
  Unto my fitting place.

Some humble door among Thy many
    mansions,
  Some sheltering shade where sin and
    striving cease,
And flows forever through heaven's
    green expansions
  The river of Thy peace.

There, from the music round about me
    stealing,
  I fain would learn the new and holy
    song,

And find at last, beneath Thy trees of
    healing,
  The life for which I long.

OUR COUNTRY.

READ AT WOODSTOCK, CONN., JULY
4, 1883.

WE give thy natal day to hope,
  O Country of our love and prayer !
Thy way is down no fatal slope,
  But up to freer sun and air.

Tried as by furnace-fires, and yet
  By God's grace only stronger made,
In future task before thee set
    Thou shalt not lack the old-time
      aid.

The fathers sleep, but men remain
  As wise, as true, and brave as they ;
Why count the loss and not the gain ? —
  The best is that we have to-day.

Whate'er of folly, shame, or crime,
  Within thy mighty bounds transpires,
With speed defying space and time
  Comes to us on the accusing wires ;

While of thy wealth of noble deeds,
  Thy homes of peace, thy votes un-
    sold,
The love that pleads for human needs,
  The wrong redressed, but half is
    told !

We read each felon's chronicle,
  His acts, his words, his gallows-mood ;
We know the single sinner well
  And not the nine and ninety good.

Yet if, on daily scandals fed,
  We seem at times to doubt thy worth,
We know thee still, when all is said,
  The best and dearest spot on earth.

From the warm Mexic Gulf, or where
  Belted with flowers Los Angeles
Basks in the semi-tropic air,
  To where Katahdin's cedar trees

Are dwarfed and bent by Northern
    winds,
  Thy plenty's horn is yearly filled ;
Alone, the rounding century finds
  Thy liberal soil by free hands tilled.

A refuge for the wronged and poor,
  Thy generous heart has borne the
    blame
That, with them, through thy open
    door,
  The old world's evil outcasts came.

But, with thy just and equal rule,
  And labor's need and breadth of
    lands,
Free press and rostrum, church and
    school,
  Thy sure, if slow, transforming hands

Shall mould even them to thy design,
  Making a blessing of the ban ;
And Freedom's chemistry combine
  The alien elements of man.

The power that broke their prison bar
  And set the dusky millions free,
And welded in the flame of war
  The Union fast to Liberty,

Shall it not deal with other ills,
  Redress the red man's grievance,
    break
The Circean cup which shames and
    kills,
  And Labor full requital make ?

Alone to such as fitly bear
  Thy civic honors bid them fall ?
And call thy daughters forth to share
  The rights and duties pledged to all ?

Give every child his right of school,
  Merge private greed in public good,
And spare a treasury overfull
  The tax upon a poor man's food ?

No lack was in thy primal stock,
  No weakling founders builded here ;
Thine were the men of Plymouth Rock,
  The Huguenot and Cavalier ;

And they whose firm endurance gained
  The freedom of the souls of men,
Whose hands, unstained with blood,
    maintained,
  The swordless commonwealth of
    Penn.

And thine shall be the power of all
  To do the work which duty bids,
And make the people's council hall
  As lasting as the Pyramids !

Well have thy later years made good
Thy brave-said word a century back,
The pledge of human brotherhood,
The equal claim of white and black.

That word still echoes round the world,
And all who hear it turn to thee,
And read upon thy flag unfurled
The prophecies of destiny.

Thy great world-lesson all shall learn,
The nations in thy school shall sit,
Earth's farthest mountain-tops shall burn
With watch-fires from thy own uplit.

Great without seeking to be great
By fraud or conquest, rich in gold,
But richer in the large estate
Of virtue which thy children hold,

With peace that comes of purity
And strength to simple justice due,
So runs our loyal dream of thee ;
God of our fathers ! — make it true.

O Land of lands ! to thee we give
Our prayers, our hopes, our service free ;
For thee thy sons shall nobly live,
And at thy need shall die for thee !

THE " STORY OF IDA."

WEARY of jangling noises never stilled,
The skeptic's sneer, the bigot's hate, the din
Of clashing texts, the webs of creed men spin
Round simple truth, the children grown who build
With gilded cards their new Jerusalem,
Busy, with sacerdotal tailorings
And tinsel gauds, bedizening holy things
I turn, with glad and grateful heart, from them
To the sweet story of the Florentine
Immortal in her blameless maidenhood,
Beautiful as God's angels and as good ;
Feeling that life, even now, may be divine

With love no wrong can ever change to hate,
No sin make less than all-compassionate !

AN AUTOGRAPH.

I WRITE my name as one,
On sands by waves o'errun
Or winter's frosted pane,
Traces a record vain.

Oblivion's blankness claims
Wiser and better names,
And well my own may pass
As from the strand or glass.

Wash on, O waves of time !
Melt, noons, the frosty rime !
Welcome the shadow vast,
The silence that shall last !

When I and all who know
And love me vanish so,
What harm to them or me
Will the lost memory be ?

If any words of mine,
Through right of life divine,
Remain, what matters it
Whose hand the message writ ?

Why should the " crowner's quest "
Sit on my worst or best ?
Why should the showman claim
The poor ghost of my name ?

Yet, as when dies a sound
Its spectre lingers round,
Haply my spent life will
Leave some faint echo still.

A whisper giving breath
Of praise or blame to death,
Soothing or saddening such
As loved the living much.

Therefore with yearnings vain
And fond I still would fain
A kindly judgment seek,
A tender thought bespeak.

And, while my words are read,
Let this at least be said :
" Whate'er his life's defeatures,
He loved his fellow-creatures.

" If, of the Law's stone table,
    To hold he scarce was able
    The first great precept fast,
    He kept for man the last.

" Through mortal lapse and dullness
    What lacks the Eternal Fullness,
    If still our weakness can
    Love Him in loving man ?

" Age brought him no despairing
    Of the world's future faring ;
    In human nature still
    He found more good than ill.

" To all who dumbly suffered,
    His tongue and pen he offered ;
    His life was not his own,
    Nor lived for self alone.

" Hater of din and riot
    He lived in days unquiet ;
    And, lover of all beauty,
    Trod the hard ways of duty.

" He meant no wrong to any
    He sought the good of many,
    Yet knew both sin and folly, —
    May God forgive him wholly ! "

SAINT GREGORY'S GUEST,

AND RECENT POEMS.

TO GEN. S. C. ARMSTRONG, OF HAMPTON, VA.,

WHOSE GENEROUS AND SELF-DENYING LABORS FOR THE ELEVATION OF TWO RACES HAVE
ENLISTED MY SYMPATHIES AND COMMANDED MY ADMIRATION,
I OFFER THIS VOLUME.

SAINT GREGORY'S GUEST.

A TALE for Roman guides to tell
To careless, sight-worn travellers still,
Who pause beside the narrow cell
    Of Gregory on the Cælian Hill.

One day before the monk's door came
A beggar, stretching empty palms,
Fainting and fast-sick, in the name
    Of the Most Holy asking alms.

And the monk answered, " All I have
    In this poor cell of mine I give,
The silver cup my mother gave ;
    In Christ's name take thou it, and
      live."

Years passed ; and, called at last to bear
    Pastoral crook and keys of Rome,
The poor monk, in Saint Peter's chair,
    Sat the crowned lord of Christendom.

" Prepare a feast," Saint Gregory
      cried,
    " And let twelve beggars sit thereat."
The beggars came, and one beside,
    An unknown stranger, with them
      sat.

" I asked thee not," the Pontiff spake,
    " O stranger ; but if need be thine,
I bid thee welcome, for the sake
    Of Him who is thy Lord and mine."

A grave, calm face the stranger raised,
    Like His who on Gennesaret trod,
Or His on whom the Chaldeans gazed,
    Whose form was as the Son of God.

" Know'st thou," he said, " thy gift of
      old ? "
    And in the hand he lifted up
The Pontiff marvelled to behold
    Once more his mother's silver cup.

* Thy prayers and alms have risen, and
        bloom
    Sweetly among the flowers of heaven.
I am The Wonderful, through whom
    Whate'er thou askest shall be given."

He spake and vanished.   Gregory fell
    With his twelve guests in mute accord
Prone on their faces, knowing well
    Their eyes of flesh had seen the Lord.

The old-time legend is not vain;
    Nor vain thy art, Verona's Paul,
Telling it o'er and o'er again
    On gray Vicenza's frescoed wall.

Still wheresoever pity shares
    Its bread with sorrow, want, and sin,
And love the beggar's feast prepares,
    The uninvited Guest comes in.

Unheard, because our ears are dull,
    Unseen, because our eyes are dim,
He walks our earth, The Wonderful,
    And all good deeds are done to Him.

REVELATION.

"And I went into the Vale of Beavor, and
as I went I preached repentance to the people. And one morning, sitting by the fire, a
great cloud came over me, and a temptation
beset me. And it was said: *All things come
by Nature;* and the Elements and the Stars
came over me. And as I sat still and let it
alone, a living hope arose in me, and a true
Voice which said: *There is a living God who
made all things.* And immediately the cloud
and the temptation vanished, and Life rose
over all, and my heart was glad and I praised
the Living God." — *Journal of George Fox,*
1690.

STILL as of old, in Beavor's Vale,
    O man of God ! our hope and faith
The Elements and Stars assail,
    And the awed spirit holds its breath,
    Blown over by a wind of death.

Takes Nature thought for such as we,
    What place her human atom fills,
The weed-drift of her careless sea,
    The mist on her unheeding hills ?
    What recks she of our helpless wills ?

Strange god of Force, with fear, not
        love,
    Its trembling worshipper !   Can
    prayer

Reach the shut ear of Fate, or move
    Unpitying Energy to spare ?
    What doth the cosmic Vastness care ?

In vain to this dread Unconcern
    For the All-Father's love we look ;
In vain, in quest of it, we turn
    The storied leaves of Nature's book
    The prints her rocky tablets took.

I pray for faith, I long to trust ;
    I listen with my heart, and hear
A voice without a sound : " Be just,
    Be true, be merciful, revere
    The Word within thee : God is near !

" A light to sky and earth unknown
    Pales all their lights: a mightier
        force
Than theirs the powers of Nature own,
    And, to its goal as at its source
    His Spirit moves the Universe.

" Believe and trust.   Through stars and
        suns,
    Through life and death, through soul
        and sense,
His wise, paternal purpose runs ;
    The darkness of His providence
    Is star-lit with benign intents."

O joy supreme !   I know the Voice,
    Like none beside on earth or sea ;
Yea, more, O soul of mine, rejoice,
    By all that He requires of me,
    I know what God himself must be.

No picture to my aid I call,
    I shape no image in my prayer ;
I only know in Him is all
    Of life, light, beauty, everywhere,
    Eternal Goodness here and there !

I know He is, and what He is,
    Whose one great purpose is the good
Of all.   I rest my soul on His
    Immortal Love and Fatherhood ;
    And trust Him, as His children
    should.

I fear no more.   The clouded face
    Of Nature smiles ; through all her
        things
Of time and space and sense I trace
    The moving of the Spirit's wings,
    And hear the song of hope she sings.

ADJUSTMENT.

THE tree of Faith its bare, dry boughs
    must shed
  That nearer heaven the living ones
    may climb;
  The false must fail, though from our
    shores of time
The old lament be heard, — "Great
    Pan is dead!"
That wail is Error's, from his high
    place hurled;
  This sharp recoil is Evil undertrod;
  Our time's unrest, an angel sent of
    God
Troubling with life the waters of the
    world.
Even as they list the winds of the
    Spirit blow
  To turn or break our century-rusted
    vanes;
  Sands shift and waste; the rock
    alone remains
Where, led of Heaven, the strong tides
    come and go,
And storm-clouds, rent by thunderbolt
    and wind,
Leave, free of mist, the permanent stars
    behind.

Therefore I trust, although to outward
    sense
  Both true and false seem shaken; I
    will hold
With newer light my reverence for
    the old,
And calmly wait the births of Provi-
    dence.
No gain is lost; the clear-eyed saints
    look down
  Untroubled on the wreck of schemes
    and creeds;
  Love yet remains, its rosary of good
    deeds
Counting in task-field and o'er peopled
    town;
Truth has charmed life; the Inward
    Word survives,
  And, day by day, its revelation
    brings;
  Faith, hope, and charity, whatsoever
    things
Which cannot be shaken, stand. Still
    holy lives
Reveal the Christ of whom the letter
    told,
And the new gospel verifies the old.

THE WOOD GIANT.

FROM Alton Bay to Sandwich Dome,
  From Mad to Saco river,
For patriarchs of the primal wood
  We sought with vain endeavor.

And then we said: "The giants old
  Are lost beyond retrieval;
This pigmy growth the axe has spared
  Is not the wood primeval.

"Look where we will o'er vale and hill,
  How idle are our searches
For broad-girthed maples, wide-limbed
    oaks,
  Centennial pines and birches!

"Their tortured limbs the axe and
    saw
  Have changed to beams and trestles;
They rest in walls, they float on seas,
  They rot in sunken vessels.

"This shorn and wasted mountain land
  Of underbrush and boulder, —
Who thinks to see its full-grown tree
  Must live a century older."

At last to us a woodland path,
  To open sunset leading,
Revealed the Anakim of pines
  Our wildest wish exceeding.

Alone, the level sun before;
  Below, the lake's green islands;
Beyond, in misty distance dim,
  The rugged Northern Highlands.

Dark Titan on his Sunset Hill
  Of time and change defiant!
How dwarfed the common woodland
    seemed,
  Before the old-time giant!

What marvel that, in simpler days
  Of the world's early childhood,
Men crowned with garlands, gifts, and
    praise
  Such monarchs of the wild-wood?

That Tyrian maids with flower and
    song
  Danced through the hill grove's
    spaces,
And hoary-bearded Druids found
  In woods their holy places?

With somewhat of that Pagan awe
  With Christian reverence blending,
We saw our pine-tree's mighty arms
  Above our heads extending.

We heard his needles' mystic rune,
  Now rising, and now dying,
As erst Dodona's priestess heard
  The oak leaves prophesying.

Was it the half-unconscious moan
  Of one apart and mateless,
The weariness of unshared power,
  The loneliness of greatness ?

O dawns and sunsets, lend to him
  Your beauty and your wonder !
Blithe sparrow, sing thy summer song
  His solemn shadow under !

Play lightly on his slender keys,
  O wind of summer, waking
For hills like these the sound of seas
  On far-off beaches breaking !

And let the eagle and the crow
  Find shelter in his branches,
When winds shake down his winter snow
  In silver avalanches.

The brave are braver for their cheer,
  The strongest need assurance,
The sigh of longing makes not less
  The lesson of endurance.

THE HOMESTEAD.

AGAINST the wooded hills it stands,
  Ghosts of a dead home, staring through
Its broken lights on wasted lands
  Where old-time harvests grew.

Unploughed, unsown, by scythe unshorn,
  The poor, forsaken farm-fields lie,
Once rich and rife with golden corn
  And pale green breadths of rye.

Of healthful herb and flower bereft,
  The garden plot no housewife keeps ;
Through weeds and tangle only left,
  The snake, its tenant, creeps.

A lilac spray, once blossom-clad,
  Sways bare before the empty rooms ;
Beside the roofless porch a sad
  Pathetic red rose blooms.

His track, in mould and dust of drouth,
  On floor and hearth the squirrel leaves,
And in the fireless chimney's mouth
  His web the spider weaves.

The leaning barn, about to fall,
  Resounds no more on husking eves ;
No cattle low in yard or stall,
  No thresher beats his sheaves.

So sad, so drear ! It seems almost
  Some haunting Presence makes its sign ;
That down yon shadowy lane some ghost
  Might drive his spectral kine !

O home so desolate and lorn !
  Did all thy memories die with thee ?
Were any wed, were any born,
  Beneath this low roof-tree ?

Whose axe the wall of forest broke,
  And let the waiting sunshine through ?
What good-wife sent the earliest smoke
  Up the great chimney flue ?

Did rustic lovers hither come ?
  Did maidens, swaying back and forth
In rhythmic grace, at wheel and loom,
  Make light their toil with mirth ?

Did child feet patter on the stair ?
  Did boyhood frolic in the snow ?
Did gray age, in her elbow chair,
  Knit, rocking to and fro ?

The murmuring brook, the sighing breeze,
  The pine's slow whisper, cannot tell ;
Low mounds beneath the hemlock-trees
  Keep the home secrets well.

Cease, mother-land, to fondly boast
  Of sons far off who strive and thrive,
Forgetful that each swarming host
  Must leave an emptier hive !

O wanderers from ancestral soil,
   Leave noisome mill and chaffering
     store ;
Gird up your loins for sturdier toil,
   And build the home once more !

Come back to bayberry-scented slopes,
   And fragrant fern, and ground-mat
     vine ;
Breathe airs blown over holt and copse
   Sweet with black birch and pine.

What matter if the gains are small
   That life's essential wants supply ?
Your homestead's title gives you all
   That idle wealth can buy.

All that the many-dollared crave,
   The brick-walled slaves of Change
     and mart,
Lawns, trees, fresh air, and flowers, you
     have,
   More dear for lack of art.

Your own sole masters, freedom-willed,
   With none to bid you go or stay,
Till the old fields your fathers tilled,
   As manly men as they !

With skill that spares your toiling
     hands,
   And chemic aid that science brings,
Reclaim the waste and outworn lands,
   And reign thereon as kings !

BIRCHBROOK MILL.

A NOTELESS stream, the Birchbrook
     runs
   Beneath its leaning trees;
That low, soft ripple is its own,
   That dull roar is the sea's.

Of human signs it sees alone
   The distant church spire's tip,
And, ghost-like, on a blank of gray,
   The white sail of a ship.

No more a toiler at the wheel,
   It wanders at its will ;
Nor dam nor pond is left to tell
   Where once was Birchbrook mill.

The timbers of that mill have fed
   Long since a farmer's fires;

His doorsteps are the stones that
     ground
   The harvest of his sires.

Man trespassed here ; but Nature lost
   No right of her domain ;
She waited, and she brought the old
   Wild beauty back again.

By day the sunlight through the leaves
   Falls on its moist, green sod,
And wakes the violet bloom of spring
   And autumn's golden rod.

Its birches whisper to the wind,
   The swallow dips her wings
In the cool spray, and on its banks
   The gray song-sparrow sings.

But from it, when the dark night falls,
   The school-girl shrinks with dread ;
The farmer, home-bound from his
     fields,
   Goes by with quickened tread.

They dare not pause to hear the grind
   Of shadowy stone on stone ;
The plashing of a water-wheel
   Where wheel there now is none.

Has not a cry of pain been heard
   Above the clattering mill ?
The pawing of an unseen horse,
   Who waits his mistress still ?

Yet never to the listener's eye
   Has sight confirmed the sound ;
A wavering birch line marks alone
   The vacant pasture ground.

No ghostly arms fling up to heaven
   The agony of prayer ;
No spectral steed impatient shakes
   His white mane on the air.

The meaning of that common dread
   No tongue has fitly told ;
The secret of the dark surmise
   The brook and birches hold.

What nameless horror of the past
   Broods here forever more ?
What ghost his unforgiven sin
   Is grinding o'er and o'er ?

Does, then, immortal memory play
   The actor's tragic part,

Rehearsals of a mortal life
  And unveiled human heart ?

God's pity spare a guilty soul
  That drama of its ill,
And let the scenic curtain fall
  On Birchbrook's haunted mill !

HOW THE ROBIN CAME.

AN ALGONQUIN LEGEND.

HAPPY young friends, sit by me,
Under May's blown apple-tree,
While these home-birds in and out
Through the blossoms flit about.
Hear a story, strange and old,
By the wild red Indians told,
How the robin came to be :

Once a great chief left his son, —
Well-beloved, his only one, —
When the boy was well-nigh grown,
In the trial-lodge alone.
Left for tortures long and slow
Youths like him must undergo,
Who their pride of manhood test,
Lacking water, food, and rest.
Seven days the fast he kept,
Seven nights he never slept.
Then the young boy, wrung with pain,
Weak from nature's overstrain,
Faltering, moaned a low complaint :
"Spare me, father, for I faint !"
But the chieftain, haughty-eyed,
Hid his pity in his pride.
"You shall be a hunter good,
Knowing never lack of food ;
You shall be a warrior great,
Wise as fox and strong as bear ;
Many scalps your belt shall wear,
If with patient heart you wait
Bravely till your task is done.
Better you should starving die
Than that boy and squaw should cry
Shame upon your father's son !"

When next morn the sun's first rays
Glistened on the hemlock sprays,
Straight that lodge the old chief sought,
And boiled samp and moose meat
      brought.
"Rise and eat, my son !" he said.
Lo, he found the poor boy dead !

As with grief his grave they made,
And his bow beside him laid,
Pipe, and knife, and wampum-braid,
On the lodge-top overhead,
Preening smooth its breast of red
And the brown coat that it wore,
Sat a bird, unknown before.
And as if with human tongue,
"Mourn me not," it said, or sung ;
"I, a bird, am still your son,
Happier than if hunter fleet,
Or a brave, before your feet
Laying scalps in battle won.
Friend of man, my song shall cheer
Lodge and corn-land ; hovering near,
To each wigwam I shall bring
Tidings of the coming spring ;
Every child my voice shall know
In the moon of melting snow,
When the maple's red bud swells,
And the wind-flower lifts its bells.
As their fond companion
Men shall henceforth own your son,
And my song shall testify
That of human kin am I."

Thus the Indian legend saith
How, at first, the robin came
With a sweeter life from death,
Bird for boy, and still the same.
If my young friends doubt that this
Is the robin's genesis,
Not in vain is still the myth
If a truth be found therewith :
Unto gentleness belong
Gifts unknown to pride and wrong ;
Happier far than hate is praise, —
He who sings than he who slays.

SWEET FERN.

THE subtle power in perfume found
  Nor priest nor sibyl vainly learned ;
On Grecian shrine or Aztec mound
  No censer idly burned.

That power the old-time worships knew,
  The Corybantes' frenzied dance,
The Pythian priestess swooning through
  The wonderland of trance.

And Nature holds, in wood and field,
  Her thousand sunlit censers still ;
To spells of flower and shrub we yield
  Against or with our will.

I climbed a hill path strange and new
　With slow feet, pausing at each turn;
A sudden waft of west wind blew
　The breath of the sweet fern.

That fragrance from my vision swept
　The alien landscape; in its stead,
Up fairer hills of youth I stepped,
　As light of heart as tread.

I saw my boyhood's lakelet shine
　Once more through rifts of woodland
　　shade;
I knew my river's winding line
　By morning mist betrayed.

With me June's freshness, lapsing
　　brook,
　Murmurs of leaf and bee, the call
Of birds, and one in voice and look
　In keeping with them all.

A fern beside the way we went
　She plucked, and, smiling, held it up,
While from her hand the wild, sweet
　　scent
　I drank as from a cup.

O potent witchery of smell!
　The dust dry-leaves to life return,
And she who plucked them owns the
　　spell
　And lifts her ghostly fern.

Or sense or spirit? Who shall say
　What touch the chord of memory
　　thrills?
It passed, and left the August day
　Ablaze on lonely hills.

BANISHED FROM MASSACHU-
SETTS.

1660.

ON A PAINTING BY E. A. ABBEY.

OVER the threshold of his pleasant
　　home
　Set in green clearings passed the ex-
　　iled Friend,
　In simple trust, misdoubting not the
　　end.
" Dear heart of mine!" he said, " the
　time has come

To trust the Lord for shelter." One
　　long gaze
　The good wife turned on each famil-
　　iar thing, —
　The lowing kine, the orchard blos-
　　soming,
The open door that showed the hearth-
　　fire's blaze, —
And calmly answered, " Yes, He will
　　provide."
　Silent and slow they crossed the
　　homestead's bound,
　Lingering the longest by their child's
　　grave-mound.
" Move on, or stay and hang!" the
　　sheriff cried.
They left behind them more than home
　　or land,
And set sad faces to an alien strand.

Safer with winds and waves than hu-
　　man wrath,
　With ravening wolves than those
　　whose zeal for God
　Was cruelty to man, the exiles trod
Drear leagues of forest without guide
　　or path,
Or launching frail boats on the un-
　　charted sea,
　Round storm-vexed capes, whose
　　teeth of granite ground
　The waves to foam, their perilous
　　way they wound,
Enduring all things so their souls were
　　free.
Oh, true confessors, shaming them who
　　did
　Anew the wrong their Pilgrim Fa-
　　thers bore!
　For you the Mayflower spread her
　　sail once more,
Freighted with souls, to all that duty bid
Faithful as they who sought an un-
　　known land,
O'er wintry seas, from Holland's Hook
　　of Sand!

So from his lost home to the darkening
　　main,
　Bodeful of storm, stout Macey held
　　his way,
　And, when the green shore blended
　　with the gray,
His poor wife moaned: " Let us turn
　　back again."
" Nay, woman, weak of faith, kneel
　　down," said he,

"And say thy prayers: the Lord
  himself will steer;
And led by Him, nor man nor devils
  I fear!"[85]
So the gray Southwicks, from a rainy
  sea,
Saw, far and faint, the loom of land,
  and gave
With feeble voices thanks for friend-
  ly ground
Whereon to rest their weary feet, and
  found
A peaceful death-bed and a quiet grave
Where, ocean-walled, and wiser than
  his age,
The lord of Shelter scorned the bigot's
  rage.

Aquidneck's isle, Nantucket's lonely
  shores,
  And Indian-haunted Narragansett
    saw
  The way-worn travellers round their
    camp-fire draw,
  Or heard the plashing of their weary
    oars.
And every place whereon they rested
  grew
  Happier for pure and gracious wom-
    anhood,
  And men whose names for stainless
    honor stood,
Founders of States and rulers wise and
  true.
The Muse of history yet shall make
  amends
  To those who freedom, peace, and
    justice taught,
  Beyond their dark age led the van of
    thought,
And left unforfeited the name of
  Friends.
Oh mother State, how foiled was thy
  design!
The gain was theirs, the loss alone was
  thine.

THE TWO ELIZABETHS.

Read at the unveiling of the bust of Elizabeth Fry at the Friends' School, Providence,
R. I.

A. D. 1209.

AMIDST Thuringia's wooded hills she
  dwelt,

A high-born princess, servant of the
  poor,
Sweetening with gracious words the
  food she dealt
  To starving throngs at Wartburg's
    blazoned door.

A blinded zealot held her soul in chains
  Cramped the sweet nature that he
    could not kill,
Scarred her fair body with his penance
  pains,
  And gauged her conscience by his
    narrow will.

God gave her gifts of beauty and of
  grace,
  With fast and vigil she denied them
    all;
Unquestioning, with sad, pathetic face,
  She followed meekly at her stern
    guide's call.

So drooped and died her home-blown
  rose of bliss
  In the chill rigor of a discipline
That turned her fond lips from her
  children's kiss,
  And made her joy of motherhood a
    sin.

To their sad level by compassion
  led,
  One with the low and vile herself she
    made,
While thankless misery mocked the
  hand that fed,
  And laughed to scorn her piteous
    masquerade.

But still, with patience that outwearied
  hate
  She gave her all while yet she had to
    give;
And then her empty hands, importu-
  nate,
  In prayer she lifted that the poor
    might live.

Sore pressed by grief, and wrongs more
  hard to bear,
  And dwarfed and stifled by a harsh
    control,
She kept life fragrant with good deeds
  and prayer,
  And fresh and pure the white flower
    of her soul.

Death found her busy at her task: one
      word
    Alone she uttered as she paused to
      die,
"Silence!"—then listened even as
      one who heard
    With song and wing the angels draw-
      ing nigh!

Now Fra Angelico's roses fill her hands,
    And, on Murillo's canvas, Want and
      Pain
Kneel at her feet. Her marble image
      stands
    Worshipped and crowned in Mar-
      burg's holy fane.

Yea, wheresoe'er her Church its cross
      uprears,
    Wide as the world her story still is
      told;
In manhood's reverence, woman's pray-
      ers and tears
    She lives again whose grave is cen-
      turies old.

And still, despite the weakness or the
      blame
    Of blind submission to the blind, she
      hath
A tender place in hearts of every name,
    And more than Rome owns Saint
      Elizabeth!

A. D. 1780.

Slow ages passed: and lo! another
      came,
    An English matron, in whose simple
      faith
Nor priestly rule nor ritual had claim,
    A plain, uncanonized Elizabeth.

No sackcloth robe, nor ashen-sprinkled
      hair,
    Nor wasting fast, nor scourge, nor
      vigil long,
Marred her calm presence. God had
      made her fair,
    And she could do His goodly work
      no wrong.

Their yoke is easy and their burden
      light
    Whose sole confessor is the Christ of
      God;

Her quiet trust and faith transcending
      sight
    Smoothed to her feet the difficult
      paths she trod.

And there she walked, as duty bade her
      go,
    Safe and unsullied as a cloistered
      nun,
Shamed with her plainness Fashion's
      gaudy show,
    And overcame the world she did not
      shun.

In Earlham's bowers, in Plashet's lib-
      eral hall,
    In the great city's restless crowd and
      din,
Her ear was open to the Master's call,
    And knew the summons of His voice
      within.

Tender as mother, beautiful as wife,
    Amidst the throngs of prisoned crime
      she stood,
In modest raiment faultless as her life,
    The type of England's worthiest
      womanhood!

To melt the hearts that harshness
      turned to stone
    The sweet persuasion of her lips suf-
      ficed,
And guilt, which only hate and fear had
      known,
    Saw in her own the pitying love of
      Christ.

So wheresoe'er the guiding Spirit went
    She followed, finding every prison cell
It opened for her sacred as a tent
    Pitched by Gennesaret or by Jacob's
      well.

And Pride and Fashion felt her strong
      appeal,
    And priest and ruler marvelled as
      they saw
How hand in hand went wisdom with
      her zeal,
    And woman's pity kept the bounds
      of law.

She rests in God's peace; but her mem-
      ory stirs
    The air of earth as with an angel's
      wings,

And warms and moves the hearts of
     men like hers,
  The sainted daughter of Hungarian
     kings.

United now, the Briton and the Hun,
  Each, in her own time, faithful unto
     death,
  Live sister souls! in name and spirit
     one,
  Thuringia's saint and our Elizabeth!

THE REUNION.

Read September 10, 1885, to the surviving
students of Haverhill Academy in 1827–28.

THE gulf of seven and fifty years
  We stretch our welcoming hands
     across ;
  The distance but a pebble's toss
Between us and our youth appears.

For in life's school we linger on
  The remnant of a once full list ;
  Conning our lessons, undismissed,
With faces to the setting sun.

And some have gone the unknown
     way,
  And some await the call to rest ;
  Who knoweth whether it is best
For those who went or those who stay ?

And yet despite of loss and ill,
  If faith and love and hope remain,
  Our length of days is not in vain,
And life is well worth living still.

Still to a gracious Providence
  The thanks of grateful hearts are
     due,
  For blessings when our lives were
     new,
For all the good vouchsafed us since.

The pain that spared us sorer hurt,
  The wish denied, the purpose crossed,
  And pleasure's fond occasions lost,
Were mercies to our small desert.

'T is something that we wander back,
  Gray pilgrims, to our ancient ways,
  And tender memories of oid days
Walk with us by the Merrimac ;

That even in life's afternoon
  A sense of youth comes back again,
  As through this cool September rain
The still green woodlands dream of
     June.

The eyes grown dim to present things
  Have keener sight for by-gone years,
  And sweet and clear, in deafening
     ears,
The bird that sang at morning sings.

Dear comrades, scattered wide and far,
  Send from their homes their kindly
     word,
  And dearer ones, unseen, unheard,
Smile on us from some heavenly star.

For life and death with God are one,
  Unchanged by seeming change His
     care
  And love are round us here and
     there ;
He breaks no thread His hand has
     spun.

Soul touches soul, the muster roll
  Of life eternal has no gaps ;
  And after half a century's lapse
Our school-day ranks are closed and
     whole.

Hail and farewell ! We go our way ;
  Where shadows end, we trust in
     light ;
  The star that ushers in the night
Is herald also of the day !

REQUITAL.

As Islam's Prophet, when his last day
     drew
  Nigh to its close, besought all men to
     say
  Whom he had wronged, to whom he
     then should pay
A debt forgotten, or for pardon sue,
And, through the silence of his weeping
     friends,
  A strange voice cried : " Thou owest
     me a debt,"
  " Allah be praised ! " he answered.
     " Even yet
He gives me power to make to thee
     amends.

Oh, friend ! I thank thee for thy timely
 word."
  So runs the tale. Its lesson all may
   heed,
  For all have sinned in thought, or
   word, or deed,
Or, like the Prophet, through neglect
 have erred.
All need forgiveness, all have debts to
 pay
Ere the night cometh, while it still is
 day.

THE LIGHT THAT IS FELT.

A TENDER child of summers three,
 Seeking her little bed at night,
Paused on the dark stair timidly.
"Oh, mother ! Take my hand," said
 she,
  "And then the dark will all be
  light."

We older children grope our way
 From dark behind to dark before ;
And only when our hands we lay,
Dear Lord, in Thine, the night is day,
 And there is darkness nevermore.

Reach downward to the sunless days
 Wherein our guides are blind as we,
And faith is small and hope delays ;
Take Thou the hands of prayer we
 raise,
 And let us feel the light of Thee !

THE TWO LOVES.

SMOOTHING soft the nestling head
Of a maiden fancy-led,
Thus a grave-eyed woman said :

"Richest gifts are those we make,
Dearer than the love we take
That we give for love's own sake.

"Well I know the heart's unrest ;
Mine has been the common quest
To be loved and therefore blest.

"Favors undeserved were mine ;
At my feet as on a shrine
Love has laid its gifts divine.

"Sweet the offerings seemed, and yet
With their sweetness came regret,
And a sense of unpaid debt.

"Heart of mine unsatisfied,
Was it vanity or pride
That a deeper joy denied ?

"Hands that ope but to receive
Empty close ; they only live
Richly who can richly give.

"Still," she sighed, with moistening
 eyes,
"Love is sweet in any guise ;
But its best is sacrifice !

"He who, giving, does not crave
Likest is to Him who gave
Life itself the loved to save.

"Love, that self-forgetful gives,
Sows surprise of ripened sheaves,
Late or soon its own receives."

AN EASTER FLOWER GIFT.

O DEAREST bloom the seasons know,
Flowers of the Resurrection blow,
 Our hope and faith restore ;
And through the bitterness of death
And loss and sorrow, breathe a breath
 Of life forevermore !

The thought of Love Immortal blends
With fond remembrances of friends ;
 In you, O sacred flowers,
By human love made doubly sweet,
The heavenly and the earthly meet,
 The heart of Christ and ours !

MULFORD.

AUTHOR OF "THE NATION" AND "THE
 REPUBLIC OF GOD."

UNNOTED as the setting of a star
 He passed ; and sect and party
  scarcely knew
 When from their midst a sage and
  seer withdrew
To fitter audience, where the great
 dead are
In God's republic of the heart and mind,
Leaving no purer, nobler soul behind.

AN ARTIST OF THE BEAUTIFUL.

G. F.

HAUNTED of Beauty, like the marvellous youth
Who sang Saint Agnes' Eve! How passing fair
Her shapes took color in thy homestead air!
How on thy canvas even her dreams were truth!
Magician! who from commonest elements
Called up divine ideals, clothed upon
By mystic lights soft blending into one
Womanly grace and child-like innocence.
Teacher! thy lesson was not given in vain.
Beauty is goodness; ugliness is sin;
Art's place is sacred: nothing foul therein
May crawl or tread with bestial feet profane.
If rightly choosing is the painter's test,
Thy choice, O master, ever was the best.

HYMNS OF THE BRAHMO SOMAJ.[86]

I.

THE mercy, O Eternal One!
By man unmeasured yet,
In joy or grief, in shade or sun,
I never will forget.
I give the whole, and not a part,
Of all Thou gavest me;
My goods, my life, my soul and heart,
I yield them all to Thee!

II.

We fast and plead, we weep and pray,
From morning until even;
We feel to find the holy way,
We knock at the gate of heaven!
And when in silent awe we wait,
And word and sign forbear,
The hinges of the golden gate
Move, soundless, to our prayer!
Who hears the eternal harmonies
Can heed no outward word;
Blind to all else is he who sees
The vision of the Lord!

III.

O soul, be patient, restrain thy tears,
Have hope, and not despair;
As a tender mother heareth her child
God hears the penitent prayer.
And not forever shall grief be thine;
On the Heavenly Mother's breast,
Washed clean and white in the waters of joy
Shall His seeking child find rest.
Console thyself with His word of grace,
And cease thy wail of woe,
For His mercy never an equal hath,
And His love no bounds can know.
Lean close unto Him in faith and hope;
How many like thee have found
In Him a shelter and home of peace,
By His mercy compassed round!
There, safe from sin and the sorrow it brings,
They sing their grateful psalms,
And rest, at noon, by the wells of God,
In the shade of His holy palms!

, 1645.) In 1651, he bade defiance to
laws of Massachusetts, and was again
lawed. He acted independently of all
and authority; and hence, doubtless,
burlesque title of "The Sagamore
Saco," which has come down to the
esent generation in the following epi-
oh:—

ere lies Bonython, the Sagamore of Saco;
e lived a rogue, and died a knave, and went
to Hobomoko."

some means or other, he obtained a
e estate. In this poem, I have taken
e liberties with him, not strictly war-
ed by historical facts, although the
uct imputed to him is in keeping with
eneral character. Over the last years
life lingers a deep obscurity. Even
anner of his death is uncertain. He
upposed to have been killed by the
us; but this is doubted by the able
defatigable author of the History
and Biddeford.—Part I. p. 115.

Note 8, page 2.

ll's Brook flows from a marsh or
the "Heath," in Saco, contain-
hundred acres. On this brook,
unded by wild and romantic
a beautiful waterfall, of more
feet.

Note 9, page 3.

omes, the first Christian preacher
ha's Vineyard; for a biography of
the reader is referred to Increase
v's account of the Praying Indians,
The following is related of him:
Lord's day, after meeting, where
oomes had been preaching, there came
Powwaw very angry, and said, ' I know
he meeting Indians are liars. You say
don't care for the Powwaws':—then
ing two or three of them by name, he
led at them, and told them they were
eived, for the Powwaws could kill all
e meeting Indians, if they set about it.
ut Hiacoomes told him that he would be
the midst of all the Powwaws in the
sland, and they should do the utmost they
ould against him; and when they should
o their worst by their witchcraft to kill
im, he would without fear set himself
gainst them, by remembering Jehovah.
He told them also he did put all the Powwaws under his heel. Such was the faith
of this good man. Nor were these Powwaws ever able to do these Christian Indians any hurt, though others were frequently hurt and killed by them."—
Mayhew, pp. 6, 7, c. I.

Note 10, page 4.

"The tooth-ache," says Roger Williams,
in his observations upon the language and
customs of the New England tribes, "is
the only paine which will force their stoute
hearts to cry." He afterwards remarks
that even the Indian women never cry as
he has heard "some of their men in this
paine."

Note 11, page 5.

Wuttamuttata, "Let us drink." *Weekan*, "It is sweet." *Vide* Roger Williams's Key to the Indian Language, "in
that parte of America called New England." London, 1643, p. 35.

Note 12, page 6.

Wetuomanit,—a house god, or demon.
"They—the Indians—have given me the
names of thirty-seven gods which I have,
all which in their solemne Worships
they invocate!" R. Williams's Briefe
Observations of the Customs, Manners,
Worships, &c., of the Natives, in Peace and
Warre, in Life and Death: on all which
is added Spiritual Observations, General
and Particular, of Chiefe and Special use—
upon all occasions—to all the English in-
habiting these parts; yet Pleasant and
Profitable to the view of all Mene.—p.
110, c. 21.

Note 13, page 7.

Mt. Desert Island, the Bald Mountain
upon which overlooks Frenchman's and
Penobscot Bay. It was upon this island
that the Jesuits made their earliest settlement.

Note 14, page 8.

Father Hennepin, a missionary among
the Iroquois, mentions that the Indians
believed him to be a conjurer, and that they
were particularly afraid of a bright silver
chalice which he had in his possession.
"The Indians," says Père Jerome Lallamant, "fear us as the greatest sorcerers on
earth."

Note 15, page 8.

Bomazeen is spoken of by Penhallow as
"the famous warrior and chieftain of Norridgewock." He was killed in the attack
of the English upon Norridgewock, in
1724.

Note 16, page 9.

Père Ralle, or Rasles, was one of the
most zealous and indefatigable of that band
of Jesuit missionaries who, at the beginning of the seventeenth century, penetrated
the forests of America, with the avowed
object of converting the heathen. The

NOTES.

Note 1, page 1.

Mogg Megone, or Hegone, was a leader among the Saco Indians, in the bloody war of 1677. He attacked and captured the garrison at Black Point, October 12th of that year ; and cut off, at the same time, a party of Englishmen near Saco River. From a deed signed by this Indian in 1664, and from other circumstances, it seems that, previous to the war, he had mingled much with the colonists. On this account, he was probably selected by the principal sachems as their agent in the treaty signed in November, 1676.

Note 2, page 1.

Baron de St. Castine came to Canada in 1644. Leaving his civilized companions, he plunged into the great wilderness and settled among the Penobscot Indians, near the mouth of their noble river. He here took for his wives the daughters of the great Modocawando, — the most powerful sachem of the East. His castle was plundered by Governor Andros, during his reckless administration ; and the enraged Baron is supposed to have excited the Indians into open hostility to the English.

Note 3, page 2.

The owner and commander of the garrison at Black Point, which Mogg attacked and plundered. He was an old man at the period to which the tale relates.

Note 4, page 2.

Major Phillips, one of the principal men of the Colony. His garrison sustained a long and terrible siege by the savages. As a magistrate and a gentleman, he exacted of his plebeian neighbors a remarkable degree of deference. The Court Records of the settlement inform us that an individual was fined for the heinous offence of saying that " Major Phillips's mare was as lean as an Indian dog."

Note 5, page 2.

Captain Harmon, of Geo York, was, for many years, the Eastern Indians. In one of his up the Kennebec River, at the party of rangers, he discovered the savages asleep by a large tiously creeping towards them u was certain of his aim, he ordered to single out their objects. The f charge killed or mortally wou whole number of the unconscious

Note 6, page 2.

Wood Island, near the mou Saco. It was visited by the Monts and Champlain, in 1603. lowing extract, from the journa latter, relates to it : " Having Kennebec, we ran along the coast westward, and cast anchor under island, near the mainland, where twenty or more natives. I here vis island, beautifully clothed with a growth of forest trees, particularly oak and walnut ; and overspread vines, that, in their season, produce ex lent grapes. We named it the island Bacchus."— *Les Voyages de Sieur Cha plain,* Liv. 2, c. 8.

Note 7, page 2.

John Bonython was the son of Richa Bonython, Gent., one of the most efficier and able magistrates of the Colony. Joh proved to be " a degenerate plant." 1635, we find, by the Court Records, th for some offence, he was fined 40 *s*. 1640, he was fined for abuse toward Gibson, the minister, and Mary his Soon after he was fined for disorderly duct in the house of his father. In the " Great and General Court adj John Bonython outlawed, and incapa any of his Majesty's laws, and proc him a rebel." (Court Records of th first religious mission of the Jesuits, to the savages in North America, was in 1611. The zeal of the fathers for the conversion of the Indians to the Catholic faith knew no bounds. For this, they plunged into the depths of the wilderness ; habituated themselves to all the hardships and privations of the natives ; suffered cold, hunger, and some of them death itself, by the extremest tortures. Père Brebeuf, after laboring in the cause of his mission for twenty years, together with his companion, Père Lallamant, was burned alive. To these might be added the names of those Jesuits who were put to death by the Iroquois, — Daniel, Garnier, Buteaux, La Riborerde, Goupil, Constantin, and Liegeouis. "For bed," says Father Lallamant, in his *Relation de ce qui s'est dans le pays des Hurons*, 1640, c. 3, "we have nothing but a miserable piece of bark of a tree ; for nourishment, a handful or two of corn, either roasted or soaked in water, which seldom satisfies our hunger ; and after all, not venturing to perform even the ceremonies of our religion, without being considered as sorcerers." Their success among the natives, however, by no means equalled their exertions. Père Lallamant says : " With respect to adult persons, in good health, there is little apparent success ; on the contrary, there have been nothing but storms and whirlwinds from that quarter."

Sebastian Ralle established himself, some time about the year 1670, at Norridgewock, where he continued more than forty years. He was accused, and perhaps not without justice, of exciting his praying Indians against the English, whom he looked upon as the enemies not only of his king, but also of the Catholic religion. He was killed by the English, in 1724, at the foot of the cross which his own hands had planted. This Indian church was broken up, and its members either killed outright or dispersed.

In a letter written by Ralle to his nephew he gives the following account of his church, and his own labors : "All my converts repair to the church regularly twice every day ; first, very early in the morning, to attend mass, and again in the evening, to assist in the prayers at sunset. As it is necessary to fix the imagination of savages, whose attention is easily distracted, I have composed prayers, calculated to inspire them with just sentiments of the august sacrifice of our altars : they chant, or at least recite them aloud, during mass. Besides preaching to them on Sundays and saints' days, I seldom let a working-day pass, without making a concise exhortation, for the purpose of inspiring them with horror at those vices to which they are most addicted, or to confirm them in the practice of some particular virtue." *Vide Lettres Edifiantes et Cur.*, Vol. VI. p. 127.

Note 17, page 12.

The character of Ralle has probably never been correctly delineated. By his brethren of the Romish Church, he has been nearly apotheosized. On the other hand, our Puritan historians have represented him as a demon in human form. He was undoubtedly sincere in his devotion to the interests of his church, and not overscrupulous as to the means of advancing those interests. "The French," says the author of the History of Saco and Biddeford, "after the peace of 1713, secretly promised to supply the Indians with arms and ammunition, if they would renew hostilities. Their principal agent was the celebrated Ralle, the French Jesuit." — p. 215.

Note 18, page 13.

Hertel de Rouville was an active and unsparing enemy of the English. He was the leader of the combined French and Indian forces which destroyed Deerfield and massacred its inhabitants, in 1703. He was afterwards killed in the attack upon Haverhill. Tradition says that, on examining his dead body, his head and face were found to be perfectly smooth, without the slightest appearance of hair or beard.

Note 19, page 13.

Cowesass ? — tawhich wessaseen ? Are you afraid ? — why fear you ?

Note 20, page 15.

Winnepurkit, otherwise called George, Sachem of Saugus, married a daughter of Passaconaway, the great Pennacook chieftain, in 1662. The wedding took place at Pennacook (now Concord, N. H.), and the ceremonies closed with a great feast. According to the usages of the chiefs, Passaconaway ordered a select number of his men to accompany the newly-married couple to the dwelling of the husband, where in turn there was another great feast. Some time after, the wife of Winnepurkit expressing a desire to visit her father's house, was permitted to go, accompanied by a brave escort of her husband's chief men. But when she wished to return, her father sent a messenger to Saugus, informing her husband, and asking him to come and take her away. He returned for answer that ne had escorted his wife to her father's house in a style that became a chief, and that now if she wished to return, her father must send her back in the same way. This Passaconaway refused to do, and it is said that here terminated the connection of his daughter with the Saugus chief. — *Vide Morton's New Canaan.*

NOTE 21, page 18.

This was the name which the Indians of New England gave to two or three of their principal chiefs, to whom all their inferior sagamores acknowledged allegiance. Passaconaway seems to have been one of these chiefs. His residence was at Pennacook. (Mass. Hist. Coll., Vol. III. pp. 21, 22.) "He was regarded," says Hubbard, "as a great sorcerer, and his fame was widely spread. It was said of him that he could cause a green leaf to grow in winter, trees to dance, water to burn, &c. He was, undoubtedly, one of those shrewd and powerful men whose achievements are always regarded by a barbarous people as the result of supernatural aid. The Indians gave to such the names of Powahs or Panisees."

"The Panisees are men of great courage and wisdom, and to these the Devill appeareth more familiarly than to others." — *Winslow's Relation.*

NOTE 22, page 20.

"The Indians," says Roger Williams, "have a god whom they call Wetuomanit, who presides over the household."

NOTE 23, page 22.

There are rocks in the river at the Falls of Amoskeag, in the cavities of which, tradition says, the Indians formerly stored and concealed their corn.

NOTE 24, page 23.

The Spring God. — See *Roger Williams's Key,* &c.

NOTE 25, page 25.

"Mat wonck kunna-monee." We shall see thee or her no more. — *Vide Roger Williams's Key to the Indian Language.*

NOTE 26, page 26.

"The Great South West God." — See *Roger Williams's Observations,* &c.

NOTE 27, page 26.

The celebrated Captain Smith, after resigning the government of the Colony in Virginia, in his capacity of "Admiral of New England," made a careful survey of the coast from Penobscot to Cape Cod, in the summer of 1614.

NOTE 28, page 26.

Lake Winnipiseogee, — *The Smile of the Great Spirit,* — the source of one of the branches of the Merrimack.

NOTE 29, page 26.

Captain Smith gave to the promontory, now called Cape Ann, the name of Tragabizanda, in memory of his young and beautiful mistress of that name, who, while he was a captive at Constantinople, like Desdemona, "loved him for the dangers he had passed."

NOTE 30, page 27.

Some three or four years since, a fragment of a statue, rudely chiselled from dark gray stone, was found in the town of Bradford, on the Merrimack. Its origin must be left entirely to conjecture. The fact that the ancient Northmen visited New England, some centuries before the discoveries of Columbus, is now very generally admitted.

NOTE 31, page 36.

De Soto, in the sixteenth century, penetrated into the wilds of the new world in search of gold and the fountain of perpetual youth.

NOTE 32, page 41.

TOUSSAINT L'OUVERTURE, the black chieftain of Hayti, was a slave on the plantation "de Libertas," belonging to M. BAYOU. When the rising of the negroes took place, in 1791, TOUSSAINT refused to join them until he had aided M. BAYOU and his family to escape to Baltimore. The white man had discovered in Toussaint many noble qualities, and had instructed him in some of the first branches of education ; and the preservation of his life was owing to the negro's gratitude for this kindness.

In 1797, Toussaint L'Ouverture was appointed, by the French government, General-in-Chief of the armies of St. Domingo, and, as such, signed the Convention with General Maitland for the evacuation of the island by the British. From this period, until 1801, the island, under the government of Toussaint, was happy, tranquil, and prosperous. The miserable attempt of Napoleon to re-establish slavery in St. Domingo, although it failed of its intended object, proved fatal to the negro chieftain. Treacherously seized by Leclerc, he was hurried on board a vessel by night, and conveyed to France, where he was confined in a cold subterranean dungeon, at Besançon, where, in April, 1803, he died. The treatment of Toussaint finds a parallel only in the murder of the Duke D'Enghien. It was the remark of Godwin, in his Lectures, that the West India Islands, since their first discovery by Columbus, could not boast of a single name which deserves comparison with that of Toussaint L'Ouverture.

NOTE 33, page 43.

The reader may, perhaps, call to mind the beautiful sonnet of William Wordsworth, addressed to Toussaint L'Ouverture, during his confinement in France.

" Toussaint ! — thou most unhappy man of men !
Whether the whistling rustic tends his plough
Within thy hearing, or thou liest now
Buried in some deep dungeon's earless den ;
O miserable chieftain ! — where and when
Wilt thou find patience ? — Yet, die not, do thou
Wear rather in thy bonds a cheerful brow ;
Though fallen thyself, never to rise again,
Live and take comfort. Thou hast left behind
Powers that will work for thee ; air, earth, and skies, —
There 's not a breathing of the common wind
That will forget thee : thou hast great allies
Thy friends are exultations, agonies,
And love, and man's unconquerable mind."

NOTE 34, page 43.

The French ship LE RODEUR, with a crew of twenty-two men, and with one hundred and sixty negro slaves, sailed from Bonny, in Africa, April, 1819. On approaching the line, a terrible malady broke out, — an obstinate disease of the eyes, — contagious, and altogether beyond the resources of medicine. It was aggravated by the scarcity of water among the slaves (only half a wineglass per day being allowed to an individual), and by the extreme impurity of the air in which they breathed. By the advice of the physician, they were brought upon deck occasionally ; but some of the poor wretches, locking themselves in each other's arms, leaped overboard, in the hope, which so universally prevails among them, of being swiftly transported to their own homes in Africa. To check this, the captain ordered several who were stopped in the attempt to be shot, or hanged, before their companions. The disease extended to the crew ; and one after another were smitten with it, until only *one* remained unaffected. Yet even this dreadful condition did not preclude calculation : to save the expense of supporting slaves rendered unsalable, and to obtain grounds for a claim against the underwriters, *thirty-six of the negroes, having become blind, were thrown into the sea and drowned !*

In the midst of their dreadful fears lest the solitary individual, whose sight re-mained unaffected, should also be seized with the malady, a sail was discovered. It was the Spanish slaver, Leon. The same disease had been there ; and, horrible to tell, all the crew had become blind ! Unable to assist each other, the vessels parted. The Spanish ship has never since been heard of. The Rodeur reached Guadaloupe on the 21st of June ; the only man who had escaped the disease, and had thus been enabled to steer the slaver into port, caught it in three days after its arrival.— *Speech of M. Benjamin Constant, in the French Chamber of Deputies,* June 17 1820.

NOTE 35, page 61.

The Northern author of the Congressional rule against receiving petitions of the people on the subject of Slavery.

NOTE 36, page 70.

Dr. Thacher, surgeon in Scammel's regiment, in his description of the siege of Yorktown, says : " The labor on the Virginia plantations is performed altogether by a species of the human race cruelly wrested from their native country, and doomed to perpetual bondage, while their masters are manfully contending for freedom and the natural rights of man. Such is the inconsistency of human nature." Eighteen hundred slaves were found at Yorktown, after its surrender, and restored to their masters. Well was it said by Dr. Barnes, in his late work on Slavery : " No slave was any nearer his freedom after the surrender of Yorktown than when Patrick Henry first taught the notes of liberty to echo among the hills and vales of Virginia."

NOTE 37, page 76.

The rights and liberties affirmed by MAGNA CHARTA were deemed of such importance, in the thirteenth century, that the Bishops, twice a year, with tapers burning, and in their pontifical robes, pronounced, in the presence of the king and the representatives of the estates of England, the greater excommunication against the infringer of that instrument. The imposing ceremony took place in the great Hall of Westminster. A copy of the curse, as pronounced in 1253, declares that, " by the authority of Almighty God, and the blessed Apostles and Martyrs, and all the saints in heaven, all those who violate the English liberties, and secretly or openly, by deed, word, or counsel, do make statutes, *or observe them being made,* against said liberties, are accursed and sequestered from the company of heaven and the sacraments of the Holy Church."

WILLIAM PENN, in his admirable political pamphlet, "England's Present Interest considered," alluding to the curse of the Charter-breakers, says : "I am no Roman Catholic, and little value their other curses ; yet I declare I would not for the world incur this curse, as every man deservedly doth, who offers violence to the fundamental freedom thereby repeated and confirmed."

NOTE 38, page 91.

"The manner in which the Waldenses and heretics disseminated their principles among the Catholic gentry, was by carrying with them a box of trinkets, or articles of dress. Having entered the houses of the gentry and disposed of some of their goods, they cautiously intimated that they had commodities far more valuable than these, — inestimable jewels, which they would show if they could be protected from the clergy. They would then give their purchasers a Bible or Testament ; and thereby many were deluded into heresy."— *R. Saccho.*

NOTE 39, page 107.

Chalkley Hall, near Frankford, Pa., the residence of THOMAS CHALKLEY, an eminent minister of the Friends' denomination. He was one of the early settlers of the Colony, and his Journal, which was published in 1749, presents a quaint but beautiful picture of a life of unostentatious and simple goodness. He was the master of a merchant vessel, and, in his visits to the West Indies and Great Britain, omitted no opportunity to labor for the highest interests of his fellow-men. During a temporary residence in Philadelphia, in the summer of 1838, the quiet and beautiful scenery around the ancient village of Frankford frequently attracted me from the heat and bustle of the city.

NOTE 40, page 110.

August. Soliloq. cap. xxxi. " Interrogavi Terram," &c.

NOTE 41, page 112.

For the idea of this line, I am indebted to Emerson, in his inimitable sonnet to the Rhodora, —

" If eyes were made for seeing,
Then Beauty is its own excuse for being."

NOTE 42, page 121.

Among the earliest converts to the doctrines of Friends in Scotland was Barclay of Ury, an old and distinguished soldier, who had fought under Gustavus Adolphus, in Germany. As a Quaker, he became the object of persecution and abuse at the hands of the magistrates and the populace. None bore the indignities of the mob with greater patience and nobleness of soul than this once proud gentleman and soldier. One of his friends, on an occasion of uncommon rudeness, lamented that he should be treated so harshly in his old age who had been so honored before. "I find more satisfaction," said Barclay, " as well as honor, in being thus insulted for my religious principles, than when, a few years ago, it was usual for the magistrates, as I passed the city of Aberdeen, to meet me on the road and conduct me to public entertainment in their hall, and then escort me out again, to gain my favor."

NOTE 43, page 131.

Lucy Hooper died at Brooklyn, L. I., on the 1st of 8th mo., 1841, aged 24 years.

NOTE 44, page 132.

The last time I saw Dr. Channing was in the summer of 1841, when, in company with my English friend, Joseph Sturge, so well known for his philanthropic labors and liberal political opinions, I visited him in his summer residence in Rhode Island. In recalling the impressions of that visit, it can scarcely be necessary to say, that I have no reference to the peculiar religious opinions of a man whose life, beautifully and truly manifested above the atmosphere of sect, is now the world's common legacy.

NOTE 45, page 135.

"O vine of Sibmah ! I will weep for thee with the weeping of Jazer ! " — *Jeremiah* xlviii. 32.

NOTE 46, page 138.

Sophia Sturge, sister of Joseph Sturge, of Birmingham, the President of the British Complete Suffrage Association, died in the 6th month, 1845. She was the colleague, counsellor, and ever-ready helpmate of her brother in all his vast designs of beneficence. The Birmingham Pilot says of her : " Never, perhaps, were the active and passive virtues of the human character more harmoniously and beautifully blended than in this excellent woman."

NOTE 47, page 139.

Winnipiseogee : "Smile of the Great Spirit."

NOTE 48, page 142.

This legend is the subject of a celebrated picture by Tintoretto, of which Mr. Rogers possesses the original sketch. The slave lies on the ground, amid a crowd of spectators, who look on, animated by all the various emotions of sympathy, rage, terror; a woman, in front, with a child in her arms, has always been admired for the lifelike vivacity of her attitude and expression. The executioner holds up the broken implements ; St. Mark, with a headlong movement, seems to rush down from heaven in haste to save his worshipper. The dramatic grouping in this picture is wonderful ; the coloring, in its gorgeous depth and harmony, is, in Mr. Rogers's sketch, finer than in the picture.—*Mrs. Jamieson's Poetry of Sacred and Legendary Art,* Vol. I. p. 121.

NOTE 49, page 143.

Pennant, in his "Voyage to the Hebrides," describes the holy well of Loch Maree, the waters of which were supposed to effect a miraculous cure of melancholy, trouble, and insanity.

NOTE 50, page 145.

The writer of these lines is no enemy of Catholics. He has, on more than one occasion, exposed himself to the censures of his Protestant brethren, by his strenuous endeavors to procure indemnification for the owners of the convent destroyed near Boston. He defended the cause of the Irish patriots long before it had become popular in this country ; and he was one of the first to urge the most liberal aid to the suffering and starving population of the Catholic island. The severity of his language finds its ample apology in the reluctant confession of one of the most eminent Romish priests, the eloquent and devoted Father Ventura.

NOTE 51, page 146.

Ebenezer Elliott, the intelligence of whose death has recently reached us, was, to the artisans of England, what Burns was to the peasantry of Scotland. His "Corn-law Rhymes" contributed not a little to that overwhelming tide of popular opinion and feeling which resulted in the repeal of the tax on bread. Well has the eloquent author of "The Reforms and Reformers of Great Britain" said of him, "Not corn-law repealers alone, but all Britons who moisten their scanty bread with the sweat of the brow, are largely indebted to his inspiring lay, for the mighty bound which the laboring mind of England has taken in our day."

NOTE 52, page 147.

The reader of the Biography of the late William Allen, the philanthropic associate of Clarkson and Romilly, cannot fail to admire his simple and beautiful record of a tour through Europe, in the years 1818 and 1819, in the company of his American friend, Stephen Grellett.

NOTE 53, page 154.

" Thou 'mind'st me of a story told
In rare Bernardin's leaves of gold."

The incident here referred to is related in a note to Bernardin Henri Saint Pierre's *Etudes de la Nature.*

"We arrived at the habitation of the Hermits a little before they sat down to their table, and while they were still at church. J. J. Rousseau proposed to me to offer up our devotions. The hermits were reciting the Litanies of Providence, which are remarkably beautiful. After we had addressed our prayers to God, and the hermits were proceeding to the refectory, Rousseau said to me, with his heart overflowing, ' At this moment I experience what is said in the gospel : *Where two or three are gathered together in my name, there am I in the midst of them.* There is here a feeling of peace and happiness which penetrates the soul.' I said, ' If Fenelon had lived, you would have been a Catholic.' He exclaimed, with tears in his eyes, ' O, if Fenelon were alive, I would struggle to get into his service, even as a lackey ! '"

In my sketch of Saint Pierre, it will be seen that I have somewhat antedated the period of his old age. At that time he was not probably more than fifty. In describing him, I have by no means exaggerated his own history of his mental condition at the period of the story. In the fragmentary Sequel to his Studies of Nature, he thus speaks of himself : " The ingratitude of those of whom I had deserved kindness, unexpected family misfortunes, the total loss of my small patrimony through enterprises solely undertaken for the benefit of my country, the debts under which I lay oppressed, the blasting of all my hopes, — these combined calamities made dreadful inroads upon my health and reason. . . . . I found it impossible to continue in a room where there was company, especially if the doors were shut. I could not even cross an alley in a public garden, if several persons had got together in it. When alone, my malady subsided. I felt myself likewise at ease in places where I saw children only. At the sight of any one walking up to the place where I was, I felt my whole frame agitated, and retired. I often said to myself, ' My sole study has been to merit well of mankind ; why do I fear them ? '"

He attributes his improved health of

mind and body to the counsels of his friend, J. J. Rousseau. "I renounced," says he, "my books. I threw my eyes upon the works of nature, which spake to all my senses a language which neither time nor nations have it in their power to alter. Thenceforth my histories and my journals were the herbage of the fields and meadows. My thoughts did not go forth painfully after them, as in the case of human systems ; but their thoughts, under a thousand engaging forms, quietly sought me. In these I studied, without effort, the laws of that Universal Wisdom which had surrounded me from the cradle, but on which heretofore I had bestowed little attention."

Speaking of Rousseau, he says : "I derived inexpressible satisfaction from his society. What I prized still more than his genius, was his probity. He was one of the few literary characters, tried in the furnace of affliction, to whom you could, with perfect security, confide your most secret thoughts. . . . . Even when he deviated, and became the victim of himself or of others, he could forget his own misery in devotion to the welfare of mankind. He was uniformly the advocate of the miserable. There might be inscribed on his tomb these affecting words from that Book of which he carried always about him some select passages, during the last years of his life : *His sins, which are many, are forgiven, for he loved much.*"

NOTE 54, page 155.

"Like that the gray-haired sea-king passed."

Dr. Hooker, who accompanied Sir James Ross in his expedition of 1841, thus describes the appearance of that unknown land of frost and fire which was seen in latitude 77° south, — a stupendous chain of mountains, the whole mass of which, from its highest point to the ocean, was covered with everlasting snow and ice : —

"The water and the sky were both as blue, or rather more intensely blue, than I have ever seen them in the tropics, and all the coast was one mass of dazzlingly beautiful peaks of snow, which, when the sun approached the horizon, reflected the most brilliant tints of golden yellow and scarlet ; and then, to see the dark cloud of smoke, tinged with flame, rising from the volcano in a perfect unbroken column, one side jet-black, the other giving back the colors of the sun, sometimes turning off at a right angle by some current of wind, and stretching many miles to leeward ! This was a sight so surpassing everything that can be imagined, and so heightened by the consciousness that we had penetrated, under the guidance of our commander, into regions far beyond what was ever deemed practicable, that it caused a feeling of awe to steal over us at the consideration of our own comparative insignificance and helplessness, and at the same time an indescribable feeling of the greatness of the Creator in the works of his hand."

NOTE 55, page 161.

The election of Charles Sumner to the U. S. Senate "followed hard upon" the rendition of the fugitive Sims by the U. S. officials and the armed police of Boston.

NOTE 56, page 164.

The storming of the city of Derne, in 1805, by General Eaton, at the head of nine Americans, forty Greeks, and a motley array of Turks and Arabs, was one of those feats of hardihood and daring which have in all ages attracted the admiration of the multitude. The higher and holier heroism of Christian self-denial and sacrifice, in the humble walks of private duty, is seldom so well appreciated.

NOTE 57, page 167.

It is proper to say that these lines are the joint impromptus of my sister and myself. They are inserted here as an expression of our admiration of the gifted stranger whom we have since learned to love as a friend.

NOTE 58, page 171.

This ballad was originally published in a prose work of the author's, as the song of a wandering Milesian schoolmaster.

In the seventeenth century, slavery in the New World was by no means confined to the natives of Africa. Political offenders and criminals were transported by the British government to the plantations of Barbadoes and Virginia, where they were sold like cattle in the market. Kidnapping of free and innocent white persons was practised to a considerable extent in the seaports of the United Kingdom.

NOTE 59, page 172.

It can scarcely be necessary to say that there are elements in the character and passages in the history of the great Hungarian statesman and orator, which necessarily command the admiration of those, even, who believe that no political revolution was ever worth the price of human blood.

NOTE 60, page 175.

"Homilies from Oldbug hear."

Dr. W——, author of "The Puritan," under the name of Jonathan Oldbug.

Note 61, page 187.

William Forster, of Norwich, England, died in East Tennessee, in the 1st month, 1854, while engaged in presenting to the governors of the States of this Union the address of his religious society on the evils of slavery. He was the relative and coadjutor of the Buxtons, Gurneys, and Frys; and his whole life, extending almost to threescore and ten years, was a pure and beautiful example of Christian benevolence. He had travelled over Europe, and visited most of its sovereigns, to plead against the slave-trade and slavery; and had twice before made visits to this country, under impressions of religious duty.

Note 62, page 188.

No more fitting inscription could be placed on the tombstone of Robert Rantoul than this : " He died at his post in Congress, and his last words were a protest in the name of Democracy against the Fugitive-Slave Law."

Note 63, page 200.

"Sebah, Oasis of Fezzan, 10th March, 1846. — This evening the female slaves were unusually excited in singing, and I had the curiosity to ask my negro servant, Said, what they were singing about. As many of them were natives of his own country, he had no difficulty in translating the Mandara or Bornou language. I had often asked the Moors to translate their songs for me, but got no satisfactory account from them. Said at first said, ' O, they sing of *Rubee* ' (God). ' What do you mean ? ' I replied, impatiently. ' O, don't you know ? ' he continued, ' they asked God to give them their *Atka* ? ' (certificate of freedom.) I inquired, ' Is that all ? Said : ' No ; they say, " Where are we going ? The world is large. *O God ! Where are we going ? O God !* " ' I inquired, ' What else ? ' Said : ' They remember their country, Bornou, and say, *"Bornou was a pleasant country, full of all good things ; but this is a bad country, and we are miserable !* " ' ' Do they say anything else ? ' Said : ' No ; they repeat these words over and over again, and add, " O God ! give us our *Atka, and let us return again to our dear home.*" '

" I am not surprised I got little satisfaction when I asked the Moors about the songs of their slaves. Who will say that the above words are not a very appropriate song ? What could have been more congenially adapted to their then woful condition ? It is not to be wondered at that these poor bondwomen cheer up their hearts, in their long, lonely, and painful wanderings over the desert, with words and sentiments like these ; but I have often observed that their fatigue and sufferings were too great for them to strike up this melancholy dirge, and many days their plaintive strains never broke over the silence of the desert." — *Richardson's Journal.*

Note 64, page 201.

One of the latest and most interesting items of Eastern news is the statement that Slavery has been formally and totally abolished in Egypt.

Note 65, page 213.

A letter from England, in the *Friends' Review,* says : " Joseph Sturge, with a companion, Thomas Harvey, has been visiting the shores of Finland, to ascertain the amount of mischief and loss to poor and peaceable sufferers, occasioned by the gunboats of the Allied squadrons in the late war, with a view to obtaining relief for them."

Note 66, page 226.

A remarkable custom, brought from the Old Country, formerly prevailed in the rural districts of New England. On the death of a member of the family, the bees were at once informed of the event, and their hives dressed in mourning. This ceremonial was supposed to be necessary to prevent the swarms from leaving their hives and seeking a new home.

Note 67, page 235.

"Too late I loved Thee, O Beauty of ancient days, yet ever new ! And lo ! Thou wert within, and I abroad searching for thee. Thou wert with me, but I was not with Thee." — *August. Soliloq.,* Book X.

Note 68, page 235.

" And I saw that there was an Ocean of Darkness and Death : but an infinite Ocean of Light and Love flowed over the Ocean of Darkness : And in that I saw the infinite Love of God." — *George Fox's Journal.*

Note 69, page 243.

The massacre of unarmed and unoffending men, in Southern Kansas, took place near the Marais du Cygne of the French *voyageurs.*

Note 70, page 254.

Read at the Friends' School Anniversary, Providence, R. I., 6th mo., 1860.

Note 71, page 264.

See English caricatures of America :

Slaveholder and cowhide, with the motto, " Have n't I a right to wallop my nigger ? "

NOTE 72, page 266.

It is recorded that the Chians, when subjugated by Mithridates of Cappadocia, were delivered up to their own slaves, to be carried away captive to Colchis. Athenæus considers this a just punishment for their wickedness in first introducing the slave-trade into Greece. From this ancient villany of the Chians the proverb arose, " The Chian hath bought himself a master."

NOTE 73, page 270.

This ballad was written on the occasion of a Horticultural Festival. Cobbler Keezar was a noted character among the first settlers in the valley of the Merrimack.

NOTE 74, page 283.

Lieutenant Herndon's Report of the Exploration of the Amazon has a striking description of the peculiar and melancholy notes of a bird heard by night on the shores of the river. The Indian guides called it " The Cry of a Lost Soul " !

NOTE 75, page 361.

Eleonora Johanna Von Merlau, or, as Sewall the Quaker Historian gives it, Von Merlane, a noble young lady of Frankfort, seems to have held among the Mystics of that city very much such a position as Annia Maria Schurmaus did among the Labadists of Holland. William Penn appears to have shared the admiration of her own immediate circle for this accomplished and gifted lady.

NOTE 76, page 363.

Magister Johann Kelpius, a graduate of the University of Helmstadt, came to Pennsylvania in 1694, with a company of German Mystics. They made their home in the woods on the Wissahickon, a little west of the Quaker settlement of Germantown. Kelpius was a believer in the near approach of the Millennium, and was a devout student of the Book of Revelation, and the *Morgen-Rothe* of Jacob Behmen. He called his settlement " The Woman in the Wilderness " (*Das Weib in der Wueste*). He was only twenty-four years of age when he came to America, but his gravity, learning, and devotion placed him at the head of the settlement. He disliked the Quakers, because he thought they were too exclusive in the matter of ministers. He was, like most of the Mystics, opposed to the severe doctrinal views of Calvin and even Luther, declaring " that he could as little agree with the *Damnamus* of the

Augsburg Confession as with the *Anathema* of the Council of Trent."

He died in 1704, sitting in his little garden surrounded by his grieving disciples. Previous to his death it is said that he cast his famous " Stone of Wisdom " into the river, where that mystic souvenir of the times of Van Helmont, Paracelsus, and Agrippa has lain ever since, undisturbed.

NOTE 77, page 363.

Peter Sluyter, or Schluter, a native of Wesel, united himself with the sect of Labadists, who believed in the Divine commission of John De Labadie, a Roman Catholic priest converted to Protestantism, enthusiastic, eloquent, and evidently sincere in his special calling and election to separate the true and living members of the Church of Christ from the formalism and hypocrisy of the ruling sects. George Keith and Robert Barclay visited him at Amsterdam and afterward at the communities of Herford and Wieward ; and, according to Gerard Croes, found him so near to them on some points, that they offered to take him into the Society of Friends. This offer, if it was really made, which is certainly doubtful, was, happily for the Friends at least, declined. Invited to Herford in Westphalia by Elizabeth, daughter of the Elector Palatine, De Labadie and his followers preached incessantly, and succeeded in arousing a wild enthusiasm among the people, who neglected their business and gave way to excitements and strange practices. Men and women, it was said, at the Communion drank and danced together, and private marriages, or spiritual unions, were formed. Labadie died in 1674 at Altona, in Denmark, maintaining his testimonies to the last. " Nothing remains for me," he said, " except to go to my God. Death is merely ascending from a lower and narrower chamber to one higher and holier."

In 1679, Peter Sluyter and Jasper Dankers were sent to America by the community at the Castle of Wieward. Their journal, translated from the Dutch and edited by Henry C. Murphy, has been recently published by the Long Island Historical Society. They made some converts, and among them was the eldest son of Hermanns, the proprietor of a rich tract of land at the head of Chesapeake Bay, known as Bohemia Manor. Sluyter obtained a grant of this tract, and established upon it a community numbering at one time a hundred souls. Very contradictory statements are on record regarding his headship of this spiritual family, the discipline of which seems to have been of more than monastic severity. Certain it is that he bought and sold slaves, and manifested more interest in the world's goods than became a believer in the near Millennium. He evinces in his journal an overweening spiritual pride, and speaks contemptuously of other professors, especially the Quakers whom he met in his travels. The latter, on the contrary, seem to have looked favorably upon the Labadists, and uniformly speak of them courteously and kindly. His journal shows him to have been destitute of common gratitude and Christian charity. He threw himself upon the generous hospitality of the Friends wherever he went, and repaid their kindness by the coarsest abuse and misrepresentation.

Note 78, page 364.

Among the pioneer Friends were many men of learning and broad and liberal views. Penn was conversant with every department of literature and philosophy. Thomas Lloyd was a ripe and rare scholar. The great Loganian Library of Philadelphia bears witness to the varied learning and classical taste of its donor, James Logan. Thomas Story, member of the Council of State, Master of the Rolls, and Commissioner of Claims under William Penn, and an able minister of his Society, took a deep interest in scientific questions, and in a letter to his friend Logan, written while on a religious visit to Great Britain, seems to have anticipated the conclusion of modern geologists. "I spent," he says, "some months, especially at Scarborough, during the season attending meetings, at whose high cliffs and the variety of strata therein and their several positions I further learned and was confirmed in some things, — that the earth is of much older date as to the beginning of it than the time assigned in the Holy Scriptures as commonly understood, which is suited to the common capacities of mankind, as to six days of progressive work, by which I understand certain long and competent periods of time, and not natural days." It was sometimes made a matter of reproach by the Anabaptists and other sects, that the Quakers read profane writings and philosophies, and that they quoted heathen moralists in support of their views. Sluyter and Dankers, in their journal of American travels, visiting a Quaker preacher's house at Burlington, on the Delaware, found "a volume of Virgil lying on the window, as if it were a common hand-book ; also Helmont's book on Medicine (*Ortus Medicinæ, id est Initia Physica inaudita progressus medecinæ novus in morborum ultionam ad*

vitam longam), whom, in an introduction they have made to it, they make to pass for one of their own sect, although in his lifetime he did not know anything about Quakers." It would appear from this that the half-mystical, half-scientific writings of the alchemist and philosopher of Vilverde had not escaped the notice of Friends, and that they had included him in their broad eclecticism.

Note 79, page 364.

"The Quaker's Meeting," a painting by E. Hemskerck (supposed to be Egbert Hemskerck the younger, son of Egbert Hemskerck the old), in which William Penn and others — among them Charles II., or the Duke of York — are represented along with the rudest and most stolid class of the British rural population at that period. Hemskerck came to London from Holland with King William in 1689. He delighted in wild, grotesque subjects, such as the nocturnal intercourse of witches and the temptation of St. Anthony. Whatever was strange and uncommon attracted his free pencil. Judging from the portrait of Penn, he must have drawn his faces, figures, and costumes from life, although there may be something of caricature in the convulsed attitudes of two or three of the figures.

Note 80, page 366.

In one of his letters addressed to his friends in Germany he says : " These wild men, who never in their life heard Christ's teachings about temperance and contentment, herein far surpass the Christians. They live far more contented and unconcerned for the morrow. They do not overreach in trade. They know nothing of our everlasting pomp and stylishness. They neither curse nor swear, are temperate in food and drink, and if any of them get drunk, the mouth-Christians are at fault, who, for the sake of accursed lucre, sell them strong drink."

Again he wrote in 1698 to his father that he finds the Indians reasonable people, willing to accept good teaching and manners, evincing an inward piety toward God, and more eager, in fact, to understand things divine than many among you who in the pulpit teach Christ in word, but by ungodly life deny him.

" It is evident," says Professor Seideustecker, " Pastorius holds up the Indian as Nature's unspoiled child to the eyes of the ' European Babel,' somewhat after the same manner in which Tacitus used the barbarian *Germani* to shame his degenerate countrymen."

As believers in the universality of the Saving Light, the outlook of early Friends upon the heathen was a very cheerful and hopeful one. God was as near to them as to Jew or Anglo-Saxon ; as accessible at Timbuctoo as at Rome or Geneva. Not the letter of Scripture, but the spirit which dictated it, was of saving efficacy. Robert Barclay is nowhere more powerful than in his argument for the salvation of the heathen, who live according to their light, without knowing even the name of Christ. William Penn thought Socrates as good a Christian as Richard Baxter. Early Fathers of the Church, as Origen and Justin Martyr 'ld broader views on this point tha˜ modern Evangelicals. Even Augus-˜e, from whom Calvin borrowed his theology, admits that he has no controversy with the admirable philosophers, Plato and Plotinus. " Nor do I think," he says in *De Civ. Dei.*, lib. xviii., cap. 47, " that the Jews dare affirm that none belonged unto God but the Israelites."

Note 81, page 418.

This ballad, originally written for J. R. Osgood & Co.'s *Memorial History of Boston*, describes, with pardonable poetic li-c˜˜˜ a memorable incident in the annals of the city. The interview between Shattuck and the Governor took place, I have since learned, in the residence of the latter, and not in the Council Chamber.

Note 82, page 420.

This name in some parts of Europe is given to the season we call Indian Summer, in honor of the good St. Martin. The title of the poem was suggested by the fact that the day it refers to was the exact date of the Saint's birth, the 11th of November.

Note 83, page 421.

See Tylor's *Primitive Culture*, vol. ii. pp. 32, 33. Also *Journal of Asiatic Society*, vol. iv. p. 795.

Note 84, page 426.

The picturesquely situated Wayside Inn at West Ossipee, N. H., is now in ashes; and to its former guests these somewhat careless rhymes may be a not unwelcome reminder of pleasant summers and autumns on the banks of the Bearcamp and Chocorua. To the author himself they have a special interest from the fact that they were written, or improvised, under the eye, and for the amusement of a beloved invalid friend whose last earthly sunsets faded from the mountain ranges of Ossipee and Sandwich.

Note 85, page 457.

" He [Macey] shook the dust from off his feet, and departed with all his worldly goods and his family. He encountered a severe storm, and his wife, influenced by some omens of disaster, besought him to put back. He told her not to fear, for his faith was perfect. But she entreated him again. Then the spirit that impelled him broke forth: ' Woman, go below and seek thy God. I fear not the witches on earth, or the devils in hell! ' " — *Life of Robert Pike* page 55.

Note 86, page 461.

I have attempted this paraphrase of the Hymns of the Brahmo Somaj of India, as I find them in Mozoomdar's account of the devotional exercises of that remarkable religious development which has attracted far less attention and sympathy from the Christian world than it deserves, as a fresh revelation of the direct action of the Divine Spirit upon the human heart.

INDEX.